DR. GOODENOUGH'S HOME CURES & HERBAL REMEDIES

Josephus Goodenough, M. D.

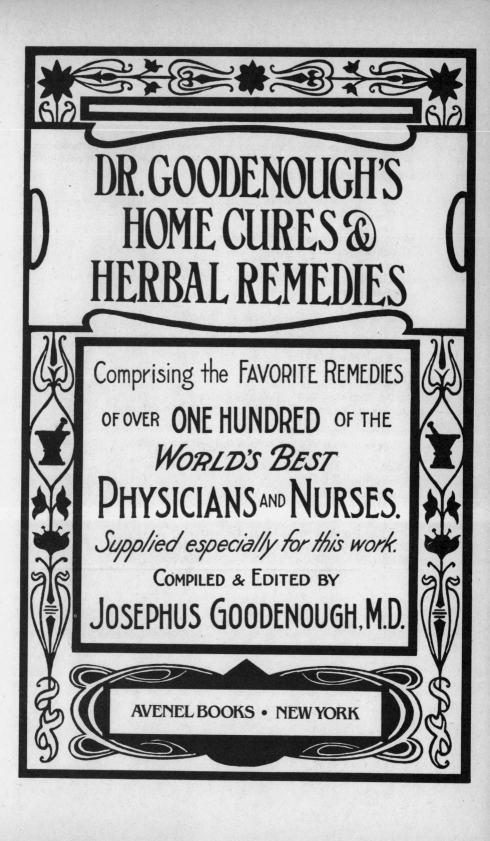

DR. GOODENOUGH'S HOME CURES & HERBAL REMEDIES

Comprising the FAVORITE REMEDIES

OF OVER **ONE HUNDRED** OF THE

WORLD'S BEST

PHYSICIANS AND NURSES.

Supplied especially for this work.

COMPILED & EDITED BY

JOSEPHUS GOODENOUGH, M.D.

AVENEL BOOKS · NEW YORK

Cautionary Notice

Brand names and formulas listed throughout the book, and particularly in Department VI are for historical interest only and are *not* for contemporary use in the form given.

———————

Copyright © 1982 by Crown Publishers, Inc.
All rights reserved.

This 1982 edition is published by Avenel Books, distributed by Crown Publishers, Inc.

Manufactured in the United States of America

This book was previously published as *The Favorite Medical Receipt Book and Home Doctor.*

h g f e d c b

Library of Congress Cataloging in Publication Data

Home cures and herbal remedies.
    Dr. Goodenough's Home cures and herbal remedies.

    Rev. ed. of: The favorite medical receipt book and home doctor. 1904.
    Includes index.
    1. Medicine, Popular.   2. Therapeutics—Popular works. I. Goodenough, Josephus. II. Title.
III. Title: Home cures and herbal remedies. IV. Title: Doctor Goodenough's Home cures and herbal remedies.
RC82.H65   1982   616.02′4   81-20655
ISBN 0-517-362430   AACR2

Table of Contents

Color Plates

FOREWORD.

Imagine living at the turn-of-the-century, in a world without anti-biotics, insulin, knowledge of vitamins, first-aid courses, and the many other modern medical drugs and techniques. When people on farms or in towns were sick they were apt to turn to the books of popular medicine, "household books," that flooded eighteenth- and nineteenth-century America.

Dr. Josephus Goodenough's home medical book, which he wrote with the added advice of many contributors, is typical of its kind, and its herbal remedies and advice to women are particularly readable. Besides these two sections, the book describes body functions and the treatment of some diseases, deals with accidents and emergencies, offers antidotes to poisons, and specifies "receipts" (recipes) for medicines, cleaning fluids, and beauty aids.

One contributor, Dr. Helen F. Warner, advises women in simple, direct language about menstruation, pregnancy (sidestepping the how of conception), childbirth (home births only) and menopause (then called "change of life"). Much of her homely wisdom is still worth pondering.

More than 325 herbal remedies, illustrated with 16 striking color plates, are described, including information such as where they are grown and their effects. This very thorough section, incorporating American Indian lore, has much that the modern herbal health devotee will find fascinating.

According to Dr. Goodenough, in his experience, a doctor might be summoned to attend the more serious cases. But otherwise, did the 1904 reader want Pink Pills for Pale People? A treatment for alcoholism? A headache liniment? The answers to all these questions were in Dr. Goodenough's book.

Some of the prescriptions are homeopathic, a nineteenth-century medical sidepath, treatment of disease by minute doses—drops or grains —of a remedy that would in healthy persons produce symptoms of the disease. In other words, the hair of the dog. Many doctors of the time felt these very small doses were an improvement over the then-current practice of drinking quarts of patent medicine.

Although the book is based on common sense and while there is value in the long, vivid descriptions of how the body works and in the 16 diagrammatic color plates, the advice in the book cannot be substituted for modern medical treatment. No layman today would try to splint the crushed finger of an accident victim. Cathartics should *not* be used in appendicitis cases. Nosebleed cannot be prevented by wearing a "bright silk ribbon around the neck." What was only dimly viewed as dangerous in the early 1900s—dosage with morphine or opium—is now recognized as damaging and addictive.

Dr. Goodenough's "household book" of 1904 is not to be taken as gospel in the 1980s but can be read with interest and amusement—and some profit in certain of the simple pragmatic remedies—as well as with wonder at the hardiness and ingenuity of our not-so-remote ancestors when faced with illness.

COMPILER AND EDITOR'S PREFACE.

Every reputable physician is to a certain extent a specialist. There are certain diseases he is most successful in treating, and for which he has his favorite remedies. The aim of this book has been to furnish its patrons with these favorite remedies—the safest, simplest and best known to the medical fraternity. To accomplish this we have gathered from many of the best physicians of this and other countries their favorite receipts, or prescriptions. The remedies thus collected cover all diseases to which the human body is subject, and have been arranged in a systematic and convenient form for the homes of this and other lands. We consulted with, and obtained these receipts from, over one hundred of the leading physicians and nurses of the world, to which has been added the combined experience and practice of the compiler and editor.

The scope of this work is entirely original, nothing like it ever before having been published. It contains complete yet simple treatises on Diseases of Women, Diseases of Children, Poisons and their Antidotes, etc., also a department on What Girls and Mothers Should Know by one of the most successful lady physicians in this or any other country. The illustrations are superior to those of any other family medical book in existence, and have been made, at great expense, especially for this work.

To gather these favorite remedies from the best physicians of many lands and arrange them in convenient form for the homes and mothers of the world, has been a long, patient, but pleasant task, and if we have succeeded in supplying our patrons with a book that will serve them faithfully "in time of need," we will be amply rewarded for our labor.

In the preparation of this work Dr. W.R. Henderson, United States Post-office Physician, at Detroit, Michigan, U.S.A., has been our constant counselor and adviser, and to him we are much indebted for his valuable contributions and suggestions.

PHYSICIANS WHOSE FAVORITE REMEDIES WILL BE FOUND IN THIS BOOK.

A number of physicians sent remedies for this book who, for professional reasons, desired that their names should not be printed. The work contains in all the choice remedies of more than one hundred leading doctors, of this and other countries, and, in addition, many home remedies of experienced and practical nurses.

1. N. L. CLARKE................ .....Mobile, Alabama.
2. F. VINSONHALER................Little Rock, Arkansas.
3. J. W. HAYWARD (Homeopathic)...Taunton, Massachusetts.
4. JOHN W. McCAUSLAND...........Fort Wayne, Indiana.
5. J. E. HANNA....................Ottawa, Ontario, Canada.
6. J. G. BROOKS...................Paducah, Kentucky.
7. CHESTER W. STRANAHAN ....Erie, Pennsylvania.
8. A. L. CLARK ....Elgin, Illinois.
9. J. F. WEATHERS................New Albany, Indiana.
10. I. G. ANTHOINE ....Nashua, New Hampshire.
11. HENRY BALDWIN, JR. ....Springfield, Ohio.
12. J. S. EATON ....Lincoln, Nebraska.
13. D. C. BROCKMAN ....Ottumwa, Iowa.
14. C. N. PALMER ....Lockport, New York.
15. C. H. MYERS ....South Bend, Indiana.
16. L. M. BERG. (Homeopathic)....Laredo, Texas.
17. W. C. CHAFEE..................Huntington, Indiana.
18. C. C. ELLIS (Homeopathic).........Somerville, Massachusetts.
19. EDWIN WALKER ....Evansville, Indiana.
20. ARTHUR T. HUDSON ....Paducah, Kentucky.
21. A. W. SCHILLER.................Salem, Ohio.
22. ARTHUR O. JONES...............Raleigh, North Carolina.
23. G. W. H. KEMPER...............Muncie, Indiana.
24. SEVERIN LACHAPELLE...........St. Henri de Montreal, P.Q.
25. W. H. HODSON ....Lockport, New York.
26. M. C. WEDGEWOOD ....Lewiston, Maine.
27. JAMES W. COKENOWER .... Des Moines, Iowa.
28. W. A. J. POLLOCK...............Pensacola, Florida.
29. J. G. KELLY........ ....Hornellsville, New York.
30. A. L. FOREMAN...... ....Stockton, California.
31. WM. KERR ....Bay City, Michigan.
32. MARGARET CALDWELL ....Waukesha, Wisconsin.
33. DANIEL LICHTY.................Rockford, Illinois.
34. ARTHUR P. GINN ....Nebraska City, Nebraska.
35. WM. H. HALL...................Saratoga Springs, N. Y.

36. J. T. JONES......................Jackson, Tennessee.
37. JOHN R. FLEMING (Homeopathic) Atlantic City, New Jersey.
38. J. N. McCOY ....Vincennes, Indiana.
39. JAS. A. HART....................Colorado Springs, Colorado.
40. SAMUEL MILLIKEN..............Dallas, Texas.
41. WM. C. WOOD...................Gloversville, New York.
42. T. E. SANDS ....Battle Creek, Michigan.
43. O. N. HOYT (Homeopathic)......Pierre, South Dakota.
44. GEO. W. CROSBY.................Atlantic City, New Jersey.
45. W. M. CAMPBELL ....Atchison, Kansas.
46. E. E. LEVERS ....Spring Valley, Wyoming.
47. D. B. WYATT ....Fond du Lac, Wisconsin.
48. NEW YORK EYE AND EAR INFIRMARY, NewYork, N.Y.
        (The largest institution of the kind in the world).
49. ROBERT W. GIBBES ....Columbia, South Carolina.
50. H. C. JONES ....Decatur, Illinois.
51. JAMES A. LANE.................Leavenworth, Kansas.
52. F. J. CAMPBELL.................Fargo, North Dakota.
53. P. I. EDWARDS ....Jackson, Michigan.
54. A. F. HAGADORN...............West Bay City, Michigan.
55. J. C. HOYE ....New Castle, Pennsylvania.
56. AMOS O. TAYLOR (Homeopathic)..Altoona, Pennsylvania.
57. WM. B. REED...................Rome, New York.
58. P. J. O'HARA ....Paris, Michigan.
59. W. C. GATES...................Rockland, Michigan.
60. N. W. CADY....................Logansport, Indiana.
61. DONALD CAMPBELL.............Butte, Montana.
62. AUGUST HEIGELMAN ....Berlin, Germany.
63. MAX VON WACHTER...........Berlin, Germany.
64. GUSTAV HUHNHOLZ.............Frankfort, Germany.
65. OTTO HUMRICH ... .Leipzig, Germany.
66. FREDERICK OBENAUER..........Potsdam, Germany.
67. CARL OESTERREICHER ....Hanover, Germany.
68. PIERRE ROSELO................Marseilles, France.
69. JULES CAMPAU... ....Bordeaux, France.
70. JOHN S. BURNS ....London, England.
71. ARCHIE S. WOODHOUSE ....Leeds, England.
72. CYRUS S. EDWARDS............Liverpool, England.
73. DOUGLAS CALVERT..............Glasgow, Scotland.
74. ARCHIBALD MacDOUGALL.......Aberdeen, Scotland.
75. PATRICK J. McMANIS ....Dublin, Ireland.
76. ITO FUCASI ....Tokio, Japan.
77. CARLOS D. GUTIERREZ..........City of Mexico, Mexico.
78. NECTAR M. KALAIJIAN..........Samsoun, Armenia.
        (Educated in the United States.).
79. JACOB SCHRECK .... Amsterdam, Holland.
80. FREDERICK MUDDER............The Hague, Holland.
81. FRITHIOF STJERNHJELM........Stockholm, Sweden.
82. DR L. W. LANDER ....Stockholm, Sweden.
83. OLAF TORDENSKJOLD............Christiana, Norway.
84. EPHRAIM J. McCOLLUM.............Tiffin, Ohio.

Department I.

DISEASES.—CAUSES, SYMPTOMS, TREATMENTS, Etc.

ABORTION.—(See DISEASES OF WOMEN).

ABSCESS.—A collection of pus or purulent matter among the tissues of the body, and in a cavity of new formation, attended with constitutional disturbance more or less pronounced according to the location and size of the tumor; and, if near the surface, noticeable by prominence, throbbing and tenderness.

Cause.—Abscesses are the result of acute local inflammation where swelling and pressure shut off nutrition until the part dies. Gradually the tissues soften, turn to pus, and the pus is discharged. This is Nature's means of elimination. Abscesses are usually acute, or *warm;* occurring in weak or scrofulous persons, they may last indefinitely, in which case they are spoken of as chronic, or *cold.*

Symptoms.—Inflammation, swelling, and pain in the affected part. When they occur in internal organs, the symptoms indicating their presence are obscure and would not be recognized with any degree of certainty by other than a practiced physician. Diagnosis in such cases is not always made during life. Occurring in the brain, may cause headache, dilation of the pupil of the eye on the affected side, vomiting and convulsions in the early stages; also respiration may increase up to a certain point or degree, and then gradually decrease to a temporary cessation (Cheyne-Stokes breathing). Paralysis may occur in the later stages.

Boils and *Carbuncles.*(see description) come under the head of *abscesses.*

TREATMENTS.—

What to Do in Advance of a Doctor.—When abscesses form near the surface, poultice with flax-seed meal or bread and milk. Open as soon as pus has formed. Keep clean with castile soap and water. Take something to purify the blood. Keep the bowels regular. For abscesses of this character it is not necessary to call a doctor, but it may be advisable in severe and obstinate cases to have them lanced by a doctor. If there are indications of an abscess on the brain, a physician or surgeon should at once be consulted.

A. In the early stage apply poultice of flax-seed until the abscess is soft to the touch of the finger, then open with a knife which has been thoroughly cleansed and dipped in boiling water. Press lightly on the sides of the incision to force out the pus, but do not press too hard. Dress the wound twice a day by washing, using castile soap, and cover with clean, soft linen.

> **B.** Dried Sulphate of Iron..................... 1 drachm.
> Sulphate of Magnesia..................... 4   "
> Elixir Vitriol................................. 6   "
> Syrup Ginger.............................. ½ ounce.
> Add enough water to make the whole 3   "
>
> *Mix.*—Take a teaspoonful in a wineglassful of water after meals.—(19).
>
> *Note.*—Where the patient has a healthy color, the Sulphate of Iron should be omitted.

C. Where the abscess is slow, take Hepor Sulphur or Sulphide of Calcium in 2-grain pills. This hastens suppuration and the healing process.—(12).

D. When forming, poultice with flax-seed or bread and milk, and open freely as soon as pus has formed. After opening apply clean linen, or absorbent cotton pad wet with solution of Carbolic Acid, teaspoonful to pint of boiling water. Change as often as soiled. *Never poultice an abscess after it is open.*—(13).

Remark.—A poultice of ground flax-seed or ground elm bark is recommended by Dr. J. T. Johnson.

E. Open and syringe out with boiled rain or filtered water, containing 20 drops strong Carbolic Acid to the teacupful. Keep a clean cloth wet with the same over the part. Renew when soiled. Syringe out daily.—(14).

ABDOMINAL DROPSY.—(See *Ascites* under DROPSY).

ACNE.—(See SKIN DISEASES).

ADDISON'S DISEASE.—(See BRONZED SKIN DISEASE).

AGUE.—See *Intermittent Fever* under MALARIAL FEVERS).

ALBUMINURIA.—(See KIDNEY DISEASES).

ALCOHOLISM.—The physical and mental phenomena induced by the use of alcohol, of which *drunkenness* is an acute form and *delirium tremens* an incident of the chronic form.

Drunkenness.— *Symptoms.* — Intoxication begins with a period of exhilaration. The ordinary case does not go further than this, the effects passing away in sleep. In the more acute form, produced by imbibing an excessive quantity of alcoholic stimulants, the exhilaration is followed by a delirious stage, which is in turn succeeded by a state of coma not unlike that in *apoplexy*, the breathing being sonorous in character and the face bloated and congested. (See page 470.)

Chronic Alcoholism.—The continued indulgence in alcoholic drinks brings about morbid changes in the various organs and tissues of the body. Dyspepsia, diseases of the heart, liver and kidneys, organic brain diseases and epilepsy may be brought about through this cause.

Symptoms.—Dyspepsia, usually vomiting in the morning, sleeplessness, restlessness, and an increasing muscular tremor. All the functions of the mind become perverted, and the individual comes in time to have an imbecile expression added to bloated and repulsive features.

TREATMENTS.—

A. Continue the use of liquor, for a time at least, but restrict to a certain amount. Take perhaps two ounces a day, in the form of sling, and the balance of the time, or whenever there is a desire for liquor, drink Scullcap tea (see chapter on herbs) freely. If this is continued, the nerves will become toned up and the taste for alcoholic drinks will gradually die out.

It is also claimed that the dried root of Angelica (see chapter on herbs), taken in doses of 15 to 20 grains, will cause a disgust for all spirituous liquors.

A tea made from Stramonium (see chapter on herbs) leaves is claimed not only to cure or relieve the appetite for alcohol, but also for tobacco. This tea may be given in ordinary tea or coffee, oftentimes without the patient's knowledge.

B. Those wishing to stop the use of intoxicating drinks will find the following a most excellent substitute. It will relieve the catarrhal condition of the stomach, aid digestion, and give vigor and tone to a weakened or shattered nervous system:

> Strychnine Sulphate...................... 1 grain.
> Fowler's Solution.......................... 2 drachms.
> Lloyd's Hydrastus.......................... 4   "
> Tincture Chloride of Iron.............. 3   "
> Glycerine..................................... 2 ounces.
>
> Add enough water to make 4 ounces. *Mix*, and take one teaspoonful before or after each meal.

C. Aromatic Spirits of Ammonia, a teaspoonful or two in a glass of water, helps to sober up and overcome the depression following excesses. May be repeated in half an hour or an hour. (14.)

D. Hot bath daily; bowels kept open by the use of salts; Aromatic Spirits of Ammonia, a teaspoonful in a little milk every two or three hours.

E. Bromidia in teaspoonful doses in water every hour. To produce sleep and quiet nervousness, ¼ grain of Morphine Sulphate by hypodermic injection is good if some one can be depended upon to give it. Do not tell the patient he is being given Morphine.—(9.)

Note.—Morphine is only to help the patient to get sobered, and is not to be continued.

F. Bromide of Soda............................. 10 grains.
    Bromide of Potash....................... 10   "
    Bromide of Ammonia...................... 10   "

    Mix.—Dissolve in water and take every two or three hours until relieved.– (22).

G. Total abstinence, with 20-grain doses of Bromide of Potash every three hours more or less often as needed to control the nervous system.—(7.)

H Celerina (proprietary).............. 3 ounces.
    Comp. Tincture Cinchona......... 3   "
    Tincture Nux Vomica............... 2   "
    Fowler's Solution.................. 1½ drachms.

    Dose.—Teaspoonful in water three times a day, before meals.

                or,
    Peacock's Bromides....................... 4 ounces

    Dose.—Teaspoonful in water three times a day, between meals and at bedtime.—(20.)

I. Sulphate of Iron.......................... 1 drachm.
    Magnesia 2   "
    Peppermint Water................... .. 12   "
    Nutmeg 12   "

    Dose.—Two teaspoonfuls, twice daily, after breakfast and supper.

This is a tonic and stimulant, and has proven beneficial in numerous cases. –(70.)

Note.—Dr. Burns states, in giving this remedy, that it cured of drunkenness the father of no less a personage than the celebrated divine, Rev. Newman Hall.

Dutchman's Temperance Lecture—Short, but Sound Common Sense.—"I shall tell you how it vas I drunk my lager; den I put mine hand on my head, and dere vas one pain. Den I puts mine hand on my body, and dere vas pain. Den I puts my hand on my pocket, and dere vas notting. So I jine mit de Demperance. Now dere is no pain in my head, and de pain in my body vas all gone away. I put mine hand on mine pocket, and dere vas 20 dollars. So I stay mit de Demperance beeples."

Delirium Tremens.—This is an incident in *chronic alco-holism*, and occurs in consequence either of unusual excesses or the withdrawal for a short time of the accustomed stimulus. It is the result of exhaustion of the nerve functions and consequent irritation of the brain.

Symptoms.—The delirium itself is usually preceded by two or three days of mental depression and restlessness, during which the patient is peevish and irritable and his sleep disturbed; or he may suffer from loss of appetite and nausea, and perhaps vomit occasionally. He is greatly dejected, and is haunted with a sense of impending danger or misfortune. As delirium develops he talks incessantly, mingling the real with the imaginary, his ravings frequently becoming unintelligible through a trembling of the tongue. There is a rapid pulse, a tremor of the muscles of the limbs, a fidgeting of the hands, a constant activity of the body and utter sleeplessness. Bodily and mentally he is busy day and night. He suffers from one delusion after another, being haunted with spectres, threatened with dangers, attacked by enemies, and at times covered with loathsome objects, as reptiles, vermin, etc., which he is unable to shake off. These symptoms continue until sleep is produced or the patient sinks from exhaustion. If he is unable to obtain refreshing sleep in four or five days, the disease is likely to terminate fatally.

TREATMENTS.—

What to Do.—Put the patient to bed and keep him as quiet as possible. It is a good idea to give a little hot sling—just enough to keep the brain slightly stimulated—but not to give it more than once a day. Bromide of Potassium may be given in from 5 to 10-grain doses, or a doctor may be called for further treatment.

In cases where delirium comes on while a man is still carrying on his long-continued debauch, there will generally be a greater determination of blood to the head than in the ordinary cases arising after a debauch has been discontinued for a short time. In this case there must be the most active derivative treatment to draw the blood away from the head, such as the feet in water as hot as it can be borne, with mustard in it, mustard plasters to the feet and back of the neck, sponging with strong cayenne whiskey, an active cathartic, etc., this to be followed with quieting treatment. A warm bath continued from three hours even to ten hours, with cold applications to the head, has proven a very successful remedy, patients often falling asleep in the bath.

A person suffering from delirium tremens is not to be trusted alone for a moment, as he is liable to injure himself by jumping out of a window, or in some other way, to free himself from his imaginary enemies.

A. Force feeding with strong coffee, soups and milk or beef tea. Get patient in quiet place and to sleep if possible. If stomach will hold, give 20 grains of Bromide of Potash every two hours till quiet. Keep bowels open. Give ginger and pepper tea. No whiskey. Or give teaspoonful Tincture of Cinchona Compound in water every two or three hours.—(No. 13.)

B. Teaspoonful doses of Tincture of Capsicum. Milk diet. 20-grain doses of Bromide of Potash, taken in water every three or four hours.—(No. 7.)

ALCOHOL.

In making the following statements concerning the effects of alcohol upon the human system, the aim has been to confine the thought entirely to the diseased changes produced upon the various tissues and organs by the continued use of alcoholic stimulants. The statements are not overdrawn, the object being to give the facts.

Alcohol is absorbed from the stomach into the circulation. No change takes place in the alcohol in the stomach; it circulates in the blood as alcohol, and in this diluted state it comes in direct contact with the tissues and inflames them. Its first effect is upon the nervous system.

Nerves of the Blood Vessels.—The nerves which govern the size of the blood vessels become paralyzed, the small vessels become relaxed and dilated, and the organs are flooded with blood which they do not need. The cells and organs receiving this increased blood supply become larger and, as a result, new cells begin to form. They develop by a division of the parent cells, and thus there is an increase in tissue. This new growth lacks quality, as alcohol is never a true tonic. The individual is bloated and the flesh is flabby. The effect is deceitful and superficial, and the alcohol steadily saps the vital forces and undermines the constitution.

Connective Tissue.—The new tissue mentioned is a form of connective tissue. As naturally supplied, connective tissue develops with the growth of the individual and acts as a framework for all the structures of the body. When resulting from inflammation, however, it invariably contracts. As the contraction continues, the unyielding pressure on surrounding tissues causes a shrinkage in the size of the organ it envelops, and the functions of that organ are correspondingly interfered with.

The Stomach.—Commencing with the stomach, where the first effects of alcohol are produced, the little glands of the lining membrane, which collect from the passing blood stream certain materials and transform them into digestive ferments (see *Diges-tion*), are squeezed and pressed out of shape. Some are entirely obliterated, others are closed, the openings of others are narrowed or closed, and they become useless. Many glands that are not destroyed may have some of their secreting cells destroyed. The stomach may be dilated and may contain more or less fluid, but the secretions are changed in quality and the digestive fluids are lessened. It contains too much mucus, and chronic dyspepsia is the result. This is proven by the morning vomiting of drunkards and by post mortem examinations.

The Liver. — The same change takes place in other parts : First in the liver, because the alcohol is carried direct to that organ from the stomach. The changes in the liver are practically the same as in the stomach, *i. e.*, first overgrowth of connective tissue and then shrinkage of the organ, and the cause is the same —chronic inflammation. The shrinkage of the liver prevents more or less the return of the blood that passes through it. This return circulation comes from the stomach, digestive tract, spleen, etc.; and as the blood is forced back to these organs, the changes in the stomach are increased and congestion and inflammation of other organs follow. There results diarrhea, enlarged spleen, piles, abdominal dropsy, or more than one of these conditions may exist at the same time. This disease is called *cirrhosis*, or *sclerosis* of the liver, meaning a hardening. It is also called *hob-nailed liver*, *rum-drinker's liver*, *whiskey liver*, etc. With the single exception of syphilis, this disease can only be produced by alcohol and is frequently met with in habitual drunkards.

During the early stages of inflammation, liver abscess may form, and death may occur before the liver has had time to shrink.

The Kidneys.—The effect of alcohol upon the kidneys is much the same as upon the liver, and is the most chronic of all forms of kidney disease. The blood vessels supplying the kidneys are large in proportion to the size of the organs. This subjects them to a proportionately large amount of the irritating effects of alcohol, hence their great liability to disease.

The whole organ becomes shrunken, and the outer portion is nearly obliterated. This is also called *sclerosis*. It is one form of Bright's Disease and is most often produced by alcohol.

The Heart. — Blood cannot circulate freely through the kidneys, as many small vessels have been destroyed, hence it is crowded into other channels. This renders them full and tense, and the heart beat is increased in proportion. The heart is enlarged, and the muscle fibres of the small arteries throughout the whole body are increased as a result of the extra strain upon them.

Fatty Degeneration of the heart may and does follow the low form of inflammation produced by alcohol. Gradually the cells of which the organ is formed lose their vitality, degenerate and are changed more or less into fat. The muscle fibres become indistinct, and the tissues are soft and easily torn.

The Arteries.—Degeneration of the walls of the arteries takes place, *i.e.*, many cells change more or less to fat. While in this condition the cells constituting the arteries are unable to exert their selective power, and lime salts are frequently deposited. These salts are always present in the circulation, but in health are prevented from entering the walls of the blood vessels. Any disturbance of the nervous system leaves the tissues without proper support, and the individual cells are unable to absorb proper nourishment. The larger arteries are comparatively free from danger, because their walls are thicker and stronger. The medium-sized arteries are most affected—those of the upper and lower extremities and those supplying the brain. Ultimately some of these vessels become changed into a hard, brittle tube, like the stem of a clay pipe.

In amputation such arteries are secured with difficulty, as the ligature or thread with which they are tied is liable to cut through. This condition of the arteries is the principal cause of *apoplexy*, as in their diseased condition any strain, heavy lifting, or sudden bending forward, may so increase the blood pressure as to cause rupture of such vessels in the brain. Aneurism (see *Aneurism*) or Aortic Stenosis (see *Stenosis*) may also occur.

Brain and Spinal Cord. — Upon the brain and spinal cord alcohol produces the same effect as upon other organs or tissues : First, congestion; second, a low form of inflammation, followed by an overgrowth of connective tissue. The contraction of this tissue produces hardening here as elsewhere.

The contraction of the connective tissue in the brain and cord causes pressure upon the nerves, nerve cells and surrounding tissue, obliterates many small vessels, interferes with nutrition, and the result is hardening and loss of function. The hardening is called sclerosis. This is responsible for many forms of spinal paralysis, and may be caused by alcohol or other irritants.

Bronchial Tubes, etc.—Alcohol also produces a low form of inflammation of the mucous membrane lining the bronchial tubes and air cells of the lungs. This is called chronic bronchitis. Alcohol produces the same changes here as elsewhere. At first the mucous membrane is congested and thickened, the calibre or size of the air tubes is lessened, and the secretions are increased by reason of the increased amount of blood. This produces irritation and cough, and more or less expectoration of thick, tenacious mucus.

The same catarrhal condition may be produced in the mucous membrane of the digestive tract, causing chronic diarrhea. Chronic catarrh may also result.

Absorption of Water. —Alcohol absorbs water from every part of the body, and this is the reason so much water is needed after drinking liquor. Alcohol also extracts water from the blood corpuscles, leaving them shrunken. The absorption of water causes condensation and hardening of all the tissues. This is most marked in the brain because the brain requires so much blood and contains so much alcohol. The brain is the seat of reason, judgment, memory, emotion, sympathy, charity, love, etc., but the effects of alcohol bring these noble qualities to the brute level.

Delirium tremens is caused by alcohol, which absorbs so much water from the brain tissues. As the brain shrivels and shrinks, and the vessels become irregular, the optic nerve, or nerve of sight, becomes so drawn and bent that it transmits to the brain tortuous, grotesque and frightful objects, while the excitement of the victim is the result of the poison acting as an irritant. For a time the user of alcohol lives fast in a physical sense, and enjoys animal exhilaration, but while he is doing this, the changes already described are taking place—slowly, but surely. It is true that it may require several years to produce the change in some people, while in others the same condition is produced in a shorter time; but sooner or later these changes occur in all who continue the use of alcohol.

AMENORRHEA.—(See under DISEASES OF WOMEN).

AMYLOID DEGENERATION. — (See DISEASES OF LIVER).

ANÆMIA.—In this disease there is a deficiency in the number of the red corpuscles of the blood. The corpuscles present contain the normal amount of coloring matter, but for some reason their number is diminished. There are two forms of this disease —*Anæmia* and *Pernicious Anæmia*. *Ischæmia* is localized Anæmia. The last is generally due to the sudden shutting off of the blood supply.

Causes.—Anæmia may result from deficient food supply or improper food, lack of fresh air, want of sunshine, a scrofulous tendency or disposition, overwork, unhygienic surroundings, or indigestion followed by a catarrhal condition of the stomach and bowels; or may follow protracted fevers, ulcer of the stomach, or Bright's Disease. See *Pernicious Anæmia*, following.

Symptoms.—The patient is pale, weak and irritable; the lips look bloodless, and the conjunctiva, or mucous membrane which lines the eyelids, is pale and white looking; there is loss of appetite, dyspepsia, and may be acid fermentation in the stomach and eructations; at times there may be nausea and vomiting. There may also be dizziness or fainting, or palpitation of the heart. The palpitation, when it occurs, is sympathetic, and is the result of the condition of the stomach. The heart and stomach lie in close relation and the same nerves supply both organs.

TREATMENTS.—

A. In this disease the blood lacks the normal elements as a result of indigestion and constipation, and contains many impurities; hence the treatment consists wholly in regulating the condition of the bowels and in nourishing food, never forgetting an abundance of fresh air and regular habits. The remedies which may be used in this disease are Iron, and Fowler's Solution. Blaud's Pills in 5-grain doses after meals are recommended by some, and are undoubtedly of value. We recommend as an excellent combination the following :

Lloyd's Hydrastus.........................	3	drachms.
Tincture of Chloride of Iron...........	6	"
Fowler's Solution..........................	2	"
Glycerine....................................	1½	ounce.
Simple Elixir, enough to make......	4	"

Mix, and take one teaspoonful three times a day, after meals.

Iodide of Arsenic is also a good remedy; if substituted for the foregoing, the dose should be 1-50 of a grain, taken between meals and at bedtime.

If the *heart* is troublesome, give 2 drops of Fluid Extract of Digitalis three or four times a day, or less often; or give 2 grains of Caffeine every three hours, or as needed. Give either one of these often enough to keep the heart regular.

For the *digestive tract*, give 10 grains of Salol after meals and at bed time—four doses a day.

If *constipation* is present, give 15 drops of Fluid Extract of Cascara in the morning, or morning and night. This amount may be increased or diminished to suit the case. Before giving the Cascara, give 1-5 of a grain of Calomel every hour until two grains have been taken, and if while giving the Cascara the liver seems to be inactive, give an occasional ¼-of-a-grain dose of Podophyllin. This amount may be given every night, if necessary. It will not be necessary to continue the Calomel.

If there is *headache* or *dizziness*, give one pill or tablet of Aconitine Amorphus, 1-100 grain, every one or two hours.

If there are *neuralgic pains*, give one pill or tablet—1-250 of a grain—of Gelsemine every thirty minutes until it takes effect. If the eyelids become heavy and droop, it is from the effects of the Gelsemine, and if continued, the amount of the dose should be decreased or taken less often.

B. The successful treatment of anæmia demands pure, dry air; a wholesome, mixed diet, adapted to the digestive powers; daily moderate and cheering exercise; a daily stimulating and cleansing bath; and the employment of such medicines as strengthen the digestive organs and improve the quality of the blood. Flannel should be used next the skin, and should be changed frequently. The following may be used with advantage:

Caulophyllin.	2 scruples.
Ptelea...	2 "
Strychnia....................................	1 grain.
Extract Dandelion......................	2 scruples.

This should be mixed and formed into about forty pills, one of which should be taken three times a day, an hour before eating. In connection with this take the following:

Ammonia-Citrate of Iron............. ½ ounce.

Dissolve in two ounces of water, and add two ounces of Lemon Syrup. Take a teaspoonful half an hour after each meal.

This treatment should be persevered in, especially the Iron, for sometime after all anæmic symptoms have disappeared.

ANÆMIA, PERNICIOUS OR PROGRESSIVE.—In the pernicious form all of the conditions which produce the ordinary anæmia are exaggerated.

Cause.—There has never been any cause given for this disease, yet we wish to state what seems to us to be a reasonable cause for this ailment. First, however, we will enumerate the

Symptoms. — The disease comes on without warning. First there is languor and constipation, followed by palpitation of the heart, difficult breathing, dizziness, fainting, poor appetite, nausea and vomiting; later there is fever and disturbance of sight. The patient is thin and weak. There are degenerative changes in the arteries and in the marrow of long bones, fatty degeneration of the liver and spleen, and rupture of small vessels just beneath the skin causes hemorrhage and gives the skin a mottled appearance. There are also hemorrhagic spots in the liver and kidneys, and degeneration of the heart muscles.

This condition and all of these symptoms indicate a lack of nourishment from some cause—poor food, dyspepsia, or bad hygiene. We believe the greatest cause to be the unhealthy condition of the digestive tract. There are four avenues of elimination for the waste material in the body: One is the lungs, poison being eliminated by the air cells and tubes. Carbonic acid gas is given off through this channel, also 1½ pints of fluid in the form of watery vapor, every 24 hours. This vapor contains many poisons, the nature of which is not known. Another avenue is the skin. Many waste materials are eliminated through the pores of the skin. Another avenue is the kidneys. The kidneys eliminate many waste products, the principal one being urea, a deadly poison. The remaining channel for elimination is the digestive tract, but elimination by this route is checked, and the constipation allows degenerative changes to go on, resulting in the production of many poisons. These are absorbed more or less into the circulation, gradually the system becomes permeated with the impurities, and gradually the patient is brought under their lowering tendencies. This condition would not only account for pernicious anæmia, but for typhoid fever, consumption, cancer, softening of the brain, and any and all chronic diseases. The primary, or first cause, is dyspepsia, followed by constipation and lack of elimination, as stated.

TREATMENT.—

First, cause thorough elimination by the digestive tract by means of cathartics, and also flush the bowels with large injections of warm water. Give ten doses of Calomel, 1-5 of a grain each, every 30 minutes, and follow with one or two tablespoonfuls of Laxol (see *Index*). Arrange for good ventilation, see that the surroundings are all made clean and wholesome, and give frequent feedings of the most nutritious food. If there is evidence of dyspepsia, give artificial digestants (see *Index*). Give 1 teaspoonful of Bovinine with each meal, increasing the dose to 2 or 3 teaspoonfuls if the patient does not object. Give 1-50 of a grain of Iodide of Arsenic three times a day, between meals and at bedtime, or perhaps a better remedy would be the following:

Tincture of Chloride of Iron .... ½ ounce.
Fowler's Solution........................ 3 drachms.
Glycerine................................... 2 ounces.
Simple Elixir, enough to make 4   "

Mix, and take 1 teaspoonful after meals.

Give 10 grains of Salol four times a day. Give frequent baths, keeping the skin clean and healthy. Following the baths rub the surface lightly each time. Cod Liver Oil may be applied to the skin after each bath, or, if the odor is objectionable, Sweet Oil instead. This will relieve the friction and allow massage to go on to greater lengths; also the oil that is absorbed is digested and appropriated by the system.

ANASARCA.—(See under DROPSY).

ANEURISM.—Aneurism is a tumor formed by the bulging of an artery. The artery may become weakened at some point, as described under *Atheroma*, or aneurism may be the result of violent exercise or heavy lifting. The force of the circulation may be brought so direct as to cause slight bulging, which gradually develops into a large tumor. This sac formation, small at first, gradually becomes larger, as with each heart beat the blood is driven into it with greater force. It may occur on any artery, but usually occurs on one of the larger arteries.

Cause.—Aneurism may be caused by diseased arteries, such as result from syphilis, alcohol, old age, or any condition where there is mild inflammation long continued, as described under atheroma. It may also result from Bright's disease, from violent exercise, from heavy lifting, or from the formation of an abscess near an artery.

Symptoms. — The most prominent symptom of aneurism is a pulsating tumor. By making pressure upon the artery above the tumor, that is, on the side toward the heart, the tumor will disappear, showing that the blood has drained away; by making pressure below the tumor, or on the side farthest from the heart, the tumor will become larger as the blood is gradually pumped into it. These tumors also produce a peculiar whirring sound. They may form on the aorta, that is, the large artery that is given off from the lower left cavity of the heart and which is the beginning of the arterial system. If the tumor forms in the chest cavity, it may cause pressure upon the nerves which supply the lungs, and will cause cough; if it presses upon the nerve which supplies the heart, it may excite or depress the heart's action; if it presses upon the nerve that supplies the organ of voice, it will cause hoarseness. The same nerves supply all of these organs. They pass down, one on either side of the neck, and enter the chest cavity. Aneurism may exist for a limited time without noticeable symptoms, but as the tumor grows it presses upon and wears away any and all tissues with which it may come in contact. It wears away bone as well as soft tissue.

Treatment:—

The first object should be to secure quiet. The patient should rest as much as possible. If the aneurism is not large, the patient can be around, but lying down several hours a day will be of great benefit. When we remember that the number of heart beats is from 20 to 30 less to the minute while lying down, we can readily understand the advantage of this suggestion, because the whole object is to lessen the circulation and lessen both the frequency and force of the heart beat. It is only by this means that any relief can be secured. A very low diet is also of great benefit. Veratrum and Aconite are given internally in 1-drop doses every hour with a view to slowing the heart's action and lessening the force of the pulse. Mechanical pressure is also used. When the aneurism is favorably located, by making pressure above it, on the side toward the heart, the circulation is brought to such a low ebb that the aneurism remains nearly empty. If the disease is the result of syphilis, anti-syphilitic treatment should be given. If the artery is on an arm or a leg, and all other means fail, the artery may be tied above the aneurism, thus shutting off the blood pressure. Should gangrene follow the tying of an artery, amputation would be necessary.

ANGINA PECTORIS. — (See under DISEASES OF THE HEART).

DISEASES OF THE ANUS.

The anus is the lowest part, or termination, of the bowel. It is surrounded by muscular fibres, called *sphincter ani*, which keep the orifice closed when the bowels are not to be evacuated. It is subject to

Fissures,
Fistulas,
Hemorrhoids, or Piles,
Prolapsus Ani.

Itching.—An annoying itching is often felt at the anus, for which the best treatment is to keep the parts very clean with good soap and water, and to take internally Sulphur and Cream of Tartar. Also the application of an ointment made of Carbolic Acid in the proportion of ½ teaspoonful of Carbolic Acid to ½ pound of fresh lard, will stop the itching and burning so common in diseases of the anus.

FISSURE OF THE ANUS.—An ulceration of the anus.

Cause.—There are various causes which may result in such an abscess, among which are constipation and piles.

Symptoms.—In case of a *fissure* the pain attendant upon evacuation continues for several hours instead of a short time, as in the case of piles.

TREATMENT.—

Fissure should be treated by a physician. The treatment recommended below is the proper one, but really requires a physician to make the application.

A. Clean the parts thoroughly and touch up the cracks with Nitrate of Silver. If this does not cure, have the parts stretched under Ether. (1C).

FISTULA.—An unnatural passage leading from the skin or mucous membrane to any other surface. Occurring in the bowel, it is simply the track of an unhealed ulcer.

Cause.—In a rectal fistula the ulcer is the result of constipation or injury; usually the former. The pressure from the dry and hardened fæces produces irritation and inflammation to such an extent that an ulcer forms. This may be one, two, three or four inches above the external opening; usually it is about two and one-half inches above. Suppuration continues, extending toward and usually appearing upon the surface. Where the pus burrows through until an opening is made on the surface, the fistula is spoken of as *complete;* if it does not reach the surface, it is spoken of as a *blind* or *incomplete* fistula.

Symptoms.—The most prominent symptom is the passage of fæces through the false opening. There is also a feeling of uneasiness and, sometimes, more or less pain, although the pain and burning sensation are not so marked as in fissure.

Treatment.—

The first part of the treatment only belongs to the patient to perform for himself, and consists in taking an active cathartic, and, after the bowels have moved thoroughly, to wash out the lower bowel with an abundance of water—two or three quarts. A physician will then pass a groove-director through the external opening into the bowel, cut through to the surface and make provision for dressing the wound.

HEMORRHOIDS—PILES. — Piles are tumors situated about the anus or just within the rectum. The former are *external piles*, the latter, *internal piles*. Both varieties may exist at the same time. In some cases these tumors break and blood is discharged from them, in which case they are spoken of as *bleeding piles;* if there is no discharge of blood, and they remain internal, they are spoken of as *blind piles*.

Cause.—What seems to be an imperfection in the anatomical structure of the veins surrounding the rectum is the primary cause of this trouble. The veins throughout the body and lower extremities are well supplied with little valves which prevent a return of the blood, but for some unknown reason those surrounding the rectum are not thus supplied. The absence of these valves favors congestion, and the veins gradually bulge until small sacs are formed. Everything that irritates the lower bowel, as strong physics, habitual costiveness and any of the causes which tend to produce it, as straining at stools, etc., will cause an increase of blood in this part and a consequent congestion, and piles are the usual result.

Symptoms. — Pain, often a burning sensation, and a protrusion of the pile. Usually there is hemorrhage, which may be slight or very profuse. If the hemorrhoids are large and remain internal, there will be a constant desire to evacuate the bowels for the reason that the sensation is the same as though the mass consisted of fecal matter. An examination will reveal the true condition.

TREATMENTS.—

All conditions are benefited by the free use of intestinal antiseptics: 10 grains of the Sulphocarbolate of Soda in tablet form, or the same amount of Salol, either in tablet form or powder, should be taken four times a day. To insure greater regularity of bowel movement, avoid meats and all heavy foods for supper It is a well established fact that by eating light suppers difficulties of constipation are more readily overcome.

Local Applications:

A. The following ointment will be found of value in many cases of piles:

Vaseline.. 1 ounce.
Nut-Galls, pulverized........ .... 80 grains.
Pulverized Opium........................... ½ drachm.

Put on a plate and mix together thoroughly with a case-knife or something of the kind. Use after each movement of the bowels.

If the bowel comes down, put it back, carrying it up with the index finger as far as possible. This will cure simple piles, but in case of fistula or hemorrhoids it will be necessary to have a surgical operation.

B. Tincture of Iodine........................... 10 drops.
Carbolic Acid.................................. 10 "
Morphine Sulphate....................... 5 grains.
Nut-Galls, powdered...................... 80 "
Lanoline, enough to make........... 1 ounce.
(80).

C. Flour of Sulphur........................... 2 ounces.
Nut-Galls, powdered..................... 1 "
Opium, powdered........................ 1 drachm.

Add lard enough to make a paste and mix thoroughly. (63.)

D. Tannic Acid................................. 15 grains.
Borax, powdered........................... 10 "
Carbolic Acid............................... 20 drops.
Vaseline....................................... 2 ounces.

Mix, and apply to piles two or three times each day. Keep bowels regular with mild laxatives. (42.)

E. Take the inner bark of the white oak tree, boil and strain, and boil again until you obtain ½ pint of the extract, very thick; then add ½ pint of oil of the oldest and strongest bacon you can procure; simmer together until a union takes place when cold. Apply by the finger up the rectum every night Abstain from strong and stimulating diet.

While the foregoing remedies are recommended as the most satisfactory methods of palliative treatment, a cure cannot be promised by their use. After the sacs have once formed, local treatment is uncertain. In many cases it will relieve, and possibly in some cases effect a cure. The only *sure* treatment, however, is the injection method or removal with the knife. The latter requires anesthetics and two weeks in bed; the injection method requires neither, and does not interfere with the occupation whatever it may be. The injections are made by the use of a hypodermic needle, and the treatment would, therefore, almost necessarily belong to a physician to perform.

PROLAPSUS ANI.—A falling of the lower intestine, which is sometimes protruded from the body at great length.

Cause.—This trouble occurs in weak and delicate children and is the result of general debility. The whole system is relaxed, and the sphincter muscle, which in health guards the external opening to the bowel, loses its sensitiveness and power to control. The connective tissue support is relaxed and weakened along the digestive tract, and the prolapse is simply the result of gravitation.

TREATMENT.—

The bowels should be kept regular, and a small quantity of cold water should be injected into the rectum each time before the bowels move. This contracts the tissues, is stimulating in its effects, and tends to prevent the trouble. When prolapse occurs, the part should be carefully replaced; usually this may be done without much trouble. The child should lie down with the hips elevated, and Sweet Oil or Vaseline be applied, as it will facilitate movement. Now carry the part inward carefully, by the finger. If this does not succeed, wrap a thin, soft cloth about the finger. The surface of the bowel adheres to the cloth, hence is more rapidly replaced. If the bowel is exposed for any great length, the part should first be bathed with cold water. This contracts the tissues. Now apply the Sweet Oil, elevate the hips, and stand the child on its head, if necessary; but usually there is no trouble.

APHASIA.—Aphasia means partial or complete loss of the power of expression. The patient may not be able to recall words, or may not be able to comprehend words, either written or spoken. In that variety of Aphasia known as *ataxic*, the patient is unable to control the muscles of the face and mouth. This disease, or these difficulties result from some lesion or imperfection in the brain. There is no danger to life, and they are not amenable to treatment other than good hygienic surroundings and the usual attention to proper habits and principles.

APHONIA.—Aphonia means the loss of voice, partial or complete. Partial loss of voice may be caused by any interference with the nerves that supply the larynx, or organ of voice. This is a branch of a nerve that rises in the back part of the brain, passes down the neck into the chest and supplies the lungs, heart and stomach. Interference with this nerve, or with the branch that supplies the organ of voice, may be caused by tumors, by an aneurism, by tuberculosis of the vocal chords, or by cancer of the throat. A temporary cause may be, and usually is, the paralysis that follows diphtheria. In the absence of some local cause, the lesion or difficulty must be in the brain.

TREATMENT.—

Tuberculosis of the vocal chords may be benefited by treatment, but this treatment would have to be applied by a physician. There might be a temporary relief afforded in *cancer* of the throat by spraying with antiseptic solutions. The *aneurism* (for treatment, see under ANEURISM) or the *tumor* would be found in close relation to the jugular vein, either in the neck or high up in the chest cavity.

For a *tumor*, the probable treatment is removal, or tying of the arteries that supply it. This would necessitate an operation. Before resorting to surgical means, however, the following treatment may be given a trial:

Local applications of Iodine should be made and the patient should take large doses of Iodine internally, as 2 teaspoonfuls of Syrup of Hydriodic Acid between meals and at bed time; or, 12 to 15 drops of Tincture of Iodine in ½ glass of milk taken instead. The dose of Acid or Iodine should be increased until the eyes present a catarrhal condition. This is an indication that the patient is taking all the system will bear. He should then go back to half the dose and gradually increase as before. If there is no improvement at the end of four weeks, an operation is justifiable.

APOPLEXY.— A disease characterized by the sudden loss of the power of sense and motion. The name is derived from certain Greek words which mean a striking or knocking down, inasmuch as the subject of it falls to the ground unconscious as if he had received a violent blow.

Cause. — It is caused by pressure on the brain substance, resulting from the rupture of an artery. Men are more subject to it than women, and those attacked usually have short necks and corpulent figures. Excesses in diet and alcoholic drinks are predisposing causes, also Bright's disease and syphilis.

Symptoms. — There are three forms of attack. A person seized with the first form falls suddenly in a state of insensibility, breathes heavily with a snoring sound, pulse full and strong, face generally flushed, body covered with a clammy sweat, veins of the head and temples standing out as though overfilled, and the eyes fixed and bloodshot. Sometimes convulsions occur, foam issuing from the mouth. The face is drawn toward one side.

In the second form the disease begins with a sudden pain in the head; the patient becomes pale, sick and faint, and usually vomits; the skin is cold and the pulse feeble; occasionally there are slight convulsions; the patient may or may not fall, but is likely to recover soon from all the symptoms except a headache, which will continue until after a time the patient becomes oppressed, forgetful, unable to connect ideas, and finally sinks into insensibility from which he never rouses. In some cases this form is accompanied with palsy of one side; in other cases no palsy occurs. While this form of attack does not appear so frightful as the first, it is of more serious import.

The third form is the sudden loss of power on one side of the body, also a loss of speech but not of consciousness; or, if the first attack is accompanied with stupor, it soon passes off. The patient appears rational and endeavors to answer questions and indicate his desires by signs. This may be called paralytic apoplexy, and in some cases it passes into apoplexy proper and the patient dies. In other cases, under proper treatment, he may recover rapidly, or the recovery may be gradual; or he may live for years with imperfect speech and the loss of the use of an arm or a leg.

TREATMENTS. —

What to Do Till the Doctor Comes. — Send for the doctor, and while waiting for him loosen the clothing, especially about the neck, raise the windows to give free circulation of air, prevent crowding about the patient, put the feet in hot water, as hot as ought to be borne, and apply a mustard plaster to the calf of the legs and along the spine, and, if the patient can swallow, give a large dose of Castor Oil or some active cathartic.

A. Keep patient in semi-erect resting posture. Apply cold to head and heat to extremities. If possible, give something to act thoroughly on the bowels. Mustard to back of neck. Send at once for doctor.—(14.)

B. Apply cold application to the head. Put cord around arm, three inches above elbow, and draw it down tightly. When the large vein just below the cord is tense and full, cut with a sharp pointed knife, and when one pint or a pint and a half of blood is taken, remove cord and put a compress on the wound, or hold with finger pressed on it. Use a clean knife.—(9.)

C. Tincture of Aconite, 15 drops in ½ a glass of cold water. Give 2 teaspoonfuls every half hour until improvement sets in, then every hour or two hours. I have been very successful with this for over thirty years.—(18.)

Persons who have a tendency towards apoplexy, and especially those who have had one stroke, should avoid highly seasoned food and stimulating drinks. If an immediate attack is feared, use frequent cathartics, say twice a week, eat plain food, drink no spirits, use cool baths for the head and hot ones for the feet, and take plenty of out-of-door exercise, but avoiding fatigue, excitement, or over-exertion.

APPENDICITIS.—The appendix is a narrow tube, usually from two to four inches in length, and in diameter about the size of a goose quill, or a little larger. It is situated in the abdominal cavity, rather low down and toward the right side. It is attached to the back part of the cæcum. The cæcum is the somewhat dilated commencement of the large bowel. Appendicitis is inflammation of the appendix. The attached end of the appendix opens into the cæcum and the outer end is closed. Sometimes appendicitis occurs more than once in the same person. This is called *recurrent appendicitis.* The appendix consists of a mucous lining, an outer and inner muscular coat and a peritoneal covering. These are all continuous with the structures of the cæcum, in fact, the appendix is merely a branch or offshoot of the cæcum, and its structure is the same. There is localized peritonitis in appendicitis, and in severe cases the tendency is toward the formation of an abscess.

An abscess always renders the case more grave, yet an abscess is the exception and not the rule, and even when it forms it is often, though not always, absorbed, that is, carried away by the circulation, and complete recovery follows. There is altogether too much excitement and fear regarding appendicitis. This is the natural result of the extravagance in operative procedures. If the price of operation was brought down to a reasonable limit, at least seventy-five per cent of the operations would cease at once.

Cause.—Many statements have been made and many theories advanced regarding appendicitis, yet the cause is not so mysterious. The first cause of appendicitis is indigestion; following this is unhealthy blood and an unhealthy condition of the digestive tract. Constipation results, with the production of many poisons and irritating substances. This condition produces a low form of inflammation, which extends along the digestive tract and into the appendix, and the secretions of this organ become unhealthy. The result may be simply a catarrhal condition which is so mild as to give no symptoms other than a few colicky pains, or the attack may extend all the way from this state to a more severe form, and even to death. Injury to the appendix, irritation from external causes, or any condition producing congestion and lowering the vitality of the organs will aid in producing appendicitis. It has been stated that the cæcum is the somewhat dilated commencement of the large bowel, and that the appendix is attached to and opens into the cæcum. When the food does not digest, it ferments, gases are formed, and the cæcum becomes dilated. When the cæcum dilates, the opening into the appendix is enlarged and the pressure of gases may force many substances into the appendix that never would have entered if this part of the digestive tract had been healthy. If the surgeon operates at this time, he makes the startling discovery that appendicitis was caused by—well, whatever he happens to find. Some irritating substance finding its way into the appendix may act as an exciting cause, but the *real* cause is excessive irritation produced by a diseased digestive tract. This results in inflammation, and, if the appendix is involved, it is appendicitis. Usually the attached end of the appendix remains open and the products of inflammation are discharged into the bowels. This is why ninety per cent of the cases recover without operation.

The condition of the mucous membrane of the appendix in appendicitis is the same as that of the bowel in diarrhea. The only danger is that the membrane may become so swollen that the attached end will be closed, in which case there would be no opportunity for drainage and the swelling and pressure would soon shut off circulation. This is the first step towards the formation of an abscess. The swelling and pressure may be so rapid and the circulation shut off so suddenly that gangrene will result in patches. This accounts for those exceptional cases where rupture occurs during the first 48 hours; the rupture follows the gangrene. These cases are fatal. An operation could have been performed early enough to save life, but the trouble is that a rupture is not expected so soon. These cases seldom occur.

Symptoms.—The symptoms are:

First, sudden onset of pain. This may occur in the region of the appendix, or anywhere in the abdominal cavity.

Second, nausea and, usually, vomiting.

Third, elevation of temperature, or fever.

Fourth, the localizing of the pain over the seat of the appendix, though later, in severe and even fatal cases, both pain and fever may disappear and the patient feel and appear comfortable. *Continued pain and soreness is not evidence of a severe case*; on the contrary, it is evidence that the case is not severe. The pain is the result of neuralgic conditions, while the soreness is simply evidence of a diseased digestive tract. When the appendix is attacked, the abdominal wall or muscles over that region may be more or less tense. This is Nature's effort to protect the parts beneath, yet these symptoms amount to little because this tension or resistance may be entirely wanting within a few days and yet the case prove a fatal one. *After the first onset the most severe and dangerous cases are attended with the fewest symptoms, as will be shown.*

When an abscess forms, there is usually thrown out a false membrane, forming a sack, which surrounds the appendix and encloses the pus. An abscess increases in size by the destruction of tissue from within outward, first destroying the walls of the appendix. In like manner the inflammation keeps extending further back, and always keeps outside the pus. This inflammatory zone constitutes the sack already mentioned which surrounds the appendix. If there should be an abscess within the appendix, and the appendix should rupture, the newly formed sack would hold the pus for a few days, when, if absorption did not take place, that is, if the pus was not carried away by the circulation, the sack too would rupture and allow the contents to pour into the cavity of the abdomen; the poison would then cause general peritonitis, and death would result. Sometimes the sack is wholly impervious, that is, completely retains the contents, which renders the disease purely local. In these cases, instead of the usual symptoms of abscess, such as chills, fever, etc., there are no marked symptoms; the temperature is about normal, there is no pain, and the patient may feel able to attend to his accustomed duties. These abscesses may escape detection from even the most experienced surgeon. Such cases should be operated upon, yet in many of these the real condition is not understood. The patient may seem to be making rapid progress toward recovery, when suddenly there is a change; the abscess has ruptured, the patient has collapsed, and in a few hours death closes the scene. We are aware that some surgeons may criticise our statement that they cannot always detect an abscess in the abdominal cavity when it is present, yet the foregoing is the result of our experience in the field of operation and we feel it our duty to state the facts.

Some physicians claim to cure all cases by medication; others contend that even after the abscess forms it is better to wait for one week, and then, if absorption does not take place, to operate; still others can see only one form of treatment for all cases, that is, operation. While the first is depending upon his medicine, and the second waiting for absorption, rupture may suddenly occur, with the results already described. In the case of the man who always operates, death may result from the operation itself, that is, the removal of the appendix from a healthy man will cause death in two or three per cent of cases.

If an operation reveals an abscess, and the appendix and surrounding structures are found firmly bound by inflammatory adhesions, it is good practice to wash out the abscess cavity and drain, and not persist in the efforts to tear the appendix loose, as such efforts might cause rupture into the abdominal cavity and this would be liable to result fatally.

TREATMENTS.—

What to Do Till the Doctor Comes. — As the pain in appendicitis is very severe, it is assumed that a doctor will be sent for immediately. In the meantime, however, much may be done to relieve the patient.

If a severe pain is felt in the right side of the abdomen, put a mustard plaster over the pain, and give injections of water as hot as can be borne, the water to be made slippery with soap— soft soap is really better for this purpose than castile. Or, take a tablespoonful of Turpentine and the yolk of two eggs, beat thoroughly together, put into a quart of hot water, and use that. The latter makes an excellent injection as it serves to draw the gas from the bowels. Also give warm drinks—some balm tea. Catnip tea, or something of that kind, is soothing and quieting to the nerves, and gets the patient to sweating. Of course, he will be put to bed. In place of the mustard plaster, cloths may be wrung out of a hot decoction of some bitter herb (as Smartweed, Wormwood, Tansy, etc.), and applied hot.

A. Perfect quiet and a good physician.—(4.)

B. Take a tablespoonful of Epsom Salts in a goblet of hot water. Apply hot fomentations and send for a doctor. Keep constantly in a reclining position.—(14.)

C. Send for a surgeon. In the meantime Epsom Salts, tablespoonful in water every three hours until bowels move freely. Do not give an opiate.—(19.)

APTHÆ.—(See under DISEASES OF CHILDREN).

ASCITES.—(See under DROPSY).

ASTHMA.—Asthma is paroxysmal, and is usually a chronic disorder or disease of the organs of respiration (breathing).

Cause.—The exact cause of this disease has never been satisfactorily determined. It is believed by some to be hereditary, but it may start from diseases of the lining membrane of the nasal passages. It may be caused by sudden changes from a dry to a damp atmosphere. It is seldom entirely cured.

Symptoms.—It is characterized by extreme difficulty in breathing and an oppressive sense of suffocation. There is wheezing, and a distressing tightness about the chest. The trouble usually comes on quite suddenly, sometimes in a few hours. After the first attack the sufferer has warning symptoms of its approach. These warnings are the symptoms proper, only in a milder form. During the attack the face is usually flushed, and spasm of the respiratory muscles may exclude the air from the lungs to the extent that *cyanosis* may result. In cyanosis the patient turns blue, the eyeballs become prominent, and the respiratory muscles, especially those of the neck, become distended. In some cases respiration becomes a mere gasp as the poor victim struggles for breath. The attack may last for a few hours only, or for a whole day or night, or both.

TREATMENTS.—

What to Do Before a Doctor is Called.—If one is subject to asthma, he should have on hand, to take when a paroxysm occurs, the following:

> Ipecac, powdered (or the crushed root)...................................... 1 drachm.
> Bloodroot, powdered (or the crushed root)............................ ½ "
> Lobelia Seeds, crushed (or the leaves)..................................... 2 "

Mix these three ingredients together, then fill a coffee cup (about one-half pint) one-third full of white sugar, or say half full, drop in the mixture and stir all together thoroughly with a spoon. Fill the cup nearly full of boiling water. Pour it out of a teakettle that has been boiling, turning it in slowly and stirring thoroughly with a spoon at the same time. Continue to stir it occasionally as long as the water remains warm, then set it to one side and let it settle. When thoroughly settled, strain. During a paroxysm, take a teaspoonful of this liquid every fifteen or twenty minutes until sick at the stomach. By that time the lungs will have relaxed and the person be comfortable. Probably the second dose will be sufficient to relieve him.

NOTE.—If the above mixture is put into a bottle, corked tight and set in a cool place, it will keep four or five weeks. By adding one or two ounces of Glycerine to each pint, the mixture, bottled, will keep for months.

A. The following is a most excellent remedy to take between the attacks of asthma:

Nitrate of Strychnine..................... ⅓ grain.
Sulphate of Atropine..................... 1–20 "
Glonoin... 1–10 "
Glycerine...................................... 2 ounces.
Simple Elixir............................... 2 "

Mix, and take one teaspoonful before meals and at bedtime.

In case of threatened attack, take one teaspoonful every hour until the throat is dry or the face flushed; then take one teaspoonful every two or three hours for a few doses.

The Strychnine is a systemic or general tonic; the Atropine dilates the small vessels, brings the blood to the surface, relieves congestion, and is one of the best remedies to relieve muscular spasm. Glonoin produces the same effect on the circulation and is also a powerful heart stimulant, but has no direct action upon the muscles involved.

This remedy has recently been tried by us in some severe cases, and been uniformly successful. It is by reason of this success that we feel justified in recommending it to our friends across the water. (62.)

B. Pulverized Lobelia....................... 1 drachm.
Sulphuric Ether.......................... 1 ounce.

Mix, and let stand two weeks, shaking the mixture every day.

Use.—Pour 15 or 20 drops on a handkerchief and inhale through mouth and nose. Should relieve asthma in three minutes. If not, repeat the inhaling process. (58.)

C. Dried Mullein leaves, soaked in a strong solution of Nitre (Saltpetre) and again dried. Smoke in a pipe and inhale the smoke, or inhale from a saucer.

To an adult, 25 drops of Laudanum. Inhalation of steam. Keep room well ventilated. (14.)

D. Oil of Lobelia.............................. 1 drachm.
Potass Iodide............................. 3 "
Water... 3 ounces.
Syrup... 3 "

Mix and dissolve.

Dose: A teaspoonful three or four times a day. (8.)

E. Inhalation of fumes from Jamestown weed. (60.)

F. If the spasmodic action is very considerable, and has arisen soon after a full meal, let an emetic (see *Emetics*) be at once given. Probably the best emetic in this case would be

Ipecac, the dose of which would be one teaspoonful of the powder, or a teaspoonful of the fluid extract, or from one to three teaspoonfuls of the syrup; to be taken every fifteen minutes until the spasm is relieved. In the meantime get the feet into hot water for fifteen or twenty minutes, followed with Mustard to the feet, to divert the blood from the lungs. Warm water, or some warm herb tea may be drank with the Ipecac (or other emetic that may be used) to assist its action.

G. No one thing will be found to cure absolutely in all cases, because there will be found complications of other diseases, differing in different persons, but permanent cures in some cases are claimed to have been effected with the following preparation:

Lobelia Seed	½ ounce.
High Cranberry Bark	½ "
Stramonium Seed	¼ "
Capsicum	¼ "
Alcohol	1 quart.

Mix, and let stand for two weeks, shaking daily.

Dose: From one-half to one teaspoonful three or four times a day as a cure, and every thirty minutes for relief.

Bathing daily is believed by some to be absolutely necessary to enable the system to resist the tendency to take cold, which is almost certain to bring on an attack of asthma with all who are subject to the disease. Begin by using warm water, but gradually use cooler water until able to bathe in cold water, keeping this up until the little changes in the atmosphere do not have so quick an effect on the system. For those for whom a daily cold bath would be too severe, the following is recommended: a daily sponging with a tincture of Cayenne, ¼ ounce of the Cayenne to one quart of whiskey, sponging the whole surface before dressing in the morning; and with this sponging, a cold or tepid bath two or three times a week.

In connection with either of these forms of bathing, some internal remedy (as recommended above) should be persevered in if permanent relief is expected. One difficulty with asthmatic patients in not being able to effect a cure, or at least a very considerable benefit, is that they do not continue the use of a remedy sufficiently long to make a lasting impression. To work an alterative effect, the remedy must be taken three or four times daily for a month, or two or three months, as the previously short or long establishment of the disease would seem to call for.

Following are a few cases given by Dr. Ray, who uses Ferrocyanuret of Potash—more commonly called Prussiate of Potash—in the treatment of asthma. A full history of each case is given:

1. "Mrs. S., aged 48, has suffered for many years from palpitation of the heart, with dyspnœa (difficulty of breathing) and asthma, had often been under treatment by different medical men of some notoriety, but without permanent benefit, all of which was made known on my first visit. Prescribed as follows:

Ferrocyanuret (Prussiate) Potassa... 1 ounce.
Water .... 2 "
Simple Syrup................................. 6 "
Sulphuric Ether .... 1 drachm.

Mix. Dose:—One teaspoonful five times a day for a period of three or four months, with entire relief both of heart symptoms and of the respiratory organs."

2. "M. M., aged 60, male, feeble from long indisposition and much medication, subject to chronic bronchitis of long standing, expectorated freely a tough and glairy mucus, sometimes streaked with blood, making constant efforts to clear his throat, troublesome cough at night and much irritability of the throat. Called at my office and gave the above history, stating that he had lost all hope of relief, having often been treated before. Prescribed as follows:

Ferrocyanuret of Potassa................. 1 ounce.
Alcoholic Extract of Hyoscyamus... 1 drachm.
Water .... 2 ounces.
Simple Syrup................................. 3 "

Mix. Dose:—One teaspoonful 5 times a day, which was taken for some months, with gradual but permanent relief."

3. "Mrs. McD., widow, aged 30, seamstress, robust constitution, but for many years subject to severe attacks of neuralgia upon the slightest change in the atmosphere, even a change in the direction of the wind often inducing an attack. She would suffer intolerable pains, either in her face, head or limbs, the disease not confining itself to any especial organ even in the same attack. Called at my office for medical aid, and in addition to the above stated that her digestive organs were in good condition, bowels regular, catamenia (turns) appearing at regular intervals, and of natural color and duration. Prescribed as follows:

Ferrocyanuret of Potash................. 1 ounce.
Water .... 2 "
Simple Syrup................................. 6 "
Sulphuric Ether............................. 40 drops.

Mix. Dose.—One teaspoonful five times a day.

Improvement constant. No return of symptoms since. Continued treatment for two or three months. The case being one of nervous irritability, needed no other than a sedative treatment."

ATHEROMA. — Atheroma means a chronic disease of the arteries. This frequently occurs in old people as a natural result of old age; it also occurs in the young and middle aged as the result of syphilis, the prolonged use of alcohol, Bright's disease, chronic indigestion, or some form of excess. In this disease the arteries degenerate—lose their elasticity and become soft and flabby, and the coats may contain considerable fat, and during this change lime salts may also be deposited in the coats of the arteries. This is the same form of lime salts of which bone is formed. These salts are always present in the circulation, but during health he various cells of the body, including those of the arteries, select from the passing blood stream only such elements as are suited to their individual use; during the degenerative change going on in the arteries by reason of the diseased condition, the cells cannot exercise their selective power, and lime salts may be deposited. This may occur in patches, or may include the artery for some distance. In this condition and as a result of some sudden strain, as heavy lifting or bending forward, an artery may easily be ruptured. This frequently occurs in the brain and is the cause of apoplexy. Sometimes there is an overgrowth of connective tissue in the arteries, and when this contracts it hardens and becomes firm and resistant. This is called *Arterial Sclerosis*. In any of these conditions the tissues are poorly nourished.

TREATMENT.—

Give attention to diet, take nourishing food and keep the bowels regular. Guard against any symptoms of indigestion, avoid excitement, heavy lifting or athletic exercise, and take internally one teaspoonful of Syrup of Hydriodic Acid four times a day—between meals and at bedtime. Occurring in the old, care should be taken to guard against injury, as this is the condition present when dry gangrene is liable to occur, and the injury, be it ever so slight, even as the result of carelessness in the cutting of a toe nail, may excite inflammation and cause gangrene.

If the disease is caused by syphilis, give anti-syphilitic treatment; if it is the result of Bright's disease, see treatment under that head.

ATROPHY.—Atrophy is a wasting of tissues or of an organ that was originally well formed. It means a loss of weight, size and function, and is dependent upon some disorder of nutrition. What is called *active atrophy* is due to the failure of the cells or tissues to assimilate the nourishment brought to them; *passive atrophy* is understood to mean a diminished supply of nourishment. Adipose or fat tissue is merely connective tissue (see chapter on ALCOHOL for description of connective tissue).

where many of the cells are distended with fat. In atrophy the natural fat is gradually removed and the cells diminished in size, although the cells may still contain all the elements essential to normal function or activity, the fat not being necessary to the well-being of the part. Strictly speaking, however, atrophy means a decrease in the *normal* tissue elements, though as usually found it is more or less associated with fatty degeneration, that is, aside from the disappearance of the fat originally contained in the tissues, the structure proper is more or less degenerated and converted into fat. So long as waste and repair are equal and the waste is eliminated as fast as produced, health is maintained and atrophy does not occur.

Cause.—Atrophy is a natural result of old age; occurring in the young and middle aged, it depends upon diseased conditions. It may result from lack of circulation, from pressure, from inflammation, from lack of food, from lack of assimilation, from lack of exercise, and from bad hygiene. There is a certain amount of atrophy in the arteries and tissues following amputation; there is atrophy of the optic nerve after removal of the eye; atrophy may result from tumor pressure or from aneurism, or from connective tissue overgrowth. Examples of the latter are found in the kidneys in Bright's disease and in a sclerosed liver following the prolonged use of alcohol. Atrophy occurs in tuberculosis and other wasting diseases. It may occur in bone as well as soft tissue, and the cause is the same.

Order of Progression.—The first effects of atrophy are found in the disappearance of the normal fat lying just beneath the skin; second, that contained in the abdominal cavity; third, a shrinking of the muscle fibers; fourth, the same effects are found in the arteries and nervous tissue; fifth, and last, destruction of the connective tissue. It is the destruction of the nervous tissue of the brain that causes insanity during starvation.

TREATMENT.—

Barring the natural decline of old age, atrophy signifies disease, either local or general. If in the kidney or liver, see treatment under those heads; if the result of tuberculosis or other wasting diseases, see treatment as described under those heads. In the absence of any known cause, atrophy requires general systemic treatment. This includes nourishing food and attention to digestion and elimination; it includes bathing and well-ventilated sleeping rooms, daily exercise in the open air, never carried to the point of fatigue, and attention to hygienic surroundings. These cases will be benefited by 1-40 of a grain of Strychnine in pill form, taken before meals. Also by 5-drop doses of Fowler's Solution at the same time. If the patient is pale and anæmic, give 20-drop doses of Syrup of Iodide of Iron between meals and at bedtime.

BALDNESS. — Baldness may be caused by the infectious diseases, such as syphilis, or by a severe case of eruptive fever where the disease is protracted. Baldness may also be caused by some forms of ringworm (See RINGWORM). Perhaps the greatest cause of baldness is a lack of circulation in the scalp. The hair follicles are little thimble-shaped depressions in the skin, and at the bottom of each follicle is a tiny loop of blood vessels which supports the growth of the hair and nourishes the connecting gland. The gland, in turn, furnishes an oily secretion which keeps the hair and skin smooth and soft. When the circulation is interfered with, nourishment is lacking, and gradually the hair loses "tone" and eventually becomes loosened and falls out. In the majority of cases the vitality of the hair follicles is destroyed and baldness is permanent.

Many cases of falling out of the hair may be benefited or cured. Baldness resulting from a "run of fever" needs no particular treatment. Baldness resulting from a lack of circulation requires stimulating applications, as any of those following. Massage regularly and persistently applied will improve the circulation and aid materially in the support of the hair. Pilocarpine is credited with the power of producing a new growth of hair where the hair follicles are not destroyed. This remedy is very expensive and we cannot speak from personal experience. If used, it must be taken internally and continued for a long time. The dose must be governed by the effect in each individual case. If it causes an increase in the flow of saliva, this will indicate that the dose must be lessened; if this symptom is not present, the amount can be continued and increased to the point of effect. Perhaps the average dose would be 1-10 of a grain four times a day.

The discovery that Pilocarpine would cure baldness was accidental. Patients who had been kept for several months in some of our hospitals and given Pilocarpine for other causes, had, in case of baldness, noticed the hair began to grow. This surprised both patients and physicians. The latter became interested, and by comparing notes it was discovered that very many cases of baldness had been cured by the prolonged use of Pilocarpine; at least, there was no other known cause.

Pilocarpine increases the secretions of the whole body, including those of the scalp. During the course of treatment, where the Pilocarpine is given, the hair follicles and their connecting glands always contain an increased amount of secretions. Putting the two facts together, that is, the increase in the secretions and the growth of hair in those cases that had been bald for years, the only intelligent solution that could be arrived at was that the new growth of hair was due solely to the Pilocarpine.

TREATMENTS.—

A. Take a small handful each of the bark of Witch Hazel and Bittersweet. Put this into an iron dish and pour on to it one quart of boiling water. Let it simmer (not boil) down to one pint. Strain and add four ounces of Bay Rum and ½ ounce of Glycerine. Rub thoroughly into the scalp once a day, shaking the bottle well each time before using. If the hair follicles are not destroyed, this will promote a growth of hair.

Of course, the scalp must be kept clean. Wash occasionally with soap—about one ounce of the tincture of Green soap added clear, a little at a time—rub the scalp gently, rinse thoroughly with clear water, and then apply the above wash.

B. Alcohol...................................... 2 ounces.
Water of Ammonia........................ 1½ drachms.
Glycerine.................................... 1 "
Salts of Tartar.............................. 1 "
Castile Soap, powdered .... 8 grains.
Water, enough to make................. 5 ounces.

Mix, and rub well into the scalp two or three times a week.

C. A most excellent application is the following:

Resorsin..................................... 4 drachms
Listerine .... 2 ounces.
Glycerine .... 20 drops.
Rosewater enough to make........... 8 ounces.

Apply to the scalp twice a week.

D. Friction of the scalp with a moderately stiff hair brush, and application of an ointment made of Carbolic Acid and Vaseline in the proportion of 1 part Carbolic Acid to 48 parts of Vaseline; or Oil of Tar 1 part to 24 parts of liquid Cosmoline. (7.)

E. Frequent shampoo and massage with Tar soap. (5.)

F. Tincture Spanish Fly................ 1 drachm.
Castor Oil .... ½ ounce.
Purified Beef Marrow................ 1 "
Lemon Juice............................. ½ "

To be rubbed into the scalp morning and evening. (27.)

G. Tincture Cantharides................ 2 drachms.
Quinine Sulphate...................... 1 "
Rum.. 8 ounces.
Rosewater sufficient quantity to perfume..................................

Rub a small quantity well into the scalp once a day.—(21.)

H   Sulphate of Quinine.................. 1 drachm.
    Tincture of Spanish Fly 1   "
    Liquid Vaseline......................... 1 ounce,
    Aromatic Spirits of Ammonia..... ½   "
    Bay Rum, enough to make......... 8   "

   Mix together and use with a wet brush twice
a day, rubbing in well,—(53.)

BARBER'S ITCH.—(See RINGWORM OF THE BEARD).

BED SORES.—*Bed Sores* mean sores that are occasioned
by lying too long in one position.   Sometimes only the skin is
destroyed, sometimes the deeper structures.   Lesions of this kind
are most apt to occur in old people, and are very difficult to heal.
Circulation is poor and nutrition is at a low ebb, and there is but
little to stimulate the healing.

Cause.—Failure of nutrition due to low vitality and pressure.
These sores occur at points sustaining the greatest weight.   The
pressure shuts off the blood supply, partially or completely, the
tissues die and, in severe cases, slough away.

Symptoms. — The skin may first assume a brighter red, then
gradually changes in color and becomes darker.   Death may occur
at one point in the center and spread, or may occur simultan-
eously at several points and gradually unite.

TREATMENTS.—

In case of long illness, especially of old people, bed sores are
very apt to occur, and those having the care of them should
employ

Preventive Treatments. — The position of the patient
should be frequently changed.   Bathing and friction should also
be used daily, and especially over the surface where the greatest
pressure occurs. This will improve the circulation and aid largely
in keeping up a healthy condition.   Clean sheets should be kept
on the bed, and the sheets and mattress upon which the patient
lies should be kept as smooth and free from wrinkles as possible.
Great protection may be had by placing under the patient pillows,
cushions, or soft quilts folded together.   Air pillows are used in
many cases.   These are simply circular hollow rubber tubes filled
with air.

Under *Preventive Treatments* the following applications are
recommended for suspected or exposed parts.

A. Tannic Acid .... ½ ounce.
    Glycerine.................................... 4   "
    Alcohol 4   "

B. Prevent by keeping patient changing from side to side. Do not let him lie in one position too long. Sponge back and hips three or four times a day with the following:

> Alum... 1 drachm.
> Alcohol .... ½ ounce.

Pad back with soft cotton so as to keep pressure off tender places.—(13.)

C. To prevent bed sores, bathe exposed parts three or four times a day with clear alcohol.—(8.)

Applications for Sores.—The surface should be thoroughly cleansed at least twice a day—morning and evening—with warm water and Castile soap, after which any of the following applications may be made:

> A. Oxide of Zinc................................ 1 drachm.
> Ichthyol 2   "
> Vaseline, enough to make .... 1 ounce.
> *Mix* well, spread on a muslin and place over sore.

B. Two per cent solution of Formaldehyde, which is made as follows:

> Formaldehyde................................ 10 drops.
> Water... 1 ounce.

> After bathing, as above directed, wet a soft cloth in the solution and lay it over the sore, covering the cloth with a light bandage.

BELLYACHE.—This is a term somewhat loosely applied to the various pains that may occur either in the stomach or bowels. These pains are the result of indigestion, constipation, or pressure from the formation of gases, either in the stomach or digestive tract. They are sometimes "colicky" in nature. They all indicate practically the same condition, indigestion, either from overeating or eating too fast, and may also be influenced by sedentary habits as these tend to a sluggish condition of the digestive organs. It is a form of neuralgia, the same as rheumatism, lumbago, etc. Neuralgia is not a separate disease, but a painful reminder of our errors.

TREATMENTS.—

A. A cathartic should be given, and the individual should be more careful regarding his diet. He should eat less for a few days and drink more water between meals. This will render the digestive tract more active and digestion will be improved, also elimination. Many of these cases call for better ventilation.

B. Give some warm tea freely, as Peppermint, Spearmint, etc.

C. For babies, Catnip tea with a little Anise seed added. If bowels are too close, use Elder blows (Sweet Elder flowers), in place of Catnip.

Adults: Ten drops Essence Peppermint and 4 or 5 drops Spirits Camphor in form of hot sling. (14.)

D. A teaspoonful of Paregoric for adult, followed by oil or salts. In children the dose of Paregoric should be gauged to suit the age of patient: a child one year old should have 10 drops; a child ten years old, ½ teaspoonful. Never awaken anyone to give him Paregoric, or Opium in any form, such as Morphine or Laudanum. (9.)

E. For baby, strong Peppermint water without sugar, or Catnip tea. If hands and feet are cold, wrap up. Warm flannel over stomach.

Older children same, with suitable doses of Paregoric, according to age. Give careful diet. Watch out for tender point over the appendix on right flank. (13.)

F. Paregoric... 1   ounce.
Tincture of Capsicum................... 1   "
Spirits of Camphor........................ 1   "
Syrup of Rhubarb......................... 2   "
Spirits of Chloroform.................. ½ drachm.
Simple Syrup.............................. 4 ounces.

Mix, and take one teaspoonful in warm water every hour until relieved.

Note.—While *Paregoric* has been and is a very common remedy for children, we wish to remind the reader of two things: First, Paregoric contains Opium, and its effect is the same as to give Laudanum diluted; second, small children and babies do not bear Opium well. Codeine will quiet nervousness or irritability and is perfectly safe. 1-60 to 1-40 of a grain would be a suitable dose for a child one year old.

BILIARY STONE.—(See GALL-STONES).

BILIOUSNESS.—See LIVER, CONGESTION OF).

BLACK-HEADS.—(See under SKIN DISEASES).

THE BLADDER AND ITS DISEASES.

The bladder is a membranous sac designed as a receptacle for the urine. It is situated in the pelvic cavity. Its position is subject to great change, according to the amount of its distention, also according to the condition of the surrounding structures. The bladder has four coats. The lining mucous membrane forms the inner coat, next is connective tissue, then the muscular coat, and last the serous coat. The connective tissue unites the mucous membrane to the muscular coat. The serous or outer coat is formed of the peritoneum (the lining membrane of the abdomen) and does not entirely cover the bladder. The ureters lead from the kidneys into the back wall of the bladder near the bottom. The bladder may be considered simply as a dilatation of the ureters. What is called the neck of the bladder, the point of outlet, is surrounded by the prostate gland, and it is at this point that the urethra begins.

DYSURIA.—The meaning of this term is *painful urination*. It is not a disease of itself, but there are three conditions especially that are liable to produce it: the first is inflammation of the bladder, the second is stricture, and the third, which is less severe, arises from an enlarged prostate gland. Any of these conditions may result in complete retention of urine, in which case distention of the bladder soon follows and the pain is agonizing.

TREATMENT.—

Depending upon inflammation, it is amenable to early treatment (see BLADDER, INFLAMMATION OF). In case of stricture or an enlarged prostate gland (see under those diseases), the conditions are overcome with difficulty and require prolonged treatment. In case of complete retention relief can only be had by use of the catheter, an instrument designed to be introduced into the bladder to draw off the urine. After one application by the doctor a soft catheter can be applied by any one.

Retention of Urine.—Take corn silks and pumpkin seeds, make a tea and drink freely of it, and place wheat bran poultices as hot as can be borne over the bladder. If these fail, use catherer.

35

BLADDER, INFLAMMATION OF.—The bladder is subject to inflammation from the following causes:

The injudicious use of irritating drugs, especially Cantharides and Copaiba.

External injury.

Extension of inflammation from surrounding structures.

From local irritation, as in the formation of stone.

It may result from taking cold.

It may be caused by the urine when it contains too much acid. This acid is the result of indigestion.

It may be caused by tumors or cancer.

It may be either acute or chronic.

Acute Form.—

Symptoms.—The onset is sudden. There is moderate fever and burning pain in the region of the bladder, and especially along the urethra following urination. The pain is increased by pressure. The mucous membrane is red and swollen and there is an almost incessant desire to urinate. This is not done freely and is accompanied with great distress. The increased blood supply results in an overproduction of new cells on the surface of the mucous membrane, and these drop away into the urine and are eliminated. The natural secretions of the mucous membrane are changed to a thick, tenacious form, and if the inflammation is severe enough small vessels will rupture and *blood will also appear in the urine.* At first the urine may be clear, but as the result of new cell formation and the thick, ropy mucus, it soon becomes cloudy and undergoes decomposition. If the inflammation is in the neck of the bladder there may be complete retention of urine (see DYSURIA), and great pain in the perineum as well as great distress in the bladder.   If continued, this would result in distention of the kidney and blood poison.   The bladder lies in close relation with the rectum, and sometimes the irritation causes a frequent desire to evacuate the bowels.   This is called *tenesmus.*

TREATMENTS.—

What to Do Till the Doctor Comes.—Put the patient to bed and use hot applications to ease the pain until the doctor can arrive. Cloths may be wrung out of hot water, but are more effective wrung out of a decoction of Smartweed. They should be put across the abdomen as hot as the patient can bear them and changed often enough to keep the surface hot. Or an excellent way is to put the Smartweed into two sacks, steep them up, wring one out at a time and lay across the patient, changing as often as necessary.

The hot applications tend to evacuate the bladder, but if the case is too obstinate for relief to be afforded by such means, it will be necessary for the doctor to attend to this on his arrival. In calling the doctor he should be informed of the nature of the difficulty in order that he may bring the necessary instruments with him.

A. Give a large dose of Castor Oil or other active cathartic, and put the patient to bed. Absolute quiet is necessary. If the urine is highly acid, which is indicated by a high color, give a teaspoonful of the following every two hours:

Acetate of Potash .... ½ ounce.
Tritica .... 4 "

If the urine is alkaline and contains thick ropy mucus, give one teaspoonful of the following mixture every two hours:

Benzoate of Soda............................ ½ ounce.
Glycerine .... 1 "
Water... 3 "

Mix together.

or,

Salicylate of Soda............................ ½ ounce.
Glycerine .... 1 "
Water... 3 "

Mix, and take one teaspoonful every three hours.

or,

Salol 10 grains every three hours.

B. Tea made of corn silks—green silks if in season. May be drank freely.

Quinine in 3-grain doses four times a day in connection with the remedy mentioned above. Avoid eating acids or anything sour. Drink alkaline waters after meals.—(9.)

C. Benzoic Acid.................................. 1 drachm.
Borax .... 1½ "
Water .... 8 ounces.

Mix, and take tablespoonful every two hours until relieved.

D. Tartar Emetic .... 2½ grains.
Epsom Salts.................................... 2 ounces.
Sulphate of Morphine .... 2 grains.
Tincture of American Hellebore ... 1½ ounces.
Aromatic Sulphuric Acid.............. ½ drachm.
Syrup Ginger................................ 2 ounces.
Water.. 10 "

Mix. Dose:—A tablespoonful every two, three or four hours.—(20.)

E. Treatment depends upon conditions and causes, and requires investigation by a medical man to be intelligently treated. —(14.)

F. Give watermelon or flaxseed tea, and inject Laudanum and warm water into the bowel.—(6.)

Chronic Form.—Inflammation of the bladder may become chronic. This is more liable to occur in old people, and may be caused by stricture or by stone, but is more often due to an enlargement of the prostate gland, which surrounds the neck of the bladder and in an enlarged state keeps up a constant irritation. This is followed by congestion, a low form of inflammation and an overgrowth of tissue. The walls of the bladder may become one-half inch thick. The desire to pass water is unduly frequent, and the bladder never entirely empties itself. (See PROSTATE GLAND ENLARGED.) The urine presents a cloudy appearance, is alkaline and contains a large amount of mucus and pus. On standing, it deposits a thick, ropy sediment, and often gives offensive odor because the retained urine undergoes decomposition. Chronic inflammation of the bladder is also accompanied with a dull pain and more or less emaciation and weakness.

TREATMENTS.—

A. Give 10 grains of Salol four times a day, or 10 grains of Benzoate of Soda four times a day. The bladder should be completely emptied several times a day. Eat plain food and drink large quantities of pure water. If chronic inflammation continues until the walls of the bladder become thickened, there is no cure. Avoid active exercise, walking or riding, as these tend to aggravate the case and increase the inflammation.

B. One ounce best Gum Arabic dissolved in a glassful of water.

Dose.—A teaspoonful every two or three hours.

Especially useful in chronic and sub-acute cases.—(8.)

What is called ammoniacal decomposition of urine may present a cloudy appearance. This may occur without inflammation of the bladder. Normal urine has what is called an acid reaction. If a piece of blue litmus paper is thrust into it, it will change to red. After the decomposition mentioned this change will not occur, but the urine will now change red litmus to blue. This form of fermentation is caused by the small trace of mucus that is always present, and other organic matter in the urine acting as a ferment converts the urea, which is normally present, into Carbonate of Ammonia. This form of decomposition can be detected by the odor. If the litmus paper which has been changed to red is allowed to dry, the original blue color will return as soon as the Ammonia has evaporated.

BLADDER, GRAVEL or STONE IN. — Gravel may be present in the bladder, having been carried through the ureters from the kidneys. As stated under DISEASES OF THE KIDNEYS,

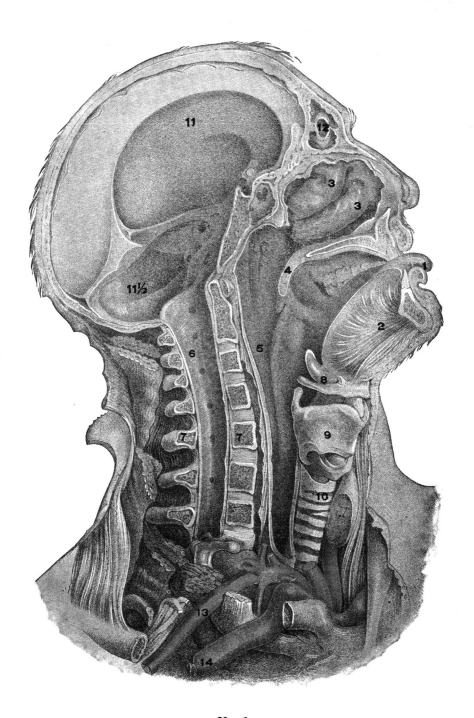

No. 1.

1, Tongue.   2, Muscles of Tongue.   3, Bones of Nose.   4, Soft Palate.
5, Gullet   6, Spinal Canal.   7, Vertebræ.   8, Opening to Wind-Pipe.   9,
Thyroid Cartilage.   10, Wind-Pipe.   11, Upper Brain.   11½, Lower Brain.
12, Eye Cavity.   13, Artery.   14, Vein.

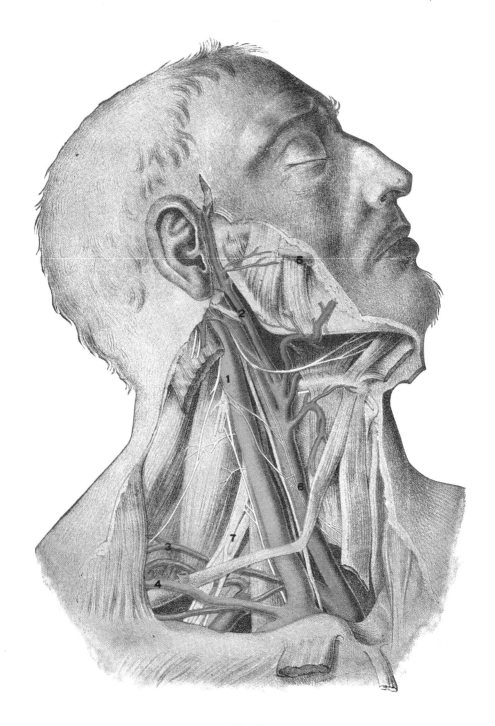

No. 2.

1, Jugular Vein. 2, Artery supplying Face and Scalp. 3, Artery, 4, Vein.
5, Salivary Duct. 6, Large Artery of Neck. 7, Nerves.

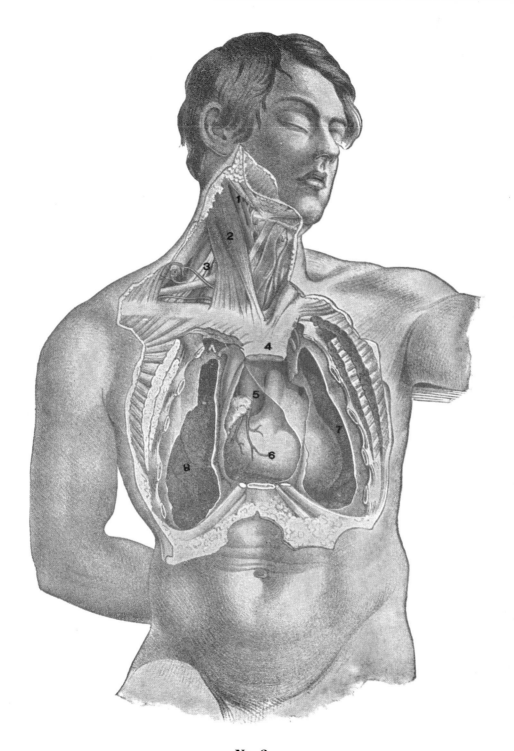

No. 3.

1, Artery of Neck.   2, Large Muscles of Neck.   3, Large Nerve.
4, Upper End of Breast Bone.   5, Large Artery coming from Heart.
6, Heart (with sac partly removed).   7, Left Lung.   8, Right Lung.

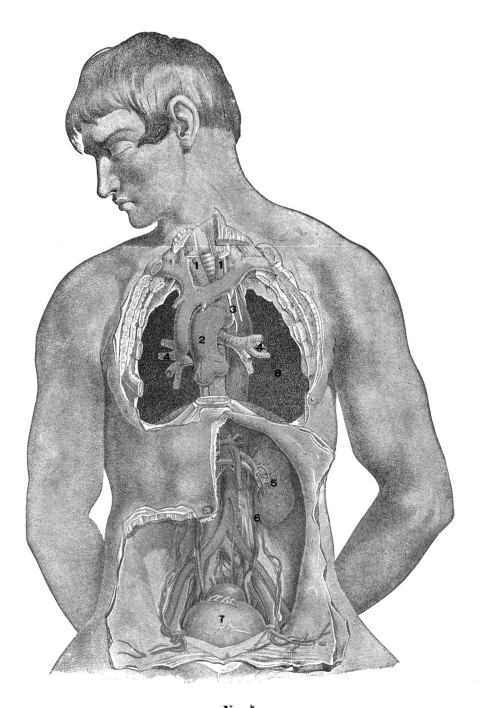

No. 4.

1, Arteries supplying Neck and Brain.   2, Large Artery arising from Heart (which is removed).   3, Nerves.   4, Bronchial Tubes (cut off). 5, Left Kidney.   6, Left Ureter.   7, Bladder.   8, Left Lung.

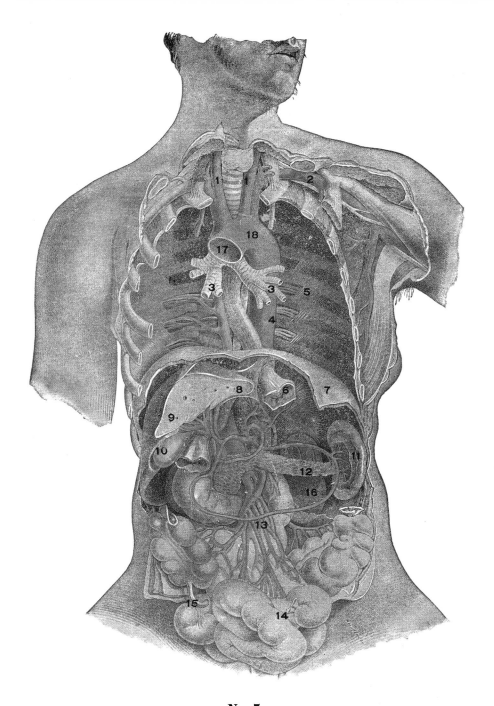

No. 5.

1, Large Arteries of the Neck.   2, Large Artery of Side and Arm.
3, Bronchial Tubes (cut off).   4, Descending large Artery.   5, Lung Cavity.
6, Termination of the Gullet (Stomach removed).   7, Diaphragm.   8, 9,
Liver.   10, Gall-Bladder.   11, Spleen.   12, Pancreas.   13, Blood Vessels from
the Membranous Covering of the Bowels.   14, Large and small Intestines.
15, Appendix.   16, Kidney.   17, Artery cut off at Junction of the Heart.   18,
Arch of the Aorta.

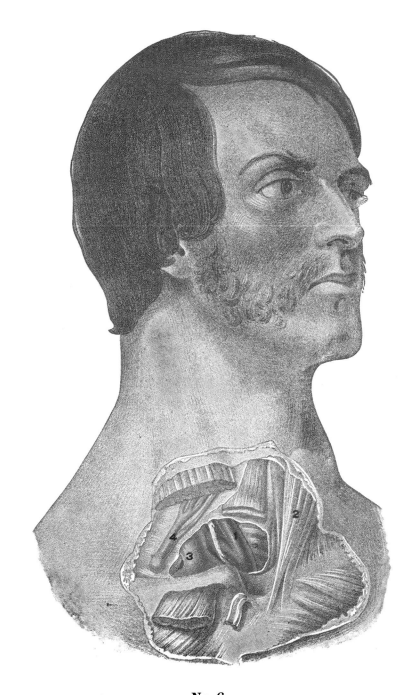

No. 6.

1, Arteries.   2, Muscles of Neck.   3, 4, Veins.

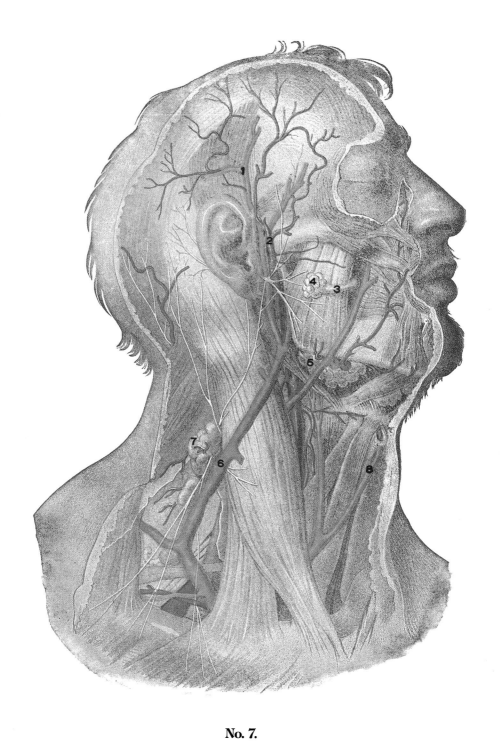

No. 7.

1, Vein.   2, Artery.   3, Salivary Duct.   4, 5, Salivary Glands.   6, Vein.
7, Lymphatic Gland.   8, Vein.

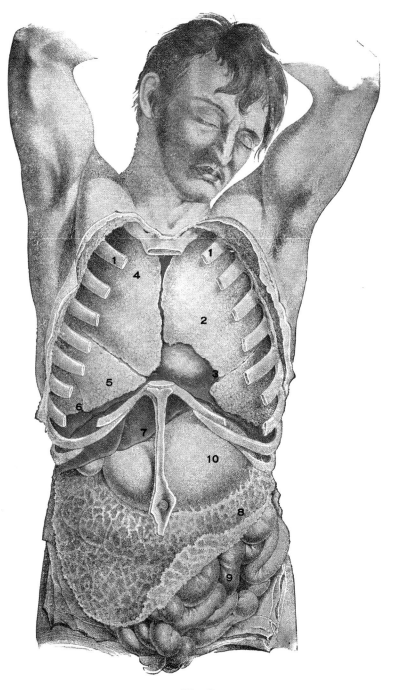

No. 8.

1, First Rib (cut off).   2, Left Lung.   3, Apex of Heart.   4, Right Lung, upper lobe.   5, Right Lung, middle lobe.   6, Right Lung, lower lobe.   7, Liver.   8, Membranous covering of the Bowels.   9, Bowels. 10, Stomach.

this gravel is clusters of uric acid crystals. Gravel may be more abundant in the bladder because there is more room for it. It may collect in such quantities as to cause irritation. In the case of an enlarged prostate gland where the bladder is not entirely emptied, the accumulations may continue to the formation of one or more stones of large size.

Cause.—The cause of gravel is fully stated under Diseases of the Kidneys. Stones may originate in the bladder, but are usually discharged from the kidney into the bladder where they continue to grow in size. Stone may result from alkaline urine following inflammation of the bladder. In this case, as in the kidney, the stone would be formed of phosphates.

Symptoms. — Stone in the bladder first produces uneasiness, followed by a dull pain in the region of the organ. The desire to urinate is more frequent, especially during the day, or when the patient is exercising. Walking and riding increase the irritation and pain. Urination may increase the pain, because it is apt to disturb the stone, which is sometimes drawn over the entrance to the urethra and effectually stops the flow. By changing position, the stone may be removed and the bladder empty itself. If the stone is rough, with sharp edges, it produces severe pain when brought in direct contact with the sides of the bladder as it is being emptied. There is usually more or less mucus present in the urine, and blood may also be present at times. A stone that is perfectly smooth may reach large proportions and produce no symptoms at all.

TREATMENTS.—

A. For medical and general systemic treatment, see *Stone in the Kidney*. If medical treatment fails, an operation will be called for. It should be remembered, however, that the symptoms of stone in the bladder may be caused by other conditions, and an operation should never be made until an examination has demonstrated the presence of stone. This examination is made by passing a *sound* into the bladder, and by careful manipulation bringing it in contact with the stone. The contact must be both heard and felt. This leaves no room for doubt and is the only sure method of diagnosis.

B. Drink freely of Gravel Weed tea (*see chapter on herbs*). If this does not dissolve the stone, and the trouble continues, consult medical aid. The stone may have to be crushed with instruments.

BLEBS.—*Blebs* are *water blisters*, varying in size from a bean to an egg, which form on the skin. They are characteristic of a skin disease known as *pemphigus*. (See PEMPHIGUS).

TREATMENT.—

A. Open them and apply an ointment made as follows:

Carbolic Acid.. 1 part.
Lard, or Cosmoline........................... 20 "
(7.)

BLISTER.—A thin bladder raised on the skin, containing a watery fluid. It may be caused by some injury, as burns, unaccustomed friction, etc. Blisters are sometimes raised with plasters over the seat of a severe pain as a means of relieving the pain. The *vesicles* that form in *small-pox* are small water blisters. If the fluid in a water blister, or vesicle, becomes purulent, that is, changes to pus, it is then called a pustule.

TREATMENTS.—

A. For a severe blister take cabbage leaves, soften them by putting in warm water, take out stems, and apply warm over the blister. If the cabbage leaves are not at hand, dress the blister with bread and milk poultice.

B. Draw a coarse thread in blister with a needle, cut thread and leave ends protrude at least half an inch from blister. (4.)

C. The blister should not be molested so long as there is any sensation of the burn, but when the pain has subsided, puncture near the base, but be careful not to rupture the skin of the blister as it acts better as a covering for the raw surface than any artificial dressing that can be substituted. (9.)

BLOOD BLISTER.—Blood blisters are caused by a slight injury, as a light blow, or pinching the skin. When these effects are severe enough, some of the little vessels that are just beneath the skin are ruptured, blood escapes, the outer layer of the skin is raised, and this constitutes a blood blister. If these are opened they should be opened with a sharp needle, which should enter the skin a short distance from the base of the blister and be pushed through to where blood is contained. This allows free drainage and does not disturb the outer layer of the skin.

BLOOD POISONING.—This means poison in the circulation. It is not understood to mean blood poisoning resulting from contagious diseases, such as scarlet fever, diphtheria, small-pox, etc., but includes only those cases of blood poisoning resulting from an unhealthy or infected wound, where poison is being absorbed into the circulation. Medical writers divide blood poisoning into several separate forms, as follows: *Septicæmia, Sapræmia* and *Pyæmia*. Septicemia is frequently spoken of as *Septic Infection*, and Sapræmia as *Septic Intoxication*.

These divisions are largely theoretical. The cause, symptoms and treatment are practically the same in all. In treating a case of blood poisoning, neither the doctor nor the public consider the conditions indicated by the foregoing terms. It is treated simply as a case of blood poisoning.

Cause.—The cause of blood poisoning is the absorption into the system of a specific virus or poison, usually from a poisoned wound. It may follow a case of confinement where the after-birth or some part of it is allowed to remain in the uterus, or it may result from abscess formation in the body—bone abscess, abscess of the kidney, of the liver, ulcers formed in the digestive tract during typhoid fever, abscess of the lung or abscess of the middle ear. Any of these conditions may produce blood poisoning, and the cause is the same—the absorption into the circulation of a specific poison or virus. In some cases there is also absorption of pus or other putrid matter. The absorption of both the specific poison and the putrid matter is called *Pyæmia*, meaning pus in the blood.

Symptoms.—The symptoms of blood poisoning commence soon after the introduction of the diseased matter. When following confinement it usually makes its appearance four or five days after labor. In many cases there is a chill or sense of chilliness, restlessness, high temperature, nausea, vomiting and, later, diarrhea. The eliminations may contain blood, and hemorrhage may occur in spots beneath the skin. There is a dry, coated tongue, headache, weak, rapid pulse, scanty, high-colored urine, loss of strength and emaciation. If the disease continues, the temperature falls below normal, there is a gradual failing of respiration, increasing heart failure, unconsciousness and death. Delirium may occur during the progress of the disease. In what is called Pyæmia, small abscesses may form in different parts of the body, hence in these cases the symptoms may vary slightly, as, a chill may follow the formation of each new abscess, and following the chill a few hours later there may be profuse sweating, the result of weakness.

TREATMENTS.—

The treatment is the same in all cases. If the poison has been absorbed from a wound, first thoroughly cleanse the part. If on the surface, make a large opening and wash out carefully with a strong antiseptic solution, and secure thorough drainage. Dress the wound with antiseptic cloths and bandages. This will cut off the supply, and the patient has now only to get rid of the poison in the system.   If the wound is on the hand or foot, and red lines extend towards the body, it is evidence that resistance is being overcome and that the poison and inflammation are extending.   These lines, which are the veins, gradually assume a darker hue.   They should be cut open at frequent intervals and the poisoned blood be allowed to escape.   Wash thoroughly with antiseptics and use antiseptic dressings.   The wound should be dressed once or twice a day, as the case demands.   Thorough cleanliness must be maintained or success will not follow the treatment.   If the foot, hand or arm is badly swollen and the inflammation is extending toward the body, the limb may be wrapped with a loose bandage and kept wet with a solution of Corrosive Sublimate, 15 grains to one quart of water.   If the disease is the result of a poisoned uterus, the uterus should be thoroughly washed out with warm water containing 20 grains of Carbolic Acid to the pint.   If any portion of the after-birth is present, it must be removed by mechanical means.   Like the wound, the uterus may need washing out once or twice a day for a few days.

These cases need stimulants.   Some use large quantities of Whiskey and Quinine; others depend upon 1-30 of a grain of Strychnine or 2 drops of Fluid Extract of Digitalis about once in three hours.   These remedies are especially strengthening to the heart.   Give an active cathartic, secure thorough movement of the bowels once or twice a day, keep the skin active by means of baths and brisk rubbing, feed the patient at frequent intervals with the most nourishing foods, secure good ventilation and give abundance of pure water.   If this general treatment is well observed, there will be less danger of heart failure.   If there is much vomiting, put a large mustard plaster over the stomach or give small quantities of milk and lime water, equal parts.   The lime water must be fresh.   The following is also good:

Carbolic Acid.................................. 1 drop.
Subnitrate of Bismuth.................... 2 drachms.
Lime Water.................................. 2 ounces.

Mix, and take ½ a teaspoonful every twenty or thirty minutes more or less often as needed, or give, as one dose,

Lactopeptine .... 10 grains.
Bismuth 10   "

every thirty minutes or every hour.   In many cases crust coffee is more effectual in checking vomiting than any other treatment.   It should be given without sugar or milk.

The points to be remembered in treating blood poisoning are:
First, thorough cleanliness.
Second, free elimination and nourishing food.
Third, give stimulants as the case requires.

BLOODY FLUX.—(See *Dysentery* under DIARRHEA).

BLOODY URINE. — This is not a disease, but is a condition that may be present in inflammation either of the bladder or kidneys. Its presence would indicate some trouble of this kind, and an investigation into the cause of it should be made. It may also be due to injury.

BOIL.—A boil is an acute affection of the skin in the form of a circumscribed inflammation. It starts as a small pimple and gradually increases in size until it attains certain dimensions, when it suppurates and casts out pus, and a tough, whitish mass of dead matter called a "core." A boil is about a week in developing sufficiently to discharge its contents, after which the part heals.

Cause.—A vitiated condition of the blood.

A. Keep constantly covered with Carbolized Vaseline. Go to your doctor for internal medicine.—(14.)

B. Boils are local troubles and do not come from bad blood, as supposed by many. Some foreign matter finding its way into the skin alongside of a hair is the origin of a boil. Boils need poulticing until they contain pus, and should then be opened with a clean knife. Do not bruise the flesh by pressing after opening. Apply soft oiled cloth after the boil is open.—(9.)

Note. — The above statement as to the cause of boils is somewhat contrary to the opinion popularly held, but it is the opinion held by one of the physicians represented in this book, and we desire to give all sides of a question so far as the scope of the present volume will admit.

        C. Carbolic Acid.................................. 10 drops.
           Cocaine, 10 per cent solution........... 5   "
           Fluid Extract of Ergot .... 1 drachm.

        Mix. Put 5 drops on a plaster made of the yolk of one egg and one teaspoonful of salt. Apply twice daily.—(22.)

BONE DISEASES.

Bones are two-thirds lime salts and one-third soft tissue. There are 200 separate bones in the human body not counting the teeth. They act as a framework and support other structures. The surface of bones is firm and compact; the inner portion is somewhat porous, that is, contains many openings, which extend in various directions. These accommodate the passage of blood vessels and nerves for the purpose of nutrition. All bone is surrounded by a thin firm membrane called *periosteum*. It is through the periosteum that the blood vessels are distributed, and from there they enter the various channels and divide throughout the bone substance; hence, whenever the periosteum is destroyed, or torn loose by accident, that portion of bone which it covered may die from lack of nourishment. Bone is subject to disease the same as soft tissue. *Abscess*, *caries* and *necrosis* are preceded by inflammation. In inflammation of bone the pain is intense because the bone is resistant and unyielding, hence the pressure is greater.

INFLAMMATION OF BONE.—When this occurs in the center of a long bone, it is called *myelitis;* when occurring on the surface, it is called *ostitis;* when it includes the whole bone, it is called *osteo-myelitis;* when occuring in the periosteum, which surrounds the bone, it is called *periostitis*. (*itis* means inflammation.)

Causes.— Injury, syphilis, extension of inflammation from other tissues. When digestion is poor, the blood contains many irritating substances. Such irritation may, and often does, cause inflammation of the kidneys, liver or lung, and may also cause inflammation of bone. In the young and healthy, injury is the most frequent cause. Inflammation of bone may terminate in caries, suppuration or necrosis.

Symptoms.—In acute inflammation of bone the pain is always severe. It is deep, "boring," and at times agonizing, because the structure is firm and resistant and there is no room for swelling as in soft tissue. This is why a bone felon is so painful. The pain is usually worse at night, and is also influenced by damp weather. If pus forms, there are one or more chills, and later there is redness and swelling on the surface.

TREATMENT.—

In acute inflammation of bone put the patient to bed, elevate the affected part, put on a bandage as tight as can be borne, and wet with the following solution:

Sugar of Lead	4 drachms.
Laudanum	2 ounces.
Water	2 quarts.

Give an active cathartic. Give Morphine or Opium internally, if necessary. If the disease has existed for some time, apply heat instead of Lead, water and Laudanum. Also apply counter-irritants. A large mustard plaster wrapped around the limb would answer for this purpose. If unable to control the case, cut the tissues clear to the bone, including the periosteum. This will relieve the pressure and also the pain to some extent. If there is evidence of pus, continue the opening into the bone, and if pus is discovered, give free drainage and dress as directed under *necrosis*. Any surgical measures would require the services of a physician.

BONE ABSCESS.—Abscess of bone is a chronic disease. Bone abscess was first described by Sir Benjamin Brodie, hence is sometimes called Brodie's Abscess. It usually occurs near the ends of long bones, as those of the leg or arm. These bones are larger and contain more blood; again, they are subject to greater strain, hence to greater irritation.

Cause.—The cause is inflammation resulting from injury. At first there is an increase in the blood supply. This is followed by an increase in bone tissue. The pressure from the newly formed cells and from the congested and inflamed vessels continues until circulation and nutrition are shut off and the structure dies. The death of the first cells occurs at any point where the pressure is greatest. The surrounding bone thickens and hardens by reason of the inflammation of the periosteum. Pus usually breaks through at the end of the bone because the ends are not covered by the periosteum, hence there is less resistance at this point. The cause of abscess in bone is the same as in soft tissue and the changes are the same. See abscess in *Appendicitis.*

Symptoms. — There is pain, which is usually worse at night and which is aggravated by dampness. The pain is localized and persistent. Later there is discoloration of the skin. Motion or dependent position or any slight injury causes violent attacks of pain. The nearest joint is especially subject to pain, the cause being the sensitiveness of the synovial membrane. This membrane surrounds the joint and is the part first affected in inflammatory rheumatism.

TREATMENT.—

We have stated before that wherever pus is discovered the abscess should be opened at once. There is no exception to this rule. In opening bone abscess open at the point of greatest tenderness. Give free drainage, scrape away dead bone, and by means of a syringe wash out the cavity with any antiseptic solution. Maintain absolute cleanliness. Dress the wound every day, more or less often as needed. Of course the treatment also includes attention to the general system, to food, ventilation, elimination, etc.

ULCERATION OF BONE.—CARIES.—Ulcer in bone is the same as ulcer elsewhere. The only difference between ulcer and abscess is that an ulcer opens on the surface and an abscess does not. Caries is death of bone resulting from ulceration or suppuration. This is sometimes called *molecular death*, meaning that only molecules or minute particles of bone are destroyed at a time: it is a gradual destruction. Caries of bone excites some inflammation around the diseased area, and some new tissue forms. This new tissue protects the healthy bone, and at the same time some of the new tissue is destroyed by inflammation and pressure and aids in the formation of pus, which is discharged.

Causes.—It may be caused by syphilis, scrofula, tuberculosis, or any condition where there is lowered vitality and a lack of nutrition. Caries may also be caused by mercury or phosphorus; it may also be caused by freezing or by burns; it may follow scarlet fever or typhoid fever where the disease is protracted, as in that case the health of the patient becomes very low and the system debilitated. It usually occurs in the young. Injury is probably the exciting cause, that is, the immediate cause.

Symptoms. — This form of bone disease commences on the surface of the bone, hence the pus can readily escape through the skin. In abscess the disease commences below the surface and within the substance of the bone. The symptoms are the same as those of inflammation of bone, though less severe. There may be some soreness, and enlargement or swelling due to the pus may be noticed. If not opened, the pus breaks through and is discharged. The pus from caries, or slow death of bone, contains small particles of bone matter and feels gritty. This is positive evidence that the bone is diseased. The odor from this kind of abscess is very foul. A probe inserted through the bone and coming in contact with it causes a dull sound. A healthy bone would give a clear note. The surrounding bone is softened, and oftentimes the probe can be pushed through it. If not treated, the opening from caries does not heal and the discharge becomes chronic.

TREATMENT.—

If due to syphilis, give anti-syphilitic treatment ; if it is the result of scrofula or tuberculosis, give treatment described under those diseases ; if it has been caused by the fumes of mercury or phosphorus, those employed in factories where these are used should change their occupation. The opening through which the pus passes out should be enlarged, the dead bone scraped away and the cavity swabbed with some strong antiseptic solution, even pure Carbolic Acid, and then washed out with pure water. The greatest care should be exercised to maintain cleanliness, both in the cavity and out. New dressings are usually required once or twice a day for a time, but may be lessened as the condition improves. General systemic treatment is required.

SOFTENING OF BONE.—OSTEO MALATIA.—MOLLITES OSSIUM. — In this disease the bones become gradually softened, are dissolved, and are carried away by the circulation. The urine contains an excessive amount of bone salts. This change commences toward the center of the bones and extends toward the surface.

Cause.—The cause is said to be unknown, although some believe it is the presence of lactic acid in the blood. Undoubtedly the cause of bone softening is a lack of nutrition, which means poor food, indigestion, lack of elimination, bad air, etc.

Symptoms.—There may be light pains, rheumatic in character. Fractures occur as the result of very slight cause. Later, the bones may bend out of shape and various deformities thus result.

TREATMENT.—

Mechanical support in the way of splints. Try to strengthen the system by means of nourishing foods and good hygienic surroundings.

DEATH OF BONE. — NECROSIS. — Necrosis means death. Gangrene is necrosis. When applied to bone, necrosis means death of a portion or portions large enough to be seen.

Cause—Tearing off or destroying the periosteum may be the cause. The vessels which supply the bone are first distributed through the periosteum, hence destruction of this membrane cuts off nutrition ; inflammation may be the cause, as inflammation destroys or shuts off the circulation and the tissues die for want of nourishment ; it may be caused by taking Mercury or Phosphorus; it may die from injury or may follow a burn or freezing; or it may follow scarlet fever or typhoid fever where the inflammation is slow and the patient becomes greatly emaciated.

Where a shell of bone dies and becomes separated from the surrounding healthy bone, it is called a *sequestrum*. The dead bone is light in color because it contains no blood and because bone is naturally white. The dead bone is a foreign body and the surrounding healthy bone is greatly inflamed, the same as any soft tissue following gangrene, and this line of inflammation would correspond to the line of demarkation as described under *Gangrene;* the periosteum surrounding the dead bone is also greatly inflamed; there is a production of new tissue, the same as that following inflammation elsewhere. This new tissue breaks down and causes suppuration, and this leaves a space between the dead bone and the living. The dead bone cannot escape, and if the pus is not absorbed it breaks externally and the dead bone is left in the cavity. The surrounding case of healthy bone is called an *involucrum*, meaning a sheath of bone. The opening through which the pus escapes is called a *cloaca*, meaning a canal.

Symptoms. — The first symptom is that of inflammation of bone. The pain stops when the pus escapes because the pressure is relieved. A probe inserted through the cavity will strike the healthy bone, which will be hard, and which, on tapping lightly, will give a clear note; in caries the sound is dull, because in caries the-surrounding bone is more or less affected and is soft. These openings do not heal.

TREATMENT.—

The treatment consists in making a large opening and giving free drainage. Scrape the cavity, if necessary, and swab it out with a strong antiseptic solution. Clear Carbolic Acid is recommended by some. Pack the cavity with Iodoform gauze and dress with a bandage. These abscesses require daily dressing— the dressings should be frequent enough to maintain thorough cleanliness of the surface. Remove the dead bone as soon as it becomes loosened. These cases usually require special attention to food and careful hygienic surroundings. If the disease is caused by syphilis, give anti-syphilitic treatment; if the result of phosphorus, change the occupation.

HYPERTROPHY OF BONE.— This means an overgrowth.

Cause.—Increased blood supply. This may result from a low form of inflammation; said to result in some cases from excessive use of the part; may also result from injury in the young and robust as this might cause chronic inflammation. There is slight overgrowth following the healing of bone abscess or the repair of fracture.

TREATMENT.—

Local treatment is not needed for hypertrophy or overgrowth of bone. If the cause is removed, that is, if the injury heals or the inflammation is checked, the overgrowth will remain a permanent addition to the bone. If the overgrowth is the result of a low form of inflammation long continued, it will eventually end in abscess, ulcer, softening or death of bone. Constitutional treatment may do much to prevent this result. Much depends upon diet, fresh air and proper exercise.

ATROPHY OF BONE.—(See ATROPHY).

BOWELS, INFLAMMATION OF.—Inflammation of the bowels is confined to the mucous membrane lining the digestive tract, and is accompanied with soreness, diarrhea, fever and more or less prostration. The conditions in inflammation of the bowels are inseparably connected with those resulting from diarrhea and dysentery. Diarrhea and dysentery are different stages of the same inflammation, and the treatment for any one of these three

conditions is only a modification of the treatment for the others. The three can be more intelligently treated under one heading, and the reader is therefore referred to the subject of *Diarrhea*.

DISEASES OF THE BRAIN.

The brain, which is the acknowledged medium of communication between mind and matter, is incased in three distinct membranes and inclosed within the skull. Both the brain and its membranes are subject to disease. Any disease of the brain causes a disturbance of the mental faculties, the acute form being characterized by delirium and the chronic form by the loss or perversion of some or all of the mental faculties. All diseases of the brain have a tendency towards convulsions and paralysis. Owing to its inclosed position its diseases can be diagnosed only by symptoms, and in cases of abnormal changes in the structure of the brain the diagnosis is seldom made during life, although improved surgical methods now reach and relieve or cure many cases of abscess and other local lesions.

Diseases Particularly Affecting the Brain.—Alcoholism, chronic dyspepsia, Bright's disease and syphilis bring about morbid changes in the structure of the brain which not only render it more liable to disease, but to impairment of the mental faculties.

ACUTE MENINGITIS.—The term *meningitis* refers expressly to an inflammation of the membranes covering the brain. It runs a rapid course. Death may result in a few days, or the fever may continue for two or three weeks.

Causes. — It may occur during the course of acute infectious diseases, *i.e.*, scarlet fever, measles, etc. Continued sleeplessness, exposure to the sun, syphilis and delirium tremens are among other causes.

Symptoms. — The earlier symptoms are: intense pain in the head ; redness of the face and eyes, the latter being wild and brilliant and sensitive to light, and the pupils much contracted ; dryness of the skin ; thirst ; lack of sleep; sensitiveness to sound; costiveness; vomiting; convulsions; and delirium, which, as the fever develops and increases, becomes violent.

In a few days, or perhaps hours, an entire change of symptoms takes place: light and sound no longer affect the patient, his vision and hearing now being dull and perverted; the pupil of the eye from being contracted now expands unnaturally ; instead of being wildly delirious he is likely to lie in a semi-unconscious state, muttering indistinctly; there is a twitching of the muscles, and local paralysis may occur in any part of the body.

If the patient recovers, these symptoms gradually disappear, yet the paralysis may be obstinate or even permanent, or there may be a permanent impairment of the vision or hearing. If the patient does not recover, he sinks into a state of coma, succeeded by death.

TREATMENTS.—

What to Do Till the Doctor Comes.—When there is indication of serious brain trouble, send immediately for your doctor. In the meantime the point is to recall the blood from the upper to the lower extremities. For this purpose apply heat to the feet and cold to the head. The feet may be put into hot water, or cans of hot water laid to the feet and along the limbs. For the head, the nicest thing, if there is a butcher's shop anywhere around, is to get a beef's bladder, fill it about half full with crushed ice, tie it so it cannot drip, and lay the head on that. It makes a cool, soft pillow, does not allow dampness to spread to the bed or clothing, and will sometimes keep for twenty-four hours without melting. If the patient is in a stupor, this is all that can be done till the doctor comes; if he is not in a stupor, and is wild, a little Laudanum, say from 5 to 10 drops, according to age, may be given. For a child, use Paregoric in place of Laudanum.

A. Keep head cool by cold applications. Quiet, darkened room, moderate temperature, Mustard to neck. Send for a doctor.—(14).

B. For further treatment, see *Cerebro-Spinal Meningitis* (inflammation of the brain and spinal cord). The same treatment will be found most satisfactory for *Inflammation of the Brain* alone.

There is another form of this disease where the inflammation attacks the coverings of both the brain and spinal cord. This is called

CEREBRO-SPINAL MENINGITIS.

Symptoms.—A typical case begins without previous symptoms or warning. The attack is sudden and frightful. There is vomiting, an agonizing headache, dizziness and an overwhelming sense of weakness. The vomiting is peculiar; there is a forcible ejection of the contents of the stomach without apparent effort, called projectile vomiting. With children there may be convulsions, loss of consciousness, and rapidly rising temperature—103 to 105. Within a few hours the muscles of the back of the neck and back contract and become rigid. The head and shoulders are drawn backward, while the feet and lower limbs are drawn in the same direction. Only the heels and back of the head touch the bed. There is great pain in the slightest effort to move. Sleep is absent, and, if a child, its screams may be heard for some distance. The whole body has now become extremely sensitive, and the nervous manifestations seem past all control.

Cramps or spasms of individual muscles may occur; this trouble usually takes place in the lower limbs. Usually within twenty-four hours there is a slight rash of a bluish red color on the face and upper eyelids, especially the latter, hence it is sometimes called *Spotted Fever*. The head is hot, the feet cold. There may be dark spots along the spine, caused by an excess of blood and the rupture of some small vessels just beneath or into the skin.

Altogether Cerebro-Spinal Meningitis presents a degree of suffering seldom met in any other disease. In some cases there is early collapse, that is, great prostration of the vital powers, followed by rapid death, which may occur within 48 to 72 hours. Where recovery takes place, the disease passes into a convalescent state in from ten days to two weeks.

The foregoing symptoms are not overdrawn, but are taken from actual experience. In like manner the following suggestions regarding treatment are not only prompted by that same experience, but are the most effective in checking the disease.

TREATMENT.—

For a Child.—Place the child in a tub of warm water. If he is old enough to sit upright, there should be water enough to cover the shoulders; if an infant, he must be supported so that his face will be kept above the surface. Pin or hold a quilt around the child's neck and allow it to fall over the tub. This will retain the heat and aid materially in producing sweating. Pour in hot water from time to time—pour it against the side of the tub and keep the water within the tub moving so as to prevent the hot stream from striking the child. Gradually increase the temperature of the water in this way until quite hot. Allow the child to remain in the water until profuse sweating takes place, say from thirty minutes to one hour—two or three hours will do no harm if the child is quiet. The relief is so great that the child often falls asleep in the water.

In a severe case, according to our experience, the hot bath is required once in about fifteen hours for two or three days, then less often.

For an Adult.—The same treatment applied to an adult will meet with equally satisfactory results, but cannot always be accomplished as conveniently. The bath may be substituted by artificial heat, as bottles or jugs filled with boiling water placed around the patient. Also hot herb drinks may be given. These are not likely to cause nausea, and aid in producing perspiration, which is the object of the treatment. The patient should be kept well covered.

How does this benefit the patient? Simply by *equalizing the circulation.* Just beneath the skin is a dense network of blood vessels estimated to be capable of holding one half the blood in the body. The heat from the warm water dilates these small vessels, and they are immediately filled with blood; this relieves the brain and spinal cord. The treatment should be repeated often enough to keep the patient quiet. The need of it will be indicated by contraction of the muscles and increasing pain. The head will be hot and the feet cold.

All physicians understand that drug medication is of little value, and may do actual harm by irritating the stomach, which is *extremely* sensitive, and thus increase the vomiting.

Absolute quiet must be maintained as far as possible. When the appetite returns, the question of feeding is an important one, as any interference with digestion may cause alarming symptoms and even a relapse. Only the most nourishing and easily digested food should be allowed, and this in small quantities at first.

TUBERCULAR MENINGITIS–This disease is an inflammation of the membrane covering the brain. During the disease the under surface of this membrane is covered more or less with small elevations or tubercles about the size of a millet seed, hence the name—*Tubercular Meningitis.*

The tubercles are situated mostly on the under side of the membrane, that is, next to the brain substance. They follow the small arteries, and this obstructs the circulation and causes pressure, and there follows an escape of the blood into the brain substance. The ventricles or lymph spaces are distended, which increases the pressure still more. This pressure accounts for the over-sensitiveness and delirium which are often present, also for the insensibility, deepening into coma, which precedes death.

Cause.—This disease is caused by irritants in the blood. These may be the result of scarlet fever, measles, typhoid fever, or may result from improper food and indigestion. The reason children are especially liable to this disease is that the brain is not well developed and lacks the power of resistance.

Symptoms. — Irritability, poor appetite, child loses flesh, abdomen may be enlarged, loss of sleep, sudden screaming of the child either day or night. The head is often thrown backwards or rolled from side to side, the child may keep its hands more or less about the head, and there may be vomiting. All of these symptoms gradually grow worse. The child is very sensitive to noise. Later the symptoms subside, the fever disappears, there may be delirium or stupor, and the child lies motionless, taking no food. The result is always fatal.

TREATMENT.—

There are some remedies recommended for this disease, but without much hope of cure. The only treatment seems to be symptomatic. Make the child as quiet and comfortable as possible, secure good ventilation, give the most nourishing food, etc. Syrup of Iodide of Iron is recommended by some, also small doses of Quinine, or Cod Liver Oil if the child can take it. Salol is also a good remedy.

Of the Syrup of the Iodide of Iron, the dose for a child one year old would be from 3 to 5 drops taken in a little sweetened water four or five times a day between feedings; of the Quinine, 1-5 of a grain dose four times a day; of the Cod Liver Oil, a teaspoonful of the clear oil of good quality may be taken three times a day. The Salol is intended for the bowels, the dose for a child one year old being from one to two grains four times a day. If the bowels are free from offensive odor, give one grain; if not, increase the dose until there is an improvement and then return to the original dose.

For this disease we wish to recommend the treatment under *Cerebro-Spinal Meningitis.* We would suggest three baths every day, allowing the child to remain in the water at least one hour each time.

SOFTENING OF THE BRAIN.—When softening of the brain occurs, it usually follows diseased arteries. It may result from a weak heart. Diseased arteries and a weak heart are the natural results of old age. Softening of the brain may follow Bright's disease, or accident or injury where from hemorrhage or blood clot the circulation is shut off. It may follow mental overwork, aneurism, or inflammation, where swelling and pressure interfere with nutrition. When occurring in the young or middle aged, it is the result of alcohol or syphilis. These produce chronic inflammation of the arteries and the vessels become soft and flabby, lose their elasticity, and change more or less to fat; this constitutes *Atheroma.* The arteries are formed of three coats or membranes. The inner coat is composed of a single layer of flat cells joined together edge to edge, like a tile floor. This layer of cells has the power to prevent the coagulation — clot formation—of blood. In the inflammation following syphilis or the prolonged use of alcohol, the inner coat is sometimes destroyed in places, and wherever this occurs blood clots form. These may be broken loose by the circulation and carried to the brain, when, on reaching some artery too small for their passage, they completely shut off the circulation, and for want of nutrition that part of the brain supplied by such an artery will die and degenerate. The diseased artery may occur in the brain and be followed by blood clot. In this case the symptoms are of a more chronic nature. In the plugging of an artery in other portions of the body the congestion and exudate are usually absorbed, or may become organized, that is, bands of connective tissue may form and later be followed by arteries. In this case the circulation and nutrition of the part gradually improves, and the diseased area returns to its normal state, barring the contraction of the new tissue formation, which resembles a scar; but in the brain, softening generally results. The muscles and skin are the most resistant to degenerative changes, and the brain and bowels the least. When through a lack of circulation the brain is deprived of nourishment, it readily undergoes degenerative changes, the tissues softening. Softening of the brain means death of the part. The dead area is not circumscribed, but passes insensibly into the surrounding tissues. The brain is composed of nerve cells and their prolongations, the nerve fibres, all held together by a form of connective tissue called *neuroglia*. The cells are dark and situated on the surface; the fibres are light in color and are situated beneath the surface. The cells are first affected, though the fibres first show degenerative changes. Later the cells degenerate, and finally the connective tissue and the arteries, and together these break down in a granular mass containing much fat, hence may be called fatty degeneration, though is generally called softening. As the tissues soften they change in color to red, yellow or white, the color being governed by the amount of blood in the vessels and the amount of exudate. Softening of the brain is named in accordance with the color of the tissues. The so-called yellow softening is simply a later stage of the red softening where the color of the blood has gradually faded. Where the circulation is shut off suddenly, as by a blood clot, the color may remain white, or white softening may become red as a result of hemorrhage into the diseased area; hence we see that these divisions are of little value. Brain softening is most common in the aged as a result of narrowing of the arteries following chronic inflammation and a weak heart.

The brain is supplied by two sets of arteries. Both arise from the same source, yet in their distribution they are entirely separate. One set supplies the surface and outer portion, and the other supplies the central portion. There is no communication between them, hence there is a borderland of diminished blood supply; and this accounts for some cases of softening, especially in the aged.

Symptoms.—Where the circulation is shut off suddenly, as the result of a blood clot or hemorrhage, there would be dizziness, fainting and unconsciousness. Occurring less suddenly, there would be pallor, more or less loss of power, dizziness, headache, and occasionally fainting might occur. This condition and these symptoms would follow disease of the arteries from old age, alcoholism, syphilis, Bright's disease, or any condition where there was general debility. In these cases softening of the brain would be secondary and there would be other evidences of disease before the degenerative change in the brain had made its appearance.

TREATMENT.—

Since the degenerative changes in the brain are secondary to other diseases, the treatment must be directed to the general system. If from syphilis, give anti-syphilitic treatment; if due to alcohol, stop the use of alcoholic drinks; if from Bright's disease, see treatment under that head. Whether from these causes or from old age, the treatment consists practically in diet, tonics, and the internal administration of some of the Iodides. The Iodides in any form are simply a means of administering Iodine, which cannot be taken in the pure form (or raw state) because it is too irritating. Iodine is valuable following chronic inflammation because it is one of the best known remedies to liquefy the products of inflammation and render them in a condition to be more rapidly taken up and carried away by the circulation. Iodine is also a most excellent antiseptic, thus aiding the blood in overcoming the morbid influences of disease and putrefactive changes. In treating this condition, elimination must receive special attention. If there are any evidences of indigestion, artificial digestants should be given. If the bowels are inactive, give Podophyllin in ¼-grain doses at bedtime. Also give 10-grain doses of Salol four times a day. Regarding the choice of Iodine preparations, Iodide of Arsenic may be given in doses varying from 1-100 to 1-50 of a grain four times a day, between meals and at bedtime; or one teaspoonful of the Syrup of Hydriodic Acid four times a day may be substituted. Iodide of Potash is equally as valuable, but its taste is decidedly unpleasant. If the patient is pale and anæmic, Iodide of Iron would be the best preparation—1-50 of a grain four times a day, between meals and at bedtime. Only the most nourishing and easily digested food should be allowed. The amount of exercise will depend upon the condition of the patient. If the brain trouble is the result of a blood clot or hemorrhage, if the pulse is full and the temperature elevated, an active cathartic should be given, followed by small doses of Aconite until the condition is changed. The same treatment should follow inflammation of the brain. Absolute rest and mental quiet would also be indicated.

BRAIN, HARDENING (Induration) **OF.**—In cases of chronic inflammation, a directly opposite effect may be produced, the brain matter hardening instead of softening.   Such chronic inflammation may follow any of the infectious diseases, or be the result of rheumatism, etc.

Cause.—The hardening process is the direct result of new tissue growth.   This tissue as naturally supplied acts as a framework for all the structures of the body, including the brain, but when resulting from inflammation it invariably contracts, and the natural tissue is either pressed upon or caught in the mesh of the contracting fibers and destroyed.

Symptoms.—In the early stages hardening of the brain matter causes convulsions because of the pressure.

TREATMENT.—

What to Do Till the Doctor Comes.—It is assumed that in case of convulsions a doctor will be called.   In the meantime put the patient in bed, surround by hot packs, cover with quilts, and, if able to swallow, give hot drinks—hot teas of herbs that possess sweating properties, as Pleurisy Root, Golden Seal, etc., would be best.   Sweating relaxes the system and, if the disease has not progressed too far, relief may be had in a short time.   It will readily be seen, however, that the conditions are such that only temporary relief is likely to be afforded.

BRAIN, CONCUSSION OF.—Due to a shock or injury to the brain, as a fall from a horse, etc.   In accidents of this kind the brain substance is liable to be ruptured or torn.   This result may follow when there is no fracture of the skull, or fracture may occur without serious injury to the brain substance. Fracture where there is no displacement of bone may be overlooked.

Symptoms.—The patient usually lies in an unconscious condition.   He may partially recover and indulge in incoherent, rambling talk, or may lie and moan; periods of delirium may occur.   Also vomiting may occur, according to the part of the brain affected.   Injury to the base of the brain will produce vomiting.   Any brain injury sufficient to produce unconsciousness should be considered dangerous.

TREATMENTS.—

What to Do Till the Doctor Comes.—Get the patient out of an exposed condition, either from a hot sun or from cold, as soon as possible.   It would be a good idea to put the feet into hot Mustard water and to put a Mustard plaster to the nape of the neck. If the surface is cold, apply artificial heat by any means.   If he is in a stupor, this is all that can be done till the doctor comes; if he has revived and is delirious, a little Laudanum, say from 5 to 10 drops, according to age, may be given. If a child, give Paregoric in place of Laudanum.

A. The recumbent posture; ice cap to the head. 2-drop doses of Tincture of Aconite every three hours. Sips of hot water to relieve vomiting, if present. (7).

BRAIN, ABSCESS ON.—(See ABSCESS).

BRAIN, TUMORS ON.—Tumors may form on the brain which do not suppurate, that is, do not become abscesses. The effect produced, however, is very much the same, that is, characteristic of brain lesions. These lesions (changes brought about by disease or injury) of whatever nature, if produced by constitutional disease, as syphilis, etc., are benefited by constitutional treatment.

BRAIN, WATER ON.—(See *Hydrocephalus*, under DROPSY). _____

BREASTS, DISEASES OF.—(See under DISEASES OF WOMEN).

BRIGHT'S DISEASE.—(See under KIDNEY DISEASES).

BRONCHITIS.—(See under LUNG DISEASES).

BRONCHOCELE.—(See GOITRE.)

BRONZED SKIN—ADDISON'S DISEASE.—This is a constitutional disease, consisting of a peculiar anæmic condition. It is characterized by a coloring of the skin that has given rise to the term, "bronzed skin disease." It first affects the supra-renal capsules—small organs situated at the upper margin of the kidneys.

Cause.—Diseased conditions of the blood, as from scrofula or syphilis.

Symptoms.—It begins insidiously. There is a gradual lessening of vital force, causing a feeling of languor and indisposition. The person is easily fatigued, is troubled with shortness of breath and some palpitation of heart. There is loss of appetite, indigestion, depression of spirits and an inclination to sleep a great deal. The skin at first presents a pale appearance, the pallor extending also to the mucous membrane of the mouth, then gradually turns dark, later becomes jaundiced, and finally changes to a mulatto or bronze hue. In persons of fair complexion, probably the first noticeable change would be a darkening of the skin. The tendency of the disease is towards death, which usually occurs within a year or two.

TREATMENTS.—

What to Do.—In diseases of this kind that creep on stealthily, a doctor is not usually consulted until the disease is too far advanced to give him a fair opportunity to do anything for the patient. Therefore, if a person is not feeling well, he should try to improve his condition by taking care of himself and taking the simple home remedies that seem to fit his case; but if after a reasonable trial there is no improvement, he should see his doctor without further delay.

> **A.** Compound **Syrup** of Stillingia..........4 ounces.
> Iodide of Potassium.......................1 drachm.
> Shake, and let dissolve.
> *Dose.*— 1 teaspoonful three times a day, between meals and at bedtime. Take an alkaline bath twice a week.

B. Fresh Sulphurous Acid should be frequently applied. Get small vial at a time and keep well corked, as it otherwise absorbs Oxygen and becomes Sulphuric Acid, which irritates and excoriates.—(14.)

C. Perfect rest and freedom from care and mental worry. Good, nutritious diet. Stimulation with coarse towels after a hot bath. By using a little Sweet Oil on the surface the rubbing, or massage, may be carried on indefinitely without irritation, and more than that, it produces a soft, healthy texture. Any portion of the Oil that is absorbed goes to nourish the system. Also give 1-20 grain doses of Arsenic after meals, and 10-drop doses of Tincture of Iron three times a day after meals.—(7).

BUNIONS—BURSA, ENLARGED.—A bursa is an irregular cavity formed in the loose connective tissue around joints, being situated between the tendons. The bursa is filled with a fluid which is poured out over the surface of the tendons to facilitate their movements and prevent friction. A bursa may be either superficial or deep. The superficial are those that protect the small tendons in their movements over light joints near the surface, as, for instance, the ball of the great toe; the deep bursa is to protect the large tendons in their passage over rough bony prominences situated around large joints, as, for example, the hip joint. Continued pressure from tight shoes excites a mild inflammation of the bursa over the great toe joint and increases its secretions. This constitutes a bunion and, if continued, results in an overgrowth of the bone, causing permanent deformity.

TREATMENTS.—

A. Turpentine externally and poultices of hot Flax seed at night. Chloroform liniment to relieve pain.—(7.)

B. Put cloths saturated with Turpentine over the bunion on retiring. Bandage to keep cloths in place.

C. Get shoes to fit. Apply bunion plaster.—(13.)

D. Paint with Tincture of Iodine. When very painful, apply hot fomentations of Smartweed and Wormwood. Avoid irritating part.

CANCER.—There are two principal varieties of cancer, one called *sarcoma* and the other called *carcinoma.* The first usually occurs before forty years of age, and the second, after that period. These two forms of cancer differ only in the appearance (as shown under the microscope) of the cells of which they are formed, and in the kind of tissue in which they occur. Practically there is no difference, for, unless successfully removed, either is destructive to life.

Cause.—There are two theories regarding the cause of cancer: One is that it is caused by a germ, and the other that it is the result of degenerative changes going on in the body. While there are a number of investigators who hold to the germ theory, although unable to discover the germ, the majority believe that cancer is the result of the retrograde changes mentioned. That standard authority, Green's Pathology, page 249, states that the germs or parasites found, which are claimed to be the cause of cancer, "apparently are not parasites, but are degenerate cells or products of cells. In the few cases in which parasites have been present in the tissues, they may have been there as a secondary infection." Page 256 states, "Some cancers seem to be due to irritation in people whose resistance is diminished."

First, let us remember that the human body, all parts, tissues and organs, are composed of small particles of matter called cells. The life work of these cells is to take up nutrition, to constantly build up their own structure and to eliminate waste material. The failure from any cause to take up nutrition is the first step in the chain of malignant tissue growth that leads to cancer. In health the blood contains elements of nutrition, which are supplied through the circulation. When nutrition is lacking, it is an indication that the blood is unhealthy,—the result of poor food, or of indigestion from some cause. In health the tissues and individual cells are under the intelligent guidance of the nervous system and for a time can successfully resist the morbid influence or effects of unhealthy blood, but when this condition exists too long, or the amount of poison in the blood increases beyond a certain limit, it will cause congestion; mild at first and perhaps unnoticed, yet after a time, at some point where the resistance is least, the nerve fibres become more or less paralyzed, and this allows the congestion to increase, lessens nutrition and leaves the tissues without proper control. In health the nervous system controls the function of the cells and retards decay and death; but with this power or influence lessened and the tissues gorged with unhealthy blood, the cells at that point multiply more rapidly and deviate more or less from the normal. This is the beginning of cancer.

The conditions from which cancers arise, then, may be enumerated as follows, remembering that inflammation always depends upon an irritant which excites an increased blood supply:

First, an unhealthy digestive tract, lack of nourishment and the formation of many poisons.

Second, the absorption of the poisons, which act as irritants.

Third, the irritants produce first, congestion, and second, inflammation.

Fourth, the result of the inflammation is an increase in the blood supply, and the tissues at that point being overfed, the cells first enlarge, then divide and subdivide, first one and then another, and thus new tissue forms. But the blood is unhealthy, the vitality low, and the morbid effects of the degenerative changes which are constantly going on in the new growth renders the cells malignant and the blood more impure, and in turn the inflammation and growth are increased.

In health the cells constituting the different organs and tissues of the body have a certain well defined size and shape, not all alike, but each peculiar to the organ or part to which it belongs, and which under the microscope can be recognized just as a man can be recognized by his appearance. But as a result of the conditions described the cells constituting the growth lose their identity, and this is the reason that there is no specific cancer cell, that is, no particular size or form. The cells may be large or small and variously shaped, due to their malignancy and mutual pressure upon each other. As a result of rapid growth and from lack of vitality, they break down easily. The cells constituting "proud flesh" may be large or small like the cancer cells, but they too lack vitality and break down easily. When the general system is unhealthy and the surrounding tissues offer but slight resistance, the growth is rapid. The new cells do not have time to develop, but remain small and the growth soft. The softer the growth the more numerous the blood vessels, hence more blood and lymph are supplied. These are the reasons why this form of cancer is more rapidly fatal. If the vitality improves, the resistance improves also, and the growth is checked in proportion. Cancerous growths have a framework of connective tissue the same as other organs. This connective tissue is strong and fibrous. It pervades and supports all the organs and structures of the body. The growth of the malignant cancer cells may be lessened, and the inflammation may still continue to cause an increase in this connective tissue. But connective tissue resulting from inflammation always contracts and hardens. This is the condition when a large, hard, slowly growing lump appears in the breast or elsewhere. Rapid increase in tissue cells always results in a diminution, or loss, of vitality. Most cancers grow so rapidly that the cells do not have time to mature; their vitality is low and pressure upon each other aids in their own destruction; they break down easily. They are constantly undergoing this change, and furnish the phenomena known as suppuration. If on the surface, as the nose, face or lip, it breaks externally and the acrid discharge corrodes the skin if allowed to come in contact with it; or when situated internally, the poison excites inflammation around the growth. Dead and dying tissue always excites inflammation, and the inflammatory zone aids in checking its spread. This is Nature's method of localizing disease. A more common example of Nature's effort to check disease is found in the inflammatory zone which surrounds every abscess, and the red line which separates the living from the dead in gangrene; in gangrene it is called the line of demarkation.

Yet in spite of efforts to localize the disease, the morbid effects of the malignant growth gradually pervade the system and digestion and assimilation are reduced to a low ebb. This is why the patient grows so thin and weak, and this is why the disease ends fatally.

The individual cells of the body need stimulation the same as a man needs exercise. Such stimulation is the natural result of repair and waste. The cells are actively engaged in taking up new elements from the blood and reforming and refitting them into their own structure; these elements become living matter. In health there is given off an equal amount of waste. This is a natural action and produces a natural stimulation. All life's forces depend upon this stimulation. Besides the work mentioned, many of the cells manufacture new products which are necessary in maintaining life and health: The liver cells manufacture bile; those of the salivary glands, ptyalin; those of the thyroid gland, iodine; and those of the stomach manufacture pepsin. These products all act as ferments and aid digestion. (See *Digestion* under STOMACH DISEASES.) The pancreas also furnishes four ferments which aid in the same work. The kidney cells eliminate urea, and those of the lungs and skin eliminate many other poisons. This aids still more in stimulating the organs, but when irritation from impure and poisonous blood renders these changes excessive, it is called inflammation. This lowers the powers of resistance and disease results, hence the statement in Green's Pathology, "Cancer seems to be due to irritation in people whose resistance is diminished."

Symptoms.—A cancer growing within the body may present no early symptoms. The first evidence of its presence may be a gradual loss of appetite and of weight. Among the early symptoms are stinging, darting pains. Later, as the growth develops, the pain becomes more constant. By this time, if the cancer is situated in the breast, stomach or abdominal cavity, it can be felt. When in the stomach, the appetite is affected earlier than when in other situations, and sooner or later there is vomiting. In some cases vomiting is delayed until three or four weeks before death. If on the surface—face or lip—there is first a small, hard lump, which bleeds easily and does not entirely heal. This may develop to the size of a small pea and then remain stationary for some months, when it begins to grow again and soon forms a slowly extending ulcer. The edges of such an ulcer are hard and ragged or irregular. The discharge is foul-smelling and irritating, and destroys the skin if allowed to come in contact with it. In cancer of the breast the inflammation extends to the skin, giving it a puckered appearance. The skin looks dark and congested.

TREATMENTS.—

In many cases cancers are treated by surgical means only, that is, are removed by the surgeon's knife. Those who follow this method of treatment claim that by making liberal allowance for the growth,—"cutting wide of the mark",—complete removal is assured, and that, if the operation is made early, it is the only safe and intelligent method of dealing with this otherwise fatal malady. On the other hand, there are those who treat cancers by local applications—plasters—and who believe that in all cases where the growth appears on the surface, it can be successfully treated in this way. Statistics favor this claim. Certain it is that many a cancerous growth treated in this way has been lifted out *whole*, with the fibres, or roots, unbroken, the part from which it has been removed showing all the various avenues into which these roots penetrated. The danger in using the knife is that some of these roots may be cut off, and should the least portion of one of them remain, the cancer is almost certain to grow again. The applications named below have been used with great success; in action they seem to follow up the various branches of a cancer, and to seek out and destroy its uttermost parts.

The following are a few of the more important remedies used and recommended by leading doctors. The list includes the treatment employed by Doctor Lombard, the noted "cancer doctor."

A. The first remedy is one recommended by F. W. Brewer, M. D., and reported in the Chicago *Medical Times*, as follows:—

Chloride of Zinc	½ ounce.
Powdered Blood Root	½ ounce.
Flour	½ ounce.

Make into a paste with Aromatic Sulphuric Acid. Spread on a soft cloth and apply. Continue the application until the growth is destroyed. Then dress with any mild application, as Vaseline containing ten drops of Carbolic Acid to the ounce.

B. The second remedy is used by W. N. Sherman, M. D., and reported in the *Medical World:*

Chloride of Zinc............................	5 grains.
Powdered Alum	5 grains.
Tannic Acid.................................	2 grains.
Persulphate of Iron........................	3 grains.
Glycerine sufficient to make a paste.	

Apply as above. The after treatment is the same.

C. Dr. J. L. Horr says, in the Boston *Medical and Surgical Journal:*

"Having, without solicitation on my part, become possessed of the knowledge of the secret remedies employed by the late Doctor Lombard, the famous 'cancer doctor' of Maine, I feel it my privilege, as a member of the scientific profession that has only for its object the advancement of knowledge and the relief of suffering, to make a simple statement of the remedies and methods which were employed in the so-called 'treatment of cancer.' The remedy employed, if the cancer was small, was the dried juice of the leaves of Phytolacco (Poke Root), which was applied in the form of a plaster until sloughing took place. The after treatment was some simple dressing, like simple Cerate.

"If the tumor had obtained considerable size, Doctor Lombard first used a paste composed of Chloride of Zinc and pulverized Blood Root until a scar was produced, and then used the same dressing as before until the mass sloughed away.

"The knowledge of these remedies was given to me by Doctor Lombard himself while I was attending him during his last illness, but a few days before he died."

D. There are many other remedies used for the removal of cancer. Chromic Acid, melted on the end of a glass rod and applied direct, or made into a paste and applied to the growth, is used by many. The juice of fresh Sorrel, dried down to a paste and applied, will prove equally satisfactory.

CANCRUM ORIS.—(See under MOUTH, DISEASES OF).

CAPILLARY BRONCHITIS.—(See under LUNG DISEASES).

CARBUNCLE.—A carbuncle is an inflammation of the deeper layer of the skin, and includes more or less of the tissue beneath the skin. The swelling or inflammation strangulates the circulation more or less, nutrition is shut off and the tissues destroyed, hence pus is formed. A carbuncle differs from a boil as it is divided into many sections or parts by a framework of connective tissue, giving to the whole structure a honeycombed appearance. It is larger than a boil, has a flat top, and when suppuration takes place it discharges from several openings, which correspond to the number of its divisions. They appear most frequently in persons above middle age. They occasion great suffering, and sometimes prove fatal. They usually occur on the back and posterior portions of the neck, but upon the head or neck they are more dangerous than in other situations.

Cause.—Carbuncles are due to irritation from unhealthy blood. The irritation becomes excessive and is followed by inflammation; the inflammation becomes localized, swelling and pressure interfere with nutrition, the tissues break down and pus forms. Like inflammations elsewhere, a carbuncle is enclosed by an inflammatory zone which prevents the spread of the pus.

Symptoms.—There is burning, throbbing, deep-seated pain, and a decided loss of strength and energy. Constitutional symptoms, as chills and fever, are also present.

TREATMENTS.—

To Abort.—When a carbuncle first begins to come, paint it over with the Tincture of Iodine twice a day until the surface becomes sore, and attend to the general health. For instance, if the bowels are constipated, regulate them with Castor Oil, with Senna steeped up, or with some mild cathartic pill, and take the following for a blood purifier, which is also good for boils:

> Burdock root.
> Yellow Dock root.
> Wild Cherry bark.
> Dandelion root.

Take a small handful of each, add a quart of hot water and steep in an iron kettle. Simmer until the strength is out of the roots, strain, and then boil the liquid down to a pint. Sweeten, if preferred, and take a tablespoonful three times a day.

Do not meddle with the carbuncle itself. Do not squeeze it, do not pick at it, but paint it over when it first starts with Iodine, and if it is not aborted (prevented from developing) by the above treatment, that is, if pus begins to form, poultice it. Bread and milk with Catnip leaves stirred into it thoroughly, makes a soothing poultice.

> A. Alcohol... 1 ounce.
>   Glycerine 1   "
>   Boracic Acid.................................... 2 drachms.
>   Corrosive Sublimate .... 1 grain.
>   Water... 8 ounces.

> *Mix*, and apply locally on wet cloth, keeping parts continually moist.—(46.)

B. Carbolic Acid..................................20 drops.
Glycerine.................................... 1 ounce.

Apply on cotton.—(6.)

C. Should be opened early and freely and dressed with Carbolated Vaseline to which 10 drops of Turpentine has been added.—(14.)

D. Silicea, 12th dilution, applied night and morning. When opened, wash frequently with Permanganate of Potash in solution—2 grains of the Potash to 1 ounce of water. This wash will stain, and clothing should be protected from it.—(3)—Homeopathic.

CARIES.—(See under BONE DISEASES.)

CATALEPSY.—An hysterical state in which the mind, or intellect, seems for the time being to be cut off from the body. All movement ceases and the trunk and limbs remain fixed in the position in which they were when the fit occurred. If moved by another person, they remain as placed. The breast does not rise and fall, and the person does not seem to breathe, but a professional ear can detect a slight beating of the heart. The eyes are fixed and staring and the subject of the fit is said to be *in a trance.* The fit may be brief or may continue indefinitely, a peculiarity being that when consciousness is regained the person immediately completes the act that he was about performing when his senses were arrested.

TREATMENTS.—

What to Do Till the Doctor Comes. — During the fit hold Hartshorn to the nostrils, rub the head and back part of the neck with a Turpentine liniment, put Mustard to the feet and calf of the legs—may also be applied to the spine. Give Catnip tea or Asafœtida pills .

A. Keep the person warm and apply Mustard to the feet.

CATARRH.—This disease is an inflammation of a mucous membrane, from which a fluid is discharged.

Cause.— It is induced by "taking cold." The lining of the nose, throat and bronchial passages are especially liable to attack as the result of a cold in the head. Catarrh may be either *acute* or *chronic.*

Symptoms.—*Acute Nasal Catarrh* is attended with a cough, thirst, lassitude, chilliness followed with slight fever, watery eyes, feeling of fullness in the nostrils, dull pain in the forehead and a discharge from the nose. This discharge is at first watery and later purulent in character. The air passages leading into the throat also become inflamed and the discharge is ejected by the mouth or swallowed.   If constant care is exercised, however, in keeping the nostrils open and the mouth closed, the patient not permitting himself to breathe through the mouth, the inflammation is less likely to extend to the throat and bronchial passages.

TREATMENTS.—

A. Take the root of Colt's-Foot (for a description of this plant see A CHAPTER ON HERBS), wash, dry in the sun or by the fire, and powder. Sift, and use same as snuff. Salt and water snuffed up the nose is also good. Take 3 grains of Sulphite of Soda and 6 grains of Chlorate of Potash, dissolve in a glass two-thirds full of warm water. Snuff up both nostrils, draw through to the throat and spit out.

> **B.** Camphor....................................... 15 grains.
>   Menthol (crystal)........................... 15   "
>   *Mix* until of clear appearance and add
>   Vaseline to make........................... 1 ounce.
>   Make into an ointment.

When having this ointment made up, secure from the druggist a small glass tube, about as big around as a pipe stem. Dip this into the ointment, taking up a small quantity, and pass the tube well up into the nostril. Hold the other nostril closed, and also press the nostril around the tube so as to exclude the passage of air; then give a hard snuff and the ointment will be drawn from the tube well up into the head. It not only clears the passages, but heals the mucous surface. It may be used several times a day (too often may cause nausea as some of it will pass through into the throat). A fresh cold in the head will often be entirely overcome, and it will give relief in the most stubborn case of catarrh.   Probable cost, thirty cents.
From a head and throat specialist of Milwaukee, Wis.

C. To half a pint of water use one ounce of Glycerine, ten drops of Carbolic Acid, and a half teaspoonful each of baking soda and salt, to which add a teaspoonful of Listerine. This will always relieve cold or catarrh in the head.

CATARRH, CHRONIC NASAL.— When catarrh becomes chronic, the air passages are widely dilated, and both bones and cartilages may be more or less destroyed. The mucous membrane which lines the cavities, once thick and swollen, has now become thin, firm and resistant as a result of the contraction of the newly formed connective tissue. The sense of smell is more or less interfered with—in some cases is entirely lost. The natural secretions are changed both in quality and quantity; they are unhealthy and ill-smelling, and sometimes of a greenish color. The secretion, reaching the surface, forms crusts or scales, which must be removed before successful treatment can be instituted.

TREATMENTS. —

    A. Boracic Acid................................. 1 ounce.
       Pure Water .... 1 quart.

Dissolve the acid in the water, pour in a fountain syringe and hang syringe on the wall at some convenient place. The patient should bend the head well forward, place the tip of the syringe in the nostril, first one, then the other, and allow the solution to pass through the nasal openings and out through the mouth, which should be kept open. This will thoroughly saturate, loosen and remove the crusts which form in chronic nasal catarrh, and when you have rendered the surface clean and wholesome, you have cured the disease. Any mild antiseptic may be used in place of the Boracic acid.

    B. The following may be used morning and evening, and will be found most satisfactory in all cases not too far advanced:

      Menthol.............................. 5 to 10 grains.
      Oil Eucalyptus..................... 10 drops.
      Oil Wintergreen .... 2 "
      Liquid Alboline.................... 1 ounce.

      Mix, and use in Atomizer morning and evening. When using the atomizer, draw in the breath, and be sure the vapor passes through the nasal cavities into the throat.

    C. Ely's Cream Balm is a catarrh remedy that is well known and has for years been sold throughout the country. See PATENT PREPARATIONS.

    D. Use the following as a nasal spray three times daily:

      Camphor Gum .... 30 grains.
      Menthol...................................... 10 "
      Liquid Alboline.......................... 1 ounce.
                      —(46).

    E. Castile soap and water snuffed up the nose from the hand will always improve, and often cure.—(12).

    F. Iodine .... 10 grains.
      Alcohol..................................... 1 ounce

      Put into a 2 oz. vial, and when the Iodine is dissolved fill the vial with soft water Inject a little of the mixture into the nostrils with a small syringe 3 times daily. An alterative containing Iodine, taken internally, will be a desirable thing in treating an obstinate case of chronic catarrh.

      The above has been a very successful treatment.—(65).

CATARACT.— (See under EYE, DISEASES OF).

CEREBRO-SPINAL MENINGITIS. — (See under BRAIN, DISEASES OF).

CHANGE OF LIFE.—(See under WOMEN'S DISEASES).

CHAPPED HANDS.—REMEDIES.

A. Quince Seed................ .... ½ ounce.
Borax...................................... ¼ "
Glycerine.............................. 2 "
Water..............................12 "

Add the Quince seed to the warm water and let stand until it becomes quite thick. This may require several hours. Strain, and carefully dissolve the Borax in a little of the mixture, add the two together and lastly add the Glycerine; add perfume as desired. This makes a preparation that will keep the hands soft and free from all roughness. It dries in a few minutes, and kid gloves may then be put on with ease.

B. Flostilla is a remedy for chapped hands that is widely known throughout the country. It will be found among the PATENT PREPARATIONS. It is a very satisfactory preparation and will please all who use it.

C. Sweet Oil...................................... 3 ounces.
Spermaceti................................... 4 "
Pulverized Camphor...................... 1 "

Heat gently in a clean earthen vessel, stirring to prevent scorching, and apply, after warming a little, night and morning. Butter just churned and unsalted may be substituted for Sweet Oil—same quantity.—(79).

D. Deer's Tallow................................ 4 ounces.
Glycerine...................................... 1 "
Pulverized Camphor...................... ½ "
Honey... ¼ "

Carefully incorporate together by gentle heat, or by rubbing with a knife or spatula on a plate, or in a mortar.

Makes a very healing ointment for chaps, sore lips, etc., also for chafing from trusses.—(79).

E. Wash clean at bedtime with warm water containing a liberal amount of wheat bran, and after wiping apply Glycerine and rub dry. (17).

F. Pulverized Orris Root.................... 1 drachm.
Water (warm).............................. 4 ounces.

Let stand 24 hours, strain through fine gauze, and add:

Glycerine...................................... ½ ounce.
Bay Rum......................................2 "

Mix, and apply often, thoroughly washing and drying before using.—(3).—Homeopathic.

G. Wash at night in corn meal water or bran water till soft; rub dry, then rub in Cosmoline thoroughly and sleep in old clean gloves. Keep the hands out of water during day and repeat every night until well.—(13).

CHICKEN-POX.—(See under ERUPTIVE FEVERS).

CHILBLAINS. — Chilblains are inflammatory swellings affecting the hands and feet, and are produced by exposure to cold. The swellings are of a purplish or bluish color, and are accompanied by an unbearable itching. They may blister, or, in severe cases, be attended with ulceration and sloughing.

REMEDIES.—

A. Twenty grains Carbolic Acid to one ounce Vaseline; apply to parts.—(14).

B. Rub every night with Turpentine, or get Citron ointment, one ounce, and apply to chilblains at night.—(13).

C. Keep feet dusted with Boracic Acid. It will relieve the most obstinate case.—(18).—Homeopathic.

D. Carbolic Acid............................... 1 drachm.
Tincture Iodine............................ 2   "
Tannic Acid................................. 1   "
Simple Cerate .... 4 ounces.

Mix, and apply twice daily.—(46).

E. Hydrochloric Acid......................... 1 drachm.
Rainwater...................................... 7 ounce.

Wash the feet two or three times daily, or wet the stockings with the preparation until relieved.—(81).

F. Tincture of Iodine........................ 1 ounce.
Soap Liniment............................... 1   "
or,
Turpentine.................................... ½ ounce.
Ether.. ½   "
Oil of Thyme................................. ½   "

Sometimes little water blisters form. These may be painted over with Balsam Peru or Collodion, ½ drachm.

G.—Paint chilblains freely with Muriate Tincture of Iron.

CHILL.—A disagreeable sensation of coolness accompanied with shivering.

TREATMENTS.—

A.—Immediate relief by surrounding patient with hot water bottles and giving internally from 1 to 2 ounces of Whiskey. Rectal injection of hot salt solution—2 teaspoonfuls of salt to 2 quarts of water.—(60).

B. Cover warmly, give warm drinks and get to sweating. After sweating is produced give, for an adult, 3 to 5 grains of Quinine every four or five hours.

C. Keep the surface of the body warm with hot blankets and hot drinks. Take Quinine after the chill to prevent a recurrence.—(7).

D. Drink hot lemonade until chill passes off, and then take Quinine.—(17).

CHILLS AND FEVER.—(See *Intermittent Fever* under MALARIAL FEVERS).

CHLOROSIS.—(See under WOMEN'S DISEASES).

CHOLERA.—This disease is characterized by vomiting and purging as the essential symptoms, also by griping, and spasms in the legs and arms. *Asiatic Cholera* is the more malignant form.

ASIATIC CHOLERA.—This form of *cholera* is of oriental origin. Epidemics are known to have occurred for several centuries, but it was not until the early part of the nineteenth century that the attention of European physicians was generally directed to the disease. This was occasioned by a violent epidemic which broke out in India.

Cause.— Due to unhealthy surroundings, poor food, bad air. The eating of unripe fruits and indigestible foods and drinking of alcoholic liquors all predispose to an attack in time of an epidemic. The statement has been made that "With pure water, pure air, pure soil and pure habits, cholera need not be feared."

Symptoms.—The beginning of this disease is marked by a derangement of the digestive organs, impaired appetite, thirst, lassitude, chilliness, and especially by a painless diarrhea; there may also be twitchings of the calves of the legs. These indispositions, which might easily be occasioned by other causes, continue from a few hours to several days. Or the attack may be quite sudden and marked with profuse evacuations.

The characteristic feature which distinguishes cholera and marks the beginning of the disease itself, is the vomiting and purging of a colorless fluid which looks almost like rice water. This is accompanied with increasing thirst and with cramps of the calves of the legs and other muscles, but if the attack is not a severe one, it may be arrested at this stage. If not arrested, the cramps become severe and exceedingly painful, and soon attack the bowels and stomach. At this stage the breathing is hurried, with distress about the heart, and the secretion of urine is greatly diminished or entirely stopped.

The discharges, which consist largely of serum (the watery portion of the blood), leave the patient in a state of great prostration from which he seldom recovers. The pulse is hardly perceptible, skin cold and clammy, and the patient presents a frightful appearance of emaciation; yet there is a sense of great heat in the stomach accompanied with intense thirst. The emaciation or shrinking of the tissues is the result of draining the water from the system through the digestive tract.

The foregoing symptoms represent a typical case of cholera. These cases are seldom met at the present. With attention to cleanliness cholera is fast becoming a disease of the past, and to-day we do not fear it.

TREATMENTS.—

What to Do Till the Doctor Comes.—Cholera proper is preceded by a relaxed state of the bowels, that is, by a mild diarrhea. In time of an epidemic, or in sections regularly visited by cholera, a looseness of the bowels, however mild, should not be neglected for a moment. An excellent remedy for the looseness is the following:

> Capsicum (Cayenne Pepper) .... 20 grains.
> Gum Camphor (powdered) .... 10 "
>
> Put into a teacup, fill two-thirds full of hot water and stir thoroughly. Take a teaspoonful of the solution every hour, or oftener, if necessary, until the diarrhea is controlled. If this solution does not seem to have a controlling effect, secure medical aid without delay.

A. For Cholera, Cholera Morbus, Colic or Painful Diarrhea:

> Oil of Cajeput .... 1 ounce.
> Oil of Cloves................................. 1 "
> Oil of Peppermint.......................... 1 "
> Oil of Anise .... 1 "
> Alcohol .... 4 "
>
> *Dose.*—From 10 to 15 drops every 30 minutes; or ½ teaspoonful every hour. It should be taken in simple syrup, mucilage of slippery elm bark, or hot brandy and water sweetened.
> In epidemics of cholera, as much as a teaspoonful of this mixture has been given every fifteen minutes, one or two such doses generally succeeding in relieving the pains and spasms. —(76).

B Chloroform............................... 1 drachm.
> Tincture of Camphor .... 1 "
> Tincture of Capsicum .... 1 "
> Tincture of Opium .... 1 "
> Tincture of Ginger...................... 1 "
>
> *Mix.*
> *Dose.*—Teaspoonful every hour.—(7).

CHOLERA MORBUS.—*Cholera Morbus*, or *Simple Cholera*, is a disease that is prevalent in warm weather.

Cause.—This disease occurs in summer and fall. It is influenced by extreme heat, and perhaps by hard work which lowers physical power, or the power of resistance; also caused by eating unripe fruit and vegetables and by drinking cold water. In other words it is caused by acute indigestion when the system is relaxed.

Symptoms.—This form usually comes on suddenly, with retching, distension and flatulency of the stomach, griping pain in the bowels, and vomiting and purging of irritating matter. The patient is tormented with thirst, but water is rejected by the stomach as soon as swallowed. There is also heat, quick breathing, a frequent but weak and fluttering pulse, and, in very severe cases, cramps of the legs. When the disease is violent, there is great loss of vitality, with cold, clammy sweats and coldness of the extremities, sometimes ending in death. Usually the symptoms, pretty severe for a few hours or for a day or two, gradually lessen, leaving the patient in a state of great debility. The features are sunken and the eyes look "hollow," due to the amount of water that has been drained from the tissues.

TREATMENTS.—

What to Do Before Calling a Doctor.—Usually due to overloading the stomach. Give Brandy sling; or make a Camphor tea by dropping into hot water a few drops of the Spirits of Camphor and sweetening. Peppermint tea is also good. For griping add, for an adult, from 15 to 20 drops of Laudanum. Usually there are from three to six evacuations of the bowels and vomiting, and then the patient is entirely relieved, although left very weak; but if the attack is not controlled within a few hours, then call a doctor.

If a person is attacked violently in this way, it is advisable to send for a physician at once. In the meantime, put hot applications over the abdomen—cloths wrung out of hot water or the hot decoction of some bitter herb—and give hot sling, or any of the simple remedies mentioned.

A. The one thought to bear in mind is to bring the blood abundantly to the surface. The vomiting and the continued evacuations of the bowels is the result of prostration brought on by the cause given above. The circulation near the surface of the body is feeble, while the internal organs are congested, the congestion being the result of the irritation produced by the acute indigestion. This is why the surface is pale, cold and clammy. If the blood can be drawn to the surface, immediate relief will follow. For this purpose apply external heat; and give, for an adult, Atropine in $\frac{1}{100}$-grain doses. If there is severe pain, add from 20 to 40 drops of Laudanum. Repeat the dose of Atropine every hour until the surface is flushed, which will mean that the circulation has been equalized and the internal organs relieved. Atropine internally and artificial heat externally are the best possible means of bringing about favorable results.

B. Paregoric...................................... 1 ounce.
Tincture of Capsicum.................... 2 drachms.
Subnitrate of Bismuth.................. 2   "
Simple Syrup............................. 4 ounces.
  Mix. and take teaspoonful every hour until relieved.—(46).

C. Wash out stomach with hot water. For adult 10 drops Laudanum in strong Peppermint water every hour till relieved. Children may take appropriate doses of Paregoric in strong Peppermint.—(13).

CHOLERA INFANTUM, or SUMMER COMPLAINT OF INFANTS.

—This is a disease to which children are subject during the summer months.

Cause.—The conditions are the same as those described under *Cholera Morbus.*

Symptoms.—It begins with restlessness, pain, vomiting and diarrhea. The eliminations from the bowels are foul-smelling and often contain undigested food. The pulse is rapid and feeble and the surface cold. Sometimes there is but a limited amount of diarrhea, and at the same time the bowels are distended with their contents. More or less gas may be present, and in this case the abdomen is bloated and tender. In a well-developed state the child lies in a stupor, taking no notice of the surroundings. There is but little or no fever. Where the bowel eliminations are frequent, with abundant watery discharges, the features of the child look shrunken and wasted as a result of the water that has been drained away.

TREATMENTS.—

What to Do Till the Doctor Comes.—This is a dangerous disease and a doctor should be called early. In the meantime, an excellent thing to give is the following:

Rhubarb (powdered)................... 1 teaspoonful.
Bicarbonate of Soda (baking soda) ½   "
White Sugar............................. 2 tablespoonfuls.

  Mix well and add twenty drops of Essence of Peppermint. Put this into a teacup and pour two-thirds full of boiling water, stirring at the same time you are pouring in the water. Set to one side and let settle. Dip from the surface. For a child one year old, half a teaspoonful every hour; three years old, a teaspoonful every half hour. A warm bath may be given, and injections of hot water are also beneficial. If the child is very fretful and distressed, a few drops (from five to ten) of Laudanum may be added to the injection. Bitter herbs, as Hops, Smartweed, etc., may be steeped up, enclosed in flannel and laid across the bowels. If there is nothing else to give before the doctor can arrive, teaspoonful doses of hot sling will not be out of place.

A. This trouble occurs from various causes and requires treatment accordingly too grave for guess work. Send for your doctor at once; may give a few drops Paregoric pending his arrival. Salted water often stops vomiting.—(14).

B. Stop all food for twenty-four hours. Keep the child quiet. In some cases the movement of the bowels may be slight or absent. In any event it is a good plan to add one tablespoonful of warm water to an equal amount of Glycerine, mix well and inject into the bowels, and with a soft cloth hold the injection for five or ten minutes. Repeat the injection if results are not satisfactory. The discharges are usually offensive; for this, give the following:

Sulphocarbolate of Zinc............... 20 grains.
Glycerine.................................... 4 teaspoonfuls.
Water 6   "

Dissolve the Sulphocarbolate in the Glycerine and water and give one teaspoonful every two hours.

The same amount of Salol may be given if the Sulphocarbolate cannot be had. Place the Salol on the tongue dry, and give water with teaspoon. During the disease the drinking water should be boiled and cooled and given to the child freely. If the child is pale and cold, apply external heat. Equal parts of powdered wood charcoal and Lactopeptine should be mixed and 5 grains given every hour or two.—(74).

C.—Stop all feeding and give liberally of hot water into which a few live coals of wood have been dropped. Send for doctor.

D. Tincture Nux Vomica............... 2 drachms.
Dilute Nitro-Muriatic Aci d........ 2   "
Subnitrate of Bismuth............... 2   "
Lactopeptine 2   "
Tincture Red Pepper................. ½ teaspoonful.
Simple Syrup........................... 4 ounces.
Sherry Wine............................ 4   "

Mix together and take one teaspoonful in water three or four times a day.—(53).

CHOREA.—(See under CHILDREN'S DISEASES).

CHORDEE.—(See under VENEREAL DISEASES).

CIRRHOSIS.—This means a hardening of the tissues of an organ, and follows a mild form of inflammation long-continued. The inflammation may be the result of syphilis or of irritating matter resulting from indigestion and constipation, but is more often the result of the continued use of alcoholic liquors. This inflammation always produces an overgrowth and shrinking of tissue as described under *Alcohol.* The new tissue contracts and hardens, destroying and replacing normal tissue in proportion. This change most often takes place in the liver or kidneys, and next most frequently in the spinal cord and lungs; however, it may occur anywhere in the body.

COLIC. — An attack of pain in the abdomen, of spasmodic character, usually attended with constipation of the bowels. There is no attendant fever, and the pain is relieved by pressure over the abdomen—points which are of importance in distinguishing it from inflammation.

There are several forms of *Colic.*

BILIOUS COLIC.—Strictly speaking *Bilious Colic* means *Biliary Calculi* or *Gall-Stones*, but as the term is more or less commonly used, it is given here. As usually understood bilious colic, flatulent colic and wind colic are one and the same, and the cause is the same—undigested food. When the trouble has existed for some days and comes on in the form of an acute attack, there is nausea and vomiting of bilious matter, hence the term, *Bilious Colic.*

For treatment the reader is referred to the remedies under *Flatulent, or Wind, Colic.*

FLATULENT, or WIND, COLIC.—This form is due to indigestible matter in the intestines, which not only excites pain, but by beginning to undergo decomposition also gives rise to gases which cause a painful distension of the bowels.

TREATMENTS.—

What to do Before Calling a Doctor.—First give an active cathartic. Follow with hot applications over the abdomen and give hot drinks—hot sling, hot pepper tea, Camphor tea—or any of the remedies mentioned below.

    A. Spirits of Chloroform...................... 1 ounce.
        Paregoric....................................... 2   "
        Dose.—For an adult, take a teaspoonful in hot water every half hour,
                  or,
        Morphine, ⅛ grain every two hours for adult.

Apply hot flannels or hot bottles over bowels and stomach. If pain is in right side and there is tenderness over the appendix, it is best to have a doctor at once.—(13).

B. Laudanum.. 25 drops.
Pepper Sauce................................. ½ teaspoonful.
Spirits of Camphor .... 5 drops.

Dose.—For an adult, the whole taken in a wineglassful of hot water.—(14).

C. Tincture of Cardamon Compound.... 1 ounce.
Aromatic Spirits of Ammonia......... 1 "

Mix, and take one teaspoonful, for the adult, every hour more or less often as he need.

This prescription I have used in some most severe cases of colic of this country with the finest success. Give also a cathartic—a 5-grain dose of Calomel. The Salines or Castor Oil are not so good for bilious colic. The Calomel is better.—(77).

D. A friend who has suffered very much from colic recently obtained from a physician the following prescription, which afforded him such immediate and perfect relief that he desires to give it to the public. It is as follows:

Pulverized Opium .... 1 grain.
Sulphate of Morphia (Morphine)...... 1 "
Pulverized Camphor .... 5 "
Capsicum .... 5 "

Make into 10 pills with a thick solution of gum.

One pill will generally afford relief, but if not materially benefited after an hour or two, another may be taken. The remedy was accompanied by the following letter:

"Please find prescription, which I hope will alleviate the pains of some mortal as it has done for me. Hoping it may prove profitable to you, and, through your book, a blessing to mankind, I remain, yours, etc.

We have not permission to publish the gentleman's name.

E. A splendid remedy is the following:

Powdered Wood Charcoal............... 1 ounce.
Lactopeptin .... 1 "

Dose for adult, ½ to ⅔ of a teaspoonful; for child one year old, one teaspoonful divided into ten powders and given with a little water.

F. *For the wind colic of children*, about the nicest thing that can be given them is a tea made of soot. Take some soot from the chimney, put into a dish, pour on some hot water, and drink of it. Or a tea may be made of red pepper, or even of black pepper

—anything that is warming—but the soot tea is best as it starts the gas at once. If, however, the child is not relieved within a reasonable time, say within an hour or so, send for a doctor.

When babes are tongue-tied, they draw air into the stomach in nursing, and if a babe is constantly bothered with colic, the tongue should be examined to see if it needs cutting.

LEAD or PAINTER'S COLIC.—(See LEAD POISONING).

RENAL COLIC.—(See GRAVEL).

COLDS AND COUGHS.—Many people are troubled with colds, influenza, sore throat, lame back, etc. Prevention is the best thing for colds, as for everything else. People need not be so sensitive to colds if they would gradually accustom themselves to cold baths or cold sponging, in either case bringing the temperature of the water down gradually; and most people would soon learn to appreciate them. Finish by drying thoroughly, rubbing the skin well but not enough to produce irritation. To practice deep breathing for several minutes at a time will also be found of great benefit. Even when out in the cold, deep breathing will increase the heart action and send the blood tingling and the chills flying. The feet should always be kept warm and dry. Shoes should be large enough to allow free circulation.

Another preventative may be had by drinking plenty of water. Water flushes the small vessels, aids in keeping the bowels active and in carrying away waste.

TREATMENTS FOR COLDS.—

A. *To prevent.*—Out-door exercise and cold baths.

To cure.—Hot baths, sweats and rubbing.—(5.)

B. *To Prevent Taking.*—Rub the entire surface of the body, in a warm room on retiring, with fresh hog's lard every night, followed by bath in the morning. Do not use sweet oil or any vegetable oil. Vigorous people may take a cold sponge bath with good rubbing after and will seldom take cold.—(8).

C. If a person finds he has a cold, it is better to remain in for a day or two, take a hot foot bath, or better, an alcohol sweat at night. Take 10 grains Quinine and 10 grains of Dover's Powder. This will be all that will be needed in any ordinary attack.

D. *Lemons for Colds.*—For a fresh cold a good cathartic followed by a bowl of hot lemonade on retiring will usually prove most effective. Roasted lemon is also an effective remedy, especially in a cold of longer standing accompanied with cough. It should be roasted for thirty minutes in an oven not hot enough to blacken or dry it. When it begins to crack open, take out, press out the juice, sweeten with loaf sugar, and take a little at a time, but take often.

E. For children make an onion syrup, and give in teaspoonful doses every hour or two. Grease the nose and around the throat and chest with lard containing a little Turpentine.—(67).

F. Hot foot bath and 10 drops Tincture of Gelsemium at bedtime. Take Cathartic the following morning.—(46).

G. In case of an adult, take 6 grains Quinine, drink one pint of water, bathe feet in hot water and go to bed. From ten to twenty-four hours in bed after the above treatment will usually terminate any ordinary cold. A cold should not be regarded as a light matter as it may be the forerunner of serious troubles.—(9).

H. A good cathartic—tablespoonful of Salts. At night take a hot foot bath and a strong cup of hot Ginger tea, also a big dose of Quinine—from 6 to 10 grains—get into a warm bed and get up a good, heavy sweat. This will break up an ordinary cold.—(13).

Ancient Method of Cure.—The *Evening Post* says the following plan for the cure of Colds has been in use since 1340:

> Put your feet in hot water,
>   As high as your thighes;
> Wrappe your head up in flannelle,
>   As low as your eyes;
> Take a quarte of rum'd gruelle,
>   When in bedde, as a dose;
> With a number four dippe,
>   Well tallow your nose.

This will be found as valuable and practical at the present time, except perhaps as to the depth of the foot bath and the amount of "rum'd gruelle." Perhaps a pint of that would be sufficient now-a-days, if made tolerably strong, repeating the treatment one or two nights until the cold is broken.

REMEDIES FOR COUGHS.—

A. A most excellent and satisfactory cough mixture may be made as follows:—

> Fluid Extract of Ipecac.................... 1 ounce.
> Chloroform...................................... ¼ "
> Tincture of White Pine.................... 4 "
> Water... 14 "
> Sugar... 28 "
> Tincture of Gelsemium.................... ½ "

First dissolve the sugar in the water, next add the Ipecac and the Gelsemium, and last the White Pine and Chloroform.

Dose: One teaspoonful every two or three hours, as needed.

This prescription was used by an old physician who had practiced many years and had learned to depend upon it in all cases of ordinary coughs and colds. It will not disappoint any who use it.

B Syrup of Ipecac.............................. 1 ounce.
Syrup of Tolu .... 1 "
Syrup of Rhubarb.......................... 1 "
Spirits of Nitre............................... 1 "
Paregoric....................................... 1 "

The dose for an adult is one teaspoonful every two to four hours; for a child one year old, give 5 drops. Dose may be increased, if necessary.

This is a very simple remedy and the results are satisfactory in nearly all cases.—(67).

C. Paregoric and Hive Syrup, one part of the former to two parts of the latter, taken in 30-drop doses every four hours.—(7).

D. Fluid Extract Tolu......................... 1 ounce.
Wine Antimony .... 1 "
Paregoric...................................... 1 "
Fluid Extract Grindelia Robusta..... 1 "

Mix, and take one teaspoonful three or four times a day,

or,

Dilute Hydrobromic Acid........... 3 drachms.
Fluid Extract Grindelia Robusta 1 ounce.
Paregoric................................... 1 "
Syrup of Tolu............................ 1½ "
Glycerine, add to make.............. 6 "

Mix, and take one teaspoonful every three or four hours.

E. *For Cough and Sore Lungs.*—To one quart of water add one large handful of strong hops. Let the water boil till reduced to one pint, then thoroughly strain, rinse out kettle and replace hop water. Carefully stir in one pound of heavy brown sugar and bring to a simmering heat, then remove from the fire and, when cold, add from one-half to one pint of the best Jamaica rum.

Dose, from one to two teaspoonfuls as often as required.

F. We have used the following cough mixture for many years with the most satisfactory results. We have also given the formula to a number of physicians who have been equally successful.

No. 1. Wild Cherry bark, cut fine...... 2½ ounces
No. 2. Ipecac Root, powdered........... 2½ drachms.
Blood Root, powdered............ 3 "
Squills, powdered................... 1½ "
Licorice Root, powdered......... 2 "
Anise Seed, ground................. ½ ounce.
Fennel Seed, powdered........... 1 drachm.
Sulphuric Acid.....................15 to 20 drops.
Fresh Orange Peel..................½ to 1 ounce.
Alcohol................................... 1 pint.

Put No. 1 into a large bottle and add one pint of water, allowing it to stand for one week. Of No. 2, first add the Sulphuric Acid to the Alcohol, then add the other ingredients. Also allow this mixture to stand one week, then mix No. 1 and No. 2 together and allow to stand for one week or ten days more. Each bottle should be shaken before the mixtures are added together and the bottle containing the two should be shaken. At the end of ten days, after the two solutions are mixed, get several large sheets of filtering paper from the drug store, place two layers carefully in a funnel, set the funnel in a clean bottle and pour on the mixture, allowing it to strain through. While straining, keep well covered to prevent evaporation. By using filtering paper the solution will come out clear and bright. Now add 10 ounces of sugar and dissolve by shaking the bottle. More sugar may be added if desired. Three or four grains of Sulphate of Codeine should be added to each 4 ounces when it is used. This preparation will keep for any length of time.

Dose, one teaspoonful. It is perfectly safe to give to children of any age as it contains neither Opium nor Morphine. For a child five years old the dose would be ⅓ teaspoonful. For adults where the cough is severe and there is a good deal of pain, if the mixture does not control the condition ⅛ of a grain of Morphine may be added to each dose for two or three doses.

Winter Cough Remedies.—

A. Zinc Sulphate, ½ grain dissolved in a teaspoonful of water. To be taken every one, two or three hours. Take no water or anything right after it as you want its local effect.
This is the best remedy on earth. Try it.—(30).

> **B.** Ammoniated Tincture of Guiacum.
> *Dose.*—5 drops on a little sugar every half to one hour. Let it slowly dissolve in the mouth and swallow it. Take nothing right away after it. This is a good one also. These cheap remedies are really superior to the expensive cough syrups.—(30).

> **C.** Liquor Ammonia Acetatus.......... 2 drachms.
> Syrup of Squills Compound........ 2 "
> Fluid Extract of Licorice........... 6 "
> Syrup of Wild Cherry enough to
> make..................................... 3 ounces.
>
> *Dose.*—One teaspoonful every hour or two.—(34).

COLOR BLINDNESS.—(See under Eye, Diseases of).

CONGESTIVE CHILL—CONGESTIVE FEVER.—
(See *Pernicious Fever* under Malarial Fevers).

CONSTIPATION, OR COSTIVENESS.—This is a common disorder. It is due to a sluggish state of the liver and bowels, the bowels retaining the fæces longer than is warranted by a state of health. Constipation means the production of many poisons in the digestive tract which are absorbed into the system and produce a chronic state of disease.

Cause. —It may be due to the character of the food taken, or to the habits of the individual, especially habits of neglect. Some have held the theory that constipation is due to a lack of development in the thickness of the muscular walls of the digestive tract; others, that it is due to imperfect nerve supply and poor circulation; still others argue that it is congenital, that is, exists from birth. But such claims seem to be more a matter of theory than of practical demonstration.

TREATMENTS.—

A. Try to overcome it by diet and habit. Eat graham mush and graham bread, corn bread, coarse food of all kinds, prunes, figs, baked apples, fruit, etc. Drink lots of water before bedtime—a pint every night—and a glass of hot water the first thing in the morning twenty or thirty minutes before breakfast. Have a regular time to have bowels move, say the first thing after breakfast.

If medicine is needed, take 10 to 20 drops of Fluid Extract Cascara Sagrada once or twice a day. Massage over bowels will cure many cases.—(13).

B. The Aloin Strychnine, Belladonna and Cascara pills kept by druggists will give excellent satisfaction in relieving constipation, taken one or two at bedtime, as needed. These pills are a tonic, and there is absolutely no danger in their continued use in chronic constipation. If used with judgment, and regular habits observed, they will result in a permanent cure.—(46).

C. Teaspoonful of Epsom Salts in a glassful of water the first thing in the morning. This treatment should be long continued.—(11).

D. A teaspoonful of corn meal in a glass of cold water on getting out of bed in the morning. A teacupful of very hot water sipped from a teaspoon on sitting down to breakfast. Fruits usually good. Prolonged rubbing and kneading of the bowels, and especially the cultivation of a fixed time or habit in movement of bowels.—(8).

E. A fresh egg beaten in a gill of water and drank on rising in the morning, and at each meal, for a week or ten days, has cured obstinate cases. It might be increased to two or three at a time as the stomach will bear.—(68).

F. Drink liberally of cold water at bedtime and of hot water as soon as you arise. Then attend to nature's calls "religiously." Let nothing hinder.—(17).

CONSUMPTION.—(See under TUBERCULOSIS).

CONVULSIONS.—Convulsions are due to nervous manifestations. The body is drawn into violent spasmodic contractions, the spasm being confined to the external or voluntary muscles. There is usually loss of consciousness.

Cause.—Convulsions may result from different causes, as uræmic or puerperal convulsions, due to the retention of urea in the system. Infantile convulsions may be due to teething or to worms. With children convulsions are most often caused by indigestion; in this case the trouble is confined to the stomach, hence a dose of Ipecac is always in order. Convulsions also occur in *Epilepsy*. (See EPILEPSY).

Convulsions in Children.—

A. Put babe in warm water—temperature of 105—*i. e.*, comfortably warm for hand. As soon as possible give him full dose of Castor Oil, and inject the bowels with warm water or soap suds. Keep body and extremities warm.—(13).

B. Give the patient a dose of Salts or Oil for laxative purposes. If necessary protect the tongue from the closure of the jaws by inserting a cork, piece of wood or knife-handle between the teeth. If severe, a doctor might administer a little Chloroform.—(7).

C. In children little to be done during the convulsion. As soon as possible give ½ to 2 teaspoonfuls of Castor Oil, according to age. The cathartic relieves the head and also the digestive apparatus, which is generally the locality at fault. If the head remains drawn back after the spasm, look out for spinal meningitis, which is very fatal.—(14).

CORN.—A hardening of the outer layer of cells of the skin of the toes or other portions of the foot. A kernel is developed in the calloused portion, about the size of a small pea and cone-shaped. At times it is soft instead of hard, forming what is called a soft corn. This occurs on the side of the foot or between the toes, and is caused by the part being continually moist with sweat.

Cause.—Long-continued pressure or friction caused by ill-fitting shoes.

> **A.** Salicylic Acid.............................. 30 grains.
> Extract Indian Hemp.................... 20   "
> Collodion....................................... ½ ounce.
>
> *Mix*, and apply with a soft brush once daily for six days, then soak corn in warm water. Repeat the application if necessary.—(46).

B.—Get felt corn plaster at drug store and place over corn. Then apply on top of corn the following:

Salicylic Acid............................... ⅛ ounce.
Collodion .... ½   "
First soften corn, every night, with Glycerine or soaking in hot water, then make above application. Wear properly fitting shoes and corns will disappear.—(13).

C.—Remove the pressure by change of foot gear. Remove hard part of corn and cover with an ointment made by thoroughly mixing together equal parts of cooking Soda or Saleratus and Mutton Tallow or Vaseline. The corn will soon disappear.—(14).

D. Take Sheep Sorrel, mash, press out the juice, spread on a plate and dry down to a thick salve. Mix a little pulverized Potash with this salve and bind on a very little of the mixture for two or three nights, or until the corn turns black, showing that it has been killed, then leave it to come out.

or,

Potash, powdered.......................... 1 ounce.
Salt of Lemon, powdered...............½   "
Mix, and bind a little on corn for four or five nights.—(70).

E. Warm a stick of Lead Plaster and rub on to a bit of white silk, which bind on to corn and wear until kernel can be pulled or picked out.

F. Wet lint or batting with Spirits of Turpentine and bind over corn.

CRAMPS.—Cramps are caused by irritation of a nerve or nerves controlling one or more muscles. The irritation is the result of waste products in the system. All life's forces are kept up by irritation (see *Cancer*, cause of), but when this irritation is carried too far, the condition is usually indicated by pains or cramps. Irritation is but another term for stimulation. At first over-stimulation increases the nerve forces with the result that one or more muscles become spasmodic. When these spasms relax and contract, it is called *clonic;* when the muscle remains rigid, it is called *tonic* spasm or cramp.

TREATMENT.—

Usually change of position and massage applied to the affected parts will relieve the trouble. Like other painful conditions, cramps are an indication that more careful diet and more thorough elimination are necessary. Cramps may be influenced by too much hard work, by a lack of exercise or a lack of fresh air. Cramps, pains in the stomach and bowels, rheumatism, acute or chronic, lumbago, neuralgia in any form, sciatica, headache, and all other forms of aches and pain require the same general treatment, *i. e.*, diet, elimination and fresh air.

CROUP, SPASMODIC.—This disease is a mild degree of catarrhal inflammation of the larynx associated with spasm. It does not often occur before the age of six months nor after the fifth year.

Causes.—It occurs in the otherwise healthy as well as the sickly. Some children seem predisposed to it, and those who have had it once are likely to have it again. Those who have large tonsils and catarrhal throats are more subject to it, the immediate cause being a cold or a fit of indigestion.

Symptoms.—The attack is usually preceded by cold or hoarseness. The child plays around by day and in the evening there is a hollow, barking cough. Towards midnight there is an increase in severity; the breathing becomes more difficult and may be heard in an adjoining room, the child struggles for breath and is in great distress, and the cough is hoarse and ringing. In a few hours the breathing becomes easier, the attack passes away and the child falls asleep. In the morning he is apparently well, but for some hoarseness, and plays as usual. Next night there is a fresh attack, usually little different from the first night. The third night it will be mild or absent. Many children have such attacks several times during the cold season. This disease is very alarming to parents. until the child has come through two or more attacks, but is never dangerous.

A. For spasmodic croup keep child warm and hot flannels about neck and over chest. Give ½ teaspoonful Syrup of Ipecac every ten or fifteen minutes till child vomits freely. Give plenty of warm water to wash out stomach. If there is any diphtheria in country, look upon every croup case with suspicion.—(13).

B. For spasmodic croup, nothing is better or more prompt than flannels wrung out of cold water and applied to throat, and then covered with heavy dry flannel cloth. Renew every ten minutes.—(60).

C. Alum pulverized, ½ teaspoonful in a little Molasses, is a simple remedy and one that is almost always at hand. One dose seldom fails to give relief, but if it should, it may be repeated in an hour.

D Oil of Wintergreen...........................10 drops.
Oil of Lobelia.................................10
Dilute Alcohol................................ 1 ounce.

Mix, and give from 1 to 10 drops every fifteen or twenty minutes until the paroxysm passes off, which it usually does in a very short time.—(82).

E. Inhale steam from lime while it is being slacked. Give ¼ grain of Calomel every two hours.—(9).

CROUP, MEMBRANOUS.—(See under DIPHTHERIA).

DANDRUFF.—This affection is a disorder of the sebaceous glands, technically known as *seborrhea*. Seborrhea may affect the skin of any portion of the body, but the term *dandruff* is understood to mean the scurfy deposit which forms on the scalp.

Cause.—Dandruff depends upon a diseased condition of the oil glands which open into the hair follicles. The glands become irritated and furnish too much oil, which dries on the surface and forms the crusts or scales commonly known as dandruff. The disease is constitutional, the same as eczema, and the irritation mentioned is caused by irritants in the blood.

TREATMENTS.—

A. Put one tablespoonful Flour of Sulphur in a quart of rain water, and use once a day, after shaking well, as a wash to the scalp. Do not wet your hair with anything else and you will soon cure your dandruff.—(13).

B.—Wash scalp in salt water, use brush and avoid the use of fine combs. Do not use metallic combs. Apply Vaseline twice a week, rubbed well into scalp.—(9).

Those who object to Vaseline by reason of its being too greasy, may find a valuable substitute in Glycerine and Rose Water. The advantage of Glycerine lies in its easy removal. It readily unites with water, therefore may easily be washed off. The Vaseline would cover over and mask the symptoms and allow the condition to become worse. It is in cases like these that Coke Dandruff Cure, or any good antiseptic, is especially valuable.—(See under PATENT PREPARATIONS).

C. Bay Rum and rain water, equal parts.

For shampoo use two or three fresh eggs. When the head is clean, apply the Bay Rum and rain water, rubbing into the scalp with the balls of the fingers.—(50).

D. Shampoo head with white of an egg, and afterwards rub scalp thoroughly with Vaseline.—(46).

DEAFNESS.— There is so much of enjoyment and happiness dependent upon the ability to hear well, that a considerable anxiety arises at once on inability to hear the slightest sound; and although there are but few who are entirely deaf as compared with the mass who can hear, yet there are quite a good many whose hearing is more or less affected.

Cause.—Inflammation of the middle ear is the general cause of deafness. It may follow taking cold, or may follow the infectious diseases, especially scarlet fever.

Symptoms.— The symptoms, or sensations realized, on the approach of an inflammation and consequent deafness, if the inflammation is not subdued, will be a feeling of fullness of the parts, uneasiness, singing noises, and pain, more or less severe. If not relieved, ulceration may follow.

TREATMENTS.—

A. Let an active sweat be taken, and let this be repeated at least once a day in acute cases and once a week in chronic cases until relief is obtained. There is no plan quite equal to the spirit, or hot-air bath, but according to the choice of the patient or the conveniences at hand. In connection with the sweating process, a diaphoretic, or sweating medicine, must be given that will have a tendency to keep up a little perspiration, such as a tea of the Virginia Snake-Root and of Pleurisy-Root, equal parts, say ¼ ounce of each, to water, 1 pint, drank in the course of the day, and continued as needed. Active cathartics should also be given; this is of first importance.

Such active systemic treatment is particularly necessary when the inflammation is acute, the result of such treatment being to draw the blood away from the inflamed part, equalize the circulation, and thus prevent the danger of the formation of an abscess, which is liable to follow an acute attack of inflammation of any part.

B. Deafness is not infrequently caused, or at least a partial loss of hearing, by the accumulation of the natural secretions of the ear (ear wax). In some cases this secretion is excessive. In these cases there is a mild local inflammation from some cause, and the result is not only an increase in the secretion, but the moisture evaporates more rapidly, leaving the exudate (discharge) a dry and hardened mass. This is continually surrounded by a fresh supply, which keeps the surface unirritated and the condition unnoticed by the individual. This accumulation is in the external canal and can be easily removed. Lay the sound ear on the table, and with a small syringe fill the affected ear with the following solution:

Baking Soda	1 teaspoonful.
Glycerine	8 teaspoonfuls.
Water	8 teaspoonfuls.

Mix, allow the solution to remain in the ear ten or fifteen minutes, let it drain and plug with batting.

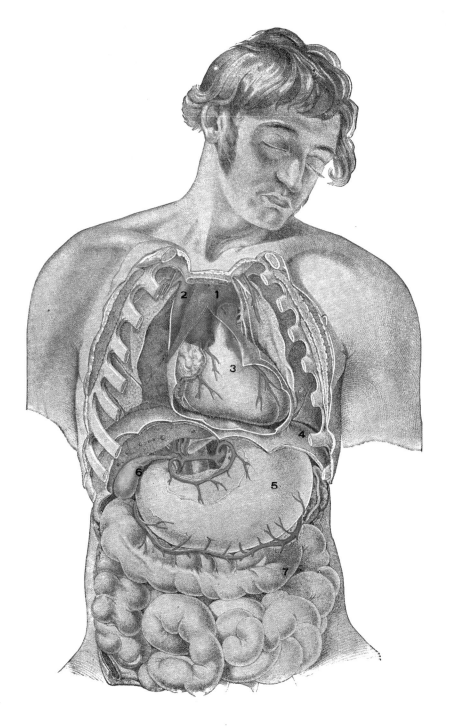

No. 9.

1, Large Artery coming from Heart.　2, Large Vein.　3, Heart (uncovered).　4, Diaphragm.　5, Stomach.　6, Gall Bladder. 7, Bowels.

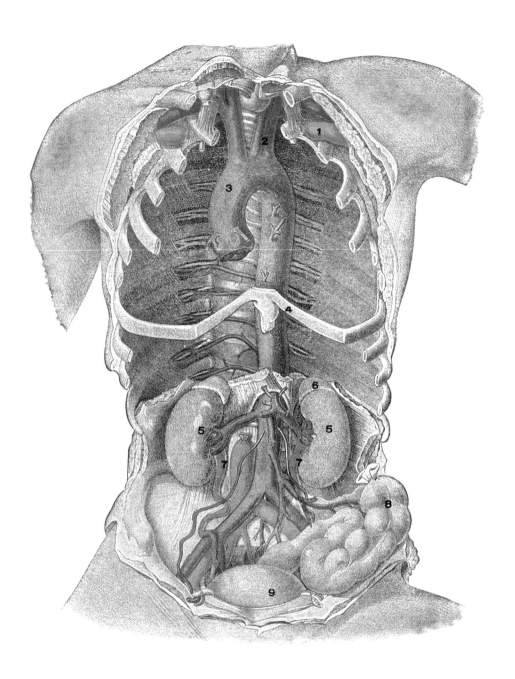

No. 10.

1, Vein.   2, Artery.   3, Large Artery from Heart.   4, Diaphragm (cut off).   5, Kidneys.   6, Supra-renal Capsule.   7, Ureter.   8, Large Intestine.   9, Bladder.

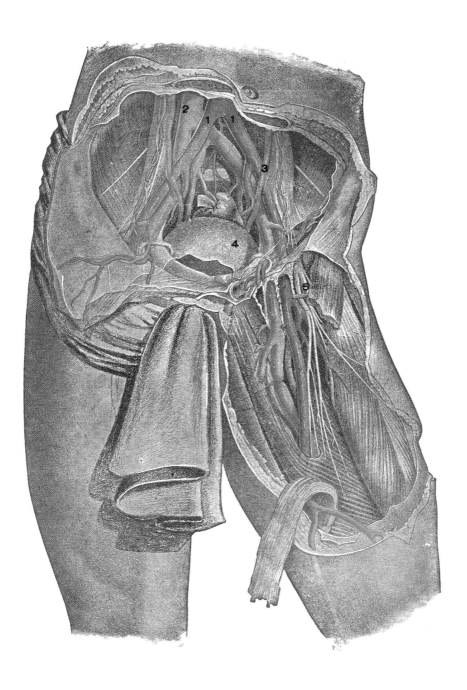

No. 11.

1, Large Arteries.　　2, Large Vein.　　3, Ureter.　　4, Bladder.
5, Nerves.

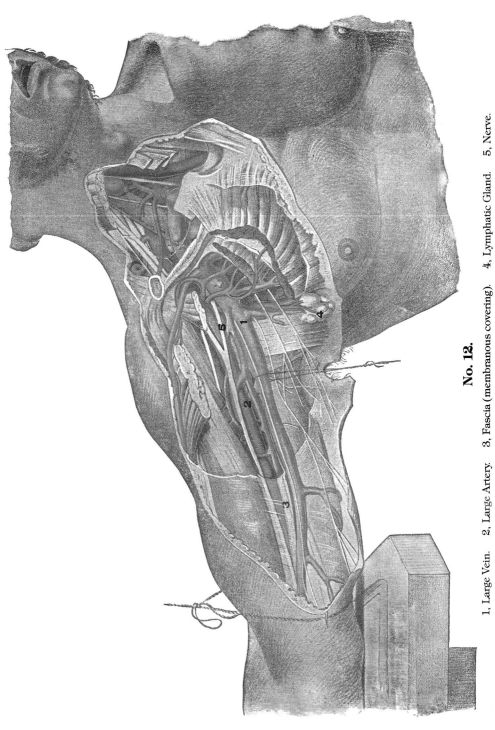

No. 12.

1, Large Vein.   2, Large Artery.   3, Fascia (membranous covering).   4, Lymphatic Gland.   5, Nerve.

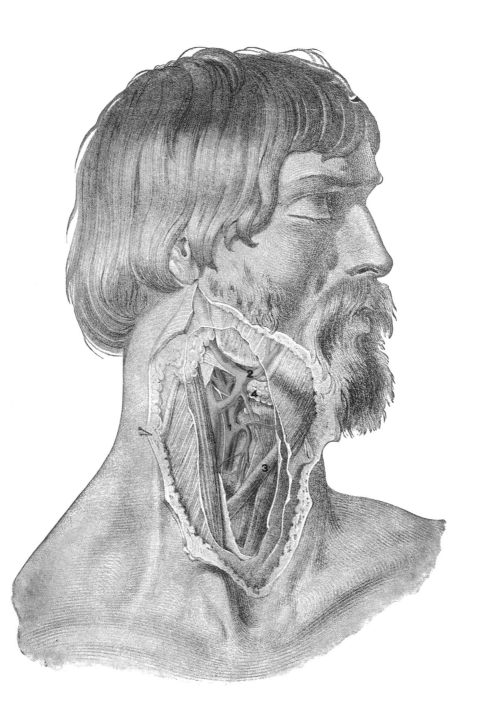

No. 13.

1, Artery.   2, Vein.   3, Muscle.   4, Salivary Gland.

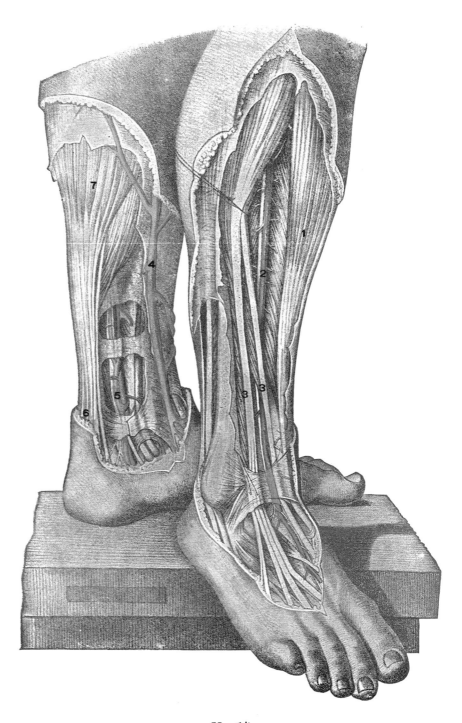

No. 14.

1, Muscle moving Foot.   2, Arteries.   3, Tendons of Muscles.
4, 5, Veins.   Tendon of Heel.   7, Muscles of Calf.

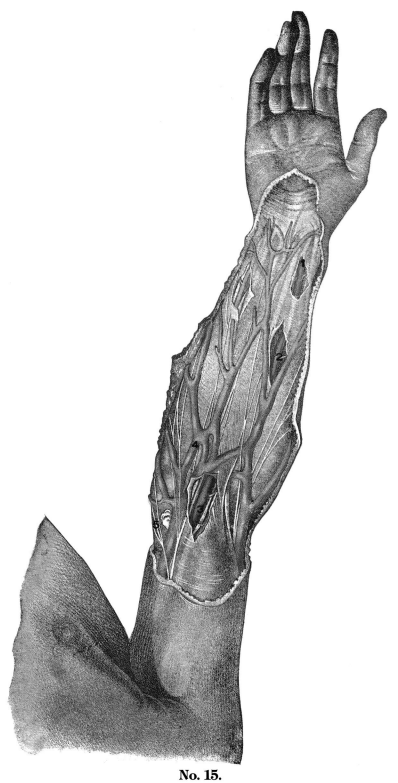

No. 15.

1, 2, 3, Arteries.   4, Veins.   5, Nerves.

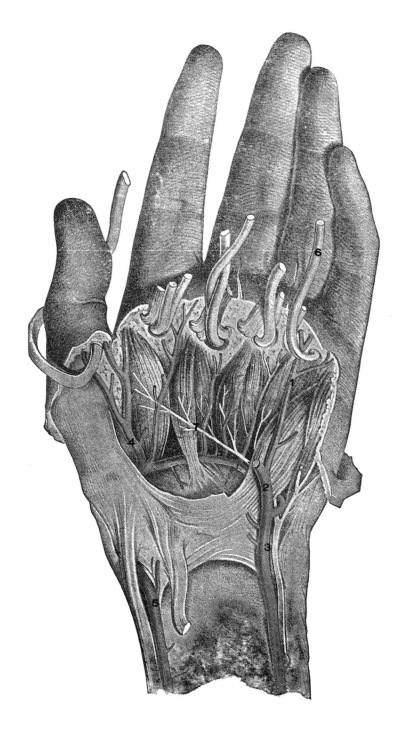

No. 16.

1, 2, 3, 4, 5, Arteries.   6, Tendons.   7, Nerves.

Repeat twice a day for two or three days, then syringe out with soap and warm water. This will remove any accumulations, and in cases where deafness is the result of such accumulations, hearing will be restored.

C. Hen's Oil, 1 gill; and a single handful of the sweet clover raised in gardens stewed in the oil until the juice is all out; strain it and bottle for use.

Where deafness is recent, it will be cured by putting three or four drops daily into the ear; but if of long standing, much relief will be obtained if continued a sufficient length of time. Syringe out ears with warm soapsuds twice a day—morning and evening.

DELIRIUM.—The term *delirium* means a wandering of the mind dependent upon some disease, as a fever, and so distinguished from insanity. In a delirious state the ideas of a person are wild, irregular and unconnected.

TREATMENTS.—

What to Do Till the Doctor Comes.—Give a few drops of Paregoric to quiet and produce sleep: If a child, from 15 to 20 drops; if an adult, a teaspoonful of the Paregoric, or from 15 to 20 drops of Laudanum. As a general thing, delirium is produced by fever, and a doctor is visiting the patient every day; but sometimes illness comes on in that way—a person may be taken delirious—and the above is the thing to do until the doctor comes. The feet may be immersed in warm water, as the object is to draw the excess of blood from the brain.

A. Reduce the fever with cold sponging and cold cloths to head. Keep feet warm. Keep quiet. Do not let in any company. Give an adult 20 grains Bromide of Potash in water if there is no contra-indication. Always consult doctor. (13).

DELIRIUM TREMENS.—(See under ALCOHOLISM).

DIABETES.—There are two varieties of this disease, *Diabetes Mellitus* and *Diabetes Insipidus.*

DIABETES MELLITUS.—This is a disorder of nutrition in which fruit sugar accumulates in the blood and later is carried from the system with the urine, which is greatly increased.

During digestion the starch contained in the different food products is converted into glucose or grape sugar. This is absorbed and carried by the veins direct to the liver, where some of it is converted into a substance called glycogen. The glycogen is stored up by the liver cells and delivered to the circulation as the system requires. In health it unites with the oxygen from the air we breathe and is oxidized. This produces heat and aids in maintaining the bodily temperature; but the system cannot oxidize the amount present in diabetes, hence its appearance through the kidneys.

Cause.—While there are a number of theories advanced regarding the cause of *Diabetes Mellitus*, all investigators are agreed that the disease is preceded by some disordered state of the nervous system. Undoudtedly the first cause is indigestion and constipation. Both are present. The return circulation from the digestive tract passes through the liver, the latter becomes unhealthy and unable to convert the glucose into glycogen, in which case more glucose is left in the circulation than the system can oxidize. Passing through the circulation, the glucose irritates and weakens the kidneys until some of it finds its way into the secreting tubes and is carried off with the urine. Primarily this is called *Diabetes;* later it causes *Bright's Disease.*

Symptoms.— The onset of this disease is nearly always stealthy, and is unnoticed by the patient. The first thing noticed in many cases is excessive thirst or a large increase in the amount of urine, or it may be unusual weakness. The urine is pale in color, very acid, the specific gravity is increased, and sugar is constantly present. At times the appetite is voracious, and at the same time there is a loss of flesh.

The normal amount of urine daily is about fifty ounces, or three pints. In this disease the amount varies from six or eight pints in mild cases to thirty or forty pints in severe ones. The tongue is usually dry, red and glazed. The skin is dry and harsh.

TREATMENTS.—

What to Do.—Keep the patient on a strict diet. Avoid all starchy foods, and also those that contain sugar.

Drink as small a quantity of fluids of all kinds as possible. A cold, *weak* infusion of common tea is the most harmless, and at the same time quite as efficient in quenching thirst as any drink that can be taken. Patients may be allowed to take a swallow of this every hour or two.

Attention to the skin is also a matter of importance. Frequent bathing is desirable. The warm alkaline and spirituous bath may be used before going to bed, and the cold sponge bath in the morning before dressing. Both should be followed with a brisk friction, especially on the spine. To prevent irritation apply Sweet Oil.

A compound Taraxacum and Podophyllin pill should be given every night and morning, or in such quantity as will at least secure one evacuation from the bowels every day. Other valuable remedies for the constipation which is always present are: the well-known Aloin, Strychnine and Belladonna combination in pill form; or the Fluid Extract of Cascara Sagrada in 10-drop doses morning and night, more or less, as needed.

As a tonic, a decoction of Ptelea and Wild Cherry may be given in wineglassful doses three times a day.

A. Milk diet. Avoid sugar or starchy foods.

Basham's Mixture in teaspoonful doses 3 or 4 times a day.—(7).

B. Abstain from sugars and starch and reduce mental work and worry.—(3.)

C. Avoid sugars and starches in diet. Diet alone will sometimes cure, but must be continued for a long time.—(50).

D. *Dr. King makes the following report:* "I have treated four cases of Diabetes Mellitus successfully by the internal administration of Nitrate of Ammonia in doses of from 10 to 20 grains repeated three times a day and given in solution. In conjunction with this agent I also employed the following pills, alternating them every four weeks:

"No. 1. Citrate of Iron and Strychnia....... 45 grains.
        Quinine Sulphate........................ 45 "
        Opium................................... 60 "

    Mix, divide into 90 pills, and give one pill three or four times a day.

"No. 2. Bromide Potassium..................... 270 grains.
        Extract Conium Maculatum......... 90 "
        Extract Aletris.......................... 90 "

    Mix, divide into 90 pills and give same as above, giving No. 1 for four weeks and then giving No. 2 for the next four weeks, and so on."

Rennet wine was prescribed to be taken after the breakfast and dinner meals, and the usual attention bestowed upon the skin, kidneys, bowels, diet, etc.

E. Carbonate of Ammonia............ 90 grains.
     Phosphate of Ammonia............ 90 "
     Carbonate of Soda.................... 2 drachms.
     Tincture of Ginger.................. ½ ounce.
     Glycerine.............................. 1½ "
     Simple Elixir enough to make.. 4 "

    Dose, a teaspoonful in water three times a day.

    This mixture is very grateful to the patient. It relieves thirst and mitigates the morbid appetite. The tongue gradually becomes moist, and the urine diminishes in quantity and contains less sugar.—(74).

DIABETES INSIPIDUS.—This disease usually comes on slowly. Increased secretion of urine and great thirst are the chief symptoms. The amount of urine may be from twenty to forty pints a day and even more. It is extremely pale and watery, and of low specific gravity. The low specific gravity and absence of sugar in the urine will distinguish this disease from *Diabetes Mellitus.*

In many instances *Diabetes Insipidus* does not interfere with the general health, the greatest inconvenience being frequent passing of water and constant thirst. If the primary cause of this trouble is some organic disease, the health may be much impaired. Where there is no other disease, the patient may have good health indefinitely, or nature may restore him to normal health.

TREATMENT.—

The treatment is the same as that for *Diabetes Mellitus.* True, sugar may not be present, but the danger is that this form will run into *Diabetes Mellitus* prcper; hence the advisability of following the treatments outlined above.

DIARRHEA.—The *Alimentary Canal* is about 30 or 32 feet long and begins in the mouth. It is lined throughout with mucous membrane. The different portions of this tract have been given different names, as follows:

First, the mouth.
Second, the throat.
Third, the æsophagus, which leads from the throat to the stomach and which is about nine inches in length.
Fourth, the stomach, which is from 10 to 12 inches in length and is capable of holding from 3 to 8 pints, according to the amount of distension.
Fifth, the first part of the small bowel, called the duodenum, which is 10 to 12 inches in length.
Sixth, the small bowel, which is about 25 feet in length and is capable of holding about 15 pints.
Seventh, the large bowel, which is 5 or 6 feet in length and is capable of holding about 8 pints, but, moderately distended, will hold twice that amount.

The mouth is designed for the mechanical division of food and the first step in digestion, called *insalivation.* The æsophagus conveys the food to the stomach. The stomach is simply a dilatation of the canal, being that part of the tract where some of the principal digestive changes are produced and in which the partial reduction and solution of the food takes place. In the small bowel the digestive changes are rendered more complete and the nutritive principles of the food are separated and absorbed into the circulation, the unused portion being passed on into the large bowel as waste material and, in health, eliminated from the system. Excessive and rapid eating, drinking of strong tea and coffee and the excessive use of the various alcoholic liquors, followed by indigestion and a lack of elimination together with consequent degenerative changes and the absorption of many poisons, are responsible for most of our ills.

The glands of the mouth furnish one kind of digestive ferment, those of the stomach three kinds, and those of the small bowel several other kinds. (See DIGESTION). There is little or no digestive fluid furnished by the glands of the large bowel.

The mucous membrane which lines the digestive tract and the various glands which it contains is a delicate structure, and was not designed by Nature to suffer the abuse and neglect to which it is often subjected. The coats of the small bowel are very thin. Commencing just below the duodenum, or about one foot below the stomach, the small bowel is so thin that a newspaper may be read through it.

The digestive tract is subject to many diseases, which are usually described under separate heads, but which for convenience and clearness are here described together. Strictly speaking, they are not different diseases, but different stages of the same disease—different stages of the same inflammatory process —and that is why it seems advisable to group them together.

The following are some of the different terms applied to the different stages of the disease found in the digestive tract:

Diarrhea.—This is a morbid condition marked by frequent movements and an increased amount of fluid eliminated. The mucous membrane is congested and presents a catarrhal condition.

Inflammation of the Bowels.—This is a catarrhal inflammation of the mucous membrane of the bowels accompanied with fever, soreness and frequent movement. It is sometimes called *Catarrhal Diarrhea*. It is said to be confined more to the large bowel, but, like dysentery, it includes more or less of the small bowel. The mucous membrane is swollen and presents a catarrhal appearance. The swelling may be so great that vessels rupture and blood appears in the eliminations. The glands are swollen and elevated and show a strong tendency to ulcerate. The condition of the mucous membrane may be considered a stage between diarrhea and dysentery.

Dysentery.—This is an inflammation of the mucous membrane of the large bowel particularly, but also includes more or less of the small bowel. Dysentery is sometimes called *Bloody*

Flux, because during these attacks some small blood vessels in the mucous membrane may rupture and blood appear in the eliminations, but this same evidence of inflammation may and often does occur in bowel difficulties which are known by other names. This is only an aggravated case of diarrhea. The disease extends all the way from a mild form of inflammation to the more serious condition where the inflammation is so great that nutrition is shut off, ulcers form and parts of the mucous membrane slough away.

Cause.—The cause of diarrhea is indigestion, constipation, or both. Diarrhea usually occurs during the summer months because the system is weakened and relaxed by the heat. This is especially true of children as they have not sufficient vitality and physical strength to withstand its effects. Again, people drink more during the summer; this favors free action of the bowels, and may interfere with digestion, especially if taken soon after meals. Another important reason is found in the amount of unripe fruit that is eaten. Unripe fruit contains starch, which is converted into glucose or fruit sugar during the process of ripening. A considerable quantity of this sugar in some kinds of fruits is what gives them their sweet taste. Uncooked starch is not digestible and acts as an irritant in the digestive tract, thus stimulating increased activity. This form of diarrhea is usually acute, but the inflammation is mild and tends to early recovery. At other seasons of the year constipation is the rule, because the heat is replaced by a bracing atmosphere and the many varieties of green fruit are not indulged in.

The stages of diarrhea known as *Inflammation of the Bowels and Dysentery* are the result of unhealthy conditions that have existed for some time. First, the morbid effects cause only congestion, and this passes unnoticed into a mild form of inflammation before the diarrhea begins. The mucous membrane has become unhealthy to the extent that degenerative changes have made their appearance. Distributed throughout the mucous membrane are little thimble-shaped depressions called glands, which open into the bowel. Before dysentery begins these become swollen and choked with unhealthy secretions until they are ready to break down and ulcerate. With the increased inflammation there is increased distension of the blood vessels and increased exudate from the swollen glands. When the unhealthy secretions from the diseased glands and other products of inflammation reach a certain point, the irritation, acting as a stimulus, causes increased action, resulting in dysentery. These cases do not recover as rapidly as simple diarrhea because a greater derangement precedes the attack, yet, as stated, all of these so-called diseases are but different stages of the same inflammatory process. Following constipation, there is more pressure, hence more soreness, and the disease is of longer duration because it comes on gradually and the morbid changes in the mucous membrane reach greater proportions before giving evidence of the conditions present.

Symptoms.—The symptoms in a mild case of Diarrhea may be colicky pains and a little nausea, and there may also be some headache and a feeling of languor; the inflammation is slight as there has been no structural change in the mucous membrane, and the symptoms largely disappear with thorough elimination. With simple diarrhea there is no fever present in the beginning. This form of the disease usually lasts three or four days. The movements are frequent and include large quantities of water, showing the distension of the blood vessels from which the water was drained. The odor is bad. In many of these cases food, showing but little or no effects of digestion, is eliminated. This is due to the unhealthy condition of the bowel. The mucous membrane lining the bowel is swollen and presents a catarrhal condition. There is no rupture of small vessels and blood does not appear.

If there is a burning or scalding sensation, it shows that the inflammation has progressed a step further. The eliminations now present a greenish appearance, the odor is increased, and the mucous secretions thicken more or less as the disease advances.

This disease occurring in children makes them irritable; they cry a great deal, are peevish, fretful, and appear to suffer considerably. They vomit easily, and the eliminations contain undigested food, also curdy lumps if the child drinks milk. These lumps are formed of that part of the milk called caseine, or milk albumen.

Chronic Diarrhea may follow frequent attacks of acute. In chronic diarrhea the symptoms are all aggravated, and the change in the mucous membrane resembles that found in dysentery. Both the mucous membrane and the submucous or deeper tissues present a catarrhal condition. There is an abundance of mucus furnished by the glands mentioned. Many of these glands break down and small ulcers form, hence pus may also appear. Chronic diarrhea, inflammation of the bowels and dysentery are most marked in the large bowel, although more or less of the small bowel is included.

As any of these forms of disease continue, the whole thickness of the mucous membrane becomes involved and the number of glands that are broken down and converted into ulcers are increased, and not only the mucous membrane, but the outer portion of the bowel may become involved and form adhesions to the surrounding structures.

First the mucous membrane, and the connective tissue beneath which joins it to the muscular layer, slough away in large patches, and the whole thickness of the bowel becomes infiltrated with blood and serum, which presents more or less a dark hue by reason of the continued congestion and inflammation. The bowel is swollen and thickened as the result of new tissue growth. Later the contraction of this tissue tends to close the ulcers, thus permanently destroying many of the glands, and the walls of the bowels are more or less thinned as a result of the contraction of the new tissue and the destruction of the natural. The contraction is not uniform, hence the bowel presents an unequal diameter; in some places it is narrowed, and in others, dilated. It contains mucus, pus, and other products of inflammation.

TREATMENT.—

The treatment of any and all forms of diarrhea or dysentery is not difficult, and is practically the same, because all forms present characteristics more or less in common. Dosage should be regulated according to age, but otherwise the treatment for infant, child or adult is the same.

First, secure thorough elimination. For this purpose Castor Oil, Epsom Salts or Rochelle Salts are most frequently used, and their frequency is in the order named. One large dose of either may be given, although several small doses of the Salts frequently repeated will perhaps act more thoroughly. The Castor Oil is most rapid and certain in its action, therefore would be preferable if the case was urgent. Castor Oil, however, is very nauseating to many, hence we recommend in its stead Laxol (see Index), which is nearly 100 per cent. pure Castor Oil, with the taste of the Oil disguised. Those who prefer to buy it will find it at any drug store.

With the Salts the action depends more upon the large amount of water they attract into the bowel from the congested or inflamed mucous membrane, hence their effects are more cooling, and for this reason they would be the better remedy in inflammation. The Salts also produce more or less nausea. For some years past we have used in their place the Seidlitz Salts manufactured by the Abbott Alkaloidal Co. of Ravenswood, Chicago, Illinois. This preparation is 98 per cent. Epsom Salts, the other two per cent. being of such a nature as to render the compound effervescing and pleasant to take. From a teaspoonful to a tablespoonful of the Salts may be taken every morning, or as needed.

Calomel is another excellent remedy. In making this statement we realize that there is much prejudice against this drug. It may be taken in one dose of 5 to 10 grains, or $\frac{1}{4}$-grain doses may be taken one hour apart until the bowels move freely.

The laxatives mentioned are for the purpose of freeing the digestive tract of irritating substances, and should be followed by antiseptics. For this purpose we especially recommend the following:

Ten grains of Salol every three hours, or the same amount of the Sulphocarbolates of Lime, Zinc and Soda combined; or if the movements are very frequent and it is desired to control this particular feature, give Sulphocarbolate of Zinc alone—5 grains every two hours. The preparation of Zinc is astringent while the combination or Salol is not; otherwise there is no difference. In either case the purpose is to render the digestive tract clean and healthy. These remedies stop fermentation and render ulcers and other unhealthy surfaces clean and wholesome. As soon as there is improvement, give less often—perhaps two or three times a day.

The main thought to keep in mind is cleanliness. Ulcers or any degenerative changes in the digestive tract should be treated the same as on the surface. For this purpose, the Sulphocarbolates of Lime, Zinc and Soda combined, or Salol, are the best remedies. Regulate the dose and the treatment for infants, children and adults is the same.

Arsenite of Copper is another remedy of value and may be given in doses of $\frac{1}{100}$ of a grain every two to four hours. Half this amount, $\frac{1}{200}$ of a grain, may be given either with the Sulphocarbolates or the Salol. The tablets are most convenient.

The following remedy will check fermentation, relieve the congestion of the mucous membrane and free its surface of unhealthy secretions, stimulate digestion and regulate movement. It is a valuable remedy for many cases of bowel troubles that occur in summer, and especially so with children:

> Carbonate of Soda...... .... 1 drachm
> Wine of Ipecac............................. 1   "
> Fluid Hydrastus........................... 6   "
> Syrup of Rhubarb sufficient to make 4 ounces.

> *Dose.*—One teaspoonful every 2 to 4 hours, as indicated by the condition of the bowels. Give a dose of Laxol before commencing this remedy.

Fever may be present with both inflammation of the bowels and dysentery. If it is, the foregoing treatment will be ideal, as it is aimed directly at the cause, *i. e.*, the unhealthy condition of the bowels. Additional treatment for the fever consists of Aconite and Veratrum in one-drop doses every hour or two. A better remedy for fever resulting from inflammation of the bowels is the following:

Fluid Extract of Ipecac...................	10 drops.
Tincture of Aconite	10 "
Glycerine.......................................	½ ounce.
Water enough to make	4 "

Dose:—1 teaspoonful every hour.

If there is much pain and restlessness with children, give Codeine. For a child one year old, $\frac{1}{30}$ of a grain two or three times a day is usually sufficient. For adults where there is pain and soreness due to inflammation or dysentery, give one grain of Opium. One or two doses a day are usually sufficient. Opium is constipating and this effect must be overcome by Laxol, Seidlitz Salts, or some other remedy. It is generally understood that in inflammation of the bowels and dysentery the pain and soreness are marked. We have seen many cases where the pain and soreness were severe in an ordinary case of diarrhea, and have seen chronic cases free from both.

In many cases of bowel trouble there is rapid emaciation, because digestion and assimilation are interfered with to such an extent that the patient receives but little nourishment; hence the question of diet is an important one. In simple diarrhea, if all food is stopped for 24 hours it will be of great benefit to the patient, and then only such food should be allowed as is easily digested, and should be taken in rather small amounts for a few days. Milk, or milk and lime water, equal parts, is perhaps best of all. Next are toast, boiled rice and meat broths. The less solid food taken the better. In chronic cases, toast, meat broths, soft cooked eggs and other concentrated foods that are easily digested should be taken.

Diarrhea.—Remedies Recommended.—

A. Give a little hot brandy sling. Take the bark of Black-berry roots and leaves and steep up and make a strong decoction. Drink this freely, but avoid other drinks as much as possible, especially cold water. A little grated nutmeg may be put into the tea, and it may be sweetened with loaf sugar if desired.

B. Paregoric....................................	4 drachms.
Aromatic Syrup of Rhubarb	3 "
Aromatic Spirits of Ammonia........	2 "
Subnitrate of Bismuth..................	2 "
Blackberry Wine enough to make..	4 ounces.

Dose; 2 teaspoonfuls (bottle well shaken) in a little water every three hours.—(22).

C. Arsenate of Copper	$\frac{1}{100}$ grain.
Water...	8 ounces.

Dose: 1 teaspoonful every ten to twenty minutes till relieved,

or,

Paregoric.............................. ...... 1 ounce,
Tincture Red Pepper..................... 1 drachm.
Subnitrate of Bismuth.................. ½ "
Syrup.. 4 ounces.

Mix, and take teaspoonful every half hour until relieved.—(46).

D. Tincture of Rhubarb .... 1 ounce.
  Spirits of Camphor .... ½ "
  Laudanum.................................... ½ "
  Tincture of Ginger. .... ½ "
  Essence of Cinnamon..................... ½ "
  Tincture of Capsicum .... ¼ "

Mix, and shake when using.

Dose: One-half teaspoonful, on sugar or in a little sweetened water. In severe cases repeat every 30 minutes until relief from pain is obtained, then every hour or two as needed until the evacuations are lessened and improved in appearance.

E. Tincture of Aconite............... 5 to 10 drops.
  Tincture of Ipecac................. 15 drops.
  Water .... 4 ounces.

Dose: 1 teaspoonful every hour.—(77).

F. Dr. Owen reports a case of a friend of his who cured himself of a most obstinate diarrhea of several months standing, after trying everything else he could hear of, simply by eating once a day, as his dinner, a slice of raw bacon, a raw onion and plenty of salt, and bread. It required only two weeks to effect the cure. The doctor adds: "The remedy is not bad to take if one is hungry."

Diarrhea of Old Age.—Sometimes with old people there is a relaxed condition of the bowels that causes diarrhea. These cases are not frequent, but are occasionally met, and the treatment especially recommended for them is as follows:

Sulphate of Strychnine.................. ½ grain.
Hyoscyamine...............................1-10 "
Sulphocarbolate of Zinc................. 24 "
Glycerine.................................... 2 ounces.
Simple Elixir.............................. 2 "

Mix, and take one teaspoonful every two or three hours until there is improvement, then less often.

Inflammation of the Bowels.— REMEDIES RECOMMENDED.

What to Do Till the Doctor Comes.—Evacuate the bowels, if possible, with an injection of soapsuds, as hot as can be borne. Put the patient to bed and cover the bowels either with cloths wrung out of the hot decoction of some bitter herb, such as May-weed or Smartweed steeped up, or with a poultice made of Flax-seed meal. Or cloths may be wrung out of hot water alone. The hot applications afford relief, but if the pain is very severe and there is any Laudanum in the house, from 8 to 12 drops may be given, if an adult.

A. Warm poultices to the abdomen. Half teaspoonful doses of Epsom Salts every two hours till the discharges are frequent. Milk diet. Laudanum or Paregoric to relieve pain.—(9).

B. Keep the bowels moving, and apply hot flannel cloths with flannel binder around the abdomen.—(17).

C. Give tablespoonful of Epsom Salts in goblet of hot water. Apply hot fomentations. Insure absolute rest in bed and send for a doctor.—(14).

Dysentery.—Remedies Recommended.

What to Do Before Calling a Doctor.—In the first place give Castor Oil according to age: for a child, a teaspoonful with 1 to 2 drops of Laudanum; for an adult, a tablespoonful of the Oil with from 10 to 15 drops of Laudanum. Hot brandy sling is good. A most excellent remedy is a tea made from Blackberry roots: Take a small handful of the roots, put into a dish and steep, and let the patient drink freely of it. If for a child, it may be sweetened by adding loaf or white sugar.

In country districts remote from a physician the physic may be followed with a tea made of the bark of White Oak—the young growth, or saplings. Steep it, add a few drops of the Spirits of Camphor, and give a teaspoonful to a dose, repeating every three or four hours. The Oak tea should not be given until the physic has operated. The Blackberry tea may be given from the start.

The diet should be of the mildest and most nourishing kind, as boiled milk with a bit of flour thickening, making a kind of porridge, or thickened milk, rice boiled in milk, or rice flour, if it can be obtained, scalded with water then boiled in milk, or boiled milk with bread crumbled in it, until the strength begins to mend, then avoid everything likely to produce a relapse, which is almost always worse than the first attack.

A. Dover's Powder .... ½ drachm.
Subnitrate of Bismuth .... ½ ounce.
Salol .... ½ drachm.

Mix, divide into twelve powders and take one every hour or two.—(46).

B. Empty bowels by Oil or Salts in small doses. Give adult 5 to 10 drops of Laudanum in one teaspoonful of Castor Oil every two to four hours.—(13).

C. Give hot starch injections and encourage free perspiration.—(5).

D. 10 drops of Laudanum in a tablespoonful of Castor Oil. Very plain diet. Drink hot salt water (teaspoonful to the pint). Wash the bowels out with hot soapsuds.—(7).

E. *Dysentery of Small Children.*—Dr. Hall reports his success with dysentery of small children. His treatment is so uniform that it is only necessary to give one case to have a general understanding of it. "A child of eight months had diarrhea, commencing in the morning, but in the evening the stools became small and bloody, attended with tenesmus (straining). Pulse 130 and hard, surface hot, very restless, nausea with occasional retching. Discharges about every ten minutes. Child regarded by the parents as in a dangerous condition, one having died in the same house from the same disease the week previous.

"Prescribed at 11 p. m.:

Tincture of Aconite.........................	5 drops.
Tincture of Ipecac...........................	15 "
Water	4 ounces.

Dose.—A teaspoonful every hour.

"No dysenteric discharges after 4 a. m. next morning, and the child was well the second day."

The Ipecac is believed to be certain, or *specific*, in its action upon mucous surfaces—the internal surface of the intestines is mucus—and the Aconite lowers the circulation and thus reduces fever. A child 2 to 4 years old might be given twice the amount. An adult might take a tablespoonful as a dose.

DIPHTHERIA. — Diphtheria is an acute communicable disease characterized by the formation of a false membrane upon certain mucous surfaces, especially of the tonsils and throat. Like other inflammations it varies in severity, ranging from a mild to a severe form. In the mild forms there is little constitutional disturbances; in the severe forms there is great prostration and heart weakness. It is often followed by paralysis of the throat. A severe case is one of the most dreaded diseases of childhood. Though often epidemic, it is always present in large cities.

Cause.—Diphtheria is due to a certain specific poison. Some claim this poison is the result of germ action, and others claim that it is a constitutional disease.

The period of inoculation is from two to five days. Second attacks are very common.

Symptoms.—There is considerable variance in the intensity of the symptoms and the development of the disease. It may begin mildly with a sensation of chilliness followed by slight fever, indisposition, and some uneasiness in swallowing. Or the onset may be severe, a chill being followed with great febrile reaction, swallowing becoming painful, the limbs aching and the prostration being marked.

The first local symptom is a redness of one or both tonsils, accompanied with a swelling of the glands at the angle of the jaw. After this redness comes an exudation which gradually forms a membranous tissue covering more or less the surface of the tonsils. The membrane may extend to the nasal passages, giving rise to an offensive discharge from the nose of a thin, serous fluid, slightly tinged with blood. The disease may also extend from the throat along the Eustacian tubes to the middle ear and cause deafness. In such cases the tympanum, or outer membrane, may be perforated, and there may be caries (death) of the bones of the ear. The membrane formed in the throat is usually of a grayish or leathery color, which, if removed, *leaves a raw and bleeding surface—a characteristic feature of a diphtheritic membrane as distinguished from whitish patches that may form in the throat in other affections.* Not infrequently portions of this membrane are expectorated, and in severe cases ulceration and sloughing also occur. The odor arising from the putrid secretions in *diphtheria* is exceedingly offensive.

Nausea, vomiting or bleeding at the nose, when occurring late in the disease, paralysis before the exudate (membrane) disappears, subnormal temperature and all complications are unfavorable. Also convulsions occurring late are unfavorable, while as ushering-in symptoms they are of no especial significance. Diphtheria paralysis is usually recovered from, though paralysis of the heart may occur when least expected. Even after the danger seems past, the child while at play may by reason of sudden effort topple over dead, and for this reason should be kept quiet during convalescence. Paralysis of the muscles of respiration or of the diaphragm give rise to grave symptoms. Complications may prove fatal by their attack upon other organs, as the kidneys, liver or brain. Paralysis of the muscles of the throat may cause fluids to pass out through the nose. Imperfect closure of the epiglottis may allow food to enter the trachea (windpipe).

TREATMENTS.—

What to Do Till the Doctor Comes.—Diphtheria is generally confined to childhood. If the disease is prevalent and any member of the family complains of "sore throat," be on guard. It may prove to be only a sore throat from taking cold, but diphtheria generally commences in that way. The first thing the child complains of is that his throat feels sore, that it hurts him to swallow, or perhaps that his throat pains him. First give a cathartic.

Squeeze out the juice from lemons and stir in sulphur until you have it about the consistency of thick cream. Give the child a little 'in his mouth every half hour and have him swallow it. Keep watch of the throat, and if the lining membrane, that is, the inside of the throat, assumes an ash-colored hue, put him to bed, in a room by himself, and keep others away; keep him warm and send immediately for your doctor. Bathe the throat with Camphorated Oil, putting on the Oil pretty freely and afterwards wrapping with a flannel cloth. Give all the lemonade he can drink.

An excellent gargle for diphtheric sore throat is made of the Chlorate of Potash and the Sulphite of Soda, put up in powders of twenty grains of the Potash to ten grains of the Soda. Put one of these powders into a common goblet, fill two-thirds full of hot water, so as to dissolve it, and gargle the throat every two or three hours. Have the child gargle as low down as possible, and occasionally let him swallow a quarter of a teaspoonful—just enough to moisten the membranes of the throat—especially if he cannot gargle well. If he cannot gargle and it is necessary to use a swab, take Glycerine and Carbolic Acid, 15 parts Glycerine to one part Carbolic Acid, or say 15 drops of Carbolic Acid to one ounce of Glycerine, and swab the throat with that.

> **A.** Carbolic Acid, full strength .... 15 drops.
> Chlorate of Potash........................... 1 drachm.
> Tincture of Myrrh........................... 1 "
> Oil of Wintergreen......................... 5 drops.
>
> *Mix*, and add slowly by trituration (stirring rapidly) four ounces of honey.
>
> *Dose.*—Give child one tablespoonful every half hour, if the case is severe. This remedy has proven very successful in the treatment of diphtheria and those who use it will find the results most satisfactory.

The food should be of the most nourishing kind, milk, eggs, beef, broths, toast, etc. Small amounts must be given at frequent intervals day and night.

If there is discharge from the nose, spray the cavities with Peroxide of Hydrogen, and spray the throat with the same remedy. Sleep should not interfere with treatment, either medicinal or feeding.

Antitoxin is considered by many a specific for diphtheria, and is quite generally used, but can be administered only by a physician.

B. Bathe the throat internally and externally with ordinary coal oil. Give Sulphur mixed in molasses, and if improvement is not soon apparent, send for your doctor.—(17).

C. Iodide of Potash.......................... 2 drachms.
　　 Whiskey.................................... 4 ounces.

Mix, and give teaspoonful every four hours.

Give Antitoxin as soon as the disease is diagnosed.

Give teaspoonful of Salt in ½ glass of warm water every three to four hours, and at the same time give 3 to 10 drops of the Tincture of Digitalis in water three times daily, according to age.—(46).

Note.—If the salt solution causes nausea, lessen or omit that part of the treatment.

D. Diphtheria Antitoxin, first and last. Throat disinfected with Hydrogen Peroxide sprayed, full strength.—(60).

E. Antitoxin. Calomel cathartic—from 1 to 5 grains of Calomel, according to age. Use disinfectant gargle. Patient ordinarily well in four or five days.—(54).

F. Iodide of Mercury, first dilution. Give 2 tablets every two hours. Chlorinated Lime Water, give 2 drops in water every two hours. Alternate the two remedies. Use Alcohol for gargling, and as strong as possible. Make patient eat the most nourishing foods. Do not use Antitoxin unless it is *known* to be fresh and pure.—(18)—Homeopathic.

G. Report of two cases where Phytolacca was used as treatment:

1. "Mrs. B., 31. Nov. 16th. Throat commenced to feel sore in morning, followed by high fever all day, right tonsil very much swollen; at noon commenced to see substance forming on the tonsil. Was called 10 P. M., found right tonsil covered completely with pseudo-membrane, fauces and soft palate very much inflamed, deglutition almost impossible, loss of appetite, great frontal headache, bowels moved every two hours, with severe pain in umbilical regions, great prostration, vertigo" (dizziness) "so great she could not walk. Pulse 127, soft. Gave Phytolacca 4 drops every hour, and a gargle of same every hour, consisting of 50 drops in tumbler water. 18th, very much better; pulse, 100, throat did not feel near so sore, false membrane began to come off, back and limbs ached but slightly, headache nearly gone; continued same treatment three days. Discharged her cured. Diarrhea stopped second day."

2. "Mrs. G., 21, nursing a babe. Dec. 11th, throat commenced to feel sore, very restless night. 12th, slight headache with severe pain in back and legs, very chilly all the time, throat very sore, both tonsils very much swollen and covered in patches with dark-colored pseudo-membrane, deglutition" (swallowing) "very difficult, face very much flushed, great prostration, could not sit up any, so faint and weak, bowels regular. Gave Phytolacca

4 drops every ½ hour, with gargle of same. 13th, felt very much better; fever all gone, back and legs did not ache any, throat felt very sore, tonsils very red and swollen, covered in patches with the pseudo-exudation, deglutition very painful. Continued same treatment once an hour. 14th, felt quite well; pseudo-membrane off from both tonsils, large holes eaten into tonsils, could swallow quite well. Continued same treatment every two hours, discharged her cured next day. Babe nursed her throughout, did not take disease."

LARYNGEAL DIPHTHERIA—CROUP, TRUE OR MEMBRANOUS.—For many years the medical fraternity has been divided as to the identity of membranous croup and diphtheria, but to-day most physicians consider them one and the same.

The **treatment** and general care of the child is the same as that already given under *Diphtheria*.

DROPSY.—Dropsy is not a disease, but a symptom. It is a result of disease and indicates a serious condition of the health. It consists of an effusion of the watery part of the blood into a cavity, or into the loose connective tissue which envelops the body and lies just beneath the skin. In the latter case it is called *Anasarca.* Occurring in the abdominal cavity, it is called *Ascites;* in the chest cavity, *Hydrothorax;* in the brain, *Hydrocephalus;* in the sac which surrounds the heart, *Hydro-Pericardium.* The two latter seldom occur. *Hydrocephalus,* or *Water on the Brain,* is a disease of infancy. Swelling is the universal evidence of dropsy. Dropsy always depends upon obstruction of the return circulation. The obstruction may be due to tumors, inflammation acute or chronic, or may be due to a weak heart. When due to tumor or inflammation, it is localized, that is, the return circulation being blocked, the blood is forced back, oozes out through the veins, and is found in the nearest cavity or tissue. Dropsy may result from Bright's disease. In health the kidneys contain a large amount of blood. During inflammation the blood cannot circulate through them, but is forced back toward the heart. At first the force of the heart beat is increased to overcome the extra demands made upon it, but later the heart may become diseased and weakened, when the return circulation will be correspondingly slow. *Oedema* is a term often applied to swelling or localized dropsy occurring just beneath the skin. Inflammatory swellings are sometimes spoken of as *oedematous.*

Dropsy may also affect other smaller cavities of the body, deriving its name therefrom, as *Dropsy of the Testicle,*called *Hydrocele.*

TREATMENTS.—

A. If due to tumor, remove the growth; if due to inflammation, weak heart or Bright's disease, see treatment under those heads. In all cases relieve as far as possible by keeping the bowels active. Water may be drawn from the abdomen, chest or any other cavity by inserting a *trocar*. This is a hollow needle and the water drains through it. It will be understood, of course, that this simply relieves the patient but does not cure. The only cure is removal of the cause, and this may be difficult or impossible.

B. One of the best remedies for any form of dropsy is Dwarf Elder (see chapter on herbs for description and directions). Of course, when dropsical symptoms appear, consult a doctor as to their nature and cause.

In the chapter on HERB REMEDIES will be found many herbs that produce a free discharge of urine, and thus help to relieve, and in many cases have cured dropsy in some of its forms.

C. Jalap.. ½ ounce
Cream of Tartar............................ 1   "
Elaterium, powdered........ .... 4 grains.
Capsicum .... 1 drachm.

Mix, and divide into 20 powders.

Dose.—Take one powder in a little syrup or molasses, morning, noon and night, and if this does not cause as free a cathartic action as the patient can well bear, take another at late bedtime, until a free and full cathartic action has been brought about, which may be repeated every three or four days, as needed.

D. Is only a symptom of some diseased condition, which, if it be possible to remove, the dropsy will disappear.—(14).

E. Purgative doses of Salts and a purely milk diet. No liquor or stimulant drinks.—(7).

F. Hydrocele.—Draw off the water and inject into the sac Tincture of Iodine, diluted one-half with water.—(10).

G. Hydrocele.—Rest in bed, with support of the parts, and cathartic doses of Epsom Salts.—(7).

H. Hydrocephalus.—For a child a year old, one grain Iodide Potassium in a tablespoonful of water, three times a day, between meals.—(14).

DYSENTERY.—(See under DIARRHEA).

DYSMENORRHEA.—(See under DISEASES OF WOMEN).

DYSPEPSIA. (See under STOMACH DISEASES).

DYSURIA.—(See under BLADDER DISEASES).

THE EAR AND ITS DISEASES.

The ear consists of three parts—the external, middle and internal.

The External Ear.—The external ear is formed of cartilage and bone and is covered with skin; the expanded portion is formed of cartilage without bone and is popularly recognized as "the ear." The border of the external ear gradually verges or approaches towards the opening which leads to the middle ear. This opening, called the external auditory canal, is about 1½ inches in length. The first half inch is formed of cartilage; the remaining portion is situated in bone, and all is covered or lined with skin which becomes more modified as it extends inward. It is supplied with numerous glands which secrete or furnish an adhesive yellow and bitter substance, the purpose of which is supposed to be the entanglement of insects, dust and other foreign bodies. The direction of the external canal is inward, forward and a little downward. It is narrower in the center than at either end, which makes it difficult to remove foreign bodies that may become lodged in it. It is separated from the middle ear by a membrane called the *tympanic membrane*. This membrane is composed of three layers: The outer layer is skin, the middle layer is connective tissue and forms the framework, and the internal layer is mucous membrane.

The Middle Ear.—The middle portion of the ear is hollow and is called the *tympanum*, meaning a drum. As stated, it is separated from the external ear by the tympanic membrane; it is separated from the internal ear by a bony partition. This partition is covered with mucous membrane and contains two openings, one round and the other oval, and these openings are lined with a delicate membrane. Extending across the middle ear is a chain of three very small bones held together by a delicate structure of cartilage. The inner end of this chain fits into one of the openings in the bony partition, and the cartilage blends with that lining the opening. The mucous membrane which covers the partition is reflected over and covers the entire chain, and blends at the outer end of the chain with the tympanic membrane. By means of the mucous membrane and the cartilage which supports it, the chain is allowed to vibrate back and forth, thus when wave sounds are received any jarring of the delicate structures of the internal ear is prevented.

105

Leading from the middle ear to the throat is a small tube or canal called the *Eustachian tube* after its discoverer. This tube is formed of connective tissue and cartilage, and is lined with mucous membrane which is continuous with the mucous membrane of the throat.

The Internal Ear.—This portion of the ear is sometimes called the *labyrinth*, meaning a winding passage. It is divided into three parts: first, the vestibule, or common opening, situated next to the middle ear; second, three small canals, each forming a half circle with both ends opening into the vestibule; third, the *cochlea*—so-called from its resemblance to a snail shell—which also opens into the vestibule. The cochlea is about ¼ of an inch in length and consists of a central column of bone. This column tapers from base to top and is surrounded by a spiral canal which makes 2½ turns. The canal, which is divided lengthwise into two parts by a thin layer of bone and delicate membrane, is about 1½ inches in length. Its termination resembles the half of an inverted funnel cut in two lengthwise. The two parts communicate at the top. The lower end of one opens into the vestibule, and the lower end of the other extends to the round window in the bony partition between the internal and middle ear, but is prevented from opening into the middle ear by reason of the mucous membrane which covers the window. The vestibule, the three half circular canals and the spiral canals of the cochlea, are lined with mucous membrane.

Each of the spiral canals contains a closed membrane in the form of a tube. This tube about one-third fills the space. Surrounding it and filling the balance of the space in the canals is a fluid called *perilymph*. The same kind of fluid fills the tube, and is here called *endolymph*. Covering the outer surface of the wall of the cochlea or snail shell is a delicate membrane which follows the whole length of the spiral canal. It is composed of cells whose arrangement somewhat resembles the key-board of a piano. These cells are supplied with delicate hair-like processes. The base of the cochlea is about 1 inch in breadth and contains numerous openings for the passage of the branches of the auditory nerve, or nerve of hearing. Upon entering, one-half of this nerve goes to supply the vestibule and half-circular canals, and the other half ascends the spiral canal in the cochlea and divides into delicate filaments or fibers which join the hair-like processes of the cells. The different sound waves traveling along the external canal are transmitted across the middle ear by the chain of bones, communicate with the internal ear and are received by the cells forming the key-board. This produces the different tones, and the various impressions are conveyed to the brain.

EARACHE.—Earache is a trouble usually met with in children. It may follow taking cold, and is one of the symptoms in congestion, inflammation, or suppuration of the middle ear. As usually met with, earache is not a serious condition. However, it should be remembered that the ear is a very sensitive organ, and it requires but very slight pressure to cause pain. As stated in the foregoing, the middle ear is lined with mucous membrane which is continuous from the throat, passing along the Eustachian tube, therefore inflammation of the throat may and often does extend to the middle ear and cause earache. Inflammation or abscess in one of the cavities of the mastoid process (see *Abscess of the Mastoid Process*) may cause earache.

TREATMENTS.—

A. Earache as ordinarily met should be treated with hot applications; hot cloths should be applied to the side of the head, or better, cloths wrung out of hot water, or apply hot poultices, because moist heat can be applied at a higher temperature than dry heat.

Give internally 5 grains of Bromide of Potash and $\frac{1}{800}$ of a grain of Atropine every one or two hours. This dose is suitable for a child five years of age. Children are usually restless and worry a great deal with this trouble, therefore $\frac{1}{15}$ of a grain of Codeine should be added to the Atropine and Bromide. In the proper dose these remedies are perfectly harmless for small children and even babies. If the child is quiet, omit the Codeine; if the face flushes or the pupil of the eye dilates, stop the Atropine.

If there is evidence of pus, the abscess should be opened at once and thoroughly washed out. It will require washing two or three times a day with water containing a few drops of Carbolic Acid, or some other antiseptic. While opening an abscess in the middle ear is a very simple procedure, it requires the services of a physician, and he would instruct regarding the antiseptics and the after treatment.

B. Laudanum poured into the ear. A drop is sufficient.—(7).

C. Equal parts of Tincture of Opium and Tincture of Belladonna. Drop 5 drops warm into the ear every hour or two if necessary. For infant, 2 drops will be sufficient.—(45).

D. Laudanum and Sweet Oil, equal parts, warm, dropped into the ear. Hen's Oil or Glycerine will do equally as well in place of the Sweet Oil. Apply hot salt bag, or bag of hops very hot.—(9).

E. Hydrochlorate of Pilocarpine $\frac{1}{24}$ grain. To be given by the mouth. Repeat every hour until there is an increased flow of saliva. This is evidence that the child is under the effects. —(2).

Note.—Pilocarpine is preferable to Laudanum, or Opium in any form, in treating children, because it does not produce convulsions, and sometimes Opium, even in small doses, does produce this trouble. It should be remembered that Opium is not a suitable remedy for small children.

F. Mix equal parts of Glycerine and Laudanum, warm, drop 3 or 4 drops into the ear and apply local heat.

If child is very restless and there is much pain, give 5 drops of Paregoric, or ¼ of a grain of Codeine.

CATARRH OF THE EAR.—In health the middle ear is filled with air, which is received through the Eustachian tube. Respiration creates a constant change of this air. During an attack of catarrh the mucous membrane lining the Eustachian tube may become so swollen as to completely close the opening. Should this occur, the air in the middle ear is sometimes absorbed, producing the condition known as *Dry Catarrh* of the middle ear. Or, when the tube is closed and swollen, the membrane lining the middle ear may continue to pour out a catarrhal exudate which is sometimes converted into pus. This would constitute an abscess. This may be absorbed or may break through the external membrane and discharge through the external canal. This is the condition present when people tell you that "the ear runs." See treatment "A" under EARACHE.

ABSCESS OF THE MASTOID PROCESS.—Situated just behind the middle ear is a prominent bone, called the *mastoid process*. This is filled with large spaces which open into and communicate with the middle ear, Eustachian tube and throat. Sometimes the catarrhal conditions extend from the middle ear into one or more of the large cavities of this bone and form an abscess. This would call for the assistance of a surgeon, who may find it necessary to make an incision behind the ear, drill through the bone and allow the pus to escape. The danger of an abscess at this point is that the internal bony partition might be destroyed and the inflammation and suppuration penetrate to the brain.

ECZEMA.—(See under SKIN DISEASES).

ENDOCARDITIS.—(See under HEART, DISEASES OF).

ENTERIC FEVER.—*Enteric Fever* means fever caused by diseases of the digestive tract. The term may be applied to any of the inflammatory processes where fever is present. *Typhoid Fever* is sometimes spoken of as *Enteric Fever*.

EPILEPSY.—Epilepsy, often called *Falling Sickness*, is a disease of the nervous system, characterized by attacks of unconsciousness with or without convulsions, usually with.

Cause.—A large per cent of the cases begin in childhood, and many are of hereditary origin. Chronic alcoholism in the parent is believed to be an important factor in producing this disease.

Disorders of digestion, depression of spirits, loss of vigor, a feeling of languor, an unhealthy system and cloudy brain, are common in epileptics, thus giving evidence of a lack of nourishment. Occurring in children and infants, this lack of nourishment may be the result of indigestion from improper feeding; or it may be the result of hereditary taint—the vitality of the child may never have been quite up to the normal. In the latter case digestion and assimilation would be lowered, and the nervous system would be still less able to withstand a faulty diet and the irritating effects of retained waste. Lack of nutrition robs the blood of its natural elements. The higher forms of digestion are carried on in the circulation, and when the blood is improperly nourished, poisons in the form of uric acid, lactic acid, etc., remain in the system and produce irritation.

Especially does this affect the brain as one-fifth of all the blood in the body goes to nourish that organ. Receiving five times as much blood as any other organ of its size, it must follow that any habit or indulgence which impairs digestion and causes unhealthy blood must produce a morbid influence upon the brain and nervous system, hence the enormous production of nervous debility, monomania, hypochondria, insanity, idiocy, and many minor ailments, such as rheumatism, neuralgia, headache, mental stupor, lack of resolution, etc. Indigestion and retained waste irritate the nervous system and produce the different mental, nervous and emotional states known as hysteria, nervousness, melancholia, and other depressions and hallucinations. This is the foundation upon which epilepsy·stands. Dynamite may be struck once or a thousand times if the blows are light enough, but sooner or later it will explode: The irritation produced by dyspepsia may be stored up for a time, but sooner or later it too will explode. It will accumulate in the central nervous system, the brain and spinal cord until they are surcharged, and at the first opportunity it will break forth and its power for a time be irresistible, as in an epileptic fit.

Symptoms.—As a rule epileptic fits come on without warning symptoms. In some cases, however, they are preceded, perhaps for a day or two, with a feeling of fullness in the head, giddiness, and specks floating before the eyes; in other cases the attack is preceded by a voracious appetite. There may be no immediate warning, or there may be a sharp cry or an unusual, animal-like sound. The patient falls unconscious and sometimes writhes in convulsions. In some cases the patient is conscious of a tingling sensation, or a feeling like a cold draught, which seems to start in the fingers or toes and works its way rapidly upward, unconsciousness coming on as it reaches the throat or head. The countenance is livid, swollen and distorted; the tongue is often thrust from the mouth, and not infrequently lacerated with the teeth; respiration is impeded; foam issues from the mouth; the eyelids are partly open, the eyeballs starting out, and the pupil is fixed and insensible to the stimulus of light.

These symptoms, which indicate a severe attack, remit presently, but may be followed with another and perhaps severer fit, or with a succession of fits; or the convulsions and other symptoms may gradually diminish after the first fit, leaving the patient in a state of stupor from which he sinks into a deep sleep, awakening as from ordinary slumber and without consciousness of what has occurred.

There is little probability of a cure if the disease has run for a number of years, or if the patient has been afflicted since birth; but the attempt should be made in all cases.

TREATMENTS.—

A. Take a solution of the following:

> Bromide of Potash .... 2 grains.
> Bromide of Ammonia 2   "
>
> Dissolve in a tablespoonful of water and repeat three times a day. Or, take an ounce of each of the above, put into a dish that will hold a quart, pour in warm water and dissolve, and give a tablespoonful three times a day, which will be about two grains of each to the dose.

B. The bromides and other sedatives may be valuable in many cases of epilepsy, and undoubtedly exert a temporary benefit upon all cases, yet it is doubtful if their continued use is helpful. They cover over, but do not remove the cause; their use produces a temporary effect only. Taken habitually, they slowly, but surely, weaken the nervous system, lower vitality, and aid in reducing physical strength.

Those who have studied the question of epilepsy believe that with attention to diet and elimination a cure may be effected. We all know that drug medication is disappointing and that operations are useless. All forms have been tried. If injury should drive a sliver or bone into the skull, or cause other brain pressure, an operation might relieve and effect a cure; but epilepsy is seldom caused by injury.

ERUCTATIONS.—Eructations are the result of gases formed in the stomach and indicate that there is undigested food present, which means dyspepsia. The gas, not being able to escape along the digestive tract, is expelled by the mouth. Those troubled with eructations should pay close attention to diet and, if needed, some artificial digestant may be taken for a short time. Regarding diet, if the eructations are sour, avoid starchy foods as they produce acids; if there is a greasy taste in the mouth, avoid fats; if there is an odor indicating any article of food eaten or drank, such articles should be avoided.

TREATMENT.—

For the indigestion we recommend the following:

Scale Pepsin (1 to 3000) .... 2 drachms.
Hydrochloric (Muriatic) Acid ...... 15 drops.
Glycerine .... 1 ounce.
Simple Elixir .... 2 ounces.

Mix, and take one teaspoonful after each meal.

ERYSIPELAS. — Erysipelas is an acute inflammatory disease, usually confined to the skin, but may affect the deeper tissues. When extending to the deeper structures, it is called *phlegmonous.*

Cause.—Due to a specific ferment. See cause of *Small-Pox.* The disease is not contagious.

Symptoms.—The disease usually comes on with a chill, though in many cases the chill is absent. There is moderate fever, full pulse, and there may be headache. The affected part becomes red and swollen. The swelling may be smooth, tense and glistening, or may begin as bright red spots which join as the swelling increases. The swelling is so great and the circulation is interfered with to such an extent that it has a peculiar dark hue. The face is quite a usual seat of the disease, and when occurring there the swelling frequently closes the eyes. The inflamed surface may be covered with a rash; vesicles of quite large size may appear and become filled with a watery fluid; the urine may contain albumen. The disease usually lasts about one week.

TREATMENTS.—

What to Do.—If it is a bad case, send for a doctor. In the meantime, wring cloths out of sour buttermilk, or, what is still better, make a cranberry poultice and bind on. To do this, simply crush the cranberries and bind on with cloths. Paint around the outside of the eruption with Tincture of Iodine.

A. Painting the surface with Tincture of Iodine is said to check the spread of the disease in some cases. Some claim that active cathartics followed by Pilocarpine in ⅛ grain doses every hour until there is free perspiration, is a specific treatment. The

Pilocarpine should be continued until the symptoms disappear, the dose being lessened as the disease subsides. *Pilocarpine should only be given when the patient is strong and robust.*

B. We believe the best treatment for Erysipelas is the following: First wash the inflamed surface with soap and water, then with Boric Acid and water—25 grains of Boric Acid to the ounce of water. Wipe dry and apply equal parts of Ichthyol and Glycerine, and cover with a light bandage. Dress twice a day, washing the surface clean each time before making the application of Ichthyol. Internally, give 5 drops Fowler's Solution four times a day. The advantage of using the Glycerine and Ichthyol is that both are easily removed before making a new application. Ichthyol and Vaseline, or other excipient, may be used if desired. If there is sleeplessness, Sulfonal in from 5 to 10 grain doses, Phenacetine in from 5 to 10 grain doses, Chloral in from 10 to 20 grain doses, or the Bromides in from 20 to 40 grain doses, may be given. The Chloral or Bromides should be given in plenty of water. If Glycerine or Sugar is added to the water, it will improve the taste. In the strong a low diet is advised. Sometimes erysipelas attacks the weak and emaciated, those suffering from chronic disease. In this case the eruptions are pale, temperature low and vitality depressed. These cases need stimulants and tonics. Give 20 to 30 drops of Tincture of Chloride of Iron after meals. The diet should be nutritious. Ichthyol and Fowler's Solution may be used in all cases.

C. Ichthyol Ointment .... 1 ounce.
Vaseline 1   "

Mix, and apply locally.

Give 10 drops Tincture of Iron internally every two hours. Keep bowels open with Salts.—(46).

D. Ichthyol .... 2½ ounces.
Colodion, flexible 2   drachms.

Mix, and apply every three or four hours. *Be sure* to have application extend one inch beyond the inflammation.

Tincture of Chloride of Iron .... 2 ounces.
Tincture Poison Oak (Rhus Tox-
icodendron) .... 2 drachms.

Mix, and take 35 drops in water every two hours. Keep bowels regular, and give milk, beef tea and eggs.—(53).

ERYSIPELAS, PHLEGMONOUS.—When erysipelas attacks the deeper structures, the disease assumes altogether a different form; the swelling is much greater and the discoloration is of a deeper and darker hue. This is accompanied with high fever, rapid pulse, throbbing pain and prostration. There are irregular chills, followed by sweating, the result of poisons absorbed. The swelling may be so great that the circulation may be entirely shut off and gangrene result. By extension through the loose connective tissue just beneath the skin this form of erysipelas may include or cover a large surface, as a whole arm or leg.

TREATMENT.—

Keep the bowels and skin active and healthy. Give 10 grains Salol every three hours and the most nourishing diet. Give from a teaspoonful to a tablespoonful of Bovinine in a glass of milk every four hours. Put two ounces of rice in one pint of water, boil for three hours, adding sufficient water to maintain the original pint, mix two eggs and a half pint of cream and add to the boiled rice, then add all to one pint of hot beef tea, (see *Beef Tea* under MISCELLANEOUS MEDICAL RECEIPTS), and feed to the patient every one, two or three hours, according to the severity of the case. Should there be danger of suppuration or gangrene, incise at once. Cut deep enough to allow free drainage. This will reduce the swelling and relieve the circulation. It may be necessary to make frequent incisions. Wash the wounds with Peroxide of Hydrogen, full strength, Carbolic Acid water, or other antiseptics. Allow free drainage and dress with gauze soaked in antiseptics. Give abundance of fresh air.

EXCORIATION.—(See under CHILDREN'S DISEASES).

THE EYE AND ITS DISEASES.

The eye rests in a bony cavity or socket and is embedded in fat. The fat protects it from jarring, while the surrounding wall of bone protects it from injury.

The eyeball consists of two parts, which may be compared to a large and a small marble—the large one about one inch in diameter and the small one about one-sixth as large. Sinking the small marble about two-thirds of its diameter into the larger would give a general outline of the eyeball. The small marble would represent one-sixth, and is called the *cornea*. It is placed in front. Its size compares to that portion of the eye that gives color—black, blue or gray. The larger part would represent the five-sixths and is placed in the orbital cavity. It is the portion that we can see but partially. It constitutes the white of the eye and meets the cornea at the border of the color line.

The muscles which move the eye are attached by their inner ends to the apex or inner point of the orbital cavity, and the front or outer ends are attached to the outer surface of the eyeball a little back of the cornea and a little behind the circle where the large and small marbles join. The muscles are placed above, below, on either side and obliquely, so that the eye may roll in all directions.

The eyeball is composed of three coats—the inner, middle and outer. The inner coat of the eyeball is called the *retina*, meaning a network. It is formed by the expanded fibers of the optic nerve, or nerve of sight. This nerve has its origin in the brain. It passes out of the skull through a little opening in the apex or orbital cavity, and immediately its fibers divide and radiate in all directions, forming a thin membrane. The fibers are held in position by a delicate connective tissue framework. These fibers terminate at the junction of the cornea with the large part of the eye, as represented by the junction of the large and small marble. The artery which supplies the eye rests within the substance of the optic nerve at its point of entrance into the orbital cavity, and, like the nerve, branches of this artery expand in a radiating manner, forming a close network of vessels which are held together by delicate fibers of connective tissue. This constitutes the middle coat and is called the *choroid*, meaning a membrane of vessels. On the inner surface of this membrane, lying next to the expanded nerve fibers, is a layer of dark cells. These cells absorb the light, which otherwise would be reflected from side to side and cause confusion. This dark layer corresponds to the black lining of the photographer's camera. The outer coat or membrane is called the *sclerotic*, meaning hard. Covering the brain and lying next to the inner surface of the skull is a firm membrane of connective tissue, called the *dura-mater*. When the optic nerve leaves the brain, a sheath of this dura-mater goes with it, and when the optic nerve expands and forms the inner membrane of the eyeball, the sheath of dura-mater also expands and forms the outer membrane. The outer membrane or coat completely surrounds the eyeball in front and, being hard and fibrous, aids in maintaining the eye in the form of a globe. It is white and glistening and forms the *white of the eye*. In front it is somewhat modified and forms the cornea.

At the junction of the cornea with the larger part of the eyeball, the choroid, or middle coat, somewhat modified, makes a sharp bend inward and forms the *iris*, which is a thin curtain stretched vertically across, near the front of the eye, at the junction of the large and small marbles. Iris means many colors, hence the term. The colors—blue, black, gray, etc.—are caused by the various shades of coloring matter found in the layer of cells which covers the back part of the iris. With the Albino race there is little or no coloring in this layer of cells, hence the light color of their eyes. The iris contains two sets of muscle fibers: One set radiates from the center to the surface like the spokes in a wagon wheel; the other set is circular. This gives it the power to contract and dilate, thus changing the size of the pupil. The pupil is simply an opening in the center of the iris for the admission of rays of light. When light is very bright, the pupil contracts, shutting out some of the rays; when light is dim, the pupil dilates, allowing more light to enter. The lids also aid in controlling the amount of light that enters the eye.

As stated, the choroid or middle coat makes a sharp bend inward at the point indicated by the junction of the two marbles, and being here supplied with circular and radiating fibers, forms the iris. The iris is flat, the cornea is oval, hence between the cornea and iris is a space, called the *anterior chamber*. Behind the iris and close to the pupil is the *lens*. This is a transparent double-convex body which aids in focusing the rays of light. The lens is about one-third of an inch in diameter from side to side, and one-quarter of an inch in diameter from before backwards. The lens is oval, the iris is flat, hence the iris recedes from the lens towards its circumference, leaving a space. This space is called the *posterior chamber*. The two chambers or spaces communicate through the pupil, or opening in the iris.

Both the front and back chambers are filled with a liquid called *aqueous humor*. This is composed of about five or six drops of water, holding in solution a trace of alkaline salts. Within the walls of the retina or inner membrane, and filling the whole of the space behind the lens, is a jelly-like substance called *vitreous humor*, so named because it resembles melted glass. The vitreous humor aids in focusing the rays of light. Surrounding the vitreous humor is a thin, transparent membrane called the *hyaline membrane*, meaning transparent. In front it encloses the lens, forming a capsule around it. This capsule is attached to the surrounding structures and aids in holding the lens in position.

Light enters the eye through the cornea, aqueous humor, pupil, lens and vitreous humor in the order named, and is focused on the retina or inner membrane of nerve fibers, the impression or picture made on the retina being conveyed by the optic nerve to the brain.

The Lachrymal, or Tear, Apparatus.—The junction of the upper and lower eyelids is called the *canthi*, meaning corners of the eye. The inner canthus is somewhat prolonged inward, forming a triangular space. This space contains what is called the *caruncle*, meaning a fleshy elevation. On the apex or highest point of this elevation is a small opening. This is the commencement of the *lachrymal,* or tear, *duct.* This opening extends inward towards the nose for a short distance and terminates in what is called the *lachrymal sac.* This sac is the dilated upper portion of the lachrymal duct. It is called the nasal duct because it opens into the nose. From the inner canthus or inner angle of the eye, this duct, which is about three-fourths of an inch in length, passes inward, backward and downward and terminates in the nasal cavity. Situated at the inner angle of the eye, and on the margin of the lid, is a slight elevation called the *lachrymal papilla.* The apex or highest point of this papilla is also pierced by a small opening. The glands which furnish the tears are situated just outside the orbital cavity and above the outer canthus or junction of the eyelids. The under surface of the glands rest upon the convexity of the eyeball. Each gland is supplied with from ten to twelve ducts, which convey the tears over the surface of the eye. The tears pass along these ducts, which converge to the single opening in the papilla already described, and next enter the canal which leads to the nose. That is why the latter needs frequent wipings during the act of crying. If the tears flow too fast, they do not all enter or pass through the nasal duct, but overflow and run down the cheek.

Each eyelid contains a thin piece of cartilage about one inch in length. This aids in maintaining form. Between the cartilage and the mucous membrane which lines the lids are a number of small glands, about forty in the upper lid and thirty in the lower lid. They are embedded in grooves on the under surface of the cartilage, and by means of straight tubes or ducts each gland opens upon the margin of the lid. These glands secrete a sebaceous or oily substance which prevents the lids from adhering together. Sometimes the opening of a gland becomes closed, and, the gland continuing to secrete, quite a large tumor may form. It is sometimes necessary to remove this with a knife.

DEFECTS OF VISION.

Hyperopia — Far-Sightedness. — Rays of light should focus exactly on the retina, that is, meet at the same point on the inner membrane that is formed by the expanded fibers of the optic nerve. This is called perfect vision or stigmatism. But the eye is subject to deformities the same as other parts of the body. Sometimes the globe of the eye (eyeball) is too short, so that the rays of light from an object held at an ordinary distance do not focus on the retina, and this results in confusion; if the rays could continue backward, they would meet behind the retina. This is called *hyperopia,* or *far-sightedness,* because it is necessary that the rays of light should come from an object held at some distance. These enter the eye more on a straight line and do not need so much power to concentrate, hence may focus on the retina or inner membrane. Hyperopia is congenital, that is, exists from birth. Convex glasses correct this trouble because they aid in bringing the rays of light together at the proper point.

Myopia—Near-Sightedness.—Sometimes the globe of the eye is too long, and the rays of light focus in front of the retina. This is called *myopia*, or *near-sightedness*, because it is necessary that the object should be held near the eyes. This causes the rays of light first to diverge, or enter the eye more at an angle, and this brings their point of meeting farther back. The cause of myopia is not known. Concave glasses will correct this trouble because they aid in diverging the rays and bring their point of meeting farther back where they may reach the retina.

Presbyopia—Far-Sightedness of Old Age.—In middle life and old age the lens becomes slightly opaque—less transparent—the density is increased, elasticity is diminished and the power of accommodation is correspondingly lessened. This is called *presbyopia*, or *far-sightedness of old age*. This trouble may be corrected by artificial lenses of sufficient strength to serve as an equivalent or substitute for the loss of the natural lens.

Color Blindness is due to lack of development or paralysis of some of the fibers of the optic nerve. The defect may include one or both eyes.

Strabismus means *cross-eyed*. When the eyes turn in, it is called *convergent;* when they turn out, *divergent*. One or both eyes may be affected. The cause is unequal strength of the muscles controlling the eyes, the stronger overcoming the weaker. By over-exertion the weak muscles may be able to hold the eye in position, yet this constant strain causes headache. This condition is frequently met with in school children and may be wholly corrected by glasses.

TREATMENT.—

A. Defects of vision which are not produced by disease of the eye are remedied by having the eyes fitted with suitable glasses. A competent oculist should be consulted. For those who are unable to pay there are free clinics connected with all medical colleges.—(48).

DISEASES OF THE EYE.

OPHTHALMIA.—This is a term somewhat loosely applied to any and all forms of inflammation of the eye, but more especially to those forms which attack the mucous membrane lining the lids.

TREATMENTS.—

A. Bathe the eye with warm water containing 10 or 15 grains of Boracic Acid to an ounce, protect the eyes from light, if very painful remain indoors for a few days, and drop the following mixture in the eye four or five times a day:

Sulphate of Zinc	1 grain.
Morphine	2 "
Camphor Water	2 drachms.
Boracic Acid	10 grains.
Water sufficient to make	1 ounce.

—(81).

B. Put one teaspoonful of clean, whole Flax seed into 1 ounce of water. Stir frequently and allow to stand until a mucilage is formed. To relieve painful inflammation, drop 2 or 3 drops into the eye every twenty to thirty minutes. The pain is relieved by the mechanical protection afforded the inflamed surfaces.

C. Boracic Acid powder, 1 ounce. Dissolve ½ teaspoonful of the powder in a glass of hot water, allow it to cool and bathe the eye several times a day by dipping absorbent cotton into the solution and squeezing solution from it into the eye.—(48).

D. Blue Vitriol	1 grain.
White Vitriol	1 "
Fine Table Salt	1 "
Loaf Sugar	1 "
Morphine	1 "
Soft or Distilled Water	1 ounce.

Mix, and when all is dissolved, strain through fine muslin. Apply three to five times daily, according to the severity of the case.

E. Common table salt, 2 to 5 grains to an ounce of water. This makes a good wash for weak and inflamed eyes.

F. Sulphate of Zinc	¼ grain.
Muriate Cocaine	⅛ "
Sulphate Morphine	⅛ "
Water	1 ounce.

Mix. Drop in the eye every two hours more or less often according to pain.—(47).

G. Boracic Acid	10 grains.
Muriate Cocaine	4 "
Rosewater	1 ounce.

Mix. Drop in the eyes every two hours.—(34).

H. Pith of Sassafras	1 drachm.
Soft Water	1 ounce.

This is a soothing preparation to inflamed eyes.

I. Hops and Poppy heads thoroughly mashed and boiled in water make a good poultice in inflammation, and the water in which they have been boiled is also useful as a wash for the eyes.

J. White Vitriol .... 5 grains.
Table Salt .... 5 "
Morphine .... 2 "
Lard, unsalted................................. 1 ounce.

Mix, and apply by rubbing a little between and upon the lids. Freshly churned and unsalted butter may be used in place of the lard.

INFLAMMATION OF THE LIDS.—CONJUNCTIVITIS.

—The mucous membrane which lines the eyelids is reflected over the front of the eyeball as far as the cornea. This membrane is called the *conjunctiva*. Inflammation of the conjunctiva is called *Conjunctivitis*. If there is much watery discharge, it is called *Catarrhal Conjunctivitis*. Sometimes the discharge becomes thick and contains a little pus; this is called *Muco-Purulent Conjunctivitis*. If the inflammation is the result of gonorrheal infection, it is called *Purulent Conjunctivitis*. If the inflammation is the result of injury, or of a foreign body, it is called *traumatic*, meaning the result of injury. (See under ACCIDENTS AND EMERGENCIES). Sometimes there is a formation of small hard elevations which cause friction and give the sensation of a foreign body in the eye, the eye becoming bloodshot as the result of the irritation; this is called *Granular Conjunctivitis, Trauchoma or Granulated Lids*. Sometimes during an attack of diphtheria when the disease affects the nasal cavities, it also extends to the mucous membrane lining the eyelids and a false membrane appears on the lids the same as in the nose and throat. This is called *Diphtheritic Conjunctivitis*. Diphtheria may make its first appearance in the eyes.

It will be noticed that each of the foregoing forms of inflammation is confined to the mucous membrane lining the lids and does not affect the eye proper. Some of these inflammations, if allowed to continue, may by extension invade the eyeball and become more serious, affecting and even destroying the sight. This is particularly true of purulent conjunctivitis.

Conjunctivitis, Simple.—The most common disease of the eye is inflammation of the conjunctiva. Usually it is of a mild nature and soon recovered from.

Catarrhal Conjunctivitis and **Muco-Purulent Conjunctivitis** are only different manifestations of *Simple Conjunctivitis*. The same treatment is applicable to all.

Causes.—Such inflammation may result from the same conditions which cause rheumatism, *i. e.*, acids and other irritating substances in the blood. It may result from injury or from foreign bodies in the eye, or from the infection of diphtheria or gonorrhea. It precedes an attack of measles. It more frequently results from atmospheric changes that produce influenza, colds and catarrh of the nasal passages.

Symptoms.—Usually, the symptoms are not marked. The mucous membrane may be slightly swollen and thickened; the eyes look red, there is a slight catarrhal condition, and the individual may not be able to bear strong light.

TREATMENT.—

See washes and applications under *Ophthalmia.*

Conjunctivitis, Granular — Granulated Lids.—This is inflammation of the conjunctiva in which the membrane becomes studded with small elevations, some of which later join together and become larger and more resistant. The roughened lids produce irritation, the cornea becomes vascular, that is, blood vessels form in that portion of the mucous membrane covering the eyeball, the eye becomes bloodshot, and the cornea loses its luster and becomes more or less opaque, or non-transparent. The disease tends to run a chronic course.

Symptoms.—If the disease comes on in acute form, there is first redness and swelling with profuse discharge of thick secretions. At first the swelling may completely hide the granulations, but later it diminishes and the elevations are visible. Usually the disease comes on more mildly and may be unnoticed until the granulations are quite large. In either case the granulations produce a sensation of a foreign body in the eye, due to irritation. There is fear of light, as in other diseases of the eye.

TREATMENT.—

If the eye is very sensitive, dissolve 2 grains of Cocaine in ¼ ounce of water and drop into the eye every three to five minutes until the pain ceases, then take the margin of the lid between the thumb and finger, carefully lift it up and apply a pointed crystal of Sulphate of Copper—Blue Vitriol. Pass the crystal quickly and gently over the granulated surface and immediately wash out with Boric Acid solution—20 grains of Boric Acid to 1 ounce of water. Apply this treatment twice a week, and apply a crystal of Alum in the same manner every second day. If this does not destroy the granulations, apply the Sulphate of Copper crystal every other day for a few days. A convenient piece of either the Sulphate of Copper or Alum may be obtained at any drug store. With a sharp knife shave one end down to a point, and finish by dipping into water and rubbing the surface until perfectly smooth. These crystals can be obtained properly shaped for this purpose and fitted with handles.

Granulated lids may also be successfully treated with electricity.

Any form of treatment will be more successful if the eyes are protected from light. When out of doors, colored glasses should be worn.

Conjunctivitis, Purulent.

—This inflammation is much more dangerous, and is also contagious. It usually affects the new-born, though adults sometimes have it. It is met with most frequently in cities. The disease commences from thirty-six to forty-eight hours after infection, runs a long and tedious course, and may affect the cornea (eyeball) and destroy the sight.

Cause.—This disease is caused by a specific poison. It is the result of gonorrheal infection, and in the new-born is contracted during birth.

Symptoms.—The disease may not be noticed sometimes for two or three days atter birth, when the lids will appear red, somewhat swollen and glued together. Examination shows a thick, purulent secretion, which escapes when the lids are raised. There may be but little pain at first, but later the lids become more swollen and the discharge thinner and more abundant. There is loss of appetite, restlessness from increased pain, the cornea or eyeball may become ulcerated, and perforation may follow. In this case the lens escapes, and when the inflammation subsides the eyeball shrinks and the child is blind. If the eyeball remains sound, the eye gradually returns to the normal and sight is restored.

TREATMENT:—

Cleanse the eyes thoroughly with a saturated solution of Boric Acid and water—25 grains of the acid to an ounce of water. If discovered early, keep cold compresses on the eyes, being careful not to press the lids against the eyeball. Keep the eyes as free from the discharge as possible with bits of absorbent cotton wet in the Boric Acid solution. If the disease does not respond to treatment, turn the lids outward, hold them firmly, and brush them with a 4 per cent. solution of Nitrate of Silver—20 grains to the ounce—once a day, and wash off at once with warm Boric Acid solution, or warm solution of salt and water followed with the Boric Acid solution. When using the Silver solution, be careful to apply to the lids only and do not touch the eyeball, and *wash off at once.* Should the eyeball become involved, add 3 grains of Atropine to one ounce of water and drop in the eye three or four times a day, or often enough to keep the pupil well dilated.

Note.—In using Atropine, allow excess of the solution to drain from the outer angle of the eye so as to avoid its passage through the tear duct into the nose and throat.

Conjunctivitis, Diphtheritic.—This is diphtheria of the eyes. The tissue affected is the mucous membrane lining the lids. A false membrane forms and constitutional symptoms are present, the same as in diphtheria of the throat. The disease may be the result of diphtheria in the nasal cavities, having traveled through the tear ducts, or it may make its first appearance in the eyes.

Cause.—The same as that which causes diphtheria in the throat.

Symptoms.—The mucous membrane of the lids becomes swollen and painful. At first there is an increase in the secretions, or tears, and within twenty-four to thirty-six hours the false membrane makes its appearance. This membrane is the same as that which appears in the throat. The color is the same —dark and leathery—with a well defined border, that is, the junction of the false membrane and mucous membrane is distinct. As the disease progresses the lids become greatly swollen, and may become purplish in color by reason of interference with the circulation. The skin is tense and glistening. The pressure of the swollen lids upon the cornea may cause the latter to lose its luster and become hazy in appearance. Constitutional symptoms are also present.

TREATMENT.—

If seen early, keep cold packs over the eyes. Dissolve 20 grains of Boric Acid in 1 ounce of water. Keep small pieces of cloth or cotton saturated with this constantly applied. If the lids are already greatly swollen, the application should be hot instead of cold. The solution should also be dropped into the eyes several times a day. The constitutional treatment is the same as that given under *Diphtheria.*

INFLAMMATION OF THE MARGIN OF THE LIDS—BLEPHARITIS.— Blepharitis is an inflammation of the border or margin of the eyelid. The disease is due to blocking up of the hair follicles and the small glands connected with them. The inflammation may also extend to the lids.

Symptoms.—The symptoms of blepharitis are irritation and redness along the margin of the lids, and usually the formation of scales or crusts. The natural secretions produced by the hair follicles and associate glands are increased by the irritation. These dry on the margin of the lids and produce the scales mentioned.

TREATMENT.—

Cleanse the lids thoroughly, washing with hot water and Castile soap. If the surface is inflamed, mix Yellow Oxide of Mercury, 3 grains, with 2 drachms of Vaseline, and apply twice a day. Maintain thorough cleanliness and the disease will soon disappear.

INFLAMMATION OF THE IRIS—IRITIS.—There
are several causes for Iritis. It may be caused by syphilis, may result from injury, or it may be caused by the same conditions which produce rheumatism, that is, acids and other irritating substances in the blood. It is well to remember that inflammation always depends upon an irritant in some form. This is true of inflammation everywhere. Suppurative iritis is so called when the products of inflammation turn to pus. This form is most apt to occur in those who are poorly nourished.

Symptoms.—Pain, which is usually severe. The iris looks cloudy. The fluid in front of the iris is changed as a result of its contamination with inflammatory products, and this interferes with sight. It will be remembered that the iris is stretched across just in front of the lens; during inflammation it may grow fast to the lens. This would cause unequal dilatation and interfere with light entering the eye. The mucous membrane that is reflected over the front of the eyeball may become congested and more or less inflamed, and surrounding the cornea may be seen dark red lines, the result of distended vessels.

TREATMENT.—

One danger in iritis is that the iris may grow fast to the lens, in which case, even if no other damage results, there will remain unequal dilatation of the pupil and permanent interference of sight. To prevent this, dissolve 4 grains of Atropine in an ounce of water and drop a little in the eye every thirty minutes until the pupil dilates. After that perhaps three times a day will be sufficient. (See note under *Purulent Conjunctivitis* for use of Atropine.) When the pupil is widely dilated, its inner border surrounds the lens and there is no danger of contact or adhesion. The bowels should be kept active, and in those usually healthy a low diet should be maintained. Also take 1 teaspoonful of Syrup of Hydriodic Acid three times a day, *between meals*. The patient should be kept in a dark room, as bright light irritates the iris and increases the trouble. After improvement the patient should wear colored glasses for a time to prevent, if possible, a return of the trouble. It is also good practice to give 2-drop doses of Tincture of Aconite or Fluid Extract of Veratrum every hour for a day or two. This has a tendency to equalize the circulation and relieve the congested vessels about the eye. Sometimes pain is relieved by keeping hot applications on the eyes. This may consist of small pieces of cotton wet in hot Boric Acid water, 10 or 20 grains of the acid to the ounce, changed every five or ten minutes. Any case of iritis that does not respond readily to treatment should receive the most skilled attention, for if not relieved, serious consequences may follow.

CATARACT.—A cataract is an opacity or non-transparency of the lens of the eye. It frequently occurs as the result of old age, but sometimes occurs in the young, and is also sometimes present even in infants.

Cause.—When not resulting from injury, inflammation or suppuration, cataract results from a lack of nourishment. Usually the cataract includes the whole lens. This is generally true in the form met with in old age. Sometimes, however, and more especially in the young, the opacity is confined to the central part of the lens and the outer surface remains normal. This is called *nuclear cataract.*

Symptoms.—The first symptom of cataract is a gradual dimness of vision. The patient can see better on a dark day or in the twilight. The reason is that the pupil dilates and admits more light. There is no pain or evidence of trouble in any way except the interference with sight. When the patient tries to read, it is found necessary to hold the book very close to the eyes. This causes the rays of light to radiate and enter the eye more on an angle, and by this means they find their way into the eye by passing around the border of the lens. By dilating the pupils with Atropine, the opacity of the lens may be plainly seen. It looks white or very light in color. This is seen by looking through the pupil. It will be remembered that the lens is situated directly behind the pupil, enclosed and supported by a little transparent membrane.

TREATMENT.—

The treatment is removal of the lens and fitting the eyes with artificial glasses. This is an operation of considerable delicacy. For nuclear cataract enlarging of the pupils is advised. In this form the outer border of the lens remains natural, and by enlarging the pupils the light may be readily transmitted. The opaque center does not extend or become larger, but remains stationary throughout life. Soft cataract is so-called because the lens is soft, opaque and non-transparent to light. This form is usually met with in the young—children and infants.

Secondary Cataract is where the capsule in which the lens was enclosed becomes opaque or non-transparent after the removal of the lens.

STY, or HORDEOLUM.—Under the description of the eye it was stated that the lids were supplied with a flat layer of cartilage or dense connective tissue to aid in maintaining their form, and that on the under side of each plate of dense tissue were a number of glands. A duct leads from each gland to the free margin of the lid. Sometimes one of these ducts or openings becomes closed, and as the secretions of the gland continue, a bulging is caused. This is called a *Sty*.

Cause.—Irritation from unhealthy blood; in other words, the cause is constitutional. This is why there are usually a number of these affections. The irritation causes an increase in the secretions of the glands with the result that one of the ducts becomes closed, and as the gland continues to secrete, the part swells, bulges forward, and becomes inflamed and painful.

TREATMENT.—

As a rule these affections are stubborn, the same as eczema and dandruff, and do not respond readily to treatment. This shows that the cause is not local, but constitutional. Usually the inflammation continues three or four days, pus forms, the tumor ruptures, the contents are discharged and the part heals. The treatment consists in trying to prevent pus formation, and also to prevent other tumors and swellings of a like nature. Small hot poultices may be laid over the lids, or a solution of hot Boric Acid may be applied on a soft cloth or small piece of cotton and changed frequently. If there is evidence of pus, the tumor should be opened at once. In place of the poultices or hot applications the following ointment is sometimes used:

> Yellow Oxide of Mercury.............. 3 grains.
> Vaseline....................................... 1 drachm.
>
> *Mix* thoroughly and apply to the affected lid two or three times a day. If this ointment is found irritating in any case, add more Vaseline.

With the first appearance of a sty, an active cathartic should be given and the patient should be careful about the diet.

PTERYGIUM (Terigium).—This is a thickening of the mucous membrane which commences at the inner angle or junction of the lid and extends over the eyeball. It is a fleshy, wedge-shaped growth. The apex or point is directed toward the pupil, while the base remains at the point of origin, that is, corresponds to the fleshy eminence at the inner angle of the lids. In the description of the eye this eminence is described as the *caruncle*.

Cause. — Long-continued irritation, the result of irritants in the blood. This results first in congestion, second in inflammation, and third in overgrowth of the membrane, the result of increased blood supply.

Symptoms. — A fleshy growth commencing at the inner angle of the eye, the outer end pointed and extending toward the pupil. If allowed to continue, it reaches and may nearly cover the pupil.

TREATMENT.—

Removal with a knife.

FAINTING.—A temporary suspension of the vital functions and mental powers, in some cases occurring suddenly, and in others preceded by a distress about the heart, a swimming of the head and a sense of general helplessness; also sometimes preceded by sickness at the stomach and coldness of the feet and hands.

Causes.—The causes of fainting are many: Pain, injuries, loss of blood, fatigue and weakness, fright, confinement in crowded places where the heat is great and ventilation poor, tight lacing and distressing sights. Organic diseases of the heart may occasion fainting in those who are afflicted with them.

TREATMENTS.—

A. Bathe the temples and around the nostrils with Camphor; sprinkle a little cold water in the face; get the patient into fresh air; give a little sling.

B. Lay the patient on the back on a bed, the floor, or the ground. Compel bystanders to keep away so that fresh air can be obtained. Never raise the patient up to a sitting or standing position.—(8).

C. Assume horizontal position; head a little lower than body.—(54).

D. Horizontal position on back. Cold to the head. Aromatic Spirits of Ammonia to nose for inhalation.—(10).

Faintness.—Give patient plenty of fresh air and also give brandy sling. Rub arms and limbs thoroughly. Wet cloth in Aqua Ammonia and let patient inhale it, being careful not to hold it close enough to strangle.

FATTY DEGENERATION. — (See under HEART, DISEASES OF).

FELON.—An abscess on a finger or thumb is termed a *felon*, but a felon proper is an inflammation of the membrane covering the bone. It occurs usually in the last joint of either a thumb or finger.

Symptoms.—The pain, at first deep and throbbing, soon becomes excruciating in the extreme, and the joint affected presents a swollen and inflamed appearance.

TREATMENTS.—

A. The usual method of relief, and the safest, is to have the finger lanced freely, the incision reaching to the bone. If this is not done, the ulcerating process goes on within the membrane until the bone itself is very likely to be destroyed. If the felon is not lanced, the application of poultices not only affords some degree of relief and comfort, but hastens suppuration.

B. Poultice with bread and milk or Flaxseed. Lance it as soon as possible. After it is lanced use a Slippery Elm poultice.

C. Take a handful each of the roots of Indian Turnip and of Blue Flag, and stew them in hog's lard sufficient to stew well. When done, strain and press out, and add Tar, 4 tablespoonfuls, and Castile soap half as much; simmer together, and apply this until the felon breaks.

D. Venice Turpentine, 1 ounce. Put into ½ teaspoonful of water and stir with a rough stick until the mass looks like candied honey, then spread a good coat on a cloth and wrap around the finger. If the case is only recent, it will remove the pain in a few hours.

E. A Poke Root poultice on a felon cures by absorption, unless matter is already formed; if matter has already formed, it soon brings it to a head and thus saves much pain and suffering.

F. Blue Flag and Hellebore roots, equal parts. Boil in milk and water, then soak the felon in it for twenty minutes, as hot as can be borne, and bind the roots on the parts for one hour. This has cured many felons when commenced in time.

G. Felon Ointment. — Take sweet Oil, ½ pint, and stew a small plug of tobacco in it until the tobacco is crisped; then squeeze it out and add Red Lead, 1 ounce, and boil until black; when a little cool, add pulverized Camphor Gum, 1 ounce.—(79).

H. Felon Salve.—A salve made by burning 1 tablespoonful of Copperas, then pulverizing it and mixing with the yolk of an egg, is said to relieve the pain and cure the felon in twenty-four hours; then heal with cream two parts and soft soap one part. Apply the healing salve daily after soaking the part in warm water.—(79).

FEVERS.

Fever is evidence of a disordered system—evidence of systemic disease. Its chief symptom is elevation of temperature. The cause may be local or general. The name corresponds to the location and conditions which cause it and to the characteristic symptoms, as *typhoid* where there is stupor, *scarlet* meaning a flush, *intermittent*, or fever and ague, etc.

Fever is divided into three stages: first, that of chills or chilliness; second, heat and elevation of temperature; third, the sweating stage. It is also divided into two groups, idiopathic and symptomatic. Where the fever is self-generating, as in small-pox or scarlet fever, it is termed idiopathic; but where it is dependent upon local conditions, as absorption from an infected wound, it is called symptomatic.

Cause. — The arteries are controlled by two sets of nerve fibers, one set tending to dilate and make them larger, and the other set tending to contract and make them smaller. This opposite effect during health keeps the arteries a natural size. Poisons paralyze more or less the nerve fibers which control the arteries and allow them to dilate. The large arteries are affected but little; the small ones may be greatly enlarged. Just beneath the skin is a vast network of vessels which are estimated to be capable of holding one-half the blood in the body. These vessels become dilated, and an unusual amount of blood is brought to the surface. This is why the face is red during a fever. Every chemical change produces a certain amount of heat; this is a universal law. The tissue change, repair and waste, which is constantly taking place in the body, is a chemical change, and the heat thus produced maintains bodily temperature. The change depends upon the circulation; the blood furnishes the repair in the form of nourishment, and carries away the waste. During health the two sets of nerve fibers control the circulation so nicely and the tissue change is so well governed that an even temperature is maintained. When poison is present from any cause, it first paralyzes the nerves which contract the arteries and allows them to dilate; this brings a large amount of blood to the surface and tissue change is increased, hence an increase in temperature, or fever. We can see the wisdom of this when we remember that it causes the patient to sweat, as elimination through the pores of the skin aids materially in giving relief.

This is Nature's plan. This is why the nerves that dilate are allowed to control, and this is why the blood is brought to the surface. Whether the poison is generated in the system, as in scarlet fever, or whether it is absorbed from a poisoned wound, makes no difference; the results are the same. The poison may also be absorbed from bad air, poisonous gases or bad water; or fever may result from nervous conditions, without poison.

Symptoms of General Fever.—After languor, weakness and restlessness for a day or two, or more, as the case may be, the first striking symptom of an approaching fever will be a *chill* of greater or less severity and continuance according to the greater or less disturbance of the system. The chill will to a certain extent indicate the severity of the oncoming disease. If nothing is done to relieve the attack and the chills continue, the skin becomes pale, the features shrunken and haggard, and the patient is led to think that streams of cold water are being poured down his back. As soon as this chilliness begins to subside, the circulation begins to increase; greater or less heat of the surface is produced, the strength is gradually diminished, and considerable thirst is manifested, the pulse also being increased in *frequency* and *hardness*. By a *frequent* pulse is meant one faster than in health, which is from *sixty-five* to *seventy-five;* and by a *hard* pulse, one that resists the examiner, as though it was bound to pass under the finger no matter how hard the pressure. There may be considerable distress about the stomach and other internal organs, also great aversion to making the least exertion of body or mind. The patient is willing to lie down, and seems to care but little whether anything is done for his relief or not; but it should be remembered that the greater his *indifference*, the greater the necessity for *immediate* attention to the case.

TREATMENTS.—

What to Do. — The treatment should be directed to the removal of the cause, if possible. If an infected wound, first cleanse thoroughly with soap and water, then use antiseptics—shut off the supply of poison from this source, and then the patient has only to get rid of the amount in the system. If from bad air or foul gases, secure a change of surroundings, and in all cases keep the eliminative organs active—a dose of Castor Oil or Salts taken internally, and frequent bathing to keep the skin active. If the surface is dry and hot, sweat the patient. Aconite and other fever remedies may be useful. If the patient is weak, give stimulants. For typhoid fever, give antiseptics internally. A light diet is usually of advantage for the first day or two, but give an abundance of pure water. A thorough action of the bowels will cure many cases of fever. If this does not succeed, and the patient grows worse, send for the doctor.

TYPHOID FEVER.—While this disease may occur at any season of the year, it is most common in the autumn, especially at the close of a hot, dry summer.

Cause.—Typhoid fever is the result of an unhealthy digestive tract which is brought about by a long train of conditions, hence the great number of symptoms. First there is indigestion and lack of elimination from some cause, and this is followed by degenerative changes and the production of many poisons. Some of these poisons are absorbed, and gradually the system is brought under their morbid influence, vitality is lowered and resistance lessened. This accounts for the languor, headache, fever, loss of appetite, etc., which precede the disease. The condition of the bowels causes congestion of the lining mucous membrane, and this congestion extends to all mucous surfaces, hence there may be nosebleed. At the lips the mucous membrane is continuous with the deeper layer of the skin, and there is congestion of this layer also, so that hemorrhage may, and in many cases does occur on the surface of the body. This hemorrhage is more apt to occur over the abdominal cavity, and those seeing it for the first time are, of course, frightened. The various glands situated in the mucous membrane of the bowel are abundantly supplied with blood vessels, hence the congestion, which gradually increases to inflammation, is greatest at these points. The swelling and pressure continue until nutrition is shut off or reduced to such a low ebb that ulceration takes place, the same as in dysentery. The changes in the mucous membrane are: first, congestion; second, inflammation; third, ulceration. If allowed to go on, ulceration will continue until all of the glands have been invaded. That is why the disease used to last from four to eight weeks. To-day there seems no excuse for such duration.

Symptoms.—The disease is developed insidiously. The patient does not feel well, but does not know to what to ascribe his bad feelings. He tires easily, is perhaps dizzy at times, may bleed at the nose, and suffers from headache, particularly pain in the back part of the head. His digestion is disordered, his sleep disturbed, his spirits depressed, his intellect dulled; and while he usually continues about his work, his weakness grows upon him until he is attacked with slight chills or shiverings. As the onset of this disease is so insidious in character, it is difficult to determine the time when fever develops.

During the first five days after the onset of the fever the temperature increases in a characteristic manner, being about two degrees higher in the evening than in the morning, and increasing one degree each day. During this time, in fact, during the whole of the first week, the patient complains of pain in the head and nausea, although the greater portion of the time he is listless and indifferent, lying with his eyes closed as if asleep. The tongue is heavily coated. Diarrhea is believed by some to be a characteristic symptom of this disease, but in many cases the bowels are constipated. The discharge is at first of a dark color, but during the second week becomes yellowish and more fluid and ill-smelling. The abdomen is somewhat distended, and upon pressure over the right groin gives a gurgling sound. In some cases between the seventh and ninth days an eruption of rose-colored spots occurs in clusters upon the abdomen, chest or back. They disappear on pressure (returning, of course, when the pressure is removed) and last for several days.

During the second week all the symptoms of the first week are exaggerated; the former listlessness of the patient gradually changes to stupor, interrupted by delirium; deafness is developed; also the teeth become coated with an unhealthy accumulation.

Towards the end of the second week, or some time during the third week, in the majority of cases the patient grows worse; his prostration is extreme, and his stupor so great that he is roused with difficulty; the tongue is covered with a dark-colored crust and is dry and cracked. Hemorrhage of the bowels may also occur at this time.

If the patient survives the period just mentioned, during the fourth week the symptoms remit and, greatly emaciated and debilitated, he passes into a slow convalescence.

Variations in Symptoms.—In the strong and robust, morbid conditions of the digestive tract which cause typhoid fever may be held in check until the system is so overwhelmed with poison that the disease breaks forth suddenly and with great force. These cases present none of the symptoms mentioned. We have seen a few cases of this kind.

The reader should remember that in typhoid fever, as in all other diseases, the symptoms vary greatly. Many of the symptoms may be absent, or so modified as to attract but little attention. It is seldom that the symptoms are all present or occur in regular order as usually given by medical writers. Those who care for the sick must exercise a reasonable amount of judgment independent of what are usually called symptoms. An unhealthy condition of the digestive tract may give all the symptoms of typhoid fever, yet the disease may not be present. Fever, headache, loss of appetite, nausea, coated tongue, pains in different parts of the body, dull feeling, loss of vigor extending all the way from slight indisposition to inability to perform manual labor, bloating and soreness along the digestive tract, and many other symptoms and conditions may be present, and yet there may be no typhoid fever. Thorough elimination and internal antiseptics for a day or two, with a restricted diet, will clear up the great majority of these cases, and the individual feel as well as ever.

An error that is constantly being made is that of confounding typhoid fever with other typhoid (depressing) symptoms. The word *typhoid* means *stupor*, therefore, strictly speaking, any condition of stupor where fever is present may be called *typhoid fever*, and some doctors do apply the term to many low conditions accompanied by fever.

The very nature of typhoid fever renders diagnosis extremely difficult. If a typhoid patient lives until the end of the second week, there will be ulcers along the digestive tract. The evidence of this condition may easily be detected by the stools, as they will contain both mucus and pus. Ulcers may occur without typhoid; in fact, any and all the symptoms of typhoid may and undoubtedly do occur many times when the disease is not present.

Scattered throughout the small bowel are numerous small glands. These are placed in the mucous membrane and have no excretory ducts. Their use is said to be unknown, yet they undoubtedly aid in digestion, as they are the largest, or most developed, during the digestive period. In places these glands are clustered together, forming little groups. These groups are called "Peyer's patches" because first described by Dr. Peyer. There are from twenty to thirty of these groups in the small bowel, varying from one-half an inch in width to three, four or more inches in length. The mucous membrane surrounding them is highly vascular, that is, abundantly supplied with blood vessels. The normal blood supply being greater than in the surrounding mucous membrane, inflammation is more intense, therefore they are a good field for degenerative changes, ulceration, etc., and that is the reason ulceration occurs at these particular points.

Typhoid Fever, To Prevent—Great Value of Lemon Juice.—Lemon juice will destroy typhoid fever germs in water. This important discovery is the result of recent experiments made in bacteriological bureaus in European capitals. One experimenter recently dropped a little lemon juice into a culture tube containing typhoid germs. To his amazement he found the acid shriveled up and killed the germs. This discovery is timely and valuable, especially for localities where typhoid fever is prevalent.

Dr. Asa Ferguson, a practitioner of London, has just published an article in which he gives the results of experiments made by European scientists. Commenting upon the lemon juice test, Dr. Ferguson says: "Typhoid germs must be taken into the stomach in order to cause typhoid fever. If, therefore, people will put a teaspoonful of lemon juice into the water they drink, they will avoid typhoid fever."

TREATMENTS. —

What To Do Till the Doctor Comes.—Give an active cathartic. Put the patient to bed, keep him warm and give him warm drinks. Get him to sweating, if possible. After thorough elimination give 10-grain doses either of Salol or the Sulphocarbolates, as directed nnder *Internal Antiseptics* following. If no improvement within a day or two, send for a doctor.

How to Help the Doctor.—An important part of the treatment of typhoid fever consists of nourishment and cleanliness, and especially should the latter be applied to the digestive tract. All eliminations, even the sputum, should be deposited in a solution of Carbolic Acid or a solution of lime in water of the consistency of whitewash, and allowed to stand for one or two hours. It should then be emptied at a good distance from the house and well and always in the same place, and occasionally a quantity of lime thrown over this.

The drinking water should be pure.

Good ventilation should be secured at all times; it is necessary to pay particular attention to this feature.

Daily baths should be given, even if the temperature is not high, as they will aid in elimination and give a sense of relief and general improvement.

Typhoid fever patients should be fed every one, two or three hours, depending upon the amount taken. Sleep should not interfere with feeding if the patient is low; this is important.

The food should consist of milk, soft cooked eggs, beef tea made at home, meat broths, rice boiled for three hours, vegetable soups strained and the liquid only given (nearly all patients like soups made in this way), etc. Boil two ounces of rice in one pint of water for three hours, adding water sufficient to maintain the original amount; mix two eggs with one-half pint of cream, add to the rice, and add this to one pint of hot beef tea. No patient should be compelled to take food that is not agreeable. Fruit juices are excellent in all stages of this disease.

If the food is not well digested, artificial digestants should be given, but the doctor will attend to this.

A. Initial dose of Calomel, followed by frequent small doses of same combined with intestinal antiseptics, will greatly modify and cut short the disease.—(31).

Internal Antiseptics for Typhoid Fever.—First, secure thorough elimination by means of Calomel, Castor Oil or Salts. Ten grains of Calomel, followed in six or eight hours by 2 tablespoonfuls of Epsom Salts or of Seidlitz Salts, is best. Enough of the Salts should be taken every morning to cause at least one movement during the day. The Calomel should not be continued for fear of salivation. Salol or the Sulphocarbolates of Zinc, Lime and Soda combined are the best antiseptics for the digestive tract, and should be given from the first, commencing as soon as the laxatives have operated. The dose of either is from 5 to 10 grains every two hours. When the eliminations improve, the amount should be lessened. Salol and the Sulphocarbolates possess marked advantages over other preparations of this kind because their antiseptic influence extends for a greater distance along the digestive tract.

In some cases diarrhea is troublesome. Where this condition is present, Sulphocarbolate of Zinc alone is the best remedy because of its astringent properties. Otherwise, it does not differ from the others. The Sulphocarbolates may be given in tablet or solution, as desired by the patient. The taste is not pleasant, hence tablets are often preferred. There is no taste to Salol, therefore it may be given in tablet or powder. It will not dissolve in water; the Sulphocarbolates will. If the Sulphocarbolates are dissolved, a little Glycerine may be added. This will help to cover the taste and the Glycerine itself is a good antiseptic. But its influence does not reach far beyond the stomach. If there is much pain with diarrhea, a pill containing one grain of Opium and one grain of Acetate of Lead may be given once or twice a day.

A weak heart, high temperature, stupor, delirium, foul odor, etc., are indications that the patient is being overcome by poisons generated in the digestive tract, and call for more intestinal antiseptics. Internal remedies for fever should be avoided as they weaken the patient. With plenty of pure water, fresh air, thorough elimination and a liberal use of antiseptics there will be little need for severe treatment, such as fever remedies or ice packs, and but little danger of hemorrhage. Atropine is one of the best remedies for dangerous hemorrhage if it does occur. In the event of hemorrhage, if the physician is not at hand and the case seems urgent, any of the following may be given:

Atropine .... 1-50 grain,
or,
Tincture of Iron, a small teaspoonful, well diluted,
or,
Fluid Extract of Ergot...... 1½ teaspoonfuls,
or,
Morphine .... ½ grain,
or,
Opium.............................. 2 grains.

The Morphine and Opium are valuable, but will not act so quickly, and are somewhat dangerous if the patient is very low. Artificial heat is also valuable as it aids in bringing the blood to the surface, and thus relieves the internal organs.

TYPHUS FEVER.—What is called *typhus fever* bears a close resemblance to *typhoid fever;* in fact the two were separated only a few years ago. Some claim that in typhus fever the Peyer's glands do not ulcerate; in typhoid fever they do. This effort at separation is unimportant. Typhus fever is clearly a filth disease, the result of bad surroundings. With our present knowledge of sanitation both typhus fever and typhoid fever are fast disappearing. Typhus used to be prevalent on shipboard, in jails and in army life, and for that reason was often called *Camp Fever* or *Jail Fever*.

TREATMENT.—

The treatment recommended under *Typhoid Fever* will apply with equal force to *Typhus Fever*.

YELLOW FEVER.—This is a disease of low districts, usually near the sea. It does not occur above an elevation of 2500 feet above the sea level, nor in a temperature below 70 degrees.

Cause.—The cause is bad hygiene. Yellow fever is clearly a filth disease. For one hundred and forty years there had been deaths in Havana from yellow fever during the months of June and July; but when the Americans went over and removed some of the heaps of ancient rubbish and emptied the overflowing cesspools, yellow fever vanished. There were no deaths from this disease during the months of June and July in the year of 1901, and there was comparatively little sickness during the months named, yet the country was filled with American soldiers, not yet acclimated, or accustomed, to the heat of the country.

Symptoms.—First there is sudden onset, with severe pains in the stomach or bowels, back and lower limbs, and severe headache. The vessels about the stomach are gorged with blood; there is a rapid rise in temperature, the face is flushed, the pulse is rapid, and there is loss of appetite, nausea and vomiting. If the patient lives, there is improvement within two or three days; he becomes more comfortable and may recover. If recovery does not follow, the relapse shows all the symptoms exaggerated. The ejections from the stomach become darker, and in some cases almost black, hence the name "black vomit." There is great prostration. The skin becomes yellow. This is said to be due to the destruction of the red blood corpuscles. There are degenerative changes in the liver and kidneys. The temperature is subnormal. These symptoms are followed by collapse and death. Deaths have occurred in 24 to 48 hours.

TREATMENT.—

In severe cases there is not much that can be done with drugs. 5 or 10 grain doses of Calomel may be given, and any of the usual means to prevent vomiting. If the patient is cold, apply artificial heat and give Tincture of Belladonna—20 to 30 drops to a dose. Repeat every hour or two until the surface is warm and the face is flushed. In cases that are less severe, treat as an ordinary case of biliousness. With the thorough sanitation that is now being instituted in yellow fever districts, the disease will soon become rare.

ERUPTIVE FEVERS.

The eruptive fevers, as measles, scarlet fever, etc., have many features in common. All have a period of incubation, that is, a time from exposure to the manifestation of the disease; all are accompanied with a fever of more or less intensity preceding the eruption; each fever has an eruption which is peculiar to itself; and each is contagious and occurs most commonly in childhood, rarely attacking the same person twice.

CHICKEN POX. — This is a mild, contagious, eruptive disease, confined almost exclusively to children, and to which the system is subject but once. It is neither distressing nor dangerous, but is not infrequently confounded with a light case of *small-pox* as the symptoms of the two diseases are similar in some particulars.

Cause. — A contagious poison to which children only are subject.

Symptoms.—Slight indisposition, impaired appetite, constipation and mild febrile symptoms, followed, probably within twenty-four hours, with an eruption on the *body* and *extremities* (rarely on the face) in the form of vesicles (little blisters or sacs). These vesicles are not preceded by pimples, as in *small-pox* (see small-pox symptoms), and are not hollow in the centre. They are transparent and vary from the size of a pin-head to a split pea. On the fifth or sixth day they begin to dry, a process which is rapidly accomplished. Scabs then form and fall off as in *small-pox*, but they rarely leave a permanent scar.

TREATMENTS.—

Treatment Without a Doctor.—For chicken-pox all that is necessary to do is to keep the child in the house. Give warm drinks to bring the rash out, and keep him from the air and out of draughts. In all eruptive diseases exclude fatty foods, that is, fat meats, etc. (Butter is not a fat.) Restrict to a diet of broths, beef tea and vegetables as much as possible.

No particular treatment is needed, but until the rash appears there may be quite a little fever, and for this Aconite may be given. Put 6 drops of Aconite into a glass of water and give a teaspoonful every three or four hours. After the rash appears, give three times a day.

A. Dust surface with flour or starch to stop itching, keep bowels open and avoid taking cold. Treat each sore as needed for any small sore. Avoid rubbing or picking about face.—(13).

SMALL-POX, or VARIOLA.—*Variola*, the technical name for this disease, is derived from the Greek word *varus*, meaning a pimple. The disease itself is an acute inflammation of the skin, characterized by febrile symptoms and an eruption in the form of pimples. These pimples first feel like shot under the skin, but later develop, become watery, change to pus, and finally scabs form which drop off, leaving pits in the flesh. The time of incubation is from ten to sixteen days. It is a highly contagious disease.

Small-pox is divided into four varieties: The modified or *varioloid*, a very mild form; the *discrete*, where the pocks remain separate; the *confluent*, where the pocks spread and join together; and the malignant. The last form seldom occurs. Such a case is evidence that the system was very unhealthy before the disease began.

Cause.—A specific ferment which sets up fermentation in the system. When digestion, oxidation or elimination are interfered with, there is more or less waste present; this is admitted by all. The specific ferment sets up fermentation in this waste just as the specific ferment, yeast, sets up fermentation in starch in bread making. The severity of the case is governed by the condition of the system. In a healthy man the specific ferment produces no result because there is no waste. That is why some escape the disease while others have it. Some of the products of fermentation are poisonous to the system; some of the products of yeast fermentation are poisonous. In bread making the yeast fermentation produces Carbonic Acid, which is a deadly poison to all animal life. It is the different poisons resulting from different ferments that produce contagious diseases. The various poisons resulting from these ferments produce different effects upon the system, as shown in small-pox, erysipelas, measles, etc., and this accounts for the different infectious diseases.

These principles were taught by the late Prof. W. B. Carpenter, recognized as the world's greatest physiologist.

The varieties of small-pox as here described represent the disease rather as it occurred years ago, when hygiene was neither known nor practiced. To-day small-pox is not considered so dangerous a disease. These forms are seldom met, and, if we are to judge the future by the past, then we must conclude that with clean and wholesome surroundings, while there may be variations in its severity, it will not again prove so destructive to human life as in those days when its path was marked by suffering, misery and death. The *Plague* once swept over and devastated whole countries; to-day the plague is but a relic of the past. *Leprosy*, once so dreaded, we have learned to look upon only as a filth disease, hence we do not fear it. *Malaria* is controlled by surroundings, and to-day we hear little of it. *Yellow Fever* had been prevalent in Havana for many years, but, as stated elsewhere, when the Americans went over and emptied the overflowing cess-pools and carried away the ancient rubbish, yellow fever vanished; and we think it but reasonable to believe that with attention to fresh air and cleanliness small-pox will go the way of leprosy, yellow fever and the plague. What applies to these diseases will apply with equal force to other diseases.

All understand that there are many cases of small-pox so mild that they are diagnosed with difficulty. This has always been true in this disease. The symptoms given below are intended to represent well-developed cases, *i. e.*, severe cases.

Discrete Form. — The patient is taken suddenly with a violent chill, followed by high fever, a rapid pulse and intense headache. As the fever comes on he is subject to nausea and vomiting. Vomiting at this time is characteristic of the disease, and another very characteristic symptom is a severe pain in the back, extending also into the lower limbs. Convulsions may occur, especially in children, or the patient may be delirious. About the third day the rash makes its appearance, first about the mouth and on the forehead, or about the roots of the hair, but soon noticeable on the wrists, neck, breast, etc., spreading over the entire body in the course of a few hours, and continuing to come out (the spots increasing in number) for two or three days. *With the appearance of the eruption the fever and all febrile symptoms abate*, and the patient is, for a season, comparatively comfortable, while in a case of the measles the fever *increases* when the eruption appears.

The rash has at first the appearance of coarse red spots, not unlike the eruption in measles, for which it is sometimes mistaken. Soon, however, the center of the spots harden and become slightly prominent, and are distinct to the touch, particularly at the wrists, where they "feel like shots under the skin." The prominence develops into papulæ (pimples), and about the sixth day of the disease these become filled with a clear, watery liquid; they are now termed vesicles. The vesicles attain to about the size of a small pea, but continue separate and distinct, and become slightly depressed in the center. This depression is an unmistakable sign of small-pox. Another symptom is the following: First let us remember that small-pox vesicles are divided into many chambers, giving them a honeycombed appearance. By taking a needle and carefully opening a vesicle upon one side, it will be found that only a small part of the secretions escape and that the elevation feels as firm and resistant as before. In other words, the vesicle is not emptied, but only the single chamber pierced by the needle. Gradually the liquid contained in the vesicles loses its clear appearance, and by the ninth day they have become pustules (the so-called "pocks"), filled with a yellowish matter from which a very offensive odor is emitted. The pustules, which are encircled by a band of red, become greatly inflamed and swollen, giving a distorted appearance, the features being almost unrecognizable if the eruption is thickly set. This is the most critical stage of the disease. The fever returns and is attended with prominent nervous phenomena, the patient becoming wildly delirious, or perhaps coma resulting. On the eleventh or twelfth day, in favorable cases, the pustules, which by this time are so filled with matter that the central depression is lost and they have become pointed instead, show signs of drying up, or many of them may burst. This stage of the disease is attended with great itching of the skin. Scabs now begin to form, the secondary fever declines and convalescence is established.

Not only is the external skin affected in small-pox, but certain portions of the mucous membrane also, particularly the lining of the mouth and throat. The swelling in the throat presses upon the glands and causes much discomfort. The inflammation extends also to the lining of the nasal passages, is not infrequently communicated to the eye, and may affect other of the mucous membranes.

Confluent Form.—The same general symptoms characterize this variety of small-pox that are exhibited in the discrete form, but all are much severer: The invasion is more violent, the fever runs higher, the patient is more prostrated, the eruption makes its appearance the *second* day instead of the *third*, and the pocks, instead of being single, run together and form great blisters. This is more particularly true on the face than of the eruption elsewhere, the disfigurement of the features thus caused being shocking to witness. The mucous membranes, too, are affected with proportionately greater severity, and dangerous complications are more liable to result. The death rate in the confluent variety is fifty per cent.

Malignant Form.—From this variety none recover. The course of the disease is short and violent; the patient is apparently overwhelmed from the start.   Hemorrhages are frequent and livid spots appear on the flesh; but death usually occurs, either by convulsions or coma, before the characteristic eruption appears.

Modified Form, or Varioloid.—In this form all the symptoms are modified.   It is a mild form.   Its course is shorter, it is not attended with a secondary fever, and it is rarely fatal.   In some cases it amounts to an indisposition only rather than an illness.

TREATMENT.—

What to Do.—If the disease is prevalent or a person knows he has been exposed, the usual course is to be vaccinated the first thing, even though he may have been vaccinated before.   In case of exposure the house should be quarantined and he should retire to a room by himself.   No other members of the family, nor any one else, should hold direct communication with him inside of nine days.   The first symptoms are pain in the back and head, and when these symptoms appear the doctor should be called and, if possible, some one who has had the disease engaged to act as nurse.

A. A mild case of small-pox may be treated the same as a case of scarlet fever, *i. e.*: Isolate the patient; secure an abundance of fresh air; if the patient feels hot, maintain a low even temperature and give cool sponge baths, as these produce a feeling of rest and quiet; give light, nourishing diet; for the fever, give Aconite—a 1-drop dose of the Tincture of Aconite every hour while the fever lasts; give an abundance of pure cold water; give some mild antiseptics to keep the bowels healthy, as, 5 grains of Salol every two or three hours, or, 5-grain doses of the Sulphocarbolates of Lime, Soda and Zinc combined; if the patient feels chilly and the surface is cold, increase the temperature of the room, apply artificial heat, and give hot drinks—stimulants.

Where the case is graver, where there is depression of the vital forces from the absorption of pus during the suppurative (pus forming) stage, the conditions will not admit of fever remedies without they are supported by stimulants, which may be given in the form of hot sling, Tincture of Capsicum in hot water, or red pepper tea well diluted with hot water and sweetened with sugar.   When there is great prostration, with low muttering delirium, increase the antiseptics, that is, the Salol or Sulphocarbolates; also give Tincture of Belladonna in 10-drop doses every hour until the circulation is improved and the surface is warm. The nasal cavities, mouth and throat should be sprayed two or three times a day with Marschand's Peroxide Hydrogen diluted with an equal amount of water, or, in very severe cases, used full strength.

It is to prevent conditions like the last named that we wish to speak particularly. We believe that primarily small-pox presents no serious morbid changes or difficulties; and that if it could be arrested before the watery fluid in the vesicles changes to pus, the disease would be comparatively mild and harmless and the name small-pox lose its terrors. *To prevent pus formation the following treatments are recommended:*

1. Make a saturated solution of Epsom Salts, for example, one pint, and add to this one-half ounce of Aromatic Sulphuric Acid. About the fifth or sixth day, or before evidence of pus makes its appearance, heat the mixture and sponge the patient thoroughly with it morning and evening. Repeat the bath, or sponging, the next day, or any time thereafter if there is evidence of suppuration.

2. Make a 10 per cent solution of Corrosive Sublimate, or add 6 drachms of the Corrosive Sublimate to one pint of water, heat quite hot, see that the Corrosive Sublimate is thoroughly dissolved, and sponge the patient as above directed. Use this solution only when there is danger of pus formation, and only on such part or parts of the body as the danger appears.

Important.—The Corrosive Sublimate solution is the stronger of the two, and while we recommend this treatment, its application should be under the direction of a physician. The bottle containing the Sublimate should be labeled "*poison.*"

In applying either wash be careful to protect the eyes, that is, not to let any of the fluid get into them.

These and other strong antiseptics will prevent the watery fluid in the vesicles from changing to pus, and render the discharge absolutely harmless. When we remember that it is the formation and absorption of pus that poisons the patient and produces the secondary fever, aggravates all the symptoms and renders the disease so dangerous and fatal, we can readily see that if this change can be intercepted, or prevented, the disease will be rendered mild and harmless.

VACCINATION AND ANTI-VACCINATION.

Vaccination has been established and practiced in many countries for many years—centuries in fact, and those who support this practice claim that those who have been successfully vaccinated need have absolutely no fear of small-pox. They claim that vaccination produces the disease in a mild form and after this the system is immune. The vaccine used to vaccinate people is obtained from cows suffering with a disease called cow-pox. The vaccine is taken from the sores which appear on the cow, and by scarifying the skin (usually of the arm) the vaccine is applied and enters the circulation. Those who support these principles claim that the cow-pox and small-pox are one and the same disease, and that is why the system is rendered immune after the light attack following vaccination.

Those who oppose vaccination claim that it does not protect from small-pox. They claim that cow-pox and small-pox are not the same; that the poison or vaccine does not produce the same disease and that is why vaccination does not protect. They claim that grease from the horse's hock will produce the same vesicles and the same disease as the vaccine from the cow, and at one time Jenner himself claimed this to be true and used grease from the horse on a large scale; it was in general use in many European hospitals. This part of their claim is a matter of history. Many medical men admit that " vaccination is by no means harmless, but that it is the lesser of two evils." The anti-vaccinationists claim that scrofula, chronic eczema and erysipelas follow vaccination more or less frequently. This is also admitted by many of the medical profession. Ulcers, abscesses, syphilis, loss of sight, and other diseases also follow some cases of vaccination. The many recent fatalities in New Jersey and other states following vaccination has given the practice a hard blow.

We do not wish to be understood as advising for or against vaccination; the reader must judge for himself. Since the practice has existed so long, and there is still so much dispute, we think it but simple justice to briefly mention the claims of both sides.

Note.—It is generally understood that Edward Jenner discovered vaccination, yet vaccination was practiced in very ancient times—2,000 years before our Christian era. The Sanskrit contains a clear description of vaccination, which has been translated by Dr. Michea.

MEASLES.—This disease, which is characterized by catarrhal symptoms and an eruption of the skin, is both contagious and epidemic. As an epidemic it makes its appearance usually in January and lasts until about May, but individual cases may occur at any time of year. As persons are subject to it but once one epidemic is not likely to be followed by another for a number of years, although there are generally a number of cases the next season after an epidemic among those who escaped the preceding year. The disease is, as a rule, contracted in youth, and the young are attacked with less severity than persons of more mature years.

Cause.—A contagion which is particularly communicable to children.

Symptoms.—From ten to fourteen days elapse from the time of contracting the disease before the patient begins to "come down" with it. During the last few days of this period he is likely to feel more or less indisposed. About the tenth to fourteenth day a feeling of chilliness comes on, and he has the appearance of having contracted a severe cold in the head. There is some fever; the catarrh, which extends to the eyes, continues. They become red and the lids swollen; also a hoarse cough is developed; there is muscular soreness all over the body, and may be headache, or the patient may exhibit drowsiness. On the fourth day the rash appears, first on the forehead and face, in the form of red dots. These dots generally run together and spread all over the body. They are very slightly elevated and rough to the touch, but the skin not covered with the rash is natural in appearance, whereas in scarlet fever it is uniformly red. In scarlet fever, too, the eruption comes on earlier and there is no catarrh. With the apbearance of the rash the fever, mild at first, increases, and the catarrh is aggravated. After the second day the eruption begins to grow dull—more brownish—and by the ninth day or earlier, has disappeared altogether, followed, if the attack has been severe, by a peeling off of the skin in minute flakes. The patient's eyes remain weak, and the cough is likely to continue for a time.

One of the most important considerations in a case of measles ls the care that should be taken, both during incubation (if the patient knows he has been exposed) and recovery, not to become exposed to draughts, cold, etc., as the catarrhal condition mentioned extends along the bronchial tubes, and the danger is the tendency towards lung diseases, especially in those of scrofulous constitution. Measles may also be followed with inflammation of the eyes, impaired hearing, or chronic catarrh.

TREATMENTS.—

What to Do.—The first symptom in measles is that of a common cold, accompanied with a dry, hacking cough. So if the disease is anywhere around, the parent should be on the lookout for this symptom, and when the child begins coughing, keep him in the house. With the appearance of the rash soak his feet in warm water, as warm as he can bear, put him to bed and give him warm herb drinks—Saffron tea is best. Let him drink of it freely. Get him to sweating and see that he does not cool off too soon. Keep him moist and do not allow cold air to strike him, though in all cases the room should be well ventilated. For the fever that precedes the rash, take Aconite (see *Chicken-Pox*). If the rash comes out nicely, it is not necessary to have a physician unless as a matter of satisfaction to the parent; but the greatest care must be taken to prevent chilling, in which case the rash will in all probability be driven back, and a doctor should then be immediately summoned. The cough is aggravating and will last for a week or two after the measles have disappeared and the child gets out. An excellent thing for this cough is Hoarhound. Steep it up, sweeten it, make a syrup and give freely. The throat may be quite sore, and, as in other fevers, the patient is very thirsty. Let him have all the cold water or lemonade he wants to drink. The room should be darkened as light is painful to the eyes.

A. Keep the patient well housed and warm in well-ventilated room, and give all the cold water he can drink. This treatment well attended to will be all most patients will need.—(30).

B. For racking cough and restlessness, put ¼ grain Morphine in ¼ glass of water. Give one teaspoonful after cough—perhaps each hour—to give rest. Don't give it except needed to quiet, and don't give to infants.—(43).

For the Itching That Sometimes Accompanies This Disease.—If the fever is high and there is much irritation and restlessness, give a bath once a day; twice if necessary. If this does not relieve the trouble, apply pure Sweet Oil, or Vaseline containing 5 drops of Carbolic Acid to the ounce.

A uniform temperature should be maintained, not only through the disease, but during convalescence, as this lessens the danger of taking cold, and in many cases the child is more easily managed as the skin is particularly sensitive at this time.

For Measles Cough.—If the cough is troublesome, or lingers after the disease disappears, give the following:

> Sulphate of Codeine.......................... 1 grain.
> Tincture of Nux Vomica.................. ¼ drachm.
> Syrup of Wild Cherry...................... 1 ounce.
> Water enough to make all............... 2 ounces.
> *Dose.*—Teaspoonful three or four times a day,

or,

> Put 1½ ounces of Fellows' Syrup of Hypophosphites into a 4-ounce bottle and fill the bottle with Maltine. Mix by shaking together, and give one teaspooful at meal time and one at bedtime. Give small doses oftener, if needed.

FALSE MEASLES.—Also called *German Measles, Rotheln, Roseola*, etc.—This is a trivial affection, resembling measles, but lacking the pronounced catarrhal and other severe symptoms. No complications arise and no ill effects follow it. The patient may feel mildly indisposed for a day or two before the rash appears— perhaps has a sore throat and a mild fever. The eruption appears first on the upper part of the body in red dots. By the time it reaches the limbs it is beginning to fade where it first made its appearance.

TREATMENT.—

Give first a cathartic, and follow with either the Sulpho-carbolates or Salol in the proper dose four times a day—after meals and at bedtime. A dose of either for a child five years old would be 2 grains. Restrict the diet, give an abundance of pure water, secure good ventilation and *prevent taking cold.*

Note.—There are those who believe *Measles* and *German Measles* are the same disease—that the so-called *German Measles* are but a mild form of *Measles* proper.

SCARLATINA, or, (as commonly called), **SCARLET FEVER.**—This is usually a disease of childhood, although grown people may have it, and even die of it. It is an acute inflammation of the skin and mucous membrane, characterized by a diffused scarlet flush and rash covering more or less of the whole body and extending along the mucous membrane of the mouth, throat, air tubes of the lungs, digestive tract, middle ear, the collecting tubes of the kidneys, etc.

Three varieties of scarlet fever are recognized, and it may be said in this connection that if the child's system is unhealthy before the attack, whether from bad surroundings, improper nourishment, constitutionally or otherwise, the disease is more likely to assume a malignant type.

Scarlatina Simple.—This is a light form with no complications.

Scarlatina Angina.—This name is given to a variety where the symptoms are all increased, especially those of the throat. In this variety the swelling and pressure of the throat structures cause great pain, the patient swallowing with the greatest difficulty. The swelling may be so great as to shut off the circulation and produce local death—gangrene. This is the condition present in the disease called *Black Diphtheria.* This, however, seldom occurs.

Scarlatina Malignant. This is a form in which the condition is still more grave. The eruption is delayed, nervous disturbances are marked, and the pulse is rapid and feeble due to weakness from the poison in the system.

The circulation being feeble, the surface of the body receives but little blood, the skin is pale, and there is little or no rash. The temperature may be below normal, and collapse and death may soon follow. If eruption occurs in this variety, it may be in patches and of a purplish hue, showing that the circulation is sluggish. There is no distinct dividing line between the three forms of scarlatina. They may merge one into another as day passes into night. The malignant form seldom occurs.

Symptoms.—Following are the symptoms of scarlet fever, yet it should be remembered that some of the symptoms may be absent, and some or all may be so modified as to render the case doubtful.

Scarlet fever begins suddenly, sometimes with a chill or chilliness. With children there may be convulsions; these are more liable to occur in weak children. There is frequently nausea and vomiting, though this is not severe. High fever is one of the early symptoms. The glands of the neck are swollen, the throat is red and inflamed and the tongue coated. There is frequently delirium, but this is usually mild and lasts but a short time.

The rash.—In twenty-four to thirty-six hours there is a bright rash, first appearing in the roof of the mouth, on the tongue, face, neck or breast, and spreading rapidly over the body. The rash first appears as a scarlet flush, with pin-point eruptions. These are not perceptibly raised, and the inflammation extends between them, so there is no healthy skin where the rash appears. The rash is intensified by heat. With its appearance the patient may suffer from a burning sensation over the whole or parts of the body. The throat is also more painful; the tongue is heavily coated, the papillæ of the tongue are elevated, and both the papillæ and border of the tongue are of a bright red.

On the fourth or fifth day the fever declines and the eruption fades. If there has been but little rash, the eruption may fade earlier. From the sixth to the eighth day scaling of the outer skin commences; this continues for one week or more. In mild cases scaling is not perceptible.

TREATMENTS.—

What to Do Till the Doctor Comes.—If the disease is prevalent, or the child has been exposed, when he commences to complain or the parent thinks he is coming down with it, begin giving warm drinks so as to bring out the rash as quickly as possible. Some herb tea is the best thing. If the rash is at all delayed, send immediately for the doctor; or if the child is taken violently ill, for instance, has convulsions, it is best to call the doctor at once.

The rash appears first in the roof of the mouth. As soon as it appears on the surface the best thing that can be done is to grease the child all over, from the hair to the soles of the feet and the inside of the hands, with the rind of bacon or other smoked meats. Do this about twice a day, night and morning, and be sure to exclude the air while doing it so that a chill will not result. If no smoked meat is at hand, the rind of salt pork may be used, but it is not so good on account of the creosote contained in the smoked article. The rind should be held by a stove or grate and warmed before applying. The fleshy or greasy side, of course, is the side to apply. This stops the intense itching and is one of the best remedies that can be used. Or Sweet Oil or Vaseline, which make a more agreeable application, may be used instead.

No other children should be allowed to communicate with the patient. The disease may also be carried in clothing, in the hair of adults or in the hair of a dog with which the child has played, especially when peeling.

How to Help the Doctor.—Frequent bathing with water slightly warm will aid largely in controlling fever and producing a feeling of quiet. Bathing also helps to control burning and itching. Cover lightly in bed, and give abundance of fresh air and pure cold water; or lemonade may be given, and is greatly desired by some children. For the digestive tract, attend to the eliminations and give some mild disinfectant, as Salol, from 1 to 3 grains every two or three hours; or, in mild cases three times a day would be enough. This dose is suitable up to five or six years of age, and may be increased for older children. See if the kidneys are active. If the fever is high, maintain a low, even temperature. If the surface is cold and the skin pale, apply external heat and give stimulants in the form of hot drinks to produce sweating. This will aid in bringing out the rash.

A. Tincture of Aconite, ½ drop. Repeat every half hour until skin becomes moist. Plenty of fresh air and pure water.—(29.)

B. Give child a hot bath and put it to bed, keep it quiet and call the doctor.—(38.)

If fever is high, give a cold sponge bath every one or two hours. Keep bowels open, and give patient all the water he can drink. If throat is sore, use gargle or spray of:

Boracic Acid.................................. 1½ drachms.
Peroxide of Hydrogen.................. 4 ounces.
Rub patient with Olive Oil twice daily.—(61).

What Scarlet Fever May Be Followed With.—The majority of those having scarlet fever make a rapid and complete recovery. Occasionally, however, the child is left with some chronic affection. Chronic inflammation of the middle ear may follow; or an abscess may form in the middle ear during the progress of the disease. This usually breaks through the outer membrane and discharges externally, though it may in rare instances penetrate to and cause abscess of the brain. Inflammation of the ear without abscess may result in more or less deafness. Chronic sore throat not infrequently follows the fever; or it may be followed with chronic inflammation of the eyelids, or inflammation of the eyeball, causing blindness, or chronic diarrhea, rheumatism, Bright's disease, heart disease and dropsy.

After-Effects, to Guard Against.—Intelligence should be exercised along these lines, even without instructions from the doctor. The mother's care and judgment should be sufficient to meet indications of difficulty as they arise, and relieve all possibility of chronic ailments following upon this disease.

Itching of the Skin in Scarlet Fever.—Under the treatments for measles it is stated that the skin is sensitive for a time. This condition applies more particularly to scarlet fever. The scaling or peeling of the outer skin leaves the deeper layer (true skin) more or less unprotected, and for this reason, as well as to prevent taking cold, the child should be kept in a uniform temperature. If there remains a sense of heat or itching, apply pure Sweet Oil, or Vaseline containing five drops of Carbolic Acid to the ounce. Either is harmless, and will usually overcome the difficulty and render the condition one of quiet and satisfaction.

Chronic Inflammation of the Kidneys.—Care should be exercised for some time in feeding. Any evidence of indigestion should be met with a more careful diet. The bowels should be kept regular. Small doses of antiseptics should be given for ten days or two weeks. For this purpose give 2 or 3 grains of Salol three times a day. This may be given in pill or powder. It is tasteless and a child will take it without difficulty. Give plenty of pure water for some time after the disease, as this aids in flushing the small blood vessels, and is really one of the best means of preventing congestion or inflammation of the kidneys. Evidence of indigestion may often be found in the urine. If it is scanty or high-colored, or if there is "brick dust" sediment, it is evidence that the digestion is interfered with and that the kidneys are called upon to do extra work in eliminating waste material. This excess would have a tendency to precipitate Bright's disease, hence the need of attention at this particular time.

Chronic Inflammation of the Throat.—The throat should be sprayed or gargled with Peroxide of Hydrogen diluted with an equal amount of water.

Indication of Weak Heart.—If the child tires easily and there is shortness of breath, it is an indication that the heart needs strengthening. For this trouble give 2-drop or 3-drop doses of Tincture of Digitalis three times a day.

If the child continues pale, it is evidence that too much blood remains in the internal organs, and this increases the danger of throat and kidney troubles. For this give from 3-drop to 5-drop doses of the Tincture of Belladonna every three hours until the skin is flushed and the color healthy. Repeat this treatment whenever needed. If there is no change after a few doses, increase the amount or give the same dose oftener. Remember that as long as the circulation is uniform there is no danger of inflammation or chronic after-effects, and there is no remedy better suited to control the circulation than Belladonna. Also remember that the pale face may be due, not so much to a lack of circulation as to a lack of blood to circulate. Especial attention should always be given to nourishment in these cases.

MALARIAL FEVERS.

Malarial Fevers are supposed to be caused by an animal parasite which enters the system and passes its cycle of development, or period of life, in the blood cells. The cycle of development varies from twenty-four to seventy-two hours. The parasites pass through the whole period of their existence in this time, at the end of which the parent, or mature parasite, subdivides into ten to twenty parasites, each one of which attacks a new blood corpuscle to repeat the story of its parent's existence. The period between the paroxysms of chills and fever corresponds to the life period of the parasite in the blood.

The malarial parasite is hidden in countless millions in marshy districts and decaying vegetable matter ready for entrance into the human system. It is believed to be carried into the system by water or by the air we breathe. Of late it has been proven that mosquitoes, etc., frequently carry the parasite. Hot weather, hot climate and low elevation aid the spread of the disease, while cold weather, cold climate and high elevation check it almost entirely.

Under the head of malarial fevers may be classed *Intermittent* (fever and ague), *Remittent*, *Relapsing*, *Typho-Malarial* and *Pernicious*. All of these fevers excepting intermittent fever, however, may be due to bilious conditions as well as to malaria. The evidence of malaria is the regular recurrence of the paroxysms of chills and fever. With this exception there is no distinct dividing line between the fevers mentioned. Fever means poison in the system, and, while primarily poison may be the effect or result of bad air (malaria), it is also the effect and result of retained waste. Unhealthy surroundings may institute the first effect by producing a general morbid condition, thus rendering all the organs sluggish. Tissue change—repair and waste—is interfered with. There is indigestion, thus increasing the amount of eliminative work, but elimination is checked and gradually the system is overcome.

The evidence of this condition manifests itself differently in different individuals. With some the symptoms may appear early, while with others they may be held in abeyance until the system is so overpowered that they break forth with sudden and overwhelming effect. This is more likely to be the result in the strong and robust because their vitality is stronger.

TREATMENT.—

The treatment is the same: elimination and tonics. Secure thorough elimination by the bowels; keep the kidneys active, or, if there is danger of congestion of these organs, apply hot poultices across the back, changing them often; give plenty of pure water; give frequent baths to insure free elimination by the skin; rub the surface until it is in a bright glow, which will aid in relieving congestion by equalizing the circulation; give nourishing food; give intestinal antiseptics—from 2 to 10 grains of Salol every two to four hours, according to age and condition of the bowels. Offensive odor calls for more antiseptics; if odor is absent, give less.

For internal treatment nothing is better than Quinine and Fowler's Solution—2 grains Quinine and 5 drops of Fowler's Solution before meals and at bedtime. In severe cases this dose may be increased. Fowler's Solution is only a means of giving Arsenic. The solution contains one per cent of that drug. Arsenic is eliminated by the skin, hence in the process of elimination it is brought intimately in contact with all the tissues. Again, Arsenic has the power of protecting seven thousand times its own weight of tissue from degenerative changes; in other words, rendering the tissues healthy. Arsenic is also believed to possess a special nutritive action on the heart. If digestion is interfered with, be more careful about the diet, and, if needed, give artificial digestants.

INTERMITTENT FEVER.—Consists of febrile attacks at regular intervals, between which attacks the patient is free from fever. It is commonly spoken of as "*fever and ague,*" or "*chills and fever.*"

Cause.—Intermittent fever is supposed to be due to the parasite of malaria, as mentioned in the preceding description of *Malarial Fevers.*

Symptoms.—There is a succession of symptoms, which may be divided into three stages, as follows:

The Cold Stage.—The attack usually comes on with a pain in the head and loins, a desire to yawn and stretch, and a coldness of the extremities. These symptoms are followed by shivering, which generally develops into violent shaking accompanied with a chattering of the teeth.

The Hot Stage.—This stage follows the cold stage, and is characterized by high fever. The change from the one to the other is usually gradual, the chilly sensations being alternated with flashes of heat until a fever is developed. The change, however, may be quite sudden. The skin, which before was pale, now becomes flushed and extremely hot and sensitive. A severe pain in the head and intense thirst are marked symptoms of this stage.

The Sweating Stage.—As the fever passes off the skin becomes moist, and this moisture increases, frequently, to a profuse sweat; the body returns to its normal temperature, the pains and aches disappear, and the patient falls into a refreshing slumber. He awakens free from any symptoms of the disease, but, of course, more or less exhausted from the effects of the paroxysm.

There are variations from these symptoms. In the so-called *"dumb ague"* the chill is slight or unnoticeable, but the other symptoms are apparent. The attack may consist of any one of the three stages—the chill, the fever or the profuse perspiration —or there may be a regular recurrence of pain in some part of the body, one side of the head or some feature of the face. The regular return of such symptoms indicates malarial origin.

Ague Cake.—During the cold stage the blood is driven inward from the surface and particularly oppresses the spleen, which, in cases of long standing, becomes swollen and permanently enlarged. This swelling may be distinctly felt, and is often quite perceptible to the eye.

TREATMENTS.—

A. A person need not be troubled with the ague very long who will take the following remedy:

> Quinine.................................... 1 drachm.
> Capsicum.................................... 15 grains.
> Iron (ferri sub carbonus)............. ½ drachm.

> Have this mixed and put up in doses of 10 grains each, taking every four hours. Or, if it is not put up in regular doses, take of the mixture what you can hold on the point of a case-knife every four hours.

B. Give 15 grains of Quinine five hours before the expected attack. Give Fowler's Solution of Arsenic in 10-drop doses after meals, also give 3 grains of Quinine at the same time.

C. Give 16 to 20 grains of Quinine at one dose five hours before the expected chill, followed by smaller doses, say 3 grains four times a day.—(51).

D. Quinine, three 5-grain doses taken every day till cured. Also put a handful of rusty nails into a gallon jug of hard cider and take a wineglassful after meals till all is taken.—(14).

E. Boneset tea; then Quinine to full effect—buzzing in the head.—(6).

F. Open bowels freely with Compound Cathartic pills. Give 3-grain Quinine capsules every three hours till chills are broken, then give 3 grains two or three times a day for a week. Keep bowels open freely every day.—(13).

G. Quinine Sulphate in 2-grain doses every three hours.

In malaria the next best thing to Quinine is a thorough elimination bath every other day.—(42).

H. Adults should be treated with Quinine Sulphate at the rate of one grain for every hour in the 24 for about two days. Best administered by the mouth in 4 to 6 grain doses. After the paroxysms are broken, preventive doses of 1 or 2 grains three times daily should be administered along with Iron tonics to restore the blood.—(31).

I. Take Quinine, 5 grains every four hours, commencing as soon as the sweating stage comes on. Open bowels freely with cathartic—best Compound Cathartic pills, three at a dose. After chills are broken the following pills:

Strychnine Sulphate........................ 1 grain.
Arsenous Acid................................. 1 "
Quinine Sulphate............................ 1 drachm.
Extract of Gentian enough to make pill mass.
Divide into 30 pills.

A pill after each meal. Quinine should be stopped after chills are broken, but taken again as above on the 6th, 7th, 13th, 14th, 20th and 21st days.—(35).

REMITTENT or Bilious FEVER.—*Remittent Fever* and *Intermittent Fever* have a succession of paroxysms that are nearly identical, the differentiation being in the third stage of the paroxysm, which in the one is *remittent* and in the other *intermittent*. Remittent fever is the more severe. The bilious fever mentioned here is not to be confounded with the condition known as biliousness.

Cause.—The malarial parasite; or changes from heat to cold, by which the secretions are lessened, or checked; are supposed to be the causes of derangement in the liver and other organs by which a large amount of bile is retained in the system, causing this variety of fever. It is generally quite mild in the North, especially where the general surface of the land is dry and rolling; but in the South, and where the general surface of the land is low and flat, it is severe, and often of a congestive or pernicious character.

Symptoms.—Remittent fever begins with a *chill* and pain or uneasiness in the upper part of the abdomen. The chill is followed by a *hot stage* during which there is persistent vomiting, also pain in the head and limbs. The temperature rises, sometimes to such a degree as to be attended with delirium. The bowels are costive, the evacuations being dark-colored and ill-smelling, and the urine is high-colored and scanty. The skin has a *jaundiced* appearance. The hot stage in the remittent form lasts considerably longer than in the intermittent form, sometimes continuing for twenty-four hours. As in intermittent fever, the hot stage is succeeded by a *sweating stage*, but in the remittent form, as indicated by the name, there is a *remission* of the febrile symptoms only; the fever does not entirely abate and the sweating is very slight. A second chill does not usually occur, but after two to eight or ten hours the hot stage again returns, and is succeeded, as at first, by a remission. The disease usually runs from seven to fourteen days.

TREATMENTS.

What to Do Before Calling a Doctor.—First give an active cathartic, and if there is evidence of undigested food in the stomach, give an emetic to vomit the patient. An excellent remedy to follow with is a tea made of Pleurisy root (see chapter on herbs). Take the roots of this herb and crush them if dry, or break them if green, put them into a dish, pour boiling water on them and let them simmer, and have the patient drink freely of this tea until he is sweating well. Continue to keep the bowels open, and give 10 grains of Salol four times a day; also give 5 drops of Fowler's Solution together with 3 grains of Quinine three times a day. After 24 to 48 hours give plain, nourishing and easily digested food in rather limited amounts for a few days.

If there is no improvement under this treatment, a doctor should be called.

A. Antikamnia and Quinine Tablets, 10 of them.
Give one every three hours.—(20).

TYPHO-MALARIAL FEVER.—It not infrequently happens in a case of remittent fever that the remissions cease and the fever becomes continuous. When this occurs the patient becomes greatly prostrated, either lying in a stupor or being delirious. His condition resembles that of a typhoid patient, hence the name, *typho-malarial.*

TREATMENT.—

We think that no case of remittent fever would, under the treatment recommended under that head, run into a typhoid form. If it did, other treatment than that recommended by a physician who was in personal attendance would hardly be of avail.

RELAPSING FEVER.—This fever, as its name indicates, is characterized by *relapses.* It is also known as *Bilious Typhoid Fever;* also as *Famine Fever*, from the fact that the conditions of poverty, filth and overcrowding are favorable to it, and that it is frequently the accompaniment of famine. During the course of the fever the blood contains organisms of spiral form that keep constantly twisting, a sort of cork-screw movement, from which the disease is also known as *Spirillum Fever.*

Symptoms.—The onset may be abrupt or gradual. There is high fever, the temperature rising progressively until about the sixth day. During this time there is nausea and vomiting, also pain in the head and limbs, particularly in the calf of the leg. The liver and spleen become swollen, giving rise to a feeling of fullness, and jaundice is usually present. On the seventh day, or from the fifth to the seventh day, the fever ends about as abruptly as it began, but *returns again* about the fourteenth day. There may be several such relapses. The patient becomes greatly emaciated and recovery is tedious.

TREATMENTS.—

What to Do Till the Doctor Comes.—Send for a doctor. In the meantime move the bowels with injections, soak the feet in warm water, put to bed and, if possible, get to sweating. If there is any delay in getting the doctor, the following treatment may be resorted to: Count out 10 teaspoonfuls of water, put into a glass, add 30 drops of Tincture of Aconite, and take of the solution a teaspoonful every four hours. Alternate this with Quinine in 3 grain doses, giving the Aconite and Quinine two hours apart.

General Treatment.—Like other lingering fevers, *Relapsing Fever* is largely influenced by surroundings. All fevers of this kind must be treated on general principles. Drug medication is subordinate. First, attend to the surroundings. Remember the cellar, well, drains, offensive cess-pools, dark and illy ventilated sleeping rooms, quality of food, etc. Give all of these proper attention. Put the patient into a large, well-ventilated room; secure thorough action of the bowels; give a bath every day; give properly cooked, easily digested and nourishing food every two to four hours, according to the strength of the patient; give 10 grains of Salol, or of the Sulphocarbolates, three times a day, or, if odor of eliminations is bad, give every two hours until natural, then three times a day; and give of the following one tablespoonful four times a day:

> Fowler's Solution........................ 1½ drachms.
> Fellows' Syrup of Hypophosphites 4 ounces.
> Maltine. or a good extract of milk. 8 "
> *Mix*, by shaking the bottle.

We read and hear much about prophylactic remedies or medicines (meaning medicines to preserve against disease), but as preventive measures there is absolutely no treatment and no remedies equal to the foregoing. Every one can institute preventive measures of this kind, and prevention will relieve the necessity of treatment.

It is stated elsewhere in this work that, lying just beneath the skin and covering the whole outer surface of the body is a dense network of vessels capable of holding one-half the blood in the system; and that the lungs contain six hundred million air cells whose combined surface is more than seven times greater than the whole outer surface of the body. This is indisputable evidence that the Divine Architect designed an abundance of fresh air and free surface circulation. Again, the tissues of the body contain phosphorous. If exposed to the air, phosphorous immediately unites and spontaneous combustion is the result, producing great heat. The brain is estimated to contain one ounce of this element. One-fifth of all the blood goes to nourish the brain, hence one-fifth of all the oxygen absorbed from the air we breathe is carried direct to the brain and unites with the phosphorous contained there in order that our thoughts may breathe and our words may burn. The presence of so large an amount of phosphorous in the brain and the readiness with which it unites with oxygen, is another evidence that Nature has designed that we should exercise freely in the open air, and that our lungs should be capable of full expansion in order that we may inhale an abundance of oxygen. This keeps the fire burning, sends a glow to the cheek, a fire to the eye, and lights up the whole countenance with an expression that medicine does not, cannot give.

A former health officer of Philadelphia stated publicly that *he never met a case of malignant disease where the conditions could not be traced to bad hygienic surroundings.* We do not wish to dwell too long upon this subject, but if we can impress our readers with the fact that the foregoing is a safeguard against disease, especially *malignant* disease, we shall feel that our effort has not been in vain. *With proper hygiene and physical training, the word "malignant" would soon disappear from our text books.*

PERNICIOUS FEVER—CONGESTIVE FEVER.—

This fever, as its name indicates, is of a malignant character. It is an intense variety of malarial fever, and may be either *remittent* or *intermittent.* A case of either may suddenly develop the malignant form. Pernicious fever is also known as *Congestive Fever,* the chill with which it is ushered in being spoken of as a *congestive chill.* It is due to a high degree of malarial poison.

Symptoms.—As stated in the foregoing, simple remittent or intermittent fever may develop into the malignant, or pernicious, form; and, in the majority of cases, the *first* succession of cold, hot and sweating stages is of the ordinary type.

Pernicious fever is characterized by severe congestion of some internal part, and the symptoms vary according to the location of the congestion. Not infrequently the congestion affects two sets of organs, the symptoms characteristic of each being combined. There are, however, general symptoms characteristic of most cases. For instance, there is great restlessness, a cold, clammy surface with raging internal fever and intense thirst, features shrunken and countenance anxious; pulse weak except in *cerebral* variety (where brain is congested).

If the stomach and bowels are the seat of the congestion, there is nausea, vomiting, straining and purging, the evacuations being thin and mixed with blood.

In the *thoracic* variety (the congestion affecting the organs of the chest) there is difficulty in breathing, the patient gasping for air and troubled with an annoying cough.

If the brain is congested, the patient is wildly delirious, the delirium being succeeded with convulsions and a state of stupor not unlike that of apoplexy, the breathing being slow and stertorous (snoring), the pulse full and the countenance flushed or livid.

There is another variety, beginning with either of the simple forms, in which internal congestion is developed affecting both the organs of the chest and the abdomen. There is nausea, vomiting, quick, short breathing, and pain over the liver and kidneys. These symptoms continue for a few hours, when the skin suddenly turns yellow, followed by the passing of bloody urine. After this there is the abatement of symptoms characteristic of all malarial fevers. This may be a remission or an intermission according to the nature of the simple form from which it was developed.

In still another variety the surface is intensely cold and covered with a cold sweat, while at the same time the patient, as he expresses it, is "burning up inside" and suffers from intense thirst. The voice is feeble and indistinct and the countenance pinched and deathlike, but the mind remains clear.

It must not be supposed that in the malignant malarial form there is a succession of paroxysms such as characterize the simple form. It is the effort of the physician to prevent a second malignant paroxysm, as the patient, with his reduced vitality, is very likely to succumb to it; and a third malignant paroxysm is almost invariably fatal. Indeed, it is not of infrequent occurrence that death occurs during the *first congestive chill* before febrile reaction has developed. After one malignant paroxysm, however, the disease may be partially controlled so that succeeding paroxysms which occur will be of the simple form.

It will be readily apparent after a study of the causes of malignant malarial, or pernicious, fever, and the gravity of the disease, that even a simple case of *fever and ague*, or *chills and fever*, should not be permitted to go without treatment, as the malignant form may be lurking in the virus of the simplest case if no counteracting agent is employed.

Pernicious, or *Malignant*, *Fever*, does not often occur, and when it does it is evidence that bad hygiene has existed for some time. It is also evidence that there has been a lack of intestinal sanitation. It means, in a word, that the individual was loaded with poison before the disease came on. Perfect digestion and elimination will relieve the danger of *Pernicious Fever*.

TREATMENTS.—

What to Do Till the Doctor Comes.—Send for the doctor immediately, and in the meantime do everything possible to get the patient out of the chill. Soak the feet in hot water, into which may be thrown a tablespoonful of soda and a little handful of salt. Bathe to the knees, rub thoroughly, and put to bed. Give warm drinks, and put around the patient bottles of hot water, hot bricks, or stones heated hot; or take ears of corn, boil them up, take them out of the water, roll them up and put around the patient. In a congestive chill the surface is dark colored or purple, and unless the chill can be broken up, death results.

If the Doctor is Delayed.—If for any reason the doctor cannot or does not come, the treatment should be continued after the chill is broken. Elimination, fresh air, and a nourishing diet are the keynotes in conditions of this kind. Keep the bowels active.

Give no article of food that disagrees with the digestion. Rice boiled for three hours, soft cooked eggs, beaten raw eggs in milk, dry toast, oatmeal boiled for three hours and strained, using only the liquid part, meat broths, vegetables boiled and strained, using only the liquid part—any of these are valuable. Give 10 grains of Salol three times a day. If the eliminations give offensive odor, give the Salol every two hours for one day, and at frequent intervals for a longer time if necessary. Give a hot bath every day, and each time sweat the patient profusely. Give a $\frac{1}{100}$-grain of Sulphate of Atropine one hour before taking the daily bath. Provide good ventilation. An abundance of fresh air is of the utmost importance. Give 3-grain doses of Quinine four times a day. The following mixture should also be given:

> Fowler's Solution........................ 2 drachms.
> Nitro-Muriatic Acid..................... 4   "
> Glycerine................................. ... 2 ounces.
> Water enough to make................. 4   "
>
> Take one teaspoonful after meals.

A. The object is to get up a *reaction*, and all efforts must be directed to this end, and that too with all possible speed.

First.—It is not amiss in any chill to put the patient's feet into *hot* water, as hot as it can be borne; but in a congestive chill it is almost absolutely necessary to place the whole body into *hot water*, keeping it as hot as it can be endured without scalding, for 20 to 30 minutes; but if there is no bathing convenience in the house, have sheets wrung out of hot water and wrapped around the whole body, then hot irons, bricks, or stones, or boiled ears of corn, or small bags of corn, or oats, placed all around the patient, to get up and keep up as much heat as possible until the chill is overcome and reaction established; at the same time give strong tea of Cayenne, Ginger, or even Black Pepper as freely as can be and if there is Quinine in the house, or near, give three or four doses of 4 to 6 grains every half hour. Rubbing one hand and arm, and one foot and leg at a time with Cayenne, or Mustard, if help is at hand, would be of great assistance also in *re-establishing* the circulation.

Second.—After the patient has revived and the difficulty passes off, give at least 3-grain doses of Quinine every three or four hours, to prevent the return of the chill, which is fully as likely to return as in common ague; and also continue a *tonic* and cleansing course of treatment for several days to aid in re-establishing general health, and thereby keep off the disease; but, in case of the continuation, or return of the chill, the treatment will be the same, following closely with mild cathartics, tonics, etc.— (75).

Fever Summary.—Fevers given under so many different names or headings are confusing, therefore we wish to remind the reader that, with the exception of malaria, all fevers, regardless of their name or nature, are the result of the same cause—an unhealthy system. They are but different stages or different manifestations of the same diseased condition, and the treatment is the same, with the exception that some require less and others more. As the diseased condition continues, some organ, tissue or part less able to withstand the morbid effects, becomes debilitated and weakened until it presents evidence of a special or separate disease, after which it is given some particular name. It may be typhoid fever or abscess of the liver, enlarged spleen or consumption of the lungs. Fever is present in these and many other diseases, yet all might have been prevented if the directions for *General Treatment* under RELAPSING FEVER had been thoroughly applied. Such treatment does not belong especially to relapsing fever, but belongs to any and all conditions where the general health is interfered with.

FEVER SORE.—A fever sore is an ulceration of bone. For description and treatment see under BONE DISEASES. The following treatment has also been recommended.

Such a sore often breaks out on the shin of children after a fever.

TREATMENT.—

Fresh Butter .... 1 pound.
Oxide of Zinc .... 1 ounce.
Iodoform.................................... 1 scruple.

Work the mixture with a knife, or something of the kind, to get, the Zinc and Iodoform mixed thoroughly through the butter. Spread a little on linen and cover the sore.

Compound Stillingia Syrup............ 4 ounces.
Iodide of Potassium...................... 1 drachm.

Take from ½ to 1 teaspoonful three times a day, depending upon the age. This will act as an antiseptic to the blood and aid in healing the sore. Unless something is taken for the blood, the sore will not heal.

The treatments recommended under *Fungus Disease* would also be applicable here. See FUNGUS DISEASE.

FISH SKIN DISEASE.—(See under SKIN DISEASES).

FISSURE.—(See under ANUS, DISEASES OF).

FISTULA.—(See under ANUS, DISEASES OF).

FITS.—(See Convulsions).

FLOODING.—(See under Women's Diseases).

FRECKLES.—(See under Skin Diseases).

FUNGUS DISEASE. — *Fungus* is a spongy, morbid growth or granulation in animal bodies, as the proud flesh of wounds or some forms of cancer growth that break out.

Treatment.—

The treatment of fungus growths consists of the local applications of caustics. Under the head of *Caustics* in the Miscellaneous Department will be found a number of such remedies.

The following is also recommended:

> **A.** Sulphuric Acid.............................. 1 ounce.
> Nitric Acid .... ½ "
> Corrosive Sublimate...................... ¼ "
>
> *Mix*, by first putting the Sulphuric Acid into a porcelain dish and then carefully adding the Nitric Acid. When the effervescence ceases and it becomes cold, put into a strong bottle and add the Corrosive Sublimate.

This is a fine thing for destroying proud flesh and for dressing all lacerated or bruised wounds. Cuts and penetrating wounds may be treated by dipping a feather into this solution and drawing into the wound. Of course this treatment would not be needed in the case of a healthy wound, but will be found most excellent for indolent and sloughing wounds or sores that show no tendency to heal.

After a thorough application of the foregoing, the wound should be washed out with pure water. Where sores of this kind exist, it is evidence that constitutional treatment is also needed.

B. Carbolic Acid, full strength, applied daily.—(7).

GALL-STONES.—This is a disease of middle life, and more common in those of corpulent figure.

Cause.—Crystallization of certain properties of the bile, which form the nucleus (beginning) of a gall-stone. Other particles from time to time adhere to this nucleus until finally a stone is formed which sometimes reaches the size of a hickory nut. So long as gall-stones remain in the gall bladder they occasion no inconvenience and their presence remains unsuspected, unless they become so large as to produce ulceration, in which case local peritonitis is likely to occur. Usually, however, they are discharged through the duct which leads from the gall bladder to the intestine.

Symptoms.—The instant a gall-stone passes into the biliary duct, which is small and consequently stretched and drawn by the passage of the stone, the patient is seized with a piercing pain in the region of the gall bladder. The pain spreads over the abdomen, the muscles of which cramp and become sensitive to the touch, and extends to the right side and shoulder. Nausea and vomiting usually occur, and the agony may be so great that the patient faints or is thrown into convulsions. Remissions from the violence of the pain may take place, but the patient does not experience entire relief until the passage of the stone into the intestine is effected; this may be accomplished in from one to several hours, or may take several days. When the stone is discharged into the intestine, which is larger than the biliary duct, the pain ceases and only a soreness and exhaustion remain. Remission of pain may also be experienced by the stone falling back into the gall bladder.

On account of the stoppage of the flow of bile during the passage of a stone, jaundice is caused. Even after the passage of a small stone, which has been effected in an hour or two, the skin will have a slightly yellow appearance, which, however, soon disappears.

In our experience we met one case of gall-stones which had evidently formed in the gall duct, not in the gall bladder. There were five of these stones, and the duct had gradually distended until it had reached enormous proportions and presented itself against the abdominal wall in the form of a large tumor. An operation revealed a duct 1¼ inches in diameter and about 6 inches long. Adhesions had drawn the duct forward, tense and firm, hence the appearance of the tumor. The greater part of the duct was removed, the wound closed and the patient recovered. If a stone forms in the gall bladder and is too large for passage through the duct, inflammation may follow and the gall bladder become adherent to the digestive tract, that is, the gall bladder and the bowel grow together. Ulceration may follow, and the stone be discharged into the bowel through the track of the ulcer. This seldom occurs.

TREATMENTS.—

What to Do.—In cases of gall-stones, for immediate relief give Olive Oil—the pure, genuine oil. If one is subject to this distressing complaint, Olive Oil should be kept on hand, and when the trouble comes on, take tablespoonful doses of it every two or three hours until relieved. Consult a doctor for the treatment applicable to the case.

A. Drink a gill of Olive Oil a day for a month.—(14).

B. To relieve pain:

Chloroform	2 drachms.
Tincture of Capsicum	½ "
Laudanum	1 "
Spirits Camphor	1 "
Good Wine	3 "

Mix, and take 10 drops every hour or two in water.—(53).

C. Take one teaspoonful of Sodium Phosphate in glass of warm water an hour before each meal and at bedtime.—(46).

D. Phosphate of Soda, teaspoonful in glass of hot water two or three times daily, long continued, has been more satisfactory than anything else.—(45).

E. A teaspoonful of Epsom Salts every two hours until the bowel is emptied. Paregoric in teaspoonful doses every half hour until pain is relieved. Operation is indicated when the surroundings are favorable.—(9).

F. Five drops of Chloroform three or four times a day for months; also, best Sweet Oil two teaspoonfuls three times a day. The above to prevent the formation of biliary stones.—(8).

G. This disease, when it occurs, produces such intense pain and suffering that, aside from our own experience, we have consulted those high in authority, and in offering the following remedy we will say that we believe it to be the best treatment that can be administered in these cases:

Valerianate of Strychnine	$\frac{1}{67}$ grain.
Glonoin	$\frac{1}{250}$ "
Hyoscyamine	$\frac{1}{250}$ "

The above makes one dose, and the dose should be given, either in capsule or pill form, every thirty minutes until the face flushes.

The Strychnine stimulates muscular contraction and aids in forcing the stone through the duct, or canal, into the bowel. The action of the Hyoscyamine harmonizes with the Strychnine by relaxing the muscular spasms brought on by the pain. The Hyoscyamine also dilates the small arteries all over the body and allows the blood to flow away from the congested gall bladder. This aids in relieving the pressure and pain. The Glonoin aids in dilating the arteries and acts as a powerful heart stimulant, thus strengthening the patient and preventing fainting or collapse, which is liable to occur. With this treatment, if it is still found necessary to use Morphine for the relief of pain, the amount required will be comparatively small.

The foregoing remedies are decidedly tonic in their general effect, and this fact, together with the relief from the trouble and small amount of Morphine used, will result in a rapid and most satisfactory cure.—(62).

GANGRENE, or MORTIFICATION.—Gangrene is the death of a part from lack of nutrition. It is a putrefactive change occurring in a dead limb, or in any dead tissue. Either gangrene or mortification means death. Gangrene is understood to mean death of a part in a live body, while mortification is a term more often applied to a dead body.

Cause.—Gangrene may result from either too high or too low a temperature, as a burn or freezing. It may also result from a strangulated hernia, or any condition where the circulation is shut off. It may result from injury, erysipelas, diabetes or old age. The last two forms depend upon constitutional conditions. The other varieties depend upon local causes.

Constitutional Gangrene depends upon systemic disease, such as diseased arteries, or diabetes.

Senile (or Dry) Gangrene, which is also constitutional, is a drying up or shrinking of a part from poor circulation. This form is usually met with in the aged, and is due to a weak heart. There is but little interference with the venous (return) circulation; the trouble is, there is but little blood sent to the part, and with good drainage the part becomes dry and dies. This form is comparatively harmless.

Moist Gangrene results from external injury, or from inflammation where circulation and nutrition are suddenly checked and the part dies. In this case there is no opportunity for drainage and the moisture remains. This is a very dangerous form. When occurring from injury if the inflammation is extensive, as in a bruised or mangled leg, it may first appear in the foot or lower part of the limb and extend toward the body so rapidly that in a few hours dark spots may cover the surface in many places. If it reaches the body, the case is hopeless. Surgical interference is the only treatment for this form of gangrene.

Embolic Gangrene is due to a sudden plugging of an artery with a blood clot, shutting off the supply of blood and nourishment.

Hospital Gangrene results from bad hygiene and lack of antiseptics. This form is now seldom heard of.

Phlegmonous Gangrene results from erysipelas. Where the disease affects the different structures, death of the tissues results from pressure due to swelling.

Symptoms of Dry Gangrene.—In senile gangrene, or gangrene of old age, there is a weak heart, poor circulation and diseased arteries. The disease usually occurs in the part farthest distant from the heart, as the foot or hand, because the circulation is more feeble there. The first symptom may be a sensation of coldness or numbness of the part. Any slight accident or injury may cause inflammation which is out of proportion to the injury. Sooner or later a dark spot appears, a blister may form and a little bloody fluid be discharged. In cases of this kind there are no constitutional symptoms other than those that existed before. There may be a sensation of heat and pain for a short time when the disease first begins. When a large area, as an arm or a leg dies, there will be fever, pain, sleeplessness, exhaustion and rapid death.

Symptoms of Moist Gangrene.—When gangrene follows an injury, there may be no symptoms until dark spots appear. These spread rapidly. The part will be greatly swollen, and feels soft and boggy from the contained fluid and formation of gases resulting from decomposition. The odor is horrible. Gangrene may result from tying a large artery in some operation. In this case the symptoms would be as follows: The pulse is absent, the limb becomes greatly swollen, the surface is cold, and blisters containing a bloody fluid may appear. The pain is mostly confined to the part where the artery was tied. In gangrene the adjoining healthy tissue is greatly inflamed. This is the battle line between the living and the dead; it is called the line of demarkation. It is not present in gangrene resulting from accident, as described, but is present in senile gangrene, and may occur in gangrene caused by tying an artery, in which case amputation should be made some distance above this line.

TREATMENT.—

Dry Gangrene.—The treatment consists in keeping the part clean, antiseptic dressing, such as cloths wet with Listorine laid over the affected part, or the part sprinkled with Iodoform; good food and tonics. If the disease shows a tendency to spread, apply heat to the part. Amputations are not recommended in aged people.

Moist Gangrene.—The treatment in moist gangrene following injury is to amputate at once. The patient should receive the most nourishing diet. Stimulants are required, and, later, tonics, good ventilation, etc.

Phlegmonous Gangrene.—For the treatment of gangrene following erysipelas, see ERYSIPELAS PHLEGMONOUS.

Embolic Gangrene.—Usually occurs in the liver, lungs or brain, hence is not amenable to treatment. Should it occur in an arm or leg, wait for the line of demarkation, and, if extensive, amputate the same as for gangrene resulting from tying an artery.

Hospital Gangrene.—This would require the same treatment as for moist gangrene, or embolic gangrene, or for that form resulting from tying an artery. Hospital gangrene, however, is a form that is nearly extinct and needs no particular mention.

For *Omphalitis*, or *Gangrene of Infants*, also *Cancrum Oris*, or *Gangrene of the Mouth*, see under DISEASES OF CHILDREN.

GIN LIVER.—(See under LIVER, DISEASES OF).

GLANDERS—FARCY.—This is a contagious disease. Primarily it affects the horse, but may be communicated to man. At first the disease is confined to the mucous membrane of the nose and air passages. It is accompanied by a pustular eruption which causes profuse discharges.

Cause.—The cause is a specific ferment which sets up inflammatory changes in the mucous membrane and skin.

Symptoms.—The disease commences with a catarrhal inflammation and nodular (knotty) swelling of the mucous membrane of the nose, and extends along the air passages. Suppuration and ulceration of the nodules soon follow, and thus a purulent nasal discharge is established. When the mucous membrane is affected most, the disease is called *Glanders;* when the skin is affected most, it is called *Farcy.* As the disease continues, however, these two conditions become more or less associated with each other. First, the nodules form. These may be the size of a pea, smaller or larger. They are poorly supplied with blood vessels, hence soon degenerate. The degeneration is followed by more or less suppuration. The odor of the discharge is foul, and the ulcers show no tendency to heal. The glands of the neck and other lymphatic structures are swollen. The poison from the suppurative surfaces enters the blood and the whole system becomes affected. There is inflammation of the skin, mucous membrane of the air passages, stomach and digestive tract. Abscesses form beneath the skin in the joints and in other structures. The condition is one of blood poisoning. Inflammation of the skin may occur in large patches, and the inflamed area be covered with large vesicles which soon turn into pustules, break down and discharge. The disease usually runs a rapid course and is generally fatal. However, there are said to be some cases that are chronic; a chronic case usually recovers.

TREATMENTS.—

A. The treatment consists in rendering the ulcers as healthy as possible, and in freeing the system of poison. The ulcerous patches on the mucous membrane cannot be reached directly. This renders the situation graver because there is constant absorption of poison from these surfaces. The bowels, kidneys and skin should be kept active in order to eliminate as much of the poison as possible. Large doses of Fowler's Solution—20 to 30 drops—should be taken four times a day, at meal time and on going to bed; and 40-drop doses of Syrup of Iodide of Iron taken between meals and at bedtime—three doses a day. ' The last dose of each may be taken together. Salicylate of Soda in 20-grain doses every three hours is also valuable; or take internally 3 or 4 drops of Carbolic Acid, well diluted with water, every three hours, and also take $\frac{1}{30}$ grain of Strychnine with each dose.

B. Nasal ulcers may be treated by snuffing up the nose Iodoform and injections of Carbolic Acid or Nitrate of Silver. A general tonic, nutritious diet and abundance of pure air and water are of the greatest importance. Alcoholic stimulants have been used with advantage. Ulcers occurring externally may be treated by the application of Carbolic Acid.

GLEET.—(See under VENEREAL DISEASES).

GOITRE, BIG NECK, or BRONCHOCELE.—This is an enlargement of a gland (thyroid) in the front of the neck. It is an endemic disease, that is, peculiar to certain localities. It is much more prevalent in some districts of Europe than anywhere in America, yet there are few parts of the world where it may not be found. It is sometimes cured by removal from a goitre district, and it may be contracted by settling in such a district.

Cause.—It has never been ascertained just why certain localities should be favorable to this affection, but it is believed to occur in persons of a scrofulous tendency.

Symptoms.—The enlargement begins, usually in early life, as a soft tumor, which increases in size, hardens in the course of time, and generally becomes irregular in shape, the enlargement on the right side being larger than that on the left. The growth is unattended with pain, but after the tumor has attained a certain size it begins to press upon the windpipe and gullet, thus interfering with breathing and swallowing and causing headaches and other disagreeable feelings.

TREATMENTS.—

A. Wash externally with a solution of Tincture of Iodine diluted in ½ the amount of Alcohol. Repeat every evening until it disappears.

B. Iodide of Potassium...................... 2 drachms.
Iodine .... 1 "
Water... 2½ ounces.

Mix, shake a few minutes and pour into two vials, one for internal use and one for external application.

Internal Dose.—5 to 10 drops, between meals, to be taken in a little water. Do not take for two hours after eating.

External Application.—With a feather wet the enlargement night and morning until the swelling disappears.—(69).

C. Paint the neck with Tincture of Iodine every second day. —(7).

GONORRHEA.—(See VENEREAL DISEASES).

GOUT. — This is a disease that exceeds rheumatism in the severity of the pain occasioned, but instead of affecting the large joints, it is confined usually to the smaller ones. The first joint of the great toe is most frequently affected.

Cause. — The tendency to *gout* is generally inherited, but is usually caused directly by high living or over-indulgence in wine and malt liquors. Where the disease has been *acquired* by such indulgences it does not make its appearance until after about thirty-five years of age; if inherited, it may come on early in life. Men more than women are subject to it.

Symptoms.— An acute attack may be preceded for several days by a derangement of the digestive organs, especially a sour stomach, but the gouty pain comes on suddenly, usually soon after midnight. The pain is wrenchingly severe, and the part hot, swollen and sensitive to the touch. The whole limb (if it is the toe joint that is attacked) is affected with swelling and painful muscular contractions, and the veins are congested. The patient has a chill at the beginning of the paroxysm, followed with fever. There is an entire or partial remission of the symptoms about daylight, but they come on again at night, decreasing in severity, however, until after a few days the patient becomes convalescent. After recovery he is in better general health than before the attack.

A second attack may not occur for three or four years, or may occur in one year. After the first attack it is prone to return, but of course much depends upon the manner of living. The time between the second and third attack is less than between the first and second, in fact, the time between each succeeding attack lessens.

The characteristic of this disease is a deposit about the affected joints of a chalky substance. which increases with each attack until the joints present a knobby and deformed appearance.

TREATMENTS.—

A. The patient should restrict himself in the matter of diet. As a remedy, there is nothing better than Wintergreen. If the wintergreens can be obtained, boil them up, make a strong tea, and drink freely.   If not, take the Oil of Wintergreen, a few drops on loaf sugar, three times a day.   Or take a tea made of Virginia Snake root and Wintergreen, equal parts.   Another excellent remedy is Black Cohosh, taken either in decoction or tincture.

The great value of the Wintergreen Oil is found in the fact that it contains a large percentage of Salicylic Acid, and this acid is one of the most valuable remedies in all forms of gout or rheumatism.   It should not be given clear, however, as it is too irritating.   Salicylate of Soda is another safe way of administering Salicylic Acid.   In either case the acid circulates in the blood as a free agent, and is one of the best of all known remedies to prevent fermentation and degenerative changes, which are always more or less present in rheumatism and gout.

Salicylic Acid is eliminated by the kidneys, hence is a good antiseptic to these organs and also to the bladder.

B. For Chronic Gout.—Take hot vinegar and put into it all the table salt which it will dissolve, and bathe the parts affected with a soft piece of flannel.   Rub in with the hand, and dry the part by the fire.   Repeat this operation four times in the 24 hours, 15 minutes each time, for four days; then twice a day for the same period; then once, and follow this rule whenever the symptoms show themselves at any future time.

The philosophy of the above formula is as follows: Chronic gout proceeds from the obstruction of the free circulation of the blood (in the parts affected) by the deposit of a chalky substance, which is generally understood to be a carbonate and phosphate of lime.   Vinegar and salt dissolve these, and the old chronic compound is broken up.   The carbonate of lime, etc., become acetate and muriate, and these, being soluble, are taken up by the circulation and eliminated.   This fact will be seen by the gouty joints becoming less and less in bulk until they assume their natural size.   During this process the stomach and bowels should be kept regulated by a gentle purgative.   Abstinence from alcoholic drinks; exercise in the open air, and especially in the morning; free bathing of the whole surface; eating only the plainest food; and occupying the time by study or useful employment, are very desirable assistants.

C. *Gout Tincture.*—

Veratrum Viride.......................... .. ½ ounce.
Opium .... ¼   "
Wine........ .... ½ pint.

Let stand for several days.

Dose.—15 to 30 drops, according to the robustness of the patient, at intervals of two to four hours.

A French officer introduced this remedy in gout some sixty years ago, and it became so celebrated that, incredible as it seems, it sold as high as from five to ten francs a dose. It is considered valuable also in acute rheumatism. In gout it removes the paroxysms, allays pain, *reduces the pulse and abates fever*, and procures rest and sleep.—(68).

GRAVEL, or STONE.—(See under KIDNEY DISEASES).

GREEN SICKNESS.—(See under WOMEN'S DISEASES).

GURGLING OF THE INTESTINES.—This is the peculiar sound caused by gas in the digestive tract. During the fermentive condition of the bowels following constipation, in typhoid fever and inflammation of the bowels, this condition is greatly increased. True it sometimes occurs in those who miss a meal, or who are not seriously troubled with constipation or disease of any kind; yet we are inclined to believe that this condition whenever present is dependent wholly upon the formation of gas, and indicates an unhealthy condition of the digestive tract.

TREATMENT.—

If actual disease is present, see treatment under the various heads. In the absence of any well defined disease, take 10 grains of Salol three times a day. Take the meals regularly, exercise great care regarding the diet and keep the bowels regular.

HAEMOPHILIA—BLEEDER'S DISEASE.—This is an abnormal condition of the blood vessels in which hemorrhage is a frequent symptom. It occurs upon the slightest occasion. Any slight accident or injury may produce troublesome bleeding. The extraction of a tooth or removal of a tonsil is liable to cause dangerous hemorrhage.

Cause.—The cause is not well understood. Evidently it is a lack of normal development of the vessels.

TREATMENT.—

Guard against injury as much as possible and avoid operations of all kinds. When an injury or wound has occurred, cleanse the wound and take absolute rest. If in a favorable locality, pressure on the artery should be employed. The diet should be light and supporting. After a serious attack of bleeding the patient should take Iron and Cod Liver Oil until the health seems restored. The Cod Liver Oil should be taken in tablespoonful doses three times a day before meals, and 10 drops of the Muriate Tincture of Iron in a teaspoonful of simple syrup after meals. When possible, a residence in the South during the winter is advisable as most cases are aggravated by cold weather, and in any case care must be taken in guarding against cold and wet.

HAY FEVER (*Hay Asthma, Hay Cold, Rose Cold*).—So called because it usually occurs during the haying season. The only difference between asthma and hay fever is that in hay fever there is a slight rise in temperature and a catarrhal condition of the eyes, nasal cavities, throat, and air tubes of the lungs, but mostly in the air passages of the head. At first the mucous membrane may seem dry, but this is followed by an increase in the secretions. In some cases there is a profuse watery discharge. Hay fever may, and sometimes does, assume all the seriousness of asthma. There is no dividing line between them. The catarrh is the most prominent symptom which divides the two.

TREATMENTS.—

A. Change of climate affords the greatest relief, but the remedy is Lobelia tea (see chapter on herbs). Drink until the lungs are relaxed.

Remark.—Northern Michigan climate is a positive relief for hay fever sufferers. It is doubtful if a permanent cure can be effected.

B. Artemesia Vulgaris, sixth dilution. Take in pill form or 1-drop doses four times a day during the months of freedom from the disease.—(3)—Homeopathic.

HEADACHE.—There is no one ailment to which humanity is so universally subject as headache. It is a symptom of nearly every disease, and no disorder so slight that it does not have its accompanying headache. There is the *nervous headache* to which so many women especially are subject, the *catarrhal headache* and the *neuralgic headache;* there is the warning and unpleasant fullness in the head of those subject to apoplexy or epilepsy; there is the distressing accompaniment to organic disease within the brain; and there is the positive illness called *sick headache.*

SICK HEADACHE.—*Causes.*—There is a variety of causes which may produce sick headache. Usually it is due to disturbances of digestion and is spoken of as *bilious headache.* Exacting mental labor, worry, or insufficient sleep may induce an attack of sick headache by interference with digestion or elimination. Defects of vision not corrected by the use of lenses (glasses), or the wearing of lenses that have not been properly fitted to the eyes, is the cause of much headache, and, in cases of severe eye strain, of sick headache. Irritation of the ovaries or womb is another cause of headache.

Symptoms of Sick Headache.—The pain in the head is very sharp and severe, and is attended with a feeling of nausea that is aggravated by movement, and by periods of faintness and giddiness. If vomiting or an evacuation takes place, the patient is relieved for the time being; but such relief is likely to be only temporary, and is soon succeeded with another paroxysm of pain, nausea, faintness and giddiness. Ordinarily the attack lasts but a few hours. Usually it is impossible to take anything in the way of nourishment during its continuance, and for a little time after the stomach will not bear anything but light foods. The patient is weak for a day or two after such an attack.

TREATMENTS.—

A. *Nervous Headache.*—Hot pack, dark room, bed and anodyne—something to quiet the nerves.

Sick Headache.—Hot water internally, or emetic.

B. Acetanilid .... 1 ounce.
Citrate Caffeine............................. 15 grains.
Bicarbonate Soda.......................... 1 drachm.
Sulphate Strychnine...................... ¼ grain.
Cocoa, sufficient quantity.

Mix, and take from 5 to 10 grains every two hours until relieved.—(46).

C. Acetanilid..................................... 60 grains.
Monobromate of Camphor .... 30 "
Citrate of Caffeine .... 30 "

Mix, and divide into 30 powders. Take one powder every half hour until relieved.—(53).

D. A prompt cathartic, and teaspoonful doses of Bicarbonate of Soda every three or four hours.—(7).

E. *Bilious Headache.* — Give Boneset tea until the patient is sick at the stomach and vomits; or, if there is no Boneset at hand, tepid (warm) water will do. Have him drink just as much as he can, and if that does not produce nausea and vomiting, wait a little while and have him drink again. He should try to drink enough to give the stomach a good rinsing out.

F. *Headache from Biliousness.*—Take Mandrake and Culver's Root, dry them, powder and sift. Take of the powder, 2 grains Culver Root and 1 grain Mandrake. Mix in water and take every night at bedtime until bowels move thoroughly. After bowels move take ½ ounce inner bark of Willow and steep in ½ pint of water. Take tablespoonful three times a day before meals.

G. *Arising from Dyspepsia*, or other deranged conditions of the stomach, give a cathartic, put the feet into hot Mustard water, using at least one tablespoonful of Mustard, and give freely of

Pennyroyal or Sage tea, which will produce vomiting and relieve the stomach. Afterwards apply a Mustard plaster to the stomach and back of the neck.—(66).

H. *Arising from a Determination of Blood to the Head*, known by throbbing pain and flushed face, put Mustard plasters to the feet and drink freely of strong Ginger tea as hot as it can be borne, go to bed and cover well. This will usually give immediate relief. From 10 to 15 drops of the Tincture of Gelsemium may be added to the tea, which will aid in quieting the agitation and relieving the pain.—(66).

I. *Periodical Headache.*—There are those who have sick headache coming on at periods of from a few weeks to two or three months, lasting two or three days, accompanied with nausea, and occasionally with vomiting. In these cases after using an emetic to relieve the present attack, take the Cathartic Syrup next following:

Cathartic Syrup.—

Best Senna Leaf	1 ounce.
Jalap	½ "
Butternut, the inner bark of the root, dried and bruised	2 "
Peppermint Leaf	½ "
Fennel Seed	½ "
Alcohol	½ pint.
Water	1½ "
Sugar	2 pounds.

Put all into the spirits and water, except the sugar, and let it stand 2 weeks, then strain, pressing out the dregs, add the sugar and dissolve without heat. If it should cause griping in any case, increase the Fennel Seed and Peppermint leaf.

Dose.—One tablespoonful once a day, or less often if the bowels become too loose, up to the next period when the headache might have been expected, and it will not be forthcoming.

This is a mild purgative, and especially pleasant. Most persons, after a trial of it, will adopt it for their general cathartic, and especially for children. Increase or lessen the dose according to the effect desired.

THE HEART AND ITS DISEASES.

The heart is a hollow, muscular organ, conical in shape. It is situated obliquely in the chest cavity, and towards the left side. Its base extends upward and to the right as high as the second rib. The center of the base corresponds to the center of the body, and lies near the surface just below the chest bone. The apex extends downward and to the left to a point between the fifth and sixth rib, three and one-half inches to the left of the median line, or center of the body.

Internally the heart is divided into four cavities, two upper and two lower. A longitudinal partition divides it into a right and a left cavity. The right and left cavities do not communicate. The heart is again divided by a transverse partition into four chambers, two upper and two lower. The upper and lower cavities communicate through small openings which are guarded by valves. The left and right heart are really two organs moulded into one — Nature's means of economizing space and power.

The duty of the heart is to force the blood through the circulatory system. The veins carry the dark venous blood from all parts of the body and empty it into the right side of the heart. From there it is sent through the lungs for oxidation. Many of its impurities are eliminated through the bronchial tubes, the effect of the oxygen being to purify the blood and render it a bright red before it is returned to the left side of the heart and sent out through the general circulation.

Symptoms of Disease of the Heart.—Diseases of the heart are characterized by shortness of breath, frequently amounting to a choked or stifled feeling, palpitation, pale, unhealthy skin, and eventually by dropsy, the swelling usually beginning in the feet and ankles. It is not, however, conclusive evidence that a person has some organic disease of the heart because he may have some of these symptoms. Over-exertion will produce shortness of breath, but if there is a growing tendency in this direction and it is produced by less and less exertion, there is, of course, room for apprehension. Palpitation, which is tumultuous beating and a pain or sense of oppression in the region of the heart, may be due to dyspepsia. It may also result from nervous conditions. Dropsical symptoms also arise from other causes. (See DROPSY).

173

However, a reliable physician should early be consulted if there are any symptoms to indicate a possible affection of the heart, in order that the nature of the affection may be determined and exciting causes removed or abstained from.

TREATMENTS:—

A. Heart Disease.—Nutritious diet. Bicarbonate of Soda in teaspoonful doses three or four times a day.—(7).

B. Palpitation.—Tincture of Ginger in a half-teaspoonful dose every hour.—(7).

C. Shortness of Breath.—

Iodide of Potash............................ 1 drachm.
Seng.. 4 ounces.

Dose.—A teaspoonful in a little water three times a day, between meals.—(28).

D. Heart Failure.— Hypodermic injection of $\frac{1}{80}$ grain Strychnia. Repeat in an hour if necessary.—(45).

E. Heart Failure.—

Tincture Digitalis........................ 3 drachms.
Simple Elixir.............................. 4 ounces.

Dose.—For an adult, a teaspoonful every four hours.

F. Diseases of Circulation.—Drink hot water and employ friction along the limbs. Open the bowels by purgative medicines.—(7).

G. Diseases of Circulation.—Stop coffee, tea and tobacco. Get stomach in good condition. Take careful diet.—(13).

ANGINA PECTORIS.— Also called Neuralgia of the Heart (see NEURALGIA).

Cause.—It may be either of nervous or organic origin.

Symptoms.—This affection, like others of neuralgic character, occurs in paroxysms and comes on suddenly. The patient is attacked with a pain in the region of the heart that is so intense and is attended with a feeling of such fear of death that he holds rigidly to the position he first assumes, breathes slowly, and seems afraid to move. The chest is fixed and the pain extends also into the left shoulder and arm. A sense of coldness is always present in one of these paroxysms, and the patient often breaks out into a cold sweat. Great exhaustion follows such an attack. Death may occur during the paroxysm or from the exhaustion which follows it, or the patient may survive a number of attacks.

TREATMENTS.—

What to Do Till the Doctor Comes.—This is a serious thing and a doctor should be called immediately in case of an attack of severe pain about the heart. In the meantime, give a hot sling —brandy, if you have it—*and have hot water on hand when the doctor arrives;* he may want it. Put the patient to bed, keep him quiet and get him warm if possible. Repeat the sling as often as he can bear, say every fifteen or twenty minutes.

> **A.** Tincture Aconite........................... 40 drops.
> Bromide Soda.............................:............... 1 ounce.
> Simple Elixir............................. 4 ounces.
> *Mix*, and take one teaspoonful three times a day between the attacks.—(46).

B. Give 2 to 4 tablespoonfuls of whiskey, properly diluted, and 20 or 25 drops of Laudanum, and send for a doctor. Apply Mustard to chest and back.—(14).

C. Tablets of Nitroglycerine $\frac{1}{50}$ grain each. Let one dissolve on the tongue. If not relieved in fifteen minutes, use another one the same way.—(20).

Note.—Sometimes a full dose of Nitroglycerine proves such a sudden and powerful stimulant that the heart, which is diseased, or laboring under difficulties, is unable to respond, and the over-stimulation, instead of supporting the organ, paralyzes it; it grows rapidly weaker, and death soon follows. We have seen a few cases of this kind, where $\frac{1}{50}$ grain of Nitroglycerine was given and the heart immediately responded by giving a few irregular and spasmodic throbs and bounds, then gradually grew weaker and the patient died within a few hours. Remember that over-stimulation produces death.

We recommend from 5 to 10 drop doses of Fowler's Solution between attacks, taken three times a day, say for three weeks, then skip a week and take a week, and so on.

D. Those who are troubled with neuralgia of the heart will not only find the following suggestion convenient, but in case of a sudden and unexpected attack it will prove a great benefit as a means of relief from this most distressing disease.

Secure a drachm vial, which can be carried without inconvenience, and put into it a few tablet triturates of Glonoin, or Nitroglycerine, $\frac{1}{250}$ of a grain each. The triturates are better than pills because they dissolve readily. When an attack comes on, place a tablet on the tongue; it will dissolve immediately. Repeat the dose in ten, twenty or thirty minutes, or as needed.

E. Glonoin, 2d dilution. Take in drop doses or pill form every twenty or thirty minutes until relieved.—(3)—Homeopathic.

Pseudo Angina. There is also a false angina, hysterical in character, afflicting nervous women and children. It is attended with neuralgic pains in the chest and near the heart, and with general hysterical phenomena. It is not dangerous to life.

FATTY DEGENERATION, or FATTY HEART.—In this disease the fibers of the muscles of the heart are gradually replaced by fat, thus causing a degeneration of the muscular tissues and a corresponding inability of the organ to perform its functions properly.

Cause.—In most cases it is the result of some chronic state or disease, as prolonged anæmia, dyspepsia, alcoholism, scrofula, cancer, tuberculosis. Elderly people are sometimes subject to it. It is always the result of impaired nutrition.

Symptoms.—The heart, being enfeebled, the circulation is weak; the pulse is slow and there is a shortness of breath. There is distress of a neuralgic character about the heart, and attacks of *angina pectoris* occur. The various organs of the body are reduced to an anæmic state, one organ being more susceptible in one individual, and another in another. In some the brain is particularly affected, dizziness and swooning being characteristic; in others the lungs are more susceptible, and this is marked with a dry, hacking cough; dyspepsia and constipation are characteristic of anæmia of the gastric system; and derangements of the urine, ending in dropsy, where the kidneys are affected. The foregoing are all symptoms of a weak heart, from whatever cause. A peculiar and characteristic symptom of *Fatty Degeneration* is a constant sighing. *Arcus senilus*, a light ring surrounding or partially surrounding the pupil of the eye, is claimed to indicate fatty heart.

TREATMENTS.—

A. Diet. The food that is eaten should be nutritious, but with a fleshy person where anything of this kind is suspected, all fatty foods should be avoided.

As a remedy, Strophanthus may be taken three times a day. *See note below.*

B. Avoid starchy foods and take 3 drops of Fowler's Solu tion after meals.—(72). *See note below.*

Note.—In *Fatty Heart*, drugs that have a direct action on this organ, as Digitalis, or a powerful action, as Nitroglycerine (Glonoin), must be given with caution, because to increase its work means over-exertion and, if this is carried too far, more harm than good will result.

As a heart tonic, we would recommend any one of the following, given at the beginning in a very small dose, as indicated, *i.e.*:

Strychnine, $\frac{1}{60}$ grain dose three times a day,
or,
Caffeine, 1-grain dose three times a day,
or,
Tincture of Strophanthus, 3-drop dose three times a day.

Fowler's Solution, while not classed as a heart tonic, is still believed to give special support to this organ. More than that, it is one of the best aids to digestion and assimilation, thus increasing nutrition and strengthening the vitality of the patient. While its influence is not so direct, its general effect is of far greater importance.

PERICARDITIS.—Acute Form.—The heart is enclosed

in a membranous sac which blends with the outer coats of the great vessels—arteries and veins—a short distance from their junction with the heart. This sac may be considered a dilatation of the outer coats of these vessels, which expand and surround the heart. Below the membrane is attached to the diaphragm and aids in forming what is called the central tendon; in front it is partially covered by the margin of the lungs, and above it lies near to the chest bone; behind it are the bronchial tubes, the æsophagus and the thoracic or descending aorta; its sides are surrounded by the pleura, the delicate membrane which encloses the lungs.

As the outer coats of the vessels expand to form this membranous sac, they separate, or divide into two layers. The inner layer, which is more delicate in structure, invests and is adherent to the surface of the heart. The two layers lie in close relation to each other. They are smooth and glistening and furnish a thin fluid which serves to facilitate movement and reduce friction to a minimum. An inflammation of this sac is called Pericarditis.

Cause.—Such an inflammation rarely occurs except as it develops in the course of some other disease, as acute rheumatism, Bright's disease, pneumonia, diphtheria, scarlet fever, etc.

Symptoms.—The general symptoms are distress in the region of the heart, short cough, difficulty of breathing, usually nausea, vomiting and palpitation. (See ENDOCARDITIS).

TREATMENT.—

What To Do Till the Doctor Comes.—If nausea occurs, a little weak Camphor sling may be given. For distress about the heart, use hot applications—cloths wrung out of a hot decoction of some bitter herb, as Smartweed, Mayweed, etc., are best. Warm drinks may also be given. A little hot sling is always admissible in such a case. In the meantime the doctor should be summoned to learn the cause. Have hot water on hand when he arrives.

Those attending the sick in any acute disease should keep calm and avoid any betrayal of anxiety or excitement. To alarm the patient is about the worst thing a nurse can do, and may, where there are heart complications, result fatally.

ENDOCARDITIS.—Acute Form.

—The endocardium is a thin, delicate membrane which lines the cavities of the heart. It is composed of a single layer of flat cells joined edge to edge, like a stone pavement. It is continuous with, and is the same in structure as the lining membrane or inner coat of the arteries. As the outer coats of the large vessels leading to the heart expand to form the sac which enclose it, so the inner coat expands and lines the heart cavities. Inflammation of this membrane is called *Endocarditis.*

Cause.—This inflammation is usually developed in the course of some other inflammation. It is difficult, or impossible, to make a distinguishing diagnosis between *Endocarditis* and *Pericarditis;* usually an inflammation of the one communicates itself to the other. An acute inflammation of either may end in chronic inflammation, when will be found the symptoms covered under DISEASES OF THE HEART, *Symptoms of.*

TREATMENT.—See under PERICARDITIS.

HYDROPERICARDIUM.—(See under DROPSY).

HYPERTROPHY, or HYPERPLASIA.

—This is an increased growth in the tissue of which the heart is formed; the walls are thicker and the organ is larger and heavier.

Cause.—Any condition which obstructs the outflow of blood or otherwise increases the heart action may cause *Hypertrophy.* It may be caused by alcohol, tobacco, tea or coffee. Each of these, if taken in quantity or continued, acts as a stimulant or irritant and causes an increase in the heart action. The disease may be caused by chronic bronchitis, or by some forms of Bright's disease; the first interferes with the circulation through the lungs, and the second interferes with the circulation in the kidneys and thus forces the blood back toward the heart, thereby increasing its work. Hypertrophy may be caused by a shrinking or other defect of the valve which guards the opening into the aorta, or large artery leading from the heart. This is called *Aortic Stenosis.* Such defect would allow the blood to flow back into the cavity of the heart, and this would call for extra work to pump it out again. The lower left cavity could not entirely empty itself; this would force the blood back into the upper cavity, and it would become dilated. The upper left cavity is also dilated when the valve guarding the opening between these two cavities is defective; the blood flows back and the result is the same. In either case the lungs become congested, the blood is forced back to the right side of the heart, and the walls of the latter become thickened from overwork. This does not occur until late in the disease. The right side may also become affected from any condition of the lungs which obstructs the flow of blood through them. *Emphysema* might cause it. In emphysema the air cells are distended and this obstructs the circulation. Sometimes the walls of the air cells are broken down and air escapes into the intervening or surrounding tissue. This is called *Vesicular Emphysema.* Emphysema is caused by prolonged and forcible respiration, as blowing wind instruments. Emphysema would increase the pressure and check the circulation still more. In Pericarditis the outer membrane surrounding the heart may become adherent to the inner membrane—the one which is adherent to the heart (see PERICARDITIS). This prevents the gliding action of the membranes and results in increased effort. This would cause hypertrophy of the whole organ. A heart thus enlarged may weigh from ten to twenty and even thirty pounds. The normal weight is ten to twelve ounces, or less than one pound.

Symptoms.—The symptoms are increased heart action. The arteries are distended, the pulse is full and strong, and the arteries at the side of the neck may be seen throbbing. There is headache from blood pressure, ringing in the ears from pressure of over-distended vessels supplying those organs, and the face and eyes are flushed from the over-distended vessels. There is cough and difficult breathing from pressure in the lungs. A full, strong heart beat may be easily detected. The lower point of the heart is below its normal position and farther to the left.

TREATMENT.—

But few remedies are needed for this disease. If caused by alcohol, tobacco, tea or coffee, stop their use. The patient should lie down several hours a day, should not indulge in active exercise, in straining or heavy lifting, and should give particular attention to the diet. The remedies used are those that will slow the heart action—Aconite and Veratrum in 1-drop or 2-drop doses three or four times a day would be best for this purpose. Bromide of Potash in 20-grain doses four times a day would also prove valuable.

DILATATION OF THE HEART.—In this disease the heart cavities are enlarged without any increase in the muscle tissue or thickening of their walls. On the contrary the walls may be thinner than normal.

Cause.—The cause may be any of those which produce *Hypertrophy.* The nerve supply is feeble and the heart is weak. Over-straining causes dilatation without a corresponding increase in growth. This disease occurs in the young and feeble. In this disease the right side of the heart is usually affected first because it is naturally weaker and less able to stand the strain.

Symptoms.—The heart beat is weak, the pulse is feeble, and the veins are enlarged as the force of the heart beat is not sufficient to control the return circulation. There is headache from lack of blood and nourishment, coughing, difficult breathing from distension and pressure of the vessels in the lungs, dyspepsia from a sluggish circulation around the stomach, constipation from a sluggish circulation along the digestive tract, the urine is scanty from a lack of circulation in the kidneys, the mind is dull, and vitality and ambition are lacking. The patient may be troubled with dizziness and fainting from poor circulation in the brain.

TREATMENT.—

Nourishing diet, bitter tonics—usually Iron is needed—moderate exercise, laxatives to keep the kidneys and skin active, and for a weak heart, Digitalis, Caffeine, Strychnine and Strophanthus are valuable.—See note under *Fatty Degeneration.*

STENOSIS AND REGURGITATION.—These conditions have already been referred to. The aorta is a large artery and forms the great trunk of the arterial system, as already stated. The lower left ventricle or cavity of the heart opens into this artery, and in health this opening is guarded by the aortic valve. This valve may become inflamed, the inflammation may cause new tissue growth, and new tissue growth resulting from inflammation always shrinks when it matures. Small blood vessels and nerve fibers are destroyed and also more or less of the natural tissue, and the result is a firm and inelastic growth. As a result of inflammation in the valve mentioned, lime salts may be deposited, the same as in the formation of bone (see BONE DISEASES), and this would also render the valve firm and unyielding. In either case the valve cannot be pressed back, but remains constantly in the way of the current and interferes with the amount of blood sent out. This is called *Aortic Stenosis.*

In health the mitral valve guards the opening between the two cavities in the left side of the heart, and the same changes may occur in this valve as those just described in the aortic valve. These valves are formed of the picked-up folds of the delicate membrane which lines the heart cavities. When there is new connective tissue and the new tissue contracts, the valve becomes shrunken and will not fit the opening. When the valve fails to open and thus interferes with the current, it is called *Stenosis*, or narrowing. When the openings are improperly closed and the blood is allowed to flow back past the shrunken valve, it is called *Regurgitation*. The change described in the mitral valve is one of the most frequent affections or diseases of the heart, and the change in the aortic valve is second.

The valves in the right side of the heart are seldom affected, because the right side of the heart has only to receive the blood from the return circulation and send it out through the lungs, while the left side receives it back from the lungs and must then force it through the whole arterial system; hence there is more strain on the left side and more liability to disease.

While the diagnosis and treatment of *Stenosis* would call for the services of a physician, we make the following suggestions concerning

TREATMENT.—

It will readily be seen that any remedies or conditions that increase the action of the heart are to be avoided; drug medication is unimportant in these conditions. First, the amount of fluids taken should be reduced as far as consistent with health and strength, because this lessens the amount of blood and correspondingly lessens the work of the heart. This is best controlled by a concentrated diet of easily digested foods, drinking very little water, and no tea, coffee or alcohol. Tobacco should not be used. Fowler's Solution is a remedy that has been highly recommended in valvular diseases of the heart, probably because it aids digestion and assimilation. 5-drop doses should be given at meal time. Heart tonics may be used for a time, but should not be relied upon because they cannot permanently increase the strength of the heart; their continued use may be compared to whipping a tired horse. Many of the heart tonics contract the small blood vessels. These would do more harm than good for the reason that they would force the blood back toward the heart and necessarily increase its work. Strophanthus is a remedy of considerable value for these troubles as it produces no effect upon the size of the small vessels. Strophanthin, the active principle, is a convenient form. From $\frac{1}{300}$ to $\frac{1}{200}$ of a grain in pill or tablet form, or, later, Caffeine in 2- or 3-grain doses is recommended.

HEARTBURN.—What is called heartburn is the result of indigestion (see *Indigestion* under STOMACH, DISEASES OF). Especially is this true of indigestion caused by starchy foods, as these result in the formation of many acids, and these acids produce a burning sensation which extends along the æsophagus into the chest cavity and is felt just behind the chest bone. Heartburn may be attended with an inclination to vomit.

TREATMENTS.—

A. Nitromuriatic Acid. 5 drops of strong acid in a glass of water after meals.—(54).

B. Teaspoonful doses of Bicarbonate of Soda (common baking soda) every three hours.—(7).

HEMORRHAGE.—The rupture of a blood vessel gives rise to a discharge of blood called *hemorrhage*. Apoplexy is caused by the rupture of a blood vessel in the brain.

A hemorrhage from the lungs is of a bright red color, frothy, and expectorated after coughing. Many cases of supposed hemorrhage from the lungs are not from the lungs at all, but are caused by the rupture of small blood vessels along the upper part of the trachea, or large air tube. They follow a fit of coughing when the mucous membrane is congested and swollen from taking cold, or from some other cause. These cases are apt to occasion a great deal of anxiety and fright, yet they are as harmless as nosebleed. We have also known the sudden rupture of small vessels in the stomach to result from the same cause, and produce the same effect. All these cases require is a little rest and the same treatment that would be given any case of congestion.

Hemorrhage of this kind may be distinguished from hemorrhage of the lungs from the fact that *the blood is not frothy*.

Hemorrhage from the lungs seldom occurs, and the blood is frothy by reason of its containing air. Hemorrhage from the stomach contains no air, and the contents of the stomach are mixed with the hemorrhage. Also, quite large quantities of blood may be coughed up in the morning as a result of nosebleed during the night, in which case the blood is clotted and dark.

Streaks of blood or slight hemorrhage from the bowels during diarrhea or dysentery is no cause for alarm. When hemorrhage follows tyhoid fever or cancer of the bowels, its nature and importance will be readily understood. With the free use of intestinal antiseptics and good hygienic surroundings, hemorrhage will not occur in typhoid fever.

Always look at these cases from a common-sense standpoint. Use ordinary home remedies, or the case may need no treatment at all. In many cases the individual is benefited, because the hemorrhage has relieved the congestion. Ulcer of the stomach or tuberculosis will give a history long before hemorrhage occurs.

TREATMENTS.—

The following remedy is equally valuable for any and all forms of hemorrhage, whether from the lungs, stomach, wound or wherever.

> Sulphate of Atropine.................... $\frac{1}{100}$ grain.
>
> Repeat in thirty minutes if necessary. If this does not control the hemorrhage, send for a doctor.

As a drug store may not be at hand, and this remedy not be obtainable, the following home treatments are recommended in cases of emergency:

Hemorrhage from the Lungs.—

What to Do Till the Doctor Comes.—Keep the patient quiet and raise the shoulders with pillows. The best remedy is Capsicum (red pepper), but salt is good. If hemorrhage occurs and nothing else is at hand, give salty water at frequent intervals. Follow the salt with Capsicum. The Capsicum may be made into a strong tea and drank along at short intervals, or 3-grain capsules may be given every half hour until the hemorrhage is controlled. If the hemorrhage should be a violent one, and especially if the patient is not subject to them, send for a physician. *Always have hot water on hand on the arrival of a physician.* He may not need it, but if he does, no time will be wasted waiting for it to heat.

Spitting of Blood.—Cracked ice, small piece on tongue every few minutes, will help to control it.—(31).

Hemorrhage from the Stomach.—

What to Do Till the Doctor Comes.—Salt is good for this, also Alum water. Take a little pulverized Alum, dissolve it in warm water, and take a teaspoonful of the solution every little while. For an adult, give 15 to 20 drops of Laudanum. If the hemorrhage is a violent one, send for a doctor; or if not violent enough to make this necessary, consult him as to cause. The patient should lie down and keep perfectly quiet.

Intestinal Hemorrhage.—

What to Do Till the Doctor Comes.—Intestinal hemorrhage is a symptom which usually demands prompt attention, no matter how slight it may be. In many cases the enforcement of absolute rest and quiet, with the administration of cold drinks, and of opium in from ⅛ to ⅓ grain doses, given once in three or four hours to diminish the activity of the bowels is all that is needed. A good remedy is an injection of a decoction of peach and raspberry leaves with 15 or 20 drops of Spirits of Turpentine added, repeated every two hours. If this fails to stop hemorrhage, the doctor should be sent for. *Always have hot water ready on the arrival of a physician.*

Hemorrhage from Injury.—(See "Bleeding from," under ACCIDENTS AND EMERGENCIES, DEPARTMENT III.

HEMORRHOIDS.—(See DISEASES OF ANUS).

HERNIA, or RUPTURE.—By hernia is meant the protrusion of a part of one of the internal organs from its natural position. The term "rupture" refers especially to a displacement of the bowels or membranous covering. This displacement occurs most frequently in the groin, or at the navel.

When hernia occurs it is not because the abdominal wall has been ruptured. The opening through which the hernia passes is a natural one and is always present. In fœtal life the testicles are situated in the abdominal cavity. Before birth they descend into the scrotum, and these natural openings are the tracts through which the testicles passed. An egg is surrounded by a thin film which is quite strong and would retain the egg if the shell were carefully removed. If a small opening were made in the egg shell and the egg then suddenly and forcibly moved in the right direction, the film could be made to bulge through the opening in the shell. The film of the egg may be compared to the peritoneum which lines the abdominal cavity, and the opening in the shell to the unclosed tract through which the testicle passed. As the result of sudden or violent movement the peritoneum may be forced through this opening, and the bowel may also protrude. Either one or both would constitute a hernia. Usually both are present. (See page 451.)

Causes.—Occurring at the navel, it comes on usually soon after birth, being due to weakness at the point where the umbilical cord was attached to the fœtus. Generally, however, hernia occurs in adults as the result of a strain or from some violent exercise.

Forms of Rupture.—There are three varieties of rupture: In the first the bowel or membrane can be forced back into place by pressure, called *reducible hernia;* in the second the displacement cannot be forced back into its normal location, called *irreducible hernia;* and in the third the displacement of the bowel is such that the part displaced is constricted so as to shut off the circulation. This is called *strangulated hernia.* The last named is accompanied with nausea, vomiting, a twisting, burning pain, pain on pressure, and no impulse, or swelling out of the tumor, on coughing. The treatment of a strangulated hernia admits of no delay, as, unless relieved, mortification sets in in a few hours and death results. An irreducible hernia may become strangulated.

For further description of *internal* and *strangulated hernia*, see under INTESTINAL OBSTRUCTION.

TREATMENTS.—

A. A suitable truss, applied early and adjusted by a physician or experienced druggist. If constipated, keep bowels reasonably open with some mild physic, as Cream of Tartar and Salts—a teaspoonful of each taken night and morning.

B. It has been proven beyond any doubt that hernia or rupture can be permanently cured by the Fidelity method—the injection of a fluid into the hernial canal and wearing a well-fitting truss for about three months. From four to eight injections are usually required. This method is nearly painless, and the patient can work every day during treatment if he wishes to do so.—(10).

Note.—The medical profession is divided regarding the injection method. It is upheld and condemned with equal force.

C. Lay patient on back, with head a foot or two lower than heels. Apply cloths wrung out of cold water, and let nobody but a physician attempt reduction by pressure. After reduction, get suitable truss applied and wear it.—(60).

Note.—In strangulated hernia if reduction is impossible, an operation is the only hope.

HERPES.—(See under SKIN DISEASES).

HICCOUGH.— Hiccough is a symptom of disease that in most cases is easily recovered from. There are some cases, however, that assume serious and even dangerous proportions.

Causes.—The diaphragm is a thin membrane which divides the chest from the abdominal cavity and aids in respiration, rising and falling with each breath. The stomach is placed just beneath the diaphragm. The diaphragm passes obliquely backward and downward, hence it is not only above but partially behind the stomach. During indigestion the stomach may become very irritable. The constipation which follows causes bloating and pressure, and this increases the trouble. The stomach is forced backward and irritates the diaphragm.

The *solar plexus* is a large collection of nerves situated just behind the stomach. Irritation may communicate through this bundle of nerves, as it receives branches both from the stomach and the diaphragm. Any condition which irritates the diaphragm may result in hiccough, as the irritation causes contraction of the diaphragm downward. This is so sudden that it causes a vacuum in the chest. The outside air attempts to rush in and fill the lungs, but is prevented by the sudden closure of the glottis —the space between the vocal chords through which the air passes. This produces the peculiar sound known as hiccough. Why does the glottis close at this time more than during ordinary breathing? Because the spasmodic action of the diaphragm against the stomach causes spasm of this organ also. The same nerves which supply the stomach supply the vocal chords, hence every spasm of the diaphragm is first conveyed to the stomach, then flashed over the nerve fibers to the vocal chords, and they contract, closing the space between them as described. Hiccough usually stops without attention, though sometimes the trouble is persistent and is said to cause death. It is not, however, the hiccough, but the septic or unhealthy condition of the digestive tract that causes death. Free elimination will usually relieve the trouble.

Hiccough may be caused by inflammation of the upper part of the spinal cord, as that part of the cord situated in the neck sends out the nerves which pass downward through the chest cavity and supply the diaphragm, and inflammation of this part of the spinal cord might so irritate and excite these nerves as to cause spasmodic action, as described.

Tumor in the lungs may cause pressure upon these nerves and result in irritation and spasms. The same nerves which supply the lungs also supply the stomach and, through the *solar plexus*, communicate with the nerves which supply the diaphragm, hence irritation from a tumor in any part of the lungs may cause spasms and hiccough.

Hiccough may result from a *strangulated hernia*, because the nerves which supply the digestive tract also communicate with the *solar plexus*, and this with the diaphragm.

Peritonitis, or inflammation of the thin membrane which surrounds the bowels, may produce spasms and hiccough in the same way.

TREATMENTS.—

A. As nearly every case of hiccough is caused by indigestion and constipation, it may be successfully treated by giving one or two tablespoonfuls of Castor Oil followed by $\frac{1}{250}$ of a grain of Atropine every half hour until the throat is dry or until the face is flushed. When hiccough results from inflammation of the spinal cord, from a tumor in the lungs, from strangulated hernia or from peritonitis, it will be readily understood that different treatment will be required. If inflammation of the spinal cord, the usual fever remedies may be given; tumor in the lungs would probably prove fatal; a strangulated hernia demands an operation; the treatment for peritonitis is described under that heading.

We offer our own personal experience in support of the statement that nearly every case of hiccough is caused by indigestion and constipation. Our experience extends over many years and includes a large number of cases, and, barring peritonitis, hernia, inflammation of the spinal cord or tumor growth, hiccough has invariably been relieved by active cathartics and antispasmodics, of which Atropine and Hyoscyamine are among the best. Some cases of hiccough are caused by hysteria, but the hysteria is usually the result of indigestion. A little Croton Oil, followed by a cold bath, a brisk rub, and a few doses of Atropine, has a wonderful effect in disposing of hysteria.

B. Take a little Camphor sling or Peppermint sling. Sometimes Soda water is effective.

C. Lemon juice, mixed with sugar to make it palatable, and taken freely.—(76).

D. Frequent drinks of hot water with Ginger, Mustard or Soda stirred into it.—(7).

E. I have stopped with Belladonna cases that have been given up by many physicians. I use one drop of the tincture every half hour.—(18)—Homeopathic.

Note.—Belladonna contains Atropine. See Treatment "A."

HIVES.—(See under SKIN DISEASES).

HYDROCEPHALUS.—(See under DROPSY.)

HYDROCELE.—(See under DROPSY).

HYDROPHOBIA.—This disease is characterized by great disturbance of the central nervous system, difficulty in swallowing, dread or fear of water, severe muscular contraction, convulsions and death.

Cause.—Hydrophobia is caused by a specific poison which is found in the saliva of rabid animals. It is usually conveyed to the human system by the bite of a dog.

Symptoms.—The symptoms may be slight at first. There is pain at the point of the wound. If the wound has healed, there is swelling at the same place and the scar appears red. The wound may re-open and discharge. There is general uneasiness or restlessness, anxiety, headache. chilliness, and perhaps a feeling of stiffness or lameness. The patient may be low-spirited; the vessels about the neck become congested, and expectoration is increased; the difficulty in swallowing also increases until the sight of water or some sound or sharp noise may startle the patient and bring on convulsions. During these attacks the mind is usually lost and the patient may rave, or strange hallucinations may be present. There is also moderate fever. Death usually occurs in four or five days.

TREATMENTS.—

A. The first object should be to prevent absorption of the poison. If the bite has been on a limb, a stout cord or handkerchief may be tied around the limb and twisted with a piece of wood until circulation is arrested. Sucking the wound is usually effective in withdrawing the poison, and can convey no additional danger to the person bitten. If the patient cannot reach the wound with his own mouth, another may volunteer to suck it, although this is dangerous; but the danger may be largely obviated by applying a solution of Carbolic Acid to the wound before sucking. The use of caustics should not be delayed. A hot iron in the form of a nail, poker or other available instrument at a white heat, should be brought in contact with all parts of the wound. If the poison has been absorbed, one of the best remedies is what is commonly known as Red Chickweed (see *Chickweed* in Chapter on HERBS). It is prepared by boiling about one ounce of the dried plant in two quarts of strong beer or ale until it is half evaporated. Strain the liquid and add two drachms of Tincture of Opium. For an adult, the medicine should be given in ½ gill doses every morning for three mornings. If the symptoms are fully developed, the whole of the preparation may be taken in one day. The dose for children should be in proportion to their age. Persons bitten should bathe the wound with the same liquid. Those about the person who has been bitten should preserve a calm and cheerful demeanor, and avoid all allusions to the occurrence. He should be protected from all excitement, and should not be allowed to see that he is an object of solicitude.

B. If the wound from a rabid dog is on an extremity, as a finger or toe, and it is possible to sever the member at once by a single blow from a large knife or hatchet, the treatment, while it may seem a little harsh, would be effectual. The next best thing to do, if the remedies are at hand, is to apply a Caustic (See CAUSTICS)—alkalies or acids. A strong alkali, as a stick of Potash, would be better than an acid because its effects go deeper. Other means of arresting the poison are by shutting off the circulation, sucking the wound or application of hot iron, as mentioned elsewhere. According to past teachings, if the poison gains entrance into the system, there is no known remedy that will do more than to relieve the symptoms; in other words, symptomatic treatment is about all that can be applied. For this purpose Chloroform, large doses of Morphine, etc., are recommended.

While we have not had experience with this disease, we wish to suggest a treatment that certainly seems rational, and one that we should speedily adopt if occasion ever required. The remedies we should use would be Atropine and Pilocarpine. Give at once ⅓ of a grain of Pilocarpine and $\frac{1}{100}$ of a grain of Atropine with a hypodermic needle. This will speedily bring the blood to the surface and cause profuse sweating. In order to aid perspiration, apply artificial heat by any means, and keep the water literally pouring out of every pore of the skin. This is simply a means of elimination, and one of the quickest and most thorough that could be adopted. The object, of course, is to relieve the system of the poison. Give large quantities of pure water. Let the patient drink this by the pint. Not all at once, of course, yet in a few hours a large quantity of pure water can be taken in this way and cause no inconvenience. Atropine aids materially in bringing the blood to the surface, but will not produce sweating. It is also a powerful stimulant; it stimulates the heart, the circulation and the respiration. This is of particular benefit since the Pilocarpine is a depressant; but while ⅓ of a grain of Pilocarpine has a tendency to weaken the patient, it is one of the quickest remedies to effect elimination. These are desperate cases and need heroic treatment. While this work is going on, and at the very beginning, give a large and active cathartic— something that will cause large, watery evacuations, as 10 grains of Scamony and 10 grains of Jalap. The large amount of water taken will not only aid in keeping up the sweating, but it will dilute the poisons and aid materially in keeping the bowels active. This same treatment applies to any other case of blood poisoning.

Note.—We believe also that Treatment "B" under LOCKJAW would be ideal if the patient was sufficiently manageable to apply it.

Hysterical Hydrophobia.—There are cases of hysteria that are said to simulate hydrophobia so nearly that, judging from the symptoms, no distinction could be made. The hysterical patient may mimic animals, such as the cat or dog; there may be spasmodic and highly emotional periods, where the patient is unable to swallow, has a fear or dread of water, etc. There are also those who claim that there is no such disease as hydrophobia. This claim is supported by some of our best physicians. While hysterical patients may give all of the symptoms of hydrophobia, such a claim would not cover the conditions met in the lower animals. Surely we cannot charge these cases to hysteria, and to our minds this is proof positive that hydrophobia is a distinct and separate disease. Hydrophobia does not occur from the bite of rabid animals nearly so often as many suppose. Less than ten per cent of those bitten by mad dogs have the disease. This statement is supported by James Howard Thornton, M.D., Fellow of the King's College of London, and by many other eminent physicians.

HYPOCHONDRIA.—This is an affection of the nervous system characterized by the belief that one has some bodily ailment or disease. The patient has spells of moodiness. It is similar to *Melancholia*. *Monomania*, or insanity upon one subject, is another evidence of the same condition. Rheumatism, headache, mental stupor, lack of resolution, hysteria and many other depressions and hallucinations are the result of the same cause; so is insanity.

Cause.—A gradual loss of nerve control resulting from the irritating effects of indigestion and retained waste. A lack of proper nourishment reduces the vitality and physical force below par, and the patient is unable to exercise proper control of himself. The brain becomes clouded and dull, and intelligent guidance is more or less disturbed, *i. e.*, the individual is unable to exercise proper control of his actions. The various conditions mentioned are simply different manifestations of the one cause.

TREATMENT.—

The treatment suggests itself. It consists of attention to diet, digestion and elimination, also an abundance of pure water, fresh air, sunshine and proper exercise. This is the best treatment for conditions of this kind. Drug medication is unimportant, although in severe cases may be required for a short time. Chloral, the Bromides and Asafœtida are probably the best remedies.

HYSTERIA.—As a disorder of the nervous system it is generally confined to women, usually occurring in paroxysms, but in very nervous women approaching a chronic state. A paroxysm may vary from moaning and gesticulation to violent struggling. There may also be slight twitching of the muscles, and in some cases general convulsive movements. Consciousness is never wholly lost, and the paroxysm is believed to be more or less under the control of the patient, who, if instead of giving way to her feelings would endeavor to control them, might possibly escape a paroxysm altogether. Hysteria may, however, be developed during the course of an organic disease, when, owing to a weakened condition, the patient is certainly less accountable for lack of self-control. The severer forms mentioned are not often met.

A. A 5-grain pill of Asafœtida taken three times a day will generally control hysteria. Or a fine thing for nervous disorders of any kind is a tea made of Scullcap, or of English Valerian, or of American Valerian (common ladyslipper). See chapter on herbs for description and directions. Any treatment to be effective must be long-continued.

> **B.** Tincture of Valerian................ 3 drachms.
> Asafœtida............................... 30 grains.
> Water .... 4 ounces.
> *Mix*, and take one teaspoonful every two hours.—(46).

INFLAMMATION.—Inflammation is a morbid or diseased process in some part of the living body. There are present heat, pain, redness and swelling. The conditions present in inflammation and in fever are the same, and the cause is the same. However, inflammation is generally understood to be localized, as inflammation of the liver, lungs or kidneys, or inflammation of a joint in rheumatism. Inflammations are spoken of as *adhesive* or *fibrinous*, *plastic* or *corpuscular*, and *aplastic*. Adhesive inflammation is where a wound heals without suppurating—without the formation of pus; in plastic inflammation the wound heals less rapidly; in aplastic inflammation the wound shows a strong tendency to suppurate with no tendency to heal. These conditions are sometimes spoken of as healing by first, second and third intention.

Cause.—The cause is an irritant. The blood may contain irritants as a result of indigestion and result in inflammatory rheumatism. Inflammation may result from an accident or injury, as a sprain, dislocation, cut, or penetrating wound; or it may result from a poisoned wound. Chronic inflammation may result from chronic dyspepsia, the prolonged use of alcohol, syphilis, tuberculosis, etc.

Symptoms.—The symptoms are both local and constitutional. The local symptoms are those already mentioned—heat, pain, redness and swelling. The constitutional symptom is fever. The conditions and changes present in the blood vessels and circulation are the same as those described under fever.

TREATMENT.—

See *Fevers.* If from a poisoned wound, see *Blood Poisoning*. If from inflammatory rheumatism or accident, see treatment under those heads. If resulting from tuberculosis or other chronic disease, see treatment accordingly.

INFLUENZA.—LA GRIPPE.—Through custom we are in the habit of calling any and all kinds of acute catarrhal conditions by this term. Influenza has long been recognized by medical writers. It usually occurs in epidemic form. The majority of cases resemble an ordinary cold, yet there are some attacks that present a striking contrast, *i, e.*, a sudden onset, followed by debility and prostration which seem to be out of all proportion to any known cause. This is more particularly true with the old and those not physically strong. There are but few deaths resulting directly from this disease, yet other diseases, such as pneumonia, chronic bronchitis, consumption, etc., may follow, and for this reason those who have had a severe attack ought to take every precaution and remain indoors until the danger is past. It is not always necessary to have a doctor, perhaps seldom, yet good judgment and care should be exercised in every case.

Cause.—By some it is believed to be caused by a germ. Perhaps the great majority believe it is caused by atmospheric changes. The reason for this belief is that it occurs in widely separated districts at the same time.

Symptoms.—The onset is sudden with chills or chilliness, followed by fever and a weakness that in some cases amounts almost to prostration. Headache is present, especially frontal headache—over the eyes. The reason is that situated over each eye in the frontal bone is a cavity which is lined with mucous membrane, being continuous through and opening from the nose. The catarrh may close the opening, and the pressure from the swollen membrane and the exudate will cause pain. Catarrhal symptoms are abundant. The mucous membrane of the nasal passages, throat, bronchial tubes, etc., all furnish a profuse secretion, which is at first thin and watery, but later becomes thick and tenacious. The patient feels sore and lame, and in some cases there is a deep, dull pain throughout the body. The appetite is destroyed. In lighter attacks sneezing is frequent, the eyes are watery, the tongue may be coated, and the discharge from the nose keeps the patient busy giving special attention to that organ.

TREATMENTS.—

A. Mild cases may be treated successfully without a doctor, as follows:

For the catarrhal and nasal discharge take the following:

> Atropine.. $\frac{1}{50}$ grain.
> Morphine... ½ "
> Calomel... 1 "
>
> *Mix* intimately and divide into 8 powders. Take 1 powder every two hours until the throat is dry or the face is flushed, or until the catarrhal symptoms disappear; then continue every three hours, or three times a day. If the amount of Calomel is not sufficient to move the bowels, take a dose of Seidlitz Salts, Castor Oil, or any other convenient laxative.

Another most excellent remedy is the following:

Acetanilid...................................... ½ drachm.
Salicylate of Soda.......................... ½ "

Mix intimately, and divide into 12 powders.
Take one of these every two hours until the
ears "sing." After that take one powder every
three hours, or three times a day.

The Acetanilid powders have no effect in controlling the
nasal catarrh, while the Atropine powders are directed especially
to that condition, hence these remedies may be taken alternately.
This would bring the doses one hour apart. Take until the face
is flushed or the ears "sing." When the face flushes, the Atropine powders should be taken only three times a day, as directed
above; when the ears "sing," the Salicylate of Soda powders
should be taken only three times a day. It is not our purpose to
recommend remedies that are not supported by our personal experience, hence we are confident that the above treatment, applied
according to directions, will prove satisfactory in the great
majority of cases.

The patient should remain indoors for a few days, and in
those cases that are more severe should remain in bed for a day
or two. Keep an even temperature and good ventilation. This
will undoubtedly hasten favorable termination, and is advised in
all cases where circumstances will permit.

In those cases that are *very* severe, where, following a sudden
onset, there are chills and debility amounting almost to collapse,
put the patient to bed, apply external heat and give hot drinks.
If there is vomiting, put a large Mustard plaster over the stomach,
put the feet into hot water, and give a cathartic and stimulants.
The Salicylate of Soda powders are applicable to these cases, and
will prove the very best remedy that can be given.

Following these cases, mild or severe, there is often a troublesome and persistent cough: Malto Yerbine, given in teaspoonful
doses six or eight times a day is often a specific for this cough.

Where the severer form attacks old people, supporting treatment in the form of nourishing food and tonics is always needed,
and even the same precaution taken by those of younger years
will prove of benefit by hastening a more complete and satisfactory
cure. For those cases needing a tonic, give the following:

Fellows' Compound Syrup of Hypo-
   phosphates................................ 3 ounces.
Maltine....................................... 6 "

Mix together by shaking the bottle, and
take in tablespoonful doses before or immediately after meals.

This will prove one of the most nutritive and satisfactory remedies that can be taken. Following a severe case, great care should be exercised to guard against exposure, as the second attack is liable to be more disastrous than the first.

B. If in mild form this seldom requires medical attendance. Keep the patient in the house and, if possible, on the bed or sofa for two or three days. Meat should be avoided and the diet restricted to simple and easily digested food. Moderate quantities of cold drinks should be taken, such as fruit juices, lemonade, raspberry vinegar, etc. Quinine in moderate doses should be taken from the first. The tickling cough calls for steam inhalations, and the air of the room may be kept moist by the evaporation of water kept boiling in a broad, shallow vessel. If the case is severe, a physician should be called.

C. Take for the head and backache 5 to 10 grains Phenacetine. For an adult follow with doses of 1 drop each of Tincture of Aconite and Spirits of Camphor every two hours.—(8).

D. Five grains of Quinine every four hours, with 1 grain of Dover's Powder and 1 grain of Camphor with each dose.—(7).

E. Quinine... 1 drachm.
　　Dover's Powder........................ ½ "
　　Capsicum................................. 30 grains.
　　Calomel.................................... 1 "
　　　Mix, divide into 12 powders and take 1 every two to four hours.—(46).

F. Soak the feet, put to bed and give warm herb teas to produce sweating. Move the bowels with a mild cathartic, such as Rhubarb Syrup, which for an adult may be given in dessertspoonful doses three or four times a day. Also give from 3- to 5-grain doses of Quinine every four hours. As additional nourishment, if the appetite is poor, give the following:

　　Milk.................................. 10 tablespoonfuls.
　　Good Brandy or Whiskey... 5 "

Add to this the white of an egg, thoroughly beaten, and 2 tablespoonfuls of white sugar. Give a tablespoonful, say every four hours.—(71).

INSANITY.—While some cases are violent, it should be remembered that many cases are mild. Insanity does not necessarily mean a dangerous condition of the mind, and no strictly dividing line can be drawn between sanity and insanity. It is well known that from time to time sane people have been placed in insane asylums. It is also well known that in each case before being removed, the *prisoner* was examined by those supposed to be capable judges. So long as a man's speech and actions conform to the general standard, his right to individual citizenship is unquestioned. His manner may be overbearing, may be pleasing or displeasing, may be mild or energetic; his habits may be cleanly or unhygienic; he may resort to sharp practices, or be easily led by others; his dealings may be questionable or honest; his conduct may be strange, or may be within the limits of good judgment; his temper may be mild or vicious; but so long as he does not pass beyond a certain limit, he will not be molested. His self-control may be the result of far-sighted cunning, or the result of legitimate business and moral principles; that makes no difference regarding the question of sanity so long as the instincts of propriety dominate. So long as this is true, the man is safe from the charge of insanity. By a failure to fully develop our faculties, by perverted instincts through bad company and bad habits, we all contain, perhaps, elements of insanity.

Insanity is caused by indigestion, whether resulting from the prolonged use of alcohol or other cause. This is followed by the morbid influence of unhealthy blood. We all understand that this condition produces disease of the liver, kidneys, heart, lungs, etc.; it also produces disease of the brain. The organs mentioned undergo structural changes. One-fifth of all the blood in the body goes to nourish the brain. For this reason the brain is much more exposed to the morbid influence of septic blood, and it is no wonder that it also undergoes structural changes. If the morbid influence continues, there is a molecular change in the brain substance, *i. e.*, its chemistry is altered. It cannot be otherwise. Unhealthy blood never did and never will produce normal, healthy tissue in the brain or anywhere else. Again, the lack of normal or uniform development of the nervous system, while it may not cause insanity, may cause the individual to commit rash, immoral or illegal acts. Any and all of these conditions are made worse by bad company, which tends to develop low, vicious habits.

The controlling center of the nervous system is the brain and spinal cord. The brain is situated in the skull, and the cord in a canal formed in the spinal column. The nerves escape through little openings called *foramen*. All of the tissues of the body, including the brain, are composed of small particles of matter called cells. The cells vary in composition according to the part or organ in which they are placed, and according to the duties which they perform. In the brain these cells are situated externally, or on the surface. They are gray in color and form a layer about one-quarter of an inch deep. The surface of the brain is marked by deep fissures or grooves, and these are also filled with the gray cells—Nature's method of economizing space. With the fissures or convolutions unfolded, or spread out, the surface of the brain would measure about four square feet. The gray cells, or the outer surface of the brain, furnish the source from which all human power is supposed to emanate. Internally the brain is composed of nerve fibers. The nerves are lighter in color and, as stated elsewhere, are no more nor less than prolongations or long-drawn-out thread-like processes of the nerve cells. All are held together by a framework of delicate tissue called connective tissue, or neuroglia. In the spinal cord the gray cells are located internally and the fibers externally.

The brain is the center of the nervous system. In health it is the seat of judgment, reason and memory; in a word, the seat of government. Pain, injury or any trouble is at once transmitted to the brain by the nerve fibers, just as a message is sent by means of a telegraph wire. The brain is the central station, understands all messages, and instantly forms a complete conception of the situation or condition, understands the wish, desire, danger or trouble, and sends back the order of action. The outer covering of the brain, or nerve cells, is the seat of reason, judgment, emotion, sensation, pleasure, pain, and all that we see, hear, enjoy or suffer; but with the molecular or elementary change above described, these cells are unable to receive, analyze or transmit thought and action intelligently. Instead the mind becomes clouded, dull, stupid or vicious, and insanity results. The function of the nerve fibers differs from that of the nerve cells, as it is the duty of the fibers to convey such thought, sensation, etc. The nerve fibers are only the material substance through which thought and sensation are expressed, just as wire is the material substance through which a telegraphic message is expressed. In the same way the nerve cells are the material substance through which intelligence is made manifest, just as the steel of a magnet is the material substance through which magnetic influence is made manifest. The nervous system with its five senses is but the marvelous expression of the one great power. The five senses are evidence of the wisdom of the Creator: The sense of touch is more acute in the fingers than on the elbow or the nose, because it is more convenient to feel with the hands; the sense of taste is left to the mouth, because that is where the food must be placed before being eaten; the eyes and ears are placed in the head so that we can see and hear while we are using our hands and feet; the sense of smell is placed in the nasal cavities because the air is constantly passing through them to the lungs, hence we are able to detect the first symptoms of decay, bad air or foul odor.

While the brain is the great center of the nervous system, the spinal cord also contains many subordinate nerve centers. Many nerve fibers extend downward from the brain and join with those of the spinal cord, and the subordinate centers thus formed may be compared with a switch-board in large telegraph offices where messages are received by one system and transmitted by another. So also in the nervous system: Messages are received by one system and sent to the brain by another, hence the centers in the cord are under the control of the brain. Life, force and intelligence pervade the nervous system everywhere, and it is this unseen influence which conveys impressions and controls our actions.

The nervous system is divided into the *cerebro-spinal* and *sympathetic*. The cerebro-spinal includes those nerves which have their origin in the brain and spinal cord. The sympathetic is so called because it is believed to produce sympathy between the different organs and tissues of the body. The cerebro-spinal nerves are under the control of the will. They supply the voluntary or external muscles—those under our control. The sympathetic nerves are connected with the brain and spinal cord indirectly, and are not under the control of the will. They supply the involuntary or internal muscles—those of the stomach, heart, liver, kidneys, etc. The sympathetic nerve fibers have their origin just in front of the spinal column; they are connected with the cord indirectly, and also continue up into the brain. The sympathetic system forms large ganglions, or bundles, of nerve fibers in different parts of the body. One of the largest is situated just behind the stomach and is called the *solar plexus*. This is why a sharp blow or injury over this point produces such a shock, and why, if severe enough, unconsciousness, collapse, and even death may follow. When we refer to the "pit" of the stomach, it is this bundle of nerve fibers that has been disturbed. Like the centers in the spinal cord, these groups of nerve fibers communicate with and are under the control of the brain.

As stated, a lack of development of the nervous system is often the cause of crime. This is the reason some persons commit crime while others do not. It has also been stated that a lack of development may be the result of bad company, bad habits or low moral surroundings. These influences tend to develop only the baser elements of human nature, while the higher and nobler instincts are allowed to remain dormant. Children and young people otherwise bright may lack development in some particular. This may lead to drink or dishonesty in early life, and be wholly overcome in later years when experience has taught them that which they did not know. A lack of development may render it easy or difficult to be moral. One class scarcely needs the restraining influence of the law; another class becomes criminals in spite of the law. Mental traits and characteristics reside in the subtle force expressed through the nervous system. When there is improper or imperfect development, we should by proper influence raise the unfortunate, if possible, to honest citizenship, rather than be so fierce in our thirst for their punishment. Man can be led, but he cannot be driven.

INSOMNIA.—Insomnia is a disease of the nervous system in which there is inability to sleep. This may exist alone or be connected with some other affection. It is a sign of disease even if there is no pain or other evidence of suffering. It may be the result of mental overwork.

TREATMENTS.—

A. If an accompaniment of other disease, the treatment should be directed to the disease proper; if due to mental overwork, Chloral or the Bromides are the best remedies. Of the Chloral, 20 grains, well diluted in water, may be given at one dose; of the Bromide of Potash, 40 grains, also well diluted in water, may be given at one dose. Or better, 20 grains of each may be given together. If sleep is not produced in two or three hours, one-half the dose—10 grains of each—may be given. If eight or nine hours' sleep can be secured, it will greatly refresh and strengthen the individual and lessen the danger of a recurrence of the trouble on the succeeding night. He should be released from his daily cares to as great an extent as possible, should take out-of-door exercise, and give special attention to diet, eliminations, etc.

B. A hot bath for twenty to thirty minutes before going to bed.—(45).

> **C.** Trionol... 1 drachm.
> Sulphonol.................................... 1 "
>
> *Mix*, divide into 12 powders and take one at bedtime.—(46).

D. A brisk cathartic, followed by 10-grain doses of Bromide of Potassium every three hours.—(7).

INTERMITTENT FEVER.—(See under MALARIAL FEVERS).

INTESTINAL OBSTRUCTION.—Intestinal Obstruction is a condition in which natural movement is prevented by mechanical means. It may follow inflammation resulting from injury. The obstruction may be partial or complete, acute (sudden) or chronic. Acute obstruction is due to the sudden narrowing or stoppage of some portion of the bowel; chronic obstruction is due to the gradual narrowing or stoppage of some portion of the bowel. A chronic narrowing may at any time become acute. When the obstruction also includes the shutting off of the circulation, it is called *strangulation.* Strangulation may follow an internal hernia. The small bowel is driven through some narrow internal opening, which may be the result of inflammation of the peritoneum at some previous time. The peritoneum lines the whole abdominal cavity and also surrounds the stomach and bowels. As a result of inflammation this membrane may have grown fast at different points, thus forming openings between the attached surfaces. Following a mild form of appendicitis, the outer end of the appendix may have grown fast, leaving a narrow slit or space beneath; following inflammation of the tubes or ovaries, there may have been adhesions leaving small openings; inflammatory conditions of tumors may result in adhesion and small clefts or openings. Through any of these a loop of the small intestine may be driven. This would constitute an *Internal Hernia,* and if the pressure was severe enough to shut off the circulation, it would be called *strangulated.* The only difference between an internal and an external hernia is that the external hernia gives positive signs of its presence by the swelling produced, while the presence of an internal hernia is suspected only from the symptoms, and the symptoms may closely resemble other forms of obstruction.

Causes.—Mechanical obstruction of the bowels may be due to any of the following:

Internal Hernia, Volvulus, Intersusception, pressure from *Tumor Growths, Enlarged Spleen,* partial *Paralysis,* with corresponding loss of peristalsis, *Stone — Enteroliths,* or foreign bodies in.

The most frequent cause of obstruction is constipation, as this causes a gradual absorption of the fluids, leaving the contents of the bowel a dry and hardened mass.

Internal Hernia, Obstruction from. — *Symptoms.* — The attack is sudden and severe, and usually follows some violent exercise. Vomiting begins early and is continuous, and soon becomes stercoracious, that is, some of the contents of the bowel are ejected. There is bloating, soreness comes on in a few hours, the pulse is rapid and feeble and the temperature is subnormal, the patient grows faint and, if relief is not had, collapse and death soon follow.

TREATMENT.—

Tincture of Nux Vomica	1½ drachms.
Tincture of Belladonna	2 "
Laudanum	2 "
Glycerine enough to make	2 ounces.

Give one teaspoonful of this mixture every thirty minutes until the face is flushed. The Nux Vomica will increase peristalsis—the natural movement of the bowels. Belladonna will relieve the spasmodic condition that is always present at the beginning, and the Laudanum will quiet the pain. This remedy is as good as any, yet it is dangerous to depend upon medicine in cases of this kind. Usually an operation is needed, and the earlier this is performed the better.

Volvulus.—This means a twisting of a section of the bowel, forming a kink. It usually occurs low down in the large bowel, or rectum. Or two intestinal coils of the small bowel may become twisted together; this occurs high up in the small bowel. Either may cause obstruction.

Cause.—The most frequent cause is constipation.

Symptoms. — If the small bowel becomes twisted, the symptoms correspond to internal hernia. When occurring low down in the large bowel, the condition is usually preceded by constipation, and one of the early symptoms is sudden pain. If vomiting occurs, it is late—after several hours or a day—and is not severe, only the contents of the stomach being ejected. There is no fever; the temperature may be subnormal. If not relieved, there is bloating and soreness, commencing in the left side. The pulse is rapid and feeble. Serious symptoms, as collapse, are not likely to occur early.

TREATMENT.—

If due to constipation, which is the most common cause, thorough elimination is the treatment. Give 10 grains of Calomel, or other active cathartic, and give large injections of warm soapy water regularly every hour, elevating the hips of the patient and having the ejections retained as long as possible each time. Gently kneading the bowels while giving the injections is of benefit. The pain may be overcome with a few drops of Laudanum. If the patient is pale, cold and weak, give stimulants—hot drinks, hot pepper tea, whiskey sling, artificial heat—any means of bringing the blood to the surface. If improvement does not soon take place, send for a doctor.

If the small bowel becomes twisted, an operation will probably be necessary. Medicinal treatment would be the same as that for internal hernia, or perhaps in such case 6 ounces of Sweet Oil given internally would be better.

Intersusception.—This is a slipping of one portion of the small bowel into another, like slipping one-half the finger of a glove into the other half.

Cause—The cause is said to be increased peristalsis, or too much activity in the movement of the bowels.

Symptoms.—Tenesmus, or frequent desire to evacuate the bowels. Mucus and blood are passed, there is a little bloating, and usually vomiting, but only of the contents of the stomach. The prolapsed bowel may extend the whole length of the digestive tract and be detected in the rectum.

TREATMENT.—

Keep the patient quiet; give 6-ounce dose of pure Sweet Oil; repeat in two hours, if needed. Control the pain with a few drops of Laudanum, and institute the usual treatment for vomiting. Large hot Mustard plasters over the stomach is one of the best means. If the patient is cold, apply heat and give hot drinks. If there is no improvement, send for the doctor. These cases generally need operation.

Tumor Growths.—Pressure from tumors of the uterus, ovaries, kidneys or other internal viscera may cause mechanical obstruction of the bowel.

Symptoms.—The symptoms from this form of obstruction come on gradually, occasional pains becoming more frequent and severe. There is a history of constipation. There may be occasional vomiting, the appetite is poor, and there is more or less dyspepsia, headache and bloating. If the tumor is inside the bowel, there will be blood and pus in the eliminations.

TREATMENT.—

Operation is the only means of affording permanent relief. See TUMORS.

Enlargement of the Spleen.—An enlarged spleen is evidence of an unhealthy system. The spleen is supplied with blood vessels which are larger in proportion to the size of the organ than those supplying other structures. This increases the danger and results in greater structural changes. The circulation is not carried on through the spleen the same as through other organs, but the blood flows through large channels or sinuses which are formed of the spleen itself. This brings the effects of unhealthy and irritating blood in direct contact with the tissues of the spleen, hence the organ is liable to a chronic form of inflammation and enlargement.

Symptoms.—The symptoms come on gradually and correspond to those described under tumor growth.

TREATMENT.—

The treatment would be general, or systemic. One of the best remedies for enlarged spleen is Hydrochlorate of Berberine in ¼-grain doses, taken four times a day—with meals and at bedtime.

Paralysis.—What is called the ulnar nerve supplies a part of the forearm. At the elbow this nerve occupies an exposed position, and sometimes receives a slight blow which causes a peculiar sensation of numbness to extend along the arm and fingers. This is the sensation when one hits his "crazy bone." This same temporary numbness and partial loss of power may be produced in the bowels by the constant pressure resulting from chronic constipation, but this condition would not properly come under the head of paralysis.

Stone, or Enteroliths.—*Symptoms.*—There will be a history of occasional colicky pains at that point, also difficulty in bowel movement with increased pain at that time. If acute obstruction occurs, there is intense pain, early vomiting and rapid pulse. The patient is pale and the surface cold.

TREATMENT.—

Six ounces of pure Sweet Oil may be given; also warm water injections every hour. If pain is very severe, give from 10 to 20 drops of Laudanum in a little sweetened water. If the patient is pale and the surface cold, give hot drinks, hot whiskey sling, and apply external heat. Any convenient remedies for vomiting may be employed, as, a Mustard plaster over the stomach. If the case does not early respond to treatment, send for a doctor.

Obstructions from Foreign Bodies.—The obstruction from foreign bodies and also from stone in the bowel occurs low down in the small bowel at its junction with the large, because that is the smallest part of the entire bowel. A stone or foreign body might cause ulceration if not removed, which would be its greatest danger. In case of a foreign body there is a history of something being swallowed. However, any article small enough to pass into the stomach is almost sure to pass through the bowel without difficulty.

Symptoms.—There is distress for days before the obstruction occurs. If the obstruction comes on suddenly and is complete, there is pain, sharp and desperate, nausea, vomiting, and weak, rapid pulse. The patient is pale, the temperature may be subnormal, and there is great prostration the same as in internal hernia.

TREATMENT.—

Treatment is the same as for *Stone* or *Intersusception.*

Important.—It should be remembered that following obstruction in any part of the bowel the symptoms are more or less alike. The symptoms of acute obstruction from any cause are much the same, and no one can say positively that it is hernia, volvulus or intersusception. In strangulated hernia, that is, where the circulation is shut off, the symptoms would probably be more severe, yet even in this case there would still remain some doubt until an operation should reveal the true situation.

IRITIS.—(See under EYE, DISEASES OF).

ITCH.—(See under SKIN DISEASES).

JAUNDICE.—Jaundice is a condition resulting from the obstruction of the bile passages. It is characterized by a yellow discoloration of the skin, preceded or accompanied by languor, and often with nausea. There is also a yellowish tinge to the white of the eye. Constipation is usually present.

Cause.—The cause is congestion of the bile ducts; or the congestion may be confined to that portion of the duct that opens into the bowels. It is a catarrhal condition, and the catarrh is the same as may exist elsewhere. There is congestion, and a greater or less amount of mucous secretions collect in the tubes and obstruct the flow of bile. The catarrh may result from excessive eating followed by indigestion, from using too much alcohol, may be caused by malaria, or may result from taking cold.

Symptoms.—The symptoms are nausea, loss of appetite and slight fever. There may be diarrhea or constipation, usually the latter. There is a yellowish color to the skin, which also shows in the whites of the eyes. There may be more or less pain in the region of the stomach and bowels. The mind becomes dull and the patient is pervaded by a spirit of languor. The urine contains bile.

TREATMENTS.—

A.—An active cathartic should be given at once, such as a single dose of Calomel of 5 to 10 grains. The patient should diet for a few days and secure an abundance of fresh air. After securing thorough action from the Calomel, the patient should take one teaspoonful of Phosphate of Soda dissolved in ½ to ⅔ of a glass of water. This should be taken one hour before each meal. The dose may be increased or diminished as found necessary. This remedy has a special action on the liver: It will relieve the congestion, dissolve the mucus and leave the bile ducts free. This insures increased activity along the whole digestive tract. Tonics may be needed for a few days. For this purpose give the following:

> Tincture of Gentian...................... 1 drachm.
> Tincture of Columbo..................... 1   "
> Elixir of Calisaya Bark, enough to
>   make.. 2 ounces.
>   *Mix*, and take 1 teaspoonful before meals.

If the trouble is due to *Malaria*, see treatment under that head.

B. Teaspoonful of Soda Phosphate in hot water before meals. Stop beer, tea, coffee and meats. Live on bread and Olive Oil. —(59).

C. Calomel...................................... ...... $\frac{1}{10}$ grain
Soda.. $\frac{1}{2}$ "
    Get in tablet form and take one every two
hours.—(46.)

JOINTS AND THEIR DISEASES.

The various bones of which the human skeleton is formed are connected together at different parts or points, and these connections are called joints.

The articular or adjoining ends of bones are covered with a thin membrane. This membrane is slightly elastic, and in places is thickened, which enables it to break the force of concussion, while its smoothness affords freedom of movement. The thickness varies according to the shape of the bone which it covers. If the surface of the bone is convex or rounded, the membrane is thickest in the center where the greatest pressure is received; if the surface is concave or hollow, it is thickest at the border.

Bones forming movable joints are held together by cartilages and ligaments, and are surrounded by what is called a capsular ligament or membrane. They are also supplied by a synovial membrane. The synovial membrane is a short, wide tube attached at either end to the margin of the articular cartilages. It invests the inner surface of the capsular ligament or membrane, and is reflected over the surface of all tendons passing through the cavity. The synovial membrane furnishes a thick fluid which lubricates the opposed surfaces and prevents friction. This fluid resembles the white of an egg, hence the name, synovial.

Joints are subject to inflammation, acute and chronic; to dislocation; to wounds, both penetrating and non-penetrating; to sprains; to a condition known as white swelling; and to ankylosis, or stiff joint. Inflammation, whether acute or chronic, is usually rheumatic. (See under RHEUMATISM). Acute inflammation may, however, follow acute inflammatory diseases. It may also occur in the course of pyæmia (blood poisoning) from any cause. In such cases it is usually confined to one joint, the hip or knee, and the fluid which collects soon turns into pus.

HIP JOINT DISEASE.—This disease is divided into three stages: *The first stage* includes an increased blood supply, or congestion, and the primary inflammation. *In the second stage* the inflammation continues, and there is an increased growth of the part due to the increased blood supply; there is also an effusion of blood serum (at first watery) into the surrounding tissue. *In the third stage* the new tissue and more or less of the surrounding structures degenerate, usually in the form of pus, which on reaching the surface escapes, the same as from any other abscess. The cause of the destruction of tissue is impure blood and pressure due to the swelling and new growth.

Cause.—Hip joint disease is due to an unhealthy system, the result of poor food, poor digestion and poor surroundings. It is most frequent in those of a scrofulous nature, in the anæmic and those poorly nourished. It may follow infectious diseases, such as scarlet fever or typhoid fever, where they are protracted, or syphilis may be the cause. The hip joint is most often affected because it is larger and more exposed, and also because it supports the weight of the body, hence is subject to pressure, strain and irritation.

Symptoms.—The symptoms of the *first stage* are slight and may not be noticed. There may be slight pain and possibly lameness. The pain may refer to the hip, front of the thigh or the knee, because this is the course taken by the nerve that supplies the hip joint.

In the second stage the lameness and pain increase, the child limps, and the symptoms are plainly noticeable. The muscles of the hip become shrunken, yet the hip may be broadened by reason of the effusion into the joint. The hip is drawn upward and forward, and the pelvis (hip bone) is tilted so as to rest the weight on the sound limb. This makes the diseased limb appear longer, yet it is not. The thigh, or leg above the knee, is flexed —drawn up. Lay the child on its back, extend the limb as far as possible, then jar the heel by a sharp blow with the hand and it will cause pain in the hip joint. This is a prominent symptom of hip joint disease. Also an attempt to straighten the limb causes the pelvis (hip bone) to tilt forward. This is due to the fact that the pelvis moves with the limb in order to prevent pain. This causes an increase in the curvature in the small of the back, called *Lordosis.* Sharp pressure inward on the hip, or any active movement of the joint, causes severe pain. If pus forms, it may break externally and form what is called abscess of the hip. If the disease continues, the ligaments about the joint are destroyed, also the membrane covering the head of the bone and that lining the socket are both destroyed. The surfaces of the bones are thus brought in direct contact, and gradually they are worn away, both by the disease and by the pressure, and the limb is correspondingly shortened.

In the third stage the head of the bone is destroyed, the large muscles about the hip draw the limb upward upon the outer surface of the pelvis, and the shortening is increased. The limb becomes more flexed—drawn up—and at this time any attempt to straighten it causes the pelvis to tilt forward, as stated. This is Nature's method of preventing pain, which otherwise would be severe.

TREATMENT.—

A. First, absolute rest. Lay the child on his back on a firm mattress. Make extension in order to relieve the pressure in the joint. A weight should be hung from the limb over the foot of the bed. This weight should be from three to eight pounds, depending upon the size of the child. Use a weight as heavy as the child can bear. Make the extension in the direction in which the limb has become flexed—bent—and gradually, from time to time, endeavor to straighten the limb and bring it to its natural position. Splints are needed, but this part of the treatment belongs to a physician. If the case is seen early, extension for three or four weeks may be sufficient. When the patient gets up, wear a high-heeled shoe on the sound limb. This will allow the weight of the diseased limb to aid in producing continuous extension, thus relieving the joints.

Internally, give Iodide of Arsenic three times a day, between meals. Give $\frac{1}{100}$ of a grain at one dose, more or less according to the age of the child. It is understood, of course, that these cases require proper hygienic surroundings, abundance of fresh air and sunshine, most nourishing food, attention to the eliminations, etc.

Another excellent remedy is the following:

> Fellows' Compound Syrup of Hypo-
> phosphites .... 3 ounces.
> Maltine.. 6   "
>
> *Mix* together by shaking the bottle, and take in tablespoonful doses before or immediately after meals.

If the case has become chronic and the joint is destroyed, extension would then be of little value; but seen early, the foregoing treatment would be the most intelligent that could be applied, and in many cases would result favorably.

WHITE SWELLING.—This form of inflammation is always chronic, and occurs only in those previously unhealthy. In more recent years white swelling is understood to mean tuberculosis or consumption. Consumption is a degenerative change which usually occurs in the lungs, but may occur in any other tissue or part. Occurring in a joint, it may first affect the bone, the membrane surrounding the joint, or any other structure entering into the joint formation. The low form of inflammation present first results in an overgrowth of connective tissue; later the new tissue and more or less of the joint structure soften and degenerate, the ligaments become relaxed and softened, and there is deformity in proportion. In some cases a large amount of fluid may collect during the earlier stages; in others there may be early degeneration of some part of the membrane surrounding the joint. This results in an opening which may continue to the surface, forming a sinus, from which later there is a more or less constant discharge of pus. In all cases the joint is swollen, and the skin is thickened and firmly adherent to the deeper structures as a result of the low form of inflammation which has existed for some time. There is no redness because the disease is chronic. Nutrition is more or less lacking, circulation is poor, and the color is lighter than normal, hence the term, white swelling. These conditions when affecting other joints are similar to that described under *Hip Joint Disease*. In these cases there is always more or less danger of general tuberculosis.

TREATMENTS.—

A. The treatment is both general and local. For general treatment, see *Consumption*. The local treatment consists first of rest. Plaster casts and other forms of splints are recommended by some and objected to by others. A common seat of the disease is the knee joint, and here extension is valuable the same as in the treatment of *Hip Joint Disease*. If there is no improvement at the end of one month, most surgeons advise injecting into the joint some form of antiseptic solution, usually a 10 per cent solution of Iodoform in Glycerine. Some advise injecting Balsam of Peru. The Iodoform and Balsam combined make a most excellent disinfectant and local stimulant. In those cases where there is a large collection of fluid, it should be removed by an aspirator.

While the above is the local treatment recommended, we must admit that it often fails to cure, and, in some cases, to afford relief. The real treatment consists in improving the system by attention to diet, elimination, fresh air, etc., as described under *Consumption*. There is always more or less stiffening of the joint in which the disease occurs. The stiffening is the result of the overgrowth and contraction of connective tissue, or the destruction of bone, tendons and ligaments, or of all combined.

B. Make a liniment of the following:

Turpentine	1	ounce.
Tincture Spanish Fly	1	"
Sweet Oil	1	"
Laudanum	1	"

Mix, and bathe the affected part night and morning, rubbing the liniment in well.—(83).

STIFF JOINT, or ANKYLOSIS.—A stiff joint is the result of inflammation followed by overgrowth and contraction of new connective tissue, or by overgrowth of the bone itself. The first lessens joint movement; the second renders the joint immovable.

Cause.—This condition may be the result of rheumatism, sprains, fractures into the joint, or any condition that produces inflammation.

TREATMENTS.—

A. Stiff joint may be benefited, but a cure is doubtful. The treatment consists of massage and an attempt to move the joint. This should be practiced daily, or at least every other day, for a long time—perhaps many weeks. Natural movement of the joint should be obtained as far as possible, never carrying the effort to extremes, or far enough to produce pain. The application of some mild liniment may also be of benefit. For this purpose we recommend the following:

Tincture of Iodine	2	ounces.
Water of Ammonia	2	"

Mix together.

At first this mixture will be dark in color, but in a few hours it will become nearly transparent. The result of the mixture is Iodide of Ammonia. This form of Ammonia is mildly stimulating, while the Iodine is one of the best remedies to liquefy the products of inflammation and render the diseased area free from refuse matter.

It must be remembered, however, that in the majority of these cases the trouble is caused by a deposit of lime salts the same as that of which the bone is formed; in other words, the bones entering into the formation of the joints are more or less solidly united as one bone, hence too much must not be expected. In case of injury to the joint, especially fracture, the condition just described should be anticipated, and passive motion be instituted at the earliest possible moment.

B. Use a liniment made of the following:

Wintergreen Oil............................. 1 drachm.
Olive Oil...................................... 1 ounce.
Aqua Ammonia............................. ½ drachm.
Oil of Lobelia............................... 20 drops.

Shake until it is mixed thoroughly, and bathe the joint just before retiring, sitting so the heat from the stove will strike the joint. If it is very stiff, at least ten minutes should be spent in rubbing it.

THE KIDNEYS AND THEIR DISEASES.

The kidneys are two small glandular organs or bodies situated in the back part of the abdominal cavity. They are enclosed in a thin membrane of connective tissue, which is attached to the surrounding structure and thus holds the organs in position. They are also supported by the arteries and veins which enter and pass through the opening at the pelvis.

Position.—If a long needle should be driven through the body 2½ inches either side the median line—the center of the body—and one inch above the umbilicus—navel—it would graze the lower end of the kidney. The kidneys extend from this point upward and a little inward for a distance of about 4½ inches. Locating them from behind, they would be found 2½ inches either side the center of the body, and covering the last dorsal and four upper lumbar vertebræ—bones which aid in forming the spinal column. Counting from above downward, this means the nineteenth and twenty-third vertebræ, inclusive. Locating them from the side, they extend from the eleventh rib nearly to the highest point of the hip bone. The one on the right side is a little lower than the one on the left, being crowded down by the liver. In size they are about 4½ inches long, 2 inches wide, and 1 inch thick. The flat surfaces face front and back, while the edges face outward and inward.

At the inner border or edge there is an opening called the pelvis. Leading from the pelvis, small tubes penetrate the organ in all directions. These tubes are lined with specialized cells which collect from the passing blood stream those elements that Nature has designed the kidneys to eliminate. Each tube terminates in a bulbous portion called *glomeruli*. The pelvis opens into the ureters and the ureters into the bladder. Really it is all one tube, varying in size and terminating in many small branches. First, the dilated portion, or bladder; next, the ureters, which are about sixteen inches long; then the small dilatation, or pelvis of the kidney; and last, leading from the pelvis, the many small collecting tubes and their branches which terminate in a dilated extremity as stated.

The arteries which supply the kidneys are very large in proportion to the size of the organs. The kidneys are but a bundle of blood vessels and collecting tubes, which from their winding course contain a large amount of blood and fluid. The importance of these organs may be better understood when it is remembered that should their action be suspended for twenty-four to forty-eight hours, death would probably result from the retained poisons.

The kidneys are subject to the following diseases:

Abscess,
Amyloid Degeneration,
Bright's Disease, or Inflammation,
Congestion, or Albuminuria,
Floating and Movable,
Stone or Gravel in,
Hydronephrosis, or distension from
    retained urine.

ABSCESS OF THE KIDNEY.— *Cause.*— An abscess may result from an injury or from a stone in the kidney, or by blocking of the ureter from any cause. Abscess of the kidney may also be caused by blood poisoning.

Symptoms. — The symptoms of abscess of the kidney are sometimes slight so far as pain is concerned, although usually there is pain which extends to the groin. With the beginning of pus formation there may be chills. In those cases which we have seen the most prominent symptoms were the loss of appetite and the general wasting of flesh. The symptoms resemble consumption, with the exception of the cough. They also resemble cancer.

TREATMENT.—

As stated elsewhere, there is but one rule for abscess; wherever pus forms, free incision should be made and thorough drainage established. This requires the services of a physician. Every attention should be paid to the general health.

AMYLOID DEGENERATION.— (See under LIVER, DISEASES OF).

In 1827 Dr. Bright, an English physician, first gave some description of the changes which occur in kidney disease, and as a result it has been the custom with some to apply the term "*Bright's Disease*" to every variety and all forms of kidney trouble. By others the term is restricted to the chronic form, that is, where the disease has progressed far enough to produce structural changes. There are still others who do not use the expression at all, claiming that it is meaningless—that it conveys no intelligent idea—that it cannot, because there are so many forms of kidney disease. Personally, we believe that to call a disease after a man's name is a very foolish habit. However, as the term Bright's disease has become so firmly fixed in the public mind, it is used here.

BRIGHT'S DISEASE—INTERSTICIAL NEPHRITIS—CIRRHOSIS OF THE KIDNEYS.—This disease is always chronic. Like other structures, the kidneys have a connective tissue framework which penetrates the organ in all directions. The low form of inflammation which is present in *Bright's Disease* produces an overgrowth of this framework, which later contracts and destroys the organ. The shrinkage is most marked on the convex or outer portion because it contains the most connective tissue. The first effects of this form of the disease upon the kidneys is upon the secretive cells which line the collecting tubes, because in their efforts to remove from the circulation the irritants which cause the trouble, these cells become overworked. The blood, which is defective, affords poor nourishment, hence the shrinkage of the collecting tubes and their dilated extremities—the glomeruli—is among the earliest changes. Following close upon these changes is the thickening of the arteries and increase of connective tissue. With such increase the capsule, or thin membrane which envelops the kidneys, becomes thickened and firmly adherent to the surface of the organs. The contraction of the new tissue constricts more or less the collecting tubes. Some may be entirely closed. Their distal or outer end may continue to secrete or collect from the passing blood stream, and, there being no escape for the fluid, the little tubes become dilated and thus small cysts or sacs are formed. These may vary in size from a millet seed to a small marble. The contracting fibers close around the glomeruli, or dilated ends of the collecting tubes: Some are pressed together in groups or bunches; some are converted into a solid mass of connective tissue, the delicate blood vessels which filled them during health having been wholly obliterated; others may show a thickening of the connective tissue capsules which enclose them. The glomeruli may contain clotted plasma from the fluid part of the blood, which now somewhat resembles starch. Some may contain pus. Some of the collecting tubes are destroyed. Others are surrounded or embedded in connective tissue overgrowth. These are irregularly dilated, the contracting fibers which surround them having drawn them outward. Some contain dead and dying cells—the secreting cells which lined them. These, having been destroyed or

dislodged by pressure, are in all stages of degeneration. The whole organ becomes shrunken. The cortex or outer portion is nearly obliterated.

Cause.—It may be produced by alcohol or by syphilis; it may follow repeated attacks of congestion; it may be caused by some of the infectious diseases, especially scarlet fever; it may be caused by irritants resulting from dyspepsia and constipation. Under the description of the kidneys it was stated that their blood supply was larger in proportion to their size than that of most organs, and irritants in the blood continually rasping through these structures will sooner or later set up a mild form of inflammation, at first unnoticed. This is why this form of disease comes on so insidiously. The same is true when it is produced by alcohol.

Symptoms.—There are no early symptoms. Perhaps an increased amount of urine is one of the first. During the disease the circulation through the kidneys is interfered with, and so much blood is forced back toward the stomach and heart that the latter beats more forcibly. This causes distension of the blood vessels and interferes with the circulation, causing dizziness, headache and nosebleed; while the congestion about the stomach may cause dyspepsia and perhaps vomiting. An examination of some of these troubles may reveal the real cause— *Bright's Disease.* All of the symptoms mentioned are the result of congestion or over-distension of the blood vessels. Urea is a poisonous waste product which in health is eliminated by the kidneys, but during Bright's disease, and especially toward the latter stages, the kidneys are unable to discharge this duty. The urea collecting in the system may produce uræmic poisoning, resulting in epileptic attacks; hence death is usually preceded by convulsions and coma, due to uræmic poisoning. Dropsy is not present. The urine may contain a small amount of albumen. During the progress of the disease the arteries may become more or less weakened and, as a result of heavy lifting or sudden bending forward, the powerful heart action may rupture a vessel in the brain, causing apoplexy. With care and proper diet the patient may live for many years.

BRIGHT'S DISEASE.—PARENCHYMATOUS NEPHRITIS.—This is another form of chronic kidney disease. In this form of the disease the kidneys, instead of being lessened in size, are enlarged. The enlargement is mostly confined to the outer portion. Under *Intersticial Nephritis* it was stated that this part contains more connective tissue. This tissue forms a loose meshwork which is capable of great distension, hence the enlargement. The enlargement is caused mostly by the exudation of

inflammatory products which pass from the circulation through the walls of the vessels and into the substance of the organs. The kidneys may become twice their natural size. Their surface is smooth, and the capsule or membrane which encloses them is but loosely attached, thus differing from the intersticial form, where it is firmly adherent. The kidneys are light in color. The collecting tubes which penetrate them in all directions are irregularly dilated and are more or less filled with the specialized cells which lined them during health. These are the cells which normally collect the urine and other waste products eliminated by this course. The tubes also contain various other products of inflammation and *debris*. The change within the tubes is more marked than in the intersticial variety. In this disease the urine is scanty and high colored, hence *there is dropsy from the beginning*. As the disease advances the dropsy increases until the abdominal cavity may become enormously distended. Albumen is present throughout the disease.

Cause.—The same as that given under *Intersticial Nephritis*.

Symptoms.—Many of the symptoms are also the same, such as headache, dizziness, loss of appetite, nausea, vomiting, etc. In the following comparative table the more important symptoms are arranged with a view of making them more easily remembered:

Intersticial Nephritis.	Parenchymatous Nephritis.
There is an increased amount of urine.	The amount of urine is lessened.
Albumen may be present in small quantities, and at times may be absent.	Albumen is always present, the amount increasing as the disease progresses.
There is no dropsy.	Dropsy from the beginning, increasing as the disease progresses.
Nosebleed, and may be other hemorrhage. In the later stages there may be hemorrhage from the brain, causing apoplexy. The reason is that the shrunken condition of the kidneys obstructs the circulation and causes congestion.	There is no hemorrhage because the kidneys remain large and the circulation is less interfered with, hence there is no congestion.
The congestion may extend from the brain along the artery that supplies the eyes and cause the latter to look red.	The eyes are not affected.
The disease occurs under forty.	Disease occurs over forty.

TREATMENT.—INTERSTICIAL NEPHRITIS.—

Avoid all alcoholic stimulants and highly seasoned foods. Food should be taken in moderate amounts, and only that which is most easily digested and most nourishing. Avoid all excitement and active exercise. Take life as easy as the circumstances will allow. It will be readily seen that the main object of treatment in this form of disease is to check the connective tissue overgrowth. Perhaps the Iodides in some form are best for this purpose: Iodide of Arsenic in $\frac{1}{50}$ of a grain dose between meals and at bedtime; or if the patient is anæmic, give Iodide of Iron —the same dose taken at the same time. Strict attention should be paid to digestion and elimination. Any article of food interfering with digestion should be discontinued. There may be times when artificial digestants are needed. Basham's Mixture or Tincture of Iron may be given after meals in the same dose as directed under *Parenchymatous Nephritis.* Basham's Mixture should be freshly made in small quantity. Frequent baths are valuable in this as in other diseases. Secure good ventilation and proper hygienic surroundings. This disease runs a chronic course. At the end of two months any form of medication that proves valuable should be discontinued for a time—perhaps two weeks—and then taken up again.

TREATMENTS.—PARENCHYMATOUS NEPHRITIS.—

What to Do.—This disease creeps on stealthily, and is usually well seated before a doctor is consulted. It would be an excellent idea for any person to have the urine tested every two or three years, in which case, if any morbid condition is present it may be discovered in time to reach it by medical aid.

A. The patient should take life easy, resting as much as possible. He should confine himself to a milk diet—one-half to one glass every four hours, taken hot and drank slowly. If other food is allowed, it should consist of a limited amount of fish, toast, apples baked or stewed, spinach, celery, lettuce, tapioca and macaroni.

Avoid tea, coffee, alcohol in any form, and all other stimulants, as they increase the inflammation and lessen the power of the kidneys to eliminate solids, of which urea is the most important because the most dangerous.

It is best to hold strictly to the milk diet until the albumen disappears, and then add only one extra dish at a time, test the urine frequently, and return to the milk diet if albumen re-appears.

Dropsical conditions are best controlled by keeping the bowels active. Cream of Tartar, Salts, Jalap, Elaterium and other active cathartics may be given. Hot baths should also be taken. No remedy or food should be given that causes nausea or interferes with digestion.

B. An excellent remedy, and one we have used with much success, is the following:

> Epsom Salts .... 1 ounce.
> Aromatic Cascara .... 1 "
> Water, add to make .... 1 pint.
> *Dose:* A tablespoonful four times a day, more or less often as needed. The dose should be increased, if necessary, to keep the bowels active.

C. Avoid taking cold. Wear heavy flannel or woolen next to the skin, winter and summer. The kidneys have but little reserve force and a cold might precipitate an acute attack, which would be only too apt to end fatally. Keep good ventilation, and improve the surroundings with proper hygienic measures.—(65).

D. Any one who has Bright's disease should have the care of a good physician, so as to meet symptoms as they appear.

I use Alkalithia, one bottle. Take a teaspoonful before each meal in water, drink while effervescing, and take a dessertspoonful after each meal of Basham's Mixture.

E. Avoid taking cold. Wear flannel next the skin, which should be kept clean and moist. Internal medication too serious for any one but a doctor to undertake.—(14).

F. Dress in flannel all the year around. Avoid catching cold or sudden chilling of surface. Drink lots of water and milk. Avoid all alcoholics, especially sour wine. Follow doctor's directions and the disease may be controlled for years.—(13).

G. Hot baths, frequently repeated. Warm flannel clothing. Milk diet, avoiding all stimulants. Tincture of Iron in 20-drop doses, well diluted, after meals and at bedtime.—(7).

CONGESTION, or ALBUMINURIA.— Albumen is an element of nutrition resulting from food products. The best example of albumen, or its purest form, may be found in the white of an egg. Albumen is always present in the blood, but in health the kidneys do not permit its passage into the urine. *Albuminuria* is a term used when there is albumen present in the urine, its presence indicating disease, which may be either mild or serious. A mild form results from taking cold or from injury. This form is called *Congestion* and usually does not last long, the kidneys soon returning to a normal condition. Occurring in a chronic form, albuminuria is known as Bright's disease. See BRIGHT'S DISEASE.

Symptoms.—In mild cases the symptoms may escape notice altogether. In a more acute stage the symptoms are as follows: Pain in the back and region of the kidneys, which may be mild or severe in proportion to the amount of congestion; fever is present, the bowels are more or less constipated, and the urine is high-colored. Occurring with or following the infectious diseases of children, the above symptoms are usually absent, and when the child returns to health the kidneys return to a normal condition.

It is taught that there are exceptional cases where albuminuria is a natural condition, that is, where albumen is constantly present in the urine without disease. The amount in such cases is small.

TREATMENTS.—

A. For a severe case, rest in bed, with hot fomentations to the small of the back and across the abdomen; active cathartics; milk diet from 24 to 48 hours, depending upon the severity of the case; if the fever is high, Aconite or other such remedies. The patient should keep quiet a few days until the pain has ceased, and the fever, soreness and other troubles have disappeared.

B. Take the silk from the ears of corn when they are first silking out, and also peach tree leaves. Put these in an earthen dish and steep as you would tea. Strain and take a tablespoonful 3 to 5 times a day. If it is not the season of the year that you can obtain the above, the following is good: Take the meats of pumpkin seeds, steep same as tea, and drink freely. Also take the inner bark of slippery elm and the inner bark of white pine, cut up into short pieces, put into a bowl, cover with water and let it stand until it is of the thickness of mucilage. Drink freely of this also. Keep the patient quiet. Give an active cathartic, and keep the bowels moving.

MOVABLE and FLOATING KIDNEY.—Some very fine theories are advanced regarding the symptoms between these two conditions. They are of little value because the same evidence is not present in all cases; in fact, in some cases there may be no evidence or symptoms at all. We know this to be true, because in trying to diagnose some of these cases we have witnessed the defeat of some noted surgeons. When the kidney wanders from its normal position and becomes fixed in some other part, it is called *dislocation*.

Cause of Movable and Floating Kidney.—Movable kidney may be caused by injury, may be due to pregnancy, to tight lacing, or may occur during some chronic or wasting disease. In the last case the tissues surrounding the kidneys may become so shrunken and wasted that the kidney may be easily displaced. Wandering kidney is always congenital.

Symptoms.—The symptoms of wandering kidney may be slight or severe. In some cases, as stated, there may be no symptoms at all. There is generally pain in the region of the kidney. This pain has a dull, dragging sensation. Sometimes, however, it is so sharp that it resembles *Renal Colic*—the pain caused by stone in the kidneys. In sitting or lying down the kidney may regain its normal position, when all of the symptoms will disappear. There may be indigestion and vomiting, also some disturbance of the heart action, as palpitation. In some cases the kidney may feel like a tumor in the abdominal cavity.

We have seen cases where the only evidence was that discovered by the patient. We recall one case of this kind in particular. The patient, a lady, being convinced that something was wrong and evidently knowing that the trouble might be caused by a misplaced kidney, tried at various times to discover the presence of the wandering organ. She continued the effort until she became so accustomed to the manner of manipulation that she was able to locate the kidney, which presented itself in the form of a small tumor in the abdominal cavity. On the strength of her own diagnosis she was advised to have an operation, and consented. Both before and after she was under the influence of Chloroform the surgeons made every effort to locate the kidney, but although she was not large, weighing only about 125 pounds, they were unable to do so. Upon operation, however, the kidney was found some distance from its natural position, was brought back and stitched in place, the patient recovered, and to-day is well.

TREATMENT.—

A tight band with a pad is said to benefit some cases, and should always be recommended before advising an operation. If this and other means fail, and the pain is severe, an operation should be made. The kidney should never be removed unless badly diseased. In this case the other kidney should be examined also, because it too might be diseased, in which case the operation would precipitate rapid death.

GRAVEL, or STONE, IN.—Gravel is a term frequently applied to small particles of solid matter found in the urine. These are uric acid crystals, which are found in the blood as the result of imperfect oxidation and are eliminated by the kidneys; or the uric acid may unite with certain salts held in solution in the blood and form what are called *urates*. The terms "gravel," "brick dust" and "sediment" are frequently applied to these deposits. These conditions are the result of excessive accumulations of uric acid in the circulation. Certain food elements produce uric acid. During health this acid unites with oxygen from the air we breathe, is changed into urea and eliminated by the kidneys; but from overeating, indigestion, constipation, lack of exercise, indoor life, bad hygiene or some other cause, this change does not take place, hence the accumulation of uric acid, as stated. This accumulation calls for extra work on the part of the kidneys, and they do what they can to relieve the trouble, hence the appearance of the urates in the urine. Many believe this condition is an indication of kidney disease, but it is not. It is the kind of kidney disease that patent medicine fakirs cure.

Sometimes this uric acid sediment in the urine assumes large proportions, forming a solid mass or stone. The stone gradually increases in size until it becomes dislodged and attempts to pass through the ureter. Stone may form from a lack of acid, or when the urine contains too much alkali. In these cases the stone is formed of phosphates.

Cause.—As above described, *i. e.*, the deposit of uric acid, or of phosphates and other sediment present in the urine.

Symptoms.—When in the form of gravel, the particles are small and readily pass into the bladder, and there may be no symptoms; or the symptoms may be a slight irritation. If a stone forms in the pelvis of the kidney, it may become quite large without producing any serious symptoms; but when a stone becomes dislodged and attempts to enter the ureter, the symptoms begin suddenly. The pain is severe, at times agonizing, and extends into the groin and thigh of the affected side. There is a frequent desire to urinate, and the urine contains more or less blood in proportion to the number of vessels ruptured by the stone. The testicle on the affected side is contracted, nausea is usually present, vomiting may occur, and the patient may collapse or become unconscious. The pain continues until the stone drops into the bladder, when it ceases as suddenly as it began. Or the stone may drop back into the pelvis of the kidney.

TREATMENTS.—

A. In treating stone in the kidney or bladder the general health must be considered. It has already been stated that uric acid is due to imperfect oxidation, or indigestion, hence the need of careful attention to diet, the digestive organs and elimination. Drink large quantities of pure water, secure an abundance of fresh air, sunshine and out-of-door exercise. Bathe frequently, observe regular habits and avoid all forms of excess.

Uric Acid Deposit.—If the urine is highly acid, it is evidence that the stone is formed of uric acid, as described, and the treatment in such cases would be alkalies in some form as these would tend to neutralize the acid and prevent formation. Liquor of Potash in 5-drop doses, well diluted with water, taken before meals and at bedtime, may be given; or 20-grain doses of Acetate of Potash in solution may be given every two or three hours until the urine is but faintly acid, and then smaller doses—perhaps 10 grains—should be continued several times a day.

Note.—All druggists keep small sheets of litmus paper—red and blue. Acid urine will change the blue paper to red, and alkaline urine will change the red paper to blue.

Alkaline Deposit.—If the urine is alkaline (see note above), it may be suspected that the stone is formed of phosphates; in such cases the mineral acids would be of benefit because they would render the urine acid. Two or 3 drops of pure Muriatic Acid, well diluted with water, should be taken after meals; or Benzoic Acid in the form of Benzoate of Soda should be given in 10-grain doses after meals and at bedtime. Enough of either should be given to keep the urine acid.

If a stone has formed and attempts to pass through the ureter, the treatment given above would have no effect on the pain and would be of no benefit at that time. For such attacks the Glonoin, Hyoscyamine and Strychnine treatment under GALL-STONES would be applicable. If this treatment does not relieve the pain, Morphine should be given. If a stone lodges in the ureter and all other means fail, an operation will be called for.

B. The best remedy that can be used for this is Gravel Weed (See chapter on HERBS for description and directions), unless the disease has progressed so far that a surgeon's attention is required.

C. Alkalithia. *Dose :* — Heaping teaspoonful in glass of water before meals and at bedtime.—(10).

D. Drink only soft water, or water which has been boiled. —(8).

E. Fluid Extract of Buchu in teaspoonful doses three or four times a day.—(7).

F. A large enema of hot water, retained as long as possible, gives more relief than Morphine in case of renal calculus—stone in the kidney or bladder.

HYDRONEPHROSIS.—Should a large stone remain in the kidney, it might prevent the passage of urine into the ureters. This would cause *Hydronephrosis*, meaning too much water in the kidney. Following this, abscess might result. It might result from any obstruction to the outflow from the bladder. This in turn would check the outflow from the kidney, and the result would be the same.

TREATMENT.—

Removal of the obstruction, if possible.

KING'S EVIL—SCROFULA.—This is a morbid constitutional condition developing in the glands and forming small, hard tumors. The glands of the neck are the most usual seat of the disease; or it may affect the lungs, as in consumption. At one time it was called *King's Evil*, as it was believed it could be cured by the touch of the king's hand. To-day we call it *Scrofula*.

LA GRIPPE.—(See INFLUENZA).

LARYNGITIS.—The Larynx is that part of the throat extending from the base of the tongue to the trachea, or windpipe. Laryngitis is understood to mean an acute inflammation of the larynx.

Cause.—The same cause that produces ordinary catarrhal colds, as atmospheric changes, exposure, draughts, wet feet, irritating vapors or dust.

Symptoms.—A slight irritation may be the only symptom, or there may be rawness and soreness. The voice may become hoarse, and there may be fever and headache. If the case is severer, there will be a sharp rise in temperature, coated tongue, dry skin, quick, strong pulse and badly swollen throat.

TREATMENTS.—

A. Give a dose of Castor Oil or other laxative, hot footbath, and wet pack about the neck—hot or cold, as desired by the patient. If the fever is very high, give 1-drop doses of Aconite every thirty minutes, or every hour. Small children require less. Keep a uniform temperature in the room—75 to 80 degrees—and at the same time provide good ventilation.

The following mixture is recommended:

Fluid Extract of Ipecac......... 10 drops.
Tincture of Aconite............... 10 "
Water .... 24 teaspoonfuls.

Mix, and give 1 teaspoonful every fifteen or thirty minutes, or less often, according to age.

or,

Tincture of Aconite..................... .. 10 drops.
Acetate of Potash .... 3 drachms.
Liquor Ammonia Acetatis............... 4 ounces.

Mix, and give 1 teaspoonful to 1 tablespoonful every fifteen or thirty minutes, or less often, according to age. When the surface becomes moist, either of the above may be discontinued.

The patient should diet for a day or two, guard against taking any more cold, and, with attention to the bowels, will usually recover rapidly.

B. For a mild case, slight counter-irritation over the throat is useful, and on going to bed the patient should apply to the throat a towel wrung out of cold water. If the case is more severe, apply a Mustard poultice over the part, followed by a hot fomentation of Hops covered with a dry flannel. For adults, tablespoonful doses of Boneset syrup may be given.

C. Laryngitis or inflammation of the throat should be treated the same as inflammation elsewhere. Counter-irritants and hot fomentations relieve by attracting the blood away from the inflamed part. Aconite and other fever remedies act in the same way, hence they may also be used in laryngitis. A gargle is often of value in this disease. The following prescription may be relied upon:

Salicylate of Soda....................... 2 drachms.
Powdered Borax.......................... ½   "
Carbolic Acid............................. 5 drops.
Glycerine .... 1 drachm.
Water sufficient to make.............. 4 ounces.

Mix, and gargle the throat every 2 hours, more or less often as needed.

D. Absolute rest of organs of voice. Inhale the following:

Compound Tincture of Benzoin........ 1 ounce.
Hot Water..................................... .. 1 pint.

And give a good Calomel purge—for an adult from 5 to 10 grains of Calomel; for a child one year old, 1 grain; the dose, if without results, to be repeated the following morning in connection with Castor Oil—from 1 to 2 teaspoonfuls of the Oil for a child; from 1 to 2 tablespoonfuls for an adult.—(45).

Note.—In giving Castor Oil, if the spoon be first dipped in sweet milk the oil will not adhere to it and is more easily swallowed.

E. Pure Bromine—Put 5 drops into a glass of cold water. Give one teaspoonful every half hour or even fifteen minutes until relieved, and *it will do it.*—(18).—Homeopathic.

Note.—As this remedy can only be obtained at drug stores, and is very volatile and difficult to handle, we suggest that the solution be made at the same time the Bromine is purchased. Ask the druggist to put 5 drops of pure Bromine into a 12-ounce bottle and fill with water.

LARYNX, OEDEMA OF.—The *glottis* is the narrow space between the vocal chords through which the air passes into the lungs. When there is swelling of the tissues immediately surrounding the glottis, it is called *Oedema of the Larynx.* It is a very dangerous disease, and usually fatal. The patient may live for a few days, or a week, or may live only a few hours. It is not a common disease.

Cause.—It is most frequently met in those who are poorly nourished and in poor hygienic surroundings. It may follow inflammation of the throat, inflammation or disease of the tonsils, erysipelas of the face, diphtheria, Bright's disease, whooping cough, tuberculosis of the throat, syphilis, aneurism, or wounds of the neck.

Symptoms.—There is a gradually increasing difficulty in breathing; there is swelling of the epiglottis, or thin layer of cartilage that guards the opening into the trachæa during the act of swallowing; there may be a sensation of a foreign body in the throat; the voice gradually grows weaker, and is finally lost; there is difficulty in swallowing, and as the disease advances there is some cough with but little expectoration; breathing becomes more difficult, the eyes protrude, the face assumes a purplish hue and, if relief is not had at once, death follows, the patient dying from asphyxia—want of air.

TREATMENT.—

The treatment consists in means that will draw the blood from the affected parts, hence an active cathartic, such as 10 grains of Jalop and 10 grains of Scammony, or ½ grain of Elaterium, should be given. If there is a history of constipation and if the bowels seem bloated, give 3 drops of Croton Oil added to a little Glycerine. Place it on the back part of the tongue, or put it into a capsule and let the patient swallow it. Give $\frac{1}{250}$ grain of Atropine every thirty minutes until the face is flushed. Sweating the patient will also aid in relieving the throat. One-third of a grain of Pilocarpine, given with a hypodermic needle, is valuable in relieving the congestion. It is also depressing and, if given, stimulants should also be given to support the patient. If other means fail, perform tracheotomy, that is, make an opening into the windpipe. This disease is always dangerous and requires the best skill and care. Fresh air is of the greatest importance. The disease just described differs from *spasm of the glottis*, or muscles which control the vocal chords, commonly called *Croup.* Simple spasm may result from nervous conditions—hysteria. Croup and simple spasm may be relieved by any remedies that are relaxing, such as Opium, Chloral or Ipecac. Fresh air is also of importance. Do not give Opium to small children, but Ipecac is perfectly safe.

LEAD POISONING.—This disease is experienced by house painters and those engaged in the manufacture of paints. The lead gains entrance into the system through the lungs and skin. Some people seem to be proof against it and to experience no evil effects after many years of exposure, while others acquire the disease very easily.

1. It is wide-spread among painters and plumbers, and those engaged in smelting lead ores.

2. Those engaged in white lead factories are particularly subject to this disease.

3. It may be accidentally acquired from drinking water from lead pipes or cisterns.

Symptoms.—The appearance of poisoning comes on gradually, the patient suffering from languor, impaired appetite, belching of wind, obstinate costiveness or dysentery and other symptoms for some time before the disease itself becomes manifest. One of the principal characteristics of the disease is a colic, which is essentially the same as the ordinary colic excepting that the pain may be more severe and may not entirely stop as in other forms.

If exposure to the poisoning influence continues, serious nervous phenomena come on—usually a palsy which affects the nerves governing the muscles of the fore-arm, giving rise to the condition known as *wrist-drop*, wherein the hand hangs from the wrist and cannot be raised voluntarily. This paralysis gradually extends to the nerves of other muscles, and while it continues the muscles affected also undergo atrophy—shrinking. This shrinking follows paralysis because nourishment is lacking and in consequence the tissues waste. Another valuable symptom, which, however, is not always present, is the existence of a blue line along the margin of the gums where they meet the teeth. This line about the gums does not usually make its appearance until the poisoning is in an advanced state.

TREATMENTS.—

A. Take 5 grains of Iodide of Potassium, dissolved in one tablespoonful of hot water, three times a day—between meals and at bedtime.

Also take, early in the morning and at bedtime, 10 drops of Dilute or Aromatic Sulphuric Acid in a wine glass half full of water.

Keep the bowels open with Epsom Salts in teaspoonful doses. Dissolve in a wine glass half full of warm water and take from one to three times a day as the case requires.

Take a warm bath every day. For this add one teaspoonful of Sal Ammoniac to warm water, and after the bath dry thoroughly with a crash towel.

B. Live largely on milk, and take the following:

Iodide Potassium .... 3 drachms.
Water... 4 ounces.
Dose.—Teaspoonful in glass of water between meals and at bedtime.—(10).

C. Laxative of Epsom Salts. Also Iodide of Potash, 10 grains in water three times daily—between meals and at bedtime.—(11).

D. Painters should drink lemonade daily to which is added 10 drops dilute Sulphuric Acid. This amount of Acid may be taken four times a day. Best taken after meals. When colic occurs, take physic of Salts.—(38).

E. Epsom Salts in doses of 2 tablespoonfuls with 10 drops of Laudanum every three hours. After relief use 5 grains of Iodide of Potash every three hours.—(36).

LEPROSY.—(See under SKIN DISEASES).

LEUCÆMIA—Sometimes called WHITE BLOOD, or ANÆMIA.—This is a disease in which there is an enormous increase in the white blood corpuscles and a diminution in the red ones. The spleen and other lymphatics are greatly enlarged.

Cause.—Unknown.

Symptoms. — There are no early symptoms. There is first *Anæmia* with enlargement of the abdomen, giving a sense of fullness. There are pains in the left side, due to the enlargement of the spleen which is situated on that side. The other glands throughout the body are also more or less enlarged. The patient grows pale and loses his appetite. There is usually diarrhea, also a gradual loss of strength, palpitation of the heart, difficult breathing and swelling of the ankles. The urine is scanty, and there are deep pains—pains in the bones, which are also sensitive to pressure. The blood becomes so light that it looks almost like milk. The spleen may become so large as to nearly fill the whole abdominal cavity. The spleen enlarges more than the other glands because its blood supply is proportionately larger, also because the blood vessels are not continued through the organ as through other structures, the circulation being continued through openings that are channeled through the spleen itself. This brings the irritating blood in direct contact with the spleenic tissue. The liver is enormously enlarged, one reason being that the veins of the spleen empty into the liver. Pressure from the spleen and liver interferes with the lung space, and thus renders breathing difficult. This also accounts for palpitation of the heart. With the loss of lung and heart power the patient is gradually weakened. Loss of strength is also partially due to a lack of nourishment.

TREATMENTS.—

A. These cases may live from one to two years. There is no known treatment that is of benefit. Make the patient as comfortable as possible in the matter of food, bathing, hygiene, pleasant surroundings, etc.

B. Put 2 drachms of Muriate Tincture of Iron into 6 ounces of Simple Syrup and take a teaspoonful three times a day after meals.

Take a small handful of each of the following:—Wild Cherry Bark, Prickly Ash Bark, Burdock Root, Narrow-leaf Dock. Boil to make a decoction and take a tablespoonful four or five times a day.

LEUCORRHEA.—(See under DISEASES OF WOMEN).

LIVER.

The liver, which is of a dark reddish color, is the largest gland in the body. Its weight is from three to four pounds.

Position.—It is situated high up on the right side close to the diaphragm. The diaphragm is a thin membrane which divides the abdominal from the chest cavity. The lower border of the liver corresponds to the lower border of the ribs in front and on the right side. In size the liver is about 12 inches from side to side and 6 or 7 inches from before backward. Its thickness from above downward is 3 inches in the median line, or center of the body, 4 inches on a vertical line corresponding to the right nipple, 4½ inches in the median line on the right side, and 4 inches behind at a point corresponding to the junction of the ninth rib with the spinal column. The upper surface of the liver is round where it lies in contact with the diaphragm; the under surface is hollow where it lies in contact with the stomach and right kidney. There is a large fissure in the under surface which divides the liver into two lobes, right and left. The right is much the larger. The left extends for a distance of two or three inches to the left of the center of the body. It should be remembered that the position of the liver changes with the position of the body.

The liver is composed of small lobules held together by a connective tissue framework. The lobules are about as large as a millet seed. The return circulation from the lower extremities and lower half of the body passes through the liver. This circulation enters the liver through a large vein called the *portal vein*. Upon entering the liver this vein divides and sub-divides into many minute branches, and these branches terminate in and around the little lobules. The lobules are hollow, with an opening in the bottom of each. Through this opening the return circulation is continued. The cavity in the little lobules is the beginning of what is called the *hepatic vein*. As the blood passes out through the openings the delicate channels unite and re-unite until all are joined, forming the hepatic vein, which leaves the liver and enters the ascending *vena cava*, a large vein which leads directly to the heart. It will be seen that the portal vein terminates in the lobules and the hepatic vein commences in them. The artery which supplies the liver with nourishment also breaks up into many minute branches, and these branches terminate in and around the little lobules, the same as the branches of the veins. The lobules also contain nerve fibers and lymphatics, so that, strictly speaking, each lobule is an independent gland by itself. The bile ducts commence in minute channels between the lobules and also in the clefts or minute spaces between the cells of which the lobules are formed. They join together, forming what is called the hepatic ducts—two in number, one from each lobe. These are about 1½ inches in length.

The *gall bladder* is a pear-shaped membranous sac, about 4 inches in length and 1 inch in breadth, and holds a little over one ounce. It is situated on the right side under the ninth rib near the chest bone. It is a reservoir for the bile. The duct leading from it is about one inch in length and joins the hepatic ducts, or those leading from the liver; together they form the common duct, and this enters the bowel about 3½ inches below the stomach. The liver cells manufacture bile, and convert glucose, or grape sugar, into a substance called *glycogen*. This is stored up by the liver cells and given to the circulation as fast as the system needs it. The glycogen readily unites with the oxygen in the circulation and aids in producing heat. The return circulation brings the blood directly from the digestive organs, hence the liver aids in producing important digestive changes that are carried on in the circulation.

The liver is subject to the following diseases:

Abscess,
Amyloid Degeneration,
Atrophy, Acute Yellow,
Congestion,
Cirrhosis, or Gin-Drinker s Liver.

ABSCESS OF THE LIVER.—*Cause.*—Abscess of the liver is caused by an unhealthy condition of the digestive tract. The veins from this tract—stomach, spleen, bowels, etc.—unite to form the portal vein. This enters the liver and breaks up into many small vessels which penetrate all parts of the organ. As they pass out they unite to form the hepatic vein which enters the ascending vena cava (see description of liver). It will readily be seen that the liver is subject to the morbid effects of indigestion as the poisons developed in the bowels are carried direct to the liver. Inflammation is the result. This lessens the amount of bile, the absence of which interferes with digestion and elimination still more, in turn more poisons are poured into the liver, and thus the abscess grows.

Symptoms.—Disturbance of digestion, poor appetite and fever, followed by vomiting and irritability, and, as the disease advances, by debility and perhaps melancholia. Later there are typhoid symptoms as a result of the unhealthy condition of the bowels. Jaundice, or yellow discoloration of the skin, is slight, as the amount of bile manufactured by the liver is lessened in proportion to the advancement of the abscess. The liver is enlarged and, as the abscess grows, the soreness in the right side increases. If the abscess breaks externally, as it nears the surface the tenderness is increased. Later, swelling and fluctuation can be detected. Abscess of the liver may break into the chest cavity and may penetrate the delicate membrane which surrounds the lungs. In this case it would communicate with the bronchial tubes and be expectorated. It may break into the stomach, into the bowels or into the abdominal cavity. Following any of these last mentioned results the external evidence would be less prominent. The situation may be more readily understood when we remember that the liver is placed in contact with each of the cavities and organs mentioned, and, as a result of inflammatory adhesions to the surfaces of any of these, destruction of tissue might follow with some one of the results mentioned.

TREATMENTS.—

A. There is one rule which has no exception, and that is, wherever pus is located, the abscess should be opened at once. This is as true with abscess of the liver as though it were located anywhere else. The treatment consists mainly in supporting measures, hygiene, food and attention to the bowels. If the fever is very high, a small dose of Aconite may be given for a limited time, say 1 drop of the tincture every hour. Internally, give 10 grains of Salol three times a day, increasing the amount if the eliminations give offensive odor. If dyspepsia is troublesome, give artificial digestants for a time, as:

Pepsin (1 to 3.000).....................	2 drachms.
Fowler's Solution.....................	2 "
Muriatic Acid (pure).................	20 drops.
Glycerine	1 ounce.
Water.	2 '

Mix all together and take one teaspoonful after meals.

Give one teaspoonful of Bovinine in half a glass of hot milk with each meal. If the patient can take it, increase the amount of Bovinine (which is exceedingly nutritious) to one tablespoonful at each meal. Every attention should be paid to a nourishing diet. Also give $\frac{1}{50}$ of a grain of Iodide of Arsenic between meals.

B. 3-grain doses of Quinine every four hours. In nearly all cases it is necessary to maintain strength by a most nutritious diet. Egg-nog may be taken at meal time, or an equal time between meals so as not to disturb the stomach by too frequent and injudicious feeding. Wine whey is nourishing, and milk and lime water have a most excellent effect on the stomach, maintaining a healthy condition. Stimulants are likely to be needed. If there should be severe pain at any time, a little Morphine may be given, say ⅛ grain combined with the Quinine.

AMYLOID DEGENERATION.—Amyloid degeneration is a term applied where the tissues of an organ present a starchy or albuminous appearance. Such degeneration usually affects the liver and kidneys, but may affect other organs.

Cause.—Amyloid degeneration is not a primary disease in the organ affected, but is the result of infiltration from without; that is, it is an evidence of chronic disease or suppuration in some other part of the body. It may result from inflammation and suppuration of bone, from syphilis, from tuberculosis, and possibly from cancer. These diseases rob the blood of the normal amount of alkaline salts, and also lessen its amount of fibrine, and amyloid degeneration found in the liver or kidneys is the result of some of these diseases. The absence of the normal amount of salts or fibrine in the blood gives to these organs the starchy or waxy appearance which characterizes the disease. Degeneration of the liver usually occurs first, and degeneration of the kidneys secondarily.

Symptoms.—When occurring in the liver, that organ becomes enlarged, and later the kidneys also become enlarged. There is no pain, but some increase in the amount of urine; the urine contains albumen. There are disorders of digestion and, later, diarrhea from similar degenerative changes in the digestive tract. There is also a general wasting of the flesh. There is but little or no jaundice for the reason that the bile ducts of the liver remain open, and for the still greater reason that there is but little bile manufactured, the amount diminishing as the disease progresses. Amyloid degeneration does not obstruct the portal (return) circulation, hence there is no abdominal dropsy. When the kidneys are involved, abdominal dropsy may be present, because the kidneys, first enlarged, afterwards become shrunken, interfering with the circulation. As the disease progresses the liver also shrinks from the same cause.

TREATMENTS.—

A. If there is a history of syphilis, give anti-syphilitic remedies. If it is the result of suppuration in bone, it calls for an operation. The bone should be thoroughly scraped and all the dead tissue removed. If the result of consumption, see the treatment under that head. In all cases there should be attention to digestion, ventilation, proper exercise, clothing, etc. If due to suppuration in bone or to consumption, early treatment would probably prove successful. If the disease is well developed, there is but little hope.

B. The primary cause should be ascertained and, if possible, relieved. The following alterative treatment is recommended:

Take a small handful each of Wild Cherry bark, Prickly Ash bark, Dandelion root and Culver's root, steep to make a decoction, sweeten with rock candy if desired, and drink freely. Wear warm clothing and apply counter-irritants, such as Mustard plasters, etc., over the liver. Bathe in hot water in which has been put a little salt and Muriate of Ammonia and a tablespoonful of Mustard, mixed well with the water before bathing.

ACUTE YELLOW ATROPHY — MALIGNANT JAUNDICE.

—This is a disease of the liver resulting in rapid destruction of that organ. The disease runs a rapid course—the patient is jaundiced. Duration, a week or ten days; termination, death.

Cause.—While there is no cause given for this disease, we believe that it is caused by the retention of poisons in the system. The vitality of the patient may hold out until the system is so thoroughly overcome that collapse and rapid death are the result;

and we think the condition of the patient supports this view. It is not the liver alone that is affected; we believe the primary cause to be in the digestive tract. The return circulation from the digestive organs goes direct to the liver. The large vein which carries the venous blood divides on reaching the liver, and subdivides into minute branches which penetrate all parts of the organ, and thus the poison is brought into direct relation with the whole structure; hence it is not strange that it may be so overcome by the morbid influence of septic blood as to pass through the rapid degenerative changes mentioned. With the increase in the liver trouble, the circulation is checked. This increases the congestion of the stomach and bowels, hence the vomiting of blood which may occur in this disease. In health the return circulation from the spleen passes through the liver. During the progress of the disease the circulation is checked and the poisoned blood is dammed back, hence enlargement of the spleen occurs.

Symptoms.—The first symptom is the catarrhal condition of the stomach and bowels; the tongue is badly coated, there is headache, vomiting and nausea, quick pulse and a little fever. The jaundice rapidly increases, the spleen becomes enlarged, the urine contains bile and albumen, and a lessened amount of urea is eliminated. Nausea is followed by vomiting of blood dark in color, showing the congestion of the stomach; the eliminations from the bowels show the desperate state of disease in the digestive tract; yet the return circulation carries the poisons from both stomach and bowels and empties them into the liver. This supports our belief that disease of the liver is secondary. The liver degenerates rapidly. Its structures break down and it becomes very small.

TREATMENT.—

Medical works contain no treatment of this disease excepting symptomatic, *i. e.*, make the patient as comfortable as possible by treating the symptoms. We wish, however, to recommend the treatment given for *Hydrophobia*. If there is anything that will help in this disease, it is thorough and *early* elimination. Stimulants should be added as the case requires. We would also recommend the addition of $\frac{1}{10}$ of a grain of Calomel every half hour for ten doses, then every hour for ten doses; also the most nourishing food to be given at frequent intervals. For the vomiting, a large Mustard plaster should be placed over the stomach, and equal parts of milk and lime water given frequently in small quantities. Crust or corn coffee is also excellent in case of vomiting, and may be readily prepared.

CONGESTION OF THE LIVER—BILIOUSNESS —"LIVER COMPLAINT."

—"LIVER COMPLAINT."— In this disease the vessels of the liver contain too much blood and the organ may be slightly enlarged on this account. There is a sense of fullness on the right side, and there may be a feeling of soreness.

Cause.—It may be caused by the liberal use of alcohol. The most frequent cause is indigestion and constipation. It is also supposed to be influenced by taking cold.

Symptoms.—The symptoms depend upon the amount of congestion. If slight, the symptoms are slight; if the congestion reaches the point of inflammation, the symptoms are severer. In a mild case of congestion there may be headache and a dull feeling, there may be fever, the patient may experience slight pains throughout the system, the tongue may be coated and the appetite interfered with; an increase of this trouble would constitute catarrhal jaundice. There is no strictly dividing line between the two. In severer cases, in addition to the symptoms given there would be nausea, vomiting, pain in the right side, and the skin and white of the eye would show a yellowish tinge. There would also be pain in the right shoulder. The last symptom belongs to catarrhal jaundice, and would not be met with in a simple case of *Biliousness*, or *Congestion of the Liver.*

TREATMENTS.—

A. Give an active cathartic. Castor Oil or Salts may be used, but we believe in these cases that 5 to 10 grains of Calomel should be given at night, followed the next morning by a tablespoonful of Castor Oil or Salts. Seidlitz Salts (see *Index*) may be used instead of the Epsom or Rochelle Salts. The patient should diet for two or three days and, if the action of the liver is sluggish and there is a tendency to constipation, should continue the Seidlitz Salts in one or two teaspoonful doses every morning; or take one teaspoonful of Phosphate of Soda in half a glass of water one hour before meals, more or less as needed. Phosphate of Soda is not so pleasant to take as the Seidlitz, and it is not so effectual in its action in the digestive tract, but it is a better liver stimulant. With ordinary care these cases recover in a few days, and usually a doctor is not needed.

B. Apply a Mustard plaster over the region of the liver. Make a syrup of Wild Cherry and Prickly Ash bark and give tablespoonful doses four or five times a day. If the case is persistent—if there is jaundice, digestive disturbances, pain, soreness and enlargement on the right side, keep the bowels active and give proper attention to diet. If there is fever, give 1 or 2-drop doses of Tincture of Aconite or Fluid Extract of Veratrum every two hours.   If the evidence of abscess continues, apply large hot poultices to hasten its formation, and open early.

C. *Bilious Tonic.*—

Oil of Wintergreen	1	teaspoonful.
Oil of Peppermint	5	drops.
Oil of Lemon	15	"
Alcohol	½	pint.
Water	½	"
Sulphuric Acid	30	drops.

Mix well, and add the following:

Red Peruvian Bark, finely pulverized	2	ounces.
Rhubarb Root, finely pulverized	1	ounce.
Simple Syrup, or Molasses, enough to make all together	1	quart.

Those who are acted upon easily by cathartics cannot bear more than half this quantity of Rhubarb. Let such have it made accordingly.   The object of its use is to keep the bowels just solvent, not loose like diarrhea.

The oils and acid should be put into the Alcohol first, then the water, and afterwards the bark and Rhubarb. Allow to stand for ten days, shaking the bottle two or three times each day; then strain carefully through muslin, or filter through filtering paper, which may be obtained at any drug store, and add the syrup or molasses.

Dose.—For an adult 1 to 2 teaspoonfuls four times daily, at meals and bedtime; for a child of twelve years, half this dose. If very bilious and costive, take a full cathartic dose of Rhubarb, or such other cathartic medicine as you are in the habit of using, to move the bowels freely.

This will be found a valuable tonic in all cases requiring one. Especially recommended as a spring tonic. Also valuable in agues and remittent fevers. Repeat at intervals of a week, two or three times if needed.   In nearly every case a permanent cure will be effected if the medicine is taken three or four days at each repetition.

D. Sulphate of Quinine	1	drachm.
Syrup of Rhubarb	4	ounces.
Simple Elixir, enough to make	8	"

Dissolve the Quinine in the Elixir and add the Rhubarb.

This preparation is needed only when there is constipation present.

Dose.—The average dose would be a teaspoonful two or three times a day. Enough must be taken to cause normal evacuation —at least one movement of the bowels every day. It will be necessary for each one to gauge the dose according to his individual needs.

CIRRHOSIS OF THE LIVER—GIN DRINKER'S LIVER—CHRONIC INFLAMMATION.

—As stated in the description of the liver, the organ is formed of many little lobules held together by a framework of connective tissue. This disease consists in an overgrowth of this framework, which later shrinks and destroys the organ. As stated under ALCOHOL, connective tissue resulting from inflammation always shrinks. During the early stages there is congestion, and later there is a low form of inflammation. This, with the increased growth of the connective tissue, causes the liver to enlarge. The edges of the organ are rounded, smooth and thickened. The cells of which the organ is formed may also be swollen and contain more or less fat. With the increase in the connective tissue new blood vessels form. These are derived from the artery which supplies the liver. If a cut surface of the liver could be examined at this time, connective tissue overgrowth would be visible to the naked eye. The remaining lobules of which the liver is formed would so contrast with the new tissue as to present a granular appearance. Jaundice is usually slight, as the bile capillaries, or channels through which the bile flows, are interfered with but little. In health these capillaries or channels have their origin between the lobules and between the cells of which the lobules are formed. Gradually these cells are obliterated, and thus the bile channels are made larger. A greater reason for the absence of jaundice is the destruction of the cells which manufacture bile. Such destruction is the result of pressure from the new tissue growth and, later, its contraction. The new tissue fibers enclose within their meshes the little lobules of which the liver is formed, and the contraction of this tissue destroys them. Their more active cells maintain their individuality longest, but finally disappear.

Contraction of the new tissue not only destroys the liver cells, but obliterates the vessels, and the digestive work which in health is carried on by the liver is interfered with. A loss of nutrition results, and gradually the whole system suffers. The organ decreases in size, such decrease being in proportion to the amount of the new tissue and its contraction. This shrinkage is called *Atrophy*. The surface is shrunken irregularly and the edges are nodular (lumpy), the hardening being most marked along the front edge because it is thinner, and more in the right lobe than in the left because it is larger. The shrinkage of the liver prevents more or less the return of the blood that passes through it. The return circulation comes from the stomach, digestive tract and spleen. The blood is forced back to these organs and congestion and inflammation follow. The patient may vomit blood (seldom). There may be chronic dyspepsia, diarrhea, enlarged spleen, piles or abdominal dropsy, or more than one of these conditions may exist at the same time. This disease is called *Cirrhosis* or *Sclerosis*, meaning a hardening. It is also called *Hob-Nailed Liver*, *Rum Drinker's Liver*, *Whiskey Liver*, etc.

Cause.—The continued and prolonged use of liquor. With the single exception of syphilis, it is claimed this disease can only be produced bv alcohol. It is frequently met in habitual drunkards.

Symbtoms.—During the early stages of inflammation, liver abscess may form; or death may occur in the earlier stages before the liver has had time to shrink. There are no early symptoms. The first evidence of this disease is dyspepsia and the morning vomiting of drunkards. Later there may be diarrhea, or there may be traces of blood in the ejections from the stomach or in the eliminations from the bowels. As the disease progresses there is abdominal dropsy, the abdomen eventually becoming enormously distended.

TREATMENT.—

There is no treatment that is of benefit. By increasing the activity of the bowels the dropsy may be overcome to some extent. It is necessary to exercise judgment in regard to food —to avoid those things that disturb the stomach, etc. Sooner or later it will be found necessary to tap the abdomen in order to draw off the amount of fluid. This process will need to be repeated from time to time. The disease is fatal.

Alcoholic liquors should be entirely given up, and the use of tea, coffee, and highly seasoned animal foods discontinued. Fats, and foods containing large quantities of sugar, should be avoided. Juicy plants, such as lettuce, celery, cabbage, etc., should be substituted for starchy vegetables. A diet largely composed of skimmed milk is nutritious. A good remedy is equal parts of Mandrake root and Culver root mixed and taken in 3-grain doses from one to three times a day, or sufficiently often to keep the bowels open.

LOCKJAW—TETANUS.—This is a formidable disease, caused by involuntary, persistent, independent and painful contractions or spasms of certain muscles, usually the muscles of the jaw, neck and throat. However, a great number of muscles may be involved, including nearly the whole body.

Cause.—A certain specific poison, which is thought most often to follow penetrating wounds—those made by rusty nails, etc. The poison is also sometimes communicated by vaccination. Its source is not always known.

Symptoms.—First noticed in the muscles of the neck and jaw; the neck becomes stiff and the jaw is moved with difficulty. Swallowing becomes difficult, because the muscles controlling the action become more or less involved. Gradually this feeling of stiffness increases until the muscles become rigid and the jaws are firmly closed. In exceptional cases the muscles of the back may be involved, drawing the head back, the feet are drawn in the same direction, the body forming an arch; or the body may be bent sideways or forwards. Usually this does not occur. The diaphragm may be more or less involved, producing what are called *girdle pains*. These and other pains produced by this disease are sharp and agonizing. Any slight noise, or a sudden draft striking the patient, may produce convulsions. This increases the pain and suffering. There is usually constipation, the amount of urine is diminished and there is moderate fever. Sleeplessness may be a troublesome feature. The mind remains clear. If the muscles of respiration, or those controlling the glottis—the small space between the vocal chords through which the air passes—become involved, the case is serious at once. When death occurs, it usually is within one week.

TREATMENTS.—

A. It is sometimes necessary to extract a tooth and feed the patient through a tube. If there are already any teeth missing, the extraction will not be necessary. Strict attention must be paid to ventilation, avoiding all drafts. Watch the action of the kidneys; if they fail to excrete the normal amount of urine, other means of elimination must be resorted to. Increase the activity of the bowels; give large doses of Jalap and Scammony because they produce copious watery evacuations. These remedies can be given in solution by the same method as that of feeding. To relax the system, Bromide of Potash, Chloral, Morphine, Physostigmine, Opium, Chloroform, Apomorphine, Hyoscyamine, Indian Hemp, Aconite, Tartar Emetic, Curare, Anti-tetanic Serum and other remedies have been recommended; but to relieve the necessity of choosing from this formidable array, we can assure the reader that they are without value. The Atropine and Pilocarpine treatment given for *Hydrophobia* will not only relieve, but will unquestionably cure many of these cases.

B. Another, and we believe a better, treatment is sweating by artificial heat as described under Cerebro-Spinal Meningitis, and for the same reasons. In Lockjaw the pain is due to the great muscular tension. Heat relieves this condition, eases the pain and eliminates the poison. Heat should be applied until sweating is profuse, and applied often enough and continued long enough to give relief. To dabble with Lockjaw Serum or Antitoxine is a crime against the patient.

C. If there is a wound, wash frequently with Turpentine. Pour Turpentine into the wound, or if it is a hole caused by a nail, inject the Turpentine with small syringe. This is to prevent lockjaw.—(38).

D. Specific Gelsemium, 5 drops every hour until the whole system is relaxed, then gradually reduce the dose. Midway between every dose give full doses of Specific Passaflora. Continue this treatment until the spasms cease.—(30).

> **E.** Gelsemium, fluid extract............... ½ drachm.
> Hyoscyamus, "   "   3   "
> Lithiated Hydrangea...................... 4 ounces.
>
> *Mix*, and give ½ teaspoonful every three or four hours.—(47).

LOCOMOTOR ATAXIA.—This is a chronic inflammation of the spinal cord. The inflammation is followed by an overgrowth and contraction of the connective tissue framework, and a corresponding degeneration of the natural tissue—nerve cells and nerve fibers. The disease is usually divided into three stages, yet these stages are not altogether separate, but merge one into another; or some of the symptoms under one stage may be present earlier or later than here indicated. In the first stage there are sharp pains in the lower extremities, sometimes spoken of as *lightning* pains. The optic nerve is easily affected. In the second stage there is inco-ordination, that is, inability to control or harmonize the action of certain groups of voluntary muscles in the lower extremities. The third stage is that of paralysis. The disease runs a chronic course, lasting for years. There may be quite long periods of time when it seems to remain stationary, and then it progresses a step further. It may last ten or fifteen years.

The first evidence of the disease is manifested in the lower extremities, because the disease commences in the lower part of the spinal cord and it is in this part that the nerves governing the lower extremities have their origin. As the disease progresses the inflammatory and degenerative changes extend up the cord. When it reaches the cervical portion of the cord, or that portion situated in the neck, the arms and hands experience a condition similar to that first experienced in the lower extremities, because the nerves governing them have their origin in that part of the cord situated in the neck. The disease ultimately proves fatal.

Cause.—The cause is the same as that given under paralysis.

Symptoms.—Before any of the symptoms present themselves there is evidence of dyspepsia. There is nausea, and may be vomiting; there are also neuralgic pains in the stomach and bowels. This is evidence that the digestive organs are primarily at fault.

First Stage.—The first noticeable symptoms are absence of the knee-jerk, pains extending down the lower limbs, and unequal dilatation of the pupils of the eye. If the reader will place one limb over the opposite knee, and with the edge of the hand strike a light, sharp blow across or just below the knee-cap, there will be a slight convulsive jerk of the suspended foot. The absence of such jerk constitutes the sign or symptom mentioned. This is called Westphal's sign. The first effects of inflammation are those of a stimulus, hence the pain and inco-ordination. The patient is unable to control his movements by reason of the constant presence of the disease. The stimulus first manifests itself in the lower part of the cord and extends higher up. When affecting that part just below and between the shoulder blades, there is pain and a feeling of constriction about the chest, because the nerves supplying the chest muscles have their origin in that part of the cord. These pains are sometimes called *girdle* pains. The inequality of the pupils constitutes what is called the Argyll-Robertson sign.

Second Stage.—Inco-ordination is increased. The patient is unable to stand with the feet together and the eyes closed. This is called Romberg's sign or symptom. Later, he loses control until in attempting to walk the feet fly in all directions. In the beginning of this stage there is a sensory disturbance, *i. e.*, a loss of sensation, which commences in the soles of the feet. First there is a sense of numbness, which gradually extends along the limbs. This condition, or change, continues to increase until paralysis is complete.

With the loss of sensation sores are apt to occur on the affected surface. The joints may become swollen and the swelling be followed with degenerative changes. If the patient lies in bed, bed sores are troublesome. These sores and swellings are not painful, but they cannot be cured; on the contrary, they continue to grow in size and new ones form.

Third Stage.—Paralysis, more or less complete.

The following signs are unmistakable evidence of *Locomotor Ataxia*:

Westphal's sign, or loss of knee-jerk.
Argyll-Robertson sign, or loss of pupil reflex.
Romberg's sign, or inability to stand with the feet together and eyes closed.

TREATMENTS.—

A. There is no specific treatment for this disease. Resting several hours a day is undoubtedly of advantage. The Iodides may be given in some form—1 teaspoonful of the Syrup of Hydriodic Acid three times a day, between meals and at bedtime. Tonics may be given, if needed. The greatest care should be exercised regarding diet and hygiene. If caused by alcohol, its use should be discontinued; if the result of syphilis, see treatment under that head; if there is a history of constipation or rheumatism, it will be evidence that the disease is the result of indigestion and a lack of elimination, as described under *Paralysis*.

B. One of the chief objects is to protect the patient from cold and damp. Keep him in a uniform temperature. A good and wholesome diet is necessary, and the persistent use of Cod Liver Oil is beneficial. Massage is also beneficial. Rest is useful. The patient should lie down for two or three hours each day.—(72).

C. Calabar Bean.............................. 10 grains.
　　Ginger, powdered......................... 20　"
Make into 20 pills and take 1 three times a day. Exalgine is recommended for relief of the lightning pains.—(28).

D. If due to syphilis, constitutional treatment for syphilis; if due to excessive drink or other dissipation, the proper care in such cases.
Consult the best regular and reputable physician within your means and take his advice as to treatment.—(69).

E. *External Treatment.*—Strong rubbing of the whole spine with strong sedative ointment three times a day.

Note.—See *Ointments Nos 5* and *6*, under MISCELLANEOUS MEDICAL RECEIPTS.

Internal Treatment.— Fellows' Syrup of Hypophosphites—teaspoonful after meals and at bedtime—four doses a day.—(24).

F. The following prescription has been used by the writer in over one hundred cases of Locomotor Ataxia. As a curative, nothing is better.

Iodide of Potash....... .... 5 drachms.
Corrosive Sublimate .... 1 grain.
Water...................................... 4 ounces.
　　Dose.—Take one teaspoonful after meals.—(57).

LUMBAGO.—(See under RHEUMATISM).

LUMPJAW — ACTINOMYCOCIS. — This disease is said to be caused by a parasite. It occurs in cattle, usually in the jaw, forming a large lump; hence the name, *Lumpjaw*. The disease also sometimes occurs in man.

Symptoms.—When occurring in man and on the surface of the body, it may resemble tuberculosis of the skin. If in the lungs, there is fever, cough, and wasting of flesh.

TREATMENTS.—

A. Some advise a 50 per cent solution of Carbolic Acid to be injected around the growth, when it can be reached, and repeated in three or four days. Give large doses of Iodide of Potash internally. The best treatment is complete removal of the growth by a surgeon. If the disease occurs in the internal organs, as the lungs or digestive tract, there is no known treatment that will cure.

B. Bathe affected part with Tincture of Iodine. Keep bowels open with Salts and Cream of Tartar.

Syrup Stillingia Compound......... 4 ounces.
Iodide of Potassium.................... 1 drachm.
Take a teaspoonful three times a day.

THE LUNGS AND THEIR DISEASES.

The two lungs, which are the organs of respiration, are placed in the chest cavity. They are somewhat narrow above, but broader below. The right lung is a little larger than the left because the heart is mostly in the left side, thus occupying a larger portion of that space. The average weight of the left lung is 20 ounces, and of the right, 22 ounces.

Position.—The lungs extend quite high up into the side of the neck, the highest point being from 1 to 1½ inches above the collar bone; below they extend to the sixth rib in the front, eighth rib in the side and tenth rib behind. When taking a full breath they expand and extend downward about two inches farther.

The Air Tubes.—These begin in the throat. There is one large tube, the *trachea*. Its commencement may be indicated by that prominence in the throat often spoken of as "Adam's Apple." This tube, the trachea, extends downward for a distance of nine inches, then divides into two branches. These redivide, becoming smaller until their minute subdivisions penetrate all parts of the lung substance.

The Air Cells.—At the termination of each tube there are two or three small dilatations, like little hollow beads, or like three currants on the end of a small twig if the currants and twig were hollow. These dilatations are the air cells. Both tubes and cells are lined with mucous membrane, which is continuous from the mouth and throat. The air cells vary in size, the average size being $\frac{1}{160}$ to $\frac{1}{125}$ of an inch in diameter. It is estimated that there are six hundred millions of these air cells in the lungs, and that their combined surface is more than seven times greater than the whole outer surface of the body. The air cells and air tubes are held together by elastic connective tissue, hence the power of the lungs to expand and contract.

Purification of the Blood.—The lungs are supplied by two sets of vessels: One set nourishes the organs, and the other set envelops or surrounds the air cells for the purpose of absorbing the oxygen from the air we breathe. This set is placed just beneath the delicate mucous membrane which lines the cells. Animal membrane has the power of admitting gases (oxygen) and yet remain impervious to fluid (blood). The system of vessels which supplies the lungs with nourishment and the system through which oxygen is absorbed, are entirely separate. The system which supplies nourishment has its origin in the lower left side of the heart, while that carrying the blood for oxidization comes from the right side of the heart. The blood sent for nourishment is bright red, and that sent for oxidization is dark, venous, and contains many impurities. Carbonic acid gas generated in the system is eliminated through the air tubes of the lungs, also many other poisons. It is estimated that from one to one and one-half pints of fluid (water) is eliminated by the lungs every twenty-four hours. This liquid vapor contains many deadly poisons, the nature of which is not well understood. The system of vessels through which the blood is purified, and which lies just beneath the delicate mucous membrane which lines the air cells, gives off carbonic acid gas and other poisons. These poisons escape through this membrane, and in return oxygen is absorbed through it, and by reason of this exchange the dark, venous blood is freed from its impurities and rendered bright red. It then passes on to the left side of the heart and is sent out through the general circulation to nourish the body.

Following digestion, the food elements which are absorbed into the circulation are carried by the veins to the right side of the heart, and from there are sent with the venous blood into the lungs. Meeting the oxygen which has been absorbed, these food elements undergo many important changes, hence the statement under *Epilepsy* ("C") that the higher forms of digestion are carried on in the circulation.

BRONCHITIS.—The bronchial tube commences at the throat as a single opening. The first part of this opening is called the larynx or organ of voice. It includes the vocal chords and is supported in front by what is called "Adam's Apple." This part of the opening is about 4 inches in length. The next part of the opening is called the trachea, meaning the windpipe. This is about 4½ inches in length and nearly 1 inch in diameter. This divides into two branches. The one on the right side is about 1 inch long, and the one on the left side about 1¾ inches long. These enter the lungs and divide and subdivide until they permeate all parts of the lung structure and terminate in small dilatations called air cells. The tubes, large and small, also the air cells, are lined with mucous membrane which is continuous with that lining the mouth and throat. The trachea and air tubes are formed of three membranes or coats: The external coat or covering is a layer of elastic fibrous tissue; next is the muscular coat, and internally is the mucous membrane. The trachea and its larger branches are also supported by rings formed of cartilage. These rings surround the muscular coat and are enveloped by the external elastic or fibrous coat. The rings are not complete on the posterior or back side, but are connected by the fibrous tissue.

Bronchitis means inflammation of the mucous membrane lining the air tubes, but does not include the smaller tubes or air cells. Usually the inflammation affects only the large and medium sized tubes. *Acute Bronchitis* is a disease of quite common occurrence. *Chronic Bronchitis* may follow the acute, or may result from other causes.

Cause.— The cause of *Acute Bronchitis* is atmospheric changes, the same as those which produce other forms of catarrhal colds. Just what those changes are or how they affect the system, no one knows.

Symptoms.—The symptoms of *Acute Bronchitis* are those of a common cold, which it accompanies. The catarrhal conditions of the nasal cavities and the throat extend downward into the air tubes. The voice is altered, and in a day or two expectoration is increased. Headache is often present, there is a feeling of oppression and tightness in the chest, and cough commences as soon as the disease enters the bronchial tubes. At first the cough is dry, and sometimes fierce and ringing. Later, with the increase in the secretions, the cough becomes looser and expectoration more profuse. As the disease continues, the secretions become thicker, more tenacious and yellowish in color. The cough produces pain beneath the chest bone. It also produces a feeling of soreness and rawness in the same place as the effect of inflammation in the trachea. There is usually some fever, and the pulse is more rapid than normal. Respiration is increased, because the thickening of the mucous membrane, together with the catarrhal secretions which soon follow, lessen the air space, and Nature tries to supply the needs of the system by more rapid breathing.

TREATMENTS.—

What to Do.—An acute attack of bronchitis should be avoided, if possible, by care and proper treatment during the early stages; that is, if one is subject to bronchitis he should give immediate attention to a simple "cold in the head" and try to prevent it from extending to the bronchial passages. However, if an acute attack occurs, he should be given a hot Mustard foot-bath and placed in a room where the air is kept moistened with hot vapor, as steam from a kettle of boiling water. Bathe the throat and chest freely with Camphorated Oil (oil, or even melted lard, in which Camphor Gum has been dissolved) and protect with flannels. A syrup made of Horehound, or of Horehound and Licorice combined, is an excellent remedy to give. The bowels should be regulated, and for a few days the patient should remain in a well ventilated room with a uniform temperature of 70 degrees.

A. Fluid Extract Digitalis............ .... 12 drops.
Fluid Extract Ipecac.................... 24 "
Tincture Aconite.......................... 12 "
Simple Elixir add to make............ 2 ounces.
   Mix, and take a teaspoonful every one or two hours as needed.

B. Citrate of Potash....................... 6 drachms.
Liquor Ammonia Acetatis........... 5 ounces.
Sweet Spirits Nitre..................... 1 ounce.
Fluid Extract Ipecac... .... 1 drachm.
Syrup Wild Cherry, add to.......... 8 ounces.
   Mix, and take 1 teaspoonful in water every three hours.—(46).

C. Get an ounce of Syrup of Ipecac and take 5 to 6 drops every one to three hours to loosen cough.
An adult may take the following :

Paregoric.....:............................. 1 ounce.
Syrup Ipecac............................. ¼ ounce.
Syrup.. 3 ounces.
   Take a teaspoonful every two to three hours.
—(13).

D. Syrup of Ipecac............................ ½ ounce.
Tincture of Bloodroot................. 1 drachm.
Syrup of Tolu, enough to make...... 4 ounces
    Mix, and take 1 teaspoonful every three
hours.—(12).

E. Paregoric and Whiskey, one part of the former to two of the latter, well mixed. Dose, 1 teaspoonful every three hours.—(7).

F. Camphor and Ginger jacket, applied to chest.—(6).

CHRONIC BRONCHITIS.—In *Chronic Bronchitis* there are structural changes in all the coats of the air passages. These changes commence in the mucous membrane, and later include the muscular and the external layers. Any inflammation becomes chronic when it continues until there is an overgrowth of connective tissue.

Cause.—Chronic bronchitis may be caused by the prolonged use of alcohol, or by irritating dust, as met with in factories, shops, stone quarries and iron works. It may also be caused by the inhalation of irritating vapors in those who are constantly exposed to them. It may result from Bright's disease where the blood is forced back into the lungs and heart, because this would produce congestion and later result in inflammation. It may result from the same conditions that produce rheumatism, that is, where the blood contains uric acid and other irritants. The constant presence of such irritating matter would produce congestion and, later, inflammation.

Changes Occurring in the Bronchial Tubes in Chronic Bronchitis. —In the chronic form the mucous membrane becomes greatly thickened and swollen. The inflammation reaches the deeper structures, that is, the tissues which unite the mucous membrane to the muscular coat, and there is an overgrowth of tissue. The muscular coat and external fibrous coat also become infiltrated with this overgrowth. This new tissue is a form of connective tissue which later contracts and hardens. The rings mentioned, which normally are composed of cartilage, may become infiltrated with lime salts, and thus become firm and resistant like bone. The tubes lose their elasticity and are more or less widely dilated. The dilatation may be uniform, or some parts may be more widely dilated than others, thus giving them a saculated appearance. Expectoration is profuse, especially in the morning, the secretions having collected during the night. When the secretions are profuse it is sometimes called *Bronchorrhea.* With the unequal dilatation in the tubes the secretions are difficult to dislodge, hence degenerative processes may take place, giving the breath and expectorated matter a foul odor. This is sometimas called

Fetid Bronchitis. In some cases the secretions and expectoration are diminished. This is called *Dry Bronchitis*.

TREATMENTS.—

A. Acetic Tincture of Bloodroot.......... ½ ounce.
Tincture of Black Cohosh................ ½ "
Syrup of Tolu..................... ½ "
Wine of Ipecacuanha...................... ½ "
Sweet Spirits of Nitre ....1 "

Mix, and take a teaspoonful in a little water from three to five times daily, according to the amount of irritation present.

B. *Fetid Bronchitis*.—

Fluid Extract Grindelia Robusta... 1 ounce.
Oil Eucalyptus............................. 1 drachm.
Syrup Senega............................. 1 ounce.
Glycerine..................................... 1 "
Wine of Tar, add to .... 4 "

Mix, and take 1 teaspoonful four times a day.

If the expectoration is fetid, take 10 drops of Turpentine in capsule with each dose.

C. *Dry Bronchitis*.—In the dry form the secretions may be increased by the following:

Apomorphine................................. ½ grain.
Syrup Ipecac .... ½ ounce.
Tincture White Pine .... 4 "

Mix, and take one teaspoonful four times a day. If the dose causes nausea, take less; if not, and needed, take more.

In any case of chronic bronchitis take $\frac{1}{30}$ grain of Strychnine three times a day at meal time. Also take a teaspoonful of Syrup of Hydriodic Acid between meals and at bedtime—three doses a day.

CAPILLARY BRONCHITIS.—Capillary bronchitis is a catarrhal inflammation of the small air passages or tubes of the lungs, and follows bronchitis—a catarrhal inflammation of the upper or larger air tubes of the lungs. The disease usually commences above and extends downward, and on reaching the smaller tubes it is called *capillary*, because the little tubes are small and hair-like (from *capillus*, hair). The only difference between bronchitis and capillary bronchitis is the part of the tube affected.

Capillary bronchitis is usually found in children and infants. Old people also occasionally suffer from this disease. The catarrhal inflammation extends from above downward, following the various branches of the air passages or tubes, hence all of both lungs may be affected. When the disease reaches the small tubes (capillary bronchitis) it is much more dangerous, as the catarrhal discharge may fill the little tubes and completely shut out the air from the air cells, while in the larger tubes the air can pass in and out freely.

Cause.—Dust and other irritating substances enter the bronchial tubes and cause irritation, hence the disease is sometimes met during the summer months. Colds and exposure and sudden changes in temperature from warm to cold, are more frequent causes. Weak children are particularly liable. Typhoid fever and measles always produce a catarrhal condition of the lungs, yet the catarrh produced by these diseases seldom results in capillary bronchitis except in very delicate children. In scarlet fever the rash, and in small-pox the pustules, appear in the mucous membrane lining the air tubes.

Dyspepsia, constipation, or any morbid condition of the digestive tract may aid in producing capillary bronchitis. Such conditions produce a large amount of waste in the system, and as nearly all the blood passes through the lungs once every minute, these organs are irritated, more especially since many of the poisons are eliminated by the air passages or tubes. This irritates the delicate mucous membrane which lines them, and a catarrhal inflammation is the result.

Symptoms.— The symptoms of capillary bronchitis are not always distinct, because the disease comes on gradually. A catarrhal condition has previously existed in the larger tubes. There is a gradual rise in temperature, the previous condition becomes worse, fever slowly rises to 102-3 with difficult breathing, and the respirations become rapid and shallow as the small tubes and air cells become filled. In a nursing baby there is frequent letting go of the nipple and the child worries.

The circulation through the lungs becomes more impeded. In health, with each heart beat a quantity of blood is sent from the right side of the heart through the lungs, where each air cell is surrounded with a minute network of blood vessels; but when there is inflammation of the vessels, and an exudation (discharge) through their walls, or coats, it causes interference in the circulation, and in proportion to such interference the blood is dammed back into the right side of the heart. In health the veins also empty into this side of the heart, but now they can do so but partially, hence there is congestion of the venous system throughout the body. This is why the nails, lips and face may become blue, the surface cold and the mind dull. If this condition is continued, stupor or convulsions may soon occur and the attack end fatally, caused by the failure of the blood to pass through the lungs and exchange the carbonic acid gas and other poisons for oxygen.

The ear can detect catarrhal sounds scattered throughout the lungs. There are also sounds, high or low pitched, caused by the air rushing through the tubes where the opening is partially closed by the swollen mucous membrane. Palpation, that is, placing the palms of the hands over the lungs and on the bare chest, will often locate large accumulations of mucus in the larger tubes. Rales (rattling) in the medium sized tubes, and crepitant (crackling) sounds in the small tubes or capillaries, may be plainly heard by placing the ear against the chest. These sounds are caused by the air being forced through the mucus-like secretions, and the vibration is carried to the hand or ear.

TREATMENTS.—

A. Put the child to bed, arrange for good ventilation, and maintain a uniform temperature of 75 to 80 degrees. Keep the bowels active. The air in the room should be kept moist. If the case is serious, do not let the child lie too long in one position, as the catarrhal accumulations in the air cells and small tubes may obstruct respiration to the extent of producing death. Make a cotton batting jacket large enough to cover the entire body, from the lower border of the ribs to the throat, place it upon the patient and let it remain.

The following medical treatment is valuable:

> Fluid Extract Digitalis.................. 12 drops.
> Fluid Extract Ipecac................... 24   "
> Acetate Potash. .... 3 drachms.
> Syrup Wild Cherry..................... 1 ounce.
> Water, add to make..................... 4   "
>
> *Mix*, and give ½ teaspoonful every two hours.
>
> or,
>
> Acetate of Potash........................ 1 drachm.
> Spirits of Nitre............................. ¼   "
> Fluid Extract Ipecac...................... ½   "
> Liquor Ammonia Acetate add to... 4 ounces.
>
> *Mix*, and give one teaspoonful every hour.

If there is much rattling in the lungs, showing an excess of catarrhal secretions, and breathing is seriously interfered with on that account, it is considered good practice to give an emetic and vomit the child, as active vomiting relieves the lungs more or less by forcing out the catarrhal products. During the act of vomiting the child's head should be held low as this aids materially in giving relief.

B. The foregoing is the form of treatment usually followed in *Capillary Bronchitis*, but we wish to give our experience along another line—a treatment which in the hands of those who have followed it for many years is recommended to meet every requirement. Those who adopt this method may do so with every confidence of success. We have seen cases that were otherwise hopeless treated by this method, the child making a rapid and complete recovery. It is a **Home Treatment,** as follows :

Take a piece of cloth and make a loose waist for the child; make it large so that it will cover from the lower border of the ribs to the throat and allow a lap of 4 or 5 inches in front. Take a quantity of onions and chop them fine, add 3 or 4 table-spoonfuls of fresh lard, put in an iron kettle, stir to prevent burning, and heat thoroughly. In the bottom of the crib place a large soapstone, quite hot, and over this place several layers of quilts. Lay the waist in the crib, or on the table, and cover with the hot onions to a depth of ¾ of an inch. Remove all the clothing from the child, place the poultice in the crib, lay the child on it, wrap it firmly about the body, and cover with one or more pieces of quilts; also place some hot flat-irons along the sides of the crib. By means of the soapstone and other artificial heat, the poultices will not need changing oftener than once in four hours. How does this benefit the child? The same as explained under *Cerebro-Spinal Meningitis*—by equalizing the circulation bringing the blood to the surface, causing profuse sweating, and in this way relieving the lungs. This treatment may seem a little harsh, but it is not, and of the many cases we have seen treated in this way, we have never yet known or experienced the slightest difficulty in keeping the child perfectly quiet and contented. As with any other line of treatment, the bowels should be kept regular, the child should receive a nourishing diet, given in moderate amounts at reasonably short intervals, and temperature and ventilation maintained as before mentioned.

The above treatment was first suggested by Mrs. Ellen Cronkrite, of Wacousta, Michigan, a nurse whose life has been spent in caring for the sick and who possesses unusual intelligence in all matters pertaining to home treatment. The suggestion seemed to contain so much merit that, under the instructions of Mrs. Cronkrite, its application was immediately secured in a case that seemed hopeless. Such flattering results followed that we feel justified in recommending it in all cases of *Capillary Bronchitis*, and assure those who administer the treatment that they can do so with every confidence.

CIRRHOSIS OF THE LUNGS.—(See under TUBERCULOSIS).

CONGESTION, *Hyperemia, Oedema of the Lungs* and other terms are used to denote an abnormal fullness of the vessels in those organs. We do not deem it necessary or advisable to treat these conditions separately, as it would be confusing and often misleading. Engorgement of the vessels in the lungs may follow the use of alcohol. Too much blood is present when the return circulation is checked, as in liver disease, because much of the return circulation passes through the liver. This interferes with the outflow and the blood is dammed back into the lungs. Over-fullness is present in Bright's disease for the same reason— interference with the outflow. Over fullness or congestion is also present as described under HEART DISEASE.

HEMORRHAGE OF THE LUNGS.—(See uuder HEM-ORRHAGE).

PNEUMONIA.—Pneumonia is an inflammation of a part of one or both lungs. It is seldom that both lungs are involved. The right lung is divided into three lobes and the left into two. An acute localized inflammation of one or more entire lobes is called lobar pneumonia. The diseased area may include a part, a whole lobe, or more than one lobe.

Lobular Pneumonia.—Sometimes the little air cells and small bronchial tubes are affected with a catarrhal condition accompanied by a low form of inflammation. This is called lobular pneumonia. It is also called capillary bronchitis, and is described under that head. This is usually a disease of the old or the very young.

Bronchitis is a catarrhal inflammation of the large or bronchial tubes, the smaller tubes and air cells not being affected. Inflammation of the smaller bronchial tubes is always present more or less in lobar pneumonia.

Croupous Pneumonia is attended with the formation of a membrane in the bronchial tube.

Pleuro-Pneumonia is so called because the pleura, a thin membrane which surrounds the lungs, is included in the inflammatory process. Probably this always occurs to some extent.

Typhoid Pneumonia is a term employed when the disease is accompanied with typhoid symptoms.

Bilious Pneumonia is so called because the disease is complicated with congestion of the liver.

Broncho-Pneumonia affects both tubes and lungs, and is caused by the inhalation of dust and other irritating substances. It is usually found in stone cutters, millers, and those who work in planing mills and factories where dust is plentiful. This is a chronic form, and by extension downward the small tubes and air cells are affected. At first the vessels supplying the mucous membrane of the air passages become congested and contain too much blood. This narrows the opening through the smaller tubes, and also narrows the diameter of the air cells. The increased blood supply results in an increase of the connective tissue framework in the lungs. As this new tissue growth matures, it contracts as elsewhere. With the contraction of the newly formed tissue many small tubes and air cells and many blood vessels are obliterated. As the disease progresses the lungs become hardened and shrunken, and the powers of respiration are much diminished.

Summer Bronchitis is synonymous with hay fever.

Lobar Pneumonia.—This is the form usually spoken of as pneumonia. In this form the affected portion of the lung becomes solid and firm, no air passing through it. Double pneumonia is usually fatal. The air cells are merely the dilated extremities of the air tubes. From three to five of these dilatations are usually found on the end of each tube. Both tubes and cells are lined with mucous membrane. Pneumonia is an inflammation of the air cells, and cannot exist without producing bronchitis, *i. e.*, inflammation of some of the smaller tubes; though bronchitis can and usually does exist without pneumonia, the inflammatory process stopping before it reaches the smaller tubes and cells.

Cause.—The irritation produced by any of the conditions which cause chronic bronchitis may assume an acute form and produce pneumonia. Pneumonia is always the result of an unhealthy system. The blood contains an excess of irritants, and now there is only needed an exciting cause, such as wet feet or a cold, to precipitate acute inflammation of the lungs. Ordinarily the wet feet or cold are easily recovered from, but with the vital forces reduced, acute inflammation may follow. Another important reason or cause for pneumonia is found in the double circulation with which the lungs are supplied, and the further fact that nearly all the blood in the body passes through these organs once every minute. See description of lungs, also CONSUMPTION. In the strong and robust any effects of an unhealthy system may be held in abeyance for a time and, later, improvement may relieve the danger; but should some exciting cause present itself before the improvement takes place, pneumonia may follow. That is why the disease may affect what was supposed to be a healthy man. All understand that the irritating effects of unhealthy blood may and do cause inflammatory rheumatism, inflammation of the pleura, or pleurisy, and may cause inflammation of the peritoneum, or peritonitis, meningitis, etc. Unhealthy blood may also cause inflammation of the lungs, or pneumonia. These and many other diseases are but different manifestations of the same cause. These conditions are governed or controlled according to our different powers to resist. Some organs or structures are stronger in one individual and others in another, hence the different diseases named above — inflammatory rheumatism, pleurisy, peritonitis, meningitis, pneumonia, etc.

It should be remembered that inflammation is always caused by or is the result of irritation, and what is better calculated to produce irritation than indigestion, constipation, and the absorption of many poisons plus those originating in the circulation as a result of imperfect oxidization? They not only produce irritation, but their increase means a proportionate loss of nutrition, strength and vitality, which may be followed by chronic disease; or the causes enumerated may precipitate an acute attack, as stated above.

Pneumonia occurs most often in the lower right lobe, because the catarrhal exudate which precedes the disease is more difficult to dislodge from the lower lobes—it must be raised from a greater depth. The right lung does not extend quite so low as the left on account of the liver, and for the same reason the lower border is a little broader, hence more of the catarrhal exudate can accumulate at this point. The second most frequent seat of pneumonia is the lower left lobe, for the reasons just given. The third most frequent location is the upper lobe. There is better drainage from the upper lobe, yet the air cells are less developed, less air passes through them, and less oxygen is absorbed by them, and without this vitalizing element they are more liable to disease and to degeneration.

The diseased area may correspond exactly to a single lobe, or may not.

Symptoms.—The disease usually begins with a chill, followed by fever and pain, which is increased by the cough which develops. The pain is also increased by pressure from the inflammation and swelling. The temperature rises rapidly. At first the pulse is full and strong, but may show early signs of embarrassed heart action. Respiration is shallow and rapid, and may increase to forty, fifty, or more per minute, according to the amount of lung structure involved. By rapid breathing Nature tries to compensate for the temporary loss of function in the diseased lung. The rapid breathing causes interrupted speech. The cough is harsh at first, and soon a frothy mucus appears. This later changes to a thick, tenacious form, due to the many new cells in the air passages which the increased blood supply has furnished. The increased blood supply also increases the secretions.

On the second or third day "rusty" sputum appears, the color being due to the rupture of small blood vessels around the air cells. The secretions continue and become yellowish, due to degenerative changes. There may be headache. Sleeplessness may be difficult to control. There may be delirium. If this occurs early, it is not important; if it occurs late, the condition is graver. Delirium is more frequent when the disease occurs in drunkards. The face is flushed and there may be nosebleed. Gastric disturbance may be more or less marked. The kidneys are less active. Prostration is marked from the first. There is more or less pleurisy, or inflammation of the delicate membrane which encloses the lung. This would be absent at first if the disease were located in the center of the lung, and would remain absent if the disease should not reach the surface of the organ. When occurring in drunkards, the disease may resemble delirium tremens. Pain, cough and expectoration may then be slight.

With children, convulsions may take the place of the chill. The spinal nerves are always liable to spasmodic action unless controlled by reason and judgment, which exist in the brain. The child's brain may not have developed a controlling influence, hence the convulsions.

The disease terminates by crisis, *i. e.*, suddenly and, usually, favorably, from the fifth to the tenth day. Within twenty-four hours convalescence is established, and recovery follows rapidly in most cases.

In the *congestion* which marks the first stage of pneumonia, the lung becomes gorged with blood, which later coagulates and renders the affected portion solid and firm. During the last stage, or from the fifth to the tenth day, the coagulation liquefies and is generally discharged by expectoration, which is increased at this time. Circulation is re-established, and the air cells are rapidly freed and return to their normal condition. This is called *resolution*. In this case the lung structure proper remains undisturbed. Some inflammatory thickening is liable to remain.

When absorption is not complete, one or more abscesses may form. If a number are present, the intervening lung substance may break down and form one large abscess, which may break into the pleural, or chest cavity, into the abdominal cavity, into the digestive tract, or may point externally. If in the lower right lobe, it may extend to the liver. If not too large, it may be absorbed. Abscess formation is described under *Appendicitis*. Abscesses usually break into the bronchial tubes and the pus is expectorated. Abscesses are rare and indicate a bad condition of the system before the attack. The lower lobes are most liable to abscess, for the same reason that they are most liable to the disease.

Gangrene is also rare and indicates an unhealthy system from the first. The unhealthy condition of the blood renders the inflammation, swelling and pressure so intense as to entirely shut off circulation, and the tissues die. A small amount of dead tissue may be cast off through the bronchial tubes. There is also intense inflammation in gangrene, as this is Nature's means of checking its spread. It marks the battle line between the living and the dead, and if the gangrenous tissue is eliminated through the air tubes, the intense inflammation may cause new tissue growth sufficient to cause pressure and interfere with the circulation a second time, and thus aid in its own destruction. Degeneration of such tissue might result in abscess.

In chronic pneumonia resolution is not complete, the air cells do not clear up, and there remains a low form of inflammation which is continuous and causes a thickening by new cell growth.

If death results, it usually occurs in the second stage, and is caused by heart failure resulting from the poison in the system.

TREATMENTS.—

What to Do Till the Doctor Comes.—Send for the doctor. In the meantime put the feet into water as hot as can be borne, afterwards rub and dry them thoroughly with a crash towel, put the patient to bed, cover warmly and keep perfectly quiet. Give hot herb drinks and apply hot applications to the chest—cloths wrung out of hot water or the hot decoction of some bitter herb, or a hot Flax seed or Mustard poultice. Get the patient to sweating.

A. Commence treatment by giving the patient an active cathartic. A large Mustard plaster may be placed over the affected lung. Some recommend a blister plaster, but we do not, because a large blister is a very uncomfortable reminder, and we think the Mustard plaster sufficient.

Put the patient to bed in a large, well-ventilated room and maintain a temperature of from 75 to 80 degrees, providing at the same time for a free exchange of air. Put an abundance of covering over the patient and give him hot drinks; sweat him profusely. To aid in producing sweating, give the following once an hour:

> Fluid Extract of Veratrum Viride.... 2 drops.
> Fluid Extract of Ipecac.................. 1 drop.
> also,
> Atropine (pill or tablet) .... $\frac{1}{250}$ grain.

The object of this treatment is to bring the blood to the surface and equalize the circulation. If this can be done, it will readily be seen that it will relieve the congestion or inflammation of the lungs.

If the patient becomes nauseated, skip a few doses of the Veratrum and Ipecac; if the pupils of the eye become dilated, skip the Atropine. If the inflammation continues, the Veratrum should be continued in 2-drop doses every two hours (or less often if it occasions nausea) for a few days. Also give $\frac{1}{20}$ of a grain of Strychnine in pill or tablet form four times a day. Strychnine is an active stimulant, while Veratrum tends to relieve the inflamed lungs.

B. Apply Mustard plaster on painful lung. Take hot drinks and bath as hot as can be borne, and go to bed. Get warm and perspire freely.—(38).

C. When first taken, or soon after the chill, put 5 drops of the Tincture of Veratrum Viride in $\frac{1}{2}$ glass of water, and give 1 teaspoonful each half hour. It will quiet the fever and congestion in twenty-four hours. Of course, if the disease has run until consolidation has taken place, Veratrum will do no good; but if given early it is an excellent remedy.—(43).

D. In the beginning—at the time of chill or a few hours after—give 1-drop doses of the Tincture of Veratrum Viride each half hour.

For hard cough put $\frac{1}{4}$ grain of Morphine in $\frac{1}{4}$ glass of water. One teaspoonful given when needed to quiet will be of real service.—(43)—Homeopathic.

E. If the fever is not broken up within forty-eight hours, the patient should receive a bath every day. Baths aid largely in controlling the temperature. This is important, as the prolonged use of fever remedies, such as Veratrum, Aconite, etc., is not recommended, because they lower temperature only at the expense of the vitality and strength of the patient. Keep the bowels active. Secure at least one thorough movement every day. Give 5 grains of Salol every three hours.

If at any time the patient seems weak or losing strength, give any additional stimulants. We do not recommend the use of whiskey in any form in the treatment of these cases because our experience is that it tends to nauseate and destroy appetite, and in cases of pneumonia the most nourishing diet is of the utmost importance. The physical strength or vitality must be maintained in as high a degree as possible. Frequent feeding of the most nourishing food is necessary. Meats or solid foods are not called for at this time, although rice boiled for three hours, soft boiled eggs, milk, toast, etc., are perfectly safe.

When the patient gets up, great care should be taken to avoid exposure, and continued attendance to the bowels and regular habits in eating are necessary.

Carbonate of Ammonia.—We are not unmindful of the reputation that Carbonate of Ammonia has in the treatment of this disease. When exposed to air, Carbonate of Ammonia readily undergoes a change which renders it worthless. To be of any value it must be hard and glistening—so hard that it cannot be cut with a knife. As usually found it is soft and readily pulverized, or at least readily shaved with a pocket knife. There may be quite a strong odor of Ammonia, yet the strength is largely gone. We have had a good deal of experience with this drug and urge a careful inspection before trusting the patient to its effects. There is so little Carbonate of Ammonia that is of value that it should be excluded from the list of remedies.

PLEURO-PNEUMONIA.— Pleuro-pneumonia means pneumonia plus inflammation of the pleura—the delicate membrane which surrounds the lungs. Probably there is always some affection of the pleura in attacks of pneumonia. If the pleura is involved to any great extent, there is more pain, the pain is much more severe, and recovery is more doubtful. The patient may fully recover from the pneumonia, but the effects may linger in the pleura and tuberculosis result. Besides enclosing the lungs, the pleura is also reflected around the inner surface of the chest cavity; thus there are two membranes. During inflammation of the membrane that encloses the lungs, the two surfaces in various places may become adherent, that is, grow fast, leaving a cavity or pocket of greater or less size. The exudate which follows the inflammation may remain unabsorbed, may contain serum and lymph, there may be some blood, and later it may change into pus, thus rendering the condition serious. If pus forms, complete recovery is doubtful, and frequently these cases proceed to tuberculosis with considerable rapidity.

Cause.—Extension of the pneumonia and involvement of the pleura. It should be remembered that inflammation of the pleura may occur without pneumonia. See PLEURISY.

Symptoms.—The symptoms are increased pain and other exaggeration of the symptoms of pneumonia. The exudate soon overspreads the affected surface of the pleura, and the two layers or membranes may become adherent, as already mentioned. If the exudate is absorbed, the points at which the two layers of the pleura have grown together may, by reason of the constant motion of the lungs, gradually separate, leaving the two surfaces attached by a band or cord of greater or less length. This is comparatively harmless, in fact, may do no harm. A little twinge of pain, or other like evidence, may remind the patient in later years that this condition exists. This condition may also result from inflammation of the pleura without pneumonia.

TREATMENT.—

The treatment is the same as that used in the usual forms of pneumonia. The pain is very severe. The membranes contained in any enclosed cavity, as the chest cavity or abdominal cavity, are called *serous* membranes. They differ from mucous membranes in being much thinner, and the secretions furnished by them are more of a serous or watery nature, hence the term, serous membranes. These membranes, wherever found, are extremely sensitive, hence in acute inflammation the pain is always severe and usually requires Opium in some form—perhaps Morphine is the oftenest used because it is the most convenient. Morphine may be given in ⅛ to ¼-grain doses as needed, or Dover's powders in 5-grain doses. Either should be given in sufficient amount to control the pain (see note below). Also attend to the bowels and give the ordinary fever remedies as needed. If the case is protracted, stimulants will also be needed; stimulants are always needed in the aged. After convalescence has been established give a teaspoonful of Syrup of Hydriodic Acid four times a day—between meals and at bedtime.

Note.—We do not recommend the free use of opiates; in fact, we are opposed to their use unless actually needed, because they cover or mask the symptoms and deceive the attendants. Again, their effects always interfere more or less with digestion, elimination and assimilation; but when pain is beyond control by other means, their results are less damaging than the debilitating effects of the pain.

MALARIAL FEVERS.—(See under Fevers).

MALINGERING—FEIGNED SICKNESS.—Sometimes after accident or injury, or possibly following some diseases or conditions, the patient pretends or feigns sickness which does not exist. In treating these cases a careful examination should always be made. If pain is complained of, make pressure at that point. The patient is very likely to say you hurt him. Make him go through some light exercise—walking, sitting, bending forward, or exercising the arms. Note if there is any muscular wasting. A careful examination always makes a favorable impression on the patient's mind. This is not only pleasing to the patient, but is a great advantage in aiding one to speak favorably of the case. It should be remembered that a careful examination cures many of these cases; but one must first gain the patient's confidence, hence the necessity of such examination. If there should be any muscular wasting, it would indicate disease of the spinal cord. The various pains the patient complains of, if they are real, are probably rheumatic in nature. It is probably advisable in these cases to give some light treatment, and as a rule the case can be discharged at an early date.

RECOMMENDED TREATMENT.—

Hypodermic injection of $\frac{1}{10}$ grain of Apomorphia for persons pretending to have taken poisons, or for hysterical fits. Relaxes the nervous system and produces prompt emesis—vomiting.— (31).

MEASLES.—(See under ERUPTIVE FEVERS).

MENINGITIS.—(See under BRAIN, DISEASES OF).

MENORRHAGIA.—(See under WOMEN'S DISEASES).

METORRHAGIA.—(See under WOMEN'S DISEASES).

MILK SICKNESS.—A number of years ago there was a disease among the cattle in this locality called *Zembles*, which disease was caused by their eating or drinking poisonous food or water. Persons eating the beef or butter or drinking the milk of the diseased cattle were very sick, and we called it "*milk sickness.*" I was called in counsel with Dr. John Martin in the case of an old lady who had vomited every few minutes for thirty-six hours and who every moment expected to die. Looking in my medicine bag I found I was out of the acids I wanted, but that I had Sulphuric Acid and Carbonate of Ammonia. I diluted the Acid and added the Ammonia and had her drink it while effervescing. We staid an hour, during which time she did not vomit, and on returning the next day found that she had not vomited and was much better—in fact, she never had another attack of vomiting to the day of her death, which was many years afterward. I have tried the same remedy many times since with the same result. The proper dose is 5 grains of Carbonate of Ammonia to 1 to 2 drops of the Sulphuric Acid, well diluted with water. This dose may be repeated if necessary.— (84).

MORTIFICATION.—(See under GANGRENE).

MOUTH, DISEASES OF.—As nearly all diseases of the mouth are affections of childhood, this subject has been placed under DISEASES OF CHILDREN. For *Syphilitic Sore Mouth*, see under VENEREAL DISEASES.

MUMPS — PAROTIDITIS.—The parotid glands are placed one on each side of the neck just in front of the ear, and at the lower border of the ear they extend back to the mastoid process—the prominent bone just behind the ear. Each of these glands weigh about one ounce. They are formed of many small lobules, held together by connective tissue. Each lobule presents many little openings or miniature glands, and each lobule gives rise to an excretory duct. These ducts unite and form a single duct, one on each side, about 1½ inches in length. The single ducts pass horizontally through the substance of the cheek, one on each side, and terminate in the mouth opposite the second double molar tooth on the upper jaw. The parotid glands are the principal ones which furnish the saliva (see DIGESTION).

Mumps means inflammation of the Parotid glands. There are other glands situated beneath the jaw which may also become affected. It is an acute, contagious disease, which develops about fourteen days after exposure and lasts about one week. One or both glands may be affected at the same time. Usually one is affected first, the inflammation of the other occurring later.

Cause. — The cause is a specific ferment or poison, the original source of which is unknown.

Symptoms—As usually described, the first symptom may be a sense of chilliness followed by a slight rise of temperature, slight increase in the pulse rate, headache, languor, loss of appetite and pain at the angle of the jaw. The pain is increased on opening the mouth or in attempting to swallow. There is a chain of glands situated on each side of the neck, and the entire chain may become swollen. The swelling may also include the side of the face. If the disease occurs only on one side, the head may be turned toward the affected side as this relieves the tension and pain. In many cases the chills, fever, increase in pulse rate and headache may be entirely absent. The inflammation continues from four to six days and then gradually declines. In rare cases the parotid glands may suppurate, that is, an abscess form. There is a small opening in the mastoid process through which the seventh cranial nerve (see NEURALGIA) passes, then continues forward through the parotid glands and supplies the muscles of the face, giving them the power of motion. It is said that in some cases the pressure of the swollen gland may cause temporary and partial paralysis of this nerve.

TREATMENTS.—

A. The bowels should be kept active and the patient avoid taking cold. A well ventilated room where the temperature is uniform is best suited for cases of this kind. Very little medicine is needed. Salicylate of Soda may be given in 5-grain doses every three hours. If necessary for the fever, give 1-drop doses of Aconite every hour. If there is evidence of pus formation, large hot poultices should be kept over the affected side of the face and neck, and the abscess opened as soon as pus is discovered. Should the patient take cold during the course of the disease, serious complications are likely to follow.

B. Keep patient on a light diet, and correct constipation, if it exists, with small doses of Epsom or Rochelle Salts. If the swollen glands are painful, a poultice of Hops will give relief; or apply Camphorated Oil and hot flannel. If complications arise, call the doctor.

C. Apply small square of Belladonna plaster to jaws. Avoid catching cold.—(38).

D. No particular treatment is necessary, but keep in the house and keep the throat done up in flannel. Warm herb drinks are good. Keep the feet warm, and particularly avoid exposure to dampness, as in case of contracting a cold by this means the swelling may spread to other glands and become a serious matter.

MYELITIS—INFLAMMATION OF THE SPINAL CORD.—It will be remembered that the spinal cord is composed of large nerve cells and nerve fibers, which are held together by delicate connective tissue and surrounded by membranes. The fibers of the cord are situated externally and divided into separate columns or tracts. Each tract is supposed to be endowed with separate functions or duties. Different diseases are sometimes limited to one or more of these tracts. The various forms of inflammation often follow a single tract, hence the various names given to *Myelitis*, or *Inflammation of the Spinal Cord*, as: *Anterior Myelitis*, meaning front part; *Lateral Myelitis*, meaning the sides; *Posterior Myelitis*, meaning behind; *Transverse Myelitis*, meaning clear across, etc.

Cause.—Acute myelitis may be caused by poisons resulting from the infectious diseases. It may follow spinal meningitis, *i. e.*, inflammation of the membrane which surrounds the cord. It may result from accident or injury.

Symptoms.—The acute form comes on suddenly. The vessels of the cord are first congested. This is followed by inflammation with rise in temperature and pain along the back. The spinal column is sensitive to the touch. First there may be pain in the lower limbs, and as the disease continues this is followed by a sense of numbness; later the limbs become more or less paralyzed. The paralysis is governed by the amount of inflammation. There is also a sense of constriction about the body; this is usually accompanied by more or less pain. There may be involuntary discharges from the bowels and bladder. Later there may be bed sores, with wasting of the muscles supplied by the nerves from the affected part of the cord. During the progress of the disease there may be spasmodic action of the muscles of the affected part. The sense of constriction about the body, sometimes called *girdle pains*, the early loss of sensation and paralysis, and the bed sores, are the most prominent symptoms of acute myelitis.

Chronic Myelitis means paralysis. See PARALYSIS.

TREATMENTS.—

What to Do Till the Doctor Comes.—To make the patient comfortable in bed is perhaps the most that can be accomplished. Sweating will aid in affording relief, and in the meantime a hot bath might be given before going to bed, or at least the feet put into hot water; also means to produce sweating after he is in bed, as cans or jugs of hot water placed around him. If the bowels have been constipated, give a cathartic. Insure quiet until the doctor can arrive.

A. Inflammation of the spinal cord is the same as inflammation elsewhere. If any means can be secured to equalize the circulation, relief will follow. First put the patient to bed. By lying on the side or face the cord is said to be somewhat relieved (doubtful). Put the feet in hot water, give hot drinks, produce sweating, give frequent baths followed by brisk rubbing, keep the skin active, give an active cathartic, and, if possible, keep the bowels regular. To aid in producing sweating small doses of Aconite may be given—one drop every thirty minutes until the skin is moist. Atropine is another very good remedy to equalize the circulation and relieve congestion and inflammation. Give $\frac{1}{100}$ of a grain every hour for two or three doses—until the throat is dry or the pupil dilates. Atropine will not produce sweating, but with plenty of hot drinks and artificial heat, sweating may be produced while giving Atropine, and both are of the highest importance in inflammation. Veratrum is another most excellent drug; however, it differs in no way from Aconite. If the inflammation is the result of syphilis, give anti-syphilitic treatment. If the patient is strong, dieting for a few days will be of benefit. Absolute quiet should be maintained. If the disease continues, nourishment and elimination are points to be especially remembered.

NAUSEA—SICKNESS AT THE STOMACH.—RE-COMMENDED TREATMENTS.

A. Give the sixth dilution of Nux Vomica either in solution or in pill form—1 or 2 drops of the solution or 1 or 2 pills every thirty minutes until relieved.—(56)—Homeopathic.

B. One or two full doses of Paregoric is all-sufficient. For adult, one teaspoonful.—(30).

C. One tablespoonful of very hot water every few minutes.

D. ½ teaspoonful of Bicarbonate of Soda in ½ a glass of water, very hot, and taken in one dose. Repeat every hour if needed.—(41).

E. Subnitrate of Bismuth, ¼ of an ounce. Divide into 24 powders and take 1 powder every two hours. Apply a Mustard plaster to the stomach. Drink a cup of hot water every two or three hours.—(42).

F. A Spice plaster over the pit of the stomach. Small pieces of ice in the mouth. Give the following:

> Subnitrate of Bismuth..................... 3 grains.
> Oxalate of Cerium............ 3   "
>
> Divide into 12 powders and take one every fifteen minutes.—(35).

G. Apply Mustard plaster over the stomach. Drink Mint tea, such as Peppermint, Spearmint, etc. Take one tablespoonful of Lime Water and put into a glass half full of sweet milk. Drink three or four times a day. Diet for a few days.

NERVOUSNESS.—This term is applied to a condition of *hyperesthesia*, or unusual sensitiveness to sound and impressions. It is also sometimes called *neurasthenia*, meaning a deficiency in nerve power—nerve exhaustion. These conditions are also called *hysteria*, *fidgets*, etc., and may result in *melancholia* or strange hallucinations.

Cause.—It may be caused by the prolonged use of alcohol, by using too much tobacco, or may be due to the climacteric period —change of life. It is probably oftenest caused by prolonged dyspepsia, where the general system becomes irritated by unhealthy blood and weakened from lack of nutrition.

Symptoms.—The symptoms are unnatural irritability, oversensitiveness, and nervous apprehension or anxiety. There is often constipation, and some disturbance of the appetite, which may be voracious at times and at other times lacking.

TREATMENTS.—

A. It will not do to tell the patient that he or she has hysterics. These cases may or may not need treatment. Unless the patient was born with some defect in the nervous system, the trouble is the result of indigestion from some cause, which has resulted in an unhealthy system. The nerves have become shattered — have lost their "tone," or vigor. If a physician is handling the case, it is necessary to make a careful examination because this makes a favorable impression upon the patient's mind. It aids in gaining confidence, and without this confidence all treatment would fail because the patient would neither follow directions nor take the medicine given. True, there may be but little medicine needed. First give attention to the eliminative organs, regulate the diet, give artificial digestants for a short time if needed, and secure proper hygienic surroundings and proper exercise. The following mixture is valuable in these cases, as in many others, for the amount of nourishment which it contains; it is not a medicine, but a food. The Maltine contains a ferment similar to the ptyaline found in the saliva, which aids materially in digestion. One part of this ferment is contained in 500 parts of the Maltine, or any good extract of Malt:

> Fellows' Syrup of Hypophosphites.. 3 ounces
> Maltine, or any good extract of Malt 6   "
>
> *Mix*, by shaking the bottle, and take 1 table-spoonful three times a day, just before meals or immediately after. A tablespoonful may also be taken at bedtime.

B. If the nervous symptoms are slight, give one pill of Aconitine Amorphous, $\frac{1}{134}$ of a grain, also one pill of Anemonine, $\frac{1}{134}$ of a grain, every hour for a few days; then once in two hours during the day. The 2 pills may be given together at the same time.

If the trouble is due to the change of life, the Bromides are more valuable. Bromide of Potash and Bromide of Ammonia, of each 5 grains, may be given two or three times a day. This amount can be increased if necessary.

In case of young girls, give Cyperipedin $\frac{1}{12}$ of a grain, and Scutillarin $\frac{1}{60}$ of a grain, every two hours. When quiet is restored, stop it altogether, until the symptoms re-appear.

When the effect is the result of alcohol, teaspoonful doses of Tincture of Capsicum well diluted, and $\frac{1}{30}$ of a grain of Strychnine may be given every three hours for a few days, then twice a day, more or less, as needed. In case of alcoholics, hot baths and a brisk rub are also advised, at the same time keeping the bowels active.

In all cases strict attention should be given to diet, alimentary sanitation and hygiene.—(72).

C. For nervousness nervines should be given. One of the best nervines is a tea made of Scullcap (see chapter on Herbs), or of English Valerian, or of American Valerian (common Lady Slipper). Or Assafœtida in 5-grain doses may be given. The use of any one of these remedies should be continued for a considerable length of time if one is subject to nervousness.

D. Regulate the diet and bowels. Eat nothing indigestible. Drink only milk and water.—(38).

> **E.** Tincture of Valerianate of Ammonia .... 2 ounces.
>
> *Dose.*—½ to 1 teaspoonful three times a day.
> —(24).

F. Celerina—made by Rio Chemical
Co., St. Louis, Mo...................... 2 ounces.
Dose.—1 teaspoonful three or four times a day in water.

or,

Peacock's Bromides........................ 2 ounces.
Dose.—1 teaspoonful three times a day in water.—(20).

G. Bromide of Potash .... 1 ounce.
Peppermint Water .... 4 ounces.
Mix. Take 1 teaspoonful in water three or four times a day, or oftener if needed.

A tepid sponge bath every day is excellent for nervousness.
—(42).

H. ¼ grain of Atropine in one glass of water. Give 1 teaspoonful each half hour until relieved.—(43).

NETTLE RASH.—(See under SKIN DISEASES).

NEURALGIA.—This is a disease of the nervous system, characterized by paroxysms of pain of a darting, stabbing character. Usually one side only is affected, whether of the body or head, the pain following the course of some sensory nerve.

The divisions given below, as, *Neuralgia of the Fifth Nerve,* etc., simply indicate the nerve affected, and the course taken by the affected nerve or nerves. These nerves have their origin in the brain and spinal cord.

Neuralgia of the Fifth Nerve—*of the face.*—The nerves that have their origin in the brain are called the cranial nerves. They are often spoken of as the *first, second, third,* etc., according to their point of origin. The one arising nearest in front is called the *first,* the next, the *second,* the *third, fourth, fifth,* and so on. The fifth is the great nerve of sensation to the head and face and the motor nerve to the muscles of mastication. The sensory branches are a very common seat of neuralgia, probably by reason of their large distribution. The nerve on the left side is the one usually affected. The pain may extend over the entire side of the face, or be confined to certain branches of the nerve, particularly to the branches that run around the eye—one just over it and one just underneath. In this case, if the pain is of any duration, the eye becomes bloodshot in appearance, "runs water," and is sensitive to the light. Also pressure on the bone just underneath the eyebrow and under the eye next to the nose causes a feeling of tenderness. At these points a fiber of the fifth nerve comes through the bone. *Megrim* and *Hemicrania* are terms frequently applied to neuralgia of the face where but one side is affected.

In severe cases of facial neuralgia there may be a convulsive twitching of the muscles on the affected side, to which the name *Tic-douloureux* has been given. The term tic-douloureux is also applied to a spasmodic twitching of the muscles of the face without pain. The muscles of the face are controlled by the seventh cranial nerve, hence in tic-douloureux the fifth nerve, the nerve of sensation, is not necessarily involved.

Cervico-Occipital Neuralgia—*of the neck and back of the head.*—The occipital nerve is also subject to neuralgia, the pain running down the back of the head into the neck as far as the collar-bone, thence upward and forward to the cheek. The affected part may become very sensitive to the touch, also an eruption may appear on the skin. In some cases there is a sensation of cracking at the nape of the neck which is very annoying. The pain comes on in paroxysms, and is either sharp and stabbing or deep and gripping in character.

Cervico-Brachial Neuralgia—*of the neck and arm.*—The nerve of the arm (brachial) may be affected with neuralgia. The pain extends from the neck down into the arm, causing a feeling of numbness and weakness in the hand, arm and shoulder, with a feeling of tenderness to the touch of all the parts affected, the tenderness extending also to the breast.

Intercostal Neuralgia—*of the side.*—Another seat of neuralgia is in the side, resulting from a nerve which follows the fifth and sixth ribs, from which it derives the name intercostal. This is frequently associated with an eruption known as *shingles*, and is characterized by tenderness at points where the nerve emerges from the bone—at the side of the chest, and in the front near the breast-bone.

Lumbo-Abdominal Neuralgia—*of the loins.*—The pain in this neuralgia differs from the forms described only in affecting a different set of nerves—those extending from the upper part of the hip to the lower part of the abdomen and contiguous parts.

Sciatica—*of the thigh.*—In this the pain follows the sciatic nerve, shooting along the back of the hip into the inner side of the thigh and down into the calf of the leg, ankle and heel. The foot loses the sense of touch, movement of the limb is accomplished with pain and difficulty, and, if the neuralgia is of long duration, a wasting of the limb takes place.

While the foregoing terms are often employed in speaking of *Neuralgia*, they are unimportant except to indicate where the trouble is located. Almost any pain may be called neuralgia. *Neuron* means nerve, plus *algos*, pain.

Cause of Neuralgia.—The conditions present in neuralgia and rheumatism (see RHEUMATISM) are the same, and the pain is Nature's voice forcibly expressed, calling attention to our errors. It is evidence that the patient has overstepped the limit of safety and now must pay principal and interest. It would be as proper to say rheumatism of the face as neuralgia of the face, but through habit we call it the latter. The term *muscular rheumatism* is not correct. If the reader should examine the fibers of the affected muscle under the microscope, such fibers would appear normal. There would be no evidence of inflammation or other trouble, showing clearly that the disease was in the nerve fiber and not the muscle fiber. When the "bones ache," the same conditions are present, but another part is affected. The part is affected first that offers the least resistance. In some resistance is less in one part or organ, and in others, in another part or organ. Pain is controlled according to our several powers to resist, and we all understand that these are not the same in each individual. Any and all of these conditions are evidence that there remains in the system irritating waste material that should be eliminated. As evidence that these statements are true, these cases almost universally give a history of constipation. Again, the urine is highly colored. This color is due to uric acid, which has been rasping through the system and which the kidneys are doing their best to eliminate. Sick headache is also an evidence of indigestion followed by the production of poison that produces local irritation in the stomach. The undigested food also aids or increases the irritation.

If further evidence is needed, let us view the situation from another standpoint. The circulation of the brain is conducted through the carotid arteries. These are situated one on either side of the neck, and lie parallel to the jugular vein. The one on the left side is more direct, hence it is shorter. The result is a more forcible circulation, resulting in greater pressure, and it follows that any irritating substances or material would produce a sharper or more acute effect. This explains the statement already made that neuralgia of the face usually occurs on the left side. The artery that supplies the left eye is a branch of the shorter carotid, and the increased pressure and irritation produce congestion of this artery. This explains why the left eye becomes "bloodshot." The middle coat of the eyeball is made up of radiating fibers of the same artery, hence the congestion causes pressure on the delicate fibers of the optic nerve, which are in contact with the artery and form the inner coat of the eye, and this accounts for the sensitiveness of the eye already mentioned. Apoplexy is caused by the rupture of an artery near the base of the brain. The ruptured artery is usually found on the left side of the brain. While this is a separate disease from neuralgia, it supports the foregoing statements regarding pressure and irritation. At the junction of the brain and spinal cord the nerve fibers cross, with the result that the right side is usually paralyzed.

There are a few exceptions to these statements, but they are rare. The foregoing conditions will cover or include nearly all cases of rheumatism or neuralgia.

Exciting Cause.—Exposure to cold or damp, anxiety or undue mental exertion, may be the exciting or immediate cause of neuralgia, as any of these tends to interfere with external circulation. This means that more of the irritating blood is retained in the internal organs, the brain and spinal cord receiving their share of the over-supply. Irritation of these structures is thus increased, hence the affection of the various nerves leading from them. The irritation also follows in the small arteries which supply the nerve fibers themselves. This aids in causing congestion, pressure and pain.

TREATMENTS.—

A. Sulphate of Morphine.................. 2½ grains.
 Sulphate of Strychnine................. ⅓ "
 Tincture of Aconite...................... 18 drops.
 Fowler's Solution........................ 1½ drachms.
 Glycerine .... 1 ounce.
 Simple Elixir, enough to make ..... 2 "

 Mix, and take one teaspoonful. Repeat in one hour, if needed.

B. Camphorated Olive Oil................ 1 ounce.
 Chloroform .... 1 drachm.
 Apply externally.

 Antikamnia .... 20 grains.
 Sulphate of Quinine .... 30 "
 Camphor, powdered .... 5 "
 Capsicum, powdered .... 10 "
 Tincture of Aconite Root............. 10 drops.

 Mix, and make 10 capsules. *Dose.*—Take one every 3 or 4 hours.—(28).

C. Take English Valerian, steep to make a tea and drink freely of it. Take from 20 to 30 drops of Paregoric two or three times a day. Counter-irritants, such as Mustard plasters, etc., placed over the region of pain are beneficial.

D. ¼ grain of Atropine in one glass of water. Give 1 teaspoonful every half hour until relieved.—(43).

E. Antikamnia and Quinine Tablets. One every 3 hours. —(20).

F. Menthol .... 45 grains.
Alcohol .... 1 ounce.
Cologne Water, enough to make..... 3   "
Mix, and apply over painful part.—(59).

G. *Megrim.*—
Antipyrine .... 1 drachm.
Spirits Ammonia............................. 1   "
Elixir Bromide Potash.................... 3 ounces.
Mix, and take one teaspoonful every 2 or 3
hours until relieved.—(29).

H. *Megrim.*—5 grains of Acetanilid every hour until relieved.
—(57).

Important.—It should be remembered that the foregoing
remedies produce only a temporary effect, and that the general
system must be improved before permanent relief can be expected.
Attention to diet, elimination, fresh air, proper exercise, etc., are
all of the greatest importance.

NIGHT SWEATS.—Night Sweats are the result of prolonged fevers, tuberculosis, or other conditions where there is
general weakness.

Treatments.—

A. Atropine in $\frac{1}{100}$ to $\frac{1}{60}$ grain doses one hour before going
to bed, or Agaricin in ¼ grain doses, taken at the same time,
are most effectual in producing immediate results. It is understood, of course, that the patient's general condition must be
improved before permanent benefit can be had. If the sweating
is the result of protracted fevers, it is evidence that poisons
remain in the system, and first these must be eliminated. Secure
thorough elimination of the bowels, and afterwards give 10 grains
of the Sulphocarbolate of Soda, or the same amount of Salol,
every four hours. If the eliminations give offensive odor, give
this dose every two hours until improvement, then four times a
day. Also give the patient 1 teaspoonful of the following
four times a day—at meal time and bedtime.

Fowler's Solution......................... ½ ounce.
Hydrochloric (Muriatic) Acid......... 30 drops.
Lloyd's Hydrastus .... 3 drachms.
Glycerine .... 2 ounces.
Water, enough to make .... 4 ounces.

With dose of the above, give 2 grains of
Quinine in pill or capsule form. If the weakness is the result of tuberculosis, see treatment
under that head. Also give the following:

Fellows' Syrup of Hypophosphites.. 2 ounces.
Maltine, or a good Extract of Malt.. 6   "

Mix by shaking the bottle, and take, for an
adult, 1 tablespoonful at meal time and bedtime—four doses a day.

B. Take 10 drops of the Tincture of Belladonna at bedtime. —(57).

C. Elixir of Vitriol—Take 20 drops in a glassful of water three times daily.—(32).

D. A teacupful of Sage tea at bedtime. —(41).

NOCTURNAL EMISSIONS—SPERMATORRHEA.
—This is an involuntary emission during sleep. Much speculation has been indulged in, many fears created, and much suffering, remorse and despair have resulted from this condition by reason of the prominence given it by quacks. To our personal knowledge many a young man has been ruined financially, and had his mind filled with horror as he tottered upon the supposed brink of insanity or an early grave. This condition is the result of keeping the patient's mind constantly upon the subject, and is exactly what the quack or advertising doctor desires and endeavors to bring about. The patient becomes so anxious that he is ready to yield up his last dollar to be free from what he supposes to be physical ruin, followed by imbecility or a miserable death. These cases are not dangerous; on the contrary, they are an indication of health, strength and vigor, and those who teach otherwise are actuated by personal greed, for the sake of which they would sacrifice health and manhood and make a foul prostitution of the practice of medicine.

TREATMENTS.—

A. The following treatment will stop the emissions. However, if they only occur occasionally in a healthy young man, no treatment is needed.

Bromide of Potash .... 1 ounce.
Glycerine 2   "
Simple Elixir, enough to make........ 4   "

Mix, and take 2 teaspoonfuls at bedtime. The dose may be increased to 1 tablespoonful, if necessary. Also take the following:

Tincture of Nux Vomica............ ½ ounce.
Lloyd's Hydrastus .... 3 drachms.
Fowler's Solution 2   "
Glycerine.............. .... 2 ounces.
Water enough to make 4   "

Mix, and take 1 teaspoonful at meal time. The last remedy need not be taken without the first one.

Keep the bowels active and have absolutely no fear of unfavorable results.

B. Fluid Extract of Black Willow—½ teaspoonful three times a day in a glass of water.—(25).

C. Specific Stavesacre—2 drops four or five times a day. Also Specific Passaflora—1 teaspoonful three hours before bedtime and also a teaspoonful on retiring.—(30).

D. Dilute Phosphoric Acid.................. 75 drops.
Fluid Extract Ergot .... 1 ounce.
Tincture of Columbo 3   "
Mix, and take 1 teaspoonful at meal time
and bedtime—four doses a day,—(23).

OBESITY — CORPULENCE — FAT. — Obesity is an accumulation of fat, usually under the skin, in the abdominal cavity, or both. This occurs to such an extent as to embarrass the activity of the individual. Obesity is an amount of fat not only incompatible with health, but may interfere with the vital powers to such an extent as to be dangerous.

Cause.—Fat meat, butter, oils, starchy food, milk and sugar are all given as the cause of obesity, and while it is true that these have a tendency to produce fat, it is also true that there are many cases of obesity where these foods are not used, or are used very sparingly. The real cause lies in the fact that the food eaten, whatever it may be, results in an over-production of fat. Why this is so has never been satisfactorily determined.

TREATMENTS.—

A. Avoidance of the foods mentioned, daily exercise in the open air, regular habits, bathing, and the avoidance of all drugs to reduce the excess of adipose tissue. Drug medication may do harm by lowering the vitality and rendering the system less capable. Mineral waters, however, are not drugs.

B. Sprudel water, alternating with Kissingen. One glassful every day.—(21).

C. Use artificial Kissingen and Vichy waters, alternately— glassful twenty minutes after meals. Avoid starches and water. —(12).

D. Avoid all food containing fat, sugar and starch, as bread, rice, potatoes, fat meat, cake, candy, pudding, beans, sago, etc. Eat lean meat, eggs, oysters, skimmed milk, turnips, soups, small amount of toast and an occasional potato.
Work enough to keep down the fat and make muscle.—(13).

E. Eat less and exercise more. Drink no water at meals. Avoid starchy diet.—(60).

F. Give Phytolacca Juice, 3 drops in water after meals. Restrict the diet and grow thin.—(18)—Homeopathic.

G. Phytolacca.—(37)—Homeopathic.

OPHTHALMIA.—(See under EYE, DISEASES OF).

OVARIES, INFLAMMATION OF, TUMOR OF, Etc.
—(See under WOMEN'S DISEASES).

PARALYSIS.—Paralysis is a partial or complete loss of the power of motion of one or more of the muscles of the body. By some it is also applied to the loss of sensation. Paralysis may be confined to a single muscle, or may include one or both limbs, or may affect one half of the body. When confined to one half of the body, it is called *Hemiplegia.* This form is the result of apoplexy. When it is confined to the upper or lower extremities, it is called *Paraplegia.* *Writer's Paralysis* is paralysis of the muscles of the wrist and fingers, due to overwork. Paralysis of the foot or one side of the face, or that following diphtheria, is termed *Local Paralysis.* *Paralysis Agitans*, or *Shaking Palsy*, is a term applied to that form where there is a constant trembling. This is a disease of middle or advanced life.

Cause.—Most cases of paralysis are due to disease of the spinal cord, and are the result of an irritant in the blood. The irritant may be the virus of syphilis, or may result from the prolonged use of alcohol or from chronic dyspepsia. Chronic dyspepsia means constipation and an unhealthy digestive tract where many poisons are generated. It seems needless to say that these poisons enter the circulation and act as irritants. A lack of exercise or poor hygienic surroundings aid in producing irritants because they render tissue change unequal. There is an excess of waste over repair. The waste is irritating and vitality is lowered. In all these conditions the blood contains many irritants and poisons which are constantly rasping through the system. The effect is always greatest where resistance is least. If in the spinal cord, it produces a low form of inflammation, followed by paralysis and death.

The spinal cord contains groups of large nerve cells and nerve fibers held together by a connective tissue framework. Long-continued inflammation, wherever it occurs, always produces an overgrowth of the connective tissue; if in the spinal cord, there is a corresponding destruction of the nerve fibers and nerve cells. As stated elsewhere, connective tissue resulting from inflammation always contracts when it matures. This contraction squeezes the nerve structures, gradually lessens circulation, causes pressure, and aids in their destruction. The nerve cells and fibers are found in different stages of degeneration, and the aggregation of the large nerve cells which form semi-independent nerve centers in the cord, degenerate and disappear more or less completely. With the destruction of the natural tissue and the contraction of the new, the spinal cord becomes hard and fibrous. Practically all forms of paralysis are the same. They consist of an increased blood supply, the result of inflammation, followed by degeneration of the nerves and nerve cells and overgrowth of connective tissue, which contracts and hardens. Sometimes one part of the cord is affected and sometimes another.

A nerve is no more nor less than a long-drawn-out process of a nerve cell. Certain cells in the brain and spinal cord send out these prolongations, and thus the nervous system is formed. The nerves of sensation arise in the back part of the cord, hence inflammation of this part is first indicated by increased sensibility, which may be in the form of pain, or of a tingling sensation; later there is loss of sensation, showing that the destruction is more complete. The nerves of motion arise in the front part of the cord, hence inflammation of this part, acting as a stimulant, is first indicated by increased muscular action. This is followed by a loss of motion and shrinking of the muscles, showing destruction and degeneration of this system. The voluntary muscles of the body and extremities are supplied with nerves from the spinal cord. Many of the nerves rising in the brain extend downward, connect with the spinal nerves and modify or control their action; but during inflammation messages cannot be transmitted through the diseased area in the cord. This leaves that portion below the disease without a break, and the spinal nerves, having escaped the control of the brain, set up a spasmodic action due to the inflammation. At first the inflammation acts as a stimulant and the nerves respond by involuntary movement. The patient cannot control his actions because of the constant excitement kept up in the cord, and because control cannot be sent from the brain. This is the condition present in *Locomotor Ataxia*. In the second stage of that disease the feet and lower limbs escape the control of the patient and fly in all directions. Later, as the disease extends upward, the hands and arms may suffer in the same way. With the destruction of the nerves of motion, paralysis is complete.

Paralysis of the lower limbs indicates invasion of the lower part of the spinal cord because the nerves governing them have their origin there; paralysis of the hands and arms indicates invasion of the cervical portion (that portion situated in the neck), because the nerves governing them arise there. Disease of the cord may begin below and extend upward, or other parts may be affected first. Chronic progressive bulbular paralysis, *i. e.* paralysis of the muscles of the throat, tongue, lips, etc., is caused by connective tissue overgrowth at the base of the brain where the nerves supplying these muscles take their origin. The nerves themselves are first hardened by inflammatory processes, and later degenerate. These changes take place gradually; so do these forms of paralysis. At first only a few cells are affected, but the number increases until function is lost, when the change takes place more rapidly. A blood clot may plug an artery supplying a group of nerve cells in the cord and cause sudden or acute paralysis. Sometimes chronic inflammation of the spinal cord may follow rheumatism, and produce permanent muscular contractions with great deformity of joints.

These changes in the cord are responsible for most forms of paralysis, and may be caused by irritation produced by alcohol, the effects of indigestion, bad hygiene, constipation, syphilis, etc., as already mentioned. Drinking hard cider may do the same thing. Hard cider not only contains alcohol, but many acids which will produce inflammation and chronic catarrh of the stomach, and this means indigestion and disease.

Volumes have been written upon paralysis and nervous diseases, yet the subject is not so difficult to understand. Long-continued irritation from septic blood in any part of the body will sooner or later produce its evil effects by interfering with the central nervous system—the brain and spinal cord. Headache is characteristic of this condition; so is neuralgia and rheumatism.

TREATMENTS.—

A. Regulate the bowels, keep the skin active, give special attention to nourishing food and to the digestive organs in general, avoid fatigue or overwork, secure an abundance of fresh air and take a reasonable amount of exercise. Internally, take 1 teaspoonful of Syrup of Hydriodic Acid between meals and at bedtime. *Do not take within two hours after a meal.* If the Syrup causes a catarrhal condition of the eyes, take less; if it does not, the dose may be increased a little. Also take 10 grains of Salol after each meal. If paralysis is due to syphilis, give treatment under that disease.

B. Use the battery, one pole being placed along the spine between the shoulders. The foot-plate should also be used. Massage is beneficial and warm clothing should always be worn. Five drops of Nux Vomica should be taken three times a day before meals, or take $\frac{1}{60}$ of a grain of Strychnine in pill form three times a day. Keep the bowels open with 1 teaspoonful of Epsom Salts in a wineglass half full of warm water, taken from one to three times a day. The diet should be nutritious. In severe cases, if the appetite is poor, and especially if the patient is not addicted to the use of stimulants, a little brandy or other liquor may be given at meal time.—(67).

C. Numb Palsy.—If this condition has existed for a great length of time, but little benefit can be expected from any treatment; but if recent, very much good will result from the following treatment faithfully followed:

Paralytic Liniment.—

Sulphuric Ether	6 ounces.
Alcohol	2 "
Laudanum	1 "
Oil of Lavender	1 "

Mix, and cork tightly.

In a recent case of paralysis let the whole extent of the numb surface be thoroughly bathed and rubbed with this preparation for several minutes, at least three times daily, and at the same time take internally 20 drops of the same in a little sweetened water. Use a large amount of friction by the hand. It is well in very recent cases to keep the parts covered with flannels. This liniment may also be used in old cases, and in many of them will undoubtedly do much good.—(67).

D. Dilute Phosphoric Acid.................. 75 drops.
Fluid Extract of Ergot .... 1 ounce.
Tincture of Columbo .... 3 "

Mix. Take 1 teaspoonful at meal time and bedtime—four doses a day.—(23).

E. Gentle friction by application of electricity (Faradic current). 3-grain doses of Iodide Potash four times a day—before breakfast, between meals and at bedtime.—(70).

Electricity in Treating Paralysis.—Electricity is recommended by a great many physicians. Success follows its use in some cases; failure in others. This may be due somewhat to the degree of confidence inspired in the patient. Many look upon electricity with a great deal of confidence, and it is good sense to believe that many times this confidence stimulates the belief in the patient's mind that he is going to get well. This belief gives energy and ambition, and every fiber becomes possessed of greater possibilities. Both digestion and assimilation are thus increased, respiration and circulation are stimulated, and these conditions may aid materially in the absorption of a blood clot, or in checking the inroads in a case of chronic or progressive paralysis.

Electricity and hope will never remove connective tissue overgrowth, but they may aid in preventing its further development and in preventing other degenerative changes: Hope and a contented mind may do this through their influence over digestion and assimilation. Hope stimulates the mind, the mind reacts upon the body, the vital powers are strengthened, physical force is renewed, and there results a determination which yields a powerful influence in checking disease.

All are agreed that these statements are true. As evidence of such agreement every doctor of experience practices these principles in treating the sick. Some doctors strive purposely to stimulate hope in the mind of their patients; others influence the mind unconsciously, their presence alone producing a confidence which medical appliances cannot give.

PEMPHIGUS.—(See under SKIN DISEASES).

PERICARDITIS.—(See under HEART, DISEASES OF).

PERITONITIS.—The *peritoneum* is a thin membrane which lines the inner wall of the abdominal cavity, is reflected around the whole length of the digestive tract and forms the outer coat of the bowels. Peritonitis is inflammation of the peritoneum. It may be acute or chronic, local or general. In the acute form there is fever, intense pain, vomiting and hiccough.

Causes.—Peritonitis may be caused by hernia, either internal or external, where there is a good deal of pressure. It may be caused by external injury, such as blows over the abdomen, or by perforating wounds into or through the abdominal cavity. There is always local peritonitis accompanying appendicitis, and by extension this may become general. It may result from inflammation of other organs, such as the ovaries, or the uterus in puerperal fever, or blood poisoning following labor. It may result from erysipelas, from ulceration of the bowels, from typhoid fever, from the rupture of an abscess into the abdominal cavity, or may follow operations upon any of the organs contained in the abdominal cavity. Peritonitis is also said to be caused by taking cold, where the blood is unhealthy and irritating and where the internal organs become highly congested. *Tubercular Peritonitis* is a chronic form.

Symptoms.—In the acute form the disease begins suddenly— usually with a chill. There is a quick rise in temperature, and the pulse is rapid—may reach as high as 140 or 150 beats per minute, and even more. The pain is severe, and the surface of the abdomen soon becomes extremely sensitive to the touch. It also becomes greatly enlarged and its muscles become rigid. The patient usually lies with the knees drawn up as this relaxes the muscles and lessens the pain. There is loss of appetite, nausea, perhaps vomiting, and hiccough usually accompanies this disease. In a severe case, the temperature, at first high, reaching perhaps 103 or 104, may soon become subnormal, the surface of the body cold, the pulse rapid and weak, and the features "pinched," the patient's face wearing an anxious expression. Where there is great distension of the abdominal cavity, the lungs, liver and heart are crowded upon more or less, and as a result the breathing may become rapid. There may be a slight cough. In peritonitis resulting from the rupture of an abscess into the abdominal cavity, there is usually, but not always,

sudden and terrific pain, weak, rapid pulse, subnormal temperature, great loss of the vital forces, collapse and rapid death. We
have witnessed but one case of this kind where there was absolutely no pain; the other symptoms were as given. In peritonitis
from the rupture of an abscess the patient usually lives only
from 15 to 24 hours, unless relieved by opening the abdominal
cavity and thoroughly flushing with sterilized water. Even with
this treatment recovery is doubtful.

TREATMENTS.—

What to Do Till the Doctor Comes.—Send for the doctor. In
peritonitis constipation is the rule, so while waiting for the
doctor, empty the lower bowel with injections. For this purpose
a quart of hot water made slippery with soap may be used, or a
more effective injection is made as follows: Take the yolks of
two eggs and a tablespoonful of turpentine, beat together thoroughly and put into a quart of hot water. After the bowel is
emptied it will be well to bathe the feet in hot water, wipe dry, and
get the patient to bed. Put hot applications across him, covering
the whole addomen. Give warm drinks, such as Mint tea, tea
of Virginia Snakeroot, White Root tea or something of the kind,
to get him to sweating freely. If the pain is extremely severe,
and especially if the doctor is at some distance, he may be given,
if an adult, from 10 to 15 drops of laudanum.

A. Commence treatment by giving active cathartics—Salts
in some form are best for this purpose because they attract large
quantities of water and thus drain the congested and inflamed
vessels. This is the first step towards relieving the inflammation.
To aid or hasten the laxative remedies, rectal injections
should be given once an hour until the bowels act thoroughly.
After this the injections may or may not be necessary. Salts in
some form should be given often enough to secure at least one
or two movements a day. Seidlitz Salts are equally as valuable
as the Rochelle or Epsom Salts, and are free from the disgust-
ing taste produced by the latter; in fact, if a little sugar is added
to a dose of Seidlitz Salts in half a glass of water, it tastes as
pleasant as lemonade.

Also $\frac{1}{250}$ of a grain of Atropine in pill or tablet form may be
given every two hours. This does not aid in elimination, but it
aids in bringing the blood to the surface and in relieving the
internal organs. It also stimulates both the heart action and
respiration, hence is one of the best remedies to prevent exhaustion and collapse, which is liable to follow. The Atropine
may be given often enough and long enough to keep the patient's
color normal. If the amount recommended does not keep the

face flushed, give every hour or oftener for a few doses; if the pupil of the eye dilates, lessen the dose, giving once in four hours.

To aid in controlling pain, hot cloths should be kept across the abdomen; cloths wet in hot water are best because moist heat can be applied at a higher temperature than dry heat. It will be necessary to change these every few minutes in order to keep the surface *hot*.

If there is vomiting, put a large Mustard plaster over the stomach and give small quantities of milk and lime water, equal parts. Only liquid food should be given, but this should be given often.

Absolute quiet should be maintained, as any excitement, or in severe cases the slightest jar, increases the pain and distress.

If the inflammation is not broken up, but becomes general, the pain will be so great that the treatment described may not control it, and it may be found necessary to give Opium in some form. Both Opium and Morphine are constipating, therefore the use of either will necessitate an increase in the amount of Salts used.

When peritonitis results from a perforating wound, or from the rupture of an abscess, an operation is necessary: If a wound, repair the damage; if an abscess, open and flush out the cavity with a large quantity of pure water.

PERNICIOUS FEVER.–(See under MALARIAL FEVERS).

PHTHISIS.—(See TUBERCULOSIS).

PILES.—(See under ANUS, DISEASES OF).

PIMPLES.—(See under SKIN DISEASES).

PLEURISY—PLEURITIS.—Pleurisy is an inflammation of the pleura. The pleura is a very thin and delicate membrane which encloses the lungs. A little above and behind the center of each lung is the point where these organs are connected to the heart. At this point also the trachea, or wind-pipe, with its various branches, enters the lungs. The lungs are connected with the heart by means of the pulmonary artery, which leaves the right side of the heart, and the pulmonary vein, which enters the left side of the heart. When the pulmonary artery enters the lungs, it divides into many minute branches, which surround the air cells. These branches again unite to form the pulmonary vein. The artery is for the purpose of carrying the venous blood into the lungs for oxidization, and the vein returns the blood purified and ready to be sent out into the general circulation. A collection of nerve fibers which supply the heart—branches of what are called the tenth cranial nerves—is also situated at the point indicated; also the ten or twelve glands into which the lymph vessels of the lungs terminate. All of the structures mentioned are supported by a framework of connective tissue, and together are called the roots of the lungs. The pleura, after enclosing each lung up to and including the "roots," is reflected over the inner wall or surface of the chest cavity and forms a complete lining; thus there are two layers of the pleura: That enclosing the lungs is called the visceral layer, and that lining the chest cavity is called the parietal layer. The space between these two layers is called the plural cavity. There is no real cavity, however, as the two layers are in close contact. If the lung should become collapsed as a result of disease, a cavity would exist. That part of the pleura which surrounds the right lung, and that which surrounds the left lung, are entirely separate; there is no communication between them. In health the adjoining surfaces of the portion enclosing the lungs and that lining the chest cavity are smooth and glistening, and supplied with a serous fluid which prevents friction. The membrane in closed cavities, like the chest and abdominal cavity, is sometimes called *serous membrane*, hence the term, *serous fluid*. As stated above, pleurisy is inflammation of the pleura. Localized pleurisy often exists with pneumonia, although it may exist without pneumonia. Pleurisy may be acute or chronic.

Changes Occurring in Pleurisy.—During the progress of the disease certain changes take place. These changes cannot be noticed by the observer, hence are not given under symptoms; yet they are of importance in conveying a more thorough and practical understanding of the disease.

First, the vessels supplying the pleura become congested, and this is followed by inflammation and an increased exudate of the serous fluid mentioned. When the exudate is slight, the pleura loses its glossy appearance, and the exudate which collects on the surface resembles a false membrane. This is called *Dry Pleurisy*. Adhesions of the two layers of the pleura, that which surrounds the lungs and that which lines the chest cavity, are apt to take place at one or more points. Sometimes there is a large amount of the fluid exudate. This compresses the lung and leaves a space between it and the chest wall. This space is filled or partially filled with the fluid. When the patient stands or sits upright, the fluid forms at the bottom and extends upward, the height depending upon the amount. The fluid causes a bulging of the chest wall at the point where it occurs. This bulging or fullness is plainly noticeable. When the patient lies down, the fluid extends to a higher point, and causes bulging on the side in which it may occur. This fluid may be absorbed or partially absorbed, and the diseased area become organized; that is, fibrous bands are sent through the diseased part as a result of new tissue growth. In this case adhesions would form between the membrane which surrounds the lung and that lining the chest cavity. Such adhesions are permanent. Later, however, as a result of constant motion, the result of respiration and other exercise, the two surfaces may be more or less separated, leaving one or more fibrous bands to indicate the point of attachment. Such bands are not apt to cause any inconvenience. In all forms of pleurisy the membrane is apt to remain more or less thickened. Where fluid collects as a result of pleurisy, it is called *Pleurisy with Effusion*. Sometimes the fluid exudate contains pus, or is converted into pus. This is called *Empyema*.

Cause.—Acute pleurisy may result from a broken rib, wounds which penetrate the chest cavity, or from pneumonia. It may follow the infectious diseases, or it may be caused by extension of pericarditis—inflammation of the membrane which enclosed the heart—or may be caused by irritants resulting from unhealthy blood, the same as that which sometimes causes acute inflammatory rheumatism.

Symptoms.— There may or may not be a chill or sense of chilliness. There is sharp pain, usually at or near the nipple of the affected side. There is a short, dry cough, which produces pain, therefore the patient coughs as little as possible. Respiration is rapid and short because breathing also increases the pain. The disease is outside the lung, hence there is no increase in the expectoration. There is moderate fever. The pain is caused by the rasping together of the two roughened surfaces of the pleura. As soon as effusion takes place (see *Changes Occurring in Pleurisy*), the pain ceases because the surfaces are separated. At first the patient lies on the sound side, because this allows the lung to drop away from the chest wall and relieve the pressure on the affected side; after the effusion he lies on the affected side, because the fluid prevents friction and this position gives him a better chance to exercise the sound lung. The disease usually occurs only on one side. If on the left side, the effusion crowds the heart toward the right; if on the right side, it crowds the heart toward the left. In either case the heart action becomes embarrassed as it is more difficult for the organ to expand and contract. With the absorption of the fluid the patient gradually enters the convalescent state. Where absorption takes place, the disease lasts from eight to twelve days; where pus forms, the disease is prolonged. The pus may break into the lungs and be expectorated, may break externally like any abscess, or may remain in the pleural cavity. In health if the ear is placed against the chest, breathing sounds can be plainly heard, because the lungs, or the pleura which surrounds them, is in direct contact with the chest wall, and with each respiration the pleura moves with a gliding motion over the inner surface of the chest cavity; but where either fluid or pus is present, such sounds cannot be detected over the area of effusion because the fluid or pus causes a separation of the affected portion of the lung.

TREATMENTS.—

What to Do Till the Doctor Comes.—Put the patient to bed and apply external heat. Give hot drinks and produce profuse perspiration. Give a large dose of Castor Oil, or other active cathartic. Place a large Mustard plaster over the affected side to act as a counter-irritant. Aconite and Veratrum are more or less common household remedies, and if at hand, give either the Tincture of Aconite or Fluid Extract of Veratrum in 1- or 2-drop doses every hour to aid in producing sweating. This treatment tends to cause active elimination both by the bowels and skin, and equalizes the circulation, thus relieving the congested and inflamed part.

To relieve the pain, some recommend a broad bandage to be bound tightly around the chest wall, as this lessens the lung action and relieves irritation. We think a better way is to take strips of adhesive plaster, about two inches wide and long enough to go a little more than half way around the body. Commence at the bottom of the lung on the affected side. Have the patient exhale all the air he can, and then quickly apply several strips of the adhesive plaster, each one drawn tightly and overlapping the one below. Repeat this until the side is firmly strapped up to and a little above the affected point. This will better control the action of the affected lung and leave the sound lung free.

In all forms of *Pleurisy* good ventilation should be secured, also good hygienic surroundings and the most nourishing food.

The foregoing treatment thoroughly applied will control many cases of pleurisy. If the case does not respond to treatment, a doctor should be called. While the reader will not be able to apply the treatment given by the physician, such treatment is presented here with a view of giving a clear understanding of the case.

A. Pilocarpine is recommended by some and may be given to the strong and robust. It is one of the most active remedies to eliminate by the skin. One-fourth grain may be given with a hypodermic needle, the dose to be repeated in one hour if free perspiration has not been obtained.

When the fluid causes pressure upon the heart, its action may become weakened. In such case some heart stimulant should be given. One-twentieth of a grain of Strychnine in pill or tablet form may be given every three hours, if needed; or 2 drops of Fluid Extract of Digitalis.

If fluid forms and is not absorbed, it should be removed by an aspirating needle. This is simply a long, hollow needle, which is plunged through the chest walls between the fifth and eighth ribs. To insure more rapid and complete absorption, the Iodides should be given—1 teaspoonful of the Syrup of Hydriodic Acid between meals and at bedtime; or, if the patient is pale and anæmic, give Iodide of Iron—$\frac{1}{50}$ of a grain between meals and at bedtime.

Whenever pus forms it should be removed at once. Where pus is present it is often necessary to make an opening through the chest wall with a knife to allow free evacuation of the pus. If the pus is fetid or foul smelling, the cavity should be washed out with some disinfectant solution. Peroxide of Hydrogen, or a weak solution of Carbolic Acid, or a solution of Boric Acid should be used, and afterwards the cavity washed out with pure water. If pus forms, the discharge is apt to continue for some time, hence free drainage is necessary. If the disease continues long, tonics are needed.

CHRONIC PLEURISY.—*Chronic Pleurisy* may result from tumor growth in the chest cavity, from tuberculosis of the lungs or other part of the body, from Bright's disease, or from the prolonged use of alcohol. If pus forms in *Chronic Pleurisy*, the treatment is the same as that already mentioned.

PLEURO-PNEUMONIA.—(See Pneumonia).

PNEUMONIA.—(See under Lungs, Diseases of).

POLYPUS.—A polypus is a small tumor with a narrow base which springs from mucous membrane. There is distension of some part of the membrane, and the distended portion is filled with a soft, gelatinous growth. Polypus is most frequently present in the nose. It is said to occur in the middle and external ear, but its presence there is not often met. Occurring in the nose it is not painful, and unless accidentally discovered the growth will escape notice until its size produces mechanical obstruction.

Cause.—The cause of polypus, when occurring in the nose, is chronic inflammation of the mucous membrane of the nasal cavities—the condition known as catarrh. Undoubtedly the condition is often largely influenced by septic or unhealthy blood.

The exciting cause may be colds or damp air. Following congestion and inflammation, there is first a thickening of the mucous membrane. Frequent and energetic blowing of the nose has a tendency to cause the membrane to bulge forward at some point where it is weakest, and that is why polypus most frequently occurs in the nasal cavities. The mucous membrane becomes separated from the tissues beneath and the space is filled with exudate from the distended vessels. The nourishment from such exudate is poor, and while Nature tries to supply the cavity with new tissue, in most cases it succeeds but partially, and the result is a soft, gelatinous formation. After the membrane becomes separated from its normal position, the distension continues at its distil or outer portion, while the point of original separation remains and forms what is called the pedicle. The shape of a polypus conforms to the shape of the cavity in which it occurs. Occasionally the polypus is of firmer growth—firmer than the variety mentioned here. It may contain considerable connective tissue and blood vessels.

TREATMENT.—

Removal, either with caustics or a knife applied to the base; or, what is usually more convenient is a loop of wire worked up over the growth to the base, or point of attachment. By tightening the loop after it is in position the growth is easily severed.

PRICKLY HEAT.—(See under SKIN DISEASES).

PROLAPSUS ANI.—(See under ANUS, DISEASES OF).

PROLAPSUS UTERI. — (See under WOMEN'S DISEASES).

PROSTATE GLAND, ENLARGEMENT OF.—The prostate is a gland consisting of two large lobes and one small one. At its greatest diameter it is about 1½ inches wide, about 1 inch long and ¾ of an inch thick. Its weight is about five drachms. It is situated beneath and partly surrounds the neck of the bladder. It is composed of connective tissue and muscle fibers, and contains numerous small glands with excretory ducts. Its under surface is in connection with the rectum. Its use is not known. In many cases in middle and advanced life this gland becomes very troublesome by reason of its enlargement. The enlargement is called *Hypertrophy of the Prostate.* The trouble is caused by the pressure of the gland upon the neck of the bladder—the commencement of the urethra. As the gland enlarges it presses upward and raises the neck of the bladder, forming a sack of greater or less dimensions and resulting in retention of urine. The pressure causes frequent desire to urinate, and at the same time the bladder is not entirely emptied. The bladder enlarges in proportion to the amount of urine retained. In some cases the opening may be so firmly closed as to cause great distension and agonizing pain. This can be relieved only by artificial means. The effects of the dilated bladder may travel up the ureter and check the flow of urine from the kidneys, causing great enlargement of these organs also (seldom).

Symptoms.—In eighty per cent of such cases the symptoms are very light and there is no serious enlargement. In the severer forms there is frequent desire to urinate, and with the amount of urine retained in the bladder it may cause inflammation. Acute inflammation does not often occur; however, the walls of the bladder may become very much thickened, and the bladder itself permanently distended. Where inflammation occurs and is severe, the urine will contain blood and thick ropy mucus, giving it a dark and cloudy appearance.

TREATMENTS.—

A. One important feature is to remain quiet. The act of walking is especially irritating to the gland and increases its size, and also irritates the bladder. Avoid extremes of heat and cold. Avoid alcohol. Give particular attention to digestion and to the condition of the bowels. If there is inflammation of the bladder, give Salicylate of Soda—10-grain doses every three hours—or Salol, 10 grains every three hours. If there is much difficulty in urination, it will be necessary to use a catheter. The patient should be taught how to use it, for with this means of security relief can be had at any time he is unable to urinate naturally; otherwise the bladder might become greatly distended before a doctor could be reached, and such distension would be followed by excruciating pain.

B. Saw Palmetto. Take in teaspoonful doses after meals and at bedtime—four doses a day.—(57).

C. Fluid Extract of Saw Palmetto—one teaspoonful three times a day.—(41).

PUERPERAL FEVER.—(See under WOMEN'S DISEASES).

PUERPERAL CONVULSIONS.—(See under WOMEN'S DISEASES).

PUTRID SORE THROAT.—This means *Diphtheria.* (See DIPHTHERIA).

PUSTULE, MALIGNANT.—This disease affects animals, and is sometimes communicated to man. In cattle it is often called *Black Leg*, because the swelling is so great and the circulation is interfered with to such an extent that the tissues become dark. It is very fatal. In man it resembles *carbuncle*, but is much more severe, and is called *Malignant Pustule*, *Anthrax* or *Wool Sorter's Disease*. The last name is given because those who handle wool, hides, etc., are more liable to take the disease. It is contagious, and the poison which inhabits the hides and wool may be conveyed to those who are engaged in this work. It affects the skin and deeper structures in the form of a gangrenous inflammation. First there appears a small swelling, which rapidly increases in size, turns dark in color and becomes gangrenous. If continued, there soon appears a fetid discharge of blood and pus.

Cause.—The cause is a specific poison or virus.

Symptoms. — The symptoms are swelling, pain, bronchitis and diarrhea, followed rapidly by a diffused gangrene. The tissues which surround the diseased area are greatly swollen, and the gases formed by the rapid decomposition of tissue produce a crackling sound. The tissues immediately joining the pustule contain vesicles filled with a bloody fluid. Constitutional symptoms are present, the same as in blood poisoning. Death usually follows in a few days.

TREATMENTS.—

A. Make as thorough and complete an excision as possible—cut out all the dead and diseased tissue that can be reached—and use antiseptics freely. Keep the bowels and skin active with a view to relieving the system of the poisons. Stimulants are also needed. The general treatment is the same as that required in blood poisoning.

Note.—When the pustule occurs on a limb, amputation is sometimes advised.

B. For local treatment make a free incision and follow with an injection of pure Peroxide of Hydrogen.

For general treatment, the following: Take twice a day—night and morning—2 drops of Carbolic Acid well mixed in a teaspoonful of Simple Syrup. The strength should be sustained by Iron and Wine, or other alcoholic beverage. The diet should be nutritious and easily digested.

C. Free incision, followed by moist or wet dressings of Corrosive Sublimate—4 grains of the Sublimate to 8 ounces of water—frequently changed.—(31).

D. First make a free incision, then introduce the point of a small syringe and inject into the wound Carbolic Acid diluted with three times its amount of water. The wound should then be syringed out with pure water.—(24).

QUINSY.—(See TONSILITIS).

RABIES.—This means Hydrophobia. (See HYDROPHOBIA).

RELAPSING FEVER.—(See under MALARIAL FEVERS).

REMITTENT FEVER. — (See under MALARIAL FEVERS).

RHEUMATISM, MUSCULAR.—Rheumatism is a painful condition of the muscles and joints. The muscles are affected most because they are subjected to greater strain, in fact, it is the muscles that move the joints. When the muscles are affected, it is called *Muscular Rheumatism*. The muscles that are used most are affected most.

Lumbago.—First come the muscles in the "small of the back," because this part or point acts as a hinge or pivot upon which the body rotates and bends. This is the part from which the body is supported, hence there is greater strain, and this increases the irritation and pain. What is called the loins extend from the lower ribs to the hips along either side of the spinal column. When rheumatism affects these parts it is called *Lumbago;* in other words, lumbago is rheumatism in the small of the back.

The next most frequent location is in those muscles supporting the most active joints, or in any muscles doing the most work.

While it is customary to speak of muscular rheumatism as we have done, it is not correct. The same general condition that produces neuralgia and other pains is the cause of rheumatism. If the reader should examine the fibers of an affected muscle under the microscope, such fibers would appear normal. There would be no evidence of inflammation or other trouble, showing clearly that the disease was in the nerve fibers and not in the muscle fibers. (See NEURALGIA).

Cause.—The first cause of rheumatism is indigestion and constipation, followed by too much acid in the circulation.

It has been stated elsewhere that the higher forms of digestion are carried on in the circulation. Certain food elements produce uric acid, and this acid, meeting the oxygen from the air we breathe, is converted into urea and eliminated by the kidneys; but as a result of overeating, too much hard work, lack of exercise, or some other cause, the change mentioned does not take place and the uric acid remains an irritating substance. Lactic acid is believed to be the product of muscle tissue. In health this acid is also oxidized and converted into carbonic acid gas and water. The carbonic acid is eliminated by the lungs, and the water by the kidneys, but indigestion lessens oxidization, and the lactic acid also remains and accumulates in the circulation. The delicate nerve fibers and other tissues being constantly bathed with these acids, become irritated, and irritation increases until actual pain exists. As evidence of the truth of this statement, we have but to remember that during an attack of rheumatism, perspiration, which is normally alkaline, is now highly acid. This is the cause of rheumatism, whether it affects the joints or muscles, or whether it is local or general, and this is why the alkaline treatment for rheumatism is so beneficial. It neutralizes the excess of acid, which relieves the irritation, and if there is inflammation present it gradually subsides.

Symptoms.—The symptoms of a mild attack or form of rheumatism are stiffness, soreness and more or less pain. When remaining too long in one position, the individual upon attempting to stand upright or move about actively finds it difficult at first. In a short time, however, the trouble passes away more or less so that free motion is established and maintained as long as the activity is kept up, because such activity tends to equalize the circulation and thus relieve the affected parts. When rheumatism occurs in a severer form, the stiffness and soreness increase to actual pain, and the affected muscles may become so painful that it will be found impossible to exercise them. Those troubled with rheumatism give a history of constipation. In the form of rheumatism here mentioned there is no fever.

Sometimes the pain is sudden, sharp and piercing, and for a few hours or a day the individual is unable to move the affected muscle or muscles. This usually occurs in the side or back, and is called a *"stitch."*

Rheumatism in the muscles of the neck often causes the head to lean toward the affected side, as this relaxes tension and lessens the pain. This is called *Torticollis*, or *Wry Neck*.

When one has rheumatism as a result of "taking cold," it simply means that the cold lessens peripheral (near the surface) circulation, hence too much blood is retained in the internal organs, in the muscles and around the joints; and this sudden increase of blood so highly charged with these acids, acting as an irritant, results in pain more or less acute.

TREATMENTS.—**Muscular Rheumatism—Lumbago.**

A. Use Smartweed tea locally.

Internally take a 5-grain tablet of Salicylate of Soda every hour until the ears ring; then the same dose every four hours until relieved.—(57).

B. Eat sparingly of meats. Keep the bowels active. Take one of the kidney cures given in the MISCELLANEOUS MEDICAL RECEIPTS, or take 20 grains of Salicylate of Soda every four hours, either in tablet or solution.

C. Green Tincture of Rhus Toxicodendron—¼ of a drop four times a day.—(37)—Homeopathic.

D. Make 10 capsules, each containing:

Antikamnia	3 grains.	
Codeine	¼	"
Salol	10	"

Take 1 every six or eight hours.—(47).

E. Continuous heat should be applied, either in dry form by the means of warm flannels, or by soft, warm Linseed poultices. Take a hot bath every night before retiring. Persons who are subject to this disease should wear warm clothing, avoid draughts and guard against strains or heavy lifting. Cases often receive benefit from visits to some of the natural mineral springs.

F. Moderate doses—3 to 7 grains—of Acetanilid every six hours to persons of a sound heart, aided by external applications of heat.

Salicylate of Soda in 20-grain doses three times a day, taken in full glass of water, is often effective.—(31).

G. Baking Soda—½ teaspoonful every four hours. Rest in the recumbent position. Very light diet.—(35).

H. Oil of Wintergreen ... ½ ounce.
Sweet Spirits of Nitre ... 2 "
Mix, and take 1 teaspoonful every three hours in ¼ glass of water.—(25).

I. Heat and counter-irritants.—(33).

J. Five grains of Muriate of Ammonia every two hours, dissolved in a wineglassful of water,
or,
Five drops Fluid Extract of Cimicifuga (Black Cohosh) in a glass of water. One teaspoonful every hour.—(41).

K. Phenacetine ... 16 grains.
Caffeine ... 3 "
Give dry on tongue. Put patient to bed. Apply heat, followed for several days with Wyeth's Salicylatis, one teaspoonful every four hours, or Potassium and Lithium tablets, 10 grains every two hours..—(26).

L. Iodide of Potash...... .... 2 drachms.
Elixir Salicylic Compound......... 4 ounces.
  Dose.—Teaspoonful between meals and at
  bedtime.—(28).

M. Citrate of Potash, 60 grains (teaspoonful) a day
in lemonade,

or,

Baking Soda, 100 grains a day.
Blister plasters shorten the attack.—(24).

N. Give, either in solution or pill form, Cimicifuga
(Black Cohosh) or Colchicine, the third dilution.—(56)—Homeopathic.

O. Take hot baths with 2 or 3 pounds of washing
Soda dissolved in each bath.—(32).

P. Salicylate of Soda, 20 grains in capsules No. 8.   One
every four hours,

or,

Tongaline liquid, 5 ounces.   Teaspoonful in hot water three
or four times a day.—(20).

Q. 20 drops Oil of Wintergreen every four hours,

or

Acetanilid...................................... 5 grains.
Caffeine Citrate............................. 1   "
  Dose to be repeated every three hours.--(41).

R. Sulphur .... 1 ounce.
Saltpetre.. ½   "
Gum Guiac .... ½   "
Colchicum root (or seed).............. ¼   "
Nutmegs....................................... ¼   "
  Pulverize and mix with 2 ounces of Simple
Syrup or molasses.

  Dose.—One teaspoonful every two hours
until the bowels move rather freely; then three
or four times daily.—(73).

Concerning the Remedies Recommended Above.—It

will be noticed that nearly all of the foregoing remedies contain
Salicylic Acid.   Both *Salol* and *Oil of Wintergreen* contain a large
percentage of Salicylic Acid.   *Elixir of Salicylic Compound,*
Tongaline and *Wyeth's Salicylates* also contain Salicylic Acid,
hence there is no difference in these remedies except the
variation in the amount of Acid.   *Baking Soda, Citrate of Potash*
and *Muriate of Ammonia* contain no Salicylic Acid, therefore
they are less valuable; yet they neutralize the excess of acid in
the circulation and in the tissues, and in this way lessen the
irritation and aid the patient in recovery.   *Colchicine* contains no
Salicylic Acid, yet it increases the eliminations of all of the
tissues of the body and of the digestive tract, hence is valuable
in freeing the system of all irritating material, and is especially
recommended for those who are fleshy and those who take but

little exercise. In this class of cases it is a valuable remedy to give in combination with the Salicylates. Acetanilid contains no Salicylic Acid, but it possesses antiseptic properties and also has a tendency to lessen the pain, therefore aids in controlling the disease. *Citrate of Caffeine* is a heart stimulant. In many cases this might be valuable in increasing the force of the circulation and aiding in giving physical power. *Spirits of Nitre* increases the activity of the kidneys, and therefore aids materially in eliminating the waste and irritating matter which cause the disease. *Hot Baths* are valuable because they aid in elimination. *Sulphur* aids in elimination both by the skin and bowels. The action of *Saltpetre* is the same as *Spirits of Nitre*. Salicylic Acid is somewhat irritating, if taken clear, hence the various forms of combination. Salicylic Acid is generally recognized to be more valuable than any other known remedy in the treatment of rheumatism, either acute or chronic, and, speaking from our own personal experience, we can heartily recommend this claim. Whenever the ears sing, take less—perhaps only half the amount.

RHEUMATISM, ACUTE ARTICULAR—INFLAMMATORY RHEUMATISM OF JOINTS. — Rheumatism

of the joints differs from muscular rheumatism. It is an acute form and very painful. Every joint is held in position by ligaments, and the joints, including the ligaments, are enclosed in a thin membrane in the form of a short, wide tube. The membrane is attached at either end to the margin of the articular surfaces of the bones forming the joint (see description of Joints). In acute rheumatism of a joint the irritation increases the blood supply, and there is swelling and redness in proportion to the increase in the circulation. The more vascular the part, *i. e.,* the more blood vessels it contains, the greater the swelling. The swelling causes pressure and the pressure causes pain. With the increase in blood supply, there is an increase in tissue change, hence the increase in the temperature, because animal heat depends upon tissue change. This gives what are called the four cardinal symptoms of inflammation—swelling, redness, heat and pain.

Cause.—The underlying cause is the same as that which produces muscular rheumatism. The exciting or immediate cause may be too much hard work, may be injury, slight or severe, or may result from atmospheric changes—damp air or rainy weather. In any case the result is the same, *i. e.,* too much blood is directed to the affected part, and blood so highly charged with acids and other irritants causes congestion and inflammation.

Symptoms.—Pain and soreness, which increase rapidly and soon result in inflammation and swelling. The temperature is high, the pulse is rapid, the perspiration is highly acid and its odor is sour; even the saliva is highly acid. The urine is scanty and high-colored, and may contain albumen. The surface over the affected joint is hot, and the normal color of the skin is more or less reddened. As the disease increases, the slightest movement causes excruciating pain.

TREATMENT.—

The inflammation and sensitiveness first occur in the membrane which surrounds the joint, and the inflammatory process extends toward the surface. The joint structures proper are not affected at the beginning of the attack, and it follows that if the disease can be checked, the joint will escape uninjured. Constipation usually exists; whether this is the case or not, give an active cathartic.

The patient should be put to bed and absolute quiet maintained. Place a rubber blanket under the affected joint, allowing it to hang over the side of the bed and into a pail or pan—something large enough to hold considerable water. Now secure a piece of flannel large enough to wrap the whole joint and so that the border will extend for some little distance above and below, and wet this in cold water—the colder the better. Wrap the wet flannel carefully, yet firmly, about the affected surface, and continue the cold by pouring cold water upon the bandage every twenty minutes, day and night. The water will drain into the pail or pan.

As soon as there is thorough action of the bowels, give 10 grains of Salicylate of Sod . every two hours until the ears sing, then every four hours. The patient should also diet two or three days—going without all food for twenty-four hours is still better. This treatment, thoroughly applied, will arrest the disease in nearly every case. If the patient is very fleshy, $\frac{1}{100}$ of a grain of Colchicine might with advantage be added to each dose of the Salicylate of Soda.

RHEUMATISM, CHRONIC.—*Chronic Rheumatism* of the joints does not usually follow the acute, but rises insidiously in people who have suffered from exposure, improper food, overwork and other hardships. In chronic inflammation the cartilages covering the articular or adjoining ends of bones may become destroyed and the exposed bones become irregularly thickened; also the capsule or membrane enclosing the joint and the ligaments which support it, may become fibrous and contract.

The prolonged irritation causes a low form of inflammation, and the same change takes place here as elsewhere. There is an increase in the connective tissue framework. Later this contracts, deforms the joints and limits motion. The contracting fibers cause pressure, aiding in the destruction of cartilage, ligament and other normal tissue; and sometimes during these degenerative changes the ligaments which support the joint soften, allowing certain muscles which are attached near the joint to contract, thus causing deformity. Sometimes tendons and ligaments about joints become filled with the lime salts of which bone is formed; this results in a stiff joint. Pus does not form.

In some cases the joint structures are not destroyed. The joint remains slightly swollen, is more or less stiffened, and the muscles which surround it are more or less shrunken and wasted; but there is no fever and no discoloration. If the joint is movable, such movement gives a creaking sound, and the tendons and ligaments of the joint produce crepitation (crackling) in the sheath or membrane which surrounds them.

TREATMENT.—

The best treatment for chronic rheumatism of joints is hot air. A temperature of 300 or 500 degrees may be applied. Hot air dilates the small vessels and brings the blood to the surface where it is applied, and thus relieves the congestion and inflammation beneath. This causes the blood to flow through the part, relieves the pressure and stops the pain. Adhesion and accumulation are also broken down and removed, thus preventing stiff joints. There is an active discharge through the skin, and the removal of waste relieves the irritated nerves. The improvement in the circulation stimulates the natural activity, nutrition is increased, the heart is strengthened and the brain relieved. Massage is also of benefit.

Massage stimulates the circulation with the same results as hot air, although it is much more limited in its effects. Electricity applied by the interrupted, or Faradic, method is only a means of massage. The advantage from the interrupted current comes from the fine, vibratory, massage-like effect; in other words, from the mechanical effect and not from the electricity. The remedies which should be used are laxatives and antiseptics. Digestion must be improved. Hot air or drug medication will be more effectual if administered by one skilled in their application, but what every one and any one can do is to guard against all forms of excess and keep the eliminative organs active, and they will not be troubled with rheumatism.

In the great majority of cases the hot air treatment cannot be applied for want of conveniences. The next best thing is the internal use of Iodides in some form. Syrup of Hydriodic Acid is pleasant to take and is as effective as Iodine in any other form. One teaspoonful may be taken three times a day—between meals and at bedtime. This may be continued for three or four weeks at a time, then skip a week or two and take again. If there is a catarrhal condition of the eyes, it is evidence that the dose is too large; in this case, take half the amount. Also take 10 grains of Salol, or 10 grains of the Sulphocarbolates (see Index), three times a day. Five-drop doses of Fowler's Solution, taken with the meals, is also valuable. At any time that there is evidence of an increase in the trouble, take any of the remedies mentioned under MUSCULAR RHEUMATISM.

RECOMMENDED TREATMENTS FOR STIFF JOINTS.—

A. The best internal remedy is Black Cohosh. Take the root and steep it and drink freely of the decoction; or, if the root is not procurable, the tincture or fluid extract may be purchased at a drug store. The dose of the tincture would be from 10 to 15 drops three times a day; of the fluid extract, from 5 to 10 drops three times a day.

For an external remedy, use the following:

> Tincture Iodine............................ 4 ounces.
> Water of Ammonia...................... 4   "
>
> *Mix*, let stand a few hours and apply, rubbing in thoroughly. The more time spent in making the application, the better.

Any treatment for Rheumatism, to be effective, must be persisted in for a long time.

> B. Oil of Wintergreen...................... 1 drachm.
> Ammonia Liniment...................... 2 ounces.
>
> *Mix* together, rub well into the joint and cover with flannel.
>
> Salol.............. .... 2 drachms.
>
> Divide into 10 powders. Take 1 every three hours.—(59).
>
> C. Ether .... 1 ounce.
> Oil of Cajeput............................. 1   "
> Benzine.. 4   "
>
> Local application,
>   or,
> External application of Gasoline.—(55).

D. John White, Harbor Beach, Michigan, had rheumatism in foot. After two doctors had failed in treating him, he used the following remedy and it cured him:

Spirits of Turpentine....	1 pint.
Alcohol	1 "
Camphor Gum.............................	1 ounce.
Saltpetre	1 "
Beef Brine...................................	1 pint.

Heat the beef brine until it comes to a boil and take off scum, then mix all together. Apply three or four times a day, rubbing it in well, or until the flesh is red. In addition take something to keep the bowels open.

E. Ten grains Salicylate of Soda every two hours. Cotton batting and oil silk to joints,—(39).

RHEUMATISM, GONORRHEAL, OF THE JOINTS.—There is another form of joint trouble, called *Gonorrheal Rheumatism*. This is not Rheumatism, however, but is caused by poisons in the blood resulting from *Gonorrhea*. It is not frequent in the early stages of gonorrhea, but when occurring is most frequent in the latter stages—in *Chronic Gonorrhea*.

Cause.—That already given—septic or poisonous material resulting from gonorrhea, carried by the circulation. The exciting or immediate cause is the same as the exciting or immediate cause for joint rheumatism proper.

Symptoms.—The symptoms are somewhat different from those of gonorrhea. In order to show the symptoms to better advantage or make them more easily understood, we give them side by side:

Gonorrheal Rheumatism of Joints.	Inflammatory Rheumatism of Joints.
Fever is slight.	Fever is high.
Lasts for several weeks or months.	Lasts about one week.
Gonorrheal has a tendency to occur again and again.	Inflammatory has not.
The perspiration is normal, that is, alkaline.	Perspiration is not normal, but highly acid; even the saliva is acid.
Heart complications are unusual.	Heart complications are frequent.
The joint may suppurate.	The joint does not suppurate
There is a history of gonorrhea.	There is no history of gonorrhea.

TREATMENT.—

Until recent years this disease was most difficult to control, in fact, there was no treatment that seemed to produce much effect. More recent developments, however, have shown that the following may be relied upon. By many who have had large experience the following remedies are said to give the most satisfactory results, and we are assured the disease may be controlled by such treatment:

Sulphide of Calcium... ½ grain, pill or tablet.

Take from four to six times a day. Give at the same time 5 drops of Fowler's Solution in a little water. If there is much effusion in the joint, it should be drawn off with an aspirating needle. If pus forms, the abscess should be opened at once, washed out with an antiseptic solution, and proper drainage maintained.

SCIATIC RHEUMATISM—SCIATICA— NEURALGIA OF THE SCIATIC NERVE.—These and

perhaps other terms are applied to painful conditions of the sciatic nerve. This nerve is the largest nerve in the body. It is a continuation of nerve fibers having their origin in the lower part of the spinal cord. At its greatest width it measures ¾ of an inch, and is said to be capable of sustaining a weight of 175 to 200 pounds. Its great size and length is the reason why affections of this nerve are so painful and persistent.

The sciatic nerve leaves the pelvic cavity through a small opening situated rather low down and toward the back part of the hip. It extends downward along the back of the thigh to a point a little above the knee, where it usually divides into two branches. It supplies the skin over the whole of the lower extremities, supplies the hip joint, the muscles along the back part of the thigh, the knee joint, the muscles of the leg below the knee, and the foot.

Cause.—The same as rheumatism and neuralgia elsewhere. It should be remembered that the nerve fibers are supplied with blood vessels, the same as other tissues of the body, and that irritating blood causes congestion of these vessels the same as elsewhere. The congestion may increase to inflammation. This congestion or inflammation means that the vessels are thickened and swollen. This causes pressure, and the delicate and sensitive nerve fibers give notice in the form of pain more or less pronounced. This is the condition in muscular rheumatism, and this is why we stated that it was the nerve fibers and not the muscle fibers that were affected. Only for the vitalizing influence supplied through the nervous system, the material body would be dead matter, therefore Nature has designed that any irritation or morbid condition that tends to interfere with normal nerve action or obstruct the vitalizing influence mentioned, shall be made manifest; hence the pain. The pain is mild or severe in proportion to the danger present. The opening through which the sciatic nerve makes its exit from the pelvic cavity is only large enough to admit the passage of the nerve. The congestion and inflammation mentioned may be communicated to the tissues surrounding this opening, and this would crowd upon the nerve at that point and increase the pain. The same congestion and inflammation may extend downward and result in adhesions of the tissues surrounding the nerve in other situations. This would cause pressure and irritation and also aid in increasing the pain. The adhesions are in proportion to the size of the nerve, and this is another reason why the disease is so stubborn and why it fails to yield to the ordinary methods of treatment.

Symptoms.—Pain along the course of the nerve. It may be most severe in the hip, at the knee, at the heel, or may include the whole nerve tract. Where the pain is severe, it usually comes on in spasms, lasting from a few hours to a day or two. In many cases the pain is not severe, but dull and more constant, leaving one point and as suddenly attacking another. Sciatica frequently follows *Lumbago*, or rheumatism in the small of the back, because the spinal cord only extends to the small of the back and the sciatic nerve is a continuation of nerve fibers having their origin at that point; hence when the pain leaves the sciatic nerve it may suddenly appear in the back or elsewhere.

TREATMENTS—Sciatica.—

A. Mustard plasters, blister plasters, and all forms of artificial heat have been used in this disease. Sometimes they give relief and sometimes they do not. Where relief is not obtained and the pain is severe, some give temporary relief with Morphine. It has been stated that the disease is the result of irritation, congestion, and perhaps inflammation, therefore we believe the best remedy is the same as would be given to relieve congestion and inflammation elsewhere, *i. e.*, 1-drop doses of Tincture of Aconite every hour; or, if the patient is strong, the same dose may be given every thirty minutes for two or three hours or more. We also recommend the following:

> Salicylate of Soda...................... 1 drachm.
> Acetanilid .... ½   "
>
> *Mix*, divide into 12 powders and give 1 powder every two hours until the ears ring.

These powders and the Aconite may be given together. We have known some very stubborn cases of sciatica—cases that have resisted all other means of treatment—to yield to the continued use of Aconite alone. Add 24 drops of the Tincture of Aconite and 1 ounce of Glycerine to 3 ounces of water. Shake the bottle and take 1 teaspoonful every one or two hours. If the patient is physically strong, he can take 1 teaspoonful every hour. If there is a sense of tingling, or a sense of numbness in the toes, fingers, hands, face or lips, it will be evidence that the patient should take less, say one-half the amount. Aconite is not recommended for those with a weak heart.

Tincture of Aconite, and, in fact, all tinctures, fluid extracts and other herbs used in medicine, owe their effects largely to a certain active ingredient often called the *active principle*. They are also sometimes called *alkaloids*, *glucosoids*, etc., according to their composition. These active principles constitute but a very small percentage of the drug. Aconitine Amorphus represents Aconite more actively than the tincture or fluid extract. This is equally true of all active principles because they are definite in amount. The Aconitine Amorphus may be given in $\frac{1}{150}$ grain doses in place of the tincture. Where it is continued for some time, it is often used, because it is prepared in pill or tablet form, hence is more convenient. We believe the Salicylate of Soda and Acetanilid powders are equally as valuable as the Aconite.

B. Croton Oil given in a full dose (from 1 to 3 drops) is the best and quickest and most permanent relief of any I have ever used.—(30).

C. A large Mustard plaster over the seat of pain along the course of the nerve.—(20).

RICKETS—RACHITIS.—Rickets may occur before birth, but usually not until after. It is a condition where the bones throughout the body become more or less softened, either from the absorption of bone matter or from a lack of deposit of lime salts; the latter is the more common cause. The disease generally occurs during the first or second year, and is usually found in cities.

Cause.—This disease is caused by a lack of nourishment, which may be the result of poor food, or of an insufficient amount of food. Another important factor is bad hygienic surroundings—bad air, lack of sunshine, unhealthy cellars, or small apartments inhabited by too many families.

Symptoms.—It will be noticed that the child is weak and poorly nourished, teething is late, or if teeth are present they may become loose and fall out. Handling the child causes more or less pain all over the body. This is caused by the condition of the bones. The child is more quiet while lying down, and cries or worries more while being handled.

Where the ribs join the chest bone there is a prominent thickening, which may readily be felt. The ribs are soft and bend easily—even breathing or traction of the diaphragm may cause the chest to become flattened, latterly or on the sides. This would cause the chest bones to bulge forward, giving the chest a narrow, wedge-shaped appearance, hence the term, "*pigeon breast.*" All of the bones lack development. The chest cavity is small and interferes with the lung power. The spinal column softens and the weight of the body may cause curvature of the spine. This curve is usually posterior, or backward, and produces the condition known as *humpback*. The bones are so soft that the periosteum, or membrane which surrounds them, can be easily removed. In standing or walking the bones of the lower limbs become bent. .The pelvic bones become deformed, and the bones of the head enlarged. If the disease is of long standing, the whole mass of bone structure becomes firm and hard. After the disease is cured, the bones of the head remain large as a result of internal pressure, and the bones of the body small from lack of development. The ribs or bones of the limbs may remain more or less misshapen as the result of muscular contractions when the bones were soft. This muscular contraction and the weight of the body causes pressure on the ends of the bones forming the joints, and they become more or less enlarged, hence the prominence at the wrist joint, elbow, ankle or knee. During the disease fractures usually occur from very slight causes. An examination of the urine will detect an abnormal amount of lime salts.

The duration of the disease is about two years. However, with good care and proper treatment a cure should be effected in less time.

TREATMENTS.—

A. The treatment consists of attention to diet and hygiene. If the child is in an unhealthy location, it should be moved—taken where it will receive an abundance of fresh air and sunshine. Every attention should be paid to a nourishing diet, frequent bathing, attention to the bowels, etc. The remedies to be taken internally are Fowler's Solution, Syrup of Lactophosphate of Lime and Maltine, or a good extract of malt. Fowler's Solution may be taken in from 1- to 3-drop doses, according to age, three times a day. Syrup of Lactophosphate of Lime may be given in 1-teaspoonful doses four times a day.

The deformities should receive mechanical support in the way of splints and bandages. Most cases may be cared for at home, but should be under the attention of a doctor.

B. *Pigeon Breast.*—When caused by rickets, give Compound Syrup of Hypophosphites with meals. Massage the chest and press the deformed bones back into place.—(40).

C. Scott's Emulsion Cod Liver Oil.—(41).

RINGWORM.—(See under SKIN DISEASES).

ROSE RASH, or ROSEOLA.—(See under SKIN DISEASES).

RUPTURE.—(See HERNIA).

ST. ANTHONY'S FIRE.—This means Erysipelas. (See ERYSIPELAS.)

ST. VITUS DANCE—CHOREA.—This is a disease of childhood, brought about by some disturbance of the nervous system resulting in irregular and spasmodic actions of certain groups of muscles. There is also more or less general weakness, lack of ambition and loss of power. The mind may be dull and the memory somewhat weakened.

Cause.—A lack of development of the nervous system, or a lack of proper nourishment and support of that system. The child becomes weak and irritable. The exciting or immediate cause may be either excitement or fright. Eye strain from too much study is also said to act as an exciting cause. There may be other conditions which bring on the first spasmodic attack. We should remember, however, that the underlying cause was present before. We realize that the foregoing is somewhat indefinite, yet they are the causes usually given for this disease. Personally, we believe the real and only cause is malnutrition, or indigestion and lack of assimilation. This may be the result of poor food, unhygienic surroundings or too close attention to school studies; or if from other causes, the result is the same. This means irritating blood and a lack of nourishment, and gradually the vitality of the child is reduced. The condition may be overlooked until, as a result of some one of the exciting causes given, the disease suddenly develops.

Symptoms.—Spasmodic and irregular movements of the voluntary muscles. The condition is made worse by an attempt to walk or perform any duty. These movements generally cease during sleep. First, there may be a general restlessness which increases until the patient loses more or less the power of coordination (see LOCOMOTOR ATAXIA), or the disease may come on suddenly, as stated above.

The disease may begin in the hands and arms, may include the muscles of the face and those of the eyes, and later extend to the lower extremities; it may include the head and body and both upper and lower extremities; or may affect the right arm and the left leg, or vice versa. When the head and body are affected, the patient moves to and fro, bending, bowing and jerking; when the lower limbs are affected, the gait is tottering and unsteady, the patient stumbling in attempting to walk; when the hands and arms are affected, the patient may not be able to feed himself. The muscles of the tongue are usually more or less affected, and this renders speech difficult and stammering. When the muscles of deglutition, or those engaged in the act of swallowing, are involved, swallowing is difficult. Watching the child or making any attempt to correct him only increases the trouble.

TREATMENTS.—

A. The child should avoid all excitement, and should not be sent to school; in fact, nothing exacting should be demanded of him. He should never be watched, harshly criticized, or otherwise severely dealt with. No attention should be paid to his actions, or such conduct as results from the disease. The symptoms should be allowed to pass unnoticed, and he should be encouraged in the belief that he is getting better. The most careful attention should be paid to diet—vegetable diet is the best. Rice boiled for two or three hours, toast, milk, soft boiled eggs, beef tea made at home (see MISCELLANEOUS DEPARTMENT), oatmeal boiled for three hours and strained, using only the liquid part, and vegetables such as used in a boiled dinner, boiled and strained, using only the liquid part, are all valuable, because they are easily digested and nourishing. The following is a valuable internal remedy:

> Fowler's Solution...................... ½ ounce.
> Fellows' Syrup of Hypophosphites 2 ounces.
> Maltine, or any good extract of
>   Malt...................................... 6   "
> *Mix* by shaking the bottle.

Give 1, 2 or 3 teaspoonfuls four times a day. Give with meals and at bedtime. The dose should correspond to the age of the child. If the appetite is not good, the child should receive more than three meals a day.

B. Fluid Extract Cimicifuga (Black Cohosh), 1 drop three times daily. Also Fowler's Solution, 3 drops three times daily. Cold douche to spine, followed by brisk rubbing.—(41).

C. Rest in bed. Not to compel the patient to lie in bed, but to allow him to rest at pleasure. Also anything to interest him and divert his mind.—(39).

SALT RHEUM.—(See under Skin Diseases).

SCARLATINA.—(See under Eruptive Fevers).

SCIATICA.—(See Rheumatism, Sciatic).

SCROFULA.—(See Tuberculosis of the Lymph Glands).

SCURVY—SCORBUTUS.—In this disease there is congestion of all mucous membrane, also of the deeper layer of the skin covering the body; hence slight hemorrhage may occur in various places, giving to the skin a spotted appearance. The gums are apt to be swollen and bleed easily. There is always languor and more or less prostration, and rheumatic pains are scattered throughout the body. What is called *"Button Scurvy"* is a disease caused by poor food and depraved nutrition. Slight growths of papules appear in the skin which are thought to resemble a button, hence the term. In all forms of scurvy there is a morbid condition of blood, always aggravated by lack of cleanliness. In the past scurvy is said to have occurred most often on ship board, although in earlier years it occurred in badly fed armies and in besieged cities.

Cause.—Long continued use of salted meats, or rather, the absence of vegetable foods. This disease is also largely influenced by bad hygiene. Absence of vegetable food and unhealthy surroundings will produce scurvy in a previously healthy man. It may follow protracted fevers. In children it is said to have been caused by some kinds of infant foods. When scurvy first appeared in the United States army, some time ago, the government issued canned fruits and vegetables to the soldiers and sailors with most excellent results. This plan or arrangement, together with better sanitation in camp life, has driven scurvy out of the field. To-day it is practically unknown to any extent.

Symptoms.—There is general weakness, languor, and lack of ambition; the skin becomes rough and pale and presents a muddy appearance; the gums are swollen and bleed easily; there may be small hemorrhagic patches beneath the skin; the eliminations from the digestive tract contain blood; the breath is offensive; the lips are pale; the eyes are sunken and may be encircled with dark lines; the face frequently bloats; the urine is high-colored and its odor is offensive; the heart is weak and fluttering, and there is shortness of breath. Occurring in children, they are anæmic and irritable and remain quiet—dislike to be handled. There is soreness about the joints, and congestion of the mucous membrane in the mouth, increasing to a profuse flow of saliva.

TREATMENTS.—

A. First, free elimination from the digestive tract, followed by antiseptics, such as Salol or the Sulphocarbolates. These cases either require a change of air or improved hygienic surroundings. The food should consist of fruit juices, fresh vegetables, milk, broths from fresh meats that are cooked but little, etc. The treatment for children and adults is the same. Where children are anæmic and very pale, Syrup of Iodide of Iron will improve the condition. This is also true with adults. In most cases but little drug medication is needed.

> B. Maltine.. 4 ounces.
> Liquid Peptonoids .... 4 "
>
> *Mix*, and take 1 dessertspoonful after meals.—(47).

SEA SICKNESS.—Sea Sickness is a distressing disease occurring on ship board. It is characterized by dizziness, intense nausea, vomiting and extreme prostration.

Cause.—The primary or first cause is the motion of the vessel—the alternate rising and falling of the bow and stern. The trouble is not so severe on vessels with heavy ballast because there is less motion. The cause is also partially explained by the condition of the system. Indigestion, an abnormal condition of the digestive tract and a lack of free circulation over the surface of the body, weaken the controlling powers of the nervous system until it is less capable of withstanding the unnatural motion of the ship.

TREATMENTS.—

A. For several days before taking passage on ship the individual should pay strict attention to diet and elimination. Keep the bowels regular in their action, eat sparingly of light food, take a bath every day and rub the surface afterward until it assumes a healthy glow.

If following the first indications of the trouble a horizontal position of the body is assumed and maintained, there is less danger; in fact, by this means many cases of sea sickness are prevented. To relieve an attack take $\frac{1}{100}$ of a grain of Atropine, $\frac{1}{60}$ of a grain of Strychnine and $\frac{1}{250}$ of a grain of Glonoin. Take all at a dose, and repeat every hour until the face is flushed; after that, take less often—perhaps once in two or three hours. Whenever relief follows, stop the treatment. We know of no better remedy that can be applied. The object is to bring the blood to the surface and maintain free peripheral circulation. If this is done, the attack will be broken up. There is nothing better for this purpose than the remedy named.

B. Have the liver acted upon thoroughly for three days previous to embarking, then whenever the nausea is felt, **touch** the tongue to the following:

Strychnine.................................... 1 grain.
Water .... 4 ounces.
—(32).

C. Sea sickness may be prevented by the following before taking the trip. See that the bowels are loose. One day previous to departure take the following:

Bromide of Potash..................... 3 drachms.
Simple Elixir............................. 2 "

Mix, and take 1 teaspoonful every five hours.—(38).

SHAKING PALSY.—(See under PARALYSIS).

SHINGLES.—(See under SKIN DISEASES).

SICK HEADACHE.—(See under HEADACHE).

SKIN DISEASES.

The skin forms a covering for the whole body and protects the deeper structures. It is usually divided into two layers: the outer, known as the cuticle epidermis, or scarf skin; and the inner, known as the cutis, corium or true skin. The corium is formed of connective tissue; the epidermis, or outer layer, is merely worn-out cells that are being cast off. The corium is well supplied with blood vessels; the outer layer has none.

The corium is covered with small elevations called papillæ. Each of these papillæ, or points, is supplied with a loop of blood vessels. It is by means of these elevations that the sense of touch is made manifest. The specialized nerve fibers which supply them are most abundant where the sense of touch is most acute, as the tips of the fingers and the soles of the feet. The true skin is continuous at the nose and mouth with the corium, or deeper layer of mucous membrane; in fact, the deeper layer of the skin and mucous membrane are the same. This sheet of membrane encloses the outer surface of the body, is continuous through the nose and mouth, and lines the cavities in the head, mouth, throat, air tubes, lungs, stomach, digestive tract, collecting tubes of the kidney, uterus, bladder and urethra.

The skin contains hair follicles, sweat glands, and sebaceous, or oil, glands.

A hair follicle is a small depression in the skin. At the base is one of the papillæ mentioned, and the loop of blood vessels which supplies each papillæ supplies the hair with nourishment. Hair follicles cover more or less all parts of the body and extremities, excepting the palms of the hands and soles of the feet.

The sebaceous, or oil, glands, commence below the surface of the skin, extend toward the surface and open into the side of the hair follicles. These glands secrete an oily substance which keeps the skin smooth and the hair glossy.

The sweat glands cover all parts of the body and extremities. They are most numerous in the palms of the hands and soles of the feet. The average amount of waste eliminated through the skin is about twenty-four ounces in twenty-four hours. This watery fluid contains from two to four per cent of solid matter.

The hair follicles, oil and sweat glands are lined with a layer of cells which, by reason of their specialized nerve supply, have the power to secrete from the passing blood stream certain materials: the hair follicles, those materials which supply the growth of the hair; the sebaceous or oil glands, those which keep the skin and hair smooth and soft; the sweat glands, those which eliminate waste. Large amounts of waste are eliminated.

In hot weather the perspiration bathes the surface of the body and keeps it cool. This is why animal life can exist in a temperature much higher than its own. When the air is moist, it does not readily take up more moisture from the body. This produces discomfort and depression, as it checks elimination. Such weather is spoken of as muggy, humid, sultry or oppressive. This is the reason the same temperature is more destructive to life in New York City or Chicago than in Minnesota or any section where the air contains less moisture. The dry air readily takes up moisture from the body and thus favors elimination through the skin. Dry clothes do not attract heat from the body; wet ones do, because their temperature is lower. This produces chilliness, and may result in taking cold. Exercise produces more heat, which meets the drain made by wet clothing.

The skin is connected with the deeper structures by a layer of connective tissue in the form of loose meshes. This is capable of great distension, as in some forms of erysipelas and other inflammations.

Birth Marks.—Enveloping the body and lying just beneath the skin, in this loose connective tissue, is a dense network of small blood vessels, estimated to be capable of holding half of the blood in the body. Many people have what are called "birth marks." These are thought to resemble a leaf, strawberry or something of the kind, and are caused by dilatation of the blood vessels in this loose connective tissue.

TREATMENT.—

Birth marks are usually so deep seated that efforts at removal should not be made.

Mole.—Sometimes this is merely a dark discoloration on the surface. In this case it is termed a mole. A mole may be slightly elevated. It is usually harmless.

TREATMENT.—

See treatment for warts. The same caustic applications will destroy moles.

Wart.—A wart is a type of papillæ of the deeper layer of the skin, but it is large. The papillæ is overgrown and contains a framework of connective tissue, blood vessels and lymphatics. Warts are sometimes called *papillomata*, meaning tumors formed by the overgrowth of a papillæ.

TREATMENTS.—

A. Apply Nitric Acid to them, being careful to touch the wart only.—(20).

B. Touch with any strong acid, or with Lunar Caustic, being careful to touch only the wart.—(32).

Note.—Lunar Caustic is Nitrate of Silver. When brought in contact with animal tissue, it decomposes, leaving the Nitric Acid free to act. Lunar Caustic, or Nitric Acid, will destroy any and all tissue with which it is brought in contact.

C. Specific Thuja applied well every day. Take 5 drops four times a day. This will cure all warts on man or animal. No failures with this treatment.—(30).

D. Apply Thuja Tincture each day for one week.—(43).

SKIN DISEASES.

What are called skin diseases are not skin diseases at all, with the exception of itch and ringworm. The other troubles are simply evidence of systemic disease. This is true of eczema, liver spots and shingles, the same as of boils, carbuncles, dandruff and other conditions of a like nature, and applies even to leprosy. True, the skin may be more or less changed in appearance and even in structure, yet it is simply the evidence of some constitutional derangement. It is a symptom, the same as pain and fever are symptoms. There may be no structural change in any tissue following the symptoms of pain or fever; while such changes may occur in the skin following systemic disease, yet they all depend upon some constitutional trouble, hence these cases need general or systemic treatment. Local treatment may relieve temporarily and make the patient more comfortable, but local treatment does not reach the real cause, and this is why it cannot cure.

Eczema is the most frequent so-called skin disease, and the treatment of this affection will be much more satisfactory if strict attention is paid to digestion, elimination, regular habits and the avoidance of all forms of excess.

ACNE.—This affection of the skin is the result of an inflammation of the sebaceous glands. It most frequently appears about the time of puberty. It is usually chronic in character.

Cause.—Authorities state that Acne is accompanied with digestive disturbances and that it is often associated with chronic diseases—anæmia, scrofula and tuberculosis are examples. Acne is an external manifestation of a general disease. It is true that in many cases there may be no actual disease, yet there is some disturbance of digestion which results in a production of irritants in some form, and these irritants affect the terminal or outer ends of the peripheral nerves—those that supply the skin. Some irritating elements generated in the system produce their effect upon the nerve terminals and some do not. The same is true with poisons that are used in medicine. Some of the Bromides, Chloral, the Iodides, Belladonna or Atropine and some other remedies produce this same irritating effect upon the terminal or end nerve fibers which supply the skin, and result in a pronounced rash. Atropine irritates and paralyzes the outer or distal end of the nerves supplying the glands of the throat; they fail to act and the throat becomes dry. It paralyzes the nerves governing the size of the vessels supplying the glands and the vessels dilate; that is why the surface becomes red. At the same time it paralyzes the terminal fibers supplying the sweat glands, and this lessens elimination. It also paralyzes the terminal nerve fibers which supply the iris; that is why the pupil dilates. It is understood, of course, that such effects are only temporary, and pass off in a few hours. The peculiar forms of poisons which produce inflammation of the sebaceous glands and result in acne may depend upon the habits, surroundings, kind of food taken, mental influence, etc., and, as stated, when they occur, being eliminated through the skin they produce their irritating effects upon the nerves supplying it. This acts as a stimulant and results in a mild form of inflammation around the sweat glands, or more especially their ducts or openings. The secretions of the glands are increased, while the inflammation and swelling of the ducts prevent more or less their escape. This causes the ducts to become dilated and their point of opening to bulge forward.

It has been stated that the effects of Atropine are only temporary. The reason is that when such effects are produced, the remedy is discontinued. The reason that the irritants which produce acne are constantly present is because such irritants are constantly being generated in the system.

Symptoms.—The oily secretion of the gland is retained, but the retention is attended with inflammation. Inflamed, ugly-looking pimples are the result. Pustules may occur among the pimples. In the pustular variety of acne pustules are the rule. The face is the part most commonly affected, although the neck, back and shoulders may be subject to this eruption.

Sometimes the color of the secretion which clogs the ducts varies from a white or yellowish to a grey or black, the last two being the result of dirt which becomes mixed with the secretions. This constitutes the condition known as *Blackheads.*

TREATMENTS.—

A. Avoid fatty foods as much as possible. Also take regularly some saline cathartic, as Carlsbad Salt in doses of from 1 to 2 teaspoonfuls in water, daily.—(63).

B. Get a can of Seidlitz Salts from the Abbott Alkaloidal Co., Ravenswood, Station X, Chicago. Take 1 teaspoonful (or a larger amount if necessary) every morning to keep the bowels regular. Bathe the face in a solution of the same Salts, say 2 teaspoonfuls of the Salts to half a glass of water. This treatment will be found most excellent. The Seidlitz Salts are effective, harmless, and pleasant to take.

C. Try the following:

    Hard Cider................................ 1 pint
    Alum....................................... size of a pea.

Keep in a bottle on your dresser and apply night and morning. Use for a long time.—(14).

D. Bathe the face often and thoroughly in good soap and hot water, and at bedtime, after bathing the face, dust on a little White Precipitate and wash it off in the morning. Keep the face protected from wind and cold.—(10).

E. Wash the affected parts two or three times a day in salt water. At night after bathing in hot water, apply the following:

    Carbolic Acid............................... 10 drops.
    White Vaseline............................. 1 ounce.

A small towel wrung out of hot water, applied on retiring, is a good remedy. The pimples should not be squeezed or pressed between the finger nails.—(9).

F. Prolonged hot bathing. Massage parts with Tar soap (not carried far enough to cause irritation), and stimulate the circulation locally with Alcohol rubbing. Keep bowels free; also kidneys and skin generally.—(14).

> **G.** Solution Subacetate of Lead......... 20 drops.
> Glycerine.................................... 1 drachm.
> Lanoline.................................... 4   "
>> Make into an ointment and rub thoroughly into the skin night and morning.—(20).

H. Keep the bowels open freely every day.—(32).

I. Diet; open bowels; fresh water.—(33).

J. Sulphur, sixth dilution. Take in drop doses or pill form four to six times a day.—(3)—Homeopathic.

Especially applicable to Blackheads.—

> **K.** Sulphuric Ether.......................... 1 ounce.
> Carbonate of Ammonia............... 1 drachm.
> Boric Acid................................. 20 grains.
> Water .... 2 ounces.
>> *Mix*, and apply locally two or three times a day.

The special value of the Ether and Ammonia is in dissolving and carrying away the greasy or oily accumulations which are apt to be present on the face, forehead, or wherever the trouble exists.

BARBER'S ITCH.—(See under Ringworm).

ECZEMA—TETTER—SALT RHEUM.—This is not a skin disease, but, like dandruff, is a manifestation of a systemic trouble. This is why it shows such a strong tendency to become chronic. The eruption is but a local manifestation of a constitutional disease. Eczema may attack all ages and classes. There is a catarrhal inflammation of the corium, or deeper layer of the skin. First there is congestion of the vessels supplying the affected part, producing redness. In this variety there is a slight exudate from the swollen vessels, and when the moisture dries it forms little scales. The scales are composed of the solid elements from the blood, of the new cells which have grown as a result of the increased blood supply, and of such other matter as may inhabit the skin where the exudate occurs.

There are several forms of *Eczema*, as, where it occurs in papules or points, where the papules contain fluid, or where they contain pus. Sometimes the inflammation and exudate cause the outer layer of the skin to become detached and it is cast off, leaving the inflamed corium, or deeper layer of the skin, exposed. This gives a red appearance, which differs from the other forms as it is a deeper red. If the inflammation is severe enough, some of the small vessels may be ruptured and blood may form part of the exudate. If the disease has existed for some time, the skin may have become thickened and hardened from increased growth as a result of the increased blood supply.

Cause.—It should be remembered that a skin lesion is merely a symptom of disease, the same as fever is a symptom. Any one having eczema must remember that his system is a little "out of order"—that more thorough elimination is needed, and more attention should be paid to diet. In some cases the use of alcohol may have been the starting point; in others, possibly tobacco. Their effects would be produced by their interference with digestion. Lack of exercise, too much hard work, laziness, or any other condition that tends to disturb the general health may produce eczema.

Symptoms.—There is always itching and burning in *Eczema.* The diseased area presents no distinct outline or border, but the redness fades gradually into the surrounding healthy skin. The papules or vesicles that occur in erysipelas may resemble those of eczema, but erysipelas presents greater swelling, more heat, and the color is a deep red, tense and shiny. The inflammation is deeper seated. If occurring about the face, the swelling may close the eyes. There is fever and frequent pulse. Erysipelas may set in with a chill, there may be nausea, vomiting, an abscess may form, or in some cases delirium may be present. Eczema presents none of these symptoms. The trouble is confined to itching, and sometimes a burning sensation, but the evidence is never severe.

TREATMENTS.—

A. In those cases where vesicles form, or where there is much moisture present, the following prescription will be found most beneficial:

> Salicylic Acid.............................. 10 grains.
> Subnitrate of Bismuth .... 1 drachm.
> Powdered Starch......................... 1 "
> Vaseline enough to make .... 1 ounce.
>
> *Mix* thoroughly, and apply two or three times a day.

This ointment will be found satisfactory in the treatment of most cases. Many cases will be controlled so that the disease will never be noticed. The most careful attention should be given to digestion and keeping the bowels regular. Ten grains of Salol should be taken three times a day.

B. Wash the diseased area with a solution of one or two tablespoonfuls of Bicarbonate of Soda in one-half to one wash bowl full of tepid water. Dry gently with a soft piece of lint or linen and apply Carbolated Vaseline—5 drops of Carbolic Acid to 1 ounce of pure Vaseline—or, better still, apply "Resinol" (proprietary) by gentle friction, and put on a piece of linen bandage.

In addition to the above local treatment, give, for an adult, 1 tablespoonful of McDade's Succus Alterans (proprietary) in a wineglassful of water three times daily.—(16)—Homeopathic.

C. Five grains of Iodide Potassium in glass of water or milk between meals; also, Fowler's Solution of Arsenic, from 5 to 10 drops in water before meals.—(10).

FISH-SKIN DISEASE.—This is an affection in which discolored crusts form on the skin. These crusts overlap each other like the scales of a fish. It makes its appearance in children at the age of one or two years and continues throughout life.

Cause.—The disease is believed to be born with the individual.

Symptoms.—The crusts do not usually extend over the skin of the entire body, but appear in patches and particularly affect the extremities. It is a rare disease in its full development. A milder form, consisting simply of a dryness and harshness of the whole surface, with a slight scaling, is much more common. This disease is always chronic.

TREATMENT.—

Add 10 drops of Carbolic Acid to 4 ounces of Sweet Oil and apply freely to the surface. This application should be kept up until the scales are all removed and the part becomes soft and pliable, resembling healthy skin. The patient should be sustained with a carefully selected diet, and every attention paid to digestion and elimination. This also includes proper hygienic surroundings.

FRECKLES, LANTIGO.—This affection consists of small, circumscribed, brownish spots the size of a pin-head, and sometimes larger. They usually occur on the face and backs of the hands. Those with light complexions are most often affected.

Cause.—The cause of freckles is the elimination through the skin of certain waste products or elements which undergo chemical changes in coming in contact with light and sunshine, resulting in discoloration. Just what the change consists of is not known, neither is it important.

TREATMENTS.—

A. Corrosive Sublimate .... 3 grains.
Diluted Muriatic Acid.................. 1 drachm.
Alcohol..................................... 1 ounce.
Glycerine .... ½ "
Water enough to make................. 4 "

Mix together and apply at night, or morning and night may be necessary. Label *Poison*, and protect the eyes when applying it. Keep the mixture out of the reach of children.

B. Another good remedy is as follows:

Citric Acid................................... 1 drachm.
Glycerine .... 1 ounce.

Apply with a soft cloth three or four times a day, more or less as needed.

C. Apply Peroxide of Hydrogen three or four times a day.—(7).

D. Rosewater.................................. 4 ounces.
Alum, pulverized........................ 2 drachms.
Lemon Juice.............................. 2 "

This will permanently improve many cases of freckles.—(75).

E. Tincture of Benzoin..................... 1 drachm.
Tincture of Tolu.......................... ½ "
Oil of Rosemary.......................... 2 drops.
Rosewater................................. 4 ounces.
—(75).

HIVES—NETTLE RASH—WHEALS—URTICARIA.

—All of these terms are applied to certain characteristic marks which appear in the skin following indigestion. The trouble is not dangerous. It usually occurs in children.

Cause.—Indigestion, and usually lack of elimination. As a result of indigestion, many irritants are present in the circulation. These irritants cause dilatation in groups of small blood vessels which supply the skin. Such dilatation is the result of the paralyzing effects of the irritants upon the nerve fibers which control the size of the vessels. The dilatation is sudden, hence the rapid appearance of the spots, large or small, the size corresponding to the amount of skin supplied by the affected vessels. The spots are usually light in the center, and a reddish, or sometimes a bright red color, around the border. They may vary from the size of a pea to a walnut, or be even larger.

Symptoms.—The sudden appearance of the spots. They may disappear as suddenly as they came, and re-appear in some other part. With their appearance there is a tingling, itching and burning sensation. Usually the child does not complain much. The spots are accompanied by digestive disturbances.

Treatments.—

A. A large dose of Castor Oil, Laxol (see Index), **Salts, or** Seidlitz Salts will cure this trouble, providing the child **is more** careful about its diet.

B. Salicylate Soda.......................... 3½ drachms.
Aromatic Elixir............... .... 4 ounces.
Mix.—Dose for child five years old, ⅓ teaspoonful in water every three or four hours; for adult, 1 teaspoonful every three or four hours.—(52).

C. Rochelle Salts—1 teaspoonful in ½ tumbler of water every half hour until bowels are moved.—(35).

ITCH—SCABIOUS.—Itch is caused by an animal parasite which burrows in the skin. These parasites multiply very fast, producing intense itching. The affection generally occurs on the hands between the fingers.

Treatments.—

A. The following application will cure this trouble:
Ammoniated Mercury (also called
White Precipitate)................. 40 grains.
Sulphur..................................... 3 drachms.
Vaseline, enough to make.......... 1 ounce.

Cleanse the hands, dry, and apply the ointment twice a day, or oftener if necessary.

B. Sulphur .... 2 ounces.
Lard .... 4 "
Mix, and apply freely at night, washing it off in the morning.—(7).

C. Make a stiff ointment by mixing Sulphur into Lard. Bathe in good strong soapsuds, dry and apply the ointment.—(17).

D. Rub with Sulphur and Lard.—(32).

E. Wash with a weak solution of Corrosive Sublimate, 4 grains to ½ pint of water. Label *Poison* and do not allow the solution to get into the eyes.—(11).

F. Use Resinol Ointment.—(30).

G. Bathe the itching parts with a solution of 1 teaspoonful of strong Carbolic Acid to 1 pint of water. Protect the eyes when using.—(8).

H. Carbolic Acid............................. 10 drops.
Water .... 4 ounces.
Mix, and apply locally.—(46).

LEPROSY.—Leprosy is endemic, *i. e.*, present **more or** less all the time, in many parts of the world—in the East and West Indies, in China, South America and southern Africa. At one time it was widely spread throughout Europe and was the most dreaded of all diseases, but to-day we do not fear it. We have learned that it is a filth disease, and modern sanitation practically disposes of it.

It is not contagious, and a case need cause no fear. Regarding the non-contagiousness of the disease, and in support of the statement that it is bred by unhealthy surroundings, we quote from that recognized authority, Green's Pathology, page 376:

"From time immemorial leprosy has been looked upon as a contagious disease, and lepers have been rigorously excluded from social communities. A very superficial examination throws doubt upon this, for in many cases lepers have been found to live in the closest associations with healthy people without communicating the disease. Many observers have maintained that the disease is communicable under certain conditions which are rarely realized. It seems more difficult to prove the contagiousness of leprosy than that of consumption, and it certainly is not so great.

"It may be noted that leprosy flourishes in all climates and upon all soils; that poor diet and salt fish do not appear to be special factors in its etiology or cause as some have thought; and that the disease does not seem to be hereditary, although Hirsch held firmly to the opposite conclusion. Children born of leprous parents in leprous places may acquire the disease, but so may outsiders entering such places. Possibly there may be some slight hereditary predisposition analogous to that believed to exist in the case of consumption.

"Observers are agreed that there is constantly present in all the recent primary lesions of leprosy a bacillus (germ) very closely resembling in its characters the tubercle bacillus.

"The bacilli are very difficult to find, both in the neighborhood of ulcerating surfaces and in the lungs. They are said to occur in definite clumps (Hansen), and to be thus distinguishable from tubercle bacilli.

"Attempts to cultivate the organism have so generally failed that the few recorded exceptions are of little value until more fully confirmed. Amid conditions under which the tubercle bacillus will flourish the leprosy bacillus will not even grow at all.

"Nor do inoculation experiments give decisive results. In the case of a criminal the disease followed inoculation—offered as an alternative to execution—but the man had up to this point been in frequent contact with lepers. Whether the infected tissue be introduced into other parts of leprous patients or into animals, the results are uniformly unsuccessful, though the bacilli themselves are not destroyed, for they can be found months afterward in the tissues.''

The external evidence of this disease is first confined to the skin, but later the deeper structures are involved, including muscle, bone and joints. In this respect it resembles what is called the third stage of syphilis. The first effects in the skin are those of inflammation, and as this continues the skin becomes enormously thickened. Sometimes tubercles form. These vary from the size of a pea to an olive. The face, chest and extremities are affected most.

Cause.—Leprosy is caused by poor food, want of clothing, filthy surroundings and a lack of elimination. Gradually the system is brought under the morbid influence of accumulated waste. The normal amount of waste is greatly increased by reason of the habits and surroundings of the patient.

Symptoms.—The first appearance is a red discoloration of the skin. The red gradually changes to dark brown, and later becomes pale, soft and flabby. The affections appear mostly upon the chest, face, ears, hands, feet, lower limbs, and the external surfaces of · the reproductive organs. At first the affected skin is painful; later it becomes insensitive. Sometimes nerve fibers become swollen. These swellings may surround the nerve for some distance, attacking first the branches that supply the skin and later the branches that supply the muscle tissue. Sometimes large eruptions make their appearance on the surface. These may either dry, leaving insensible patches, or may be followed by ulcers. Sooner or later ulcers form, leading to extensive destruction, even the dropping off of fingers, toes, or a portion of the limb. There is an overgrowth of connective tissue. Later this degenerates and breaks down, forming unhealthy matter.

TREATMENT. —

As *Leprosy* is the result of poor food, lack of elimination and bad hygiene, it follows that it is only by correcting these errors that any benefit can be obtained. Regarding internal treatment, one of the best remedies that can be used is Fowler's Solution taken in proper dose.

There is probably no treatment that will cure the disease after it has become established.

LIVER SPOTS—CHLOASMA.—This so-called disease of the skin appears in patches of a brownish color, which may be any size or shape. Liver spots generally occur in those who have wasting diseases, such as consumption, cancer, anæmia or chlorosis.

Cause.—The cause is the same as that given for freckles. Coming in contact with sunlight, a chemical change that results in discoloration is produced in certain abnormal elements eliminated by the skin. In liver spots a greater reason is the abnormal condition of the blood, hence the skin lacks the natural elements and thus aids in the chemical change produced by the sun's rays. This accounts for the change occurring in spots which correspond to the areas supplied by the terminal branches of certain arteries. Spots as large as the hand may occur, and sometimes the whole body becomes discolored.

Symptoms.—The only external symptom is the discoloration. There is no alteration in the structure of the skin, yet, as above stated, many cells lack the normal elements and contain waste, which is being eliminated. Some of this waste, upon reaching the surface and coming in contact with light, undergoes certain chemical changes which result in the discoloration. The spots are only a local manifestation of a systemic or general disease.

TREATMENT.—

The treatment is constitutional. It consists in keeping the bowels regular, in nourishing diet, good digestion, regular hours and habits, the avoidance of all forms of excess, abundance of fresh air, good ventilation in sleeping rooms, etc. The following application may be applied to the spots once a day:

> Oxide of Zinc .... 1 drachm.
> Carbolic Acid .... 10 drops.
> Vaseline .... 1 ounce.

NETTLE RASH.—(See HIVES).

PEMPHIGUS.—This is a disease of the skin of an inflammatory nature which is characterized with a succession of *blebs* (see BLEBS), or water blisters. It is associated with a debilitated condition of the general health, and occasionally results fatally. An acute attack may last for three weeks, or longer, but if the affection becomes chronic, it may run for years.

Cause.—Same as that given for *Acne*, with the exception that in pemphigus the nerves supplying the small blood vessels in the skin (vaso-motor) are affected. This allows the vessels to dilate, hence the exudation and formation of the vesicles, as stated.

Symptoms.—The acute form is attended with constitutional disturbances, the eruption being preceded with a chill and fever. The number of blebs developed vary from half a dozen to a dozen or more, and are filled with a fluid that soon turns yellowish and thickens. They usually dry up in a few days, but only to be succeeded by another crop, the *succession* being characteristic of the disease. The blisters are attended with a mild burning and itching. In very severe or malignant cases there are a greater number of the blisters, they attain to a larger size, run together, and sometimes burst, exposing a raw surface that has a tendency to ulcerate.

TREATMENTS.—

A. The treatment is constitutional as well as local. Internally, give Fowler's Solution in 5- or 10-drop doses at meal time. Care should be exercised regarding the diet, habits, hygienic surroundings, etc. The vesicles should be opened and drained as soon as formed, and the surface covered with some light dusting powder—Boric Acid or starch are often used. What is better is equal parts of Oxide of Zinc and Lycopodium. Mix intimately by passing several times through a fine sieve.

> B. Subnitrate of Bismuth.......................... 1 drachm.
> Powdered Starch 1   "
> Salicylic Acid .... 10 grains.
> Vaseline, enough to make................... 1 ounce.
> *Mix*, and apply.
> Keep the bowels open and give 5 grains of the Sulphocarbolates 4 times a day—at meal time and bedtime.

PIMPLES.—This term does not apply to any particular disease or condition. Acne or blackheads are sometimes called pimples. The rash appearing in scarlet fever, in eczema, or the vesicles which sometimes occur in erysipelas, may be called pimples. The first appearance of the rash in small-pox may also be called pimples.

TREATMENT.—

See under ACNE.

PRICKLY HEAT—MILIARIA.—This disease receives various names, according to the time of its occurrence and its appearance. It is said to be due to inflammation of the sweat glands, caused by retention of their contents, or by excessive sweating. There are two principal varieties: *Miliaria Papulosa* or prickly heat, in which only the papules appear, is one variety. These papules contain no fluid. The other variety is termed *Miliaria Vesiculosa*. Vesicles appear in this variety. The vesicles differ from the papules as they contain fluid. While this distinction is made, strictly speaking there is no dividing line between these two forms of the disease, for both papules and vesicles may, and usually do, occur in each case. First there is dilatation of the vascular system, that is, the minute vesicles about the glands become somewhat dilated and exudation is increased. The pressure prevents elimination through the ducts of the glands, and the glands may then become more or less distended. The skin contains oil glands as well as sweat glands. The exudate from the blood vessels is alkaline. It is thought by some that this alkaline exudate dissolves the oil and leaves the skin dry, and is one cause for the intense itching.

Cause.—The cause is probably the same as that which produces *Eczema*. In fact, some of these cases cannot be distinguished from eczema, or if they are, it is a distinction without a difference. Some conditions known as prickly heat may be influenced more by hot weather than an ordinary case of eczema.

Symptoms.—The disease usually comes on suddenly. Bright red papules, about as large as a pin-head, appear; sweating is profuse, and there is a prickling sensation—a sensation of heat and itching. The disease usually occurs during the summer months. It may last only a few days, or may last all summer and return the next summer. It will last until the cause is removed.

TREATMENTS.—

A. The patient should keep in a cool, well-ventilated room, should diet for a few days, pay strict attention to the eliminations, and drink a large amount of water every day. Bathe the surface with a weak solution of Lead water, say ½ ounce of Sugar of Lead to 1 gallon of water; or bathe with a solution of Carbolic Acid and water. From 2 to 4 drachms of Carbolic Acid may be added to a pint of water and the affected spot bathed with this solution; follow this with clear water. Only a small surface should be treated with the Carbolic Acid solution the first time, so that the patient may learn about how long it is safe to bathe with it in the strength given. Following the bath the surface may be sprinkled with a powder made of equal parts of Oxide of Zinc and Lycopodium. These should be intimately mixed by passing several times through a fine sieve.

B. Sponge gently with Saleratus water, then dust the body with Rice powder.—(32).

C. Bathe parts thoroughly twice a day with Distilled Extract Witch Hazel.—(38).

PSORIASIS. — Psoriasis is a term applied to designate diseases characterized by a slight redness of the skin. There is never any moisture, and the surrounding skin is natural. The small red spots which may first appear are soon covered with light, silver-colored scales. Under these scales the skin is thickened from inflammation. Psoriasis is always chronic.

Cause.—The disease is both systemic and local, and the low form of inflammation in the affected parts of the skin is due to irritants present in the circulation. As a result of the inflammation there is an excess of blood present. This causes an increase in the tissues of the part in the form of new cells, hence the thickening mentioned above. Later there is an exudation into the diseased area. This exudation may afterward be absorbed, together with many of the inflammatory products, and with proper local treatment the disease may disappear for a time; but it is almost sure to return.

TREATMENT.—

The treatment is both local and general. Internally, give 5 or 10 drops of Fowler's Solution before meals; or, what is more convenient, put 2 drachms of Fowler's Solution into a 4 ounce bottle, add 1 ounce of Glycerine and fill the bottle with water. Mix by shaking together and give 1 teaspoonful before meals. The bowels should be regulated. Also give 5 grains of the Sulphocarbolates (see Index) three times a day. Careful attention should be paid to diet and proper hygienic surroundings, and good ventilation should be provided. The patient should not try to work beyond his strength. On the other hand, where the disease affects those who perform no manual labor, or take no exercise, they should change their habits. They should take physical training, or by some means secure a reasonable amount of active exercise.

Locally, apply the following:

Pyrogalic Acid............................ ½ drachm.
Vaseline...................................... 1 ounce.
   Mix intimately.

RINGWORM.—This is a parasitic affection of the skin, causing inflammation and eruption, and called by various terms according to its location and character. It derives its name from the way in which it is developed: Beginning at a certain point, the parasitic growth spreads rapidly into a circular patch, the peculiarity being that as the patch increases in size it heals at the center, thus leaving the eruption ring-shaped. It is a highly contagious affection.

Cause.—Due to a minute animal parasite. *Tinea* means worm.

Ringworm of the Body—Tinea Circinata.—This variety begins with a spot of pimples, small, reddish and scaly. The eruption may not be circular in form at the outset, but rapidly becomes so. The pimples may remain scaly, or may change into vesicles. If there is more than one patch of the eruption, the rings as they develop may run into each other, making a patch of rings, the circles being eruptive and the intervening skin normally healthy, looking at a little distance not unlike a piece of colored embroidery work. *Circinata* is confined almost entirely to children, although adults are sometimes afflicted with a chronic and very obstinate form of the disease about the thighs which is complicated with true eczema and is attended with intense itching.

Ringworm of the Scalp—Tinea Tonsurans.—This form of ringworm is also largely confined to children. Patches of pimples come out on the scalp and increase in size, sometimes becoming as large as a silver dollar. These spots have the same characteristics as those developed in *Circinata*, with the addition of a stubbled appearance caused by the hair, which breaks off near the roots. The hair follicles, too, stand out, giving the pimpled appearance seen in a fowl from which the feathers have been plucked. It is always attended with itching, and may become chronic. Proper treatment, however, will destroy the parasites, and, this accomplished, the hair grows again.

Ringworm of the Beard—Barber's Itch—Tinea Sycosis. —This begins with the scaly, reddish pimpled patches characteristic of ringworm, but with it is a tendency of the flesh to become lumpy. These lumps do not give any pain, except upon pressure, and if a cure is effected early, they disappear altogether without leaving any scar. The hair breaks off, as in *Tonsurans*, or drops out, and the skin has a dark, purplish hue. If the disease is allowed to run, pustules form and discharge and are succeeded by thick crusts. Itching and burning are constant. It is particularly obstinate to treatment. It may be communicated by using the razor or shaving apparatus of any one afflicted with it, hence the name, *Barber's Itch*.

There is also another form of *Barber's Itch* of a purulent character. This makes its appearance in pimples of a pale yellowish color which maturate at the top, and which are found, upon examination, to be pierced with a hair. The eruption is preceded with a painful sensation of heat and tightness. If not given proper treatment, it may last for months or years.

Honey-combed Ringworm—Tinea Favosa.—This is another variety of ringworm—one that is confined almost entirely to the lower classes. It is not very common in this country. It may attack the skin, the nails, or the hair and hair follicles —usually the latter, and is sometimes called *Scald Head*. It develops in crusts of a pale yellow color. These are small and cup-shaped, and, if affecting the scalp, the common seat of the disease, are each pierced with a hair. In severe or neglected cases abscesses form under the crusts. The hair loses its luster, becomes brittle, sometimes splits lengthwise, and breaks off or falls out. If the disease is not cured, the follicles will become entirely destroyed and permanent baldness result. When the nails are affected, they thicken and become brittle and are yellowish in color. The disease has a peculiar odor, something like musty straw.

The reader can easily recognize those skin diseases which can be successfully treated without a doctor. They embrace the various forms of ringworm described, and in many respects their appearance is the same. The various forms of ringworm differ only in name and location All are caused by the same minute form of animal life, and all require the same treatment. They may commence as a small scaly surface, may be papules and later vesicles, or, if not treated, even pustules may form. All forms of ringworm differ from eczema and erysipelas as they lack the inflammatory appearance. When they occur on the scalp or in the beard, the hair is brittle and breaks off, or is easily pulled out. Eczema does not affect the hair.

The most important diagnostic feature is the well defined border presented by ringworm, barber's itch, etc. At the edge the diseased patch meets the healthy skin on a definite line. The patch rapidly grows in size and new patches appear at frequent intervals. Whenever these conditions are met, the reader can rest assured that it is ringworm in some form—which form makes no particular difference.

TREATMENTS.—

A. One application of the following will cure any and all cases: Take a piece of soft cloth and apply Formaldehyde. Be careful to apply only to the diseased surface and rub it in well. Formaldehyde can be secured at any drug store. The following ointment will also cure:

> Ammoniated Mercury (also called
>   White Precipitate)...................45 grains.
> Sulphur....................................... 3 drachms.
> Vaseline enough to make............ 1 ounce.
>
> Apply twice a day. First thoroughly cleanse the surface, rub the ointment in well and allow the application to extend a little beyond the diseased border.

B. The following simple remedy is warranted to cure any case: Take a good Havana cigar—one that makes white ashes. Smoke the cigar and spread all over the ringworm and around the edges, after first having dampened the surface so that the ashes will stick. Keep the eruption constantly covered in this way.—(70).

C. Beta Naphthol.............................. 20 grains.
   Vaseline .... 1 ounce.
   Mix, and rub into ringworm night and morning.

D. Bathe the ringworm with warm water and dry, then bathe with Acetic Acid.   Repeat next day if necessary.—(32).

Barber's Itch.—

E. Sulphur .... 1 drachm.
   Iodoform .... ½ drachm.
   Lard... 2 ounces.
   Mix well and apply once a day.—(70).

Note.—Sulphur acts mechanically.   It closes the pores of the skin and shuts out the air.   The parasites are unable to live without air, hence soon die.   Sulphur is harmless, and to insure success a liberal supply should be used—from 2 to 3 drachms to the ounce of lard.

F. Corrosive Sublimate .... 5 grains.
   Water.. 1 ounce.
   Mix.   Wet sore night and morning, following in five minutes with:
   Calomel .... ½ drachm.
   Cosmoline .... 1 ounce.

Note.—A stronger solution of Corrosive Sublimate may have to be used—up to 10 grains to ounce of water.   Always label it *Poison*, and in using be careful to protect the eyes, nose and mouth..—(13).

G. Resinol ointment applied three times daily.—(45).

H. Pack the face with gauze saturated with a solution of Corrosive Sublimate—1 part Sublimate to 250 parts water.—(10).

I. Carbolic Acid, strong solution......... 10 drops.
   Mutton Tallow .... 1 ounce.
   Mix, and rub together thoroughly.

Apply lather to face and wash off, then apply ointment. This must be done night and morning till cured.—(14).

J. Paint once daily with Tincture of Iodine until small blisters arise; then keep well anointed with Vaseline.—(4).

ROSE RASH, or ROSEOLA.—Roseola is not a term that can be applied to any particular disease.   *Erythema* or *Roseola* means a reddish discoloration.   The term can be applied to the rash in scarlet fever, or it can be applied to any condition or redness resulting from mechanical irritation.

SALT RHEUM.—(See Eczema).

SHINGLES—HERPES.—Herpes is a name given to a gradual eruption of the skin and the formation of groups of vesicles, said to be situated on an inflamed base.   The skin is inflamed and constitutes the base referred to. When the eruption takes a circular course, commencing at or near the median line (center of the body) in the back and extending around the waist to a point near the median line in front (usually on one side only), it is called *Herpes Zoster*. Herpes means creeping—the eruption comes out gradually; zoster means girdle—the eruption partially encircles the waist.

The eruption follows the course of one or more of the nerves which supply the skin over the chest or waist. These nerves have their origin in the spinal cord, follow the course of the ribs on either side and meet in front. The skin covering the course taken by the nerves is supplied by small branches, frequently given off from them.

Cause.—The cause is the same as that which produces rheumatism and neuralgia. As stated under *Sciatic Rheumatism*, the nerve fibers are supplied with blood vessels. The irritation present in the circulation first causes congestion of these vessels, and this causes pressure and pain. The same condition extends along the branches of fibers of the affected nerves that supply the skin, the vessels become congested, and a watery exudate results; hence the appearance of the vesicles.

Symptoms. — The eruption already mentioned. There is also more or less pain. In some cases the patient is decidedly nervous. The eruption may occur in groups or bunches scattered along the course of the nerve, and is accompanied by a burning, itching sensation. The fever is slight. The vesicles, which are surrounded by an inflamed area, are usually about the size of a pin-head; sometimes they are considerably larger. They may be separated, or may run together, forming irregular patches. The vesicles continue until about the fifth or eighth day, and then gradually dry up. At the end of two weeks or less they have entirely disappeared. Herpes may follow the course of other nerves and may occur in various places during an attack of neuralgia.

TREATMENTS.—

What to Do.—Exclude the air by some simple covering. Abstain from pork and all irritating articles of diet. Keep the bowels open with a teaspoonful each of Epsom Salts and Cream of Tartar, taken night and morning. Keep patient inside the house, and sponge the body with an alkaline wash, such as Soda water—1 tablespoonful to 2 quarts of water, or Muriate of Ammonia—2 teaspoonfuls to 2 quarts of water.

If patient is in great pain, give from 8 to 10 drops of Laudanum. The Laudanum may be repeated in from two to four hours, if necessary in order to keep the patient quiet.

In severe cases it will probably be advisable to have a doctor.

A. Give an active cathartic. The patient should diet for a few days. Give 10 grains of Salol or 10 grains of the Sulphocarbolates four times a day—at meal time and bedtime. Eat no meat, but restrict to a vegetable diet only ; and avoid every article of food that creates any disturbance or causes the slightest symptom of indigestion. Where evidence of digestive disturbances are present, give the following:

Scale Pepsin (1 to 3000) .... 2 drachms.
Muriatic Acid, pure...................... ½   "
Glycerine .... 1 ounce.
Fowler's Solution .... ½   "
Aromatic Cascara......................... 2 drachms.
Simple Elixir, add to.................... 4 ounces.

Mix, and take 1 teaspoonful after meals.

Also give the following:

Acetanilid................................. ½ drachm.
Salicylate of Soda......................... 1   "

Mix, divide into 12 powders, and give one powder every three hours. Fresh air is also of the greatest importance.

B. Apply to the eruption the following:

Morphine Sulphate....................... 4 grains.
Carbolic Acid............................. 6   "
Glycerine .... 1 ounce.

Mix.

Also give 5 grains of Quinine every four hours. —(35).

C. Corrosive Sublimate.................... 1 drachm.
Tincture of Chloride of Iron .... 1 ounce.

Mix. Touch the parts very slightly with a little cotton on the end of a match, then put cotton all around the waist and tie on with a bandage. Label bottle *Poison.*—(20).

TETTER.—(See ECZEMA).

SOMNAMBULISM — SLEEP-WALKING.—This is a state wherein the individual is in the habit, more or less frequent, of walking during sleep. The unusual condition of mind, or of brain, inducing such activity, prompts the individual to perform many acts that would be extremely difficult during the waking hours. The acts which are unconsciously performed during sleep, and which belong to the waking state, may include walking. riding, climbing, etc. The movements are precise and certain. They sometimes lead the individual into positions of difficulty and seeming peril, but, although unconscious, he possesses a knowledge of surrounding objects and adapts himself to the conditions with seeming ease, in fact, his senses are especially acute.

Cause.—This has never been determined, or satisfactorily explained.

TREATMENT.—

Regarding treatment, very little is said along this line by medical writers; however, we recommend the following, which is perfectly harmless and may enable the individual to overcome this unpleasant feature:

```
Bromide of Soda ........................... ½ ounce.
Chloral........................................ 2 drachms.
Glycerine ................................. ..  1 ounce.
Simple Elixir, add to.....................  4   "
     Mix, and take a teaspoonful every hour for
three hours before going to bed.
```

SPASMS.—(See CONVULSIONS).

SPERMATORRHEA.—(See NOCTURNAL EMISSIONS).

SPINAL MENINGITIS.—(See *Cerebro-Spinal Meningitis* under BRAIN DISEASES).

SPINE CLEFT.—This is a dilatation, either of the membranes covering the spinal cord, or of the spinal cord and membranes together. It is congenital, *i. e.*, exists from birth, and is usually accompanied with *Hydrocephalus*, or *Water on the Brain* (see under DROPSY). These tumors received different names, according to their size and the part of the cord of which they are formed. Sometimes they become as large as a child's head.

Cause.—Extending from the skull downward through the spinal column is an opening which contains the spinal cord. A defect in one or more of the bones forming the spinal column leaves an opening through which the cord protrudes. The trouble usually occurs in that part of the spinal column situated in the small of the back. The tumor may include only the membranes covering the cord, or may include both cord and membranes. In either case there is more or less fluid present.

Symptoms. — Presence of the tumor. Crying or coughing renders the covering of the tumor tense and firm. It is small at the point where it makes its exit through the spinal opening, its size corresponding to the defect in the bones. The membranes immediately dilate, however, and are filled with fluid the same as that contained in the spinal column. Situated in the center of the spinal cord, and extending through its entire length, is a small opening. This is called the spinal canal; it is filled with spinal fluid. Sometimes this canal may become dilated. In this case the tumor would be formed both of the cord and its coverings.

TREATMENTS.—

A. When the tumor is small, bandaging is recommended. If there is much fluid present, it should be drawn off with an aspirating needle and the tumor injected with a 10 per cent solution of Iodoform in Glycerine, or with the following:

> Iodine Crystals .... 10 grains.
> Iodide of Potash .... 30 "
> Dissolve in a few drops of water, and add
> Glycerine, 1 ounce.

The purpose of such treatment is to cause an inflammation within the walls of the tumor, with the result that permanent healing will take place.

This and other treatments are recommended, yet without much hope of effecting a cure. These cases nearly always prove fatal.

B. Take 1 teaspoonful each of Epsom Salts and Cream of Tartar three times a day to keep the bowels active. Get Buchu leaves, steep to get the strength, and strain. Drink of the tea three times a day—morning, noon and night. These remedies will stimulate the action of the bowels and kidneys and aid in draining the system of fluids, thus relieving the tumor inasmuch as it is composed largely of a watery fluid.

SPLEEN, ACUTE INFLAMMATION OR ACUTE ENLARGEMENT OF.— In this disease the spleen enlarges rapidly and becomes more or less sensitive to the touch.

Cause.— Poisons, which may result from cancer, typhoid fever, malignant pustule and other conditions where the blood becomes unhealthy and vicious.

Another reason for enlargement of the spleen, as stated elsewhere, is the large blood supply which this organ receives. The blood vessels supplying it are larger in proportion to its size than those supplying most other organs. Again, circulation is not carried on through the spleen the same as through other organs, but the blood flows through channels, or sinuses, which are formed in the spleen itself. This brings the effects of the irritating blood in direct contact with the splenic tissue.

Symptoms.— Enlargement in the left side, tenderness on pressure, and sometimes the formation of pus. In case of pus formation there would be chills and an elevation of temperature.

As a result of the inflammation, there is an overgrowth of the tissues of which the spleen is constituted. This is called *Splenic Pulp*.

TREATMENTS.—

A. If there is pus, the abscess should be opened and washed out with some disinfectant solution. Peroxide of Hydrogen would be valuable. Proper drainage should be secured and every attention given to diet and hygiene. Hydrochlorate of Berberine is said to be one of the best remedies for enlargement of the spleen. Give ¼ grain doses three times a day.

B. Steep up Boneset until it makes a strong tea, strain, and let the patient drink freely each day. Make a strong tea of Senna leaves, strain, and drink a wineglassful every three hours until the bowels move freely. A bath should be taken once a day followed by brisk friction. An irritating plaster, such as a Mustard plaster, should be applied to the side. Moderate exercise in the open air and a nourishing diet are beneficial.

Chronic Enlargement of the Spleen.—This may follow repeated attacks of the acute, and may also be caused by malaria or tuberculosis.

TREATMENT.—

If enlargement results from chronic diseases, see treatment under the proper head.

STAMMERING.—*Stammering* or *Stuttering* is a condition in which the patient in his efforts to talk hesitates, and there is a spasmodic and uncontrollable repetition of the same word or words. There is an earnest effort to speak, but persistence only increases the nervous tension and causes greater delay.

Cause.—Unknown.

TREATMENT.—

The only chance of benefiting this condition rests with the stammerer himself. He should practice speaking slowly, word by word, and cease trying to speak for a few minutes as soon as his speech becomes interrupted. Schools for stammerers have been established.

DISEASES OF THE STOMACH.

DIGESTION.

The process of digestion is one of those organic functions which are directly concerned in maintaining the life of the individual. Digestion prepares or modifies food, and renders it in a condition suitable to be passed into the circulation and appropriated by the various organs and tissues of the body. Digestion is the splitting-up of the food products into simpler forms. It is a process of fermentation which is accomplished by certain principles of the digestive tract called *ferments*.

The Salivary Glands.—These glands are six in number. One is placed on each side of the neck just beneath the jaw; one on each side of the mouth just beneath the mucous membrane; and the *parotid glands*, which are the largest and most important, are situated one on each side just in front of and at the lower border of the ear. The saliva is a product of the salivary glands, and furnishes the first ferment, *ptyalin* (tyalin), which has the power of converting starch into glucose, or grape sugar.

The Stomach.—This organ is a dilatation of the digestive tract. Its size varies in different people. Its average size when empty is about 10 inches in length and 3 inches in width, and its weight is about 4 or 5 ounces. It is capable of great distension. The stomach and whole digestive tract, including the mouth and throat, are lined with mucous membrane. The glands which supply the stomach and which furnish the digestive fluid are placed in this membrane. These glands furnish three ferments: 1, *hydrochloric (muriatic) acid*, which acts first upon the food, converting albumen into a substance called *peptones;* 2, *pepsin*, which converts the peptones into *soluble albumen;* and 3, an *unnamed ferment* which has the power of curdling milk.

The Pancreas.—The pancreas is the next organ concerned in digestion. It is from 6 to 8 inches long, about 1½ inches wide, and weighs from 3 to 6 ounces. It is placed transversely across the back part of the abdominal cavity behind the stomach. The end pointing to the left is in relation with the spleen; the end pointing to the right is in relation with the digestive tract just below the lower end of the stomach. The pancreas furnishes four ferments, which together are called *pancreatin*. Separately,

324

they are as follows: *amylopsin*, which converts starch into sugar; *tripsin*, which, like pepsin, converts albumen into peptones or soluble albumen; *steapsin*, which decomposes fats into glycerine and fatty acids; and an *unnamed ferment*, which, like that of the stomach, has the power of curdling milk.

The Liver.— This organ, which is described elsewhere, furnishes *bile*, which aids in emulsifying fats, stimulates the secretions of the small bowel, increases bowel movement and prevents decomposition.

The Small Bowel.—This part of the digestive tract has numerous glands scattered throughout its length, and these glands secrete a fluid which is called *succus entericus*. This fluid also contains digestive ferments.

The First Act of Digestion.—The first process is that of the ptyalin upon starch, the product of which is grape sugar, therefore, thorough mastication of food is of great importance. Whoever fails to thoroughly mix what he eats with saliva and its ptyalin courts dyspepsia by hindering other subsequent acts of digestion. One part of ptyalin, at the temperature of the human body, will convert two thousand times its own weight of cooked starch into grape sugar.

The Second Act of Digestion.—The food carries the saliva and its ptyalin into the stomach, where its action is continued. When food reaches the stomach, it stimulates the glands of that organ and its digestive fluid begins to flow. It appears in little drops and trickles down the mucous membrane which lines the stomach. The saliva is alkaline; the fluids of the stomach are acid. The saliva continues to act upon the food until its alkaline properties are overcome by the acid of the stomach. This is usually about three-quarters of an hour. This time is given up to starch digestion. If the saliva does not get well mixed with the food, as in rapid eating, the starch will be but poorly digested and dsypepsia be likely to follow.

The Third Act of Digestion.—This is begun when the alkali of the saliva has been neutralized by the acid of the stomach. The gastric juice exerts no influence on grape or cane sugar, starch or fat; it acts upon albumen only. When the alkali of the saliva has become neutralized, the hydrochloric acid and pepsin of the gastric fluid commence their action on the different albuminoids and convert them into peptones, which means albumen in a soluble form, that is, so that it may be absorbed into the circulation. The hydrochloric acid first partially changes the albumen into peptones, and this action is immediately followed by the pepsin, which renders the change more or less complete.

The Fourth Act of Digestion.— As fast as the stomach completes its work the resulting products are passed on and the ferments of the pancreas are called into use. These, together with the bile, enter the digestive tract about 3½ inches below the stomach. The amylopsin of the pancreatic fluid supplements the action of the ptyalin of the saliva, and converts any remaining starch into grape sugar, acting much more quickly than ptyalin.

As stated above, the fluids of the stomach convert albumen into peptones, but the change may not be complete. Tripsin, the chief of the pancreatic ferments, completes this change.

The steapsin of the pancreatic fluid, and the bile, together emulsify fats and separate the different fatty acids and glycerine (fats contain glycerine). The acids, meeting the alkalies— soda, potash, lime, etc.—contained in foods, form soapy solutions. These solutions are absorbed into the lymphatics, a system of vessels which conveys some of the products of digestion to the heart, where they are sent through the lungs for oxidation and then enter the general circulation. The bile is also a powerful aid in preventing putrefaction, and stimulates bowel movement.

The Fifth Act of Digestion.—This is taken up by the secretion, *succus entericus*, of the small bowel, which acts upon starch, fats and albumen, and aids in making digestion still more complete.

The Last Act of Digestion.—A part of the products of digestion are carried direct to the liver, where this organ further elaborates upon the digestive changes. It is aided in this work by a digestive fluid secreted in the spleen and emptied by the veins of the spleen into the liver.

Disposition of the Products.—The process of digestion completed, the resulting products are carried by the liver veins to the ascending vena cava, a large vein which empties into the right side of the heart. The products of digestion carried by the lymphatics, already mentioned, also empty into the right side of the heart, being carried by the thoracic duct, which commences just below the diaphragm and passes up through the chest cavity.

The Higher Forms of Digestion.—From the right side of the heart the venous blood containing the digested food is sent through the lungs for oxidation. This blood receives about five per cent of the oxygen from the air which enters the lungs. It is then returned to the left side of the heart and sent out through the general circulation to supply the needs of the body. The blood contains ferments which induce important digestive changes.

INDIGESTION—DYSPEPSIA.—The great majority of stomach troubles come under the head of *Indigestion* or *Dyspepsia*, meaning some disturbance of that part of the digestion carried on in the stomach. When there is an excess of acid present in the gastric fluid, it is called *Acidity of the Stomach;* when the secretions are abundant and unhealthy, it is called *Catarrhal Indigestion.*

Cause.—These and other conditions are simply the result of certain kinds of food, the excessive use of alcoholic liquors, or any other causes or conditions resulting in indigestion.

Symptoms.—The symptoms of *Dyspepsia* are loss of appetite, flatulency (wind on the stomach) with eructations, bad taste in the mouth, coated tongue, foul breath, sense of fullness, soreness and pain with a feeling of weight in the stomach, pain on pressure, and a raw or burning feeling in the stomach and behind the chest bone. In an acute attack there is nausea, and sometimes vomiting. The ejected matter may contain more or less undigested food. Loss of appetite is more marked during an acute attack; at other times it may be excessive. Constipation is generally present, or may be alternated with diarrhea.

There is drowsiness after meals, headache, and palpitation, or tumultuous heart action. Sometimes the heart is weak and fluttering. Undigested food may lie in the stomach for hours or days, and this may give the stomach control over the mental faculties and result in low spirits and evil forebodings. The sufferer becomes irritable and is unable to sleep, or is troubled with bad dreams.

Where indigestion occurs in the digestive tract, there is pain and soreness two or three hours after eating. If gas forms in the bowels, there is a sense of fullness and bloating. If long continued, the sufferer will become greatly emaciated from lack of nourishment. In some cases congestion extends along the mucous membrane lining the duct leading to the gall bladder. This checks the flow of bile and results in jaundice. If the bile cannot pass off through the natural channel, the bowels, Nature eliminates by some other means. A part is eliminated by the skin, giving the characteristic yellow color, and digestion suffers still more. Congestion or swelling of the mucous membrane lining the duct leading to the gall bladder would also prevent the flow of the pancreatic fluid, because the pancreatic duct empties into or joins the duct leading from the gall bladder just before it reaches the digestive tract; this would also interfere with digestion, and emaciation would be increased. We give below a list of remedies recommended for *Dyspepsia* or *Indigestion*, remedies that have been furnished by many representative physicians, yet we wish to state that medicinal treatment alone will not cure this trouble. The cure is largely in the hands of the sufferer, and can be expressed in one word,—*diet.*

At present physical training is being encouraged by many physicians for many diseases. Such training is recommended in place of drugs. In many cases patients are advised to abstain from food for one, two or three days, or as long as they are willing to submit, and we believe that in cases of dyspepsia, following such advice and afterward exercising care in matters of food and drink will result in more benefit than any other known method.

We recall one case in particular, where the patient suffered all the pangs and miseries ever produced by this disease, and was permanently cured by the following method: *Abstinence from all food for one week.* The patient drank a considerable quantity of Lime Water every day, which was the only thing taken into the stomach. The Lime Water was made fresh each day. The patient was a strong man, yet the treatment was a severe test of his physical strength. We saw him frequently, and have reason to believe that his claim of abstinence was true. We were also more or less associated with him during the next fifteen months, and during that time there was never the slightest evidence of dyspepsia or any form of stomach trouble.

TREATMENTS.—

A. Usually an active cathartic is of benefit. A restricted diet, and in many cases the avoidance of all food for twenty-four hours, is of great advantage. One glass of milk and Lime Water, equal parts, taken once in four hours for two or three days, will sustain the patient and insure the stomach a much-needed rest. Commence feeding by giving rice which has been boiled for three hours; or boil oatmeal for the same length of time, strain, and use only the liquid part. Also soft cooked eggs, dry toast, etc., may be taken. These should be taken at regular intervals and only in small amounts until there is a marked improvement. After each meal take 1 teaspoonful of the following:

Scale Pepsin (1 to 3000)	2	drachms.
Hydrochloric (Muriatic) A c i d, pure	½	"
Fowler's Solution......................	2	"
Lloyd's Hydrastus......................	3	"
Glycerine.................................	2	ounces.
Simple Elixir...........................	4	"

Mix together.

Or, after each meal and at bedtime take 10 grains of Lacto-peptin, manufactured by the New York Pharmacal Co., also 10 grains of Subnitrate of Bismuth—four doses a day. These may be taken together.

In all cases of indigestion, restrict the amount of food until the patient thoroughly understands the definition of the word hunger. Avoid fatigue or overwork, secure an abundance of fresh air and proper exercise and keep the bowels regular.

B. In case of weak stomach, with sluggish liver, coated tongue, bad taste in the mouth, especially in the morning, or pain after eating, there is nothing better than the following:

Tincture of Nux Vomica............ 2 drachms.
Nitro Muriatic Acid.................. 1 drachm.
Elixir Lactated Pepsin............... 1 ounce.
Fluid Extract of Dandelion........ 2 ounces.
Infusion Columbo, add to make.. 4 "

Mix, and take 1 teaspoonful diluted after each meal.

Also when there is gas in the stomach or intestines the following is very beneficial:

Charcoal....................................... 24 grains.
Pepsin .... 30 "
Bicarbonate of Soda...................... 24 "

Mix, make into 12 capsules and take 1 after eating, or whenever needed.

The bowels should be kept free with 10 to 15 drops of Fluid Extract of Cascara before breakfast, as this not only relieves but cures constipation. The dose may be increased or decreased as suits the needs of the individual.

The diet should consist of easily digested mixed foods— vegetables, stewed and roasted meats, soft boiled eggs, etc. Avoid coffee.—(78).

C. Gum Myrrh, powdered................ 1 ounce.
Columbo, " .... 1 "
Gentian, " .... 1 "
Rhubarb Root, " .... 1 "
Cubebs, " .... 1 "
Pepper, " .... 1 "
Peruvian Bark, " .... 1 "
Alcohol .... 24 ounces.
Water.. 8 "

Mix the Alcohol and water and add the powders. Let stand for ten days, shaking the bottle frequently, then strain through a piece of fine muslin. If the muslin is folded in several thicknesses, it will leave the preparation freer from sediment.

Dose.—Teaspoonful in a little water, milk, tea or coffee, twenty minutes before meals.— (66).

D. Pepsin, Fairchild's Essence ...... 2 ounces.
Pancreatin, Essence of .... 1 ounce.
Tincture Nux Vomica................. 2 drachms.
Tincture Phosphorous .... 1 drachm.
Elixir Calisaya Bark and Iron
   enough to make.................... 6 ounces.

Mix, and take 1 teaspoonful after each meal,

or,

Nitro-Hydrochloric Acid, diluted 3 drachms.
Nux Vomica, Tincture of........... 2½ "
Capsicum, Tincture of............... ½ drachm.

Mix, and take ½ teaspoonful in water before and after each meal.—(53).

E. Eat *regularly*, not to exceed three meals a day, and avoid anything that is found to disagree with the stomach. Take regular, systematic exercise—not once, but three times daily, lasting from two to three hours after each meal. To take a cold sponge bath and rub down with a coarse towel two hours after meals is the best substitute for exercise. Very little medication is needed.

F. Diluted Hydrochloric Acid............ 1 ounce.
Tincture Nux Vomica.................... ¼ "

Mix. Take 20 drops in water just after meals.—(11).

G. Tincture Nux Vomica.............. 4 drachms.
Hydrochloric Acid.................... ½ drachm.
Peppermint Water................ ... 2 ounces.
Simple Elixir .... 4 "

Mix, and take 1 teaspoonful before each meal; or take Elixir Lactopeptine—teaspoonful before meals and at bedtime.—(46).

Acidity of the Stomach.—Normally, during digestion the fluid of the stomach contains two-tenths of one per cent of hydrochloric acid. In case of acidity of the stomach it may contain many times this amount, and may also contain lactic acid, acetic acid, and perhaps many other acids. It is these acids that produce the burning sensation known as *heartburn*.

TREATMENTS.—

A. Bicarbonate of Soda................. 2 drachms.
Tincture Nux Vomica............... 3 "
Compound Tincture Gentian...... 3 ounces.
Simple Elixir, enough to make... 6 "

Mix, and take 1 teaspoonful before meals and at bedtime.

B. Baking Soda, ⅓ to 1 teaspoonful dissolved in ½ glass of water. Take all at once.—(45).

C. Dilute Nitro-Hydrochloric Acid.. 3 drachms.
Tincture of Nux Vomica............ 2   "

Mix, and take 5 drops before meals and 5
drops after meals.   Keep the bowels regular.
—(53).

D. One-half to 1 teaspoonful of baking Soda in ⅓ of a glass
of water.   Repeat in one hour until there is relief.—(9).

E. Eat slowly.   Avoid sweets.   Keep the bowels loose.
Take Milk of Magnesia (proprietary) in teaspoonful doses every
two hours until relieved.—(17).

F. Lime Water in teaspoonful doses every three hours.
Teaspoonful doses of Fairchild's Essence of Pepsin after each
meal.—(7).

Catarrhal Indigestion.—Where the secretions of the
stomach contain a good deal of mucus, showing a catarrhal condition, it is always well to start with a clear field.   Give an
emetic—1 teaspoonful of Syrup of Ipecac every ten minutes until
vomiting takes place.   When the patient vomits, have him
drink large quanties of water containing a little baking Soda—
drink a pint or a quart, if possible.   This will have a tendency
to wash out the stomach.   Next give an active cathartic—1 or 2
tablespoonfuls of Castor Oil, or the same amount of Seidlitz Salts,
or any other laxative desired, remembering that the action
should be *thorough.*   Abstain from all food for twenty-four hours,
then give the same treatment as advised under *Indigestion.*
Where the stomach contains a large amount of unhealthy
exudate in the form of mucus, the patient should drink ½ to 1
pint of *hot* water one hour before meals.

**DILATATION OF THE STOMACH—CHRONIC
INDIGESTION.**—In this disease there is an increase in the
size of the organ.   The enlargement continues until the muscle
walls lose their power to contract, and remain permanently
dilated.   In this condition the stomach contains more or less
fluid and an unhealthy mucous exudate, and chronic dyspepsia is
the result.

Cause.—Dilatation of the stomach always results from
chronic indigestion from some cause.   It follows cancer when
the cancer is situated near the opening into the small bowel, as
the growth prevents the passage of the food and the unhealthy
condition interferes with digestion.   Decomposition follows with

the production of many gases, and dilatation results. In any case of chronic indigestion the same decomposition, gas formation and dilatation may follow.

Changes That Occur During Chronic Indigestion. — When resulting from indigestion following the prolonged use of alcohol, there is first congestion of the vessels supplying the stomach, and this results in a low form of inflammation and an overgrowth of the connective tissue. The contraction of this tissue destroys the glands that furnish the digestive fluid. Some may be entirely obliterated, others are closed, and the openings of others are narrowed and their action more or less interefered with. Blood vessels are caught in the contracting fibers, circulation is lessened or shut off, the part supplied by such vessels atrophies—shrinks—and degeneration follows. At first the mucous membrane and deeper structures are thickened and swollen. The secretions are changed in quantity and quality, the natural fluids are lessened, and in places the first layer of cells covering the membrane are piled up in polypoid growths. These appear like little tumors or mounds, giving the surface an uneven appearance. In other places the mucous membrane may be largely replaced by the new connective tissue overgrowth. When these changes are complete, the walls of the stomach are thinned, as much of the natural tissue has been destroyed and the new tissue is shrunken and hardened. When dilatation of the stomach results from indigestion from other causes, the change is not so marked as when resulting from the prolonged use of alcohol. There is not so much destruction of the mucous membrane, but the membrane remains thickened and swollen and a chronic catarrhal condition results; yet in all forms the stomach may be dilated and contain more or less fluid and an unhealthy mucous secretion, also more or less undigested food.

Symptoms.—Loss of appetite, nausea, sometimes vomiting. When resulting from alcohol, there is the well-known morning vomiting of drunkards. The ejected matter is sour and ill-smelling, and often contains particles of undigested food. There is tenderness in the region of the stomach, and more or less thirst and burning at the pit of the stomach and under the chest bone. This latter is the result of the catarrhal inflammation along the æsophagus, or tube leading from the throat to the stomach. Constipation is present, and the urine is highly colored. The color is the result of waste products which these organs attempt to eliminate. Sleeplessness is a troublesome feature. This is more pronounced when occurring in drunkards. The patient may be more or less emaciated, and the physical powers are lessened because the body is not properly nourished. The skin loses its natural color and becomes pale.

TREATMENT.—

Rest and diet. Restrict the amount of starchy foods. **Give** skimmed milk and Lime Water, equal parts, soft cooked eggs, finely chopped raw beef and a little dry toast. Give from ½ to 1 pint of water as hot as can be taken, containing either a little baking Soda or 1 teaspoonful of Phosphate of Soda, one hour before meals. If this amount cannot be taken all at once, it can be disposed of in the course of twenty minutes without inconvenience.

Scale Pepsin (1 to 3000)............ 2 drachms.
Muriatic Acid, pure .... ½ "
Fowler's Solution...................... 2 "
Fluid Hydrastus .... 3 "
Strychnine.............................. ½ grain.
Glycerine............................... 2 ounces.
Simple Elixir .... 4 "
Mix, and take one teaspoonful after meals.

NEURALGIA OF THE STOMACH—GASTRALGIA.

—This is a painful condition of the stomach, the pain often occurring in paroxysms that last for an hour or more.

Cause.—Same as neuralgia elsewhere. In many cases undigested food may act as the exciting cause.

Symptoms. — The severe form usually comes on suddenly. The pain is intense and often occurs in paroxysms. During an attack of pain the heart action is weak, the patient is faint, the countenance is shrunken and the hands and feet are cold. There may be a puffiness or œdemitus condition over the surface of the stomach. The pain extends along the lower border of the ribs and into the back—usually into the small of the back. Pain is also present beneath the chest bone. The pain follows the border of the diaphragm, which is attached to the ribs and small of the back. The pain may last for thirty minutes to one hour. Sometimes there is a sudden eructation of gas and the pain ceases.

TREATMENTS.—

A. To relieve an attack of pain, take the following:

Aromatic Spirits of Ammonia......... ½ ounce.
Chloroform..... .... ¼ "
Hoffman's Anodyne..................... ½ "
Tincture of Cardamon Compound ... ½ "
Brandy................................ ½ "

Take 1 teaspoonful well diluted with water. Repeat in one hour, if necessary. Usually one dose is sufficient.

While the foregoing may check the pain, it will not remove the cause. These cases require careful attention to diet, the same as described under *Dyspepsia*. If neuralgia of the stomach has existed for some time, the attacks are somewhat persistent and there seems to be a strong tendency towards their recurrence. However, the difficulty may be overcome by regulating the diet, as stated, keeping the bowels regular, avoiding all forms of excess, and, when there are indications of indigestion, taking together 10 grains of Lactopeptin, manufactured by the New York Pharmacal Co., and 10 grains of Bismuth. Take immediately after each meal. If there are eructations of gas, also take 10 or 15 grains of Willow Charcoal. This is best taken in tablet form. The tablets can be obtained at any drug store. The Pepsin and Bismuth mentioned, or any other form of artificial digestants, should be used only when there is evidence of trouble.

B. Aromatic Spirits of Ammonia .... ½ ounce.
Hoffman's Anodyne .... ½ "
Paregoric .... 6 drachms.
Tincture of Lavender Compound..... 6 "
Syrup of Rhubarb, enough to make 3 ounces.

Take a tablespoonful every hour until relieved.—(33).

ULCER OF THE STOMACH.—*Cause.*—Ulcer of the

stomach is caused by the plugging of an artery, by a blood clot, or by some obstruction in the circulation. The part supplied by such an artery dies and degenerates.

Symptoms. — The first symptoms are those of indigestion. This trouble gradually increases. There are eructations of gas and the breath is ill-smelling. Pain, which is one of the early symptoms, soon becomes constant, and is increased one-half to one hour after eating. This is about the time the digestive fluid of the stomach changes from an alkaline to an acid condition, and it is the acid that increases the pain. There is occasional vomiting. As the disease advances, blood is contained in the ejected matter. Sometimes there is a large amount of bright red blood present. The ejected matter also contains undigested food. If vomiting occurs between meals, there is a large amount of mucus. In some cases there are occasional attacks of neuralgia. In some cases also the patient is greatly debilitated, and in others he is not. The vomiting of a large amount of bright red blood, together with the other symptoms mentioned, is sufficient evidence of ulcer of the stomach.

TREATMENT.—

The stomach should be allowed to remain as quiet as possible. When food is taken into the stomach, and during the period of digestion, the muscular coats of the organ maintain a constant churning movement, and both the food and the mechanical movement irritate the ulcer and prevent its healing. All water drank should be taken as hot as can be borne, and should contain some alkali—Phosphate of Soda, baking Soda, or Sulphate of Soda. By many Sulphate of Soda is considered the best—1 teaspoonful to a pint of water.

Regarding nourishment, those who have treated the largest number of these cases advise rectal feeding. Also bathe the surface with nutrient oils—Cod Liver Oil is perhaps one of the best. When this fails to maintain the patient and food by the stomach becomes necessary, only that that is most nourishing should be taken, and in liquid form.

CANCER OF THE STOMACH.—*Cause.*—See CANCER.

Symptoms.—During the early stages of cancer of the stomach the symptoms are those of indigestion. The patient loses in weight without any known cause. Digestive disturbances increase until there is more or less pain. The pain may be constant, or may be present only occasionally. The skin gradually changes to a straw color. In some cases the color is quite natural, especially during the first six or eight months. When the cancer is situated at what is called the cardiac end of the stomach, *i. e.*, the end into which the æsophagus opens, there is a gradual narrowing of this tube and swallowing becomes difficult; later there is regurgitation or return of the food. When it is situated at the end of the stomach opening into the small bowel, the food is prevented from passing out of the stomach. This causes the organ to dilate. The patient lives about one year. Vomiting commences at some stage of the disease—sometimes quite early, perhaps from the third to the sixth month. In other cases it does not occur until one or two months before death. Vomiting occurs soon after eating. When the growth is situated near the opening of the stomach into the small bowel and is followed by dilatation of the stomach, food may remain in the organ for from one to two or three days and then be ejected. The food is in various stages of decomposition, and blood is often present. Toward the latter stages of the disease blood is present in larger amounts, and, as a result of remaining in the stomach for some time and being brought in contact with the fluids of the stomach and the undigested food, it is dark in color and clotted. This is often spoken of as "*coffee grounds*" *vomiting*. Sometime during the disease the cancer may be felt through the abdominal wall. Usually this part of the diagnosis can be made from the sixth to the ninth month. Beginning with the symptoms, or soon after, the stomach is sensitive to touch, and during the progress of the disease this sensitiveness increases until the slightest pressure causes pain. The emaciation also increases until the patient appears like a living skeleton. Locating the growth by manipulation over the stomach, when accompanied by the symptoms given, is unmistakable evidence of the cancer.

There may be cancer of the pancreas, which is situated just behind the stomach. In this case there is less vomiting, but diarrhea is present and the eliminations contain undigested fat.

There may be cancer of the liver or gall bladder. In this case there would be evidence of digestive disturbances, but these would be less marked.

Cancer may occur in the digestive tract. If occurring at the beginning of the small bowel where it joins the stomach, the symptoms would be similar to those given, but the ejected matter would contain less blood; if occurring in the large bowel, stomach symptoms would be largely absent. The eliminations from the digestive tract would contain mucus and blood, and the odor would be foul. In all cases there is rapid emaciation, and death is the inevitable result.

TREATMENTS.—

What to Do.—As the early symptoms are the usual disorders of indigestion, correct the diet and take the ordinary remedies for dyspepsia. If the trouble continues, consult a physician.

A. If the cancer is situated where the æsophagus joins the stomach, the opening should be maintained as long as possible by dilating the part. When this fails and food cannot reach the stomach, it is necessary to insert a tube, forcing it through the constricted part, and give liquid foods. When the cancer is situated at the other end of the stomach, the usual remedies for indigestion may be given. In all cases give 10-drop doses of Fowler's Solution and 10 grains of the Sulphocarbolates at meal time—three doses a day.

Stomach Diseases—Summary.—In giving a description of the diseases of the digestive tract, we stated that those diseases given under so many different headings were confusing, that they were but different manifestations of the same diseased condition, etc. The same is true of the various forms of disease of the stomach mentioned,—*Gastric Fever, Acute Gastric Catarrh, Acidity of the Stomach, Acute Dyspepsia, Acute Indigestion, Gastralgia or Neuralgia of the Stomach.* These, and perhaps other terms, are used to denote an acute attack of *Indigestion.*

It should be remembered that this sudden manifestation of pain and other symptoms of acute trouble is not the result of a single error, but evidence of a long train of conditions, which have gradually led up to the sudden onset. For some time the patient has gone beyond the limit of safety, and the system has withstood the abuse, if we may call it such, of late suppers, late hours, excessive or rapid eating, and, in many cases, excess in drinking—whether of strong coffee, tea, ice water or alcoholic liquors makes no particular difference. Neither is it of importance whether the digestive fluids of the stomach contain a little too much acid, or are slightly alkaline; the result is the same. The small vessels supplying the mucous membrane become congested and inflamed, the digestive fluids become excessive in amount and abnormal in quality, and now Nature suddenly rebels and the patient finds himself the victim of an acute attack. These unpleasant reminders are Nature's voice, forcibly expressed. For every transgression there is now demanded full payment with interest. We should remember that if Nature's laws are broken, there will be a day of reckoning. Whether the wilful errors pertain to matters of diet and hygiene, to loss of sleep, overwork or lack of exercise, is unimportant. It would be as reasonable to expect an apple thrown into the air to remain there, as to expect abuses of the physical body to go unpunished. The only prophylactic or preventive measure against disease is a healthy system, and the only way to avoid disease of the stomach is to exercise care and judgment regarding matters of diet.

Usually when the stomach begins to give trouble, artificial digestants are resorted to. The class of people who take these patent remedies are looking for a specific—a something that will allow them to continue their indulgences and excesses and at the same time pay little or no attention to the demands of Nature. But sooner or later Nature claims her rights. It may be in the form of an acute attack, of gradual and lingering disease, some of the many deformities of rheumatism, spinal diseases, or an early death. Every one should learn that digestion cannot be purchased ready-made, that artificial digestants afford but temporary relief, and that their effects are only palliative, *i. e.*, that they quiet the symptoms without touching the cause, and that, if continued, these remedies will still further weaken the digestive organs. They do this by doing their work for them. It is well known that Nature does not waste any of her forces, nor perform any of her work in vain, and if artificial digestants are employed, the natural digestive fluids or ferments will cease to flow. The muscles of the arm would shrink if the arm were kept in a sling; a joint would refuse to act if it were kept too long in one position. When the arm and joint cease to act, Nature ceases to supply them. The same is true with the digestive fluids. If they are supplied artificially, the digestive organs will atrophy, like the muscles of the arm kept in a sling, or refuse to act, like the joint that has remained too long inactive.

Eructations in which are recognized by taste or smell anything eaten or drank, are evidence that the stomach cannot take care of that particular article, whether of food or drink. They are an indication that fermentation has occurred, the flavor or odor being thrown off with the gases of decomposition. If the eructations are greasy, avoid fats; if they are sour, avoid sugar and starchy foods, as these produce acids. If there is a bitter taste in the mouth, it is bile, and indicates congestion of the bile duct. The stomach does not rebel without a cause, and its warnings should be heeded. When stomachical digestion is perfect, we are unconscious that we have a stomach. Every organ has an individual sign by which it makes known any abnormal conditions, and it is upon the recognition of such signs that diagnosis is made.

The three great physicians of Nature are fresh air, pure water and sunshine, and these combined with healthful exercise are more effective in securing and maintaining health than drug medication. They will cure most cases of dyspepsia. If they could be bottled up and administered in tea or tablespoonful doses while people were in bed, or comfortably seated in rocking chairs, they would be more largely indulged in, and those preparing such treatment could command their millions.

When the stomach is irritable through indigestion, the condition is reflected to the brain and other organs through the connecting nerve fibers, weaving a thread of disorders which may baffle human skill. This condition produces many imaginary ailments—the blues, melancholia, irritability, nervousness, etc. These cases do not need medicine; it would be as absurd to treat such cases with medicine as it would be to give medicine for lameness caused by a sliver driven into the hand. The stomach needs rest and freedom from all irritating substances just as much as the hand needs to have the sliver removed.

It may be of interest to know that a glass of ice water lowers the temperature of the stomach 30 degrees, and this has a powerful effect in checking digestion.

STRANGURY.—This means painful urination. (See *Dysuria* under BLADDER, DISEASES OF).

STRICTURE.—Stricture means the closing of the natural lumen, or opening of any passageway, as an artery or any part of the bowel. Stricture may be partial or complete. It may affect any canal or duct, as the urethra, trachea, or wind-pipe, œsophagus, or tube leading from the throat to the stomach, or the eustachian tube, the passage leading from the base of the tongue to the middle ear. These strictures may be uniform or may be tortuous; they may be partial or complete, rendering the canal passable or impassable. They may also be recurrent, that is, returning from time to time.

Cause.—They may be caused by a foreign body, by tumors, including cancer, or may result from inflammation. The last is the most frequent cause.

TREATMENT.—

These cases require a physician.

Note.—Usually stricture is understood to mean a narrowing of the urethra following gonorrhœa (See GLEET).

STYE.—(See under EYE, DISEASES OF).

SUMMER COMPLAINT.—(See DIARRHEA).

SUNBURN.—In those unaccustomed to outdoor life, the skin over the face, neck and other exposed parts is delicate. The cells forming the outer layer of the skin are not coarse, rough and thick, because the tissues beneath have needed no particular protection. The sudden change allows the sun's rays to penetrate to the deeper structure, or skin proper. It will be remembered that it is in this layer that the blood vessels are situated. The excessive heat causes acute congestion, and, in some instances, inflammation. This accounts for the heat and swelling, and the swelling causes the pressure and pain. This condition usually lasts for a few days, more or less, according to the severity or amount of exposure.

TREATMENT.—

The best treatment is some application that will exclude the air, because it is the oxygen of the air coming in contact with the true skin that produces the sensation of smarting and burning. The application of Vaseline, Sweet Cream, Sweet Oil, or any emollient that will protect the affected area, is all that is needed. If on the hands, arms or neck, the application may be followed with a light bandage. This will insure greater protection and afford greater relief.

SWEAT GLANDS, DISORDER OF — HYPERIDROSIS.—Some persons are afflicted with excessive secretions of the sweat glands. The excess may be general all over the body, or may affect only certain parts, as the hands, arm-pits, soles of the feet, etc. It is usually accompanied with a disagreeable and disgusting odor. This is especially true when it affects the soles of the feet. Excessive sweating of the soles of the feet is not only the most uncomfortable, but the most dangerous, form of this disease. It keeps the feet wet and cold, and in many

cases is the primary step leading to chronic catarrh; or may precipitate an acute cold. The feet are kept in a sweat-bath, as it were, which causes the outer skin to peel off rapidly and leaves them tender and sensitive.

Cause.—Some irritant which excites excessive action of the nerves supplying the sweat glands and results in over-production; or the nerve supply may be unusually or abnormally developed.

TREATMENT.—

The following is one of the best remedies of prevention:

Menthol	20 grains.
Tannic Acid	40 "
Formaldehyde	20 drops.
Borax, powdered	1 ounce.
Soapstone, powdered	2 "

Mix, and dust freely inside the stockings. If there is still some sweating, add more Tannic Acid; if there is odor left, add more Formaldehyde.

The same preparation may be applied locally under the arms, or wherever abnormal sweating occurs.

Note.—The above is Allen's Foot-Ease plus Formaldehyde.

SYPHILIS.—(See under VENEREAL DISEASES).

TAPEWORM—TÆNIA SOLIUM.—This is a form of worm which sometimes inhabits the digestive tract and grows to great lengths. The variety mentioned above, tænia solium, is the one most commonly met, and varies in length from ten to thirty feet. In appearance it is flat and thin like a ribbon. There are two other varieties which are larger. The largest is said to attain a length of sixty feet. The head of the tapeworm is small and rounded, being about $\frac{1}{30}$ to $\frac{1}{40}$ of an inch in diameter. The body is composed of small segments, or joints, which vary from ⅛ to ¼ of an inch in length; the width may exceed the length. The worm is supplied with two rows of suckers, and the tænia solium is also supplied with two rows of what are called hooklets. Each worm is supplied with male and female reproductive organs. Its eggs are about $\frac{1}{1800}$ of an inch in diameter. The worm is supposed to inhabit pork, beef and fish, and to find its way into the body first in such food. It inhabits the upper part of the small bowel, and the head is firmly attached to the mucous membrane by means of the hooklets mentioned.

Cause.—The eggs, which are found in the meat mentioned. These eggs, on reaching the digestive tract, hatch and develop into the worm.

Symptoms.—The elimination of detached or disjointed segments may be the first, and is the only positive evidence of the presence of the worm. In other cases there is pain, which may be anywhere in the abdominal cavity. The appetite is more or less affected, and at times there may be nausea and vomiting. There may also be dyspepsia and constipation, and the patient may lose flesh. After eating the symptoms are apt to disappear, and are most prominent when the stomach and bowels are empty. In some cases the patient claims to feel the movement of the worm, though this may be imagination.

TREATMENTS.—

A. There are a number of remedies which are used in the treatment of tapeworm. A strong tea made from Pomegranate Root, Turpentine, Pumpkin Seed, Aspidium, Male Fern, and perhaps other remedies are used for its destruction. Of these the ethereal resin of Aspidium and the oleo resin of Male Fern are perhaps used oftenest, although Pumpkin Seed has the advantage of being cheap, effective and harmless. This is important in the case of small children, because it requires as large a dose of the remedy to destroy the tape worm in the child as in the adult, and enough of the stronger remedies to be effective might be too large a dose for the child.

In case of children, give 1 ounce of the dried Pumpkin Seed, or 4 ounces of the fresh seed. Remove the outer covering or husk, and bruise, together with chocolate or sugar. Give an active cathartic and restrict the diet as much as possible for forty-eight hours. Divide the dried seed into four doses, or the green seed into six doses, and give one hour apart. Follow the last dose with another active cathartic, such as Castor Oil. This is usually effective, and, as stated, is perfectly harmless.

For adults, give an active cathartic in the afternoon, eat a very light supper, if any, and no breakfast, and take about 1 or 2 teaspoonfuls of the oleo resin of Male Fern, or 1 teaspoonful of the ethereal resin of Aspidium. In two hours take 2 tablespoonfuls of Castor Oil and 1 drop of Croton Oil. The Tannate of Pelletierine which is the active principle of Pomegranate, is highly recommended, and may be given in from ½- to 1 -grain doses in place of the Male Fern or Aspidium.

B. Take 4 ounces of Pumpkin Seed, remove shells and bruise seeds together with two ounces of sugar and 1 pint of warm water. Let patient eat nothing for one day. The next day let him eat the Pumpkin Seed mixture, and after he has finished, give him a good dose of Epsom Salts.—(35).

C. Emulsion consisting of:

Turpentine	1 ounce.
Wintergreen Water	½ "
Gum Acacia	½ "
Simple Syrup	1 "

Mix. To be taken by an adult in one dose.—(31).

TEETH.—The teeth are subject to disease the same as other tissues, organs and structures. There may be abscess, or there may be a gradual or rapid destruction of one or more of the teeth. They are also subject to pain and tumor growths. The tumor consists of an increased amount or overgrowth of the bony tissue.

TREATMENT.—

The treatment should be preventive. This means that the teeth should receive proper care by keeping them clean. Every one should use a brush at least once a day, or, what is better, after each meal. Any evidence of decay should be investigated and cared for by the dentist. Some form of tooth powder that is cleansing and at the same time harmless, should be used occasionally, as the following:

Precipitated Chalk	1 ounce.
Orris Root, powdered	2 drachms.
Boric Acid, powdered	20 grains.

Mix, and use by applying to the brush.
Note.—Other preparations for use in cleaning the teeth will be found under MISCELLANEOUS MEDICAL RECEIPTS.

TOOTHACHE REMEDIES.—

A.	Chloral Hydrate	½ ounce.
	Gum Camphor	½ "

By gradually rubbing these two ingredients together, a liquid soon forms. This can best be done in a druggist's mortar. Keep the liquid well corked. In using take a small piece of cotton, large enough to fill the cavity in the tooth, roll it up firmly, and with the end of a tooth-pick, or some other convenient method, dip it into the solution and pack it firmly into the tooth.—(64).

Note.—The above is an excellent application.

B. Saturate a piece of cotton the size of the tooth cavity in Ammonia and put into the tooth. It will stop toothache at once. —(20).

C.	Chloroform	1 drachm.
	Oil of Cloves	1 "
	Carbolic Acid	1 "

Mix, and apply a few drops on cotton. Care should be taken not to drop any of the liquid on the lips, tongue or gums.—(36).

D. Alcohol .... ½ ounce.
Laudanum .... ½ drachm.
Chloroform, liquid measure .... 3½ "
Gum Camphor .... 2 "
Oil of Cloves .... 2 "
Sulphuric Ether, liquid measure..... 3 "
Oil of Lavender.................. .... ½ "

If there is a nerve exposed, this will quiet it.
Apply with lint. Rub freely upon the gums
and upon the face against the tooth.

E. Alcohol .... 2 ounces.
Tincture of Arnica......................... 2 drachms.
Tincture of Chloroform .... 2 "
Oil of Cloves .... 1 "

Mix, and apply to the cavity on a little
cotton.

TETTER.—(See *Eczema* under SKIN DISEASES).

THREAD WORMS.—(See under CHILDREN'S DISEASES).

THROAT, SORE.—The following treatments have been recommended. The reader is also referred to the treatments under LARYNGITIS; also, if the tonsils are affected, to the treatments under TONSILITIS.

TREATMENTS.—

A. Sage Tea, very strong..................... ½ pint.
Strained Honey .... 2 tablespoonfuls.
Common Salt................................. 2 "
Strong Vinegar.............................. 2 "

Mix, strain, and gargle the throat from
four to a dozen times daily, according to the
severity of the case —(64).

B. A pinch of the following on the tongue and swallowed,
without water, every half hour:

Cubebs, powdered........................... 1 teaspoonful.
Saltpetre... 1 "

Mix. Gargle the throat with milk. Little
or nothing to eat for 24 hours.—(35).

C. Chlorate of Potash............................ 1 drachm.
Turpentine....................................... 1 "
Syrup of Gum Arabic....................... 1 ounce.
Water .... 1 "

Mix. Take 1 teaspoonful every two hours.
—(36).

THRUSH.—(See under CHILDREN'S DISEASES).

TOE-NAIL, INGROWING. — This difficulty usually occurs on the great toe. In some cases it is very painful, so much so that the individual is unable to wear a shoe unless it is very large, or unless the part covering the toe is removed with a knife. In every case the condition is extremely unpleasant and there is always more or less soreness and pain.

Cause.—The cause is either an overgrowth along the edge of the nail, or the pressure of the nail irritates the soft tissue and results in its overgrowth. The edge of the nail either grows down into the tissues, or the tissue grows up over the edge of the nail; perhaps both conditions are present.

TREATMENTS.—

A. Very many cases may be benefited and often cured by taking a sharp-pointed knife and, by repeated strokes along the border, gradually cutting through the nail, removing a strip from one-sixteenth to one-eighth of an inch in width, and sometimes more. Where the nail grows down into the tissue it is not attached on either side, and by cutting through, the sliver of nail may be readily removed. This relieves the pressure, and for a time relieves the pain and soreness. If the trouble recurs, repeat the treatment. If successful the first time, it will be successful every time, and eventually the nail will stop growing in that direction.

The directions just given can be carried out by any one suffering with this trouble. Some cases, however, need surgical treatment.

B. *Painless Remedy.*—Henry Finch, M. D., reports, through the *British Medical Journal,* that neither cutting nor burning operations are at all necessary for the complete and rapid cure of ingrowing toe-nail. If a small, *thin,* flat piece of silver plate be bent at one edge into a slight deep groove and, after the toe has been poulticed twenty-four hours, slipped beneath the edge of the nail, so as to protect the flesh from its pressure, and the rest of the thin plate bent around the side and front of the toe, being kept in position with a small portion of adhesive plaster passed around the toe, a speedy and almost painless cure will take place; and the patient, after the first day, has the additional advantage of being able to walk. Dr. Finch has followed this method in numerous cases with uniform success.

TONGUE.—Like other tissues and organs, the tongue is subject to many diseases. There may be adhesions, including the condition known as *tongue-tie.* Such adhesions are congenital, *i. e.,* exist from birth. There may be *atrophy*—a shrinking of the organ. This may be caused by syphilis, by some disease of the brain, or by morbid growths on the tongue itself. There may be *hypertrophy* or overgrowth. This would result from a mild form of inflammation from some cause.

The tongue is also subject to ulcer, erysipelas and cancer. Barring cancer, perhaps the most serious form of disease of the tongue is acute inflammation. This is called *Glossitis.*

Acute Glossitis or Inflammation of the Tongue may result from injury—sometimes results from the sting of a bee.

Symptoms.—Sudden swelling, fever, pain and increased flow of saliva. The voice becomes changed, and speech and swallowing are difficult. The glands about the jaw enlarge and may suppurate. The swelling may be so rapid and reach such proportions as to render breathing not only difficult, but impossible.

TREATMENT.—

The same as treatment for inflammation elsewhere. Relieve the organ of the excessive amount of blood. This can only be done by draining the system of fluids and equalizing the circulation. A large dose of Pilocarpine is valuable. For a child five years old, ⅛ of a grain given with a hypodermic needle would perhaps be sufficient. This causes active elimination by the skin. Also give 1 drop of Croton Oil, either in a small capsule, or mixed with Glycerine or Sweet Oil and placed on the back of the tongue. If Croton Oil is not at hand, give a large dose of Castor Oil. Wait two hours, and if results are not obtained, give half the amount. In place of the Pilocarpine, Aconite may be given—1 drop of the tincture every hour. Also apply external heat to produce profuse perspiration. Sometimes even the most active treatment fails. In this case incisions may be made—cut deep enough to allow the blood to flow freely. This will aid in relieving the organ. In some cases it is necessary to perform tracheotomy *i. e.,* open the wind-pipe and insert an artificial tube through which the child may breathe. If an abscess forms, it should be opened and washed out the same as abscess elsewhere. These cases are always serious and require the services of a physician.

In chronic inflammation or enlargement of the tongue the disease is secondary, *i. e.,* the result of some other trouble, towards which the treatment should be directed.

TONSILITIS.—The Pharynx (farinks) commences at the back part of the mouth and terminates in the esophagus, or tube leading from the throat to the stomach. The pharynx is about 4½ inches in length. There are seven openings which communicate with it: the two nasal cavities; the two eustachian tubes, which lead to the middle ears; the trachea, which leads to the lungs; the mouth, which is in front; and the æsophagus, into which the pharynx terminates.

The upper and front part of the mouth has a bony roof covered with mucous membrane, and is called the *hard palate;* the back part is formed or composed of soft tissues only, therefore is called the *soft palate.* Arching from either side of the back part of the mouth are two folds of mucous membrane which meet in the centre; behind these are two more. The four folds contain four small muscles. These arches are called the pillars of the soft palate. They are separated at the sides of the throat, and meet in the center like the letter V. The tonsils are placed between them, thus, ⋀ , one on either side.

The tonsils are glandular bodies which vary considerably in size. During acute inflammation or chronic enlargement, they may be an inch in diameter; normally, they are very small and cannot be seen. On the surface of each tonsil there are from twelve to fifteen little openings, each extending inward and branching into many little follicles, or glandular sacs. Surrounding each of these sacs are a number of small bodies or glands with no external opening. These glands are similar to Peyer's glands in the small bowel (see TYPHOID FEVER). By means of lymphatics these ductless glands drain into the deep glands of the neck, and thus their secretions reach the general circulation. That is one reason why inflammation of the tonsils may produce such marked systemic effects.

Tonsilitis is inflammation of the tonsils. It is sometimes called *Quinsy.* As stated under *Diphtheria,* quinsy means a choking, and may be applied to any of the throat troubles where there is inflammation, swelling and difficulty in breathing or swallowing.

Cause. — The cause is the same as that which produces ordinary catarrhal colds and sore throat—probably due to atmospheric changes.

Symptoms.—In some cases the disease is ushered in with a chill, but usually it is not. There is a moderate rise of temperature, which may reach as high as 104 ; the tonsils become swollen, producing pressure and pain; there is a constant desire to clear the throat, and difficulty in swallowing ; the tonsils increase in size, and may nearly or altogether close the passage, though the act of breathing through the mouth forces an opening. In appearance at this time the tonsils are large, and deep red, and the surface may be more or less covered with whitish or yellowish points. The mucous membranes of the surrounding throat structures may be more or less swollen and inflamed. The swelling of the tonsils may be so great that suppuration will take place, in which case almost immediate relief will be afforded. Usually, however, the disease declines gradually, the fever disappearing and the tonsils returning to their normal size; or they may remain somewhat enlarged.

In inflammation and swelling of the throat it is well to remember the symptoms of diphtheria. Diphtheria may give the same early symptoms as tonsilitis, or as any case of sore throat, either mild or severe, but the typical symptom of diphtheria is the formation of a membrane, which usually appears on the tonsils at one or more points. These points spread rapidly and join together, forming a large leather-colored patch.

TONSILITIS COMPARED WITH DIPHTHERIA.

Tonsilitis.	Diphtheria.
Points first appearing are whitish or light yellow in color.	Points first appearing are of a dark, leathery color.
No membrane, but a white exudate of a downy or woolly appearance.	Smooth membrane of a dark grayish or leathery appearance.
Exudate can usually be removed with a soft cloth or swab.	Membrane is firmly adherent to the structures or tissues beneath. Cannot be removed unless torn loose.
Removal of the exudate leaves the surface natural, barring its inflamed appearance.	If membrane is torn loose, a bleeding surface is left behind.
Exudate stands out like wool on a smooth surface without any definite outline.	Membrane has a well-defined border.

TREATMENTS.—

What to Do.—Steep up bitter herbs in a closed vessel—an earthen pot or tea-kettle—and steam the patient's throat. Form a long tube by rolling up a newspaper. Place one end over the spout of the kettle, tie it in place, put the other end in or over the mouth, and have him inhale the steam as hot as can be borne comfortably. Or, add from ½ to 1 teaspoonful of Carbolic Acid to 2 quarts of boiling water, or the same amount of Turpentine, and inhale in the same way. The Carbolic Acid and Turpentine are of advantage because of their antiseptic properties; they insure cleanliness.

Give warm drinks and put to bed. If the case seems severe enough, send for a doctor. An abscess sometimes forms on the affected tonsil, and should this occur, have it opened by a doctor at the earliest moment.

A. At the first symptoms of tonsilitis give the patient an active cathartic, and give 5 grains of Salicylate of Soda every hour until the ears "sing;" after that, give every three hours. For the phlegm that collects in the throat, the following gargle will be found satisfactory:

Borax, powdered............................	2	drachms.
Salicylate of Soda	2	"
Glycerine.....................................	4	"
Water, enough to make..................	4	ounces.

Gargle several times a day, or as often as necessary.

If the fever is high, 1-drop doses of Tincture of Aconite may be given every hour, although this is unimportant; the fever is only a symptom, and if the disease is properly cared for, the symptom will disappear—so will the disease.

Another most excellent remedy for internal use is the following:

Tincture of Aconite.........................	$\frac{1}{2}$	drop.
Tincture of Belladonna Leaves.........	$\frac{1}{10}$	"
Tincture of Bryonia.........................	$\frac{1}{10}$	"
Red Iodide of Mercury....................	$\frac{1}{100}$	grain.
Sulphate of Morphine......................	$\frac{1}{100}$	"
Salicylate of Soda	1	"
Oil of Wintergreen	$\frac{1}{60}$	drop.

This combination is made in tablet form, and each tablet contains the amount given here. These tablets may be bought at any drug store.

The value of the tablet resides mostly in the amount of Salicylate of Soda it contains. Salicylate of Soda is a specific for many cases of tonsilitis. The tablets may be given one every hour, more or less often according to age. We have used these tablets and also the 5-grain doses of Salicylate of Soda in many cases of tonsilitis, and the results have been so uniformly satisfactory that we feel confident if the directions are followed, many cases of this disease can be aborted.

The patient should remain indoors for a day or two, if necessary. If the tonsils become greatly swollen, relief may be had by lancing them, cutting in one or more places. This allows them to bleed freely and relieves the congestion. If suppuration takes place, they should be lanced also. The best treatment for tonsils that are troublesome is to remove them—cut them out. This requires but a moment's time and produces no pain.

Enlarged Tonsils.—Sometimes the tonsils remain permanently enlarged. In this case it is better to have them removed. The operation is neither difficult nor painful. Until this is deemed necessary, either of the following may be used to advantage:

TREATMENTS.—

A. Chlorate of Potash................. ½ teaspoonful.
   Sulphite of Soda .... ⅓ "

> Put into a glass and fill with warm water. Gargle the throat thoroughly with a tablespoonful of this solution from three to five times a day.

Also paint the tonsils once in two or three days with the Tincture of Iodine, using a small brush. To do this, take a spoon handle, or something of the kind, and press the tongue down so that the tonsils may be treated readily. The Iodine will reduce their size by stimulating the absorption of inflammatory products.

B. Iodine .... 2 drachms.
   Glycerine................................. 6 "

Mix, and apply daily with a brush.—(45)

Note.—The object in adding the Glycerine lies in its power to attract water from the tissues beneath the surface to which it is applied. This drainage aids in reducing the size of the organ.

TOOTHACHE.—(See under TEETH).

TRANCE — MORBID SLEEP. — Trance differs from sleep both in time of duration and in the profound insensibility to external objects or impressions. Another peculiarity regarding trance is that it is more apt to follow excitement than fatigue or exhaustion. It is said to have occurred epidemically during periods of great religious excitement mingled with superstition.

A mild case resembles sleep, but there is an abnormal insensibility to external stimulation. The breathing and the pulse are quite natural. This form is called *Trance Sleep*. Or the breathing and heart action may be greatly weakened, yet perceptible. The joints remain movable, and the position of the individual can be easily changed. This condition is sometimes spoken of as *Trance Coma*, meaning deep sleep. In its severest form no heart beat or respiration can be detected. The temperature is subnormal, and the patient takes no nourishment. This form is sometimes spoken of as *Death Trance*.

Treatment.—

We have never had occasion to treat any of these cases, and so far as we know there is no satisfactory treatment that has ever been discovered. However, as a means of aid in reviving the patient we would recommend any of the following:

Inhalations of Nitrite of Amyl. Nitrite of Amyl is a liquid and is given by holding the uncorked bottle close to the nose for a few seconds at a time. While the effects last but a few minutes, they might serve to bring the individual to consciousness.

Atropine is another remedy, which does not act so quickly, but is more lasting. Place $\frac{1}{250}$ of a grain in powdered form on the tongue, and repeat this every hour for two or three doses. Under the directions of a doctor perhaps a larger dose could be given.

Glonoin, or Nitro-Glycerine, is another remedy belonging to the same class. The results somewhat resemble Nitrite of Amyl. The effects are produced rapidly and pass away within an hour.

Electricity—the Faradic current—is recommended by some. Its daily application at the same hour is claimed to have revived a patient after all other means had failed.

We wish also to recommend the rectal injection of two pints of water as hot as can be borne.

If the patient cannot be revived, the question of feeding becomes an important one. Liquid food should be given by the mouth, if the patient can swallow. Absorption through the skin is another means of conveying nourishment. Perhaps Cod Liver Oil applied to the surface once or twice a day is as valuable as any remedy that can be administered by this method.

TRICHINA WORM—TRICHINOSIS.—This disease is produced by a small worm called *trichina*. When full grown, it is from $\frac{1}{18}$ to $\frac{1}{8}$ of an inch in length. Sometimes the trichina inhabits the body of the hog, and when such meat is eaten raw or improperly cooked, this minute form of animal life finds its way into the digestive tract of man, where it multiplies very rapidly, penetrates the walls of the tract and enters the veins, or by other means finds its way into muscle tissue, which seems to be its natural place of abode. In the muscles the worms become encysted, that is, surrounded by a little membranous capsule. Later, both the cysts and the worms may become calcified, *i. e.*, lime salts are deposited, and the minute animal life appears as small white specks. They may remain encysted for months or years without undergoing any change. Should the flesh which they inhabit be swallowed by other animals, they would develop and multiply in the digestive tract, penetrate the walls of the bowels and migrate to muscle tissue, as before. They multiply rapidly

in the digestive tract, and it is the young ones that migrate to muscle tissue and become encysted. A temperature ot 170 degrees destroys this form of animal life; salting the meat also destroys it.

Rats are the most common carriers of this form of pest. It is not often that thev inhabit the body of hogs. According to some authorities they occur only in 1 to 1500 or 2000.

Cause.—Trichina finding their way into the stomach from eating pork when raw or when improperly cooked.

Symptoms—At first there is loss of appetite, nausea, perhaps vomiting, diarrhea and a feeling of languor, and there may be more or less prostration. This condition continues for a week, when the patient becomes sore and stiff and is attacked with pain, more or less severe. When the trichina enter the muscles, the pain is intense, and the slightest effort to move the affected muscle causes great pain. The pain is constant, the patient is unable to sleep, the face becomes swollen, there is fever and rapid pulse, more or less thirst, and profuse perspiration.

TREATMENT.—

Active cathartics might clear the digestive tract of the trouble, but it would have no influence upon the trichina after they became encysted. The treatment consists of food, stimulants and tonics. If only a small number of trichina migrate, the patient might recover; if a large number, the attack would prove fatal. Glycerine destroys trichina when applied to them direct. It does this by absorbing the fluids from the minute animal bodies, when they rapidly dry up and die. This remedy has been recommended in tablespoonful doses once every hour; but as the Glycerine absorbs so much water before it reaches the circulation, and becomes so largely diluted, its effects are doubtful. Alcohol has also been recommended, and its effects on the trichina are the same as the Glycerine; but it too absorbs so much water before and after reaching the circulation that its effects are doubtful.

TUBERCULOSIS — CONSUMPTION.— Consumption is a chronic, constitutional, non-contagious disease. Tuberculosis is a form of consumption in which little nodules or tubercles are formed in the affected tissues. Tubercles are small, nodular masses, about the size of a millet seed, and are produced by a low form of inflammation resulting from self-generated poisons in the system. When occurring in the lungs, the usual seat of the disease, it is called *Pulmonary Tuberculosis, Phthisis* or *Consumption*.

Consumption is a slow, wasting disease, and its primary cause is a lack of nourishment. Following, and as a result of such lack of nourishment, there is first a slight loss of vitality and lack of assimilation. The natural resistance of the tissues are lessened. The blood lacks the normal elements, and contains irritants in the form of waste material due to poor digestion and a lack of elimination. Indigestion is present in every case. The indigestion may be the result of rapid or excessive eating, poor food, unhygienic surroundings, too much hard work, or of the prolonged use of alcohol. Constipation is present more or less. This means that the digestive tract is unhealthy and that many poisons are generated there. It seems hardly necessary to state that these poisons enter the circulation, and, acting as irritants, produce a low form of inflammation. The inflammation and lack of nourishment mean that waste exceeds repair. Each organ and each individual cell of the body struggles to carry on the unequal contest, and the tissues thus become irritated and weakened and fail to appropriate the nourishment brought to them.

Those tissues and organs suffer most that are most liable to the morbid influences present. The lungs are most liable for the following reasons, hence, as stated, consumption of the lungs is the most common form. Nearly all of the blood passes through the lungs once every minute. This is not true of any other organ in the body except the heart. In the heart the blood simply passes from one cavity to another, while in the lungs the unhealthy blood must pass through the intricate network of small vessels called capillaries. This brings the morbid influences of the septic, or unhealthy blood, in direct contact with the lung tissue. Again, the lungs have a double circulation; they are supplied with two sets of blood vessels. One set supplies nourishment, and the other set is for the purification of the blood. These two systems of vessels are entirely separate. The system which supplies nourishment is given off from the lower left cavity of the heart, while that carrying the blood for elimination of the poisonous gases mentioned, and for oxidization, comes from the right side of the heart. The blood which is sent to nourish the lungs is bright red, while that sent for purification is dark, venous, and contains many poisons and impurities.

The system of vessels for the purification of the blood is placed just beneath the delicate membrane which lines the air cells. As stated elsewhere, it is estimated that there are six hundred million air cells in the lungs, and that their combined surface is more than seven times greater than the whole outer surface of the body. This surface is literally covered with small vessels through which the septic blood is constantly pouring. With every heart beat the blood is forced into the lungs, where it attempts to pass through the capillary network of small vessels; but in a morbid condition it contains many poisons, and these, acting as irritants, produce congestion, which later results in a low form of inflammation, as stated. The set of vessels which surround the air cells is so placed for the purpose of giving off waste and absorbing oxygen from the air we breathe. The mucous membrane which lines the air cells has the power of transmitting carbonic acid gas and other poisonous vapors and admitting oxygen, and yet remain proof against the passage of the fluid blood.

During the morbid conditions mentioned above more poisons are generated and less oxygen is taken into the system, and the oxidation of many products, both in the circulation and in the tissues, is interfered with. This lowers the physical force and increases the morbid effects already present. As this condition increases there is corresponding loss of weight and strength. Now some trivial occurrence, such as wet feet or exposure, may result in a bronchial catarrh, which ordinarily is easily recovered from; but with the lungs previously inflamed and their vitality at such a low ebb, the case may easily run into consumption.

Causes.—Those already mentioned. *Dyspepsia is the mother of consumption.* Every one understands that in every case of consumption the process of digestion and assimilation suffers more or less from the first. It is understood, of course, that heredity may be responsible for some cases. A child of tuberculous parents may be born with weak lungs or a weak stomach. During childhood days the lymphatic system is most liable to suffer, and undoubtedly this accounts for many cases of scrofula (see TUBERCULOSIS OF THE LYMPH GLANDS).

During that form of consumption of the lungs known as tuberculosis, the following changes take place:

Changes Occurring in Tuberculosis.—First, the irritation excites inflammation and new tissue growth. The new growth is a form of connective tissue, as mentioned under *Alcohol* and in many other places in this work. From its granular appearance it is sometimes called embryonic tissue or granulation tissue. This new tissue takes no part in the work carried on by the organs in which it occurs, but crowds out more or less the natural tissue, and the organ or organs are weakened in proportion. A dead or dying cell first becomes the center of a tubercle by exciting inflammation around itself. Dead tissue always excites inflammation; it is Nature's method of localizing disease. The inflammation surrounding the tubercle is the same as would surround a bullet, or any other foreign body that might enter the lungs. The same condition is present in every abscess. The zone of new tissue which surrounds the tubercle or abscess constitutes the battle line; it is the struggle between the living and the dead. The same conditions are present, but more prominent, in *Gangrene*. It has been stated that a dead cell forms the center of a tubercle by exciting inflammation around itself. Dust may also aid in producing tuberculosis. When the vitality of the lungs is at a low ebb, as described, a small portion of dust from a mill or factory, or that furnished by the stone cutter or iron worker, may lodge in an air cell and form the nucleus or center of a tubercle.

The tubercles do not contain blood vessels. Their lack of nourishment and failure to organize as healthy tissue leaves them without foundation or support. They are built from septic blood, have but little vitality and no duty in life, hence easily break down. Many of the new cells mentioned may die as a result of pressure upon each other, and also because they do not have time to mature. Many white corpuscles or white blood cells lodge at these points, lose their vitality and die. The blood always contains the elements of fibrine, and these elements, escaping from the swollen vessels, unite in the diseased area with the white corpuscles and other waste products and form the purulent matter which is expectorated.

It is well known that Nature never maintains a structure for nothing. Whether that structure is a whole organ or a single cell, makes no difference. When it ceases to be of use to the body, Nature immediately seeks to eliminate it. It cannot be eliminated whole, hence the various changes through which it passes to reach a liquid state. When Nature's efforts fail to liquefy and eliminate, the part becomes organized, as stated below.

In all forms of consumption of the lungs the walls of the small air tubes, and their dilated extremities, the air cells, are thickened by inflammation, and both are more or less filled with a catarrhal exudate and embryonic, or undeveloped, tissue. These changes and conditions are responsible for the consolidation present in the early stages.

Many cases of consumption are recovered from. Where recovery takes place, the diseased portion of the lung may become calcified, *i. e.*, lime salts carried by the circulation may be gradually deposited in that part. In health the little cells constituting the lung tissue do not absorb or admit lime salts into their structure, but in their diseased and weakened condition their selective power is lessened or destroyed. The diseased area may also become encysted, *i. e.*, surrounded by a thin membrane of the connective tissue already mentioned. Later the connective tissue may send fibrous bands through the diseased part, and it is then said to be organized. Blood vessels are supplied, and the healing is permanent. The natural lung tissue, however, is never replaced. Or degeneration may cause the tissue to soften and break down—liquefy—and this may be followed by absorption, *i. e.*, be carried away by the circulation; or it may be expectorated, or may be disposed of both by absorption and expectoration, and the cavity be filled with newly organized tissue, as stated. It is by such conditions as these that post-mortem examinations demonstrate that consumption has existed in some part of the lungs at some time.

Arteries last longer than lung tissue, hence they may extend through a cavity where lung tissue is destroyed. As the disease continues, they gradually become weaker until they may rupture during the act of coughing, causing hemorrhage, and sometimes, death. Or the inflammation may allow blood clots to form in the arteries, and they may be obliterated before the advancing disease can reach them. This would lessen nutrition and hasten the disease. An artery may be weakened where it is in close relation with the cavity. This would cause bulging into the cavity and constitute an aneurism (see ANEURISM). As fast as the cavity increases the aneurism may continue and fill it, until rupture occurs, which would result in fatal hemorrhage.

Quick Consumption.—In quick consumption death occurs before many of the changes have time to occur. The cause of quick consumption is, that the system is so overcome with self-generated poisons, as described, that degenerative changes occur in different parts of the body at the same time—the lungs, pleura, digestive tract, peritoneum, kidneys, liver, brain, etc. These cases prove rapidly fatal.

Symptoms.—The development of the disease is insidious and without the patient's knowledge. There may be a gradual loss of flesh and strength without any known cause. There are digestive disturbances, poor appetite, constipation, or, if constipation is not present, the digestive tract is unhealthy. There is a dry cough, a sense of languor, weariness, and sensitiveness to cold. Exertion causes shortness of breath. There is a slight rise in temperature in the afternoon, which may be preceded by a sensation of chilliness during the morning. The fever is higher in the evening and absent in the morning. With the fever there is an increased pulse rate. The patient presents a pallid appearance. There may be pain in that part of the lung first affected. In what is called the second stage, the diseased tissue commences to break down and liquefy. This is indicated by increased cough, and by more or less increased expectoration. There is also an increased loss of strength. As the disease continues and the patient grows weaker, there are night sweats and increased emaciation. In all of these conditions the patient remains hopeful.

TREATMENTS.—

A. We have had a good deal of experience in the treatment of consumption, and wish to state clearly that it is our opinion that drug medication is of but little value. We have been intimately associated with consumptives who have taken medicines for weeks and months. Many high priced remedies were used, some manufactured in this country and some coming from Germany, but the results were always the same—the disease steadily progressed. If the patient desires to take medicine, the following is recommended:

> Fowler's Solution.......................... 3 drachms.
> Fellows' Syrup of Hypophosphites.. 5 ounces.
> Maltine, or some good preparation
> of Extract of Malt .... 10 "
>
> Put into a pint bottle, mix by shaking the bottle, and take a tablespoonful just before or immediately after meals.

This aids digestion, and is more in the nature of a food than a medicine.

The most successful element in the treatment of consumption is found in improved hygienic measures, such as occupation, diet, clothing, and abundance of fresh air. Out-of-door exercise should be daily indulged in, but never carried to the point of fatigue. The patient should practice deep breathing in the open air, he should sit or stand erect, the shoulders should be drawn backwards and upwards, and the skin should be kept active by frequent bathing. Large, well-ventilated sleeping rooms should be secured. Diet should be of the most nourishing kind, as eggs, milk, meat, bread and such other food products of this nature as may be desired by the patient. Any article interfering with digestion or nutrition, however, should be promptly set aside. The patient should be strengthened by every known means, and nothing is so well suited for this purpose as pure water, good food, fresh air, sunshine, and absolute freedom of mind and body.

Digestion is always interfered with in consumption, and when food does not digest it ferments and forms many poisons which are absorbed into the system. This lowers the strength and vitality of the patient and renders him less capable of resisting the disease already present. Antiseptics to render the digestive tract free from such fermentative changes are always valuable, and for this purpose perhaps nothing is better than Salol or the Sulphocarbolates (see TYPHOID FEVER). Rendering the digestive tract healthy aids in relieving fever and night sweats. Night sweats are the result of weakness; fever is caused by the poisons in the system (see FEVER); both are a drain upon the patient. Antiseptics aid in removing this condition and increase the value of food products. This means an increase in strength and vitality.

Disinfectants, such as those mentioned, may be used in the digestive tract with a reasonable degree of certainty; but with medicines it is different. Owing to the numerous changes which medicines undergo after they enter the circulation, their effect upon the lungs is doubtful, and usually without value. It is well known that drug medication produces little, if any, effect upon the disease. Any improvement in the consumptive must be brought about by natural means, as described. The result must come through natural channels. There is no specific. The many high-priced remedies and methods are of no value.

Regarding *climate*, if going away breaks up all former associations and habits, causes business losses that cannot well be borne and renders life a burden, then the patient had much better remain at home. If the favorable influence of a better climate can be obtained in accordance with the patient's former habits and with due regard to his means, occupation, associations and contentment, then the prospects will be more hopeful.

B. Live and sleep out of doors. Get into pine woods, if possible. Never go inside of a building.—(59).

C. I will here give a specific treatment in the first stage and often in the second:

Calomel $\frac{1}{10}$ of a grain four times daily.

Tincture of Iodine—dose, 5 drops in a glass of fresh milk three times a day between meals.

Thorough massage every one or two days and anointing with Cocoanut or Olive Oil.

Proper diet, etc.

This treatment will work wonders if persevered in for weeks, and months even.—(30).

Note —The Calomel is of benefit in keeping the liver active, which is very important. The Iodine acts as a disinfectant, hence is also of value. The Cocoanut and Olive Oils are merely a means of giving nourishment.

D. Change of climate. Fresh air. Liberal diet. Rest during state of fever.--(39).

E. Creosote—8 to 15 drops in one cup of hot water after meals.

The most nourishing diet should accompany this treatment.—(26).

Note.—Like the Iodine recommended above, Creosote is believed to be of value as a disinfectant in the circulation. If unable to take in water, take in milk, in capsule, or by other means. If there is evidence that it disturbs the stomach, its use should be discontinued for a time.

F. Glycerine and best rye whisky, equal parts, to be taken freely.—(41).

CONSUMPTION—CIRRHOSIS OF THE LUNGS.

—There is another recognized form of consumption known as cirrhosis, or hardening, of the lungs. This disease is caused by irritants, such as dust, irritating gases, etc., hence is most frequently met in those who work in shops, factories, mills, stone quarries, iron works, and those who manufacture chemicals where irritating gases are produced. The disease consists of a slow process of inflammation, which begins in the upper or larger bronchial tubes, and, extending downward, enters the various branches of the air passages; hence all of both lungs are more or less affected, and therein lies the danger. The result of this inflammation is overgrowth and subsequent contraction of connective tissue. The lungs become shrunken and hardened, and the process may continue until the organs are only one-half, one third or even one-fourth their natural size.

When in this condition, or during this slow process of irritation and inflammation of the lungs, some trivial occurrence, as wet feet or exposure, may result in bronchial catarrh, which ordinarily is easily recovered from, but with the lungs previously inflamed and their vitality at a low ebb, an acute attack of pneumonia or tuberculosis may be precipitated, and under such conditions usually proves rapidly fatal.

TREATMENT.—

Since the disease depends upon irritating dust or vapors, it follows that those suffering from this trouble must secure a change of atmosphere, in fact, change to an atmosphere that is healthful and free from irritants constitutes the ideal treatment or management of a case of this kind. The capacity of the lungs has been destroyed to some extent, and a man suffering with this trouble would not have normal physical endurance even if the disease was checked; there would still remain a loss of lung power, lack of oxygen and interference with elimination, and there would be greater liability to tuberculosis and other diseases. The suggestions and treatment given under *Tuberculosis* are applicable to *Cirrhosis of the Lungs*.

After a change of atmosphere and occupation, and in order to free the lungs from inflammatory products, some of the Iodides should be taken for a time. Perhaps the Syrup of Hydriodic Acid is as good as any. Take a teaspoonful four times a day—between meals and at bedtime. If there is any evidence of a catarrhal condition of the eyes, lessen the dose, taking about one-half the amount. Any other preparation of Iodine may be taken, if preferred. It should be continued for a month or two.

TUBERCULOSIS OF THE LYMPH GLANDS— SCROFULA.

TUBERCULOSIS OF THE LYMPH GLANDS— SCROFULA.—In order to properly understand this disease, it is necessary first to give a description of the

Lymphatic Vessels and Glands.—All parts of the body are pervaded by a system of vessels called the *lymphatics*. In structure these vessels somewhat resemble the arteries and the veins, although they are much thinner—so thin and transparent that the fluid which circulates through them can be plainly seen. This system of vessels is sometimes called the *absorbents*, because they absorb certain waste material or products in all parts of the body and return them to the heart, or near the heart, where they are emptied into the veins. The veins carry these products into the heart and they are passed on through the lungs, where many of the impurities are eliminated or purified by the oxygen inhaled during respiration.

The lymphatic vessels commence, or have their origin, in certain minute spaces or clefts found in connective tissue between adjoining cells, and as this connective tissue acts as a framework for all the organs and structures in the body, it follows that the lymphatic vessels may also be found in every organ and structure. In the digestive tract the lymphatics are supposed to commence by a system of closed extremities; that is, they do not communicate directly with the digestive tract, but nourishment is taken up by them through the process of absorption.

The circulation of the lymph differs from that of the blood. The blood is sent out through one system of vessels called arteries, and the same blood, containing many impurities, is returned through another system of vessels called veins; but the lymph flows only in one direction, *i. e.*, towards the heart. Beginning as minute and delicate vessels between the little cells of the various organs and membranes mentioned, the lymphatics gradually become larger and join together, forming large trunks, which empty into the veins near the heart, as stated.

What are called the *lacteals* are the lymphatics leading from the small bowel. They are so named because they contain a light-colored fluid resembling milk; *lac* means milk, hence *lacteals*—milk-like. This fluid is also called *chyle*. It is the product of digestion which has been absorbed and is being carried from the digestive tract to the thoracic duct. The thoracic duct is a large duct or channel for all of the lymphatics of the body, except those of the right side of the head, neck, right side of the chest cavity, right side of the heart, right lung and upper portion of the liver. It is 15 to 18 inches in length, and commences close to the spinal column in the abdominal cavity near the small of the back. It passes through the chest cavity, runs parallel with the spinal column and a little below the level of the collar bone, arches forward, and empties into a large vein on the left side near the heart. The lymphatics of the right side of the head, neck, right lung, right side of the heart, right side of the chest cavity and right arm, unite to form a common duct or channel which empties into a corresponding vein on the right side.

What are called *lymphatic glands* are small oval bodies situated along the lymphatic vessels, so that the lymph passes through them in its course to the heart. Each gland has a small depression on one side where the blood vessels enter, also where the veins leave the glands. What are called glands are simply dilatations in the lymphatic vessels. The two outer coats of the vessels expand and form what is called the capsule, and from the inner surface of the capsule small processes pass from side to side, dividing the gland into many compartments or spaces. These spaces communicate with each other. The blood vessels which supply the gland are supported by the processes which pass through it, dividing it into the various spaces mentioned. Nerve fibers are also said to be found in the glands. When the two outer coats of the vessels expand to form the glands, the inner coat, which consists of a single layer of cells joined edge to edge like a stone pavement, divides into several branches, and these delicate branches are continued through the gland, re-unite at the opposite side, and pass out as a single vessel in company with the arteries and veins. Their passage through the glands is very tortuous, made so by the passage from one apartment to another. This retards the flow of lymph, and allows poisonous and morbid matter of all kinds to collect, hence the swelling of these glands from disease, as they retain many impurities and poisons.

Scrofula.—Some claim that scrofula is tuberculosis of the lymph glands; others claim that it is not. Some claim that it is tuberculosis in a latent form, and remains so until some cause or condition stimulates its active development. Probably in the majority of cases what is called scrofula is a condition rather than a disease—a condition in which the general system is unhealthy and the resisting powers are low; and the glands, by reason of their structure, as already described, are especially liable, as poisons and impurities of all kinds collect in them. Eczema, some forms of inflammation of the eye, such as granulated lids or ulcer of the cornea, chronic catarrhal inflammation of the nasal passages, also a catarrhal condition of the middle ear or outer canal, often accompany the condition known as scrofula. Surely these conditions are not tuberculous, but are rather the result of general ill health, bad air, poor food, etc. It is understood, of course, that scrofulous subjects are more liable to tuberculosis, and also to other diseases.

Scrofula is always a chronic condition. If only the superficial glands are affected, recovery is the rule and the disease is not apt to return; if the deeper glands are invaded, as those of the lungs, bronchial tubes, abdominal cavity, joints, etc., the disease becomes graver. When the joints are attacked, it may result in the condition known as *White Swelling*. It is usually a disease of childhood.

Cause.—The disease may be hereditary. One or both parents may be tuberculous, syphilitic, or for some other reason possess poor health. It may be acquired, that is, brought on by poor food, bad air, exposure and other conditions resulting in improper care of the child. It may result from faulty nutrition, as where a child one or two years of age is fed too much meat and other hearty foods, resulting in indigestion and an unhealthy system. It may result from vaccination, measles, whooping cough, and perhaps from other diseases.

Changes Occurring in Scrofula.—The glands first become swollen and inflamed. If the glands of the lungs or bronchial tubes are affected, adhesions may form and ulceration may penetrate the æsophagus or aorta. The first is the tube which leads to the stomach; the second is the large artery that passes down through the chest cavity. If the glands of the abdominal cavity are involved, adhesions may form and ulcerate into the bowels. These changes do not often occur.

The periosteum, or thin membrane which surrounds the bones, may become involved and inflamed, and the inflammation may result in suppuration, which may break through on the surface and result in a chronic discharge. The bone beneath the affected periosteum would finally be destroyed, and the discharge would become still more chronic. The center of the bone may be attacked first. The unhealthy blood may cause inflammation in the marrow of the bone, and the inflammation extend toward the surface. In this case the invasion of the periosteum would be secondary. The disease is chronic, or of slow growth, and a mild form of inflammation of the periosteum might exist for some time before it was destroyed. All bone receives its nourishment from vessels given off from the periosteum, hence the low form of inflammation would result in an increase of the blood supply and there would be an increase of the bone on the surface. This would cause the bone to become enlarged, that is, its circumference would become greater, while its central part would be more or less destroyed. The bones of the thigh, leg, arm, or those of the spinal column, may become affected. When the spinal column is attacked, the destruction of bone weakens the support and results in curvature of the spine. This is called *Pott's Disease*. When occurring near the ends of the bones and pus forms, it breaks into the joint, causing the white swelling already mentioned; occurring in the hip joint, it constitutes *Hip Joint Disease*. These affections are described under BONE DISEASES. Occurring in the middle ear, it would result in destruction of the periosteum covering the chain of movable bones, or it might extend to the mastoid process and by destruction of bone reach the brain, resulting in brain abscess.

The more serious forms here described are not often met. Usually it is the more superficial glands that are affected, and of these perhaps those of the neck are oftenest invaded.

Symptoms.—The affected glands become enlarged. At first the glands are movable, but later the inflammation extends to the skin, the skin becomes somewhat reddened and the glands more adherent. In case of suppuration the abscess might break on the surface and result in a chronic discharge, or "running sore." There is frequently, but not always, some form of skin disease, of which eczema is the most frequent. There may be a catarrhal condition of the nasal cavities. The discharge in such cases is unhealthy, the nose is swollen, and the upper lip may become involved and swollen. When the periosteum or membrane covering the bones of the nose becomes inflamed, the bone beneath dies for want of nourishment. This results in a thin, purulent discharge from the nose, which gives a very offensive odor. The tonsils are often enlarged. Unhealthy sores may occur in the skin. If the middle ear or external canal is involved, there is a chronic discharge, as in other situations. The child at the same time shows a general condition of ill health. The most prominent symptom is enlargement of the glands. Occurring in the neck, the side of the neck becomes swollen.

TREATMENT.—

The treatment should be general. Where there is suppuration, local treatment is also required. The disease is systemic— the whole system is unhealthy, and it can be readily seen that successful or satisfactory results can be obtained only with the most careful attention to diet and hygiene. The treatment required in this respect is the same as that given under tuberculosis. Where the child is pale and anæmic, Syrup of Iodide of Iron in from 5- to 10- or 15-grain doses should be given according to age. Give diluted with a little Glycerine and water between meals and at bedtime. From 2- to 3- or 5-grain doses of Salol, or the Sulphocarbolates (see Index), should also be given at meal time, and the bowels kept regular.

Cod Liver Oil is highly recommended for this and many other diseases, yet the benefit of Cod Liver Oil is simply in the nourishment that it contains. In many cases it is almost impossible to give it because of its taste. For cases of this kind we especially recommend the preparation of Cod Liver Oil found in the MISCELLANEOUS MEDICAL RECEIPTS (see Index). To be of value it must be given in large doses—from 2 to 4 or more teaspoonfuls at meal time.

Where the spine is affected, where there is suppuration into joints, or where the glands of the neck are involved, surgical treatment is required.

TUMORS.—A tumor is an overgrowth or abnormal development. Inflammatory swellings are sometimes called tumors, but tumors differ both in shape and size from the normal tissue in which they are found. The growth of a tumor is independent, that is, it is continued when the rest of the body is only being maintained in its normal state; or when the tumor is growing the body may be losing in weight. This is especially true of cancer. Those tumors which end fatally are termed *malignant;* those which are not destructive to life are called *benign*.

Tumors are named according to the part in which they are found, thus: *Chondroma* means a tumor springing from cartilage; *osteoma*, one springing from bone; *myoma*, springing from muscle; *neuroma*, a nerve tumor; *myxoma* (mucous), so-called when degenerative changes have produced a gelatinous substance resembling mucus; *lipoma*, a tumor containing much fat. Birth marks are sometimes called *angioma*, meaning a blood tumor, and are caused by the dilatation of blood vessels which lie just beneath the skin.

Benign tumors, or those not destructive to life, are common connective tissue overgrowths. Usually their only danger is their mechanical interference with the surrounding structures. However, they may rotate at the point where they are attached (pedicle), and this may cause pressure and check the return circulation. In this case the veins would become congested, and might rupture and be followed by hemorrhage. Inflammation or suppuration might follow, or inflammatory adhesion might occur, the tumor becoming attached to some of the surrounding tissues or structures. It might grow fast to the bowel and this might cause inflammation and perforation into the digestive tract, and be followed by death (seldom). Pressure might cause inflammation of the kidneys, constipation, spasms or local paralysis, or the pressure might interfere with the circulation, cause enlargement of the heart and be followed by degenerative changes. None of these conditions often occur, yet they should be considered of sufficient importance for the removal of benign tumors.

TREATMENT.—Surgical.

TYPHOID FEVER.—(See under FEVERS).

TYPHOID PNEUMONIA. — (See *Pneumonia* under LUNGS, DISEASES OF).

TYPHUS FEVER.—(See under FEVERS).

URÆMIA.—Uræmia is a condition where the blood is poisoned by the retention of urea and other waste products that are normally eliminated by the kidneys. The trouble is mostly due to the retention of urea.

Cause.—Suppression or decrease in the amount of urine eliminated; hence it may follow *Bright's Disease*, tumors that make pressure on the kidneys, *Tuberculosis*, or any condition or disease that interferes with the action of the kidneys. The more serious forms of this disease are probably the result of pregnancy where the enlarged uterus crowds upon and interferes with the kidney action.

Symptoms.—First there is a decrease in the amount of urine. Where the case is not severe, the symptoms may come on gradually in the form of headache, dizziness, drowsiness, nausea, vomiting, and chills or chilliness. The mind may become dull, stupor may result, and this may increase to profound coma.

The disease is most often encountered in cases of confinement. Here the symptoms are apt to be more sudden and severe. The first symptom may be that of convulsions, which, if not relieved, follow each other in rapid succession. The patient may scarcely regain consciousness between the convulsive attacks. If relief is not had, death soon follows (see PUERPERAL CONVULSIONS).

Some cases of uræmia may resemble apoplexy; for instance, where unconsciousness is present and convulsions are absent, *but in apoplexy there is paralysis, elevation of temperature, and deep, heavy breathing—snoring*. In uræmic coma or sleep the breathing is sharper and more rapid, the temperature is below normal, and the urine contains albumen. It should be remembered that the urine of a person suffering with apoplexy may also contain albumen. Apoplexy usually comes on suddenly; a uræmic attack may do the same. In apoplexy there are no convulsions; in uræmic poisoning convulsions are the rule.

TREATMENT.—

What to Do Till the Doctor Comes.—Uræmic poisoning always requires the services of a physician. On the first indication of such poisoning send for the doctor, and in the meantime make every effort to produce profuse perspiration.

Where there are no convulsions and the symptoms do not indicate immediate danger, give an active cathartic, put the patient to bed, cover with heavy quilts, give hot drinks, and put a large hot poultice across the small of the back over the kidneys. This should be changed frequently. Many families have what are called hot air bath cabinets, in which sweating is produced by means of an alcohol lamp. Where such conveniences are at hand they may be used in place of the hot drinks and heavy quilts mentioned. Profuse sweating is somewhat debilitating, and especially to a patient suffering with this disease, hence free ventilation or a free exchange of air should be maintained—if not during the process of sweating, it should be provided for immediately afterwards. With plenty of clothing or covering there will be no danger of taking cold. Stimulants should be given, if needed.

After free elimination has been secured both by the skin and bowels, the patient should be put on a milk diet as described under *Bright's Disease.*

When the attack is ushered in with convulsions, see treatment under PUERPERAL CONVULSIONS.

URIC ACID.—Uric acid is a product of digestion resulting principally from animal food, as meat and eggs. It is irritating to the system, and its presence is believed to be one of the causes for many diseases, both acute and chronic. When present, it is carried by the circulation and is continually rasping through the system, producing pain and inflammation.

Symptoms.—Its presence may be suspected when any of the symptoms of neuralgia or muscular rheumatism are present.

TREATMENTS.—

A. An infallible remedy is to live on vegetables, cereals and fruits. Eat no meat, and in three months all uric acid will have vanished. This never fails. If you will show me one who never eats meat of any kind, I will show you one that never has rheumatism, neuralgia or gout; yes, and no malaria.—(30).

B. Small daily doses of alkali, such as Lithium Citrate or Carbonate, together with abstemious and restricted diet.—(31).

C. Large draughts of hot water with steam or sweat baths. Some natural Lithia water is better than pure water.—(32).

> **D.** Potassium Bicarbonate............... 2 drachms.
> Citric Acid................................ 10 grains.
> Water .... 3 ounces.
>
> *Mix.* Take tablespoonful in water every four hours.—(34).

Note.—Remedies to neutralize or eliminate uric acid afford but temporary relief. So long as the acid is being continually generated in the system all treatment will fail, or at least prove unsatisfactory. Treatment to be of benefit must consist of preventive measures, and this means a vegetable diet.

URINE, INCONTINENCE OF.—(See under CHILDREN'S DISEASES.)

URINE, RETENTION OF.—(See also under BLADDER, DISEASES OF).

RECOMMENDED TREATMENTS.—

A. Hot baths aided by hot drinks to produce sweating are among the simple and very efficient remedies.—(40).

B. Hot applications over bladder. Stand behind patient and pour water from one dish to another to make a sound like that of passing urine.—(41).

C. Water-melon seed tea.—(20).

D. Hot baths to produce sweating. Cream of Tartar—teaspoonful in water every three hours until bowels move.—(39).

E. Let some one in the presence of the patient pour from one vessel to another a small stream of water. Place flannel wrung out of hot water over lower part of abdomen.—(35).

F. Injections of large quantities of very warm water per rectum.—(29).

G. Application of cloths wrung out of hot vinegar.—(55).

URINE, PAINFUL.—(See *Dysuria*, under BLADDER, DISEASES OF).

VARICOSE VEINS.—In this condition the veins are permanently dilated or enlarged. The enlargement is not uniform, being greater in some parts than others. This gives the vein a tortuous course, which is rendered still more tortuous because of the fact that the vein is considerably lengthened.

The bulging or dilatation commences wherever the walls of the veins are weakened, perhaps more often just behind the valves. Nearly all of the veins of the body are supplied with valves, which aid in the return circulation—that carrying the venous blood to the heart. Another point that is apt to be weakened is where the small veins join the larger trunk or channel. As the veins become dilated, the valves do not fit and fail to aid in the onflow of blood. This allows dilatation to increase still more. When the trouble affects the valves of the spermatic vein, it is called *Varicocele;* when affecting those in the lower rectum, it is called *Hemorrhoids* or *Piles*. It may occur in the leg during or soon after pregnancy when this condition obstructs the return flow to such an extent that dilatation of the vein results.

Cause. —There are several causes which influence this condition. The most important is a weak heart action.

Symptoms.—Dilatation of the veins, tortuous course and discoloration. The veins look darker than usual because the flow of blood is sluggish and contains an abnormal amount of impurities.

TREATMENTS.—

A. Many cases may be benefited by strengthening the heart action and by having the patient lie down several hours during the day, at the same time giving careful attention to diet, good ventilation, etc. In varicocele of the leg, the greatest benefit results from bandaging. A cloth bandage is often used. A rubber bandage about two or three inches wide is better. Best of all in this form of treatment is a silk elastic stocking. These are made to fit any part of the leg. The trouble is usually most severe below the knee. Measurement should be taken in the morning before the patient gets up. Take a tape line, draw it quite snug, and measure accurately the distance around the instep and hollow of the foot, around the heel and over the instep, around the ankle, around the largest part of the calf of the leg, and around the smallest part just below the knee. The silk stocking should be ordered to correspond to such measurement. It can be ordered by any druggist. Many cases are very satisfactorily treated by this method. Both limbs are usually affected.

Surgical treatment consists of making an incision, or usually a number of incisions, down to the vein, tying it at different points and excising or removing the part between the ligatures. In the leg the vein in most cases is easily reached because it is superficial, lying just beneath the skin. This is another reason why such veins are most often affected. They have no muscular support other than that found in the walls of the veins themselves.

In *Varicocele* the bandaging is replaced by a supensory band. If this fails, the vein is sometimes treated surgically. In case of *Hemorrhoids*, see treatment under that head.

B. In the legs, bandage from the toes up with elastic bandage. —(32).

C. Five drops Extract of Witch Hazel four times a day. Rubber stocking on limbs.—(41).

VENEREAL DISEASES.

SYPHILIS.—Syphilis is a chronic constitutional disease. It is also infectious, and may readily be conveyed from one to another. It may be hereditary or acquired; most cases are acquired. It may be communicated in many ways, as by pipes, drinking cups, or any condition or circumstance that brings the individual in contact with the poison wherever it may exist. The disease is usually communicated, however, by venereal practice, and makes its appearance about the third week after exposure and invasion.

There are said to be three stages of this disease, but the first two only properly belong to syphilis. What is called the third stage is not syphilis. The disease proper is not present. The conditions are simply those of a wrecked and wasted constitution as a result of the chronic inflammation spread throughout the system by this disease. It may be communicated in the first or second stage, but not in the third stage.

First Stage.—The first outward effect of syphilis is limited to the point where the inoculation occurs, and is in the form of a small sore called *chancre*—meaning cancerous—because of its tendency to destroy. This sore may appear any time from ten to ninety-five days after exposure—never earlier or later.

Second Stage.—This stage includes the rash, and usually makes its appearance about six weeks after the appearance of the primary sore. In this stage the disease affects the skin, mucous membrane, and various other structures of the body.

Third Stage.—This stage makes its appearance from two to five years after the beginning of the attack. In those who are physically weak, it might appear earlier. It consists of chronic lumpy or gummy growths, which may ulcerate, and which possess an inherited tendency to destroy tissue. Any or all of the important organs, such as the liver, lungs, kidneys, brain, spinal cord, etc., may be attacked. The disease also attacks and destroys bone as readily as other structures.

Cause.—The cause is a specific virus or poison, which has never been discovered, therefore cannot be described. Syphilis, small-pox, hydrophobia, scarlet fever and other diseases, are caused by a specific poison. This poison produces what is called a zymotic or diseased fermentation in the system, just as yeast cells produce fermentation in bread-making. Yeast is composed of small cells, about $\frac{1}{3000}$ of an inch in diameter. The products of a diseased fermentation in the body resulting from a specific poison or virus produce a morbid effect upon the system, and affect the appetite and the red blood corpuscles. The blood becomes diseased, and the tissues throughout the body are brought under these lowering tendencies.

Symptoms of the First Stage.—The first symptom of syphilis is the appearance of the initial sore or chancre. This occurs at the point where the inoculation took place, and is followed by what is called *buboes*—swelling of the glands in the groin. The disease is constitutional from the beginning; that is, it is not confined to the initial sore. A chancre is but a local manifestation of a systemic disease; in other words, with the first appearance of the sore the man has syphilis. Chancre is a small hard swelling, the result of inflammation. There is no pus from the chancre, though if other sores, such as chancroid, occur with chancre, pus may form. If there are more than one chancre, they all appear at the same time. A chancre disappears with the secondary symptoms, whether it has been treated or not.

Chancroid. — The name chancroid is applied to a sore that resembles chancre. This form may occur with chancre or may follow chancre, occurring at different points at different times. A chancroid appears from three to nine days after exposure, and there are usually more than one.

If more than one true chancre occurs, they occur all at once.

Chancroid is a local disease, and each succeeding sore means a new infection from the one before it.

True chancre never appears before ten days after exposure, or later than ninety-five days, —usually three weeks after.

Chancroid, or false chancre, always appears before ten days — usually from three to five days after exposure.

True chancres are hard.

False chancres are soft.

True chancres do not ulcerate, and bleed easily.

False chancres ulcerate and do not bleed.

In true chancre the glands in the groin always enlarge, but seldom suppurate. Suppuration occurs in about one case in twenty-eight.

In false chancre the glands enlarge on an average in only one-third of the cases, and always suppurate.

Enlargement of the glands in the groin may follow gonorrhea.

In true chancre the glands are movable.

In false chancre they are not.

Over true chancre the skin is natural.

With or before the appearance of the secondary stage in syphilis, the glands at the back of the neck and elbow enlarge.

Over false chancre the skin is red and inflamed.

Following false chancre, these glands do not enlarge.

Symptoms of the Second Stage.—The symptoms of secondary syphilis may occur soon after the appearance of the chancre or may be delayed for two years. At the beginning of this stage there is a rash covering the body and upper and lower extremities, and also appearing on the face and hands. Before the appearance of the rash there are usually some constitutional symptoms. The patient does not feel well, and perhaps does not sleep well. There is disturbance of the appetite, there may be slight fever and headache, and in some cases there are chills. These symptoms disappear with the appearance of the rash.

There are several forms of the rash. There may be pimples, vesicles or pustules. If a pimple enlarges and contains fluid, it is called a vesicle; if the fluid in the vesicle changes to pus, it is called a pustule. Sometimes the pimples are bright red at first, and the skin may have a reddish appearance, but the color soon becomes darker. Or there may be tubercles. The tubercles indicate a more serious condition.

Usually the rash comes out in large, coarse spots. These spots have well defined borders, that is, they do not merge gradually into the healthy skin, but the edge remains distinct and is easily recognized. The spot presents a bronze or copper color. In all forms of syphilis there is a copper-colored tinge to the rash. When pimples or vesicles occur, they are surrounded by a copper-colored ring.

Tubercles do not often appear. When they do, they are large, and of a dark, muddy, or bluish-red color. They ulcerate and give a very foul odor. The discharge may dry on the surface, forming crusts or scales, and when these are removed, ulceration will be found going on beneath. As stated, this is evidence of a very serious case.

During the secondary stage the hair may fall out. Usually the hair comes out in patches here and there, but the patient may become entirely bald. The finger nails may become loosened and drop off. The mucous membrane is also affected in this stage. Patches of mucous membrane in the nose, mouth and throat, may become inflamed and ulcerate.

Symptoms of the Third Stage. — What is called the third stage is not syphilis. The man may be shattered, debilitated, devitalized—may be a physical wreck covered with great sores which are eating their way through his body, but he has not syphilis. Syphilis is a disease that is readily communicated from one to another. It may be communicated by the blood, or by the secretions of the body. In what is called the third stage the disease cannot be transmitted to another. There is no poison or virus present in the system. The man has not the disease. His condition is simply the result of the poisons that have been present. It is simply the evidence of the terrible struggle which has been going on for months, and perhaps years. Nutrition is at a low ebb. The powers of resistance are lacking, hence the large ulcers that appear here and there, meeting with little or no opposition, make rapid and fatal inroads, destroying all structures, whether of bone or soft tissue. At this time any tissue may be attacked —the liver, lungs, brain, spinal cord, the nose, or upper jaw. Syphilis is a common cause of *Locomotor Ataxia.*

During this stage also, large gummy tumors are formed, so-called because they are soft and later break down and may ulcerate. Nutrition is so low and the tissues attacked have been so saturated with poison that the inflamed areas cannot organize, hence the appearance of the condition termed gummy. The morbid effects of these tumors or sores, when once started, easily maintain control over the surrounding tissues, and thus they "eat" their way through all structures.

TREATMENT.—

We admit we have treated but a limited number of these cases, yet we have seen the disease in its worst form, where the patient was devoid of all resemblance to a human being—nose gone, eyelids gone, lips eaten away, holes through the cheek and into the neck and arms, and necrosed patches in the skull bone. It may be said of such, however, that their tortures are but a part of the stupendous machinery of Eternal justice. The only cause for regret is that the innocent must suffer with the guilty, as the disease is perpetuated by hereditary taint. Others may be led innocently into committing a crime.

For the initial sore or chancre very little need be done. Burning or cutting out the part is of no value, and inflicts needless pain. It is of no value because, as stated in the beginning, the disease is already in the system and the primary sore is only local evidence. The spot is usually treated by keeping it clean and dusting it with equal parts of Subnitrate of Bismuth and Calomel. Iodoform is equally as good, but its odor is unpleasant. As stated, the spot disappears sooner or later with or without treatment.

The treatment for the second stage, or the stage where the rash appears, is some form of Mercury, taken internally. Any of the mercurial salts may be used, but the Bichloride of Mercury, or Corrosive Sublimate, is the one usually given. This may be given in doses of $\frac{1}{20}$ of a grain three times a day at the beginning, and increased until the patient experiences some local effect. This is called the physiological effect. It consists of diarrhea, pain in the stomach and bowels, a metallic taste in the mouth, and a soreness of the gums and teeth. The earliest evidence in the teeth may be experienced by bringing the jaws suddenly together. If any effect is being produced, the teeth will feel sore. If any one or all of these symptoms are present, they indicate that the patient is taking more than he can stand. The treatment should then be discontinued for a few days, and begun again with smaller doses. This treatment is continued for a long time—usually about six months—then the patient is given a rest for three months, and the treatment continued during the next three months.

With those who are unable to take Mercury in sufficient doses by the stomach, it is sometimes given by other means. It may be applied externally in the form of ointment, or ½ ounce of Corrosive Sublimate may be dissolved in water in which the patient takes a bath. Dissolve the Corrosive Sublimate in water enough to cover the patient in a bath tub, then cover with a quilt, allowing only the face to be exposed. Guard the eyes, nose and mouth. With those who can take large doses of Mercury baths are also beneficial, but in these cases it is not necessary to put any Corrosive Sublimate into the bath.

The most nourishing food is required, also proper clothing—wool worn next to the skin is usually advised. An abundance of fresh air should be secured, and every care should be given to the general health. If the hair commences to fall out, some stimulating application should be applied to the scalp. If ulcers form, these should be treated the same as ulcers from any other cause. If there is inflammation of the eye or interference with sight, increase the amount of Corrosive Sublimate. If the mucous membrane in the mouth, throat or nose is affected, use any means to maintain thorough cleanliness. These spots are sometimes touched lightly with pure Nitrate of Silver. Spray the affected surface with Peroxide of Hydrogen. If the teeth become loose, stop the Mercury for a time and for a few days give Atropine— $\frac{1}{250}$ of a grain every hour or two until the throat is dry, the face is red, or until the pupil of the eyes becomes dilated; then for a day or two give the same amount every three hours.

In what is called the third stage of the disease, Iodine is taken internally in some form, usually the Iodide of Potash. This is given in large doses. Some recommend 15 to 20 grains three times a day, taken two hours after meals. Some give as high as 1 drachm three times a day between meals, and even this amount is exceeded in some cases.

The foregoing is the usual routine treatment, but we wish to give a prescription that, while differing somewhat from that given, has made many a doctor famous for the treatment of this disease. It is as follows:

> Corrosive Sublimate .... 4 grains.
> Iodide of Potash............................ 4 drachms.
> Syrup of Tolu............................... 3 ounces.
> Simple Elixir .... 1 "
>
> *Mix.* Give 1 teaspoonful two hours after meals and at bedtime. If it disturbs the stomach or interferes with digestion, lessen the dose, or take less often. This treatment may be taken up at the beginning of, or any time during the second stage.

For the persistent and determined sores and ulcers that are present in what is called the third stage, use the same antiseptic treatment as in ulcers caused by any other disease. Keep them thoroughly cleansed. Wash them out with Peroxide of Hydrogen, with a solution of Carbolic Acid in water, or by other means render the surface as clean and healthy as possible.

Or, the following treatments for any form of ulcer have been recommended and are equally applicable here:

ULCERS.—

A. Wash with water colored with Blue Stone. Afterwards apply hot mutton tallow.—(32).

Note —If there is suppuration, do not cover the surface with any form of ointment.

B. One of the best dressings I have ever used for old ulcers is a mixture of Balsam Peru in Castor Oil of a strength of 5% Balsam. Of course the adjuncts of rest and cleanliness are necessary.—(31).

GONORRHEA.—This is a contagious, inflammatory state of the urethra in the male and the vagina in the female, accompanied by a discharge partly mucus and partly pus. It may extend to the bladder in the male, or to the womb and ovaries in the female, and sometimes to the rectum. It may also be transferred to the eye, setting up a most violent and dangerous inflammation. New-born children may be infected during birth, and in such cases the utmost attention is necessary to save the eye-sight. Many cases of blindness are due to this disease.

Cause.—There are two causes for inflammation of the mucous membrane of the urethra. One cause is contagion; the other is not. The non-contagious variety may be the result of the passing of sounds or instruments into the bladder, or the passage of foreign bodies—an excessive amount of gravel is an example—from urine that is highly acid, as sometimes results from indigestion. It may be caused by eczema extending along the mucous membrane lining the canal, by tuberculosis, or by an enlarged prostate. The contagious variety is caused by a certain specific ferment, which sets up inflammation.

Symptoms.—The disease usually appears in from three to five days after exposure. The first symptom in the male is at the opening or end of the urethra. This part is deep red in color and swollen. Internally, the mucous membrane is swollen, and urination is difficult as the inflammation lessens the size of the canal. There is also a slight discharge of mucus, which later contains pus. The inflammation increases for the first week, then remains stationary for another week. There is considerable pain when urinating. The inflammation then extends back-wards, and in a day or so the discharge is thick and yellow. If the inflammation reaches the neck of the bladder, there is a frequent desire to urinate. The glands in the groin may become swollen and may suppurate. In different cases the severity of the symptoms vary greatly. Occasionally an annoying feature of this disease is the condition known as *Chordee*, which means a painful erection and downward curvature of the external reproductive organ in the male.

TREATMENTS.—

What to Do.—Consult a competent physician at the earliest opportunity. In the meantime and throughout the whole course of the disease, the patient must observe certain rules. His diet should be light and cooling. No highly seasoned foods should be eaten. No alcoholic stimulants or tobacco should be used, but plenty of water should be drank. Frequent bathing of the affected parts is beneficial for their cleansing and cooling. Sexual excitement, violent exercise, dancing, late hours, etc., should be avoided. The most rigid care should be taken to destroy the discharges.

A. Add 4 grains of Permanganate of Potash to 4 ounces of water and inject twice a day, retaining the injection for two or three minutes. This, with a plain diet, the absence of all stimulants, and supporting the parts with a suspensory bandage, will in most cases result in a permanent cure,

or,

Oleo-resin of Cubebs and Copaiba, 10 drops of each, taken in capsule form three or four times a day,

or,

Ten drops of pure Oil of Sandal Wood in capsule, taken three times a day.

Note.—The injection method is the most satisfactory means of treating this disease as the remedy is thus applied directly to the diseased part. Internal medication is seldom needed, and is more or less uncertain as so many changes take place in the remedies before they reach the affected area. Again, most internal remedies used for this disease give the breath an offensive and suggestive odor.

> **B.** Sulphate of Zinc.............................. 2 grains.
> Fluid Hydrastus.............................. 5 drops.
> Water ....:........................ .... 1 ounce.

Use as an injection often.—(11).

C. Put patient to bed and use frequent douches of warm Boric Acid solution. Add Permanganate of Potash—1 grain to the ounce of water, and inject every day or two.—(3).

D. *Chordee.*—Keep the bowels active. Low diet, no meat or alcohol. Sleep in cool room. At bedtime take the following, largely diluted in sweetened water:

> Chloral .... 10 grains.
> Bromide of Potash 30   "

The dose may be increased if necessary. Do not take this unless trouble is feared. Should it occur, the application of cold water is a simple remedy, and one of the best for immediate relief.

GLEET.— Gleet means a chronic discharge from any mucous surface or membrane, but is generally understood to mean from that lining the urethra, and following gonorrhea.

Cause.— Following gonorrhea, if a perfect cure is not obtained, inflammation lingers at some point and results in an overgrowth of connective tissue. The contraction of this tissue lessens the size of the canal at that point, forming what is called a *stricture*. The efforts at urination gradually cause distension of the urethra just behind the stricture, and this saculated formation always contains urine as the stricture renders urination incomplete. These conditions serve to maintain a chronic form of inflammation, hence the chronic discharge. Or gleet may be caused by irritation from an enlarged prostate gland.

TREATMENT.—

The treatment consists of a gradual distension of the stricture by the use of sounds. Sometimes it is necessary to cut the stricture in order to render dilation more complete. The bladder should be washed out two or three times a week with pure water containing 6 drachms of Boric Acid to the pint, after which the urethra should be injected with a solution of pure water and Permanganate of Zinc—1 grain of the Zinc to an ounce of water. It will be necessary to continue both the dilation of the stricture and the medication for some time.

VOMITING.—Recommended Treatments.—

A. Salicin.................................... 1 drachm.
Subnitrate of Bismuth............... 2 drachms.

> *Mix*, and put into ½ glass of water, stir, and take 1 teaspoonful every ten to fifteen minutes.

Or,

White of 1 Fresh Egg
Common Starch.................... 1 teaspoonful.
Granulated Sugar................. 1 "

> Beat for five or ten minutes. Give patient 1 teaspoonful every ten to fifteen minutes.

Or,

> White of 1 fresh egg in ½ glass of water. Stir thoroughly and let the patient drink 1 teaspoonful every few minutes.—(61).

B. Apply Mustard plasters over the stomach. Mint tea, such as Peppermint, Spearmint, etc., may be taken in small quantities, or weak Camphor sling may be given. Crust coffee is also good.

If convenient to a drug store, get Oxalate of Cerium and give 2- or 3-grain doses every twenty or thirty minutes, as needed, until vomiting is controlled.

C. Pour boiling water over parched rice, coffee, corn or bread crust. Let stand for a few minutes, strain or let settle, and take 1 or 2 teaspoonfuls every twenty or thirty minutes. Take clear—no sugar or milk.—(32).

D. Paregoric—dose, ½ to 1 teaspoonful in a small amount of hot water, repeated every half hour, is a specific.—(30).

WARTS.—(See under description of Skin).

WATER BRASH.—This is an accompaniment of stomach troubles, and means the burning sensation in the stomach followed with sour eructations.

Treatment.—

See under Acidity of the Stomach.

WATER ON THE BRAIN.—(See *Hydrocephalus* under Dropsy).

WEN, or SEBACEOUS CYST.—This is simply an enlargement of a sebaceous, or oil, gland. It will be remembered that these glands are placed just beneath the skin, and by means of a small duct open into a hair follicle (see description of SKIN). The duct becomes closed, and the gland, continuing to secrete or furnish the usual amount of oily fluid, enlarges. The sac or membrane which forms the gland becomes thickened and tough. In size these cysts vary all the way from a pea to a walnut.

Cause.—The cause is not very clear. The wen usually occurs around joints, therefore lifting or straining may cause injury with the result that a duct becomes closed.

Symptoms—These growths come on very slowly. There is no pain or inconvenience, except such as is occasioned by their size. They are freely movable, and are filled with a fluid that somewhat resembles the white of an egg.

TREATMENT.—

Complete and thorough removal of the growth with a knife. While this is comparatively easy, it would require the services of a physician. It is not necessary to give an anæsthetic, except such as may be applied locally, and in most cases even that is not needed. The cavity is lined with a membrane which must be destroyed, otherwise the secretions will be reproduced and the trouble will return.

WHITE SWELLING.—(See under JOINTS, DISEASES OF).

WHITLOW.—This means a felon. (See FELON).

WHOOPING COUGH—PERTUSSIS.—This is a contagious disease, usually of childhood, characterized by violent fits of convulsive coughing, which recur at intervals and end with a whoop and the expectoration of a small amount of mucous secretion. It commences about one week after exposure, and usually lasts from six to eight weeks. It is seldom fatal.

Cause.—Some form of infection or poison which is unknown.

Symptoms.—The first evidence is that of a catarrhal cold. The catarrhal evidence is manifested in the eyes and nasal cavities. There is a little hoarseness, and the temperature is slightly raised in the evening. There may be a sense of tickling in the throat, which results in a short, dry cough. The first week constitutes what is called the catarrhal stage. The coughing increases gradually until it comes on in paroxysms, when the face becomes red, and perhaps dark purple, the eyes project, and the child often seizes the nearest object for support. The coughing continues until the expiratory effort of respiration is exhausted, after which there is a deep inspiratory effort which produces the peculiar whoop, caused by the air rushing into the lungs; hence the term *Whooping Cough.* These efforts are repeated two or three times, or until they are followed by the expectoration of a little mucous secretion. The disease usually disappears as gradually as it came.

During a spasm of coughing the glottis, or space between the vocal chords through which the air passes, is narrowed, and but little air reaches the lungs. The muscles of the throat are rendered tense, circulation becomes stagnant, and the pulmonary artery is congested. This is the artery through which the venous blood passes from the right side of the heart into the lungs. During congestion of this artery the right side of the heart cannot empty itself, and this dams back the venous blood in all parts of the body. This condition, together with a lack of oxygen, is what causes the child to turn so blue, or to "get black in the face."

TREATMENTS.—

A. The Bromides, Chloral, Belladonna or its active principle, Atropine, and various other remedies used for coughs and colds have been used, and perhaps are still recommended for whooping cough. There is no specific for this disease, however, and in some cases the cough is persistent and severe in spite of treatment. The child should be protected from sudden changes of weather, should receive an abundance of fresh air, have a nourishing diet, and the bowels should be kept regular. Internally, give the following:

Atropine ,	$\frac{1}{16}$ grain.
Carbolic Acid	24 drops.
Bromide of Soda	2 drachms.
Glycerine	2 ounces.
Simple Elixir, add to	4 "

Mix, and take 1 teaspoonful, more or less, according to age, every two or three hours.

Where the cough remains dry, *i. e.*, where the secretions are scanty or absent, a little Ipecac should be added to each dose— from 1 to 2 drops of the fluid extract. Where there is a good deal of irritability or nervousness present, $\frac{1}{15}$ of a grain of Codeine, for a child five years of age, should be added to each dose.

B. Give Flaxseed tea plentifully, also good care. For medicine, give the following:

Sulphate of Zinc	10 grains.
Water	30 teaspoonfuls.

Dose.—A teaspoonful, more or less, according to age, every one or two hours. Also anoint chest well once a day with Olive Oil. Goose Oil will do.—(30).

C. Use Roach's Embrocation according to the directions on the bottle. Burn Cressaline during the paroxysms.—(32).

D. Tincture Belladonna...................... 30 drops.
Chlorate Potash........................... 10 grains.
Glycerine .... 2 ounces.

Mix, and take 20 drops three or four times a day.—(47).

E. Elixir Terpine Hydrate and Codeine, 6 ounces.

Take ½ teaspoonful every three hours.—(27).

WORMS.—(For Round Worms or Thread Worms, see under CHILDREN'S DISEASES; also see TAPEWORM; also TRICHINA WORM).

YELLOW FEVER.—(See under FEVERS).

HELEN F. WARNER, M. D.

Department II.

DISEASES OF WOMEN AND CHILDREN.

WHAT GIRLS AND MOTHERS OUGHT TO KNOW.

HELEN F. WARNER, M. D.

In these few chapters I propose to give mothers some hints about the care a very young girl requires in the first crisis of her life, and to give older girls some advice about the care which they should take of their health, and of the reasons why such care should be taken.

I propose to tell the young wife and mother some things that I think it well for her to know about house sanitation, that is, about ventilation, heating, water supply, and disinfection in cases of sickness; also something about the nature of different foods, about the care of her own health, and about the care of babies and very young children.

I propose to say a few words to women approaching the second crisis of their lives, about the care it is necessary they should give themselves, and the very unnecessary alarm and dread with which many look forward to this period of their existence.

Most of this talk comes under the head of what is called *preventative medicine*, and as the old proverb, "An ounce of prevention is worth a pound of cure," is still in force, I hope it may not be without some value.

CARE OF YOUNG GIRLS.

As it is not probable that any very young girl will read these chapters — perhaps it is hardly desirable that she should — I address myself more particularly to the mothers of young and growing families.

Children are young animals in search of information in a world that to them is very new and full of puzzles. One of

380

the questions which recurs often and is asked most eagerly is, "Where do the babies come from, Mamma?" To answer the question satisfactorily without giving any information, has long been a problem among mothers. The Germans have a pretty legend that the Storks bring the babies to the happy mothers from their home in Egypt, without explaining if there is a manufactory of babies there. The more prosaic mothers in this country often tell their children that the doctor brings the baby in his satchel, sometimes subjecting him to embarrassing investigation, as I can testify. I belonged to a New England family, where the utmost reticence was practiced toward children, indeed toward all young people, and I was told merely that God sent the babies from heaven, which may be in a sense true, but which is difficult to believe of some infants. I used to wonder vaguely if they dropped through the ceiling, and why they suffered no damage and left no trace of their passage. But I was an observing child, though very reticent, and long before I reached girlhood I formed a theory of my own, from observation of the domestic animals and some women of my acquaintance, that was very near the truth.

Advice to Young Mothers.—My advice to young mothers is, when your little girl begins to notice your rounding figure, when she sees by chance the little garments about which you are busy, do not put her off with what you persuade yourself is a white lie, or tell her that children should not ask questions. If you do, she will very likely find you out in the lie—children are often very shrewd—or some older girl will tell her what she is so eager to know, coarsely, vulgarly, with sly hints and inuendoes, as if it were some unclean thing, and the sweet and holy function of motherhood will be vulgarized and profaned to her for years. *Tell the child yourself.* Explain to her that all life comes from a parent life. Show her how the mother plant ripens the seeds, which sometimes the winds and waters and birds scatter to their places, and sometimes men and women and children plant. Tell her that each seed holds a baby plant, which the warm, moist earth feeds and nourishes till it bursts its shell and the tiny plant begins to grow. Tell her—if she has the happiness to be a country child, you can show her—how the mother hen lays the eggs from her own body, and then, not trusting them to the earth, broods over them herself and keeps them safe and warm till the little chicks, which were only wee specks at first, have time to grow, and become strong enough to break their shells. Then explain to her that higher animals, mothers among the rest, nourish their babies in their own bodies till they are large enough and strong enough to live outside; that there is a new baby coming for whom mamma must make the little clothes ready, but that, though it is a very happy thing, it is too sacred and solemn to talk about to other people—just a secret which she must keep with mamma. In this way you will give your child a new interest, a new sense of the tie that binds together all created things, and a strong safeguard against evil will thus be thrown about her.

THE FIRST CRISIS.

Later, when you see from the developing figure, from the rounding breasts and from the unusual restlessness and irritability, that the first crisis in your child's life is approaching, tell her what she has to expect, and tell her plainly; tell her the truth so that she may fully understand it. Many young girls have ruined their health, or greatly injured it, in frantic efforts to stop a flow which they did not in the least understand, and which, while it greatly alarmed them, they were too shy to speak of to their mothers. Do not content yourself with telling the young girl what is coming, but keep watch over her and, when the flow actually appears, instruct her in the care she should take of herself and see that she carries out your instructions. Her whole future health hangs on this, and on this point many mothers themselves need instruction. It is of the greatest importance that she (the young, maturing girl) should be kept warm and dry during the flow, that she should avoid all violent exercise, long tramps, heavy lifting, skating, dancing, and horseback or bicycle riding. In bad weather she should be kept from school unless she can be sent in a covered carriage.

Up to this time there has been little difference in the care which the girl and her brother required, but now the differentiation commences. It is not well to push a girl at school, even one who is sluggish at her studies, during these formative years; one who is quick must often be held back. See that the girl has plenty of out-of-door air and exercise, and that she takes sufficient, wholesome food. Never allow her to go to school in the morning without her breakfast. This is the time when her appetite, which has previously been that of a healthy child, becomes fitful and irregular. Girls sometimes develop strange fancies at this time for most unwholesome things: Salt, which is all very well as a seasoning for food, but should not be taken by the spoonful, starch and chalk, are most frequently taken. If your daughter should show any such morbid appetite, you should check it at once. Talk to her kindly, but seriously, of the injury she is likely to do her health by such indulgence.

Girls in this climate generally mature at from eleven to fourteen years—thirteen is perhaps the average age. It is a misfortune if a girl menstruates before eleven, but it is no matter at all that she should be later than fourteen. So long as she shows no signs of suffering, you need not disturb yourself if she is fifteen, sixteen, or even seventeen, before the flow appears. It is not often later. The flow is often scanty at first. Do not worry about this; it is a fault on the right side. The young girl needs her blood for growth and development, and Nature does well to economize it. Then, after appearing once, the flow often holds off for months. This seems to give mothers special anxiety, but such anxiety is needless. So long as the girl seems well otherwise, let her alone, and above all do not dose her with Tansy and Pennyroyal teas, or any of the remedies for forcing Nature. You may do serious harm in this way. On the other hand, the flow when it first appears is sometimes too profuse and lasts too long. It should be practically over on the sixth day. This is not a matter to be neglected. Put the girl to bed if the flow is very free. A good household remedy for this is made by pouring a pint of boiling water over a handful of stick cinnamon. Let this steep till it is cold—do not boil it—then strain off the tea and give a wineglassful of it three or four times a day. If this, with rest in bed, fails to check the flow, send for your family physician.

If you observe these precautions, unless there is some malformation or malposition of the organs, against which, of course, you are powerless, your daughter will not suffer at her menstrual periods, and will grow up, at least as far as her sexual organs are concerned, a healthy woman. But until she is twenty she should put aside her wheel or her horse, and abjure dances, long walks or skating parties during the flow. It will often be hard for her, but it is the price of health, and if you are firm, she will form the habit of caution and cease to question the matter. Even after twenty, violent exercise should be indulged in with caution at such periods; but a healthy woman, fully developed, may take much less care than a young girl.

Dress for Young Girls.—A word, in closing this chapter, as to dress. A young girl's dress should be, of course, adapted to the season. In winter she should wear flannel from throat to heels. See that she has plenty of room to expand in. I am not a fanatical opponent of the corset. It is a comfort to many women, almost a necessity to very stout ones, and, when not tightly laced, does no harm; but a corset is an abomination for growing girls. The soft young bones yield even to slight pressure, and internal organs are forced out of place and prevented from developing properly. Let her have a loosely fitting waist, to which her skirts—the bands of which should be loose—are buttoned. The dress should not reach below the tops of her boots, so that it will not become damp and draggled even in the sloppiest weather. In cold weather she should have merino stockings and warm, stout shoes. She should have a rain coat for wet days, and, what is more, be made to wear it; and if she lives in the country, a pair of rubber boots for deep mud and snow would not be amiss.

WHAT A YOUNG WOMAN OUGHT TO KNOW.

My Dear Girl:

You are no longer a child—almost, if not quite, a woman. I want in this chapter to give you a few hints about keeping yourself well, which is much better than curing you when you are ill. I take it for granted that you want not only to be well, but to look as well as possible. To this end you must take some pains.

About Your Hair: Do not content yourself with combing out the snarls and doing it up; spend some time each day brushing it. If you have thick, heavy hair, the brush should be quite stiff, stiff enough to reach the scalp; merely smoothing down the outside hair does little or no good. Each separate hair is set in a little channel in the scalp, with one or more ducts emptying into it from glands that secrete the oil for the hair. The brush removes the dust from the mouth of these channels, presses the oil out and distributes it over the hair. That is why hair that has been well brushed takes on such a fine, silky gloss. The brush also improves the circulation of the blood in the scalp and so promotes the growth of the hair. Hair that is well brushed does not need to be washed very often, which is an advantage, because if you have long, heavy hair, washing it is a serious business. When you do wash your hair, you must be sure that it is thoroughly dry before you put it up; otherwise, you are apt to take cold.

About Your Bath: Take a cool sponge bath and a brisk rub with a coarse towel every morning. The water should be about 70 degrees. If you care to, try it with a thermometer, but it is about the temperature of a comfortably warm room. There is nothing better for the complexion. I will tell you why. The skin is full of little glands that secrete the perspiration. They carry off a great deal of waste and poisonous matter from the system, and they are at work all the time, even when you are not conscious of any perspiration. Now, if the mouths of these little glands become stopped up, or if the circulation in the skin is poor, they cannot work nearly so well. A good deal of poisonous matter that they ought to take away remains in the system, and the skin loses its clearness and becomes dark and muddy. The cool sponge and brisk rub does for the rest of the skin what the brush does for the scalp—frees the mouths of the glands and promotes the circulation of the blood. You will need only one hot bath a week. This you should take at night, just before going to bed. It is well to take a dash of cold water after it. You should not take a cold bath during the first three days of your monthly illness.

Keep Your Bowels Regular.—You should have one good evacuation of the bowels every day. This is largely a matter of habit. Go to the closet every morning after breakfast. If you are inclined to constipation, it is a good thing to take a cup of hot water just before breakfast, or a glass of cold water when you first get up in the morning. A little massage, which you can practice while dressing, will also help you. The large bowel, which contains the matter that should be evacuated, runs around the abdomen, as shown by figure "7" in cut "No. 9." If you will knead the bowel thoroughly, pressing your fingers down deeply into the abdominal wall, beginning low down on the right side, then across and down on the left, it will be stimulated to contract and empty. Do not think that it is a matter of indifference that you should go two or three days without evacuation of the bowels. The foul matters that should be evacuated are partly absorbed into the system, and you will have headache, feel dull and languid, your skin will grow yellow, and, if the condition is allowed to continue long, will become "pimpley."

As to Diet.—You should eat good, simple food. Avoid rich cake, gravies, rich pastry and preserves. Ices in moderation are wholesome enough. Eat all the fruit you want, provided it is ripe and sound, but do not eat too much candy. It would be better not to eat any, but that is too much to expect of you, for candy is a girl's greatest temptation in the eating line. Hot breads and buckwheat cakes are good to the taste, but trying to the digestion. Use tea and coffee with great moderation; they are nerve stimulants, which you do not in the least need. A cup of weak coffee you can have in the morning, if you want it, but save the tea till you are an older woman. Take plenty of time for your meals, and masticate your food thoroughly.

About Sleep.—You need at least eight hours of sleep in the twenty-four. As a child, you needed more; if you live to be an old woman, you will not need quite so much; but now, at least eight hours are needed to keep you in good condition and keep your cheeks rosy. The best time to sleep is between ten at night and six in the morning. If you are obliged to rise before six, go to bed earlier. If for any reason you are up late, learn to take a nap in the daytime.

Exercise.—Some time—the more, the better—should be spent every day in the open air. A brisk walk is excellent exercise; there is nothing better, but there are many things which girls count more amusing, such as lawn tennis, golf, bicycle riding, horseback exercise, etc. These are all good in their way, only they should not be carried to excess. Do not play matched games; in eagerness to win you are likely to overtax your strength. Basket-ball is a game with which I am not familiar, but from what I have heard of it, I should think it a very rough game and too severe exercise for most girls. These things, remember, are for exercise and recreation; they are not to take the place of occupation. Gardening is fair exercise; there is something health-giving in working in the soil, and it has the merit of being useful as well. Ordinary housework is also excellent exercise, though it has the disadvantage of being carried on in-doors. But do not make the mistake of considering driving to be exercise. Carriage exercise is only for invalids or old women. If you have been at work most of the day about the house, you may get rest and fresh air from a drive; you have had your exercise in the house.

If you practice in a gymnasium, take the advice of the leader as to what you are able to do. There is one golden rule, "Make haste slowly." Do at first only what you are able to do easily, and then do a little more each day—perhaps only a very little. You remember the story of the Spartan woman who, by lifting a calf each day from the time he was born, was able to lift him when he was full grown. I imagine even the tiniest calf would be too much for one of our girls to lift, but the lesson is just as good. You should never lift, unless in an emergency where the exertion is absolutely necessary, every ounce you possibly can, or carry for any distance a weight which is a great effort for you to lift at all. Such exertion is particularly dangerous to women because the womb and ovaries are hung in the pelvis by rather loose attachments. They easily recover from the slight changes in position produced by ordinary movements, but a sudden and violent pressure may displace some one of them so that it is unable to recover its normal position. This is more apt to happen at the menstrual period, because then the womb is heavier than at other times, and so more easily forced out of place. I shall mention this again in speaking of your dress.

Monthly Illness.—It is not necessary that you should take quite so much care at the time of your monthly illness as when you were a child, but you should still be careful at such times. Do not ride a wheel up hill, or ride it at all except for short distances; do not ride a horse at all at such a time, or play any of the violent games, as golf, lawn tennis, and especially basket-ball; croquet, you can play, though I believe that is rather out of fashion now. Do not take long tramps, though you need not be afraid of an ordinary walk. I do not ask you to stay in the house in wet weather, but you should be especially careful to change all damp clothing when you come in. If you go to a dance during your monthly illness, you should not stay late or dance all the time; sit down through at least half the dances, even at the risk of being taken for a wall-flower.

About Your Dress. — You should wear flannel next to the skin in cold weather, but if you intend wearing short-sleeved and low-necked dresses to evening entertainments, your flannel should not have long sleeves and should be cut low at the throat. I do not approve of *decollete* dresses myself, but if you will wear them, I am telling you how to do so with the least risk. Before going out sponge your neck and arms with cold water into which you have poured a little alcohol. Have some light wrap to throw over your shoulders while you are resting from the last dance, and be careful about drafts.

Do not lace your corset tight. It should fasten easily in front, and should be so loose that you can fill your lungs without difficulty. If you will look at a plate showing the internal organs, you will see how compressing the ribs—which is what a tight corset does—pushes the liver and stomach out of place and prevents the free play of the lungs; and, what is worse, but which you will not see by the plate, is that it puts too much pressure on the womb and ovaries, and is very likely to cause those displacements from which even young girls in these days often suffer. For the same reason the bands of your skirts should be loose, and if the skirts are heavy, they should be so arranged that the weight is carried from the shoulders. There is the same reason as when you were a child that you should wear a short skirt, rain coat and thick boots in wet weather, and that you should change all damp clothing at once when you come into the house.

Cosmetics, Powder, Rouge, etc. — Scorn everything of this kind. If you follow the directions that have been given you, you will need nothing of the sort. At best the effect is only temporary, and their use is likely to do your complexion lasting injury.

About Marriage. — Now I am going to speak to you on a delicate and difficult subject. You are thinking of marriage; it is right that you should. To be married to a good man, sound in body and mind, whom you sincerely love, is the best fortune that can come to you. You are limited in your choice of a husband to the men who have signified their wish to marry you, but it is better that you should die an old maid than marry a man who is "fast," as your friends say, *i. e.*, dissipated. Of course, in marriage there are many considerations besides those of health, but those of health are the only ones on which I undertake to advise you.

There are two forms of dissipation which are to be avoided in a husband on the score of health—habitual use of alcoholic drinks to excess, and the habit of association with immoral women. It is not very common for a young man to be what is called an habitual drunkard, but a man who is frequently intoxicated when young will, in all human probability, be an habitual drunkard before he is forty. If you imagine you can reform such a man, you are greatly mistaken ; he will grow worse and not better. He will not injure your health directly, only so far as misery, want and distress are likely to do it ; but your children will suffer. They are likely to have all sorts of nervous troubles, hysterics, epilepsy, and sometimes idiocy.

The second form of dissipation is even more dangerous. It is quite common for a young man of that sort to contract diseases as a result of his bad habits, which, if you marry him, would be very likely to be communicated to you or to any children that you might have by him. Do not allow yourself to become interested in such a man, even if he has beautiful eyes and fascinating manners. Choose for your associates sober, steady young men. Do not be afraid to give them a little kindly encouragement if they are shy and awkward. If a warmer interest results from such an association, it will be good, not evil fortune for you.

WHAT A YOUNG WIFE AND MOTHER SHOULD KNOW.

Many books could be filled on the subjects with which a young wife and mother should be familiar. Of late schools and universities have been very sensibly making some effort to teach the girl who hopes some day to be a wife, a few of the things she ought to know, hence the various courses on domestic sciences. Of course, in this chapter I can only give you a few hints about the various subjects on which you should be informed.

House Sanitation.—First, then, you should know something about *House Sanitation*, as it is called; that is, about the proper situation of the house, the drainage, ventilation, heating and water supply. If you are consulted about building a house in the country, try to have it on moderately high ground, which is dry. Let it face the south or east, if possible, so as to have sunlight in all the rooms. If you have a city house, try to have it on the north side of a street running east and west, or on the west side of a street running north and south, for the sake of the sunlight. In the city you may not be able to have sunshine in all the rooms, but at least there should be no dark rooms in your house. The cellar should be dry, with a good cement floor and stone walls—brick absorbs too much moisture to be used under ground. If the cellar does not extend under all the house, the remaining space should be well drained and ventilated.

Fresh Air.—There should be plenty of fresh air in your house. Air is a mixture of oxygen and nitrogen. The nitrogen serves to dilute the oxygen, which alone would be too stimulating. In breathing, the oxygen is absorbed by the blood and the carbonic acid thrown off. Carbonic acid is a poisonous gas, so you see that a person in breathing gradually poisons the air. An average man gives off a little more than half a cubic foot of carbonic acid gas in an hour when he is asleep, and nearly three times as much when he is hard at work. Women and children give off rather less. It takes very little of this—about two parts in ten thousand—to make the air unwholesome, or, as you would say, *close*. Now you see how necessary ventilation is. In summer it is very easily accomplished, as the open doors and windows give all the fresh air necessary; but in winter it is more difficult. There should be at least 1,000 cubic feet of air for each person, and the ventilation should be enough to change all the air in the room three times an hour. How can you accomplish this? It is done partly by the heating. If your house is heated by a hot-air furnace, there is, or should be, a cold-air box, so that the fresh outside air is heated and forced into the room. The foul warm air escapes through various cracks about the windows and doors if there is no special passage for it. It must escape in some way or the hot air would not come up through the register. If the house is heated by stoves, try to have in your living rooms at least one open fire. A coal grate is rather more trouble to look after, than a stove, and makes more dust, but it is an excellent ventilator. If you cannot have a grate or grates, an old-fashioned Franklin stove is not a bad substitute. With hot water or steam heating some outside opening is necessary, as there the heating does not directly assist the ventilation except that warm air is lighter than cold air, and the greater the difference in temperature, the greater the difference in weight. Now, air is a gas, and all gases of different weights have a tendency to mix, so that there is, when it is quite cold, a strong pressure of the outside air to get into the house and of the warm air inside to escape. This makes the little currents that you feel around the doors and windows. Do not cork up the bedroom windows with cotton batting, or any other windows, for that matter. Move the bed out so that you will not feel the draft. Sleeping with an open window in the room in cold winter weather is largely a matter of habit. I do not advise it in this climate for young children, who are apt to kick off their bed covering at night. Grown people in good health can follow their own inclination.

Do not have your room too warm—from 65° to 70° is warm enough for living rooms, 50° to 55° for sleeping rooms. Try to have the rooms which you occupy warmed with some degree of evenness. If you go from a kitchen where the temperature is between eighty and ninety, through a cold hall to a bedroom just above the freezing point to dress for the afternoon, can you wonder that you have a cold most of the winter?

As to the Water Supply.—If you live in the city, or even in a moderately large town, this is probably provided for by the municipal government or by a corporation more or less under its control. The quality depends perhaps somewhat upon the ease with which good water can be obtained, but much more on the care, intelligence and, sometimes, the integrity of the city fathers. I knew one Northern city where, although they had all Lake Superior to draw from, the water was for years abominably bad, and where the population suffered greatly in consequence. If, however, you live in the open country, the water supply becomes a question for each family to settle for themselves, and is one of very great importance. Cisterns are not very reliable for drinking water. It is difficult even with the greatest care to keep the water sweet, and the supply of water, depending as it does directly upon the rainfall, is apt to run short in dry weather. A well must be dug. The question is, where? The well should be on higher ground than the house, barns and outhouses. It should not be very near them. It should be protected in every possible way from surface drainage. A deep well is better than a shallow one, and it is better when a strata of fairly dense rock is passed before water is reached.

Some years ago, when I was spending my vacation in a small town among the foothills of the Green Mountains in Vermont, I went out with the village doctor one day on his rounds. In the course of the afternoon we came to a house half way up the mountain side, where there was no other house near and the air outside as pure as it is possible for air to be. Two of the family were very ill with typhoid fever, and another member was barely convalescent. The well was in a little depression between the outhouse and the barnyard, in a good position to take the drainage from both. The doctor cautioned the family, "Don't drink a drop of water from that well without boiling it." I hope they followed his advice and saved the rest of the family; but I think it more than likely that they thought the doctor was a man of fads and new-fangled notions, and the fever a dispensation of Providence, and so went on in the old way. In that small country town—two thousand would have been a large estimate for the population of the entire township—there had been that year, so the doctor told me, over one hundred cases of typhoid fever, all caused by water from infected wells. Turbid water can generally be cleared by passing it through a good stone filter, but to kill any disease germs which it may contain it should be boiled. Boiled water is not so pleasant to drink as unboiled. The carbonic acid gas, which gives it life and sparkle, has been driven out of it, and it has a rather flat taste. If you are so fortunate as to have a deep well in a good situation, this precaution will probably not be necessary.

Disinfection is considered a branch of *House Sanitation*, though it is, except in cases of sickness, a concession to human imperfection. If your cellar is light, dry, and well ventilated, if the plumbing is without a flaw, if your house is faultlessly clean and all refuse promptly removed, there should be little need of disinfection; in sickness it does become necessary.

There is a popular idea that a sick room may be disinfected by hanging up cloths wet with a solution of Carbolic Acid, or by leaving plates filled with Chloride of Lime standing about. This is a mistake. These substances may to a certain extent remove unpleasant odors, but they do nothing more. The disease germs resist the action of poisonous gases much better than we do, so to really disinfect the sick room the air must be filled with poisonous gases far beyond the tolerance of human beings. Those who have had rooms disinfected by burning Sulphur or by Formaldehyde by order of the Board of Health, will appreciate this.

The ideal disinfectant has yet to be discovered. Corrosive Sublimate might be one if it could be deprived of its poisonous and corrosive qualities, but as it is, it is out of the question for domestic use. Platt's Chloride is a very good household disinfectant. It is without color or odor and, used according to directions, is practically harmless, though it would be very unwholesome to drink. A very good solution for washing clothing, sheets or towels used about a case of contagious disease, is made by mixing four ounces of White Vitriol and two ounces of common salt in a gallon of water. For cleansing vessels and receiving discharges, a solution may be used of one and a half pounds of Green Vitriol in a gallon of water. Copperas and Permanganate of Potash are useful disinfectants, and not so poisonous as to be dangerous to handle; but they stain clothing. Chloride of Lime and Quick Lime are useful in damp and musty places; they sweeten and, to a certain extent, dry the air.

Foods.—It is very important to the welfare of your family that you should understand something of food values. I do not mean merely that you should be a good cook, though that is also very desirable and not at all to be underrated.

There are three principal classes of foods: the albuminates, found most largely in animal foods, the fats, and the starches and sugars. It may seem strange to you that starches and sugars, which do not on the surface seem to have very much in common, should be put in the same class; but all the starches are changed to sugar in the process of digestion, so that in their effect on the system they are much the same. No one of these classes will support life alone satisfactorily, and all are needed to perfect nourishment; but the proportion in which they are needed depends very much on the surroundings and circumstances of the individual to be fed. The albuminates, which are to be found in lean meat, milk, eggs, and in smaller quantities in the various cereal grains, build up the structure of the body; the fats and starches supply the heat and energy which is used up in action. Now you can see that a diet of fat pork is not suitable for a person taking but little exercise in hot weather, but is just the thing for men engaged in active out-of-door work in winter. The Esquimaux, who hunt and fish for a livelihood and are exposed most of the year to severe cold, consume great quantities of train oil and seal and walrus blubber, which a man under ordinary conditions of civilization could hardly taste without nausea. This is not owing to any peculiarity of the Esquimaux, but to the conditions under which they live, for Nansen and his lieutenant, Johansen, who were separated from their ship and supplies for nearly a year and forced to live as the Esquimaux do in the extreme North, lived and thrived on a similar diet. On the other hand, natives of very hot climates live mostly on vegetable food, and people from northern climates forced to live in the tropics would do well to follow their example. There is no doubt that Englishmen in India would suffer less from diseases of the liver if they would eat less roast beef and pastry, and live, so far as diet goes, more as the natives do. From all of which it follows that food should be adapted to the climate, the time of year and the amount of exercise taken.

Experiments have been made to ascertain the amount of energy, or working power, produced by different foods. Fats stand very high in the list; butter and fat pork are the leaders.

Then come the lean meats and cereals, oatmeal, corn meal and wheat flour. Peas and beans rank high; carrots, cabbage and potatoes, very low. Cheese stands high, though much lower than butter, but milk and eggs are surprisingly low. Poultry is low compared with other meats, and fish still lower.

There is much less waste to meat when it is cooked slowly by very moderate heat. The coarser and tougher parts of the animal may be made tender and palatable by simmering a long time slowly over a low fire. If you are obliged to practice strict economy in feeding your family, a careful study of the value of different foods and different methods of cooking, which I can only indicate here, would be of great use to you. Remember also that your table should have a certain variety and be neatly served. Spotless linen, a vase of flowers or a pretty fern add little or nothing to the expense of a meal, but they add much to its pleasure and aid indirectly both the appetite and the digestion.

There are certain substances which are taken with the food more for pleasure than for nourishment, of which I must say a word. These are tea, coffee, chocolate and various forms of alcoholic drinks. Tea and coffee are nerve stimulants, very pleasant and refreshing, and, if taken in moderation by healthy adults, I think they are practically harmless. Taken in excess, they injure the digestion, and they should under no circumstances be given to children. Chocolate has considerable food value, owing to the fat it contains, but is so rich that it can only be taken steadily by people of strong digestion. The use of alcoholic drinks is entirely unnecessary to healthy people in youth and middle life, and is so fraught with deadly danger, in our climate, at least, that alcoholics as table beverages should be entirely discouraged. Alcohol is an invaluable medicine, but should be given, like other medicines, only on the prescription of a physician.

The Pregnant State. — We come now to more personal matters—to the care of your own health under conditions which are new to you. We presuppose that you have been married a few months when you notice that you have passed the time for your monthly illness without the usual symptoms. Then you have a slight feeling of weight in the pelvis—a "bearing-down," as it is often expressed. Sometimes, not always, your breasts feel tender and mildly painful, and when you rise in the morning you have a distinct feeling of nausea. All these symptoms point to one thing, and if you do not yourself know what they mean, your mother or some older married friend will easily tell you. If the mother instinct is strong in you, as it is in the majority of women, you will feel that the news is good. Your heart will warm to the young life you are nurturing, and you will wish to take the best possible care of yourself; not only for your own sake, but for the sake of the baby that is coming, that it may make its start in life with the best possible inheritance—sweet temper, quiet nerves and robust health—that the little body may be perfect and the little soul serene.

What can you do to that end? I will tell you as well as I can. You must make up your mind to forego some pleasures. Dancing, for one thing, must be given up absolutely. It makes no difference that you have known a young woman who danced all through the earlier months of her pregnancy without disaster. It is not wise and it is not safe, even though some one person may have done it with impunity. Try as far as possible to avoid all unpleasant sights and sounds, especially the sight of deformed or disfigured people; but if you should by an unfortunate chance meet any such person, do not let your mind dwell on it with alarm. The probability that it will do any harm is after all very slight, and you can lessen it still further by resolutely refusing to let your mind dwell on the subject. Cultivate the grace of a placid and serene temper. Do not worry about things. Do not let yourself get angry even if the provocation is serious. Do not indulge in gloomy reveries. On the contrary, look on the bright side of things. This is a good receipt for keeping yourself happy; but the object is that the baby shall have a happy disposition, and in this you will find later you have been working not only in your baby's interest, but greatly in your own.

Physical Precautions.— There are also certain physical precautions that you must take at this time. Avoid all violent exercise, but at the same time keep out of doors as much as possible. Plenty of moderate exercise on the other hand is good for you, though you should stop when you find yourself decidedly tired. Do not jump from any elevation, even from a chair or carriage. Leave hanging curtains and pictures to some one else. Lifting any weight above your head is bad for you. Heavy lifting, even on a level, is to be avoided.

The advice given you in books is not by any means all good. For example, I have seen a book which advised pregnant women to eat as little as possible, and particularly to avoid meats of all kinds, because then the baby would be small, its bones soft, and the confinement in consequence easier. Now, this is very delusive. Undoubtedly if a woman is half-starved, the child will be likely to be puny and ill-nourished, though not necessarily small. Nature will nourish the baby at your expense if you try to starve it. She will take the phosphates from your bones, especially from your teeth, to build up the bones of the little one, if the food taken is not sufficient. Do not be afraid to take as much food as you can easily digest. You need more food than under different circumstances. If the early morning nausea does not persist through the day, your appetite will probably be excellent. If the nausea is troublesome, it is well to have a cup of strong hot coffee brought to your bed in the morning. Take it with a few crackers or a little bread and butter, and wait half an hour or so before you try to get up. This will commonly make a great difference in your comfort during the day. If this is not sufficient, have your druggist make for you a mixture of ½ an ounce of Bromide of Potash in 4 ounces of Tincture of Gentian Root, and take a teaspoonful of it after your meals. I have found this to answer in all but severe cases, which, of course, require the care of a physician. The nausea, even when it is severe, does not usually persist after the third or the beginning of the fourth month, though some unfortunate women suffer from it during the entire term.

Indications of Miscarriage.—If at any time after you have serious reason to think yourself pregnant, you see that you are flowing, go to bed at once and send for a physician. You are threatened with a miscarriage, which would be a serious misfortune to you. A miscarriage is a much greater strain on a woman's health than a natural confinement at term, to say nothing about the loss of your baby, which you would also feel to be a misfortune.

Plain Talk.—Right here I may say that I am well aware that there are women who would not look upon it in that light— gay young wives with the instinct of motherhood imperfectly developed, who dislike giving up the gaities to which they are accustomed, who dread the months of semi-invalidism with the ordeal at the end, and still more perhaps the confinement with and care of young children. Such women not only rejoice at the interruption of their pregnancy, but are sometimes tempted, either themselves or by the help of physicians unworthy of the name, to interrupt it forcibly. If I have any such young women among my readers, and it is very possible that I may have, I wish I could impress upon them not only the wickedness, but the danger of such a course. Would you see any great difference in the guilt of a woman who murdered a baby a month old and one who made a year-old baby her victim? Well, from the first your baby is alive. It is an old wives' fable that the life comes when you first feel it stirring. That only means that the baby has grown so large and strong that you can feel its movements through the bag of water in which it lies. And this baby, *your* baby, you are conspiring with some physician, who should be an outcast in his profession, to *murder*. This is plain talk, but it is true. No reputable physician will even think of doing this thing. He knows perfectly well what he is doing, if you do not. For a doctor it is the crime of crimes. He takes an oath on his graduation that whatever other evil he may do, he will abstain from this. He renders himself liable to the penitentiary if he is detected. A man or woman who would do this is utterly unworthy of confidence. He does not, of course, wish to kill you, because that would seriously increase his own danger; but he rarely has either the skill or the intelligence desirable, and the secrecy necessary stands in the way of the requisite precautions. The operation is a very grave one at best; and even performed by a council of physicians with every advantage, as it sometimes must be in order to save the life of the mother when it becomes impossible to save both, it is by no means always successful.

If you try experiments upon yourself, you may do yourself serious harm. Many women have killed themselves in that way. And you are very unlikely to accomplish your object. As for drugs, only a few exceptionally sensitive women are affected by them. As a rule you will materially injure your digestion, but that is all you will be likely to accomplish with drugs.

A forcible miscarriage is very much more dangerous than one occurring of itself. It is all the difference between an apple torn from the bough on which it hangs, and one from some reason dropping of its own accord before it is ripe.

This is a digression. I certainly hope the young mother to whom I have been giving advice and counsel will have no such temptation.

The Clothing Worn.—Your clothing should be loose. Do not be tempted to try to improve your appearance by tight clothing. In the first place you defeat your own object since anything that sharply outlines your figure is to your disadvantage; in the second place the pressure of tight clothing interferes with the proper development of the growing womb and may make trouble for you at the time of your confinement. The corset should be discarded after the fourth month.

False Modesty. — From false modesty some women are inclined to shut themselves up after their figure becomes decidedly noticeable. This is a mistake, and I hope you will not fall into it. You need the fresh air and the society of your friends. There is nothing whatever in your condition to be ashamed of; quite the contrary.

Symptoms That Need Attention.—It is quite possible that at about this time you may notice that your feet are somewhat swollen, particularly at night. There is nothing alarming about this if the swelling is moderate. It comes from the pressure which the heavy womb exerts on the large blood vessels. But if the swelling extends above the ankles, or if you notice that your face is puffy, especially under the eyes, or that your hands are swollen, you should see your doctor at once. These symptoms need immediate attention.

The Last Weeks of Your Term.—You are coming to the time when you feel heavy and unwieldy, when, unless you are a robust woman, it is quite an effort to move about much. Perhaps you are behindhand with the little garments for the new comer and would prefer to sit all day over your sewing. Do not yield to this temptation. You need exercise now as much as ever. It is important that you should be in the best possible physical condition to fit you for the ordeal through which you are to pass. It is at this time that many women of your acquaintance will advise you to put some astringent, as a tea of White Oak bark or a solution of Alum, on the nipples to toughen them, so that they will not become sore and tender in nursing. Do not do it. The astringent makes the tender skin brittle so that it cracks more easily. If the nipples are short or inclined to draw in, pull them out for a few minutes each day, rubbing in a little Vaseline or fresh mutton tallow. If they are very tender, you can use a solution of Tannin in Glycerine—about 5 grains of the Tannin to an ounce of Glycerine. Have the druggist mix it for you. The Glycerine prevents the Tannin from making the skin brittle.

You may also be advised to take sitz baths with a view to making the confinement easier. I never could see that such baths at this time were of any special use, but if they are not hot, only warm, they will do no harm. If the skin over the abdomen feels stretched and uncomfortable, you may get much comfort from rubbing Sweet Oil or Vaseline gently into it every night before you go to bed during the last month. Keep on rubbing gently until the Oil or Vaseline has all disappeared—been absorbed—and you will find that your underclothing will not be soiled. Of course you should only put on a little oil at a time.

Feeling of Dread.—It is natural, as the time draws near, that you should look forward to your coming trial with alarm and dread. I have even known young mothers who quite expected not to live through their first confinement. If you have any such feeling, you greatly exaggerate the danger. I am telling you the truth, not prophesying smooth things, so I cannot deny that there is a possibility of danger. But I am an old woman; I have been engaged in active practice for nearly thirty years and have never seen a woman die in childbirth, though a very few have come unpleasantly near it. I remember talking with an old doctor who had delivered more than three thousand women—a much larger number than I can boast—and he said he never had a woman die in childbirth. There is more or less danger in all the affairs of life.   Those of us who live in large towns run no small risk from electric cars, automobiles and bicycles whenever we go down town, but we do not make ourselves miserable on that account; we have become accustomed to it.   If you are a country woman, you take some risk every time you ride after a gay horse, but you like the frisky creature for all that.   Perhaps you dread the pain more than the danger.   The pain is very real in all first confinements, even if they are perfectly natural, but it is not unbearable.   You will have, or certainly should have, some Chloroform at the last, and it is astonishing how soon you will forget it when it is once over.

Preparations for Confinement.—I should perhaps tell you what preparations you should make for your approaching confinement.   If your mother can be consulted, or if you have engaged an experienced nurse, you will have all the advice on this point you need; but it is possible that you may have neither of these advantages.   You need, then, a rubber sheet large enough to cover the whole mattress except a little space at the head of the bed, about three yards of unbleached muslin for bandages—this amount will make two and is much better than anything you can make—and a paper of large safety pins.   You should have ready an old night dress, and, if it is cold weather, an under vest which you do not mind having destroyed; also a better one of each to put on when it is all over.   You should have a dozen large toilet napkins, at least four sheets besides those on the bed, and plenty of towels.   It is well to have a supply of old cotton rags, which are often useful, and remember that everything provided must be *scrupulously clean*.   This is not merely a question of good housekeeping; it is a matter of life and death.   You need a roll of absorbent cotton.   It is necessary to have a bottle of Vaseline, one of Ammonia, one of good brandy or whiskey, and a small bottle of Carbolic Acid, distinctly labeled "poison;" also a good fountain syringe.

You should have a baby basket in which is placed everything necessary for the baby's first toilet: A very soft linen rag for a wash cloth—an old table napkin if you have it—two very soft old towels, some bland, unirritating soap—*Juvenile* is very good, but white Castile will do—two papers of safety pins, small and medium sizes, a suit of the little clothes, the plainest you have, half a dozen diapers, a box of baby powder with a powder puff, a little absorbent cotton for dressing the cord and some linen bobbin for tieing it, and a pair of sharp scissors.   Of course, any stout, smooth cord will do for this purpose, but I like the bobbin because it makes a firm knot that is in no danger of slipping. There should also be a baby blanket and a square of old woolen goods—a part of an old flannel skirt will do very well—in which to receive and wrap the baby when it first arrives. Be sure the nurse, or the woman who is to be with you, knows where to lay her hand on everything, so that there will be no time lost in hunting for necessary articles when the time comes to use them.

The bed should be prepared by covering the mattress with an ordinary cover, over which is placed a sheet carefully and securely tucked in around the mattress. Over this is placed, on the middle of the bed, a sheet which is called a *draw sheet*, folded lengthwise till it is about a yard wide. This should be secured in place by safety pins. Over all this place your rubber sheet, which should also be carefully pinned in place by safety pins. Over this you can place another sheet, which had better be pinned down at the corners. When everything is over, the rubber sheet can be removed and you will have under it a clean bed for your commencing convalescence.

At the commencement of the labor you should have a warm bath and a large enema—at least two quarts of warm water made soapy with white Castile soap. Your hair should be braided and tied securely at the ends, but not put up. If the pains are now quite frequent, say once in ten minutes, you can put on the nightdress and vest you have reserved for your labor, but put on a heavy wrapper and do not go to bed until you are unable to sit up any longer. I cannot tell you how long your labor is to be. Twenty-four hours is not an unreasonable time for a first confinement, but in such cases the pains are at first quite mild and about an hour apart. In such a case, if the labor commenced in the morning, you would probably be about the house through the day, first make the preparations I have spoken of in the evening, and the baby would be born sometime during the night. This is the most common course in first labors, but sometimes the pains come on rapidly and violently from the first and the whole is over in two or three hours. I am speaking, of course, of natural labor where, as the nurses say, "everything is all right."

After Labor Is Over.—If you have had a comparatively easy labor and are yourself robust, you may feel that you are perfectly able to be up and about directly after it. On the other hand, if the labor has been severe or if you are not very strong, you will be completely tired out and find it an effort to open your eyes or answer the simplest question.

When you have had time to rest after having been bathed, have had everything made fresh and clean about you and the baby has been washed and dressed, it should be brought to you for its first meal. Most babies take the nipple eagerly from the first, but some fuss about it a good deal, tiring the mother and making the nurse much trouble. They can be taught, however, with a little patience. It is true that there is no milk in the breast yet, but the secretion that is there is very good for the baby, and it is better for you to have it drawn off.

How the Baby is Cared for.—I have said nothing as yet as to the care the baby should receive, but though you will not be able at this time to give the matter much attention, it is well that you should understand it. When the doctor has tied and cut the cord, he puts his finger in the baby's mouth to free it from any mucus that it may have taken in during the birth, and then, if it is breathing regularly, hands it to the nurse, who receives it in the square of old flannel you have provided. The baby may then be wrapped up still further and put aside until you are made clean and comfortable; but when it is washed, even in the summer unless it is in the middle of a very hot day, it should be taken to a fire. The little creature has come from a place where the temperature is between 98° and 99°, warmer than it ever is in this climate, except for a few hours perhaps in a very exceptionally hot summer's day. I have often seen babies blue and shivering with cold during the bath, and if this condition continues too long, the baby may take pneumonia, which will end its life before it is hardly begun. The baby should be anointed all over with Sweet Oil or Vaseline to soften the thick matter with which it is smeared. It should then be carefully washed with warm water and soap. It should be washed about the eyes before you put any soap in the water or on the rag, to avoid getting soap into its eyes. Remember that the baby's skin is very delicate and be gentle in all your movements, and only uncover the part of its body on which you are engaged. After the baby is clean the cord should be dressed, which is done by wrapping it in absorbent cotton and putting a small pad of the cotton over it. Then put on the band, pinning it firmly but not too tightly, then the shirt and diaper, and follow with the other clothes in their order. No pins but safety pins should ever be used about the baby, and then if he cries, no time need be spent in hunting for a possible pin which may be scratching him.

Your milk will come freely on the third day, though there may be a little milk in the breasts on the second day. It is very probable that in the first rush the baby will not be able to take it all and that the breasts will become distended and very uncomfortable. They can in that case be bandaged by putting a large towel under the shoulders, bringing it around under the arms and pinning it over the breast quite tightly and firmly. This hinders the flow of milk by pressure, supports the breasts and presses out the superfluous milk. This is also the day on which it is a time-honored custom to give a dose of Castor Oil to move the bowels. If your milk has come in slowly and scantily, this is the thing to take, as it undoubtedly increases the flow of milk; but if you have, on the contrary, too much milk, a dose of Salts or a Seidlitz Powder is better.

The flow, which was at first quite profuse, lessens as the days go by. At the end of the first week it should be less bloody and more watery than at first, and very much less in quantity. By the end of the second or early in the third week, it has generally disappeared, though some women find it reappearing after any special exertion as late as the sixth week. That is not quite as it should be. The discharge should not be offensive. There may be a faint odor to it as there often is to the menstral flow, but if the odor is decidedly offensive, there is something wrong and the doctor should be consulted.

Bathing.—You can have and should have, if you have a nurse, a sponge bath every day. You do not need any douches unless the discharge becomes offensive, and then, as I have just said, they should be given according to the direction of your physician.

Diet.—I have said nothing yet about your diet. For the first three days you should have only tea, toast and broth, gruel, or perhaps a soft boiled egg if you are quite hungry. After that you can have any simple and nutritious food. Only remember that you do not need to eat as heartily as when you were able to take plenty of exercise.

Remain in Bed.—Stay in bed ten days at least. Nothing is gained by trying to get up before that, even if you feel able to do so. The womb, which before you became pregnant was about the size of a medium sized pear and not far from that shape, has grown large enough to cover a baby weighing from six to ten pounds, not to mention the after-birth and no small quantity of water. It has become besides a powerful muscular organ with thick walls and capable of exercising great force, as you have felt during your confinement. Immediately after the labor, though it is empty and contracted, you can easily feel it in the abdomen if you are not very fleshy—a large hard ball, as large as a cannon ball or a grown person's head. It grows rapidly smaller, but it is not till the baby is six weeks old that it becomes reduced to its former size. Not till then, even if you are perfectly well, are you in as good condition for hard work as you were before your pregnancy. I do not in the least mean that it will be necessary for you to confine yourself all this time to the bed or sofa. If you are well, you can leave your room at the end of the second week, and by the end of the third can go about the house freely, or out for a short drive; but not till the baby is six weeks old ought you to take up the full round of your duties if they are at all exhausting. A little care at this time will pay in the long run and save doctors' bills, for if you try to do hard work while the womb is still heavy, you are likely to bring on some displacement which may keep you a semi-invalid for years.

CARE OF THE BABY.

The nurse, if you have one, has been engaged for a varying period of from two to six weeks. Even the longest time is soon over, and the responsibility of the baby's care falls upon you. This is an anxious time for mothers of first babies. Many a young woman has confided to me that she shed tears over the first bath she gave her baby. Few young babies enjoy their bath, and none of them like being dressed after it. The baby also resents the unfamiliar and awkward handling, and cries lustily. You feel that you are hurting your baby and can with difficulty resist the temptation to cry too. It does not really hurt a young baby to cry in moderation. It is his only way of expressing his feelings, and it is not always easy to say what feelings he is trying to express. Sometimes he is hungry, sometimes uncomfortable, as when his diaper is wet or soiled; sometimes he is tired and sleepy, and sometimes, I really think, he becomes tired of his own society and wishes to attract attention; and lastly, he is sometimes in pain. Go on with the bath and dressing and never mind the crying. You have only safety pins and so cannot prick him, as you might otherwise do. When it is over, he will be consoled by his dinner and go to sleep. In bathing him, be sure he is dried thoroughly, and then powder him carefully where folds of the skin rub together, particularly under the diaper. Never let him stay wet or mussed, and after taking off the soiled diaper, wipe him, or wash him if it is necessary, and put on fresh powder so that he will be perfectly clean and dry before you put on the clean diaper. Many babies become dreadfully chafed from neglect of this care, and must suffer very much in consequence.

Nursing the Baby.—I hope very much that you will be able to nurse your baby. It will be very much better for him and add greatly to your own comfort if you can. Do not fall into the way of nursing him whenever he cries. A young baby should be nursed every two hours—perhaps not quite so often at night, but at least ten times in twenty-four hours. He takes but little at a time and takes it very slowly. A young baby will often be fifteen or twenty minutes in taking what he wants, and will have several cat-naps in the time. Nursing is hard work for him and he has to stop for rest. When he is three months old, the time between meals may be lengthened to two hours and a half, with a still longer interval at night; at six months, every three hours, with two nursings at night; at ten months he may still be nursed every three hours, if you have milk enough for him, with but one meal at night. He now takes about eight times as much at a meal as when he was first born.

There are some precautions that you should take while nursing your baby. You may eat any simple and digestible food, but do not eat pickles nor very sour fruits, which are apt to give the baby colic. You should avoid all excitement, and not allow yourself to give way to anger. If by any unfortunate occurrence you should be greatly excited or frightened, do not nurse your baby directly after. Draw off the milk then in the breast and wait for fresh to come in before giving it to the baby. There is something in strong excitement, particularly of terror or grief, which, at least in some women, makes the milk poisonous. I knew a mother once who heard of her father's dangerous illness. She was a very devoted daughter and was greatly distressed; she prepared to go to him at once. In the midst of her preparation she stopped to nurse her baby. The baby was taken almost immediately with convulsions and died in a few hours. Cultivate a quiet mind if you wish your baby to thrive.

If the nipples become sore and tender, they may cause you much suffering. The nursing, which is ordinarily a pleasure, becomes under such circumstances positive torture. The Tannin and Glycerine mixture, of which I have spoken before, is a very good application in such cases. It should be carefully wiped off before the breast is given to the baby. Be careful not to expose the breast to cold, especially to drafts while nursing. Many broken breasts have come from carelessness in this respect.

If the baby is doing well he will increase steadily in weight —from two-thirds of an ounce to an ounce a day for the first four or five months, and about half as much for the rest of the year.

Some Hints.—Teach him to lie quietly in his crib or cradle even when he is awake; too much handling is bad for all young animals. If he is not wet nor soiled, if he is not hungry nor in pain—and you will soon learn to distinguish the cry of pain—he will learn that it is of no use to cry just to be taken up. Turn him over—babies like to change their position and when they are very young cannot do it themselves—and leave him in the cradle. Above all, do not walk with him in your arms. Why babies admire that form of exercise I do not know, but they do admire it. They do not need it, however, and it is very fatiguing to adults.

Do not keep the baby in bed with you at night. While it is still very young there is some danger that, if you are a sound sleeper, you may roll over on it and suffocate it; such things have happened. But apart trom that, it is better for the baby and for you that he should have his own cradle or crib by the side of your bed and be put back into it when he has finished nursing.

Fresh Air for the Baby.—The baby should pass part of every pleasant day in the open air, except in very cold weather, beginning from the time he is a month old if he is born in the winter; in the summer he can go out almost from the first, avoiding, of course, the heat of the sun when it is very warm. His eyes should be shaded from the light, indeed that precaution should also be taken in the house; a baby should never be allowed to stare at a bright light. He should wear a veil if it is at all cold, so that the cold of the outside air may be modified before it reaches his lungs. Do not keep him out long enough at a time to become chilled.

Teething.—At about four months the baby will begin to dreul so freely as to need a bib to protect the front of his dress, and will bite eagerly on your fingers or anything that he can put into his mouth. When he is six months old, you may begin to look for his first tooth, although many babies do not get their first teeth till a month or two later. The first tooth is usually a front one on the lower jaw, and the second follows by its side very shortly; then there is a pause for a few weeks or a couple of months, when the two corresponding teeth on the upper jaw appear almost together. The other four front teeth are apt to follow these quite closely, and then there is a long wait. The first molars appear when the baby is from a year to fourteen months old, the upper ones generally cutting through first; then come the eye and stomach teeth when the baby is from sixteen to twenty months old. The last molars may come through any time from the second to the third year.

It used to be the fashion to ascribe all the ills that a child suffered from the sixth to the twenty-fourth month to his teeth. it is now rather the mode to ignore the teeth altogether as a source of baby ills. I think the truth lies between the two extremes. That the teeth do hurt a baby more or less as they are coming through, I think there is no doubt, and he is apt to be cross, peevish and restless at such times. I have seen a few very nervous children show symptoms of convulsions—one who actually had a convulsion—but convulsions from teething are not nearly so common as used to be supposed. The liability of children of that age to diarrhea and other bowel troubles is owing to changes which are taking place in the baby's digestive apparatus fitting him to digest solid food, not to the cutting of the teeth. Babies fed at the breast are very much less liable to these troubles. It is very unlikely that your baby will have a convulsion, but if he should, put him at once into a hot bath while waiting for the doctor, and keep him in it till the convulsion is over; then take him out, dry him carefully and wrap him up in a blanket till the doctor arrives. Do not dress him as it may be necessary to put him into the hot water again.

Lancing the gums is not of the slightest use to help the teeth in cutting through. It is rather a hindrance, but I do think it quiets the nervous symptoms, probably by lessening the irritation when the gums are hot, tender and swollen.

When Shall You Wean Your Baby ?—It depends on many things—your health and his, and the time at which he was born. If you are not pulled down by the nursing, and the baby grows as he should do and seems satisfied and well nourished, you can nurse him for a year; or, if he was born in the summer, through the second summer. Do not wean him in hot weather nor when he is cutting teeth. Generally children weaned at nine months do fairly well. If the baby was born in the spring or early in the summer, and you doubt your ability to nurse him through the second summer, it is better to wean him while it is still cool, even though the year is not up.

Return of Monthly Sickness.—As a rule, women have no return of their monthly illness while nursing. To this rule, however, there are many exceptions, and you may be one of these. Should you on that account wean your baby? If the baby still thrives, I do not think it necessary on his account. It may be that the double strain is too much for you; that depends on how vigorous your health is. In that case you must balance your own interests and the baby's, and decide between them. Usually, if your health seriously deteriorates, the character of your milk will suffer; but this is not always the case. I have seen women greatly exhausted by nursing who had babies the picture of health. All their strength went to milk, as the old women say. There is another possibility which is much more serious; occasionally a nursing woman becomes pregnant. If you find that to be your case, you must wean your baby at once. It is not only best for him, but even if your milk continued good, it is the greatest injustice to the coming child to continue nursing. It is next to impossible that you should fairly nourish both.

Unless because of some such emergency as this, do not wean your baby suddenly. Begin by feeding him once, then twice in the twenty-four hours; then feed him through the day, reserving your milk for the night. In this way you accustom him gradually to the change of food, and still have your milk for him if he should become suddenly ill. Then if all is well, you can take the breast from him altogether. In this way also you will have less trouble with your breasts. The quantity of milk lessens with the lessening demand, and at the last you will have little trouble. A compress of Camphorated Oil helps to dry the milk. Press or milk out enough milk to prevent caking, and you will have no trouble. It is quite a little art to milk a woman's breast without giving pain or causing any irritation. The rubbing should be done with the tips of the fingers, and always from the edge of the breast toward the nipple. It is not easy to describe, but any experienced nurse or mother will show you how it is done.

What to Feed the Baby.—What will you feed your baby after and during weaning? Principally milk. A baby a year old, or nearly, can drink cow's milk, only it should be slightly warmed. How to obtain good milk is the next question. If you own a cow and can see to it that she has a good pasture, or a clean, well-ventilated stable, that she is in good condition and has wholesome food, you are very fortunate. If not, you must trust to the milkman. If you know something about him and his cows, so much the better; if you have serious doubts about the milk, it must be sterilized. I will describe the process later. Some authorities say that a baby a year old should have a bottle. I do not think so. Most children a year old can easily be taught to drink from a cup, and not only the trouble but the risks of nipples and bottles are saved. He does not need to be fed oftener than once in four hours, and once at night, at which times he should have as much as he wants. You may give him, if you like, particularly if he is inclined to be constipated, strained oatmeal gruel made rather thin; and a little chicken or mutton broth will not hurt him. Now and then he may have a chicken bone to suck, but the main dependence must be milk. If the bowels are too loose, the milk should be boiled.

Avoid Advertised Foods.—Do not be beguiled by the various prepared foods on the market, nor by the advertisements with pictures of most blooming infants fed exclusively on each and every one of them. None of them are to be compared to the fresh milk of a healthy cow, and with the present methods of sterilization milk can be utilized that is not perfect. If you are unfortunately so situated that you cannot procure even passably fresh milk, or the milk at your command hopelessly disagrees with the baby even after sterilization, malted milk is probably the best substitute. It has the disadvantage of being quite expensive. Condensed milk is very much used, but it is deficient in nourishing qualities, and, although babies often grow fat while using it, they are not strong.

When the baby has all his teeth but the last molars—usually when he is from one to two years old—you may begin to give him some solid food: a slice of stale bread and butter, bread and milk, a little mashed white potato, a sandwich made of rare beef scraped fine, a piece of rare beef to suck which you must watch that he does not swallow, a little oatmeal or corn meal mush, or a soft boiled egg. He will now take four meals a day and does not need to be fed at night.

Do not make the mistake of letting him taste food which he cannot have with the idea that a taste will not hurt him. It may not, but it makes him unhappy. Children will not fret for food of which they do not know the taste. It is better not to have him at the family table at this age if it can be avoided. He is too young to be taught good manners, and some of the older members of the family may not be able to resist the temptation of feeding him a little.

Food for Babies Who Cannot be Nursed.—We must now go back and speak of the baby's food in case that you are so unfortunate as to be unable from the first to nurse him. A new-born baby cannot digest cow's milk unmodified. "It is a mistake," some old doctor has said, "to think that cow's milk is the proper food for babies; it is the proper food for calves." This is certainly true of the new-born baby. What are we to do then? We must modify the milk so as to make it resemble the mother's milk as much as possible; for that it should have more fat, more sugar and much less curd. A wise Philadelphia doctor, who devoted much of his attention to children, devised a mixture which is called, after him, *Meigs' Mixture*, from which I have found excellent results; following is the receipt for a pint of it (you should have a measuring glass graduated for ounces, and then it is perfectly easy to make):

Milk	2 ounces.
Cream	3 "
Water	10 "
Milk Sugar	6¾ teaspoonfuls.

The Milk Sugar you can get at the druggist's.

If your milk and cream comes from a milkman, this mixture should be sterilized before using. You can buy a sterilizer, which consists of half a dozen bottles in a wire frame, and a pan for the hot water, which should be deep enough nearly to cover the bottles; but all you really need at this stage, if you have an ordinary steamer, is a pint bottle. Fill this bottle with the mixture, put it into the steamer over a kettle of boiling water, first corking it tightly with absorbent cotton, and let it steam twenty minutes; then take it up, before it is quite cool add a tea-spoonful of Lime Water, and put it on ice.

The baby will take from an ounce to an ounce and a half at a time. He should be fed ten times in the twenty-four hours, and you should make enough at one time to last that long. The food should always be warmed for him. You will need an alcohol lamp to warm it at night. After he is six weeks old he will take two ounces of food at a time, and need not be fed quite so often at night—eight times in the twenty-four hours will do; at three months he will take four ounces at a time and should not, if he takes all his food at each meal, need more than six meals in the twenty-four hours; at six months he will probably take about six ounces at a time and need to be fed as often; at ten months he will take eight ounces and need only be fed once at night, making five times in the twenty-four hours.

Buy a nursing bottle—one without tubing—that will hold a pint. It is hard enough to keep the nipples perfectly sweet and clean; it is practically impossible to keep fine tubing so. The bottle should be scalded each time that it is used and carefully dried. The nipples should be carefully washed and then placed in a bowl of water to which a little cooking soda has been added. The baby's mouth should be washed out quite frequently with clear water to prevent its becoming sore. It is a good plan to wash it after a meal, unless he has gone to sleep over his bottle, in which case it is a pity to disturb him.

Learning to Walk.—A healthy baby can usually sit up, if he is propped by pillows, when he is six months old; but it is two or three months later before he will sit up of himself. After that he will make decided efforts to get about, often at first by rolling over and over and then pulling himself up by sofas and chairs. Some babies will hitch themselves over the ground with considerable rapidity, and some will make efforts to creep. A baby can usually stand alone before he can creep much.

There is a great difference in the age at which babies make their first attempts at walking. Usually it is at about a year. Very ambitious and forward children will sometimes try at nine months; on the other hand, sluggish and backward children sometimes reach eighteen months without having made any effort to walk. Do not encourage the baby to walk before he is a year old, particularly if he is fat and heavy. Bow-legged children are made in that way. It is much better that he should strengthen his little legs by creeping before he puts his weight on them.

Where He is Kept.—If the baby has a nursery to himself, it should be bright and sunny, evenly warmed and well-ventilated; and this is true of any room he inhabits. On no account should there be anything like soiled or wet diapers left lying about to injure the purity of the air.

His Clothing.—The clothing should be loose and adapted to the season. It should be warm in the winter and not too warm in the summer. The child's bowels should always be protected by flannel summer and winter. In summer the flannel should be soft and light in weight. The clothing should not interfere with the freedom of the child's movements. The long dresses are usually shortened at six months; in summer this may well be done a month earlier, giving the baby a chance to kick and so strengthen his legs.

Medicines.— Give the baby as little medicine as possible, and on no account give him any sort of soothing syrup to make him sleep. This is one of the worst things you can do, making an Opium eater of him while he is still in arms.

Diseases of Children.—I have said nothing about diseases of children because that subject is ably discussed elsewhere, but I might give you a few hints in closing. Babies under a year old should be specially guarded from whooping cough. This is usually a slight ailment for children from five to ten years of age, but it is dangerous for young babies, and the younger the baby the more dangerous it becomes. Diphtheria is a scourge for old and young, but it is particularly dangerous to young children. On that account do not allow strangers to kiss or fondle your baby while it is taking its airing, and quarantine your nursery strictly against any one—man, woman or child—with a sore throat. Of the other children's diseases, scarlet fever is the only one which you need specially dread. Measles sometimes become dangerous if the child takes cold afterward and has pneumonia in consequence.

In closing this chapter, I can only wish both you and the baby long life and the best of health, and hope that following the advice I have given may contribute something to both.

WHAT A WOMAN OF FORTY-FIVE OUGHT TO KNOW.

Women approaching this age often ask questions very difficult to answer. When will the period of irregularity, rather
inelegantly called by English authors the "dodging time," begin?
How long will it last? When will the flow definitely stop? None
of these questions can be answered by positive assurance. There
is a very great difference among individual women in this respect.
One can only give something approaching a general average.
According to my experience, though I do not remember to have
seen it stated in books, the early or late closing of the menstrual
period, where it is not influenced by any disease or mental or
physical shock, is largely a matter of family habit. In some
families the married women rarely have any irregularity before
fifty, and cease menstruating at from fifty-three to fifty-five
years; in others the flow commonly ceases before forty-five.
Tait, who is the great authority on this subject, gives forty-five
years, eight and one-half months as the average date of closing.
The observations were made upon English and French women.
According to my observation, that is too early for us. Forty-
eight years seems to me much nearer the average. There is a
prevailing impression that if the menstruation begins early, it
will close early. The exact contrary is the fact; a menstruation
which begins late is more apt to finish early. There is a certain
lack of vigor in the action of the ovaries, which is shown by the
tardy appearance of the flow and which favors its early exhaustion, thus causing an early cessation of menstruation.

Married women who have borne children are, other things
being equal, later in stopping than their unmarried sisters. Some
women, not a small number, lose their courses abruptly without
any period of irregularity whatever. This is sometimes the
result of nervous shock or exposure to extreme cold at or about
the menstrual period; sometimes without any known reason.
One would naturally suppose that such women would suffer more
than others, but experience has not shown that they do. The
average length of the irregular period is a little over two years,
and the time which the various disturbances persist after the flow
has finally ceased is about the same, making a period of disturbance of rather over four years. This is, however, subject to
great variations. Sometimes it is very much shortened and, on
the other hand, it may be lengthened to ten or twelve years.

Feeling of Apprehension.—Most women look forward to this period of their lives with great apprehension, feeling sure that a great body of diseases is waiting to spring upon them at this time. This is largely a misapprehension. It is no doubt a period of strain in which the weak points in the constitution come to the front, but healthy women with well-balanced nervous systems come through the time, in nine cases out of ten, with a very moderate amount of discomfort, often hardly giving the matter a thought. "I was so busy in those days that I hardly thought of it," one woman said to me when I asked her how she had come through the change. She was not by any means robust, but as far as her sexual organs were concerned she was well. The flow, when it does appear after the irregularity begins, is apt to be accompanied by more pain than customary. It is also very irregular in duration and in quantity. I have known a slight flow—only just enough to make it desirable to wear a napkin—to persist for three months when there was no disease whatever. Such a flow, when it is so slight as not to be weakening, need cause no alarm. On the other hand, a profuse flow which tends to persist is caused, almost without exception, by some diseased condition which can be corrected by medical treatment. The most common cause is granulations of the mucous membrane inside the womb, which can be removed by scraping out the womb, or, if they are not very bad, are sometimes made to disappear by astringent applications.

Hot Flashes.—The most universal discomfort of this time which all women notice more or less, but which in some is only a slight inconvenience while in others it amounts to very positive suffering, are the *hot flashes*, so-called. These flashes are very varied in their effects. Sometimes a great wave of heat passes over the whole body, making one feel as if the room were intolerably hot; sometimes a special portion of the body, as a foot, an arm or a hand, feels as if it were on fire. These flashes ordinarily last only two or three minutes, though the time may well seem longer to the person enduring them. They are often preceded or followed by a shivering fit; more frequently followed perhaps by a drenching perspiration. There is sometimes, though I think not often, palpitation of the heart and other nervous disturbances. These flashes occur with most varying frequency—from three or four a day to the same number an hour. Most women pay but little attention to them, but to some, as I have said before, they become nearly intolerable. I know of nothing that will drive them away altogether, but Bromide of Potash, from five to ten grains two or three times a day in plenty of water—about half a tumblerful for each dose—will certainly diminish their severity and frequency.

Both women who are anxious to have children and women who are very unwilling to have them, often suppose themselves to be pregnant at the change of life. The former are much harder than the latter to be persuaded of their error. I remember one woman over fifty who had the year before lost her youngest child, a young girl to whom she was devoted. She was delighted by the prospect of another child, and I had the greatest difficulty in persuading her that she was not pregnant, though she had absolutely no symptoms of it except the disappearance of the menstrual flow. Pregnancy at an age over forty-five is rare, and the rarity increases with each succeeding year; so a woman between forty-five and fifty need not take pregnancy into the account when she notices that the monthly flow has failed to appear. It is true that it is still possible, but it is so very unlikely that it need not be considered.

Diseases Which Are Feared at This Time. — The diseases which most women associate with change of life are tumors, ovarian and uterine, and cancer. Ovarian tumors are much more common in younger women, and, far from being caused by the change of life, are rare at that time. Fibroid tumors of the womb may appear at any time, though they are more common in early middle life. In most cases they are favorably affected by the change, so that I usually advise a woman suffering from one, who is decidedly over forty and not in any present danger, to wait for the change of life before undergoing an operation; for at that time tumors of moderate size often disappear altogether, or at least shrink so as to make no further trouble.

Cancer is a disease of old age, though in some forms it is occasionally seen in young people, or even in children. There is no doubt that it occurs more frequently between the ages of forty and sixty, but it has not on that account any real connection with change of life. With men it also occurs most frequently at that age.

Nervous Disturbances.—The real troubles which are to be directly attributed to the change of life are those of the circulation which I have mentioned and which are all but universal—flooding, which, when it is severe, is almost if not quite always due to some diseased condition which can be removed by surgery; and some nervous disturbances of which I will now speak. Some women have nervous systems extremely sensitive to impressions, especially from the sexual organs. Such women are apt to be depressed and irritable during menstruation, and sometimes perhaps to have hysterical attacks at such times. They are extremely irritable and unreasonable during pregnancy, particularly towards its close, and such women are apt to suffer from nervous disorders during change of life. They are unreasonable and bad-tempered to such a degree that servants will not stay with them, and the family escape them as much as possible; or they are melancholy, sitting for hours brooding over petty annoyances hardly worth a second thought; or they suffer from a confusion of ideas, find it hard to fix their attention, lose confidence in themselves, and are often tormented by the fear of becoming insane. Very few, comparatively speaking, do become insane, and of those few, unless it is hereditary, the insanity is usually curable. Suicide is not uncommon among this class of patients.

Something may be done for these nervous disturbances by medical treatment. The bowels should be kept freely open, and a long warm bath, where the patient remains for an hour or more in the water, is an excellent sedative. Sleep should be secured at all hazards, even if it becomes necessary to give medicine for this purpose. Often change of air and scene and entire relief from household cares prove beneficial. In its beginning, in many of these cases, much may be done by the patient herself. This sensitiveness of the nervous system to the influence of other organs is a physical, not a mental condition. The impulse to speak the ill-natured word is strong, but is not, at least at first, irresistible. I have known cases of this nervous temperament combined with a strong will and sturdy common sense, where month by month and year by year the impulses were steadily fought down and the expression of them prevented, till at last the battle was permanently won. Unfortunately this combination is rare.

Other Possible Disturbances.—There is another matter to be considered. This is, as I have said, a period of special strain and, when women are not in sound health, the evils lurking in the system are apt to come to the front. A woman with defective heart valves will be apt to suffer from disturbed heart action, palpitations, fainting fits, etc. A woman whose stomach or liver is her weak point, is apt to suffer very much from digestive troubles. There is not often trouble with the lungs, for weak lungs are rather benefited than otherwise by the economy of blood gained by the suppression of the monthly flow, and the lungs do not react easily to nervous disturbances. If the bladder is irritable, it is apt to be troublesome. There will be difficulty in retaining the urine, and sometimes pain in passing it. These troubles are only indirectly owing to the change of life. They are the reaction of weak and sensitive organs to the disturbance of the whole system.

What can be done to pass this critical period with the least possible disturbance? Plenty of gentle exercise should be taken, but also plenty of rest. One should not work to the point of great fatigue, bodily or mentally. The food should be bland and not stimulating—not very much meat, only weak tea and coffee, and that in moderate quantity, and absolutely no wine or beer. The bowels should be kept freely open, and the skin kept in the best possible condition by daily warm, not hot, baths. By this means much of the used-up matter in the system is carried off and the tension relieved. Excitement should be avoided and regular hours kept.

It is very undesirable to marry at this time, particularly for women who have never been married before. The organs, already in a state of more or less disturbance, bear the unaccustomed stimulus of marriage very badly.

Caution.—I have a word of caution to give in closing this subject. It is not safe for every woman above forty to take it for granted that every disturbance of the menses comes from the impending change. In that way diseased conditions, which might at first have been easily remedied, become much more serious by neglect. The increased flow and the dribbling of blood between the periods may be the result of a polypus, which a few twists of the forceps will remove; or of a cancer, for which the only hope is in an early operation; or of some other diseased condition which needs prompt treatment. The change to which the conditions are ascribed may yet be several years distant.

A few months after the flow has definitely ceased the woman's health begins to improve, very slowly at first, and at the same time, in a large number of cases, she begins to put on flesh. The improvement persists until at the end of the second year she has quite commonly better health than she has known for years. The Indian Summer of life has commenced for her, and more often than not long years of usefulness and peace are opening before her.

DISEASES OF WOMEN.

MENSTRUATION.

In order properly to understand this subject, it is necessary first to give a

Description of the Ovaries.—The ovaries are small, somewhat elongated oval bodies about 1½ inches in length, ¾ of an inch wide and ⅓ of an inch thick. They are situated one on each side of and a little distant from the uterus. They are attached to the uterus by ligaments and by the Fallopian tubes. They are a part of the reproductive organs of the female, and furnish the ovum, or egg, which passes through the Fallopian tubes into the uterus. They consist of a large number of small bodies called the Graafian vesicles, named after their discoverer. These small bodies are about $\frac{1}{100}$ of an inch in diameter and are embedded in a framework of tissue. They contain the ovum, or egg, and both the vesicles and ovum are formed as follows:

The ovaries are surrounded or enclosed with certain membranes, and, like all other tissues, these membranes are composed of little cells. After the age of puberty the cells constituting the inner layer are constantly changing. First, they gradually enlarge, then become detached or separated from the membrane, after which they are surrounded by another delicate membrane. The cell and its membrane constitutes a Graafian vesicle. The cell continues to undergo a series of changes until it is transformed into the ovum, or egg. Later, and at regular intervals, some of these eggs rupture the membranes which enclose them and pass through the Fallopian tubes into the uterus.

The tubes which convey the eggs to the uterus are about four inches in length. They are considerably curved in their course; while the ovary is situated at the outer end of the tube, it is only about one inch distant from the uterus. The opening through these tubes is very small—perhaps large enough to admit the passage of a fine bristle. The tubes are composed of three coats. The inner coat is mucous membrane which is continuous with that lining the uterus; the middle is a muscular coat and is continuous from

415

the muscular walls of the uterus; and the outer coat is formed of peritoneum, the same membrane which lines the abdominal cavity. The tubes join the uterus at the upper or superior angles, one on each side. Really the uterus, tubes and ovaries may be considered as one organ. The different parts are designed to discharge the various duties necessary for the fulfillment of its purpose in life.

The Graafian vesicles and ovum are present in infancy, and even in fetal life. During the early years their blood supply is limited. They remain quiet until near the time of what is called puberty, when their blood supply is increased, and this excites a more active condition. They begin to enlarge, and continue to increase in size until one of them ruptures its membrane or capsule and escapes into the uterus as described. During the time these changes have been going on, the uterus has also received an increased blood supply and the mucous membrane lining its cavity has become highly congested. When the egg drops into the uterus, the vessels of the membrane rupture, there is a flow of blood, and the egg is carried onward and may or may not escape from the body. When this condition becomes established, it occurs at regular intervals and constitutes what is called

Menstruation.—This periodical condition or change naturally occurs once in twenty-eight days. However, from three to six weeks may be normal in exceptional cases. There is an increase in the blood pressure throughout the body, with special tendency toward the uterus and pelvic organs. During pregnancy menstruation is absent, though occasionally it may continue at the regular period for a few months, or in a light form throughout the term. It is also absent during the nursing period.

Cause.—This is Nature's means or method of bringing about certain conditions necessary to the propagation of the human race.

Symptoms. — When occurring normally, the symptoms are few and light. There may be a sense of fullness, heaviness and slight irritability about the pelvic organs. When occurring the first time, in exceptional cases there may be fever, restlessness, nervous phenomena, etc., but these all disappear with the beginning of the flow. When menstruation is painful, when it is excessive or when it is diminished, it is an indication of disease, either local or general.

Menstruation Diminished. — This is a condition where the flow is diminished, but not entirely checked.

Cause.—It may result from exposure, wet feet, insufficient clothing or fright; or a chronic form may result from wasting diseases.

Symptoms.—Occurring in the acute form, fever, constipation, headache, loss of appetite, etc. The symptoms may vary all the way from slight to more serious conditions, and even delirium be present. The symptoms of the chronic form are those of the conditions which produce it.

TREATMENTS.—

What to Do.—In the acute form give Aconite, or such other remedies as are used in fevers, and active cathartics; place the feet in hot water, give hot drinks, and lay hot fomentations across the abdomen. This treatment relieves congestion by equalizing the circulation. If the case becomes serious, a physician should be called.

A. If the patient is healthy, many physicians give no treatment where the flow is diminished or suppressed, but wait until the next regular period. It should be remembered that in some cases there may be considerable irregularity, even in a healthy subject, during the first year or so. Such cases need no special attention.

In the chronic form the treatment should be directed to general improvement.

AMENORRHEA.—Amenorrhea is absence or suppression of the menses. After the flow has been established it does not take place, or may be retained.

Cause.—There are several conditions which tend to a lowering of the vital forces, and this contributes to amenorrhea, as: unhealthy surroundings, poor food, indigestion, too much hard work, worry, fright, anæmia, and wasting diseases, especially consumption. By stopping the loss of blood Nature tries to reserve the forces of the patient. Amenorrhea is present during pregnancy, and after the removal of the uterus or ovaries.

TREATMENTS.—

A. What these cases usually require is that which is best calculated to restore bodily strength and vigor. Improve the hygienic surroundings, give tonics, plain, nourishing food, fresh air and sunshine. It is a mistake in these cases to give remedies merely for the purpose of producing a flow of the menses. *Restore the general system.* This will be the most certain to re-establish the menstrual period.

There is a form of amenorrhea that is congenital—exists from birth. These cases may be due to the absence or lack of development of the uterus or ovaries, or to an imperforate hymen —one without opening. If amenorrhea is accompanied by good health and a lively disposition, let the case alone. Such cases occur sometimes, and need no treatment whavever.

B. I use Lloyd's Leontin in 30-drop doses four times a day. —(30).

C. Plethoric (full-blooded) subjects may take the following:

> Permanganate of Potash .... 12 grains.
> Petroleum Jelly sufficient to fill 12 No. 2 capsules.

Take one capsule before eating until all are taken, commencing two days before the time for the expected period.—(32).

DYSMENORRHEA.—Dysmenorrhea indicates a difficult or painful menstruation.

Causes.—There are several conditions which produce this trouble or disease, such as congestion, laceration or ulcers; it may be neuralgic or rheumatic in its nature; it may be due to anæmia; or there may be mechanical interference, such as displacement or stenosis. Stenosis in this case means a narrowing of the external opening. It may be membranous, *i. e.*, the lining membrane of the uterus may be cast off in shreds; or, in exceptional cases the membrane may be expelled altogether, giving a complete cast of the uterus. In unmarried women the most frequent cause is stenosis. In this case the pain comes on a few hours or a day or two before the flow, and stops when the flow is established. In married women the most frequent cause is displacement and the inflammation which follows it.

TREATMENTS.—

A. In the case of young girls examination is not justifiable until other means have failed. Give cathartics if needed. If the patient is nervous before the periods give for a day or two 10-grain doses of Bromide of Soda together with 5 grains of Valerianate of Ammonia, every four hours. If there is much fever, give Aconite; if there is a history of rheumatism, give 20 grains of Salicylate of Soda four times a day, and keep the bowels active. If the patient is anæmic, give tonics, out-of-door exercise and nourishing diet. Morphine is seldom required. Any one of the Uterine Tonics given under MISCELLANEOUS MEDICAL RECEIPTS (see Index) will be found a specific in many cases and of great benefit in others, when not due to mechanical interference. Stenosis, prolapses or other forms of displacement, require surgical interference.

B. Put the patient to bed and apply hot water bag or hot poultice to lower part of abdomen. Give foot-bath in hot Mustard water. Evacuate the bowels as early as possible by giving 5 grains of Calomel and by rectal injection of one quart of hot soapy water.

The following combination will control pain and nervousness:

Bromide of Potash...................... 4 drachms.
Chloral Hydrate .... 2½ "
Chloroform Water....................... 4 ounces.

Give two teaspoonfuls in a little water every two or three hours.

It is unwise to give Laudanum or other opiates for the relief of this condition, because when they are once inaugurated the patient is very liable to acquire a drug habit—a condition far worse than the original disease. If these attacks are persistent and occur with each menstrual epoch, consult a good physician and allow him to dilate the uterine canal.—(49).

C. Squaw Vine, Fluid Extract........... ½ ounce.
Black Haw,   "   "   .... 1 ounce.
Dogwood,   "   "   .... ½ "
Hyoscyamus, "   "   .... ½ "
Codeine Sulphate .... 8 grains.
Simple Elixir, enough to make...... 4 ounces.

Mix, and take 1 teaspoonful three times a day for two or three days before the period commences.—(31).

D. Pulsatilla Tincture... 1 drop every half hour while the pain continues.—(41).

E. Make a tea of Chamomile plant (see chapter on HERBS) and drink three or four times daily for six weeks.—(38).

MENORRHAGIA.—Menorrhagia is a term applied to an excessive menstrual flow.

Cause.—The cause may be inflammation of the uterus, tubes or ovaries; or inflammation of the pelvic organs outside the uterus may cause it. It may be caused by tumors in the uterus or ovaries; or it may be caused by erosion, by subinvolution or by hyperplasia (see DISEASES OF THE WOMB).

TREATMENTS.—

A. Put the patient to bed and maintain absolute quiet. Give 1 teaspoonful Fluid Extract of Ergot every hour for two or three doses, or 20-drop doses of Tincture of Belladonna, or 10-drop doses of Tincture of Iron. These remedies are valuable in the order given. If the case is urgent, raise the foot of the bed on two chairs and insert small pieces of cotton into the vagina. Excessive flow without any discernible cause may be cured by a long-continued use of Fluid Extract of Hydrastis in ½ teaspoonful doses four times a day.

B. Fluid Extract Golden Seal.............. 1 ounce
Fluid Extract Ergot....................... 1   "

Mix, and take teaspoonful doses every three hours, more or less often, according to the severity of the case.—(31).

C. Fluid Extract Ergot..................... ½ ounce.
Simple Syrup enough to make...... 4 ounces.

Take 1 teaspoonful every three hours, or oftener if needed. Rest in bed is absolutely necessary if flowing is very excessive.—(42).

METORRHAGIA.—Metorrhagia is usually understood to mean an excessive uterine hemhorrage *between* the menstrual periods.

Cause.—It may be caused by some of the conditions mentioned under *Menorrhagia*, by polypus, cancer, threatened abortion, retained part of the after-birth following labor, or placenta prævia, *i. e.*, where the placenta or after-birth grows directly over the external uterine opening.

TREATMENT.—

The treatment is the same as for *Menorrhagia*. In all cases where the hemorrhage is excessive or where pregnancy is suspected, send for a physician.

GREEN SICKNESS—CHLOROSIS.—This is a term applied to a particular form of anæmia, often distinguished by a greenish-yellow coloration of the skin. It occurs in young persons, chiefly girls about puberty. It is an anæmic (see ANÆMIA) condition of a pronounced type.

Cause.—Disturbances of nutrition beginning with indigestion and constipation.

Symptoms.—The skin assumes a pallid hue, the flesh becomes flabby, and the countenance after the menses, which are either scanty or suppressed, has a greenish-yellow cast. There is no loss of flesh, instead the patient sometimes takes on fat. The feet and legs have a tendency to swell, the patient tires easily, has palpitation on slight exertion, the appetite is usually depraved, the digestion impaired and constipation the rule. *Gastric Ulcer* (see STOMACH, ULCER OF) may occur, and consumption, especially in those predisposed, is a common result.

TREATMENTS.—

The treatment consists in nourishing diet and every attention to the general health. Any of the following remedies may be taken to advantage:

A. Tincture Chloride of Iron.............. ½ ounce.
    Glycerine .... 2 ounces.
    Simple Elixir, add to................... 4   "
        Give 1 teaspoonful after meals and at bed-
        time.—(82).

B. Fellows' Syrup of Hypophosphites 5 ounces.
    Maltine, or any good preparation
      of Extract of Malt.................... 10   "
        Mix by shaking the bottle, and take a table-
    spoonful after meals and at bedtime—four doses
    a day.

C. Fowler's Solution...................... 2 drachms.
    Fluid Hydrastus......................... 4   "
    Glycerine................................. 2 ounces.
    Simple Elixir, add to................. 4   "
        Mix. Take teaspoonful four times a day—
    after meals and at bedtime.

D. Blaud's Pills—5 grains each. Take 1 at meal time and at bedtime—four a day.

E. Wyeth's Peptonate of Iron and Manganese. Dose on label on bottle.

Tablespoonful dose of Epsom Salts every morning.—(7).

CONFINEMENT, AND ATTENDANT DANGERS AND DISEASES.

Pregnancy, Signs of.—The following are the signs of pregnancy: Cessation of menstruation; a uniform development of the uterus, the organ beginning to enlarge from the fourth to the sixth week; regular and gradual enlargement of the abdominal cavity, beginning about the third month; morning vomiting, which commences about the fourth or fifth week and lasts for three months, more or less—this is sometimes absent, and sometimes very persistent; gradual enlargement of the breasts, the change occurring about the second or third month—slight soreness may be present, also change of color about the nipples, the skin becoming darker; movement of the child. It should be remembered that any of these symptoms may occur without pregnancy, even imaginary movement of the child; but when occurring together, the case is certainly suspicious and undoubtedly the condition of pregnancy exists. The only positive sign is hearing the fetal heart beat. Usually this can be heard about the fourth month.

To Calculate Time of Confinement.—The usual method is to count nine months from the cessation of the last menstrual period and add one week. This is equivalent to 280 days. The limits are said to be from 250 to 300 days. Some authorities put it as high as 317 days. There is always a period of uncertainty of one or two weeks because the exact time of conception is seldom known.

ABORTION—MISCARRIAGE.—In law and medicine *Abortion* is generally understood to mean the expulsion of the fetus from the uterus at any time before viability, or before the child is capable of maintaining life. By some abortion is applied to the expulsion of the fetus during the first three months of pregnancy. From the third to about the seventh month is called *Miscarriage;* from the seventh month to maturity or full term is called *Premature Labor*, or *Premature Delivery*. With some the term abortion is associated with the idea of criminality, that is, that abortion is brought on intentionally; hence the term has fallen somewhat into disuse and "miscarriage" has taken its place.

Causes or Conditions that Produce Abortion. — Disease or injury of the fetus; disease or injury of the mother; disease of the placenta, or what is commonly called the after-birth; hemorrhage beneath and seperation of the placenta from its attachment to the uterus; syphilis; rupture of the membrane which encloses the fetus, either accidentally or intentionally; high temperature from some forms of fever; any conditions producing congestion and inflammation of the pelvic organs and uterus; and irritation of the uterus from tumor growth. Death of the fetus may or may not result in abortion. Severe mental shock is said to produce abortion in some cases. It is sometimes produced by drugs. Perhaps one of the most common causes of abortion is inflammation of the mucous membrane lining the uterus. This membrane is sometimes called the endometrium. For cause of such inflammation see INFLAMMATION OF THE UTERUS.

Symptoms.—The symptoms are not unlike those of ordinary labor. The difference is governed somewhat by the age of the fetus. There is pain, which may be located in the back, in the front of the abdomen, in the groins, or may be most prominent in the uterus itself. These same variations often occur in regular labor. There is dilatation of the opening into the uterus. Hemorrhage is usually severe, because the placenta or after-birth is firmly attached to the walls of the uterus and is torn loose rather than separated naturally, as in the case of full term.

TREATMENT.—

The treatment in a case of abortion is the same as that following regular labor (see LABOR).

Dangers of Abortion.—During the early stages of pregnancy the membranes which surround the fetus and the placenta are more delicate in structure than the mature growth. The placenta is firmly attached to the walls of the uterus, hence the danger of some parts being torn off and remaining adherent to the walls of the organ. Such remaining tissue would die, decompose, and the poisons from it absorbed into the circulation would produce what is called *Puerperal Fever* or *Septicæmia;* in other words, blood poisoning would occur. Sometimes such remaining tissue is said to become organized, *i. e.,* surrounded and permeated by bands of new connective tissue fibers. Later, blood vessels are supplied, and the growth continues and results in what is called a *Fibroid Tumor,* meaning a tumor of hard tissue. In any case where parts of the after-birth remain, the uterus remains large and contains too much blood. This condition is described under *Subinvolution.* The inflammation resulting from retained parts of the after-birth may extend to the abdominal cavity and produce *Peritonitis.* The greatest danger exists from the third to the sixth month, because the placenta is most firmly adherent at this time.

Another reason why abortion is more dangerous than labor at full term is that it is contrary to nature; and there are many ways, impossible to describe, in which the patient may suffer from some form of weakness or disease as a result of it. This is especially true in cases where abortion occurs more than once.

To Prevent Abortion.—In case of threatened abortion the patient should lie down and remain absolutely quiet. The foot of the bed should be raised and placed on two chairs, and ¼ grain of Morphine should be given with a hypodermic needle. Visitors should be kept out of the room, and all excitement avoided. These cases need the services of a physician. If a case has progressed too far, or if the membranes have been ruptured, delivery cannot be prevented. There are other means of treatment recommended, but we have always adopted this plan with a reasonable degree of success.

When Should Abortion, or Premature Labor, Be Produced.—When the pelvis is so deformed that a full grown child cannot be delivered after the seventh month. At seven months the child may live. When the pelvis is deformed, some recommend allowing the case to go to full term, and then open the abdominal cavity and the uterus, remove the child and close up the wound. This is called *Cæsarian section* or *Cæsarian operation,* so-called because it is said Julius Cæsar was thus delivered. Premature labor is also advised by some in case of tumor growths in the abdominal cavity; when the kidneys become diseased and the urine contains a large amount of albumen; and when there is what is called *placenta prævia*, that is, where the placenta, or after-birth, grows directly over the opening into the uterus, and this condition is followed, after the sixth or seventh month, with frequent profuse and dangerous hemorrhages; also advised in some cases of Puerperal Convulsions occurring before time for normal labor.

PLACENTA PRÆVIA.—*Placenta Prævia* means that the placenta, or after-birth, grows more or less directly over the opening in the lower part of the uterus. Normally, it grows near the top. In *Placenta Prævia* there is usually more or less frequent and profuse hemorrhage after the sixth or seventh month; sometimes it occurs earlier. The later hemorrhage makes its appearance, the more favorable the case. *Placenta Prævia* does not often occur. Some authorities claim that the percentage is one to one thousand. Others claim that the percentage is even less.

Cause. — The placenta, being placed over the lower and smaller part of the uterus, it follows that, as the organ dilates to accommodate the growth of the child, and more especially since the growth of the placenta and enlargement of the uterus are unequal, the placenta is occasionally torn loose at some point; hence the hemorrhage. *Placenta Prævia* is always considered a serious condition, because the uterus dilates with the approach of labor and the placenta is torn loose, as described. Heretofore the uterus has expanded or enlarged gradually, but now it dilates rapidly and the torn vessels are left wide open. As the blood is pouring from these, others are being constantly ruptured, and the condition continues to grow worse until dilatation is complete; and even then the placenta is in the way of the child because it is below and the child is above.

Symptoms.—Hemorrhage, more or less profuse, which may occur at any time, day or night. The hemorrhage differs from that in threatened abortion from the fact that there is no pain present. The pain produced in threatened abortion is due to contractions of the uterus; in hemorrhage from *Placenta Prævia* there is no contraction. The hemorrhage is due to separation of the placenta, as stated above.

While hemorrhage is a symptom of *Placenta Prævia*, it does not necessarily follow that this condition is present, and especially if the hemorrhage occurs at what would have been the time for the regular monthly period. There are cases where the regular monthly flow occurs with more or less regularity during the whole course of pregnancy.

TREATMENT.—

In a case of labor with *Placenta Prævia*, it is usually necessary to deliver the child as rapidly as possible. It is expected that there will be a good deal of hemorrhage, and the hope cf a successful termination lies in the rapid delivery followed by contraction of the uterus. The contraction closes the torn vessels and checks the hemorrhage. It is necessary to separate the placenta forcibly and rapidly. This must be done by mechanical means. If the head of the child is presenting, apply the forceps and deliver at once; or a foot may be grasped by the hand and delivered without delay. In these cases dilating the lower part of the uterus is sometimes difficult, because, following the growth of the after-birth at this point, the uterus has become thickened and rigid and dilates with difficulty. It is needless to say that these cases require a doctor from the first. The doctor should be composed and deliberate, and at the same time energetic and thorough. Having his mind made up regarding the dangers of the case, he should proceed with energy and determination. Cases of *Placenta Prævia* are reported where no hemorrhage occurs, not even during labor. If hemorrhage occurs early and is profuse and persistent, an abortion is sometimes recommended.

LABOR.—Labor is the process whereby the child and its placental attachments are expelled from the uterus. What is called the *first stage* of labor consists of dilatation of the opening into the uterus. The *second stage* consists of the expulsion of the child, and the *third stage*, the expulsion of the placenta, or after-birth, and the contraction of the uterus. The first and second stages are largely theoretical. In the great majority of cases perhaps the attending physician does not know when one ceases and the other begins. In any event such division is unimportant and possesses no value whatever.

Symptoms.—The first indications of approaching labor are said to occur about two weeks before it actually begins. At this time the uterus is said to change its position by settling lower down in the pelvic cavity. This is said to afford great relief from previous annoyances, and that walking, breathing, etc., become easier. While the change in position probably occurs, as stated, it is our experience that such change is seldom noticed by the prospective mother.

The pains are caused by the contraction of the uterus. At first the organ is unaided in its efforts, but later the muscles of the abdominal wall are brought into action and undoubtedly aid materially in the delivery. Sometimes light pains, and even those that are quite severe, occur with considerable regularity at times for several days before labor actually begins; sometimes they do not. Usually light pains are present more or less for perhaps twenty-four hours before actual labor commences. When the time comes that Nature has designed for the uterus to free itself, or for the child to be born, the pains become more regular and severe. At first they may vary from one-half hour to twenty minutes apart, and last perhaps for one-half to one minute. Gradually they become longer, harder and more frequent.

During what is called the *second stage* the "bearing down" pains occur. During this time the patient is conscious of an effort to expel the child from the uterus, and unconsciously summons to her aid all her strength. This is generally satisfying from the belief that she is going to succeed. The pains may be most severe in the back, in front, or may seem to be confined largely to the uterus. Sometimes even during the most severe part of the trial the patient will suddenly ask for a drink or something to eat. Such requests should always be granted.

In most cases, under proper management, severe pains do not continue for more than one or two hours before the child is born. As soon as this event occurs and the child is found to be alive and normal in appearance, the cord should be tied with a strong thread about 2½ inches from the abdomen of the child. It should be tied a second time about 1 inch further distant, and cut between the knots with a pair of sharp scissors. The child should then be wrapped in a warm flannel blanket and placed in another room that has been well warmed and ventilated.

After the event is over the mother experiences a great sense of relief, and sometimes desires to be let alone for a short time. In other cases there is no particular wish or desire. After waiting about twenty minutes, if the after-birth is not expelled and there are no pains indicating that it is going to be expelled, gentle manipulation should be made over the uterus, which can be plainly outlined. One hand, or better, perhaps, both hands, may make gradual and uniform pressure upon the organ. In a short time, usually a few minutes, this will stimulate further contraction with the result that the after-birth will be separated from the inner surface of the uterus and can be easily removed. The cord should not be used as a means of delivering the after-birth, and only slight traction should be made upon it. It is probably always safe to exert a force equal to lifting a one-pound weight. Following the expulsion of the after-birth, the manipulations of the uterus should be continued until it contracts to a reasonable size—perhaps the size of a cocoanut. Such manipulation not only eliminates the placenta, but also aids in eliminating any detached parts, blood clots, etc.

Reducing the size of the uterus not only prevents hemorrhage, but renders the organ natural and places the mother beyond possible danger.

TREATMENT.—

In our experience with labor cases we have never given any particular attention to rules or theories of any kind. In caring for a large number of cases we have, with two exceptions, never spent more than two or three hours with any single case, and usually a much shorter time. We have never used the forceps— never have had occasion to do so. The following is our method of procedure:

First, instruct the nurse to give a rectal injection and secure thorough action of the bowels. Also give a vaginal douche of warm water, containing a little Boric Acid. Next, by careful manipulation gradually dilate the opening into the uterus. This effort stimulates uterine contractions, usually within a few minutes, and the contractions aid in dilation. The child and more or less water are contained in a membrane forming a sac. The water is more freely movable than the child, hence with each contraction of the uterus the water is forced against the opening, rendering the membrane tense at that point. The membrane with its contained water produces pressure from within, which not only aids in dilating the uterus, but, the pressure being uniform, insures equal expansion. As soon as the opening is sufficiently large, rupture the membrane, allowing the water to escape. The way being clear and the contractions strong and active as a result of the foregoing, delivery follows rapidly.

We understand that the claim might be made that such rapid delivery is dangerous because of its liability to rupture the external parts. However, in our experience rupture has occurred only two or three times, and then it was slight. When rupture occurs it should be repaired at once.

There are, of course, cases where, as a result of some deformity, abnormal presentation or other cause, this or any other method of managing a case might prove disastrous.

Note on Ergot.—We are aware that many physicians use Ergot in confinement cases, but we have never had a case where we thought it necessary to use this remedy. True, it may aid in the contraction of the uterus after the child is born, but if the organ has been freed from all parts of the after-birth, it will contract without it; if it has not been so freed, it will not and should not close. Ergot may contract the circular fibers about the *lower end* or neck of the uterus and thus prevent proper drainage of blood clots or any remnants of the after-birth, and prove a most dangerous remedy.

We were early taught to believe that Ergot was not only an important, but in many cases a necessary remedy in labor, but after a careful survey of the field and gathering all the information we could on the subject, we became convinced that it did more harm than good. By a study of its history we have been able to trace many cases of Child-Bed Fever to the use of Ergot; at least we were unable to detect any other cause. Certain it is that this trouble results oftenest in those cases where Ergot is used.

Caution.—Too much cannot be said regarding careful attention to physical exercise following confinement. Several weeks—perhaps two months—are required for the uterus to regain its normal size and function. Perhaps one of the greatest reasons for chronic enlargement of the uterus, accompanied with the many associate symptoms and conditions, is the direct result of getting up too soon, or more especially of resuming active duties before the physical strength is able to meet the demands of such duties. This is more apt to be the case following abortion, because with many abortions are looked upon with less consideration of their importance; in fact, we have known many cases where, following abortion, the patient was up and in the discharge of her routine duties in a few days. This is contrary to all physical law, and those indulging in such practice are sure to bring on derangement and disease.

FLOODING.—By flooding is meant hemorrhage from the uterus.

Causes.—More or less hemorrhage may result from a polypus (see TUMORS). Hemorrhage may result from *Cancer*, especially during the late stages. It more frequently results from *Abortion* (see ABORTION), from *Placenta Prævia* as explained under that head, or from failure of the uterus to contract after delivery of the child, as explained under *Labor*.

TREATMENTS.—

What to Do Till the Doctor Comes.—Place the patient on a bed, laying her on her back. Use no pillows under her head nor anything to raise it. Raise the foot of the bed by placing blocks, or something of the kind, under it. Get the doctor as quickly as possible. Have hot water on hand when he arrives.

A. *Following Confinement.*—Where there is dangerous hemorrhage following delivery, it may be almost instantly checked by making pressure on the abdominal aorta. It will be remembered that this is the large artery which comes from the heart. It passes down through the chest and abdominal cavities to about three-quarters of an inch below the umbilicus, or navel, and there divides into two branches. Pressure should be made *just at or a little above* the point of division. In many cases, by maintaining firm pressure at the point indicated for some time, the hemorrhage will not return.

Another means of treating hemorrhage is by giving $\frac{1}{100}$ or $\frac{1}{50}$ of a grain of Atropine with a hypodermic needle. As stated many times before, this dilates the small vessels all over the body and allows the blood to drain away from any congested part. Mechanical pressure may be made, as stated, while the Atropine is being prepared, administered and taking effect. However, all this requires but a short time.

Washing out the uterus with hot vinegar, packing it with ice, crowding tampons against the lower end of it and other methods are advised; but we have always used the first named, and have succeeded so well that we feel safest in recommending that treatment. In all cases it is well to raise the foot of the bed, placing the posts on two chairs.

B. When following confinement, administer one or two ounces of strong vinegar. Knead womb till contraction occurs and send for a doctor, keeping a firm hold on womb in the meantime. Raise foot of bed a foot or two.—(60).

C. Give hot salt water injections (tablespoonful of salt to quart of water) as hot as can be borne by the patient. Use large quantity. Repeat if the hemorrhage returns. Give patient Cinnamon tea to drink. Raise foot of bed to give the body slope towards the head. These means will control nearly every case by the time of arrival of the physician.—(15).

CHILD-BED FEVER—PUERPERAL FEVER—SEPTICÆMIA.

—*Cause.*—This is caused by the retention and decomposition of the after-birth, or fragments of it, following labor. The poisons produced by the decomposing remains are absorbed into the circulation, and *Septicæmia*, or *Blood Poisoning*, follows. When it occurs, it usually makes its appearance from two to four days after confinement.

Symptoms.—There is a sense of chilliness or a severe chill, and high temperature, which develops rapidly and may increase to 105 or 106, or even higher. The pulse ranges from 130 to 160. At first the face is flushed. There is no pain and the mind is clear. Among the early symptoms are soreness of the uterus and fetid odor produced by the discharges. Later the discharge is diminished and the secretions of the breasts are lessened.

The uterus is partially covered with the peritoneum that lines the abdominal cavity, hence peritonitis may follow. In this case the temperature would be slight, and might even be subnormal, though the pulse would be rapid. The abdomen would be more or less distended. Pain would be slight.

TREATMENT.—

First, clean out the uterus by mechanical means. Be sure that all placental remains and blood clots are removed, then wash out the organ with 2 quarts of warm water. Twenty or 30 drops of Carbolic Acid may be added to the water, or 3 or 4 drachms of Boric Acid. Repeat the douche in five or six hours; after this, perhaps once a day for a few days, although this part of the treatment should be governed by the temperature and by the odor of the eliminations.

The foregoing is the all-important method in treating cases of this kind. Drug medication is absolutely without avail so long as the poisons contained in the uterus are being absorbed into the system. The bowels should be kept active, the most nourishing food should be given, and every attention paid to free ventilation. Stimulants and tonics should be given if needed.

PUERPERAL CONVULSIONS.—This is a form of

convulsions that occurs before, during or after labor. In appearance the convulsions sometimes resemble epilepsy. While they are the result of uræmic poisoning, they differ from uræmic convulsions at other times, and especially if occurring during labor, the time they most frequently occur. In uræmic convulsions occurring at other times, the temperature is below normal; occurring during labor, there is fever, and the convulsions may follow each other in rapid succession; or the first one may prove fatal, the patient never regaining consciousness.

Cause.—The cause is the retention in the system of urea and other waste products usually eliminated by the kidneys. Mechanical interference from the enlarged uterus pressing upon the kidneys produces irritation and prevents their normal action with the result that they fail to eliminate the usual amount of waste material, and urea gradually accumulates in the system until convulsions occur.

Symptoms.—If the urine of a suspected patient was examined, albumen would be found present before there was any danger of convulsions. As a rule such examination is not made, and the first symptom of the trouble is the first convulsion or spasm. The body becomes rigid, the face blue, the eyes roll up in the head, there may be spasmodic twitching of the muscles of the face and hands, giving a ghastly appearance, and altogether death seems imminent. Or, the convulsions may come on gradually. There may be a gradually increasing nervousness, accompanied with spasmodic twitching of individual muscles, until suddenly the whole body is seized in one convulsive grasp.

TREATMENT.—

The only hope in these cases is elimination. The poison must be eliminated rapidly or death may result.

These cases require the services of a physician from the first. Temporary relief should be given by the inhalation of Chloroform. If labor has not terminated, it should be aided by mechanical interference and the child delivered as soon as possible. To control the convulsions any one of the following methods is recommended, and should be applied immediately after delivery, or sooner if the convulsions return.

Give ½ grain of Morphine with a hypodermic needle, and in thirty minutes give ¼ grain additional, if needed; or, give $\frac{1}{15}$ grain of Veratrine in the same manner; or, give 40 grains of Chloral by the stomach, largely diluted. The Chloral may be repeated in one hour, if needed, or, if some improvement is noticed, ½ the amount—20 grains additional—may be given.

Some claim to control convulsions best by bleeding. This also aids in eliminating poison. At least one pint of blood should be taken. This treatment is justifiable in the strong and robust, but not in the weak and anæmic. It is understood, of course, that if bleeding is resorted to the Morphine, Veratrine or Chloral will not be given.

As a means of elimination, give ⅓ grain of Pilocarpine with a hypodermic needle. Pilocarpine will produce profuse sweating, and is one of the most rapid means of elimination. This dose of Pilocarpine is depressing, however, and, if used, stimulants should be added—Digitalis, or hot sling, or other suitable or convenient stimulant. The sling will aid in sweating, the Digitalis will aid in elimination by the kidneys; either will stimulate the heart. Perhaps both may be needed.

As an active cathartic, give 3 drops of Croton Oil in a little Glycerine or water, and place on the back of the tongue; or give from ⅙ to ¼ grain of Elaterium. If these are not at hand, give a large dose of Castor Oil, or 20 grains of compound Jalap powder, or 20 grains of Scammony. Give rectal injections of hot soapy water to hasten the action of the bowels.

MILK LEG.— In this disease the leg becomes swollen and light in color, and the flesh is firm and resistant to the touch.

Cause.—It oftenest follows pregnancy, and is caused by the enlarged uterus pressing upon the veins and checking the return circulation. The trouble usually commences about ten days or two weeks after confinement.

Symptoms. — First, irregular chills, and malaise, meaning general bad feeling. This is followed by pain in the affected leg, and perhaps in the abdomen. The chills become more distinct. The limb begins to swell and there is fever, which is first remittent and later, intermittent. The limb becomes greatly swollen and the skin is hot, white and tense. Later the veins feel like cords beneath the finger, and an abscess may form in the course of a vein. The swelling is confined mostly to the layer of connective tissue just beneath the skin, hence the abscess would be near the surface and would break externally. The swelling may be so severe that gangrene results. This would cause *Septicæmia*, or blood poisoning. Or blood clots may form and be converted into pus. The effects of these clots would be carried away by the circulation, and this would result in *Pyæmia*, meaning pus in the blood. Recovery is slow and tedious, and the affected limb remains weak for some time.

TREATMENT.—

The patient should lie in bed and keep the limb elevated. Keep the bowels active. Apply Mercurial ointment and cover with a light bandage. This application should be repeated every second or third day. Internally, give 1-drop doses of Tincture of Aconite or Fluid Extract of Veratrum every hour until the temperature is lower. Sustain the patient with a nourishing diet. Give stimulants and tonics as needed. After there is improvement, give some form of Iodine—Syrup of Hydriodic Acid, Iodide of Ammonia, Iodide of Arsenic, or some other preparation. This will need to be continued for some time—weeks, and perhaps months—in order to free the system of the products of inflammation. Such a case requires the attention of a doctor. Give Seidlitz Salts freely from the first.

DISEASES OF BREASTS.

INFLAMMATION OF — ABSCESS OF — MILK FEVER—"BROKEN BREASTS."—The mammary glands for the secretion of milk in the breasts consist of ducts, ten or twelve in number each, called lactiferous, meaning milk-bearing. These ducts terminate externally at the nipple; internally, they branch into minute tubes like the roots of a tree. After delivery the increased nutrition that Nature had previously secreted in the uterus is diverted to the mammary glands for the sustenance of the child.

Cause.—If it happens that there is an excess of secretion in the breasts, the milk tubes become choked and distended with it. This may result in an inflammation of the glands, and in some cases the patient is subject to a sharp febrile attack, called *Milk Fever*. Inflammation may also result from checking the flow of the milk too early, from exposure, from mental disturbance, as worry, fright or undue excitement; also from external injury or pressure from too tight clothing.

Symptoms. — Severe local pain, increased by pressure, is caused by the inflammation, and upon examination there will usually be discovered a hard swelling. The tendency is towards suppuration, the fever increasing with the formation of the *Abscess*. If the abscess breaks, the condition is spoken of as *"Broken Breast."*

TREATMENTS.—

A. While hot poultices or heat in some form is most excellent treatment, always safe and the method usually employed, cold is also valuable if applied early. The first *real* evidence of inflammation of the breast is the presence of one or more small hard lumps. If a thin sack of ice is laid over the breast at this time and *kept there*, it will prove very effectual; in fact, applied early, it is the ideal treatment. There need be no fear about taking cold. Of course, the patient may catch an ordinary cold at this particular time, but she will not do so any more readily because of the ice pack over the breast. *A laxative should be given early.*—(82).

Note.— Where there is evidence of inflammation of the breast and poulticing is decided upon, the applications must be thorough. Gradually increase the heat as long as can be borne. The poultices must be changed often, depending upon the size—once in five or ten minutes. This work requires the undivided attention of an intelligent nurse.

If the case is seen early, the application of an ice bag, as recommended, will give most satisfactory results.

B. Sometimes the child does not take all the milk, in which case inflammation may result, and, frequently, an abscess. Use a breast pump. As soon as the milk is drawn, relief follows. If an abscess forms, treat as described under ABSCESSES.

C. Efficient support by bandage passing over opposite shoulder. Moist heat applied by poultices or by large pancakes with a central hole for the nipple. Free opening and drainage in case of suppuration.—(60).

D. Apply a breast binder that will hold up breasts. Heal sore nipples as rapidly as possible. If they show signs of gathering, apply hot poultices all over the breast, except the nipple. If an abscess forms, open at once.—(13).

NIPPLES.—The nipples during nursing are subject to excoriation, or cracking, making them extremely tender and causing much pain when the infant is nursing. These excoriations are obstinate to heal from the fact that they are constantly irritated, both by the clothing and by the action of the child in nursing. It sometimes occurs that the excoriations become ulcers if great care is not taken to protect the tender part.

TREATMENTS.—

A. Where the "cracks" occur, there is always some swelling or distension, however slight—the cells constituting the outer layer of the skin do not protect the deeper layer or true skin, and it is the exposure of this true skin to the atmosphere that causes burning and smarting. In a word, this constitutes sore nipples. All that is needed is some unirritating substance to cover over until a new layer of cells has time to form. Subnitrate of Bismuth made into a paste with water is one of the best remedies that can be applied to these painful conditions. It is non-irritating, protects the deeper layer or true skin, and gives opportunity for the natural protection to form, *i. e.*, the new layer of cells. The Bismuth is not only harmless to the child, but it is a benefit to the mucous membrane of the mouth, offering the same protection here that it does to the nipples. Another advantage in using Bismuth is that it has no taste.

B. In all cases of sore nipples the child's mouth should be washed several times a day with pure water, or, what is better, 2 ounces of water containing ¼ drachm of Boric Acid. Dust the irritated parts with Subnitrate of Bismuth.—(82).

C. Tablespoon heaping full of Catnip (use leaves and small sprigs only) and sweet cream enough to make paste. Mix and simmer for a day, then strain close and stir till cool. After nursing wash nipples with Castile soap and warm rain water and apply paste.—(14).

D. Wash nipples with Borax water after each nursing, then cover them with Zinc Ointment and protect with soft cotton till next nursing time. If this makes them hard or cracks them, use Cosmoline or fresh mutton tallow every other time. Cleanse before nursing. Let babe nurse only every three hours, and only one breast at a time. If not better soon, get nipple shield for babe to nurse through.—(13).

> **E.** Tannic Acid............................. 2 drachms.
> Glycerine...................................... 2 ounces.
> *Mix*, and apply locally every two to four hours.—(46).

BREASTS OF INFANTS, MILK IN.—Shortly after birth a secretion of milk-like fluid sometimes takes place in the breasts of infants of either sex. This occasions some inflammation and swelling, but it is a normal condition and does not require attention.

TREATMENTS.—

A. Let them alone absolutely. Avoid all rubbing, or any kind of application. Above all, do not allow any one to squeeze out the milk. They will give no trouble if let alone.—(13).

B. Let them alone. If swelled, hot or inflamed, apply a snug-fitting bandage of adhesive plaster.—(7).

DISEASES OF THE WOMB.

The uterus is subject to disease the same as other structures. Inflammation, tumor or cancer may attack this organ. Inflammation, which may be due to displacement or to other cause, is the most frequent affection. *The treatment of any of these conditions cannot be successfully applied except by a physician.*

CONDITIONS RESULTING FROM DISPLACEMENT.

Retroflexion.	The uterus is flexed or bent at a sharp angle.
Retroversion.	The uterus is slightly bent out of its natural position, usually backward.
Prolapse.	When the uterus is not maintained in its normal position, but is allowed to sink lower in the pelvic cavity by reason of weak ligaments; or when the organ is enlarged and sinks from its own weight.
Inversion.	As the name implies, the uterus is turned wrong side out. The inversion may be partial or complete. Inversion rarely occurs.
Subinvolution.	When the organ fails to contract to its natural size after labor, but remains large and contains much blood.

CONDITIONS RESULTING FROM INFLAMMATION.

Erosion.	Inflammation and ulceration of the neck of the uterus.
Hypertrophy or Hyperplasia.	This is an increase in the size of the uterus.
Atrophy.	This is a decrease in the tissue of the uterus.

TUMORS.

(Tumors are named according to their location).

Intramural.	{ Developed within the substance of the uterus.
Polypus.	{ A tumor commencing just beneath the mucous membrane which lines the uterus.
Subserous.	{ Just beneath the outer surface.

DISPLACEMENTS.

The uterus is about 3 inches long, 2 inches wide and 1 inch thick. It is shaped like a pear slightly flattened, with rather prominent rounded corners on either side toward the larger end. It is placed about the center of the pelvic cavity, and its natural position is nearly vertical, with the large end up. The lower or smaller end, called the neck, rests within the vagina, which aids in giving support.

The abdominal cavity is lined with a thin membrane called the peritoneum, which has been mentioned before. The uterus is placed below the peritoneum, yet its upper part is covered by this membrane. Stand a pear on a table with its large end up, cover with a handkerchief and allow the handkerchief to drop around the sides of the pear and its lower borders to extend outward over the surface of the table, and it will represent the peritoneal covering of the uterus. At the sides, front and back, the peritoneum is thrown into folds. These folds include fibers of the surrounding connective tissue, also muscle fibers, which are continuous from the uterus. One end of the folds is attached to the uterus, and the other end to the sides, front and back of the pelvic cavity, and constitute the ligaments which support the uterus. It will be seen that the support is not rigid and that the uterus is subject to considerable free movement. For instance, in lifting or straining the uterus would be pressed downward; when such pressure ceases, it would resume its natural position. It may also be displaced backward by a full bladder. Such displacement is perfectly natural, causes no trouble and does not indicate disease. The displacements that do cause trouble and that indicate disease are *Retroflexion*, *Retroversion*, *Prolapse* and *Inversion*.

RETROFLEXION.—When the upper end of the uterus is bent over backwards and the bend forms an angle at the junction and neck of the uterus, which corresponds to the body and neck of the pear, it is called *Retroflexion*. In this case the uterus is also rotated more or less on its long axis, so that while the upper and larger end is bent backward, the lower end projects forward.

Cause.—In most cases it is the result of a large uterus—one that did not contract properly after labor, or of getting up too early while it was still large—before the uterus had had time to contract. In such cases the ligaments mentioned are not able to give the support needed. Another cause is laceration of the lower end of the uterus during labor. The result is more or less enlargement, and this causes a relaxed condition of the ligaments. It may also be influenced by constipation or by tight lacing. It may be due to a generally relaxed condition where the body is poorly nourished. Sometimes the displacement is sudden, and is brought on by jumping out of a buggy, stepping down out of a chair, or sudden lifting or straining; but, of course, the conditions allowing such displacement existed before.

Symptoms.—When occurring suddenly, there is a sharp pain, which extends to the back. There is an irritable bladder and general bad feeling, and the patient feels that there is something wrong, but does not know what is the matter. When coming on more slowly, and in a chronic form, there is the same general bad feeling and sense of weight, dragging pain, pain in the back, headache and other symptoms given under the head of INFLAMMATION OF THE UTERUS.

TREATMENT.-

First of all, the organ must be replaced and maintained in its natural position. This requires the services of the doctor. The organ must be supported by tampons. If there is much inflammation and pain, this should be treated first and the organ replaced later. Large hot vaginal douches should be used twice a day. Saline laxatives, in the form of Seidlitz Salts or some other remedy of a like nature, should be given. The patient should avoid heavy work, lifting, straining, or anything that tends to bear down on the uterus. These cases generally need nourishing diet and attention to the general health to overcome the relaxed condition of the tissues.

RETROVERSION. — Retroversion differs from Retroflexion only in being a lesser displacement. There is no strictly dividing line between them.. The symptoms correspond to the extent of the trouble. Undoubtedly retroversion occurs more frequently than other forms of displacement. It cannot be otherwise, because retroflexion, or any other serious displacement, must necessarily follow a milder condition. There are probably many cases of retroversion, or slight displacement, that pass unnoticed. When the condition becomes more serious, an examination reveals the true state.

PROLAPSE.—When the uterus is not maintained in its normal position, but is allowed to sink lower in the pelvic cavity by reason of weak ligaments, it is called *Prolapse.* The prolapse may be partial or complete. When complete, the uterus is entirely expelled. This condition is called *Procidentia.*

Cause.—The cause of prolapse is a large uterus and weakness of the ligaments. Weak ligaments may be the result of hard work, general debility, being too much on the feet, of disease or injury, or may follow labor where the patient has not made a complete recovery and where the uterus has remained large and heavy. This is called *Subinvolution.* Perhaps this is the most frequent cause. Prolapse may also be due to the increased weight caused by tumors. It is sometimes met in old women, being the result of a general relaxation of the system. Procidentia is caused by an exaggeration of the conditions named.

Symptoms.—A sense of weight and pain in the pelvic cavity. Oftentimes the pain produces a dragging sensation, and there is a tired, worn-out feeling, a lack of ambition, pain in the back, headache, and other symptoms given under the various displacements, also those given under the head of *Subinvolution.* The symptoms vary according to the extent of the displacement.

TREATMENT.—

First, the patient should remain in bed. Take a hot douche twice a day while lying on the back, using two or three quarts of hot water each time. Dissolve ¼ ounce of Boric Acid in the water each time. Support the uterus with tampons. If the organ is large, give ½ teaspoonful of Fluid Extract of Hydrastus four times a day. The bowels should be kept active, and daily baths should be given, followed by brisk rubbing, which should be continued until the surface is a bright red. Keeping the bowels active and the blood well brought out to the surface aids largely in equalizing the circulation, and thus in relieving the congestion, also inflammation if it is present. Attention should be given to food, ventilation, hygienic surroundings, etc.

INVERSION.—Inversion is the term applied where the uterus is turned wrong side out. This may be partial or complete.

Cause.—The uterus is large, and there is relaxation or a failure to contract at some particular point. The portion first involved is usually at the highest point of the organ. It may be caused by the pulling of the cord in the efforts to remove the after-birth; it may be caused by a short cord, where, following delivery of the child, the body of the uterus would be drawn inward. It may be caused by an adherent placenta or after-birth. This may remain firmly attached at some point, and the efforts to remove it may cause the infolding of the uterus. As soon as the uterus begins to fold inward, the rest of the organ contracts upon this portion and tries to expel it, the same as it would a polypus, a blood clot, or any other foreign body.

Symptoms.—The first symptom is a sharp, sudden pain, followed by more or less hemorrhage and a dragging sensation. If the infolding is slight, the symptoms will be slight. Later there is a discharge of mucus and pus, or pus and blood. The organ remains large.

TREATMENT.—

The treatment is mechanical. Give hot douches. Support the organ with tampons. The patient should remain in bed. Attention should be given to the bowels, also to the bladder, as spasm of this organ might follow. If inversion is complete, the uterus would appear externally. In this case grasp the organ with the hand, make firm pressure with a view of lessening its size, and try to replace it. If this is impossible, some recommend waiting a month or more and then renewing the attempt; others advocate removing the organ at once. If replacement is impossible, we advise the latter.

SUBINVOLUTION.—This is the condition where the organ fails to contract to its natural size after labor—where it remains large and contains too much blood.

Cause.—It may be caused by retained parts of the after-birth, by a lack of muscular power, or by temporary paralysis due to distension and pressure. The cause may be general weakness or exhaustion, or may be the result of fright where the patient has been left alone during confinement. The last would produce a paralyzing effect upon the nervous system.

Symptoms.—The symptoms may be hemorrhage, more or less frequent and increased at the menstrual period. Examination shows the uterus to be abnormal in size. There is pain in the back, headache, and there may be palpitation of the heart and many other nervous symptoms. Constipation may be present, also more or less bloating of the abdominal cavity. There is a sense of weight in the pelvic cavity, which is made worse by the patient's being on her feet and trying to do active work. Following such efforts the symptoms mentioned will be increased until the patient may develop a seemingly unreasonable nervousness. Should the trouble become chronic, it may lead to *Hypertrophy*, or overgrowth.

TREATMENT.—

In this condition rest is of the first importance. The patient should lie down several hours each day, and should not attempt any active physical exercise or hard work; although light exercise or light work, not carried to the point of fatigue, would occupy the mind and doubtless be of advantage. Vaginal injections of hot water should be administered twice a day—night and morning—using at least 2 quarts of water each time—4 quarts would be still better. Internally take ½ teaspoonful of the Fluid Extract of Ergot, or the same amount of the Fluid Extract of Hydrastus, four times a day. These cases are usually accompanied with a general loss of strength, hence the most nourishing diet should be secured, and some time should be spent in the open air each day.

If due to retained parts of the after-birth, see CHILD-BED FEVER.

INFLAMMATIONS.

INFLAMMATION OF THE UTERUS.—*Cause.*—

Inflammation of the uterus may be caused by displacement, or may follow labor or abortion where some part of the placental membranes or after-birth is allowed to remain. It may result from unhygienic habits and an unhealthy system. This means unhealthy secretions both in the uterus and along the vaginal tract. The secretions in the vaginal tract coming in contact with the cervix or lower part of the uterus may readily extend into the cavity of that organ and increase the inflammation. Inflammation of the lower part of the uterus may follow laceration caused by child-birth. It may also be caused by gonorrheal infection.

Inflammation is usually confined to the mucous membrane which lines the cavity and is oftenest caused by displacement. In displacement the uterus is bent at a sharp angle. This causes irritation, congestion and inflammation.

Symptoms.—The symptoms of acute inflammation are slight. There may be fever, headache, slight nausea, and a feeling of weight and soreness about the organ, which is somewhat enlarged. If at the menstrual period, menstruation is increased, there is pain in the back, the organ looks swollen and its color is a deep red. The extent of these symptoms depends upon the extent of the inflammation.

One of the symptoms of chronic inflammation is painful menstruation. Blood clots are often present, and there is a chronic discharge accompanied with pain in the back, headache, disturbance of appetite and loss of strength and ambition. In such cases abortion follows pregnancy.

TREATMENT—ACUTE INFLAMMATION.—

If due to displacement, the organ should be replaced in its natural position. This, together with rest in bed for a few days, is usually all that is necessary in recent cases.

TREATMENT—CHRONIC INFLAMMATION.—

Mix equal parts of Europhen and Aristol to a creamy consistence with liquid Petroleum. Dissolve ½ ounce of Boric Acid in two or three quarts of water and with a fountain syringe thoroughly cleanse the vagina. Next warm and draw a little of the Europhen and Aristol mixture into a long-nozzled rubber syringe, exclude the air, by means of a bivalve speculum pass the nozzle of the syringe into the womb to the highest point, and inject carefully a few drops until the mixture oozes out below. This treatment should be applied every third day. This remedy cures by reason of its antiseptic properties, keeping the uterus clean and healthy. Hot douches morning and night should also be used. Use from 2 to 4 quarts of water as hot as can be borne. Dissolve ½ ounce of Boric Acid in the amount used for each injection.

If the inflammation is the result of blood poisoning from retained membranes following labor, thoroughly cleanse the uterus and use the same injection of Boric Acid and hot water. Also give the general treatment under CHILD-BED FEVER.

EROSION.—It is stated under the head of *Displacements* that the lower end of the uterus rests within the upper end of the vagina. The erosion occurs at this point, and the disease affects both the outer surface of the part projecting into the vagina and the mucous membrane which lines the lower part of the cavity. There is a gradual destruction and wearing away of tissue, and at the same time the part is enlarged because it is inflamed and swollen. Like all other organs, the uterus is composed of little particles called cells. The cells on the surface are destroyed and cast off so rapidly that the new cells cannot cover it. They are sufficient in number, but do not have time to develop. Also, the mucous membrane lining the uterus, like all other mucous membrane, contains numerous glands. Those occupying the diseased part become swollen and the secretions are greatly increased in quantity; they are also changed and thickened. Sometimes they contain pus, hence are sometimes spoken of as purulent. The mucous membrane becomes so swollen that it may dilate the lower part of the uterus and be exposed, or may roll outward and cover what naturally is a part of the outer surface. An examination reveals the mucous membrane as a red zone, varying in width and surrounding the opening into the organ. Some of the glands mentioned may become clogged and, being filled with secretions, they dilate, forming cysts which vary in size.

Cause.—It may result from unhealthy discharges from the uterus, from unhealthy secretions of the vagina which may extend into the uterus, may result from examination and the passing of instruments, from operations, or from attempts at abortion. The most frequent cause is laceration or tearing of the uterus during labor.

Symptoms.—An abundant thick, light or yellowish discharge, pain in the uterus and vagina and extending more or less throughout the pelvic cavity, a general bad feeling, a feeling of weight, pains in the back and headache. All of the symptoms are usually made worse by active exercise.

TREATMENT.—

The treatment consists of using a douche of several quarts of hot water twice a day to keep the vaginal tract clean. A little Boric Acid may be dissolved in the water with advantage. The patient should take several hours' rest each day, etc.

The uterus itself must also receive attention, but such treatment can only be applied by a doctor and by means of a speculum. There are several forms of treatment, but the following method has always proven satisfactory in our experience:

> Tincture Iodine .... 2 drachms.
> Fluid Extract Belladonna......... .. 1 "
> Glycerine, add to..................... 6 ounces.
>   *Mix* by shaking the bottle.

First thoroughly clean the lower part of the uterus with dry absorbent cotton wrapped around a small pair of forceps, and afterwards apply the solution by the same means. Pass both the dry cotton swab and that containing the solution up through the neck of the uterus. Afterwards saturate a tampon with the solution, press it up firmly against the uterus, and support it with a dry tampon. This treatment should be repeated every morning, and the tampons removed in the evening. In severe cases the tampons should be applied twice a day.

The Iodine acts as a disinfectant; the Belladonna relieves spasmodic contraction and allays pain; the Glycerine absorbs the watery part of the blood from the inflamed uterus, the drainage relieving the distension and pressure: and the tampon gives support.

Where laceration is present, an operation is needed.

HYPERTROPHY, or HYPERPLASIA.—Enlargement of the uterus where the organ fails to contract after labor is described under *Subinvolution*. In subinvolution the channels, or sinuses, through which the blood flows are dilated, and the organ is swollen and enlarged. *Hypertrophy* consists of an enlargement of the uterus due to an increased growth of the muscle tissue of which it is formed. The lining mucous membrane is also increased in thickness. There is an increase of growth over waste, the same as the muscles of an arm would increase under certain physical exercise.

Cause.—The increased growth is due to an increase in nourishment or blood supply It may be the result of chronic inflammation, may be influenced by the retention of the menses; or may result from tumor growth in the uterus, or in the pelvic cavity outside the uterus, because the increased blood supply necessary to support a tumor growth so near by would also increase the blood supply to the uterus.

Symptoms.—The symptoms correspond to the conditions which produce the overgrowth.

TREATMENT.—

The treatment should be directed to the disease or conditions which produce it.

ATROPHY.—This is a condition the opposite of *Hypertrophy*, and indicates a shrinking or decrease in the normal size of the uterus.

Symptoms.—Those of the conditions which produce it, unless surrounding structures are involved or adhesions form. The first might be followed by some form of chronic inflammation; and the second by a dragging or pulling sensation, with occasional twinges of pain, which become gradually less sharp and frequent and usually disappear altogether.

Causes.—Wasting diseases, a lack of blood supply or nourishment, injuries during pregnancy or child-birth, or following child-bed fever. Any of these conditions may destroy the mucous membrane lining the uterus and portions of the adjoining uterine walls. Destruction of the mucous membrane by curetting (scraping out the inside of the uterus with a sharp instrument) would produce the same results. The use of the cautery, *i. e.*, a hot iron or strong acids which are sometimes used in the treatment of certain diseases, will produce like results. The use of hot irons and caustics cannot be too strongly condemned. The same may be said regarding many cases of curetting.

TREATMENT.—

See under HYPERTROPHY above.

TUMORS.

As stated, among other diseases the uterus is subject to tumors. These are named according to their location. When occurring just beneath the mucous membrane which lines the uterus, they are called *submucous;* when occurring near or on the surface, and just beneath the peritoneum which covers the uterus, they are called *subserous;* occurring in the body of the organ, they are called *intramural.* These tumors are often called *fibromas* or *myomas.* Fibroma means hard and fibrous; myoma means a tumor formed in muscle tissue.

Cause.—The cause has never been given, yet we wish to state what seems to us to be a reasonable cause for these growths. The uterus, like the kidneys and brain, has a blood supply larger in proportion than other organs of the body. The arteries do not continue through the organ as through other structures, but the circulation is carried on through channels or sinuses in the uterine tissue. Whenever there is indigestion, lack of elimination, or disease from any cause, the blood contains irritating waste matter, and it is but reasonable to suppose that the morbid influence of this irritation will produce the greatest effect in those organs receiving the most blood, and more especially when brought into intimate relation with the tissues of the organ, as in the case of the uterus. The irritation is followed by congestion, unnoticed at first, but as the congestion increases to inflammation, the increased blood supply results in over-production of tissue. This is true of inflammation everywhere. It has been stated that tissue growth following inflammation is confined to the connective tissue framework. This is also true in overgrowth in the uterus, and is the reason these tumors are so hard and fibrous.

Symptoms.—Increased flow at the menstrual period, and enlargement of the organ. Examination shows a hard, lumpy growth. Many of these growths are small and give no symptoms.

TREATMENT.—

When a tumor is discovered, there should be a lessening of the blood supply of the uterus. For this purpose ½ teaspoonful of Fluid Extract of Ergot may be given four times a day, or the same amount of Fluid Extract of Hydrastus. It will be necessary to continue these remedies for some time. The patient should also keep as quiet as possible, and should lie down two or three hours every day. Tying one or more of the arteries which supply the uterus has been tried, but without satisfactory results. If the treatment fails and the growth continues, it should be removed. In this case many advise the removal of the whole organ as it lessens the possibility of cancer, which might follow.

POLYPUS.—When a tumor occurs just beneath the mucous membrane which lines the uterus, the growth is not hard, but soft. The reason is that the congestion, occurring so near the surface, causes the mucous membrane to bulge out at the point of least resistance or greatest pressure. This space is immediately filled with blood. There is no overgrowth in this case. Nature tries to supply new tissue, but the effort succeeds but partially for the reason that the mucous membrane continues to bulge forward and the size of the cavity increases so rapidly that normal tissue cannot form fast enough to fill the space; hence it is more or less filled with a soft, gelatinous growth. These growths sometimes become very large, and the uterus enlarges the same as in pregnancy. The growths are called *polypi*. They may completely fill the organ, and the mucous membrane may bulge forward and downward until it protrudes from the uterus into the vagina. The stem or pedicle by which they are attached shows the primary seat of origin.

Symptoms.—The symptom of polypus is hemorrhage, either at or between the periods. As the growth becomes larger, the hemorrhages become more frequent and there is more or less pain. The pains are the result of contractions as the uterus tries to expel its contents. The polypus excites the same contraction in the uterus that a clot of blood or any other foreign body does. In some cases there are no particular symptoms, except an increased flow at the menstrual period, until the polypus becomes large, when the hemorrhage becomes more frequent and there are painful contractions, as stated. Examination shows the condition at once. In some cases the contractions of the uterus are so strong that the growth is squeezed off —separated at the pedicle or point of attachment—and is discharged, either in parts or altogether.

TREATMENT.—

Where these growths are not expelled naturally, they should be removed.

THE VAGINA.

LEUCORRHEA.—The vagina is subject to inflammation, gonorrhea, tumors, cancer and leucorrhea. The last mentioned is caused by a relaxed condition of the surrounding tissues and of the mucous membrane, or it may result from inflammation of the uterus or other surrounding tissue.

TREATMENTS.—

A. Leucorrhea is a catarrhal condition and the treatment consists in cleanliness. This can best be maintained by injections, using a large quantity of water each time—1 gallon of water containing ½ ounce of Boric Acid. Astringents are often recommended for this trouble, such as the following:

> Sulphate of Zinc .... 1 drachm.
> Powdered Alum .... 1 　"
> Water .... 1 gallon.
>> Use all at one injection.

The great object of the local treatment is to render the surface as clean as possible. The injection should be used often enough to maintain this condition—twice a day at least. These cases usually require general treatment in the way of nourishing food. Tonics may also be needed. The following one is recommended:

> Fowler's Solution .... 3 drachms.
> Fellows' Syrup of Hypophosphites.. 5 ounces.
> Maltine, or other good preparation
> 　of Extract of Malt..................... 10 　"
>> *Mix*, and give one tablespoonful before or immediately after meals, and one at bedtime.

For a gonorrheal discharge give the same large injections twice a day, but instead of the Zinc and Alum, add 2 drachms of Permanganate of Potash or 6 drachms of Boric Acid.

If the discharge is due to inflammation of the uterus or other disease, the treatment should be directed to such cause.

B. For almost all forms of disease of the vagina the hot douche is unequalled. Use every day from a quart to a gallon of hot water with a little salt dissolved in it.—(42).

C. Use hot water douches with ½ teaspoonful of Sulphate of Zinc or Sugar of Lead dissolved in four quarts of water, or Tincture of Iodine used in the same way.—(26).

D. Creolin—20 drops in ½ gallon of warm water. Use as an injection into vagina morning and evening.—(23).

E. Free irrigations (injections) with hot solutions of Borax —hot as can be borne. Use 2 drachms of Borax to pint of water once or twice daily.—(60).

F. Wampole's Antiseptic Vaginal Cones. Introduce one at night and use injection of warm water in the morning on rising. —(9).

THE OVARIES.

INFLAMMATION OF. — The ovaries (see description under MENSTRUATION) are subject to inflammation, abscess, atrophy, or shrinking, tumor, displacement and hernia. The last two do not often occur. Inflammation is by far the most common.

Causes.—It may be caused by inflammation or abscess in the abdominal cavity, by appendicitis, blood poisoning, eruptive fevers, injury, or may result from tuberculosis, cancer or abortion. It most often occurs by extension from the uterus, passing along the Fallopian tubes, and perhaps the most frequent cause is gonorrheal infection.

Symptoms.—The most prominent symptom is pain and soreness in the region of the ovaries. If it is an acute attack, there is fever and a rapid pulse. The pain may extend around the crest of the hip down the limb. It is made worse by exercise and by the approach of the menstrual period, and is made easier by the flow. In the early stages menstruation is increased. If it continues and becomes chronic, menstruation may be lessened, or may cease altogether.

TREATMENT.—

In most cases rest is of first importance. If it is an acute attack and seen early, cold packs may be used over the diseased organ; later, hot poultices. Vaginal injections of Boric Acid solution as hot as can be borne may be used once or twice a day. If there is much fever, give 1-drop doses of Tincture of Aconite every hour, more or less often as needed. Keep the bowels regular. If seen early, give an active cathartic. The patient should remain quiet until the soreness and inflammation have disappeared. Attention should be given to the general health, ventilation, etc. With some there is a strong tendency to resort to the knife whenever there is disturbance of the general health with neuralgic pains in the region of the ovaries, or when accompanied by some nervous phenomena. This practice cannot be too strongly condemned. A great surgeon said recently, ''The tendency of the profession to appeal to the knife is the great error of the present century.'' Inflammation of the ovaries is no different from inflammation elsewhere. Inflammation of the ovaries does not often occur and, as already stated, when it does, it is usually the result of extension from surrounding structures. With some classes it most frequently results from gonorrheal infection.

TUMORS OF.—Tumors of the ovaries do not often occur. The most usual form is what is called *Ovarian Cysts*. These are caused by the failure of the egg (see description) to rupture. Instead it continues to enlarge and becomes filled with fluid. These tumors sometimes reach enormous proportions. The only treatment is removal. Where an abscess is present, it should be opened and treated the same as abscess elsewhere.

DISEASES OF CHILDREN.

INFANT FEEDING.

The Best Substitute for Mother's Milk.—If the mother is healthy, the best food for an infant is the mother's milk. When this cannot be had, cow's milk has been proved to be the best substitute, but cow's milk must be modified or changed so as to approximate human milk as nearly as possible. Mothers who are unable to nurse their infants should know how to feed them.

Infant Foods — *The Public Health Journal*, published in New York, says: "Nearly every form of infant food has been used in the New York Infant Asylums. The experience with them as foods—something for infants to thrive upon and gain weight on—has been, without exception, unsatisfactory. Many varieties are positively dangerous. Cow's milk, cream and sugar have been demonstrated to be the only reliable substitutes for mother's milk."

Deficiency of Water.—Many disturbances of digestion are to be explained by deficiency of water—certainly more than are due to an excess of it. Many infants receive water only as they get it in their milk. An infant as well as a grown person can be thirsty without being hungry. Babies who are not given water receive it only in their food, hence they are obliged to eat to satisfy thirst, and they may still suffer thirst because they cannot eat more. This also causes them to eat too much and too often.

Starch and Sugar.—Again, those having the care of babies should know that the infant's power to digest starch or cane (granulated) sugar is very slight at birth. If these are used, there is danger of setting up an acid fermentation, which may cause catarrh of the stomach and digestive tract and produce colicky pains. Cane sugar and starch cannot be digested by children under one year of age, therefore starchy foods, as bread, potatoes, etc., should not be given.

Preparation of Cow's Milk.—To render cow's milk like human milk, the appended tables may prove convenient. They also show the necessary change in the amount of ingredients which will harmonize with the child's age and growth. Very large and robust infants may require more, and weak ones less, than the amount indicated.

Sterilizing Milk.—Some prefer to sterilize milk. This may be done by pouring the milk into a clean bottle or can and placing the same in a kettle or pan of water. The cork or top should be loosened and the water boiled for thirty minutes. The cork should then be replaced and the milk set in a cool place. Before using, the milk should be slightly warmed by placing the nursing bottle in warm water.

Frequency of Nursings.—A healthy infant should not nurse more than fifteen or twenty minutes at one time. Very young infants should be allowed to nurse every two hours during the day, and the number of feedings in twenty-four hours should be ten. After the fourth or fifth week (some authorities put this as late as the third month) the infant should nurse at regular intervals of two and one-half hours during the day, and only once during the seven or eight hours during which the mother ought to sleep. From the beginning of the third month to the end of the nursing period, every three hours is often enough; after six months five to seven nursings are sufficient during the twenty-four hours, and night nursing, that is, between ten o'clock in the evening and six o'clock in the morning, should be given up. If necessary, water may be given during the night.

Disease Caused by.—Cholera infantum, various forms of rash, convulsions, brain fever and many other diseases, are brought on by unhealthy surroundings, unhealthy food and over-feeding. The stomach of the new-born babe holds only from two to three tablespoonfuls. Cow's milk contains less sugar than human milk, and about four times as much caseine, or milk albumen. During extreme hot weather less milk and more water should be given.

Time of Weaning.—Nursing babies should be weaned before they are one year old. It is better to wean them in cold weather, and when they are not cutting teeth. The mother with consumption, or very poor health from other cause, should not nurse a baby.

Hot weather kills babies by spoiling their milk and other food. The heat also lowers their vitality, or power of resistance. About one-half of all deaths in cities are young children, and about two-thirds of this number are infants under one year of age. In nearly every case the primary cause of disease commences in the digestive tract. Over one-third of the children and infants die during the months of July and August. The weather cannot be changed, but proper feeding, cleanliness and fresh air will do much to prolong the lives of children.

Preparation of Bottled Milk.—

From Birth to the Third or Fourth Month.

Milk, fresh.................................... 8 tablespoonfuls.
Lime Water, fresh (see note below).. 2   "
Water, boiled (see note below)......... 30   "
Milk Sugar, pure.......................... .. 9 even teaspoonfuls.

From the Fourth to the Ninth Month.

Milk, fresh.................................... 16 tablespoonfuls.
Lime Water, fresh........................... 2   "
Water, boiled................................. 22   "
Milk Sugar................................... 9 even teaspoonfuls.

Amount to be Given.—Enough of either of these to last for the day should be placed in a clean bottle or fruit can—one that has been thoroughly scalded—the bottle or can placed upright in a vessel containing a few inches of water, and the water heated to the boiling point (see note below). The bottle or can should then be taken from the fire, cooled quickly and kept tightly corked in a cool place. The number of tablespoonfuls of the mixture put into the feeding bottle should be as follows:

For the first week .... 2 to 3
Second to sixth week .... 3 " 7
Sixth to twelfth week......... 8 " 9
Third to sixth month .... 8 " 12
Sixth to ninth month .... 12 " 18

Note.—See INDEX for *Milk, scalded, Water, boiled* and *Lime Water,* to make.

CAPILLARY BRONCHITIS.—(See under BRONCHITIS in Department I).

CHOLERA INFANTUM.—(See under CHOLERA in Department I).

DEFORMITIES.—Many, in fact all but the more serious deformities, may be successfully treated by putting on light splints and keeping well bandaged. The treatment should commence as soon as the deformity is discovered.

EYES, SORE AT BIRTH.—(See *Purulent Conjunctivitis* under EYE, DISEASES OF, in Department I).

FRACTURES.—Fractures in children differ in no way from fractures in adults, excepting that with children the bones fracture more easily and there is less destruction of the soft tissue and less swelling, hence these cases are more easily cared for.

Causes.—Fractures may occur *in utero, i. e.,* during or before birth. Such fractures may be the result of pressure upon some of the pelvic bones during the development of the child, may result from some abnormal position during birth, or from pressure from the forceps. It is understood, of course, that fracture from the forceps is more liable to occur in a narrow pelvis, or in one that is deformed. Fractures occurring after birth are due to external violence or force, as falls, blows, etc.

TREATMENT.—

The treatment differs in no way from the treatment in the adult. In the case of a fractured limb in a child where there is little or no swelling, it is considered good practice for the doctor to put on a plaster paris bandage. This is sometimes called a plaster cast. This is allowed to remain until the fracture heals.

HARELIP.—All cases of harelip should be treated by a surgeon. The operation should be performed during infancy.

HERNIA, INGUINAL.—Under *Hernia* in DEPARTMENT I, it was stated that in fœtal life the testicles occupied a position in the abdominal cavity, and that before birth they passed down into the scrotum; also that the openings through which they pass remain and are called the inguinal canals, meaning canals in the groin. We failed to state the purpose of these canals, which is the transmission of arteries, veins and nerves that supply the testicles. The canals also contain what are called the vasa deferentia. These are two small tubes which lead from the testicles up through the inguinal canals, pass into the abdominal cavity behind and below the bladder and terminate in the urethral tract. We also stated that the canals were closed at their upper end by the peritoneum which lines the abdominal cavity, and compared the peritoneum to the film which surrounds an egg and lies beneath the shell. Sometimes in the child the abdominal opening into the canal is not properly closed, and this allows more or less free opportunity for some part of the bowel to communicate with it, the result being an *Inguinal Hernia.*

Cause.—That already given.

Symptoms.—A bulging or prominence in the form of a soft tumor along the course of the inguinal canal, which readily disappears when the child lies on its back, or which may be pressed back easily.

TREATMENT.—

The application of a properly fitting truss. These cases usually make a complete recovery later by the closure of the canal.

HERNIA, UMBILICAL.—This consists of a protrusion of some of the abdominal viscera or contents through the navel ring, which in fœtal life gave passage to the umbilical vessels that were contained in the cord.

Cause.—Incomplete closure of the ring. This may be due to crying, straining, or other internal abdominal pressure ; or may result from a lack of nourishment where proper healing has not taken place. The outer covering of skin is usually complete.

Symptoms.—A protrusion, giving the form or appearance of a small tumor, which is easily reduced by pressure.

TREATMENT.—

Take a piece of flat cork or button the proper size, cover it with soft cotton cloth, sew it in the center of a bandage, then place the cork or button directly over the tumor and secure the bandage around the body. Both the bandage and the tissues beneath should be kept thoroughly clean. Like all other forms of *Infantile Hernia*, this variety usually results in complete recovery.

INCONTINENCE. — This means an involuntary evacuation of the bowel or bladder, although it is generally understood to mean inability to retain the urine during sleep. This is a disease of childhood and is overcome with age, but may also be relieved by treatment.

Cause.—*Phimosis* (See PHIMOSIS), adhesions of the prepuce, intestinal worms, or over-sensitiveness of the urethral tract. These and other causes are given, although in many cases there can be no cause discovered. When a disease or condition exists that is not well understood, various theories are advanced as being the cause. Sometimes these theories may be correct; sometimes they may not. We think this statement applies to incontinence. Personally we believe that many cases of incontinence are due to a lack of development of the nerve fibers which supply the neck of the bladder, hence the constrictory muscle is not under proper control. Or, another way of looking at it, this nerve supply might be over-sensitive, hence the pressure resulting from a distended bladder would allow or cause an involuntary passage of the urine during sleep.

TREATMENT.—

We have always relied upon Atropine in the treatment of this trouble and have always been successful. It is good practice to give a dose of Santonine for one or two nights. If there are any worms present, it will remove them without trouble; if there are none present, it will do no harm. Again, Santonine is a remedy used by some for this trouble whether due to worms or not, and it is even claimed to be successful in some cases where Atropine fails. If Atropine is used, it should be given in several small doses frequently repeated, commencing two or three hours before the child goes to bed; or one large dose may be given. The small dose seems preferable because by that means there would be no danger of over-dosing. For a child from five to ten years old, give $\frac{1}{500}$ of a grain every hour until the pupil of the eye is well dilated, or until the face is flushed, and give at bedtime 1 grain of Santonine and 1 grain of Calomel. In some cases it is necessary to repeat the Atropine for some days. If the two or three doses of Atropine do not produce the symptoms mentioned, begin the treatment earlier the second day and continue until effect.

Retention of Urine.—In most cases with infants, retention of urine may be overcome by giving liberally of a tea made of pumpkin or watermelon seeds. Sometimes the urethral tract in the new-born male child is not complete, *i. e.*, does not reach the surface. Whenever this condition is present the doctor should make an artificial opening, being careful to have it meet the termination of the natural opening.

Note.—This same defect sometimes occurs in the digestive tract. We are acquainted with one case of this kind where an external opening was made. The opening was continued for some 2½ inches into the bowel. The mucous membrane of the bowel was brought down and stitched to the skin, and the operation was a complete success.

JAUNDICE PERNICIOUS.— This is a malignant and fatal disease of the new-born. It is a pernicious form of jaundice which differs entirely from the ordinary catarrhal variety. This form does not stain the whites of the eyes nor give other characteristic signs of jaundice.

Cause.—It is caused by defective circulation in the liver. Among the primary or earlier causes is unhealthy blood, malformation, syphilis, inflammation of the umbilical cord, imperfect circulation in the lungs, or blood poisoning from any cause. Bad hygiene and improper nourishment before birth lie at the bottom of all. *"Pernicious Jaundice"* is a misnomer because there is no jaundice present.

TREATMENT.—

The treatment is largely symptomatic. Make the child as comfortable as possible. There is no known treatment that is of value. The patient may live for a few days or for a week or two.

MOTHER'S MARK.—(See *Birth Marks* under description of SKIN in **Department I**).

DISEASES OF THE MOUTH.

Cleanliness.—Babies cannot clear the mouth of food products after eating like grown people do, and after nursing there frequently remain particles of milk in the form of curd, which may be lodged under the tongue, at the sides of the mouth, along the throat, or covering more or less the surface of the mucous membrane lining the mouth. These particles readily decompose and furnish an acid secretion which irritates and inflames the mucous membrane, and is probably the most common cause of sore mouth in infants. If the mouth is kept clean and free from the products of nursing, it will seldom get sore or give trouble.

TREATMENTS.—

A. If the mouth is rinsed out with clear water two or three times a day, or night and morning, it will be all that is needed. This can best be done by using a soft cloth wrapped around the finger.

> **B.** Peroxide of Hydrogen............... 4 drachms.
> Distilled Water.......................... 4 ounces.
> Wash the mouth with some of this solution several times a day.—(29).

APHTHÆ—THRUSH—CANKER SORE MOUTH.
—This is a disease of the mouth in which small vesicles appear. These vesicles may ulcerate. If ulceration takes place, it is called *Aphthæ*, or *Thrush;* if ulceration does not take place, it is spoken of as *Canker Sore Mouth*. It is a disease of infancy and may follow a catarrhal condition of the stomach, or may result from a lack of cleanliness of the mouth, as described.

Causes.—Those already given. It may also be caused or influenced by indigestion and an unhealthy condition of the bowels. Also said to be caused by teething.

Symptoms.—The child may refuse to nurse, and small vesicles appear in the mouth—on the tongue, gums, lips and mucous membrane of the cheek. The vesicles are first of a light color.

If ulcers form, they are quite painful. There is no odor. The child may worry a good deal, and in some cases is very troublesome.

TREATMENTS.—

A. Regulate the stomach and bowels, give good ventilation, and wash the mouth with the following mixture:

Borax, powdered........................	1 drachm.
Lloyd's Hydrastus......................	4 drachms.
Glycerine.....................................	2 "
Water enough to make................	2 ounces.

> Apply this with a soft cloth several times a day. The child's mouth should also be washed with a little warm water after nursing.

To regulate the bowels, give the following mixture:

Carbonate of Soda......................	1 drachm.
Wine of Ipecac............................	1 "
Fluid Hydrastus..........................	6 drachms.
Syrup of Rhubarb enough to make	4 ounces.

> *Dose.*—10 drops to ½ teaspoonful twice a day, according to age.

The above is applicable either to the ulcerated or simple form.

B. | | |
|---|---|
| Borax, powdered................... | ½ teaspoonful |
| Alum, powdered................... | ½   " |
| Tannin .... | ¼   " |

> *Mix* together and pour on 16 tablespoonfuls of boiling water. Stir until dissolved, add 2 ounces Glycerine and swab the mouth thoroughly three times a day. Regulate the bowels.

C. | | |
|---|---|
| Bayberry Bark, pulverized ...... | 1 teaspoonful. |
| Golden Seal, pulverized.......... | 1   " |
| Red Raspberry leaves............. | small handful. |

Put all into a dish, pour on boiling water, steep, sweeten with honey or loaf sugar, and swab the mouth thoroughly with the decoction, using a nice soft swab, three or four times a day. Be sure to brush well between the gums and cheeks and all around thoroughly.

Also splendid for nursing sore mouth.

D. Make a wash of a teaspoonful of Alum to a glass of water. Internally, one teaspoonful of Rochelle Salts every morning, taken in a glass of water before breakfast.—(7).

Note. — For infants, give Castoria

E. Add Chlorate of Potash to water until some remains undissolved in the bottom of the glass. Hold in mouth as often and as long as possible. Swallow a teaspoonful occasionally. —(14).

Note.—For an infant, swab the mouth and allow none to be swallowed.

F. "Yellow Root." Either chew the root, or make a strong tea and add equal parts of honey or Glycerine and a little Alum —(9).

Note.—For an infant, swab the mouth.

G. Gargle with solution of Chlorate of Potash—½ teaspoonful to a pint of water.—(11).

Note.—For an infant, swab the mouth.

H. Black wash composed of:

Calomel.................................... 30 grains.
Lime Water................................. 6 ounces.

Has proven very efficacious in some obstinate cases.—(60).

I. Saturate a feather in Kerosene Oil and apply to sore, is a remedy recommended by an old nurse.

J. Iodoform.. 1 drachm.
Ether... 2 "

Mix. Apply with camel's hair pencil occasionally.

CANCRUM ORIS, or GANGRENE OF THE MOUTH.—This disease usually affects children of about two years of age.

Causes. — It generally follows some severe constitutional disease, such as scarlet fever or typhoid fever, dysentery, or bad surroundings where the child has gradually become enfeebled. The child has become so weak, the blood so unhealthy, the circulation so poor, and nutrition lacking to such an extent that the part dies. Bad hygiene is believed to be the real underlying cause of this disease.

Symptoms.—About the first symptom may be one or more vesicles or blisters, which gradually turn dark. There is great swelling, but very little or no pain because the part is dead. The glands of the neck also become greatly swollen, and the cheek outside turns purplish over the diseased spot within, the skin blistering and peeling off. The gangrene spreads rapidly and affects the gums, teeth and jaw, the odor being very offensive. The disease runs a rapid course and usually ends fatally in from four to eight days. The immediate cause of death is blood poisoning from absorption of the products of the dead tissue. When recovery follows, there is more or less deformity by reason of the great destruction of tissue resulting from inflammation.

TREATMENT.—

What to Do Till the Doctor Comes. — Early and thorough removal of the dead tissue is of the first importance, and this can be accomplished only by a physician. In the meantime place the child in a well-ventilated room where he can have an abundance of fresh air, give an active cathartic, as 2 teaspoonfuls of Castor Oil, or Laxol (see INDEX), and wash the mouth thoroughly with a disinfectant—probably the disinfectant most likely to be at hand would be Carbolic Acid. Put 10 drops of Carbolic Acid into ½ pint of water and wash the mouth thoroughly every thirty minutes, making the solution fresh each time. Formaldehyde is another disinfectant, 1 drachm of which may be used to 8 ounces of water.

A better disinfectant, and one that ought to be used, especially if there is going to be any delay in getting the doctor, is the following:

Chlorate of Potash .... 1 drachm.
Muriatic Acid, pure .... 1½ "

Mix together and add

Tincture of Chloride of Iron .... 2 drachms.
Water, enough to make.................. 4 ounces.

Make a swab out of soft cloth or a small piece of cotton, and apply this directly to the diseased spot every hour.

The value of this antiseptic is found in the large amount of free Chlorine which it contains. It is well known that Chlorine is a most powerful disinfectant.

MUMPS.—(See **Department I**).

NIGHT TERROR—NIGHTMARE. — *Night Terror* is the name given to a condition which usually affects children, producing bad dreams. The child awakes in a fright with a feeling of distress or suffocation. During sleep he is attended with hideous dreams and often with inability to move, although he may be conscious, or partly so.

Cause.—In most cases the cause is the result of a too hearty supper followed by indigestion.

Symptoms.—The symptoms are restlessness during sleep, and perhaps awaking in a state of fright or with a decided feeling of fear.

TREATMENTS.—

A. These cases can always be controlled by attention to diet —eating light suppers, eating slowly and thoroughly masticating the food—and by keeping the bowels regular.

B. Keep the stomach and liver in good condition and there will never be any trouble of this kind.—(30).

PARALYSIS, INFANTILE.—This form of paralysis usually occurs between the ages of three months and three or four years.

Cause.—This is a disease of the spinal cord. It should be remembered that the spinal cord is composed of large nerve cells and nerve fibers. The fibers are merely drawn-out processes of the cells. The cells are grey in color, while the fibers are light. The fibers are located on the surface, and surrounding all is a membrane which is continuous from that which covers the brain. The grey cells are situated in the center of the cord, and their outer surface is angular in form. If the cord should be cut in two and the reader should look down on the cut end, the grey matter, or cells, would be seen to form a cross somewhat like the letter "X." In *Infantile Paralysis* the anterior projections of the grey cells are the ones first diseased, *i. e.*, the parts of the letter "X" which point forward. First there is congestion, followed by inflammation, circulation and nutrition are lessened and, if the disease continues, the part of the cord mentioned dies and degenerates. Following the destruction of the cells, their prolongations, the nerve fibers, are also destroyed because their source of supply is cut off, just the same as a tree would die if the roots were cut off. It is plainly evident that the cause of this disease is primarily a lack of nutrition. This means dyspepsia and an unhealthy condition of the digestive tract. Following this condition the blood would contain many irritants and, if continued, the irritation would produce inflammation. This is the same condition that causes paralysis in adults. The reason that it occurs so suddenly in the infant or small child is because the child's powers of resistance are comparatively weak.

Why does this condition produce paralysis in one child and tubercular meningitis or some other disease in another? Because of their different powers to resist. The same is true in the adult. In some one organ or tissue is stronger and more resistant, and in others some other organ or tissue is stronger and more resistant.

Symptoms.—First there is some fever, the appetite is poor, and there are all other symptoms that would indicate an unhealthy condition of the digestive tract. In a few days there is some improvement in this respect, and then it is discovered that paralysis exists. Paralysis may affect any one, any two, or all of the extremities. The paralyzed limb feels cold, its color is not natural but somewhat dark, or dark blue, showing poor circulation, and gradually there is a wasting of the muscles, due to the fact that the nerve supply has been destroyed.

TREATMENTS.—

A. First clear the digestive tract with a dose of Castor Oil, or Laxol (see Index). Give from 1 to 3 grains of Salol four times a day, according to age. Give from 3 to 10 drops of Syrup of Hydriodic Acid three times a day between meals. Nourishing food, fresh air, sunshine, free elimination and antiseptics for the digestive tract are points to be remembered in the treatment of this disease.

B. Take a small handful each of Witch Hazel bark, Wild Cherry bark and Skunk Cabbage, put into an iron kettle and cover with a quart of water. Boil until the strength is extracted, strain, and boil down to one pint. Sweeten this decoction and give a teaspoonful dose three to five times a day.

There is Another Form of Paralysis in which there is a shrinkage of some of the muscles and enlargement of others, with partial paralysis of all; or this condition may follow *Infantile Paralysis*.

Cause.—Those already given.

Symptoms.—The child does not begin to walk until quite late, and then with much difficulty. Walking causes pain, the gait is unsteady, and the child cannot lie down nor get up. The muscles of the chest become shrunken, and this interferes with respiration. The unequal size of the muscles gives them a knotted appearance. Later there is an increase in the curvature of the spine. This disease lasts several years and usually ends fatally.

TREATMENT.—

The treatment is the same as for *Infantile Paralysis*. Good food and proper hygienic surroundings constitute the basis. Recovery is doubtful. Paralysis of infants and small children is always a grave condition.

Paralysis of the Face.—This sometimes results from injury done by forceps at the time of delivery. These cases usually recover in a few days. Paralysis of one or more of the individual muscles about the neck and back sometimes occurs. This form is also usually recovered from.

PHIMOSIS.—*Phimosis* is a long prepuce or foreskin, rendering retraction of the skin difficult or impossible. It is usually congenital, that is, exists from birth. It may result from inflammation.

Symptoms.—Phimosis causes retention of the sebaceous matter which is usually produced, and this may cause irritation and inflammation. As the result of inflammation the prepuce may grow fast to the glands. Great irritability of the bladder may be caused, also incontinence or inability to retain the urine, or in some cases inability to retain the fæces. Disturbance of sight, loss of sleep and great nervousness may result. Nervous symptoms may be so varied that it would be difficult to enumerate all.

TREATMENT.—

Some physicians dilate the foreskin, thoroughly cleanse the surface, and instruct this to be done several times a week, keeping the parts thoroughly clean. The majority, however, advise circumcision.

SPASMS.—Nearly all cases of spasms or convulsions in children are the result of undigested food in the stomach. There is also usually an unhealthy condition of the digestive tract. Following such an experience greater attention should be paid to diet. See also CONVULSIONS in **Department I.**

TREATMENTS.—

What to Do.—Give an emetic and place the child in a tub of warm water to which 1 or 2 tablespoonfuls of Mustard have been added. After the emetic operates and the spasm has been relieved, give a dose of Castor Oil or Laxol (see Index), wrap in a small woolen blanket and put to bed. If the child has a high fever, wrap in a wet blanket; if fever is not high, a dry blanket will do.

Note.—If hot water is not at hand, give the emetic, and as soon as it operates, follow with the cathartic. The results will be the same although a little longer time may be required.

A. Immerse the child in a tub of water as hot as can be borne until improvement, then wrap in a blanket and put to bed. An emetic, cathartic or both are usually needed.

The inhalation of Chloroform dropped on a napkin will often stop the spasm, but does not remove the cause.—(20).

B. Strip the child and put into a warm bath, and let it remain in the water about ten minutes.

Also give Belladonna, third dilution—1-drop doses, in liquid or pill form, every thirty minutes till spasm is controlled.—(56). —Homeopathic.

STOMACH AND BOWEL DIFFICULTIES OF CHILDREN.—The following remedy will be found to meet the requirements in more cases of bowel derangement of children than any other preparation:

Carbonate of Soda	1	drachm.
Wine of Ipecac	1	"
Fluid Hydrastus	6	"
Syrup of Rhubarb, add to	4	ounces.

Mix. Dose.—From a few drops to 1 teaspoonful, according to age.

TONGUE-TIE.—Where the frenum of the tongue is too short, snip carefully with a pair of scissors, cutting away from the base of the tongue and towards the under jaw. If done by a physician, there is neither pain nor danger.

WORMS, ROUND.—These are the most common worm found in the digestive tract. They vary greatly in size and length. The average diameter is from $\frac{1}{8}$ to $\frac{1}{4}$ of an inch. In length they vary from 2 to 20 inches, but the average is 6 inches. They reproduce rapidly. The female is said to contain several million eggs.

Cause.—Taking the egg or the worm in minute size into the stomach with food or drink. There are a great army of parasites, including worms, which are constantly being taken into the system, but usually they are destroyed by the digestive fluids.

Symptoms.—Often there are no symptoms, even when the worms are present in large numbers. When symptoms are present, they are irritation in the stomach and bowels, occasional pains, and sometimes loss of appetite, nausea and vomiting. There may be diarrhea. Light color about the mouth, red spots on the cheek, picking the nose and disturbance of sleep are thought by many to be positive signs of worms. This is not true, however, because any and all of these symptoms might and often do result from other causes. The only positive symptom is the elimination of worms.

TREATMENTS.—

A. Santonine is the great remedy for worms, and is used more or less in nearly all worm remedies. Allow the child only a light supper, and give 1 or 2 grains of Santonine with an equal amount of Calomel. Next morning give a dose of Castor Oil or Laxol (see Index). If there are no results, repeat the treatment the next night. If no worms are present in the eliminations, it will be satisfactory proof that they do not inhabit the intestines of the child.

B. Santonine—1 to 3 grains—followed by a large dose of Castor Oil—2 teaspoonfuls, more or less according to age.—(29).

C. Santonine.................................... 1 grain.
Calomel 1   "
Soda Bicarbonate (baking soda)... 20   "

Mix intimately and divide into 10 powders. Take 1 powder every hour until the 10 are taken, and follow with a dose of Castor Oil.

D. Santonine............................. ...   4½ grains.
     Calomel...................................   4½   "
     Milk Sugar..............................   6   "
     Oil of Anise............................   1   drop.

Mix, divide into 4 powders, and take 1 at bedtime every third night.—(59).

E. Get five cents worth of Pink root and Senna leaves, steep to make a tea, sweeten with a little sugar or Glycerine, and drink freely during the morning. If the results are not satisfactory, repeat.

F. Tablets of the following:

     Santonine....................................   ½ grain.
     Calomel ....   ½   "

Take 1 tablet at bedtime, and follow in the morning with a dose of Senna tea before breakfast. One tablet is not too large a dose for a child of two years, and is sufficient up to ten or twelve years.—(31).

WORMS, THREAD or SEAT.—In appearance these look like small pieces of white thread. They inhabit the lower part of the bowel and lower rectum.

Symptoms.—The symptoms of thread or seat worms are intense itching, and also their presence in the eliminations.

TREATMENT.—

The treatment is the same as for *Round Worms.* Also make a strong solution of Quassia in water and inject into the rectum once or twice a day. Quassia comes in chips. Put a few of these chips, or small pieces, into a tumbler of water and let stand over night. In the morning inject 1 or 2 tablespoonfuls of the solution. The injection does not want to be carried high, but allowed to remain in the lower part of the tract. Follow in thirty minutes with an injection of water only—a sufficient amount to cause the bowels to move, or at least to wash out the lower part of the tract occupied by the previous injection. Or a solution of Quinine may be used. This is prepared by dissolving 5 grains of Quinine in ½ teaspoonful of Alcohol; add 2 tablespoonfuls of water and use as directed for Quassia. Or, add 20 grains of Carbolic Acid to 1 ounce of Vaseline, and apply by introducing into the lower part of the tract.

Department III.

ACCIDENTS AND EMERGENCIES.

The importance of a knowledge as to what to do immediately to prevent serious consequences from accidents and injuries, is now everywhere recognized. Keep cool, try to grasp the situation, and act promptly. Where doubt exists as to the proper thing to do, it is best to do nothing but make the patient as comfortable as possible.

Life often depends upon first treatment. A study of the suggestions given here will enable any intelligent person to determine what to do until the physician arrives.

BANDAGES.

Bandages are usually made from strips of soft cotton. They vary in width, and are rolled lengthwise, hence are sometimes called "roller" bandages. They are used for dressing fractures, wounds, etc. Their principal use is to hold dressings in place on an injured surface, but more especially to retain in position the ends of a fractured bone.

To render their application more convenient and secure, bandages are sometimes split for some distance from each end, making four strips. In the application of this form of bandage the ends may be wrapped in opposite directions around the limb, or part, and fastened; or the end of a roller bandage may be split after it is applied, and the two ends passed in different directions around the limb and secured. This is very convenient when pins or needle and thread are wanting. In applying a bandage to a limb, *always elevate the limb and commence the application at the extremity*, as the hand or foot, and wind toward the body. This will lessen the amount of blood in the part and prevent swelling.

In many cases bandages cannot be successfully applied except by one accustomed to their use. However, in emergency cases any one can apply a bandage to stop the flow of blood, or to prevent the grating of broken ends of bones, and this makes the patient more comfortable until the doctor can arrive.

SPLINTS.

In case of a broken bone, if it is necessary to move the patient some distance, some form of splint should be applied, and

463

an improvised bandage of some kind used to hold the splint in position. As stated under FRACTURES, splints may be made out of narrow, light strips of boards, pieces of shingles, small sticks, wisps of hay or grass, etc.

ASPHYXIA, or SUFFOCATION FROM GAS.

—This condition not infrequently occurs. The results, of course, depend upon the amount of gas inhaled. The victim is often found in an unconscious condition. The heart is weak, the pulse is feeble, respiration is shallow and the surface is cold.

TREATMENT.—

Fresh air is of the greatest importance in all cases of this kind. Stimulants and artificial heat—something to increase the vitality and physical power—are also needed. In some cases there is frequent and persistent vomiting, so that remedies given by the stomach may prove not only unsatisfactory, but very uncertain. Artificial heat, however, may be applied with benefit. Artificial respiration may also be needed, and may be applied the same as directed under DROWNING. A rectal injection of one quart of water as hot as can be borne is of benefit. If the condition of the stomach will tolerate, give hot drinks and stimulants. Remedies can be given with a hypodermic needle, but this part of the treatment falls upon the doctor. However, if a doctor is some distance away, the foregoing suggestions may not only revive the patient, but place him out of danger before the doctor arrives.

BLEEDING FROM INJURY.

—Hemorrhage is one of the most serious accidents that can occur. It is always a dangerous and troublesome complication for the doctor, and as the sudden loss of a large amount of blood is liable to cause death, every one should have some knowledge of the most efficient means to prevent it. Hemorrhages may come from arteries, veins, from a cut or torn surface, from the nose, stomach or lungs.

The controlling of hemorrhage may be largely aided by having the patient lie down and remain quiet, allowing the head and shoulders to rest a little lower than the feet and the rest of the body. In hemorrhage from a limb, keep the limb elevated. In all cases of severe accident or hemorrhage *a doctor should be sent for at once.*

Bleeding from an Artery.—Hemorrhage from a large artery is always dangerous, and may be recognized by its bright red color and by its coming in spurts, although the flow does not entirely cease at any time. When arteries are cut or torn, they retract within the sheath which surrounds them, and this allows greater opportunity for the blood to clot in the surrounding tissues. The inner and middle coats also contract, and this aids in forming a clot within the vessel itself. This contraction and clotting is of little importance when large vessels are wounded. When an artery is cut or torn, immediate pressure should be made with the hands. If occurring *in the arm above the elbow*, pressure should be made a little to the inner side of the front of the arm along the inner border of the biceps muscle. This is the line of the large artery which supplies the arm and hand. If hemorrhage occurs *below the elbow*, pressure may be made along the same line, or directly in front of the arm in the center of the elbow. When hemorrhage occurs *in the leg*, *if high up*, it may be controlled by making deep pressure in the center of the groin. This will compress the large artery which supplies the leg. The artery extends from that point downward toward the inner side of the knee. Pressure may be made along this line. As it extends down the leg this large artery gradually winds backward, and at the knee joint is directly in the center of the back of the leg. This point, or just above the knee, is the best place for checking hemorrhage that may occur *lower down in the leg or in the foot*, because at the knee joint the artery divides into two large branches. Pressure is most satisfactorily controlled by tying a handkerchief or some cloth about the limb, bringing the knot over the line of the artery and twisting the bandage with a stick. This is the only way in which success may be attained from the groin to the knee, because the layers of muscles are so thick and the artery is placed so deep that ordinary pressure with the hands would be of little or no benefit.

RECOMMENDED TREATMENTS.—

A. Perfect quiet, with constriction of the part by means of a rubber band or cord.—(7).

B. Tie limb between body and injury and twist the ligature until hemorrhage is checked. If about body, apply compress soaked in Turpentine, and bandage firmly until skilled assistance arrives.—(60).

C. Make out of cloth a pad larger than wound, place over wound, tie in place with handkerchief or strap, and with a stick twist till bleeding stops. Where no pad is handy, place knot of handkerchief over wound instead.

Bleeding from the Nose.—Hemorrhage from the nose in the great majority of cases is not dangerous, and quite serious cases may be controlled by plugging the nose with cotton or a soft cloth. In the more serious forms, however, this will not control the trouble. The very best means to control serious hemorrhage from the nose is by giving $\frac{1}{100}$ of a grain of Atropine. Repeat the dose in thirty minutes, and after that give once an hour. Whenever the face becomes flushed and the skin red, or should the pupil of the eye become widely dilated, this remedy should be stopped. We have treated several cases of severe hemorrhage from the nose and have never failed to control the trouble with Atropine. In some cases we have used Glonoin and Atropine together, giving $\frac{1}{100}$ of a grain of Glonoin with each dose of Atropine.

RECOMMENDED TREATMENTS.—

> **A.** Peroxide of Hydrogen...................... 1 ounce.
> Water... 1   "
>
> *Mix*. Put in an atomizer and spray the nose, or snuff up the nose from the hand.—(48).

B. From whatever cause this occurs, it may generally be stopped by putting a plug of lint into the nostrils. If this fails, apply a cold bandage to forehead, raise the head and clasp the hands underneath, so that the head will rest on both hands; moisten the plug slightly and again apply. Or you can try the simple remedies of snuffing salt and water or vinegar up the nostrils.

C. Wear a bright silk ribbon ¾ inch wide around the neck. The nose will never bleed so long as it is worn there.

I have prescribed this for thirty years, and it has never failed to prevent nosebleed.—(30).

> **D.** Antipyrin .... 10 grains.
> Water... 1 ounce.

Make a solution and apply with a piece of cotton to bleeding surface. If case is chronic, use internally Fluid Extract of Ergot in 10-drop doses, diluted in a little water, every 3 hours. —(23).

E. Take a piece of fat hog bacon just the size of the nostril, push it as far back as it can be pushed and let the patient hold a lump of ice in his mouth. The piece of bacon must be salty and three inches long. Have never known it to fail.—(20).

F. Elevate arms over head until hands meet and hold them there. Head must be elevated. Do not stoop over. Cold to bridge of nose and cold to upper part of spine.—(35).

Bleeding from Small Cuts or injuries may be stopped by cold water or ice, or pressure, until clot has had time to form. Or a bandage applied and kept wet with distilled Witch Hazel is excellent.

Bleeding from the Teeth arising from extraction: Cut a piece of clean, dry sponge, cone-shaped; compress tightly and put into cavity left by tooth.

Bleeding from the Lungs.—(See under HEMORRHAGE in Department I).

Bleeding from the Stomach.—(See under HEMORRHAGE in Department I).

Bleeding from the Bowels.—(See under HEMORRHAGE in Department I).

BLOWS over heart or lungs, or any important organ, are serious. Where patient has fainted, administer brandy frequently in small doses; rub spine with liniment.

BONES, BROKEN.—(See FRACTURES).

BRUISE.—An injury to the flesh caused by violent contact with a hard surface, as from a blow.

TREATMENTS.—

A. If a severe bruise, as from the blow of a hammer or a horse stepping on the foot, as soon as possible put the bruised part into cold water, notwithstanding it will cause an increase of pain. Keep it in the water for five or ten minutes, then take it out, dry, and put on freely any mild liniment for the same length of time. After a few minutes place it again in the water and repeat the application of liniment. The same treatment may be repeated three or four times during the first day; afterwards apply the liniment only. If the bruise is large and upon such parts as cannot be put into cold water, let cloths be wrung out of cold water and laid upon it, and from time to time apply freely a mild liniment.

Note.—The object of applying the cold is to contract the small vessels and prevent inflammation.

B. Cold water applied constantly.—(6).

C. Dissolve a teaspoonful of Sugar of Lead in a quart of distilled Witch Hazel and keep the bruised part wet with it.—(4).

Note.—The advantage of applying Sugar of Lead and Witch Hazel lies in the fact that both are astringent, hence tend to contract the small vessels the same as the application of cold water, and perhaps to a greater extent.

D. *If the injury has resulted in breaking the skin and causing an open wound.*—Steep Wormwood, wet cloths with the solution and lay over the bruised part; or apply the following ointment:

> Vaseline .... 1 ounce.
> Subnitrate of Bismuth .... 1 scruple.
> Carbolic Acid .... 10 drops.

> *Mix* well and rub over the bruise twice a day.

BURNS AND SCALDS.—The danger arising from burns will depend much upon the extent of the surface burned and the depth of the injury—if very extensive and deep, the patient may never rally; or if flame to any considerable extent has been drawn into the lungs, the probability is that the person cannot be saved. The teaching is that where a burn covers one-third of the surface, death is almost sure to follow.

The great danger from large burns is blood poisoning. All the tissues destroyed soon commence to decompose and many poisons are produced. These poisons are rapidly absorbed into the circulation, and this produces a condition of blood poisoning that may result fatally.

TREATMENTS.—

What To Do.—In the case of a severe burn or scald, if nothing else is at hand, apply cold water immediately and but little inflammation will follow. In the case of a child being burned at the table by spilling a cup of hot tea or coffee, do not wait to remove his clothing, but dash cold water on at once. This will prevent the hot clothing from burning deeper and protect the skin at the same time. Lift the clothing and pour on more water, then remove the clothing and apply cold water by wetting cloths and laying over the surface. The cloths applied must be kept wet *without removing them.* Cold milk is better than cold water because it is thicker and offers better protection.

To secure benefit from this treatment it must be applied almost immediately—quickly enough to arrest the heat before the skin has been destroyed. Otherwise it will not be so valuable as Lime Water and Linseed Oil, baking Soda and other recommended treatments.

A. For pain following burns and scalds nothing gives greater relief than the application of cold sweet milk. This may be applied on a cloth frequently changed, or, when possible, by immersing the injured surface in a vessel containing the milk. The application should be continued until there is freedom from pain, and followed by dressings of some mild, soothing antiseptic.—(1).

B. If burn is severe, cover surface with dry baking Soda and bind lightly with a soft cloth.

C. Use equal parts of Lime Water and Linseed Oil. Apply by saturating small pieces of cloth and laying over the burn. Keep cloths wet by pouring on the solution. Do not take dressing off every day. If blisters form, open at base so as to let the fluid out. Do not make a large opening. After heat is out dry Boracic Acid makes a good application.—(53).

Note.—We have stated before that the smarting and burning were caused by the destruction of the outer layer of the skin and exposure of the deeper layer. The benefit derived from Lime Water and Linseed Oil is produced as follows: The lime contained in Lime Water has a soothing effect upon the deeper tissues, while the oil acts as a covering and excludes the air.

D. Apply distilled Witch Hazel every few minutes. This will stop all smarting, even in the case of a burn from hot grease.

E. Common washing Soda or cooking Soda, 3 tablespoonfuls to a pint of water. Apply freely.—(7).

F. If clothes stick to the flesh, do not tear them off, but flood the part with Olive Oil; where clothes do not stick, apply cloths saturated with strong solution of baking Soda.

G. Apply white of eggs.

H. Lay on cloths wet in Olive Oil and Laudanum. Cloths wet in Lime Water are also good. To heal burns, apply an ointment made as follows:

Vaseline... 1 ounce.
Oxide of Zinc................................. 1 drachm.

Mix thoroughly with caseknife, spread on linen cloths and place over them.

I. In case of scalds, exclude the air at once with Soda and Flour, covering the parts and keeping them covered. — (33).

CHOKING. — (See FOREIGN BODIES IN LARYNX, also FOREIGN BODIES IN ŒSOPHAGUS).

COLLAPSE.—Collapse is an extreme and sudden prostration of the vital forces.

Symptoms.—Loss of consciousness, usually sudden, and complete relaxation of the system. Breathing may be deep or shallow. The pulse may be slow, full and strong, or rapid, small and weak. The pupils may be dilated or contracted, and the face may be flushed or pale.

Causes.—These variations are produced by the various effects on the brain, and may result from an excessive use of intoxicating liquors, from opium, concussion, fractures of the skull, apoplexy, uræmic poisoning, etc. If a man is found in an unconscious condition, a distinction should be made if possible. The most frequent causes are severe accidents or following operations.

TREATMENTS.—

What to Do Till the Doctor Comes.—The treatment of these conditions consists of stimulants to overcome the weakened condition of the heart and lowered vitality of the patient. The sluggish circulation must be aroused. Drugs for this purpose, such as Digitalis, Strychnine, Glonoin, etc., would have to be administered by a physician, but if he is delayed in coming, and especially if he is some distance away, the following suggestions carried out may place the patient out of danger before he arrives.

First place the patient in a comfortable position and give an abundance of fresh air. Apply artificial heat externally. Bottles or jugs filled with boiling water should be placed around him, and an abundance of covering should be used. This aids in bringing the blood to the surface and improves the circulation. Also inject into the rectum a pint of strong coffee as hot as can be borne. The foot of the bed should be raised so that the head and shoulders are lower than the hips. If the patient can swallow, give hot drinks.

If the patient could be placed in a warm bath and the temperature gradually raised until the water was quite hot, it would relieve the necessity of much of the foregoing treatment.

A. In almost all cases of collapse the surface is cold, the circulation is feeble and respiration is weak, and the treatment, almost without exception, is stimulants and artificial heat. In a state of collapse the patient may not always be able to swallow, but artificial heat can be applied with advantage in every case where the surface is cold.   In collapse from sunstroke (see SUNSTROKE), the treatment is radically different.

B. Apply Ammonia to nostrils on a handkerchief, so it will not be poured into nose by accident. Give a little brandy sling and apply artificial heat. As improvement occurs, give cup of hot beef tea or hot milk.—(14).

C. Keep patient perfectly quiet. Apply warm flannel to extremities. If patient can swallow, give strong coffee.

If due to hemorrhage, keep head low and stop flow of blood. —(13).

Collapse may Occur from Various Causes, a number of which are enumerated below. It should be remembered that the symptoms of the various conditions are similar, and it is often extremely difficult to differentiate. However, in most cases the previous history of the patient will aid materially in clearing up the doubt.

From Injury, or Intoxication.—Examine carefully for any injury. Alcohol is noticeable in the breath, yet a man may be stricken with apoplexy while drunk, or may fracture the skull by falling while under the influence of opium or alcohol. Again, one drink may give the smell of alcohol, but one drink will not produce collapse; so the smell of alcohol is uncertain. If it is alcoholic stupor, steady and firm pressure against the arched surface just beneath the eyebrows, to the nasal side (towards the nose) of the center, will arouse temporary consciousness.

From Epilepsy, or Uræmia.—In coma following epilepsy, the temperature is normal and the patient can be aroused. In uræmic poisoning, the temperature is below normal at first, and there are usually convulsions, dropsy and albuminaria. Examine the urine if the conveniences are at hand. In uræmic stupor the breathing is sharp and the pupils dilated. See EPILEPSY or URÆMIA.

From Apoplexy.—The breathing is slow and noisy, pulse strong and slow, face flushed, the arteries of the neck are throbbing, the pupils are uninfluenced by light, the paralyzed cheek is drawn to one side, and is usually drawn in and puffed out with each breath, and the temperature, which is at first below normal, rises later on. See treatment for APOPLEXY.

From Opium.—The pupils are contracted to a pin point, breathing is shallow, there is no paralysis, and unconsciousness comes on gradually. If enough opium has been taken to produce unconsciousness, it is an indication of opium poisoning. See treatment under POISONS, ANTIDOTES AND TREATMENTS. It is sometimes impossible to distinguish between opium poisoning and apoplexy.

From Concussion of the Brain.—There is complete muscular relaxation, the skin is pale and cold, the pulse quick and small, breathing is shallow and the temperature is below normal. Concussion sufficient to produce unconsciousness may be looked upon as serious as there is always liable to be more or less laceration of the brain substance. See treatment for CONCUSSION OF THE BRAIN.

From Compression of the Brain, as from a fractured skull, there is unconsciousness. The skin is hot, the breathing slow and noisy, both cheeks may be drawn in and puffed out with each respiration, the pulse is slow and full, and the pupils are dilated and do not respond to light.

What to Do Till the Doctor Comes.—Place the patient in a comfortable position. If it is very hot, place him in the shade; if it is cold, place where warm. Send for a doctor. While waiting, hold Ammonia to the nose occasionally, bathe the face with a little Whiskey or Alcohol in water, and, if he can swallow, give hot drinks—sling, or something of the kind.

From Hemorrhage.—In all cases maintain absolute quiet. If from an extremity, as a leg or arm, keep the limb elevated and proceed as directed under BLEEDING FROM INJURY; if the hemorrhage is from the body, stop the flow of blood by making pressure with a handkerchief or other soft cloth.   If the patient grows weak, give stimulants, as hot Whisky sling; or even hot water will improve the strength and vitality.

If the case is desperate, as following the loss of a large amount of blood, the doctor may give an injection of salt solution in the following manner:

Add ½ teaspoonful of common salt to 1 pint of warm water. Place in a fountain syringe, attach a long hollow needle to the tube of the syringe, lift up the skin from the abdominal cavity, insert the needle and allow the salt solution to penetrate the tissues.   The needle may be partially withdrawn occasionally and inserted in another direction.   In this way more of the fluid can be used.   In female patients the breast is the most successful place to inject the salt solution.   This injection increases the blood pressure, and this calls for increased heart action; in a word, it is a heart stimulant.   This is especially valuable where there has been much hemorrhage, as the salt solution takes the place of the blood that has been lost.   It is well known that following severe hemorrhage the heart action can be temporarily maintained on a normal salt solution.   Nature will not maintain her forces without a purpose.   If a large amount of blood has been lost, the heart action is correspondingly weakened because there is little work for it to do.   If the normal amount of fluid can be replaced, the heart action immediately improves to meet the extra demands made upon it, and for a time the artificial fluid injected is successful in maintaining vitality.   More than 1 pint of salt solution can be injected.

CONTUSIONS.—A contusion means a bruise. See BRUISES.

CRUSHED LIMBS.—*What to Do till the Doctor Comes.*— *Fingers and Toes* should be carefully modeled into shape, laid on a small splint, and dressed with soft white cloth soaked in cold or hot water.

Hands and Feet.—Wrap in something soft and warm.   Use cold only when bleeding is profuse.   Lay the patient down and keep the injured member elevated.   This is especially important if there is much bleeding.   If there is no hemorrhage, keeping it elevated will tend to prevent swelling.

Arms and Legs.—Treat as for hands or feet.   Do not remove clothing except to cut away, and replace by warm covering.

DISLOCATIONS.—Dislocation is abnormal displacement of one bone with another.   It may be partial or complete.   Dislocations are generally the result of accident, but may result from disease where the ligaments and other structures are relaxed or destroyed. Where the skin remains unbroken, it is called *Simple Dislocation;* where the tissues are injured and the wound reaches the surface and breaks through the skin, it is called *Compound Dislocation;* when besides the dislocation there is fracture of a bone and rupture of an important artery, it is termed *Complicated Dislocation.* Dislocations are rare in infancy and in old age, because in infancy the bones are very flexible and yield to violence, and in old age they are more brittle and fracture easily. A dislocation may be mistaken for a fracture (see FRACTURES). Dislocations *of the ankle or knee* may be forward, backward, inward or outward. Dislocations *of the hip* may be upward and downward, upward and forward or upward and backward. Dislocations *of the elbow* may include both bones of the fore-arm, or only one bone. The *under jaw* can only be displaced forward.

TREATMENT.—

The treatment for dislocation of the *under jaw* is to place the patient's head against the back of a chair, wrap your thumbs with a clean handkerchief or soft cloth, stand in front of him, place your thumbs on the lower double teeth, press quickly and firmly downward and backward, and at the same time raise his chin. This is usually effectual.

In dislocation of the *thumb or a finger*, make a loop of soft cloth and pass over it. Pull in the same line as the thumb, or finger. The sensation as well as the sound will indicate when the bone has been replaced; also the natural appearance of the joint will indicate that the dislocation has been overcome.

Dislocations of other joints always require the services of a doctor, hence will be spoken of only in a general way. They generally require extension by force until the contraction of the muscles are overcome, when the bone may be replaced in its proper position. While waiting for the doctor, make the patient as comfortable as possible, as directed under FRACTURES.

DROWNING.—TREATMENTS.—

A. Loosen clothing, if any; wipe dry; wedge mouth open and keep open. Empty the body of water by laying it on its stomach and lifting by the middle, so that the head hangs down; also jerk the body a few times, and continue this treatment as long as water flows from the mouth. After water has been got rid of, turn patient on back, placing him on level ground, and keep mouth wedged as before. Now place the left forefinger on tongue to keep it in place, and with right hand press upon the abdomen, making the pressure toward the back and head of patient; press gently at first, but increase the pressure until as much air as possible has been forced out of the chest, and then withdraw the hand so that the lungs may fill. Repeat these movements, at first making them eight or ten times a minute, then increasing to twelve or fifteen a minute. This is Satterthwaite's method. Where there are several persons to assist, Sylvester's method may be used in addition. The arms should be pressed upon the chest at the same time that the abdomen is pressed upon, and when the hand is withdrawn from the abdomen the arms should be brought up by the side of the head. *Do not give up.* People have been saved after hours of patient effort. When breathing begins, wrap patient warmly, rub limbs and body briskly, and give warm drink, or brandy in small doses at first— teaspoonful at a time.

B. If a barrel, keg or anything of that kind is at hand, lay the person on it, face downward, and roll him forwards and backwards, keeping the head *low* to force out the water. If nothing of that kind is at hand, take him by the heels and hold him up, and give the body several light jerks. After the water is all out of the lungs, place the patient on his back and work the arms up by the side of the body, above the head and down again as if you were working a pump. When the arms are brought down, press the hands firmly against the chest to expel the air; when the arms are raised, the lungs are allowed to fill. Keep the patient in a horizontal position and repeat the movements regularly and slowly—fifteen to eighteen times a minute. After he has rallied and is breathing, give a little hot Brandy sling, if he is able to swallow it. Also apply artificial heat, as this will bring the blood to the surface and aid in improving the circulation.

C. Get patient out of water as soon as possible and turn him on face. Stand astride him with your face towards his head. Put your hands under middle of body and raise it up so his head will be down, so that the water will run out of his lungs. Hold him as long as water runs, then let him down and pick him up again. Shake him till all the water is out of the lungs, then turn him on his back and go to his head. Seize his arms below the elbows, bring them out at right angles with his body and up over his head, and back again, working them back and forth in this way; and every time they are brought down, press *firmly* against the chest. These movements should be slow and regular.—(13).

EAR, THINGS IN.—Seeds or grain, sand, a pea, bead, small button, and many other articles, may become lodged at the inner end of the canal which forms the external ear. In giving a description of this canal (see EAR AND ITS DISEASES, **Department I**) it will be remembered that we stated it is not straight, but somewhat curved, and that the inner part extends downward. By taking hold of the external ear and lifting it upwards and a little backwards, the canal may be partially straightened and its termination be brought into view. While holding the ear in this position the objects mentioned, or various other articles which may have found their way into the canal, may often be grasped with a pair of tweezers or forceps and removed. Washing out the ear with warm water and a small syringe will often succeed in removing foreign bodies. If these means fail, the end of a match or toothpick may be covered with wax or a little glue, when by carefully pressing against the object it may adhere and be drawn out by this means. Sometimes it is necessary to secure the services of a doctor.

EYEBALL, INJURIES TO.—Serious injury always requires the services of a doctor at once. Place a cold wet cloth over the eye till he comes. There are many slight injuries where the eyeball may become only slightly inflamed and a little sore. In these cases keep the eye from the light; if necessary, keep it bandaged for a few days, or wear colored glasses, and use any of the Eye Waters recommended (see Index). If a foreign body becomes lodged against the eyeball, see FOREIGN BODIES IN THE EYE.

BLACK EYE.—A blow over or near the eye is liable to result in discoloration and swelling. For this condition various methods of treatment are used. Years ago it was customary to apply leeches, and perhaps that practice is still followed by some. Others recommend binding on a small piece of raw beefsteak. A good application, and one that can be quickly and easily applied, is to wet a small piece of cotton or a small piece of soft cloth with Listerine and apply over the injured surface, keeping the cloth wet with it.

EYE, THINGS IN.—(See FOREIGN BODIES IN THE EYE).

FAINTING—INSENSIBILITY.—Where patient is partially conscious, give stimulants. Ammonia or Cologne Water may be inhaled. Sprinkle cold water in face, loosen clothing, place in recumbent position and introduce fresh air into the room. No violent measures should be used to arouse a patient who may or may not be insensible. In all cases of apparent insensibility the attendants should be careful as to what they say within hearring, for while the patient can neither speak nor move, he may be perfectly conscious of what is passing around him, and the effort to speak may do him great injury; or unfavorable remarks from bystanders would naturally prove detrimental.

See also FAINTING in **Department I.**

FALLS.—If one has had a severe fall and is wholly or partially conscious, move as little as possible in case of broken bones. Place in comfortable position, loosen clothes carefully and apply restoratives. If bones are broken, see FRACTURES.

FIRE IN ONE'S CLOTHING.—Don't allow the victim out of doors or in draught. Roll him in carpet, rug, coat, cloak, quilt, or any convenient wrap. Leave only the head out for breathing. Prevent inhaling the flames.

FOREIGN BODIES—Steel, etc., IN THE EYE.— When a small piece of steel, stone or other hard substance strikes the eyeball, it may and usually does become so firmly adherent that it is removed with difficulty.

TREATMENT.—

The best way to manage these cases is to dissolve from 2 to 4 grains of Muriate of Cocaine in a drachm of water. Drop a little into the eye every two or three minutes until sensibility is relieved, and then with a sharp-pointed instrument dislodge the foreign body. It may be necessary to turn the lid upward in order to expose the cause of the trouble. To relieve the inflammation and soreness that is occasioned, mix the following:

> Sulphate of Zinc .... 1 grain.
> Morphine 2   "
> Boric Acid 20   "
> Water .... 1 ounce.
>
> Drop this into the eye from four to six times a day.

If there is much swelling and inflammation, the patient should remain in the house and keep either hot or cold packs over the eye. Dissolve 2 drachms of Boric Acid in 8 ounces of water. Saturate a small cloth or piece of cotton, place it over the eye and keep it wet with this solution.

Sometimes a small body may become lodged under the lid and it is impossible to discover it. Such cases may often be relieved in the following manner: Add a teaspoonful of whole clean Flaxseed to 1 ounce of water, stir frequently until a mucilage is formed, raise the eyelid and drop in as much as the eye will hold, allowing it to float around under the lid. By reason of its density the mucilage in coming in contact with the foreign body carries it along with it, and eventually the eye is freed from it. Whole Flaxseed is sometimes placed under the lid and the result is the same. The seeds are so smooth and oily that they cause no friction or irritation, and in coming in contact with the foreign body they dislodge it.

As a rule dirt or a cinder may be seen and easily removed with a clean silk handkerchief wrapped around the end of a lead pencil. Or, close the eye for a few minutes, allow tears to accumulate, roll the eyeball inward, and blow the nose on that side. This is sometimes all that is necessary.

FOREIGN BODIES IN THE LARYNX. — Foreign bodies, such as coins, buttons, small nails, pieces of bone or pieces of meat may become lodged in the larynx or windpipe. With children it is more apt to be peas, beans, cherry stones, small corks or carpet tacks. This makes little difference, however, as the result is the same in all cases.

Symptoms. — Violent coughing, strangling, and a feeling of suffocation with cyanosis, that is, the face becoming blue. If the foreign body is large, the struggle is desperate. If not quickly dislodged, the symptoms may become less violent, but the suffering is great, and unless the body is removed death soon results. Sometimes it is possible to locate the body from audible gurgling sounds, which correspond to the respiration. Where the body is not removed, inflammation followed by redness on the surface may point to its exact location. Should the substance be carried into the lungs, pneumonia might follow or an abscess result. If it was confined to the upper part of the air passage, adhesions might form with other surrounding structures; but unless the body is removed, death usually occurs before this has had time to take place.

TREATMENT. —

First give an active emetic. Ipecac—the powder, syrup or fluid extract of—is always safe for this purpose, and especially with children. When the patient vomits, the head should be placed *low*. While the treatment may seem a little severe, if during vomiting the patient was held by his feet with the head down, and given several light jerks, the probabilities of dislodging the foreign body would be greatly increased. Inverting the patient as described and giving the body several jerks should be tried without the emetic, if the latter is not at hand. If these means fail, surgical interference will be called for. An opening should be made into the trachea, and, if possible, the body located and removed, and the wound closed. This operation is called tracheotomy.

FOREIGN BODIES IN THE ŒSOPHAGUS. — Coins, buttons, chicken bones, and other foreign bodies sometimes find their way into this tube, which leads from the throat into the stomach. The smallest part of the tube is at the beginning. The next smallest diameter is at its junction with the stomach. Foreign bodies which get into the œsophagus usually pass into the stomach without difficulty. Should they lodge, the symptoms would correspond to the size and shape of the article, whatever it might be. If it had sharp angles, there would be stinging pain; if it was large and smooth, there would be dull pain, less acute. If the body was large, it might cause difficulty in breathing, although this symptom would be limited. Besides interfering with swallowing, the danger of a foreign body in the œsophagus would be its liability to set up inflammation. Inflammation might result in adhesion to the surrounding parts, and ulceration might penetrate into the trachea, or windpipe, into the pleural cavity, into the sac which surrounds the heart, or into the aorta, the large blood vessel which passes from the heart through the chest cavity.

TREATMENT.—

If a doctor is not immediately at hand, give an emetic. Vomiting is one of the safest, and in many cases one of the surest means of removing the trouble. A doctor may take a pair of long, smooth, curved forceps and endeavor to grasp the body and bring it out; or, if unable to draw it out, push it into the stomach. If all other means fail and the case becomes serious, the œsophagus must be opened, the body removed and the wound closed up.

FRACTURES.—By fracture is meant the breaking of a bone. This is usually the result of external force. However, it may, and sometimes does result from muscular action. The term fracture is also applied to the breaking of cartilage or tendons. Fractures may be complete, *i. e.*, entirely through the bone, or incomplete. Long bones sometimes split lengthwise for a longer or a shorter distance. A *Complicated Fracture* includes injury to the surrounding tissues. It may extend to a joint, or important arteries or other structures may be included. *Compound Fracture* is so called when the broken ends of the bone project through the skin. *Impacted Fracture* is a term applied to fracture when the broken ends of the bones are driven into each other. This may happen in fracture of one of the bones of the leg from falling heavily and striking on the feet. When the bone is badly shattered or crushed, it is called *comminuted*. Bones may be fractured easily as a result of disease.

Diagnosis.—A fracture may be distinguished from a dislocation by the free and unnatural movement. In dislocation the limb is fixed or rigid. In fracture the ends of the bone may usually be felt grating on each other; in dislocation they cannot.

Try to rotate a fractured bone and only a part of it moves; in dislocation it moves as one piece. In fracture near the ends of the bones the head remains in position; in dislocation the head of the bone is out of the socket and appears in a new position. In many cases of fracture slight movement will cause the broken ends of the bones to produce a chucking sound which may be heard for some distance. There may be shortening from either dislocation or fracture, or fracture and dislocation may occur together. Fracture with impaction, *i. e.*, where the ends of the bone are driven together, is extremely difficult to diagnose. More or less swelling follows fracture, and when this becomes extensive, diagnosis may also be difficult. In a severe bruise the pain is diffused; in fracture it is largely confined to the point where the bone is broken. Many forms of injury may include injury to the nerve supplying the part to such an extent as to cause loss of motion, hence this symptom, *i. e.*, loss of power to move a limb, may be of little value in a case of suspected fracture. The collar bone is the one most frequently broken. Next come those of the arm or leg, the ribs and kneecap.

TREATMENT.—

What to Do Till the Doctor Comes.—At the present day, even out in the country, the services of a doctor can be secured in a very short time—in an hour or two—and any efforts to relieve the patient are but temporary.

Fracture of the Collar Bone.—In fracture of the collar bone the shoulder of the injured side is lower. It is also drawn forward and inward. When the bone is separated, the outer end of the inner fragment is drawn upward and overlaps the outer fragment. When not separated, the finger can detect some irregularity at the point of fracture. The pain is mostly located at the same point. The patient supports the arm of the injured side by the sound arm and hand as this relieves the pain. The head leans toward the injured shoulder as this relaxes the muscular tension and also aids in relieving pain.

If out in the field or in the woods and the collar bone is broken, take whatever is most convenient for a sling. Place it beneath the elbow of the arm on the injured side, draw the shoulder well up and backwards and tie the support over the sound shoulder, allowing the palm of the hand on the injured side to rest upon the breast of the sound side. The patient can walk to the house.

Fracture of the Ribs.—Place the patient in bed or on a couch and have a cuspidor within reach so that the expectorations may be noted by the physician. The object of this is to detect any blood that may be present in the sputum. Blood would indicate internal injuries. It would indicate that the lung had been perforated, and that blood had followed the wound into the air cells and tubes and was being eliminated by this route. Injury of this kind would, of course, indicate a serious condition.

Fracture of the Arm.—If the arm is broken, secure some light material, such as a thin piece of board, a shingle, or a small stick with the two sides flattened, to use for a splint. In the absence of anything else, tall grass or a handful of hay equally distributed over the inner side of the splint will answer for a temporary dressing, or the hay or grass may be used for a splint. Whatever is used should be bound on reasonably tight. Regarding the bandage, it is only necessary to say that whatever is most convenient should be used for this purpose.

If the *arm is broken below the elbow*, after applying the bandage the arm should be flexed (bent) at the elbow joint and supported by a sling until the patient can reach home.

Fracture of the Leg.—In the case of broken leg the same means should be used for bandaging, but in this case the patient cannot walk, hence some means of conveyance must be provided. The most convenient is a stretcher made by securing a blanket to two sticks and placing the patient thereon. The injured limb should be handled with care and maintained in a uniform position as nearly as possible. In nearly every case of this kind conveyance can be made with a team and wagon, but a stretcher is preferable because there is less jolting and less pain.

In cases of fracture with large swelling, *neither tight bandaging nor cold should be applied for any length of time*, as gangrene might result.

Fracture of the Kneecap.—The kneecap is a small, flattened, triangular bone situated in the front of the knee joint. The outer surface is slightly oval, the inner surface is concave. It is enclosed in an expansion of the tendons of the muscles of the front of the thigh, that is, those extending from the hip to the knee. After enclosing the kneecap, the tendon continues downward and is attached to a small prominence on the tibia, or shin bone. The muscles mentioned are called the extensors because they are the ones called into action in extending the limb.

Fracture of this bone is usually the result of external violence. It is said also to result sometimes from violent muscular action. Sometimes the tissues over the kneecap become swollen and the bursa (See BURSA, ENLARGED) becomes considerably distended by an excess of fluid. This is called *Housemaid's Knee,* so-called because this condition is most frequently met in women who work on their knees scrubbing floors, etc. The same condition over the bursa situated at the back of the elbow is sometimes called *Miner's Elbow*, and results from pressure of the elbow against the rocks while using the pick and shovel.

Symptoms.—When the kneecap is fractured, the parts are widely separated and may be easily detected by the fingers. The symptoms of housemaid's knee are enlargement and swelling. In case of housemaid's knee an abscess may follow. The symptoms of abscess are those of abscess elsewhere.

TREATMENT.—

Fracture of the kneecap requires the services of a doctor. Where there is swelling and enlargement from pressure, as in the case of *Housemaid's Knee*, it seems needless to state that the patient must keep off her knees. If an abscess forms, it should be opened at once.

Fracture of the Spinal Column.—It will be remembered that the spinal cord is situated in a canal within the spinal column, therefore occupies a protected position and is seldom exposed or injured. The spinal column is composed of many small bones united together. They are arranged in three groups resembling three short columns, the neck, back, and small of the back including the portion between the hips. This renders the whole structure less liable to injury, because it requires greater force to fracture or dislocate a short column than a long one. Again, the layer of cartilage which is placed between the bones forming the spinal column acts as a cushion to aid in preventing jar or injury. If a man should fall some distance and his back should be doubled over some prominence, undoubtedly the spinal column would sustain either fracture or dislocation, although dislocation would be most liable to occur. In dislocation one bone is driven forward on another, and if such displacement was carried far enough, the spinal cord would be compressed between the two.

That part of the spinal column most liable to injury is at or just above the small of the back, because that is nearest the center. The second most frequent point liable to injury would be the lower part of the neck where it joins the more fixed part of the spinal column between the shoulders. The third most frequent point would be at the junction of the neck and head, because the bones forming the spinal column situated in the neck are more freely movable. The upper ones, called the *atlas* and *axis*, are the most liable to injury or displacement from blows applied to the head.

TREATMENT.—

In case of fracture or dislocation of the spinal column we know of no form of treatment that insures satisfactory results. Perhaps the extension method is the best, but even that is liable to fail.

FREEZING.—The part should be restored by rubbing with snow or cold water until the white color has been replaced by the natural color and pain is felt; then apply Olive Oil. For general freezing, rub with cold applications in a cold room that is gradually warmed. When patient is able to swallow, give stimulants and hot drinks, cover warmly and allow to rest.

FROSTBITE.—(See CHILBLAINS in **Department I**).

HEAT-STROKE.—This is an exhaustion due to excessive heat. A subject of heat exhaustion usually becomes unconscious. This may occur suddenly and be accompanied with tremors or convulsions, but as a usual thing unconsciousness is preceded by dizziness or vertigo. The surface remains cool and the breathing is natural, but the pulse is so feeble as to be almost imperceptible.

SUNSTROKE.—There is usually no warning in a case of sunstroke. The subject of it becomes immediately unconscious, falls in convulsions or is stricken with paralysis. The surface instead of being cool, as in a case of *Heat-stroke*, is hot and flushed, the eyes are bloodshot, and the breathing either rapid and shallow or slow and heavy.

The treatment in sunstroke as indicated by the above symptoms differs greatly from what is proper in a case of *Heat-stroke*.

TREATMENTS.—

Heat-Stroke.—*What to Do Till the Doctor Comes.*—Treatment should be prompt and administered on the spot, if possible; that is, time should not be wasted in carrying the patient any distance. Place him in a recumbent position, with the head low, loosen the clothing and keep bystanders away so that air may circulate freely about him. Give stimulants at once—whiskey or brandy in small doses, say a teaspoonful every fifteen minutes. If he is unable to swallow, inject two or three tablespoonfuls of brandy into the rectum. Bathe the temples in Camphor and apply Hartshorn to the nostrils.

A. If surface is hot and burning, strip and sprinkle freely with cold water. If surface is cold and clammy and pulse weak, give stimulants and an enema of hot salt solution.—(60).

Sunstroke.— *What to Do Till the Doctor Comes.*—Keep wrapped in sheets wet with cold water. Keep head elevated. Get a doctor as quickly as possible.

A. Ice bags to the head, and even an ice pack for the whole body if the case is a very bad one.

For internal treatment:

Bromide of Potash.........	2 drachms.
Fluid Extract Ergot...................	2 "
Water	4 ounces.

Dose.— Teaspoonful in ½ glass of water every three hours.

B. Cold water and ice to the head. Low diet. Perfect quiet in a cool place.—(7).

C. Horizontal position. Cool place. Sponge with cool water.—(17).

NOSE, THINGS IN.—Sometimes small children force buttons, peas, small corks or various other articles into one of the nasal cavities. They may be pressed so high up that their removal is difficult. In our experience in cases of this kind we have always succeeded by the following method: Make a short, sharp bend at the end of a small probe, insert the probe until it touches the foreign body, press the probe to one side and forcibly insert it past the body, then turn the probe so that the hook will be directed toward the center of the cavity, draw down on it, and the object will be brought down with it.

SCALDS.—(See under BURNS).

SHOCK.—When from accident or other cause there is great prostration of the vital forces, the condition is often spoken of as shock.

Cause.—Violent collision with other bodies, or the concussion caused by them. A sudden striking together, or against something firm and resistant, would produce shock. It is well known that a blow over the "pit" of the stomach may cause death without leaving any visible signs of injury. It is claimed that occasionally life is destroyed by sudden and powerful mental emotions, and we know personally that this may be true in those suffering with heart disease. The cause of all forms of shock is the sudden arrest of heart action due to violent disturbance of the nervous system.

Symptoms.—If the shock is a severe one, the symptoms are extreme pallor, a cold, clammy skin, feeble pulse, pinched face, dilated pupils, and bewilderment or loss of the mental faculties. In the milder forms of shock the patient may only be bewildered and talk incoherently. Nausea and vomiting are frequently associated with shock.

TREATMENTS.—

A. If a severe shock is due to injury, the shock must be treated first and the injury afterward. Artificial heat must be applied at once—to the whole body, if possible. Also the rectal injection of a quart of hot coffee, made stronger than for drinking purposes, is one of the best means of stimulating the vital powers. If the patient can swallow, stimulants should be given in small quantities at short intervals.

B. If it results from loss of blood or from severe injury, place patient in reclining posture with head lower than feet. If in bed, raise the foot a little by placing bricks under bedposts. Inject into the rectum 2 quarts of hot water into which has been thrown 1 tablespoonful of common kitchen salt. Give two teaspoonfuls of Whiskey at intervals of fifteen minutes.—(49).

C. Keep the patient quiet. Give Brandy or Whiskey. Put hot bottles to the feet and limbs.—(20).

D. Give Whiskey—one or two doses of ½ ounce each. Put hot water bottles to feet and limbs.—(41).

Electric Shock.—If insensible, strip off clothes, dash cold water on chest with some force, or proceed with artificial respiration as in drowning.

SNAKE BITES.—According to the researches of the Smithsonian Institute it appears that only ten per cent of rattlesnake bites are fatal, one per cent of copperheads, and no fatal cases from moccasin bites. From this it would seem that snake bites are not so fatal as generally supposed. It is believed the results depend largely upon the condition of the blood of the patient bitten. It is also believed by those who have made observation and studied along this line that many deaths following snake bites are due directly to fright.

Symptoms.—The symptoms of bites from all poisonous reptiles are about the same—rapid swelling and severe pain. The skin of the patient may assume a mottled appearance, and later there may be spasms, stupor or unconsciousness.

TREATMENTS.—

A. The same as that given under HYDROPHOBIA. If the bite is on an extremity, as the finger, hand or foot, apply a cord tightly about the limb in order to shut off the circulation. It would seem advisable to make several applications of this kind, and in removing the constrictions first to remove the one nearest the body, later the next one and so on. If there is prostration of the vital forces, give stimulants. Whether Whiskey or other popular remedies are used in these cases, it should be remembered that active elimination is all-important as this relieves the system of poison; hence the value of active cathartics and free elimination by the skin.

Note.—As stated under BEE STINGS, the small boy's application of black mud is believed by many to be the best treatment in those cases, and from our experience it is also equally valuable in snake bites. The following occurrence would serve to demonstrate its value in wounds of this kind, and also demonstrates the instinct of animals:

At a certain place on the banks of Pine Creek, in Pennsylvania, is a ledge of rocks which contains, or a few years ago contained, an immense number of rattlesnakes While hunting near this vicinity one day we suddenly heard the yelp of our faithful dog "Tige." This was followed in rapid succession by a number of short, sharp barks. Hurrying to the scene we found the dog surrounded by a number of rattlesnakes which bit him in many places. Suddenly the dog disappeared and we were unable to find him for several hours We finally discovered him on the bank of the creek nearly buried in soft mud. He suffered no inconvenience and gave no evidence whatever of his late exciting encounter with the rattlers.

B. Echinacea given in full doses every one or two hours is said to be a positive cure for the bite and sting of all poisonous reptiles and insects.—(30).

C. Suck the wound immediately, or cut it out.—(38).

D. Put 5 drops Tincture of Iodine in ⅔ glass of water. Give a teaspoonful every quarter of an hour for three hours, then at longer intervals as seems necessary.—(43).—Homeopathic.

SPRAINS.—A sprain is a sudden wrench caused by falling, slipping or stepping upon some loose object with the result that a joint is injured or *sprained*. The ligaments which support the joint are stretched and torn, or may be broken. The nerve fibers and muscles are more or less injured. The muscles or tendons may be injured or displaced. A sprain may be the result of a self-reduced dislocation. The ankle, knee and elbow are the joints most often sprained. The free movement of the hip joint and shoulder joint renders them comparatively free from accident. If a joint is badly sprained, it is more liable to injury afterwards; it does not regain its original strength for the reason that the torn and displaced structures cannot be arranged or replaced in their natural position. Ligaments may be torn loose or separated and fail to unite, and the joint will be weakened in proportion.

TREATMENTS.—

A. Sprains require immediate attention. The injured part should be wrapped in flannels wrung out of hot water and covered with a dry bandage. The limb should not be allowed to hang down, but kept elevated to prevent swelling.

B. Sprains of the ankle or wrist, if seen immediately after the injury, can best be treated by a simple bandage to the joint, which is left in place 24 hours. After that the joint is supported by a basket strapping of adhesive plaster.—(40).

C. Bathe parts well in hot water, afterwards bathe thoroughly with the following solution : Salt, 1 or 2 tablespoonfuls, Vinegar, Alcohol and water of each enough to make one pint. —(64).

D. Salt and the white of an egg applied forms a cast.—(37) —Homeopathic.

E. Put the part at rest and apply hot applications.—(20).

STINGS.—Sometimes the result of bee stings, or the sting of a single bee, is quite serious. However, death seldom follows unless the individual is stung many times.

Symptoms.—In most cases the only symptom is a little swelling, redness and pain. We have known those stung several times to give no symptoms or evidence at all. There are cases, however, where the results are radically different. The symptoms in a well marked case are vomiting, purging, great prostration and unconsciousness. For some distance around the sting the skin becomes spotted. This condition may be present all over the surface of the body and extremities. A bee sting on the tongue may cause rapid and enormous swelling of that organ, and swelling of the glottis to such an extent that in some cases it is said to cause death.

We were once called to treat the case of a little girl twelve years of age, who was stung only once. The bee lit on the little girl's hair and stung her on the top of the head. Either from the result of the hair or from some other cause, the wound appeared to be very slight, yet the child fell to the ground unconscious, there was rapid swelling about the head, face and eyes, also the hands and feet, and the whole surface of the body became as spotted as an adder. We applied the treatment given under "A," and it proved most successful. The spots and swelling disappeared in a few hours.

TREATMENTS.—

A. First remove the sting if it is present. The poison of a bee sting is said to be acid in its reaction, and it necessarily follows that any alkaline solution will neutralize the acid and destroy the poison, therefore, if necessary, make a slight opening in the skin with a sharp knife and apply Ammonia water or a strong solution of baking Soda in water. Aside from this the treatment would be largely symptomatic, *i. e.,* to treat whatever symptoms appear. An active cathartic might be of benefit in some cases. Stimulants might also be needed.

It is claimed that the small boy's application of black mud for bee stings, *insect* and *spider bites* is the best treatment of all. Just how this acts we are unable to say, neither does it make any particular difference. It is results we are all after rather than quibbling over a scientific diagnosis or the action of remedies applied. See under SNAKE BITES.

B. Apply Aqua Ammonia or strong Saleratus water.—(32).

STRANGULATION.—See FOREIGN BODIES IN LARYNX, also FOREIGN BODIES IN ŒSOPHAGUS).

SUFFOCATION.—(See ASPHYXIA).

SUNSTROKE.—(See under HEAT-STROKE).

THROAT, THINGS IN.—See FOREIGN BODIES IN ŒSO-PHAGUS).

WINDPIPE, THINGS IN.—(See FOREIGN BODIES IN LARYNX).

WOUNDS.—Wounds are injuries due to external mechanical force. Wounds are divided as follows:

Open Wounds: Those that are large on the surface.

Subcutaneous Wounds: Those that are larger beneath and small on the surface.

Incised Wounds: Those made with a sharp instrument where the tissues are cut clean and smooth.

Penetrating Wounds: Those resulting from a stab, bullet, nail, etc.

Contused Wounds: Where the parts are crushed, lacerated, or where the tissues are torn.

Poisoned Wounds: Where poison is conveyed into the wound.

Gunshot Wounds: If a bullet should strike some object and become flattened or misshapen and then enter the body, it might produce an open wound, a penetrating, contused or lacerated wound. Fragments of shell would do the same thing.

TREATMENT.—

If there is much hemorrhage, the first duty is to check the flow of blood. This may be done by making firm pressure with the hands or with a bandage or ligature, as described under BLEEDING FROM INJURY. Internal bleeding cannot be controlled without the services of a physician. Internal hemorrhage is always a grave and dangerous condition. To aid in checking the flow of blood the patient should remain perfectly quiet. Sometimes a bullet, nail or other blunt instrument may carry pieces of clothing into the wound. These should always be removed, but this, too, requires the services of a doctor. A bullet is more likely to push an artery aside and to cut it off. The same is sometimes true with tendons and ligaments. A bullet will sometimes glance when striking a bone. The contact may render the surface of the ball uneven or ragged, after which the wound would be much more severe if the ball should continue on its course.

If a bullet becomes lodged in the chest or abdominal cavity and does not interfere with the healing of the wound, nor produce paralysis, showing that it is not in contact with any plexis, or bundle of nerve fibers, it is better to allow it to remain. Continual probing, or an exploratory operation hunting for a ball that is doing no harm may, and often does result disastrously to the patient. A bullet that becomes lodged in the tissues and does not interfere with arteries or nerves soon becomes encysted, *i. e.*, surrounded by a membrane of new tissue. Once encysted, it may remain throughout a lifetime and produce no bad results or inconveniences.

The principal thing in caring for a wound is to *maintain absolute cleanliness*. Where the skin is broken or cut, the edges should be smoothed, if necessary, and then brought evenly together and stitched with clean silk. If about the face or neck, very fine thread or even horse hair may be used. This will prevent a scar. Wounds, especially bullet wounds, often produce great prostration of the vital forces, hence stimulants may be needed.

Department IV.

POISONS—SYMPTOMS, TREATMENTS AND ANTIDOTES.

In this chapter is given a list of all poisons which are likely to be taken, together with the most obvious symptoms, and common antidotes and treatments.

There is one general form of treatment that applies to any and all cases of accidental poisoning. *The antidote should be given first,* if at hand, as this removes the danger at once. Following this the patient should be given an active emetic to relieve the stomach of its contents. It is understood, of course, that if the antidote is not at hand, active vomiting should be instituted without delay.

If a doctor is at hand and can apply treatment immediately, perhaps an antidote would not be needed. A hypodermic injection of Apomorphine will produce vomiting usually in from three to five minutes. In this way the poison is removed before the antidote could be prepared and taken.

It is also necessary to state that if treatment is not instituted until some time after the poison is taken—after it has been absorbed into the circulation, producing its full effect—emetics are not only useless, but will work injury to the patient by aiding in destroying vitality. Rather than to give emetics in such cases, it is better to treat the condition; in other words, to treat the symptoms as they appear. If stupor is present, stimulants may be needed, although these should be given in small quantities at first.

The mineral acids are not so apt to produce dangerous or fatal effects as a result of their being taken into the circulation, but rather from their destruction of the walls of the stomach. Because of their caustic properties they are liable to penetrate the stomach walls; in other words, their effects are local. Strictly speaking, these acids are not poisons. The word "poison" applies only to such substances as produce their effect through the circulation. Carbolic Acid produces the same local effect, but destroys life by paralyzing the nervous system, particularly the heart.

489

Following corrosive poisons, such as Carbolic Acid, Corrosive Sublimate, or any of the mineral acids, some form of mucilage should be taken in considerable quantities; or the white of eggs or milk could be given with advantage. Mechanical protection is thus afforded the delicate mucous membrane of the mouth, throat and stomach, which has been more or less affected or destroyed by the action of the poison. By reason of such action the patient should receive only liquid food for some time.

The *stomach pump* is sometimes used to wash out the stomach in some cases of poisoning. We wish to state, however, that it should never be used where poisons of a corrosive nature have been taken. This refers especially to strong acids, such as Carbolic Acid, Nitric Acid, Muriatic Acid, etc. Neither should it be used where strong alkalies have been taken, such as Ammonia, Soda or Potash. The reason is that the remedies mentioned are very destructive to the mucous membrane of the stomach, and in such cases forcing a tube into this organ would only increase the damage.

Vegetable Poisons.—The poisonous principles in nearly all vegetable remedies, such as Aconite, Belladonna, Digitalis, etc., are neutralized or destroyed by Tannic Acid. This does not apply to Morphine. In the case of Morphine poisoning, Permanganate of Potash is claimed by some to neutralize the poison and act as a specific; this claim is denied by others. Tannic Acid will also neutralize some forms of chemical poisons, as Antimony, and others for which it is recommended.

Mineral Poisons.—Regarding mineral poisons, many of these may also be neutralized and their effects immediately destroyed by giving the proper antidote. For instance, dialyzed Iron, which is a very common preparation and kept in all drug stores, will immediately neutralize or destroy Arsenic when taken in any form. The dialyzed Iron and Arsenic form an insoluble compound. The white of eggs will immediately neutralize and destroy the effects of Corrosive Sublimate.

Acid Poisons.—When strong acids have been taken into the stomach they may be neutralized and their effects destroyed by alkalies, such as Soda or Potash, dissolved in water and taken in large quantities. The acid and the alkali, Soda or Potash, form a chemical compound. During their union, however, there is kept up a constant boiling process and a good deal of heat is produced. This heat may be so great as to injure the mucous membrane of the stomach and deeper tissues, hence it is believed to be a better plan to fill the stomach with pure water only. Have the patient drink 1, 2, 3 or more pints. This dilutes the acid to such an extent as to destroy its effects or render it so mild that it will do no harm. If a little ground Mustard is added to the water before the patient drinks it, it will not only dilute the acid, but vomiting will be produced at the same time.

Alkali Poisons.—In the case of poisoning from alkalies, the treatment should be the same. If it is desired to neutralize the alkali, it can readily be done by adding a liberal quantity of vinegar to the water; but the boiling and the heat would be the same as in the case of adding the alkali to the water taken for acid poisoning.

In the case of small children who are unable to drink a quantity of water, perhaps it is better to take the alkali, the Soda or Potash, in the treatment of acid poisoning, and to give vinegar as strong as can be taken for the alkali poisoning.

EMETICS.

An emetic is something taken into the stomach to cause vomiting. Below are given the most common emetics, viz., Mustard, Ipecac, Sulphate of Zinc, Sulphate of Copper and Tartar Emetic, and the proper method of taking them. Warm water is also an emetic, and warm water, water and Mustard are almost always at hand; Ipecac also is more or less frequently kept. The others mentioned probably could not be had unless obtained from a drug store, and even then might possess no advantage over the more common remedies just named. The Sulphates and Tartar Emetic not only fail to possess advantage, but in some cases they might prove a disadvantage to a dangerous degree. Sulphate of Zinc is depressing; Sulphate of Copper is irritating to the stomach; Tartar Emetic is still more depressing than Sulphate of Zinc; hence it follows that if taken in cases where the patient is extremely low, any of the three might aid in producing fatal effects.

Mustard Seed, ground.—Take a tablespoonful in a glass of wam water. If vomiting is not caused in fifteen minutes, repeat the dose.

Ipecac, Syrup or Fluid Extract of.—Take 1 teaspoonful in a little water or molasses. If vomiting is not caused in fifteen minutes, repeat the dose.

Sulphate of Zinc (White Vitriol).—Take ⅓ of a small teaspoonful of the powder (from 10 to 15 grains) dissolved in a little water. Can be repeated in twenty to thirty minutes if vomiting has not occurred.

Sulphate of Copper (Blue Vitriol).—Take a piece about the size of a common pea (3 to 5 grains) dissolved in a little water. Can be repeated in twenty to thirty minutes if vomiting has not occurred.

Tartar Emetic (Antimony).—Dissolve 6 or 8 grains in 8 tablespoonfuls of water. The dose is a tablespoonful of the mixture every ten or fifteen minutes until vomiting is caused.

MUCILAGES, OR MUCILAGINOUS DRINKS.
(TO FOLLOW CORROSIVE POISONING.)

Flaxseed tea is a common and excellent thing. Or, Gum Arabic, Slippery Elm bark or Comfrey root, soaked in water until mucilage is extracted.

Note.—Under the list of poisons a few articles are referred to others which are similar in their effects.

ACETATE OF COPPER.—(See BLUE VITRIOL).

ACETATE OF LEAD.—(See SUGAR OF LEAD).

ACONITE.—*Monk's Hood.*

Symptoms.—Nausea, vomiting, pain in the stomach; severe pain in the bowels with violent purging; cold sweats; rapid feeble pulse; color pale.

TREATMENT.—

Give ⅓ teaspoonful Tannin dissolved in water, and produce vomiting (if not already free enough) by drinking warm water, tickling the throat and giving emetics; give mucilages and stimulants, and apply external heat. Keep flat on back.

ALCOHOL.—*Rum, Brandy, Whiskey, Gin, etc.*—In large quantities a powerful narcotic poison.

Symptoms.—Inability to walk or stand, dizziness, highly flushed or pale face, noisy breathing, confusion of thought and unconsciousness.

TREATMENT.—

Cause vomiting by large draughts of warm water and by tickling the throat, or by emetics; pour cold water on the head and back of the neck; keep up motion; irritate the skin by brisk rubbing; give strong coffee. Use stomach pump. Artificial respiration may be needed.

AMMONIA.—*Spirits of Hartshorn.*

Symptoms.—Strong, burning taste in the mouth, heat in the throat and stomach, vomiting, cold clammy skin, small rapid pulse and great prostration. Death may occur in half an hour.

TREATMENT.—

Give vinegar and water, or any dilute vegetable acid; excite vomiting; give cathartics and opiates.

ANTIMONY.—(See TARTAR EMETIC).

AQUA FORTIS.—*Nitric Acid.*

Symptoms.—Strangulation in swallowing; mouth, lips and throat a yellow color; skin, cold and clammy; pulse, quick and small; retching, and vomiting of dark-colored fluids.

TREATMENT.—

Carbonate of Magnesia, calcined Magnesia, chalk or whiting in water; plaster from the wall softened with water; soap and water; wood ashes and water; milk; whites of eggs; oil. Or, as stated under *Acid Poisons* in the foregoing, drink large quantities of warm water containing 1 or more tablespoonfuls of ground Mustard.

ARSENIC.—*Rough on Rats, Paris Green, White Arsenic, Fowler's Solution, Black Oxide* (fly powder). Has little or no taste, and may be taken accidentally.

Symptoms.—Burning pain in the stomach, excessive thirst, vomiting, heat and tightness of the throat, diarrhea, slow and intermittent pulse, faintness, lethargy, palsy, convulsions, etc. Death occurs, on the average, in about twenty-four hours. Four grains have destroyed adult life.

TREATMENTS.—

A. Give 2 to 4 teaspoonfuls of dialyzed Iron; this forms an insoluble compound. Follow with tablespoonful of Syrup of Ipecac; or ground Mustard seed; or 3 to 5 grains of Sulphate of Copper; or 10 to 20 grains of Sulphate of Zinc. Give white of eggs; milk; Flaxseed tea; much warm water; or oil and Lime Water. Use stomach pump.

B. Give a good dose of iron rust, afterwards wash out the stomach and give freely of milk or cream.—(44).

Note.—It might take some time to secure a dose of iron rust and, if a drug store is within reach, a better plan would be to get an ounce of dialyzed Iron and give from 2 to 4 teaspoonfuls immediately, afterwards washing out the stomach, etc.

C. Empty the stomach as quickly as possible by thrusting finger down throat, or by giving warm Mustard water or salt water; then give milk or oil freely—Castor Oil, Linseed Oil or Sweet Oil, ½ glass; or all the milk that can be taken.—(9).

D. Dialyzed Iron in teaspoonful doses every 15 minutes. —(4).

E. Give anything to cause speedy vomiting.—(17).

F. Whites of 3 eggs, followed by copious draughts of warm water to produce free vomiting.—(19).

BELLADONNA.—(See DEADLY NIGHTSHADE).

BISMUTH.—*Oxide of Bismuth, Nitrate of Bismuth* (a white powder sometimes used as a cosmetic). *Subnitrate of Bismuth* is not a poison.

Symptoms.—Metallic taste in the mouth, heat and dryness of the throat and severe burning heat in the stomach and bowels, violent vomiting, diarrhea, pulse small and rapid, skin cold, breathing difficult, fainting and convulsions.

TREATMENT.—

Large quantities of milk; whites of eggs; oil. Cause vomiting by drinking large quantities of warm water containing one tablespoonful ground Mustard, or other emetic. Use stomach pump.

BLISTERING FLIES.—*Spanish Flies, Tincture of Cantharides.*

Symptoms.—Difficulty of swallowing and burning in the throat, violent pain in the stomach and bowels, vomiting, pain in the loins, and passage of bloody water with great pain.

TREATMENT.—

Produce vomiting by large draughts of warm water and tickling the throat with the finger or a feather; give milk or mucilaginous drinks.

BLUE VITRIOL.—*Sulphate of Copper, Blue Stone.*

Symptoms.—Strong metallic taste in the mouth, violent vomiting and purging, griping pains, frothing at the mouth, headache, dizziness, convulsions and insensibility.

TREATMENT.—

Have patient drink large quantities of water to wash out stomach, then give strong coffee, milk, whites of eggs, wheat flour and water, or mucilages.

CAMPHOR.

Symptoms.—Great excitement of nervous system, dizziness, vomiting, anxiety, small pulse, difficult breathing, fainting, cold skin, delirium and convulsions.

TREATMENT.—

Cause vomiting by drinking warm water or ground Mustard in warm water, and give mucilages, wine, and Opium or Laudanum.

CARBOLIC ACID.— This is a very frequent cause of poisoning as it is so easily obtained, and one that is generally fatal.

Symptoms.—The mucous membrane of the lips, tongue and cheeks is white, wrinkled and hardened from the action of the acid. The odor of Carbolic Acid is easily detected in the breath. There is an intense burning pain in the mouth, throat and stomach. The pupils are contracted, the skin is cold and clammy, and the pulse becomes weaker and weaker. Coma precedes death, which is sometimes accompanied by convulsions. Death may occur within an hour.

TREATMENT.—

Oil is the best application to external burns, but should not be used internally. Flaxseed tea in quantity or Mustard water given immediately by the pint or quart to dilute the acid and thus arrest its corrosive action on the tender mucous membrane of the stomach; soapy water is valuable. Stimulants may be given to prevent collapse.

CARBONATE OF LEAD.—(See WHITE LEAD).

CARBONIC ACID GAS.— Found in cellars, wells and
mines, and given off in burning charcoal and from stoves.

Symptoms. — Face swelled and more or less discolored, feeling of great weight in the head, dizziness, drowsiness, difficulty in breathing, suffocation and insensibility.

TREATMENT.—

Admit fresh air; rub the patient, especially over the lungs; cause artificial breathing (see DROWNING). Keep the head and back of the neck wet with cold water; or if the body is cold, give a warm bath, also 15 drops Tincture of Belladonna.

COBALT.—Often used as a fly poison.

Symptoms.—Pain and heat in the stomach and throat, violent retching and vomiting, cold skin, small rapid pulse, breathing rapid and difficult, diarrhea.

TREATMENT.—

Give emetics; also give freely of milk, white of eggs, wheat flour and water, or mucilages.

CORROSIVE SUBLIMATE. — *Bichloride of Mercury*.
Sometimes carelessly used as a bed-bug poison.

Symptoms.—Strong metallic or coppery taste in the mouth, burning heat in the throat, severe pain in the stomach and bowels, vomiting and purging, face flushed and swollen or anxious and pale, pulse small, irregular and rapid, skin clammy and cold, tongue white and shriveled, breathing difficult, fainting, convulsions and insensibility.

TREATMENT.—

First give the white of eggs and then cause vomiting as quickly as possible by drinking warm water containing 1 tablespoonful of ground Mustard; tickle the throat with the finger or a feather to aid in inducing vomiting; give wheat flour and water or liquid starch.

CREOSOTE.—(See OIL OF TAR).

DEADLY NIGHTSHADE.—*Belladonna.*

Symptoms.— Dryness of the throat, sickness at the stomach, dizziness, dimness of sight, pupils dilated, laughter, delirium, face red and swollen, also a scarlet eruption is often observed on the skin, convulsions, paralysis and insensibility.

TREATMENT.—

The treatment is the same as for Henbane.   See HENBANE.

DIGITALIS.—(See FOXGLOVE).

FISH (poisonous).— All kinds of fish, meats, etc., may become poisonous from disease or decay.

Symptoms.—Great thirst, weight in the stomach, vomiting, dizziness, itching, and sometimes an eruption on the skin, pulse low, hands and feet cold, twitching of the tendons; convulsions.

TREATMENT.—

Cause vomiting by drinking warm water and tickling the throat with the finger; soothing drinks and acids; recumbent position.

FOOL'S PARSLEY.— Taken by mistake for common parsley.

Symptoms. — Burning in throat and thirst, sickness, vomiting and occasional purging, cold moist skin, small frequent pulse, headache, dizziness and delirium.

TREATMENT.—

Emetics, followed by warm water, milk, Flaxseed tea or Chamomile tea; purgatives; warm bath; stimulants and opiates.

FOXGLOVE.—*Digitalis.*

Symptoms. — Irregular pulse, dizziness, indistinct vision, nausea, vomiting, cold sweats, hiccough, delirium and convulsions.

TREATMENT.—

One-third teaspoonful Tannic Acid, followed by emetics. Small doses of Opium or Laudanum (5 to 20 drops of Laudanum) may be needed to quiet the intense excitement of the nervous system. Strong coffee should also be given. Keep the patient quiet and the head low.

HELLEBORE.—*Indian Poke, Swamp Hellebore.*

Symptoms. — Violent purging and vomiting, bloody stools, great anxiety, dizziness, tremors, fainting, cold sweats, convulsions.

TREATMENT.—

Cause vomiting quickly by large draughts of warm water, molasses and water, or other emetics; also give oil and mucilaginous drinks; oily purgatives; strong coffee, or other stimulant. Opium may be given in small quantities if necessary to quiet extreme nervous sensibility.

Note.—Hellebore is sometimes used in poisonous quantities in dressing sores. In this case treatment by vomiting would be useless.

HEMLOCK (poison).— The roots have sometimes been eaten by mistake for parsnip.

Symptoms.—Dizziness, dimness of sight, delirium, and swelling of the abdomen, with pain, vomiting and purging.

TREATMENT.—

Give ⅓ teaspoonful Tannin dissolved in water, and follow with an emetic. Give warm water, Flaxseed tea, Chamomile tea, or milk; bathe the head with water and give stimulants. Use stomach pump.

HENBANE.—*Hyoscyamus.*

Symptoms. — Sickness, dilatation of the pupils, dimness of sight, dryness of mouth and throat, delirium, appearance of intoxication and insensibility.

TREATMENT.—

Give ⅓ teaspoonful of Tannin dissolved in water, and follow with strong Mustard water to produce vomiting; cold to the head; heat to the feet; strong coffee. Give stimulants as needed. Hypodermic injections of Pilocarpine may be given by a doctor.

LAUDANUM.—(See OPIUM).

LAUREL, MOUNTAIN.—Honey made from its flowers is poisonous, also birds that feed upon its buds in winter.

Symptoms. — Violent flushings of heat and cold, dizziness, sickness at the stomach, vomiting and purging, delirium, weak, rapid pulse, sweating, convulsions.

TREATMENT.—

Emetics, as warm water or molasses and water, and tickling the throat with the finger to produce vomiting; purgatives; strong stimulants, such as Ammonia and coffee. Use stomach pump.

LIME.—*Quick Lime.*

Symptoms. — Burning in the throat and stomach, vomiting, violent colic and diarrhea; sometimes constipation.

TREATMENT.—

Drink vinegar, lemon juice or any vegetable acid freely; follow with an emetic; give mucilaginous drinks; opiates if needed, warm baths, etc.

LUNAR CAUSTIC.—*Nitrate of Silver.*

Symptoms.— Burning pain in the stomach, sickness at the stomach, retching and vomiting; sometimes extreme purging; cold skin, quick, irregular pulse, difficult breathing, fainting and convulsions.

TREATMENT.—

Drink freely of common salt in water; also drink large quantities of warm water and tickle the throat to produce vomiting; or give other emetics; also warm bath; purgatives and mucilaginous drinks.

MONK'S HOOD.—(See ACONITE).

MORPHINE.—(See OPIUM).

MURIATIC ACID.—*Hydrochloric Acid.*

Symptoms.—Burning and sense of strangulation in the throat, retching, vomiting, swelling of the throat and difficulty in breathing; skin cold with clammy sweat; pulse quick and small.

TREATMENT.—

Give large quantities of water containing Mustard, Carbonate of Magnesia Calcined Magnesia, chalk or whiting, in water; soap and water; wood ashes and water; white of eggs, milk, oil, etc. *Plaster from the wall* may be beaten down to a paste with water and given, or washing soda with barley water; mucilaginous drinks.

MUSHROOMS (poisonous). — Eaten by mistake for the ordinary mushroom.

Symptoms.—Pain and sickness at the stomach, vomiting and purging; great thirst, colicky pains, cramps, dizziness, convulsions and delirium.

TREATMENT.—

Give emetics, purgatives, mucilages, acid drinks, and stimulants such as Whiskey, Brandy, Ammonia, etc.

NITRE.—*Nitrate of Potash, Saltpetre.*

Symptoms.—Great pain in the stomach, nausea, vomiting, purging, severe colic in the lower part of the bowels, difficult breathing, great prostration, fainting and convulsions. One ounce has destroyed life in three hours.

TREATMENT.—

Barley water, Flaxseed tea, warm water or molasses and water, and tickling the throat to produce vomiting; or other emetics; opiates, as 5 to 10 drops of Laudanum; stimulants, such as Brandy, Whiskey, Ether, etc.

NITRATE OF SILVER.—(See LUNAR CAUSTIC).

NITRIC ACID.—(See AQUA FORTIS).

NUX VOMICA.—(See STRYCHNINE).

OIL OF ALMONDS.—(See PRUSSIC ACID).

OIL OF CEDAR.—

Symptoms.—Heat in the stomach, immediately followed by convulsions with frothing at the mouth. Death has occurred in half an hour.

TREATMENT.—

Cause vomiting as quickly as possible by large draughts of warm water and other nauseating drinks, or by a large dose of ground Mustard seed in water. Stimulants as needed.

OIL OF RUE.—

Symptoms.—Dryness of mouth and throat, heat and pain in the stomach and bowels, thirst, headache and delirium.

TREATMENT.—

Excite vomiting as quickly as possible by large drinks of warm water containing ground Mustard seed, or other emetics.

OIL OF SAVIN.—May be taken by young women to induce menstruation—a very dangerous proceeding.

Symptoms.—Headache, delirium, general excitement, sharp pain in the stomach and bowels, nausea, vomiting and purging, convulsions.

TREATMENT.—

Cause vomiting by large drinks of warm water containing Mustard and tickling the throat; or give an emetic of Sulphate of Zinc. Follow with acid drinks and mucilages.

OIL OF TANSY.—May be taken as noted in Oil of Savin.

Symptoms.—Heat in the stomach, immediately followed by convulsions and frothing at the mouth; feeble pulse.

TREATMENT.—

Cause vomiting by large draughts of warm water containing Mustard; give acid drinks and mucilages.

OIL OF TAR.—Containing *Creosote* as its essential principle.

Symptoms.—Speedy insensibility, labored rattling breathing, cold hands and feet, watering eyes, feeble pulse.

TREATMENT.—

Cause vomiting instantly by drinking water containing Mustard, or by other emetics.

OIL OF VITRIOL.—*Sulphuric Acid.*

Symptoms.—Pain and burning in the throat and difficulty in swallowing, vomiting dark-colored fluids and shreds of membrane from the stomach, swelling of the throat, cold skin, and quick, small pulse. The lining membrane of the mouth and throat is partly destroyed and of a dark color.

TREATMENT.—

Carbonate of Magnesia, Calcined Magnesia, chalk or whiting, mixed with large quantities of water; or soap or wood ashes and water; or lime from the plastered wall made into a paste with water. The foregoing are all alkalies, and the object in giving any one of them is to neutralize the acid. Or water by the pint containing Mustard. Follow with white of eggs, milk or oils.

OPIUM.—*Gum Opium, Laudanum, Morphine.*

Symptoms.—Dizziness, stupor, drowsiness, insensibility; pulse quick and irregular at first and breathing hurried; later the breathing is slow and noisy, face flushed, pupils contracted, and the pulse slow and full. In favorable cases there is early nausea and vomiting. Death occurs in from two to twenty-four hours.

TREATMENTS.—

A. Cause instant vomiting by copious drinks of warm water containing a large quantity of ground Mustard. Keep cold water on the head and back of the neck; rub the surface with coarse towel, and *keep the person moving.* Give strong stimulants, as Brandy, Whiskey, Ammonia to nostrils, 15 drops Tincture of Belladonna, or strong tea and coffee. Use stomach pump. The stomach pump is particularly valuable in Opium poisoning, as the system may be so paralyzed that vomiting cannot be induced by emetics.

B. Give an emetic of Mustard and warm water. After the stomach is emptied make the patient drink hot strong coffee and watch the breathings.—(20).

C. Warm water by the tumblerful with Mustard in it until the patient vomits, then give strong coffee. If in a stupor, keep patient walking. Call for doctor at once.—(35.)

D. Permanganate of Potash is considered by some a safe and sure antidote for Morphine poisoning. If the case is discovered early, give the remedy by the stomach; if not, inject under the skin with a hypodermic needle.—(51).

OXALIC ACID.—May be taken accidentally from its resemblance to Epsom Salts.

Symptoms:—Hot burning taste in the swallowing and immediate vomiting, the matter thrown up being a greenish or brown color; sometimes severe pain; pulse small and irregular; numbness and spasms.

TREATMENT.—

Carbonate of Magnesia, Calcined Magnesia, chalk or whiting made into a cream with water and given freely; emetics; Lime Water with oil; mucilages.

PARIS GREEN.—(SEE ARSENIC).

PHOSPHORUS.—

Symptoms.—Hot taste of onions or garlic in the mouth, violent pains in the stomach, nausea and vomiting, convulsions.

TREATMENT.—

Fill up the stomach with Magnesia and water; give emetics, warm water, etc., to keep up the vomiting. Copper Sulphate in small doses. No oils should be used, though old Oil of Turpentine is recommended given in emulsion, from 10 drops to 1 teaspoonful.

POTASH, HYDRATE OF.—*Caustic Potash.*

Symptoms.—Burning taste in the mouth, pain in the stomach and vomiting; cold skin, small frequent pulse and great prostration.

TREATMENT.—

Give large amount of water containing ground Mustard, or Vinegar, lemon juice or other vegetable acids; rub the skin; give Oils and mucilaginous drinks.

PRUSSIC ACID.—*Hydrocyanic Acid*, the poisonous principle of the Oil of Bitter Almonds.

Symptoms.—Instant sensation of weight and pain in the head, nausea and quick pulse.   In larger doses, instant insensibility, convulsions, loss of pulse and slow breathing, death occuring in from two minutes to half an hour.

TREATMENT.—

Application of strong Ammonia to the nostrils; stimulating liniments to the chest.   Apply cold water to the head and spine. Mix 1 part Ammonia with 6 parts water and give freely.

ROUGH ON RATS.—(See ARSENIC).

STRAMONIUM.—(See THORN APPLE).

STRYCHNINE.—*Nux Vomica.*

Symptoms.—Extremely bitter taste in the mouth, muscular spasms, limbs fixed, stretched out and rigid, jaws spasmodically shut.   If the symptoms continue, there is nausea, vomiting, and difficulty in breathing.   Or, instead of the rigidity described the various groups of voluntary muscles may act spasmodically and the arms and lower limbs fly in all directions.

TREATMENT.—

Give 1 teaspoonful of Tannic Acid in water, if at hand. This will form an insoluble compound with the Strychnine. Then give emetics to produce vomiting; also give freely any fatty matter, such as Sweet Oil, lard, etc., a pint at a time, and have it vomited each time by passing the finger down the throat.   To control the spasms, give, for an adult, 30 grains Chloral Hydrate or 60 grains Bromide of Potash, or Morphine or Chloroform.   In severe cases larger doses of the Chloral or Potash may be necessary.   Or perhaps spasmodic action can be best and most quickly controlled by the hypodermic injection of Apomorphia.   These remedies would require the services of a doctor.

SUGAR OF LEAD.—*Acetate of Lead.*

Symptoms.—A burning, prickling feeling in the throat, with dryness and thirst, pain in the stomach, nausea, vomiting, constipation, cold skin, weak irregular pulse, loss of strength, cramps, numbness, dizziness, insensibility.

TREATMENT.—

Sulphuric Acid forms an insoluble compound with lead, and is best given in the form of Sulphate of Magnesia or Epsom Salts. Large amounts should be given. If necessary, Morphine may be added to relieve the spasms and pain. Give emetics, followed by mucilages, milk, white of eggs, or wheat flour with water.

SULPHATE OF COPPER.—(See BLUE VITRIOL).

SULPHATE OF ZINC.—(See WHITE VITRIOL).

SULPHURIC ACID.—(See OIL OF VITRIOL).

TARTAR EMETIC.—*Antimony.*

Symptoms.—Nausea, severe vomiting, hiccough, burning pain in the stomach due to inflammation, colic pains and violent purging, small quick pulse, cramps, dizziness and great prostration.

TREATMENT.—

Tannic Acid forms an insoluble compound with Antimony and should be given in a little water. Afterwards wash out stomach by drinking large quantity of water, and give strong tea, mucilages and warm drinks. Stimulants will be necessary.

THORN APPLE.—*Stramonium.*

Symptoms and treatment are the same as given under HENBANE.

TOBACCO.—

Symptoms.—Severe nausea, headache, vomiting, sudden weakness, cold sweats and convulsions.

TREATMENT.—

Emetics; large draughts of warm water; purgatives; acid drinks; stimulants, such as strong coffee, Brandy, Whiskey, etc., and external heat.

VERDIGRIS.—(See BLUE VITRIOL).

WHITE LEAD.—(See SUGAR OF LEAD).

WHITE VITRIOL.—*Sulphate of Zinc.*

Symptoms.—Bitter taste in the mouth with sensation of choking, severe vomiting, pain in the stomach and bowels, difficult breathing, cold hands and feet and quick, small pulse.

TREATMENT.—

Give strong alkaline drinks, as baking Soda. Follow with white of eggs; wheat flour and water; plenty of milk; emetics if needed, that is, if vomiting has not already taken place; purgatives; opiates and stimulants.

WOLF'S BANE.—(See ACONITE).

Poison Ivy.—This plant by contact, and upon many without contact, produces a violent erysipelatous inflammation, particularly of the face. The symptoms are itching, redness, burning, swelling, watery blisters and subsequent peeling of the skin. These effects are experienced soon after exposure, and usually begin to decline within a week.

TREATMENT.—

Carbolic Acid....	1 teaspoonful.
Water...............................	7 "

Mix, apply thoroughly for a few minutes and wash off with water. One thorough application of this kind will completely eradicate the poison.

Poison Dogwood.—The symptoms and treatment are similar to those of Poison Ivy.

Department V.

HERB REMEDIES.

Materia Medica is the science that treats of the substances employed in the prevention, alleviation and cure of disease; among these plant life holds the foremost place. More remedies are obtained from plants than from all other remedial sources combined, and it is the aim of this volume to give the most complete chapter on medicinal plants that has ever been introduced into any work of like character.

It has been stated by medical authority that if families would familiarize themselves with herbs and their medicinal properties and uses, many doctors' bills would be saved. Why not? Nature was the Indian's sole apothecary shop—his drugs, the plant with its leaves and flowers, the shrub with its berries and the tree with its bark. The same natural remedies, so highly esteemed by the aborigines, are in use to-day in an artificial form, labelled and placed in rows on the shelves of drug stores. We call a physician to prescribe the proper drugs. We pay the physician for his knowledge; we pay the druggist for his drugs, and in so doing we pay the chemist who compounded them and all the agencies that have been instrumental in reducing them from their natural to their artificial state.

Native plants are fully described. If there are any of these that do not grow in your vicinity, you can obtain extracts or other preparations of most of them at drug stores. Medicinal plants not growing in this country also native plants whose medicinal properties have recently been discovered and are being manufactured into various preparations, have not been described as to appearance, but the medicinal properties and uses of their products are fully stated.

There are several ways in which the medicinal properties of herbs are extracted, *i. e.*, extracts, tinctures, infusions, decoctions, bitters, etc. For domestic practice, the most common methods are infusion and decoction.

Note.—While teas, decoctions or infusions are often most convenient, and are comparatively inexpensive, we have given in an appended CHAPTER ON MEDICINES the more modern method of drug medication. The chapter is written in plain, simple language, and fully explains, not only the later forms of preparing medicines, but also explains in detail the action of each

505

remedy, including the dose, when it should be taken, and when discontinued. This is easily understood by noting the symptoms or effects produced. Such symptoms and effects are fully described, and those administering the drug can do so with intelligence and satisfaction. In the CHAPTER ON MEDICINES no attempt has been made to describe all of the remedies mentioned in this chapter, but only the more important ones.

INFUSIONS.

These are made by steeping, as tea, and are commonly called "teas." An excellent method of preparing them is to put the plant or root into a teapot (an earthen one is the better), pour on boiling water and let the pot stand for a short time where it will keep hot. Infusions are mostly made for immediate use and cannot be kept for any length of time. The strength of the plant is sometimes extracted in cold water. An infusion made in this way will keep longer than one made by steeping. An infusion may be sweetened and milk added, if desired, to make it more agreeable to the taste.

DECOCTIONS.

Decoctions are made by *boiling* substances in water for a considerable time. Vegetables or roots designed for decoction should be bruised or cut into slices so that their strength may be more easily extracted.

Decoctions may be made into *syrups* by boiling or simmering until the strength of the herb is extracted and a goodly portion of the water evaporated, then straining, adding a sufficient quantity of sugar to prevent fermentation, and heating until the sugar is all dissolved. Syrups to keep nicely should be bottled when hot, and carefully corked or sealed. The addition of one or two tablespoonfuls of Glycerine to each pint of syrup helps to preserve it and does not interfere with it in taste or otherwise.

FOMENTATIONS.

Fomentations are herbs in decoction or infusion applied locally. An excellent manner of making fomentations is to place the leaves, or portion of the herb to be used, in a bag made the proper size to cover the part desired, steep, wring the bag out of the liquid and apply hot. A bag of herbs will keep hot longer than cloths. Two bags may be made and used alternately.

OINTMENTS.

Ointments, salves and cerates are practically the same. They are composed of about eighty per cent of lard or Vaseline. The other twenty per cent is made up of some remedy. The Vaseline is merely a vehicle—a convenient method of applying the contained remedy. Like plasters, ointments, salves and cerates are named according to the remedies they contain. Thus we have Iodine ointment, Arnica salve, Resin cerate, etc. Ointments are designed for local application as palliative treatment. The nature of the drug or drugs contained in them may be astringent, stimulating or anodyne in effect.

PLASTERS.

Plasters are semi-solid substances, spread upon cloth or some other flexible material for application upon the external surface of the body. Like ointments, plasters are given different names according to the medicinal ingredients they contain, as Arnica, Belladonna, Capsicum, Cantharides or blister plaster. Plaster Paris is used for making a firm and immovable dressing for sprains, fractures, etc. Plaster Paris is so-called because it was first discovered near the city of Paris. Plaster of Paris bandages when wet with water and applied soon harden, become firm, and support the injured parts against accident or injury. The basis of all porous plasters is Gum Galbanum, found in Asia. Galbanum is stimulating and antispasmodic. Taken internally it produces about the same effect as Asafetida. The benefit of porous plasters is largely from their mechanical support.

POULTICES.

Poultices are made from various soft substances, such as ground Elm bark, ground Flaxseed, corn meal, bread and milk, etc. They are usually applied hot. They are merely a means of applying moist heat. Poultices are used to relieve pain and bring the blood to the surface, and thus aid in relieving congestion. When pus is present, they hasten the formation of the abscess and thus hasten resolution.

POWDERS

Powder is any substance composed of minute free particles in a dry state. There are many powders used for toilet purposes, such as tooth powders and the almost endless line of face powders. Used in medicine, different powders are often mixed together and divided into separate doses. In this case the powder is composed of or contains medicinal substances designed for the treatment and cure of the various diseases for which it is used.

TINCTURES.

Take the fresh or dried herb, chop and pound to a pulp, weigh, and to every ounce of the herb add two ounces of water and two ounces of Alcohol. Place the drug in a large-necked bottle, add the Alcohol and water and allow to stand from eight to fourteen days in a dark, cool place. At the end of this time the liquid should be turned off, being careful not to roil the dregs, and should be bottled. A teaspoonful of Glycerine to each four ounces of liquid will prove a valuable addition. This should be added when mixing the herb and Alcohol. Tinctures may also be made with wines or other spirituous liquors, but the principle and process remain the same.

HANDY TABLES.

60 drops make	1 fluid drachm, or 1 small teaspoonful.
8 fluid drachms make...	1 fluid ounce, or 2 tablespoonfuls.
16 fluid ounces make.....	1 pint.
1 pint equals	1 pound in weight.

(There are a few exceptions regarding weight, as Glycerine, Ether, Chloroform, Sulphuric Acid etc. These vary from the standard, which is distillled water at 60°F.)

1 Tablespoonful	equals 4 teaspoonfuls.
1 Teacup	equals 4 fluid ounces.
1 Coffee Cup	equals 6 fluid ounces.
1 Wineglass	equals from 2 to 4 tablespoonfuls.
1 drop equals...........	1 grain.
20 grains make	1 scruple, equal to ⅓ teaspoonful.
3 scruples make	1 drachm, equal to 1 teaspoonful.
8 drachms make	1 ounce, equal to 2 tablespoonfuls.

For Consumption, Lung and Liver Affections, Scrofulous Complaints, Boils

ABSCESS ROOT—*Polemonium Reptans,* called also GREEK VALERIAN, BLUE BELLS, SWEAT ROOT, etc. — Roots are fibrous, all growing from one head. Flowers are small, blue, appear early in the season and produce small seeds. Several stems often arise from the same root. Grows in damp woods to the height of one or two feet.

Employed in consumption and all affections of the lungs and liver, also in chronic complaints of a scrofulous character. The Indians used it in fevers and pleurisies to produce copious perspiration. Used in decoction, a small handful of the crushed root to three pints of boiling water, steeped down one-half. Dose, ½ teacupful every four hours. A tincture made in Whiskey, of which the dose is ½ wineglassful three times a day, will cleanse the system and blood, and is valuable to persons afflicted with boils.

ACONITE.—(See A CHAPTER ON MEDICINES).

For Vomiting, Dyspepsia, Debilitv of the Digestive Organs.

ADRUE.
Native of the Tropics,

Properties.—This remedy is of surprising worth in checking vomiting, whether it is that of pregnancy, yellow fever or indigestion. It is also a pleasant and efficient remedy in dyspepsia arising from debility of the digestive organs.

Dose.—To check vomiting, from 20 to 30 drops of the fluid extract in a little water, repeated every 10 or 15 minutes until vomiting has ceased; for dyspepsia, the same amount given three times a day.

For Coughs, Bowel Complaints, Leucorrhea, Gonorrhea, Scrofula, Gravel.

AGRIMONY—*Agrimonia Eupatoria*, called also Cockle-bur, Stickwort, etc.—This plant grows from one to two feet high and has a rounded, hairy stem which seldom branches. The leaves are oblong, pointed at both ends, and their margin is deeply and unequally notched. The flowers grow in slender spikes at the ends of the stems.

It is useful in coughs and bowel complaints, and may also be given in diarrhea, dysentery, relaxed bowels, leucorrhea and gonorrhea. The best way to take it is in a strong decoction, which may be made either of the root or the plant, and may be sweetened if desired. The dose is 4 teacupfuls every day. A tea of this plant, together with Alum and honey, is used as a remedy for tapeworm. It is also beneficial in jaundice, and, taken for a long time, is of great benefit in scrofula and gravel. The roots and whole plant are boiled in milk and used for diabetes and incontinence (involuntary evacuations) of urine.

For Neuralgia, Worms.

ALLIGATOR PEAR.

Native of the West Indies and Tropical America.

Properties. — Recommended highly by the residents of Southern Mexico in intercostal neuralgia. For this affliction rub chest and back with a dry towel until the part is well stimulated, then apply from 1½ to 2 ounces of the fluid extract, rubbing it in gently, and cover the part with a dry flannel to protect clothing from stain.

It is also highly recommended as a vermifuge, especially in the case of tapeworm. Dr. Henry Froehling, of California, reports a case in which a tapeworm with a head attached was expelled from a man within five hours. For this purpose it is given in three separate doses of a fluid drachm (teaspoonful) each in the space of one hour, and followed with a dose of Castor Oil.

Dose.—½ to 1 teaspoonful of the fluid extract.

For Tickling Coughs, Hoarseness, Scalding of Urine, Diseases of the Kidneys.

ALMOND.

Native of Mediterranean region and western Asia.

Properties.—The oil of Sweet Almonds is very serviceable in tickling coughs, hoarseness, etc.   It acts beneficially upon the urinary organs in the scalding of urine.   It is very useful, combined with other remedies, in diseases of the kidneys.   It is also much used externally, in combination with other articles, especially in preparations to whiten and soften the skin.

Dose.—Of the oil of Sweet Almonds, from 1 to 8 drachms. The oil of Bitter Almonds is poisonous.

ALOES.—(See A CHAPTER ON MEDICINES.)

For Ulcers, Sores, Piles.

ALUM ROOT—*Hencheria Acerifolia*, called also SPLIT ROCK, CLIFF WEED, GROUND MAPLE.—Has a crooked, horizontal root of a yellowish color and very small flesh-colored flowers set on a stalk.   Found in the mountainous regions of the Middle Atlantic and east Central States.

The root is used, but is seldom taken internally on account of its great astringency.   Finely powdered, it is applied to ulcers and sores in a state of discharge.   Mixed with lard, it forms a good ointment for piles, etc.

For External use on Cancerous and Ulcerous Growths.

ALVELOZ.

Native of Brazil.

Properties.—Alveloz is used as an external application in the case of cancers and ulcerous growths.   The action is irritating, producing a spreading inflammation of the skin without much pain, resulting in the destruction of the morbid tissue, which is replaced by healthy tissue.

In the northern part of Brazil the natives used to burn the wound with the juice running from a piece of broken or cut stem, after having washed it with a decoction of leaves of tobacco. M. Landowsky, in a communication to the Grenoble Congress, stated that, after applying Alveloz he places over it a dressing of Vaseline and Borax.

Preparation.—Alveloz Milk.

Use.—Apply externally as above.

For Rheumatism, Coughs, Fevers, Scurvy, Ague.

AMERICAN ARBOR VITÆ.—This evergreen attains a height of from twenty to fifty feet, and a diameter of ten to twenty feet through the greatest breadth of foliage. The branchlets are very flat and spreading. It is a beautiful tree, found in the northern part of this country and Canada, and often forms what are commonly known as cedar swamps. It grows along the rocky banks of rivers and in low swampy spots. It blossoms from May until June and matures its fruit in autumn. It assumes a conical form with such true lines as to appear "clipped," thus making a valuable high hedge tree.

An ointment made of the branchlets and pressed fruit is excellent for rheumatism. A poultice of the cones in powder with milk removes the worst rheumatic pains. A decoction of the roots or branchlets is useful in coughs, fevers, scurvy, ague, etc.

For Coughs, Debility.

AMERICAN BALM-OF-GILEAD—*Populus Balsamifera*, called also BALSAM POPLAR, etc.—This well known tree is extensively cultivated for its shade. Its buds, which possess valuable medical qualities, should be gathered in the fall of the year. They are filled with a rich balsam gum, and are good in coughs and debility. To an ounce of the bruised buds 1 pint of fourth proof spirits may be added, the dose of which is from a teaspoonful to a tablespoonful three or four times a day in sweetened water. This tincture may be applied externally to cuts and wounds.

For Appetite, Worms, Menses.

AMERICAN CENTAURY—*Sabbatia Angularis*, called also ROSE PINK, WILD SUCCORY and BITTER BLOOM.—Found in low meadows in the Middle and Southern States. Has a fibrous root, grows from one to two feet in height, and has clusters of delicate, rose-colored flowers which blossom in July and August.

Two ounces of the leaves and flowers and 1 ounce of orange peel should be infused in 2 quarts of Brandy for two weeks. One tablespoonful of this tincture taken before breakfast and dinner will create an appetite; for children having worms, 2 teaspoonfuls or more every morning. To restore the menses, pour 2 quarts of water on 2 ounces of tops, steep for half an hour, strain, add a pint of Rum, and take of this a teacupful four times a day, at the same time making hot local applications.

For Indigestion, Debility, Jaundice.

AMERICAN COLUMBO—*Frasera Carolinensis*, called also PYRAMID FLOWER.—Grows in the Western States, attains sometimes to the height of ten feet, and bears a large pyramid of crowded yellowish-white flowers sometimes three or four feet long.

Extensively used in cases requiring mild tonics, as diseases of the stomach, debility, fevers, indigestion, jaundice, etc. Infusion, 1 ounce of the bruised root to a pint of boiling water, of which the dose is a wineglassful.

For Nervous Headaches, Hysterical Disorders, Suppressed Menstruations, Colics, Indigestion.

AMERICAN DITTANY—*Cunila Mariana*, called also MOUNTAIN DITTANY, STONE MINT, WILD BASIL, etc.—This plant is peculiar to America. It has a fragrant odor, resembling that of the Marjoram. The flowers are of a reddish-blue color and blossom from July to September. It grows on mountains and hillsides, but is unknown in plains.

Dittany tea (warm infusion) is a popular remedy for colds, headaches, and for inciting general perspiration. It relieves nervous headaches and hysterical disorders. Also beneficial in suppressed menstruations, colics and indigestion. The infusion may be drank freely. The Indians smoked and chewed the leaves as a substitute for tobacco. The plant is also employed externally for bruises and sprains.

For Impurities of the Blood, Syphilitic Complaints, Chronic Rheumatism, Scrofula, etc.

AMERICAN SARSAPARILLA — *Aralia Nudicaulis*, called also SMALL SPIKENARD, WILD LICORICE, WILD SARSAPARILLA, etc.—This plant grows in deep woods and shady places. The root is creeping, twisted and many feet long. The stem is leafless, with clusters of from twelve to thirty small yellowish flowers at the end. The blossoms are followed by clusters of berries which somewhat resemble the common Elderberry.

The root of this plant may be given in syrup or infusion, and is useful in all diseases of the blood, syphilitic complaints, chronic rheumatism, scrofula, etc. Also useful in coughs, catarrhs and pains in the breast. The bruised root is used in poultices for wounds and ulcers, and also makes a useful application for erysipelas, ringworm and other skin affections.

For Cathartic Uses.

AMERICAN SENNA—*Cassia Marilandica*, called also WILD SENNA, LOCUST PLANT, etc.—The root of this plant is irregular, woody, black and fibrous. The stems are many, and grow from three to six feet high. The flowers are of a bright yellow. The fruits or pods are flat, blackish and a little hairy. They grow from two to five inches long, and hold from twelve to twenty seeds or small brown beans. It grows principally in rich soils near streams.

The Sennas are cathartics. The American Senna operates with mildness and certainty. Both the leaves and pods are used in decoction—what would lay on a tablespoon added to ½ pint of hot water, drank as needed. With mothers who are nursing babes, the cathartic principle of the Sennas passes into the mother's milk. Infants are often accidentally or purposely purged by the mother's use of Senna.

AMERICAN WHITE HELLEBORE.—(See *Veratrum Viride* in A CHAPTER ON MEDICINES).

For Debility of the Stomach and Digestive Organs, Nervous Disorders, Inflammatory Tumors.

ANGELICA—*Angelica Atropurpurea*, called also *Common Angelica.*—Found from Canada to the Carolinas, growing in meadows and marshy grounds and blooming in June and July. It has a strong odor and a warm, spicy taste.

The infusion or tea may be taken with advantage in all disorders arising from flatulence and debility of the stomach and digestive organs. It raises the spirits, strengthens the stomach and creates an appetite. Also recommended in nervous headache pains, in chlorosis, hysteria and other nervous disorders. The root may be taken in powder in doses of ½ to 1 teaspoonful, or the seeds and roots may be infused gently in water or spirits. The green root bruised and laid on inflammatory tumors will tend to disperse them. The roots when fresh are poisonous and should not be used in infusion, but after drying they lose their poisonous properties.

For Tapeworms.

ARECA NUT.

Native of Tropical Asia.

Properties.—It is an astringent and vermifuge, and is successfully used for the expulsion of tapeworms, the bowels first being cleansed by fasting and Castor Oil.

Dose.—As a vermifuge, 2 teaspoonfuls of the fluid extract, and upwards.

For Dropsies, Kidney Affections, Gravel and Stone, Heart.

ASPARAGUS.—*Asparagus Officinalis.*—A well known garden vegetable. The root and seeds are used in medicine, and sometimes a syrup is made of the young shoots. It is a native of the south of Europe, but has become naturalized in different sections of this country.

An infusion of the root, drank freely, is good in dropsy and kidney affections, particularly in stone or gravel in the kidneys or bladder. To make this infusion, keep the roots in hot, but not boiling, water for two hours, then strain. A syrup is made of the juice of the young shoots, of which the dose is from 4 to 8 tablespoonfuls. The young shoots eaten as a food have a powerful effect upon the kidneys and a sedative influence over the heart.

For Diarrhea, Obstructions of the Urine, Indigestion, Faintness at the Stomach, Consumption, Worms.

ASPEN—*Populus Tremuloides*, called also WHITE POPLAR, QUAKING ASPEN, QUIVER LEAF, etc.—Common in most parts of the country. The lightest breath of air keeps the leaves in motion, hence the popular names that have been given to it.

The bark of this tree affords one of the finest of tonics. It may be combined with other tonics. It is used in powder, decoction or tincture, and is useful in diarrhea, obstruction of the urine, indigestion, faintness at the stomach, consumption and worms. It should be taken in quantities according to its effect.

For Intermittent and Remittent Fevers, recent Colds.

AUSTRALIAN FEVER BARK—*Alstonia Constricta.*

Native of Australia.

Properties.—The action of this remedy resembles in many respects the combined action of Quinine and Nux Vomica. In a large majority of the cases of intermittent and remittent fevers it is a superior remedy. The system should be prepared for its use by the administration of the proper sedative, then Alstonia seldom fails. When Quinine fails in chronic cases, Alstonia often effects a speedy cure. In recent colds, or coryza, it is an excellent remedy.

At the beginning of an attack of this annoying trouble, 2-grain doses every two hours give prompt relief. The whole system is soon reinvigorated, the secretions and excretions which have been more or less suppressed are reestablished, and the patient feels well again. Without such aid the cold often hangs on for days and even weeks; in other words, the vital forces remain depressed and the patient feels weak and mean.

Dose.—Of the powder, from ½ to 2 grains every one to four hours, but in cases of periodical attacks, as much as 6-grain doses may be given with good results. If the dose is too large, headache with nervousness will be produced.

Of the fluid extract, from 2 to 6 drops.

For Dysentery, Chronic Diarrhea, Colic, Debility, Asthma, Sore Throat, Leucorrhea, Hemorrhage.

AVENS—*Geum Virginianum,* called also AVEN'S ROOT, EVAN ROOT, CHOCOLATE ROOT, THROAT ROOT, etc.—This plant grows about two feet high. The roots are small, brittle, brown and crooked. The flowers, which are few in number, are of a white color and grow on the ends of the stems. The fruit is a small berry, oval-shaped, brown and smooth. A decoction of Avens with sugar and milk resembles chocolate or coffee and makes a very pleasant drink.

It is useful in dysentery, chronic diarrhea, colic, debility, asthma, sore throat, leucorrhea, hemorrhage from the womb and also from the stomach. Given in weak decoction, about a pint a day may be taken, divided into three doses; or 20 grains (⅓ teaspoonful) of the powder may be taken three times daily. The roots are sometimes put into Ale and taken as a stomach tonic.

For Liver Complaint, Jaundice, Costiveness, Dyspepsia and General Debility.

BALMONY—*Chelone Glabra,* called also BITTER HERB, SNAKE HEAD, FISH MOUTH, TURTLE BLOOM, etc.—This plant is found in moist ground. It has four-cornered stems that rise from three to five feet high and are occasionally branched near the top. The leaves are five or six inches long, tapering, sharply pointed, edged with sharp teeth, and are set opposite each other. The flowers are white, and in some instances are tinged with a delicate shade of red. They form clusters, and do not bloom until late in the autumn. They are remarkable for their resemblance to a snake head, hence one of the common names. The herb should be collected in clear, dry weather, and as soon as it is in bloom, as the leaves frequently become mildewed after that time. It should be dried in the sun or in a warm, dry place.

This herb has tonic, stimulant and anti-bilious properties. It is a valuable medicine in disorders of the liver, and in jaundice will remove the yellow color from the skin and eyes. It is employed in costiveness, dyspepsia, loss of appetite and general languor and debility. A weak infusion of the plant may be drank freely.

For Catarrhal Conditions of the Lungs and Urinary Tract.

BALSAM OF COPAIVA, or COPAIBA.

Native of South America.

Properties.—The most important use of Copaiva is in catarrhal conditions of the mucous membrane of the lungs and urinary tract, but while it is undoubtedly a remedy of much value, its odor is so unpleasant that it is seldom used. At one time it was a popular remedy in the treatment of gonorrhea, but for whatever purpose it is taken internally it is eliminated partially by the lungs, hence is conveyed by the breath. As stated, this objection has practically driven it out of use. Again, it has been learned that for the venereal disease mentioned other remedies applied directly to the seat of trouble are equally as valuable.

Preparation.—Internally it is taken either in emulsion or capsule.

Dose.—From 10 to 20 drops.

For Disinfectant and Stimulating Purposes.

BALSAM FIR—*Terebinthina Canadensis.*—Native of United States and Canada. The principal source of supply for the United States is North and South Carolina. There are several species of this balsam and all forms contain a volatile oil. After the oil is distilled by means of heat the remaining substance constitutes the common resin of commerce. When first obtained from the plant or tree it is in a crude, oleoresinous state. It is then placed in a large still, heat applied, and the distilled product constitutes common turpentine, and the remaining drug, common resin, as stated.

The uses of *Turpentine* and *Resin* are too common and well known to need description. Turpentine is sometimes used internally in capillary bronchitis and in typhoid fever. It is a powerful disinfectant and stimulant. The dose extends all the way from 10 drops to 1 or 2 teaspoonfuls given in the form of emulsion.

For External Application, especially to Chronic Ulcers, and Internal Use in Chronic Bronchitis, Dysentery and Eczema.

BALSAM OF PERU—*Balsamum Peruvianum.*

Native of Brazil, and near the west coast of South America.

Properties.—Balsam Peru is a general stimulant, exerting its influence mostly upon mucous membrane, hence is sometimes used as a stimulating expectorant in chronic bronchitis, dysentery, chilblains and chronic forms of eczema. Its principal use, however, is in dressing wounds, especially chronic ulcers and other conditions where healing does not take place readily. Its principal value in these cases lies both in its antiseptic and stimulating properties.

Preparation.—When used internally the balsam is added to other ingredients forming the mixture, whether a cough syrup, a remedy for diarrhea, or other internal remedies.

Dose.—The dose internally is from 10 to 20 drops. When used for dressing wounds, it may constitute from ten to fifty per cent of the application.

For Chronic Bronchitis, Dysentery and Eczema.

BALSAM TOLU—*Balsamum Tolutanum.*

Native of Venezuela.

Properties.—The properties of Balsam Tolu resemble those of Balsam Peru. It is a stimulating expectorant. Its flavor and taste render it more valuable for internal use. It is used for chronic inflammation and, like Peru, its favorable effect is on mucous membrane.

Preparation.—The best form for internal use is Syrup of Tolu, although at the present time there is a preparation called Fluid Tolu which will readily mix with water, and this is sometimes used instead of the syrup.

Dose.—From ½ to 1 teaspoonful.

For Goitre.

BANANA ROOT.

Native of the Tropics.

Properties.—It is given internally for goitre, or bronchocele.

Dose.—From 10 to 15 drops of the fluid extract every three hours.

For Jaundice, Diarrhea, Dysentery, Fluxes, Malignant Fevers.

BARBERRY—*Berberis Vulgaris.*—A shrub rising from four to eight feet in height, with long, bending branches and many small thorns. Leaves, an egg shape inverted and bristly-toothed; flowers, yellow and many on a stalk; berries, oblong and red, and hanging in loose bunches.

The bark of the stem and root is highly esteemed in jaundice. For this purpose it is infused in hard cider and sweetened.

A syrup of the berries is also given in diarrhea, dysentery, fluxes and malignant fevers, and this syrup diluted makes an excellent drink for quenching thirst, abating heat and raising the strength, especially in bilious fevers. Of the infusion in hard cider for jaundice the dose is a fluid ounce (2 tablespoonfuls) .four or five times a day. If the powdered bark is taken as a tonic, small doses are recommended; taken as a cathartic, a teaspoonful every two or three hours until it operates. For fluxes, diarrhea, dysentery, etc., the syrup, infusion or decoction may be taken as the stomach will bear. A jam of the berries is also made for table use.

For Headache, Vertigo, Epilepsy, Spasmodic Cough, etc.

BASSWOOD—*Tilia Glabra*, called also TILIA TREE, LINDEN TREE, LIME TREE, etc.—This is a forest tree, very large and beautiful, which attains to a great size and has broad leaves and yellowish-white flowers. The wood is white and soft, and when dry will swim on the water like cork.

The leaves and bark of this tree are used as poultices, and the flowers are employed in infusion for headache, vertigo, epilepsy, spasmodic cough and other complaints. The infusion should be drank in quantities according to its effect.

For Cankers, Scrofulous Tumors, etc.

BAYBERRY—*Myrica Cerifera*, called also CANDLE BERRY, WAX BERRY, WAX MYRTLE, etc.—This plant is found growing more abundantly near large bodies of water, as, for instance, near the seashore or the Great Lakes. The flowers produce one-seeded nuts about the size of a pea, which are blackish and covered with a white waxy incrustation.

It is an invaluable remedy for removing canker from the system in all chronic cases. It is also useful in poultices for old sores, scrofulous tumors, etc. A constant drink of Bayberry and Sumach bark is excellent for scrofula in almost any stage. The bark in infusion or decoction may be taken freely internally, and is used externally in poultices.

For Diabetes, Incontinence of Urine, Ulcers, Scrofulous Diseases, Dyspeptic Affections.

BEECH—*Fagus Ferruginea*, called also RED BEECH, etc. —A decoction of the bark is used in diabetes, also for children's cases of incontinence of urine at night. A decoction of the leaves may be used with success in obstinate ulcers, skin diseases, and dyspeptic affections accompanied with weakness, headache, and low spirits. A dose of the decoction is a wine-glassful.

For Ulcerous and Cancerous Affections, Hemorrhage of the Bowels.

BEECH DROPS—*Epiphegus Virginianus*, called also CAN-CER ROOT, etc.—This plant is a parasite found growing upon the roots of the beech tree. It is of a yellowish white or brown color, and has a naked, sickly appearance. The root is bulbous and of a yellow color. The stem is from eight to fifteen inches high, has many branches, but in place of leaves is beset with short, scattering scales. It has numerous flowers, growing all along the branches just above the scales. It must be gathered before the frost touches it.

Beech drops are astringent, and are used in ulcerous and cancerous affections. The roots and tops may be powdered and the powder sprinkled on the ulcer after the use of caustics, or a tea may be made and used as a wash. They are also combined with Crowfoot and Cherry bark as a remedy in hemorrhages of the bowels. This combination also makes an excellent gargle for ulcers of the mouth.

BELLADONNA.—(See A CHAPTER ON MEDICINES).

For Wounds, Sores, Poisonous Bites, Sore Throat, Inflamed Eyes, Erysipelas.

BELLWORT—*Uvularia Perfoliata*, called also MOHAWK WEED.—The stalk rises from one-half to one and one-half feet high, and is usually divided into two equal branches at the top, on one of which is a triangular-shaped seed vessel. It has yellow flowers that come out in May. The roots are white and possess but little, taste or smell. When the plant is young, it somewhat resembles the Solomon's Seal. It grows in rich soil and is found in nearly all the Western States.

The Indians used it for wounds and sores and for the bites of rattlesnakes and other reptiles. It is also useful in sore mouth, in inflammation of the gums or larynx, and for inflamed eyes. When chewed and the juice swallowed, it is considered a cure for sore throat. The root in decoction may be taken freely, or powdered and made into an ointment or poultice for outward application. Also used in erysipelas.

For Cholera Infantum, Diarrhea, Dysentery, Affections of the Urinary Passages.

BENE-BENNI, or BENNE—*Sesamum Indicum*, called also OILY GRAIN, etc.—This plant is a native of Egypt, but is cultivated in this country. It has a branching stem, four or five feet in height. The leaves vary in shape. The flowers are of a reddish white color. The fruit is an oblong capsule, containing small, oval, yellowish seeds.

The leaves stirred into water make a fine mucilage, and this drink is much employed in cholera infantum, diarrhea, dysentery and affections of the urinary passages. One or two of the leaves stirred into half a pint of water make it sufficiently mucilaginous.

For Syphilitic and Scrofulous Complaints, Salt Rheum, Acne, Eczema, etc.

BERBERIS AQUIFOLIUM.

Native of Western United States.

Properties.— This is one of the most important of the newly discovered remedies now in use. It is a powerful alterative, and at the same time is a tonic. In constitutional syphilis and in scrofulous complaints its use is attended with remarkably good results. In the case of syphilitic ulcerations it should be combined with suitable local treatment. In such case it improves the general tone of the system with a like favorable change in the condition of the ulcer. Salt rheum, acne, eczema, scrofula and other skin diseases yields to its influence. It is also useful in "liver complaint," Bright's disease, pulmonary consumption, coughs, etc. It is also used in uterine troubles, and is combined with Cascara Sagrada in constipation.

Dose.—From 2 to 6 drops of the fluid extract.

For Hemorrhages, Lung Diseases, Asthma, Cough, Leucorrhea, Ulcers, Carbuncles, Snake Bites, after Confinement.

BETHROOT—*Trillium Purpureum*, called also Birth Root, Ground Lily, Lamb's Quarter, Indian Balm, Three-Leaved Nightshade, etc.—This plant rises about a foot in height, and has three leaves, nearly as broad as long, at the top of the stem, from between which springs a single, bell-shaped flower, purple or white in color and of a fishy odor. It grows in damp, shady places, blossoming in the Southern States in April, and farther north, in May. *See illustration.*

It is taken internally for hemorrhages—where the urine voided contains blood, hemorrhage of the womb or immoderate menstrual evacuations, spitting of blood, etc.—for lung diseases, asthma, cough. Also employed in leucorrhea. An infusion is made by adding a pint of boiling water to a tablespoonful of the powder, and may be drank freely; or the powdered root may be given in doses of ½ to 1 teaspoonful. In checking hemorrhages the powder may be added to Raspberry leaf tea instead of water, and the infusion made strong. Of this from 1 to 2 tablespoonfuls may be given at a dose and increased gradually if necessary. Externally it is used as a poultice for tumors, ulcers, carbuncles and mortifications, and for this purpose is often combined with blood root. Combined with blood root as a tonic and given after a cathartic, it is said to be a certain cure for inflamed carbuncles and ulcers. It is also claimed that chewing the root and swallowing the juice will cure the bite of a rattlesnake, either in men or cattle. The infusion was much used by Indian women after confinement. In the case of leucorrhea it should be used in injections as well as taken internally.

For Dyspepsia, Costiveness, Liver Complaint, Gravel, Dropsy, Consumptive Coughs, Asthma, Whooping Cough.

BINDWEED—*Convolvulus Panduratus*, called also MAN ROOT, MAN-IN-THE-GROUND, WILD SCAMMONY, WILD POTATO, WILD RHUBARB.—A trailing vine that grows all over the United States in loose, sandy soils. The root is milky inside and runs deep into the earth. The flowers are funnel-form, large and white with a purple tinge. The leaves are pointed, heart-shaped, and sometimes contracted near the middle, making them somewhat resemble a fiddle.

A celebrated Indian remedy. The root powdered, in doses of from 10 to 12 grains, or taken in decoction, is employed in dyspepsia, costiveness, liver complaints, gravel and dropsy. Made into a syrup with Balm of Gilead buds and Skunk Cabbage, it is very beneficial in consumptive coughs, asthma and whooping cough.

For Hemorrhage, Diarrhea, Chronic Dysentery, Leucorrhea, Gleet, Spongy Gums, Discharging Ulcers.

BISTORT—*Polygonum Bistorta*, called also GREAT BISTORT, SNAKE WEED, PATIENCE DOCK, etc.—This is a troublesome weed found in meadows. The root is creeping, woody and crooked and about the thickness of the finger, reddish within and surrounded with slender fibers of a brownish black color on the outside. The single stem rises to a height of from twelve to eighteen inches. The leaves are egg-shaped, of a bright green color, and on the under side are covered with a fine white powder, which easily rubs off. The stem ends in a spike of rose-colored flowers. The root, which is the part used in medicine, is without odor, but is very astringent to the taste.

The powdered root in doses of ½ to 1 teaspoonful is found useful in hemorrhage, diarrhea and chronic dysentery. The decoction is also employed as an astringent injection in leucorrhea and gleet, as a gargle in spongy gums and sore throat, and as a wash for discharging ulcers. The decoction is also taken internally, the dose being from 2 to 4 tablespoonfuls three or four times a day.

For Blood Purification and Bilious Diseases.

BITTER DOCK—*Rumex Obtusifolius*, called also BROAD-LEAVED DOCK and BLUNT-LEAVED DOCK.—This plant is similar in growth to the yellow or narrow-leaved dock. The leaves are broad, and spring from the stem one in a place, the same as the narrow-leaved variety. The root is thick and branching, brown on the outside and yellow within. It flowers a month later than the yellow dock. It grows about two feet in height.

It is used similar to the *Yellow Dock.*

For Use as a Tonic.

BITTER ROOT—*Apocynum Cannabinum*, called also AMERICAN IPECAC, BLACK INDIAN HEMP, INDIAN PHYSIC, etc. This plant is a native of the United States. It grows in meadows and low, moist woods. The stems are of a reddish color and grow about two feet in height. The leaves are numerous and hang on foot-stalks. The flowers form a loose, long cluster at the ends of the stems. They are whitish, similar to Buckwheat, and terminate in pods resembling cucumbers. The root is a branching tuber.

The plant is emetic, cathartic, tonic and diuretic. It is a safe and effective emetic given in doses of 30 grains of the powder; given in smaller doses, of from 3 to 4 grains at a time, it acts as a tonic—gives tone to the stomach and is useful in dyspepsia. It is also given in small doses in dropsy, in which disease it will often cause large discharges of water and copious perspiration. Its principal use, however, is as a tonic, for which purpose it may be combined with other herbs that have tonic properties.

For Scrofula and Skin Diseases, Tumors, Ulcers, Liver Complaint.

BITTERSWEET—*Solanum Dulcamara*, called also WOODY NIGHTSHADE and BITTERSWEET NIGHTSHADE.—This is an undershrub or vine, woody at the base, with soft stem, leaves in bunches at the joints, and purple flowers that blossom in June and July and are followed by scarlet berries. Usually found in moist situations, especially on rise of ground in swampy localities. *See illustration.*

This herb is not taken internally to any great extent unless combined with other remedies. Used in combination with

Yellow Dock, equal parts of each, a decoction or syrup may be made of the twigs and leaves which is very beneficial in scrofulous diseases, skin diseases, hard tumors, ill-conditioned ulcers and liver complaints. The decoction also makes an excellent wash for ulcerous sores and skin diseases.

For Intermittent and Bilious Fevers, Debility, Dropsies, Gangrene, Pulmonary Affections, Bleeding Piles, Worms.

BLACK ALDER—*Prinos Verticillatus*, called also FEVER BUSH, WINTERBERRY, etc.—Commonly grows in bunches six or eight feet in height, and is usually found in thickets on the edge of pools and marshy places. It has small white flowers, growing in tufts and appearing with the leaves. These are followed by bunches of berries of a bright red color, about the size of a pea and bitter and unpleasant to the taste. The bark is moderately bitter.

This plant has been very successfully used in intermittent and bilious fevers. It is a good tonic in cases of debility, also in dropsies, and gangrene in the early stages. A decoction or infuson may be taken in doses from ½ to a full teacupful. The decoction is made by boiling 2 ounces of the bark in 3 pints of water down to a quart. It also makes a useful wash in obstinate skin diseases. The berries infused in Brandy are used in pulmonary affections and bleeding piles, and in simple infusion or decoction are given to children for worms.

For Chronic Diarrhea, Dysentery, Cholera Infantum, Summer Complaint, Cholera Morbus.

BLACKBERRY—*Rubus Occidentalis*, called also THIMBLE-BERRY, etc.—The bark of the root of this plant made into a syrup is exceedingly valuable in chronic diarrhea, dysentery, cholera infantum, summer complaint and cholera morbus. In these diseases it often proves a sovereign remedy when all other preparations fail. Combined with Black Cohosh, it makes an excellent injection in leucorrhea and falling of the womb.

The bark of the root of this plant may be given in powder, infusion, decoction or syrup. The most common, and perhaps the best way to take it, is in decoction, which is made by adding 1 ounce of the bruised root to a pint of water. Dose, from 2 to 4 tablespoonfuls three or four times a day.

For Bowel Complaints and Digestion.

BLACK BIRCH—*Betula Lenta*, called also SWEET BIRCH, SPICY BIRCH, CHERRY BIRCH, etc.—This tree, which rises from twenty to forty feet in height, grows in low, swampy woods.

The bark in decoction is tonic and astringent, and is useful in all complaints of the bowels and cases of diarrhea. Made into a syrup with Peach meats, or Cherry-stone meats, it is an excellent remedy to promote digestion and to use as a gentle restorative.

For Confinement, Disorders of Menstruation, Rheumatism, Inflammations, Whooping Cough.

BLACK COHOSH—*Cimicifuga Racemosa*, called also SQUAW ROOT, BLACK SNAKE ROOT, RICHWEED, RATTLEWEED, etc.—This plant is found growing all over the eastern half of the United States and in Canada, and was made use of by all the Indian tribes. It is generally found in open woods and rich soils, and grows to a height of from three to eight feet. It is not common in rocky and stony places, and is very scarce in moist and swampy soils. It has a thick, brownish root with long fibers. It has but few leaves. Its flowers are scattered along stems which are from one to three feet long, and are followed by a blackish capsule which contains many seeds. *See illustration.*

It was largely used by the Indians for rheumatism, and by the Indian women in confinement, hence the name of Squaw Root. Also used by them for disorders of menstruation. A strong decoction of this plant, combined with Slippery Elm bark, forms a good poultice for every kind of inflammation. A syrup of the root is a valuable remedy for coughs. It is an astringent, and useful for bowel complaints, especially those of children. As an astringent, a strong tea or infusion should be taken. This infusion may also be used as a gargle. Cohosh is also employed as a remedy for whooping cough. For this purpose it is usually given in tincture. For a child one year old, the dose is from 5 to 10 drops four or five times a day; three to four years old, from 15 to 20 drops in a little sweetened water. The tincture is prepared by adding a pint of spirits to 2 ounces of the pulverized root. The plant may also be used in decoction.

For Uterine Tonic.

BLACK HAW—*Vibernum Prunifolium.*

Native of Eastern United States.

Properties.—Held in high esteem as a uterine tonic and sedative. It is especially valuable in threatened abortion and as a corrective of the chronic disposition to miscarry. In the latter class of cases it should be given continuously in moderate doses for at least a month prior to the usual time at which the miscarriage takes place. In dysmenorrhea due to almost every cause it may be prescribed with benefit, commencing its administration some days before the menstrual crisis. In after-pains and uterine hemorrhages it is also valuable. It is a most useful drug in menorrhagia or metorrhagia. The most common form of administering it is the fluid extract in ¼ to 1 teaspoonful doses. The principal objection to this form is its disagreeable taste, but that can be disguised in a great measure by giving it in Cinnamon water. The amount of Valerianic Acid which the fluid extract contains renders it more of a sedative than the solid extract. Where the disagreeable taste is objectionable, the solid extract may be given in doses varying from 3 to 8 grains. It is well to begin its use, in cases of menorrhagia, several days preceding the flow, and continue its administration through its duration and after its cessation.

Dose.—¼ to 1 fluidrachm (teaspoonful) Fluid Extract Black Haw several times a day.

For Tonic and Emetic Purposes, and to Cause Sweating.

BLESSED THISTLE—*Centaurea Benedicta*, called also HOLY THISTLE, SPOTTED THISTLE, SPOTTED CARDUS, etc.— This plant grows spontaneously in the southern countries of Europe, but has become naturalized in this country. It was formerly held in such high repute that it obtained the name of "Blessed Thistle" and was given for the plague, worms, and various other diseases; also in cases of obstinate ulcers and even cancers. It is now but little employed, but is a useful medicine.

A strong decoction or infusion of this plant will induce vomiting. An infusion not so strong, taken warm, produces perspiration, while 6 drachms (teaspoonfuls) of the leaves added to a pint of cold water makes a very beneficial tonic in loss of appetite and dyspepsia. It answers about the same purpose as Chamomile, which is now usually given in place of it.

The dose of the powder as a tonic is from ⅓ to 1 teaspoonful; of the infusion, 2 to 4 tablespoonfuls.

For External Application to Ulcers, Ringworms and Ill-conditioned Sores; for Internal Use as a Tonic or Emetic.

BLOOD ROOT—*Sanguinaria Canadensis*, called also RED PUCCOON, RED ROOT, etc.—This plant is found growing in low grounds among rocks, in meadows, etc. The root is a tuber about the size of the finger. It is reddish externally, and when cut a juice of a reddish orange color is discharged. *See illustration.*

This plant is capable of producing tonic, stimulant and emetic effects, according to the dose and form in which it is administered. In doses of from 8 to 20 grains it causes nausea and vomiting, and in doses not sufficient to cause nausea it acts as a stimulant and tonic. It may be applied externally, either as a powder or as a wash, to ill-conditioned ulcers, ringworm and other eruptive diseases. The powder will also remove fungous growths, and even soft polypus. It should not be given to pregnant women. A Wine tincture, made by adding 1 ounce of the pulverized root to a quart of Wine, and taken in doses of a wineglassful three times a day, is beneficial in eruptions and impurities of the blood. In malignant scarlet fever add from ½ to 1 teaspoonful to 1 quart of boiling water, strain the infusion and sweeten with honey. For a child of from two to four years old the dose is a teaspoonful, repeated every hour through the day if the child can bear it. If the surface gets broken and becomes ulcerated, wash the parts with the same infusion.

For Dropsy, Venereal Diseases.

BLUE CARDINAL FLOWER—*Lobelia Syphilitica.*—Is of the same genus as the Lobelia. Grows in moist places from eighteen inches to three feet in height, bears a long, spiked blue flower, and yields a milky juice with a rank odor. The root, consisting of white fibers, is generally used in decoction, of which the dose is from ½ to 1 wineglassful three times a day.

Used by the Indians with great success in the cure of venereal diseases. It is said the Indians combined this plant with the roots of the Mandrake and the bark of Wild Cherry in making a decoction for syphilis, and at the same time dusted the ulcers with the powdered bark of New Jersey tea. Also valuable in dropsy.

For Confinement and Female Complaints, Nervous Excitement, Hysterical Affections, Epilepsy, Dropsy, Rheumatism.

BLUE COHOSH—*Caulophyllum Thalictroides*, called also PAPOOSE ROOT, SQUAW ROOT, BLUE BERRY, etc.—Grows from one to three feet high, and has a hard, knobby, branched root that is brown outside and yellow inside. The stem divides at the top into three branches, each of which has three leaves; the flower stem springs from the same joint as the leaf stems. The flowers are small and of a yellowish or purplish green, and produce a berry of deep blue color, something like sour grapes. It grows throughout the United States, but is usually found on low, rich ground near streams, in swamps, or on islands that have been overflowed with water.

An exceedingly valuable remedy in female complaints. The Indian women make a tea or infusion of the root which they drink for two or three weeks before confinement, the effect, it is said, being to make delivery rapid and comparatively painless.

It is used in suppression of the menses, leucorrhea and similar diseases, nervous excitement and epilepsy, hysterical affections and dropsy. Usually taken in infusion or decoction, and may be drank freely. It is also made use of in rheumatism, for which a preparation is made of 2 ounces of the Cohosh root to 1 ounce of Blood Root infused in proof spirits and taken in wineglassful doses three times a day.

For Dropsy, Liver Complaint, Sore Mouth, Ulcers, Worms, Felon.

BLUE FLAG—*Iris Versicolor*, called also FLOWER DE LUCE, FLAG LILY, SNAKE LILY, LIVER LILY, etc.—Found throughout the United States in the borders of swamps and in wet meadows. Flowers in June.

The fresh dried root given in doses of 6 to 8 grains, night and morning, proves gently laxative and eradicates the most inveterate taint of the system. Given as a cathartic, the dose is about 20 grains. The root in decoction is good in dropsy, liver complaint, sore mouth and ulcers. The leaves in infusion, or a syrup made from the blossoms, is a good medicine for worms in children and for loosening the bowels. An obstinate case of dropsy was cured by an infusion of equal quantities of Blue Flag and Male Fern root taken three times a day, taking occasionally with it a little white wine. The fresh root pounded to a pulp makes one of the best poultices that can be applied to a felon.

For the Eruptive Diseases, Coughs, Sore Throat and Constipation of Children.

BLUE VIOLET—*Viola Cucullata.*—This is a well-known little plant that grows on rich, moist land, has blossoms of a blue-violet color and a small root about an inch in length.

A decoction of this plant is given to children in eruptive diseases, and a syrup made of the petals may be given them for cough, sore throat and constipation.

For Fevers, Influenza, Rheumatism, Dropsy.

BONESET—*Eupatorium Perfoliatum.*—Called also THOROUGHWORT, FEVERWORT, SWEATING PLANT, CROSSWORT, INDIAN SAGE, AGUE WEED, VEGETABLE ANTIMONY, etc.—Boneset grows most commonly in meadows and swamps near streams. It is easily recognized by its leaves, which are joined together around the stem, giving the effect of being perforated by the stem. The whole plant has a grayish-green color, and the flowers are of a pale white. The leaves are woolly beneath and rough above, and taper from where they are joined down to a sharp point, being from three to eight inches long. The seeds are black and oblong. The plant possesses little smell, but is exceedingly bitter to the taste.

Boneset is particularly valuable in fevers—intermittent, remittent and continued fevers. A cold infusion or decoction may be given as a tonic. A warm infusion may be given as an emetic, or to assist the action of other emetics. It is also recommended for influenza, and may be given with advantage in rheumatism and dropsy. It may be taken freely, a teacupful at a time.

For Bilious Disorders, Jaundice, Low Spirits, Intermittent Fevers.

BOXWOOD, or DOGWOOD—*Cornus Florida.*—This tree is found throughout the United States, but more plentifully in the Middle and Southern States. In the months of April, May and June, according to its latitude, it is covered with a profusion of large, elegant white flowers.

The bark of the root, stems and smaller branches is used (that of the root is best) and is a valuable remedy in bilious disorders, jaundice and low spirits. In the case of intermittent fevers the dose is from ⅓ to 1 teaspoonful of the dried bark, which is greatly preferable to the fresh bark as the fresh disagrees with the stomach, repeating so that from 1 to 2 tablespoonfuls may be taken between the attacks. For the infusion, take 1 ounce of the bark to a pint of boiling water. The ripe fruit infused in spirits makes an excellent tonic bitters.

For Consumption, Menses, Scurvy.

BROOK-LIME—*Veronica Beccabunga*, called also BECCA-BUNGA.—Found in ditches. Grows to the height of nine to eighteen inches. Has blue flowers, no odor, and is insipid to the taste.

The herb in infusion is used in scurvy and to purify the blood, without much regard as to dose. The fresh plant may be eaten as food, or the juice may be taken in large quantities with advantage for these complaints. It is a valuable remedy for indigestion and consumption, and in the form of bitters is good to regulate the menses.

For Urinary Complaints, Rheumatism, Dyspepsia, etc.

BUCHU.
Native of the Cape of Good Hope.
Properties.—The value of this plant as a medicine was first learned from the Hottentots. The leaves are used principally in urinary complaints, as gravel, chronic catarrh of the bladder,

etc. They are also recommended in chronic rheumatism, dyspepsia and skin affections. They may be given in powder, infusion or tincture.

Dose.—Of the powder, from 20 to 30 grains two or three times a day; of the infusion, made by adding an ounce of the leaves to a pint of boiling water, from 2 to 4 tablespoonfuls.

For Scurvy, Hypochondria, Rheumatism, Ague, Shingles, as a Tonic.

BUCKBEAN—*Menyanthes Trifoliata*, called also BITTER-WORM, MARSH TREFOIL and WATER SHAMROCK.—Grows from six to twelve inches high in swamps and stagnant waters all over the northern part of the country. It blossoms in May and June and bears many white flowers, which are tipped externally with red and fringed with white filaments within.

It is a tonic, good in scurvy, hypochondria, rheumatism, ague, also in shingles and other eruptions of a herpetic (ringworm) nature. An infusion is made of the dried leaves, 1 ounce of the leaves to a pint of boiling water, of which from 2 to 4 tablespoonfuls may be taken two or three times a day.

For Coughs, Diarrhea, Dysentery, Soreness of the Stomach and Bowels.

BUCKTHORN BRAKE—*Osmunda Regalis.*—This is found in meadows and low, moist grounds. The main root is about two inches long, and somewhat in the shape of a horn. The stems are smooth, slender and brownish, and grow about three feet high. The flowers grow in a cluster at the top of the stem, and are succeeded by numerous seed vessels which are at first green and subsequently of a brownish color. The roots should be collected in August, or about the first of April, and should be dried with care, as otherwise there is danger of their becoming mouldy.

A mucilage is obtained from the roots by steeping them in hot water, and this, with the addition of loaf sugar, Ginger, Brandy, etc., makes an excellent jelly, which is useful in coughs, diarrhea, dysentery, and soreness of the stomach and bowels; also beneficial in convalescence from any sickness. The ordinary dose is ½ wineglassful, which may be frequently repeated. The mucilage mixed with Brandy is also used as an external application for sprains and weakness of the back.

For Coughs, Consumption, Ill-Conditioned Sores.

BUGLE WEED—*Lycopus Virginicus*, called also WATER HOREHOUND, WATER BUGLE, GYPSYWORT, etc.—Found growing near water—in ditches, creeks, swamps, etc. It has white flowers that blossom from July to September. The leaves grow opposite each other on the stem, two in a place.

The leaves and stems are used in infusion, which may be drank freely. Useful in coughs, in bleeding of the lungs, and in consumption in its incipient state (the beginning of). It is also a good drink and wash for patients having ill-conditioned sores.

For Kidney Diseases, Salt Rheum, Herpes, Ulcers, Skin Diseases, Rheumatism.

BURDOCK—*Arctium Lappa.*—This plant has been naturalized in this country, and grows abundantly along the sides of roads, etc., to the height of about three feet. It is well known by the burrs or heads which adhere to the clothes.

A decoction made by boiling 2 ounces of the fresh root in 3 pints of water down to 2 pints, may be given in diseases of the kidneys and obstruction of the urine, and especially for dropsy, 1 pint to be taken in the course of twenty-four hours. It is also given in decoction in salt rheum, herpes, ulcers, rheumatism, and all diseases of the skin. The leaves bruised with a roller and moistened with hot drops form an excellent application for sprains, bruises and other external injuries. In gouty affections where the feet are swelled, the same application is of benefit.

For Poisoning by Ivy, Inflammation of the Bladder, and Kidney Diseases.

BUSH HONEYSUCKLE—*Diervilla Canadensis*, called also Gravel Weed.—Bears a yellow flower and is common all over the Northern States.

A few applications in the case of poisoning by ivy will relieve the itching and check the inflammation and swelling. A cold infusion of the leaves and twigs drank freely is a useful remedy in inflammation of the bladder with gravelly deposits, hence the name of *Gravel Weed.*

For Cathartic Purposes.

BUTTERNUT — *Juglans Cinevia*, called also White Walnut.—This is a common, well-known tree in the United States. An extract of the inner bark in doses of from 15 to 30 grains operates as an active cathartic without causing heat or irritation, and is not so liable to leave the bowels in a costive state as many other cathartics. The bark for making the extract should be procured in May or June.

For Affections of the Urinary Organs and Snake Bites.

BUTTON SNAKE ROOT—*Liatris Spicata*, called also GAY FEATHER, CORN SNAKE ROOT, etc.—This is a native of our Western prairies. It has a round stalk, sometimes growing two feet high, with leaves scattered along it, and growing from the top a ball as large as a musket ball, thickly covered with white bloom. The root consists of a knob an inch long, and appears as if decayed or rotted off. In taste it resembles the Black Snake Root.

In large doses it acts upon the urinary organs, promoting the secretion and discharge of urine. Also beneficial in chronic inflammation of the urinary organs attended with mucous discharges. For this purpose it is best given in decoction, made by boiling an ounce of the root in 1½ pints of water until reduced to a pint, which is to be drank in the course of twenty-four hours. Taken in smaller doses, it is a stimulant and tonic, but for this purpose it is better made into a tincture, prepared by adding 2 ounces of the bruised root to a pint of Wine or diluted Alcohol, the dose of which is a tablespoonful three times a day. The root, chewed and laid on the wound, is said to be an infallible cure for the bite of venomous reptiles. If this can be done when first bitten, it prevents the parts from swelling. A decoction of the plant in milk should be taken internally at the same time.

For Dropsy, Intestinal Worms, Obstructed Menstruation, Bites of Serpents.

CAINCA ROOT.

Native of Brazil.

Properties.—Cainca is mainly employed in the treatment of dropsies, for which purpose it has been found very useful. It is also recommended in the treatment of intestinal worms and in obstructed menstruation. It is much used by the natives for the bites of poisonous serpents and in rheumatic pains.

Dose.—From 1 to 3 teaspoonfuls a day of a decoction of the root.

For Nervous Diseases, Bowel Complaints, Neuralgia, etc.

CALIFORNIA LAUREL—*Umbellularia Californica*, called also CALIFORNIA OLIVE, CAJEPUT TREE, SPICE BUSH, SPICE TREE, PEPPERWOOD TREE, MOUNTAIN LAUREL, BALM OF HEAVEN, CALIFORNIA SASSAFRAS and BAY TREE.

Native of California.

Properties.—Will be found useful in nervous headache by inhaling the odor from the pressed leaves, care being taken not to continue it after relieved. Also much used in cerebro-spinal meningitis. It is useful as a stimulant, and used in bowel troubles, especially when resulting from constitutional debility. Also used in muscular cramps, chills and fever, rheumatism, neuralgia, and is very useful in stopping earache or toothache, a pledget of cotton being saturated with the fluid extract, or oil, and applied.

Dose.—10 to 20 drops of the fluid extract.

CALISAYA.—(See A Chapter on Medicines).

For Nervous Affections.

CAMPHOR—*Camphora.*
Native of Sumatra, China and Japan.
Properties.—Camphor in small doses is a mild stimulant, and may aid sometimes in relieving nervousness and excitement by increasing the physical powers. In the same way it sometimes aids in relieving headache, palpitation and hiccough. At one time it enjoyed some reputation as a remedy in epilepsy and typhoid conditions, also in cholera during the early stages, but it is not now much used internally. Given in large doses, it is depressing. It is eliminated rapidly, hence its effects are transient. Its principal use is in liniments and in the well-known Spirits of Camphor. In the form of liniment it is sometimes used in neuralgic pains. Applied in strong solution it is a counter-irritant, and is often added to other strong counter-irritants to produce blistering. When Spirits of Camphor is inhaled it seems to produce the same effect as when taken internally.

Dose.—Taken internally, from 1 to 3 grains of the Camphor "gum."

For Flatulency, Colic.

CARAWAY—*Carum Carui.*—Has a spindle-shaped root, a stalk rising to the height of about two feet, and numerous white or pale flesh-colored flowers. Cultivated in gardens.

Caraway seeds generally afford a considerable relief to persons afflicted with flatulency or liable to colic. Of the seeds in substance, the dose is from ⅓ to 1 teaspoonful. The infusion is made of 2 teaspoonfuls to a pint of boiling water. Of the oil the dose is from 1 to 10 drops.

For Wind Colic and Indigestion.

CARDAMON—*Ellettaria Cardamomum.*

Native of Malabar, Ceylon and the West Indies.

Properties.—The seeds of this plant are pleasant to the taste, and are warming and stimulating to the stomach, aiding in digestion and acting as a nervine as well. Also valuable in wind colic.

Dose.—Of the powdered seeds, from 5 to 10 grains; of the tincture, from 1 to 3 teaspoonfuls.

For Syphilis and Syphilitic Ulcers.

CAROBA—*Jacaranda Procera.*

Native of Brazil.

Properties.—Is a valuable and effective cure for syphilis. May be combined advantageously with Iodide of Potassium in cases where there are pains in the limbs. Its principal use, however, is external application to obstinate syphilitic ulcers. The leaves were used by the Indians for wounds and skin diseases, and were also used by the Portuguese for this purpose.

Dose.—¼ to 1 teaspoonful of the fluid extract.

For Kidney and Bladder Complaints—Obstructed Menses—Dysentery—Chronic Coughs—Hiccoughs—Flatulent Disorders—Ulcers and Fissures.

CARROT—*Daucus Carota.*—Called also BIRD'S NEST, BEE'S NEST, etc.—Wild carrot is a common weed in this country, growing by waysides and in old fields. It is similar to garden carrot except that the stalks are whiter and rougher. *See illustration.*

Given in strong decoction it is very useful in gravel complaints and in the passage of stone from the kidneys and bladder. Also used in cancerous ulcers and fissures of the nipples. The seeds are useful in flatulent disorders, obstructed menses, hiccough, chronic coughs and dysentery. The dose of the bruised seeds is from ¼ to ⅓ teaspoonful or more; or a strong tea or decoction of the seeds may be drank freely warm.

Of the cultivated carrot the root only is used, and, freshly scraped, is an excellent application to sloughing and cancerous ulcers.

CASCARA SAGRADA.—(See A CHAPTER ON MEDICINES).

For Debility of the Stomach and Bowels.

CASCARILLA.

Native of Bahama Islands in West Indies.

Properties.—The bark of this plant is a pleasant and stimulant stomachic, used in dyspepsia, chronic diarrhea, dysentery flatulent colic, and other cases of debility of the stomach and bowels. It is often combined with the more powerful bitters and used for the same purposes.

Dose.—Given in powder, the dose is from ⅓ to ½ teaspoonful or more, and may be taken several times a day.

For Cathartic Purposes.

CASTOR BEAN—*Ricinus Communis.*

Native of East Indies and Northern Africa.

Properties.—The seeds of the Castor Bean are expressed and yield an oil termed Castor Oil. Castor Oil is one of the most common cathartics in use, and, being mild and certain in its action, is largely used. It is excellent in relieving obstinate constipation, colic, strangulated hernia and piles on account of the mildness of its action. Taken in minute doses the oil often cures obstinate coughs. This plant is now extensively cultivated in the United States.

Dose.—For infants and small children, 1 teaspoonful of Castor Oil; for adults, 1 tablespoonful.

Note.—A preparation of Castor Oil that is now much used is Laxol (see Index). In this preparation, which is ninety-nine per cent Castor Oil, the nauseating and unpleasant taste of the oil is disguised.

For Hysterical and Nervous Affections.

CATNIP—*Nepeta Cataria,* called also CATMINT, CATWORT, etc.—Catnip is too common a plant to need description, either as to appearance or use. "Catnip tea" is given in colds and to produce perspiration, and makes a very valuable drink in hysterical and nervous affections, as well as in all diseases of the womb except inflammation. It is much given to infants to relieve flatulency and colicky pains. It is also much used externally in poultices.

For Stimulating Digestion, Checking Vomiting of Drunkards, Delirium Tremens and Local Application.

CAYENNE PEPPER, or CAPSICUM — *Capsicum Annuum.*

Native of South and Central America, Africa and Europe.

MARSHMALLOW.
(See Description.)
This herb is used externally as a poultice on Inflammatory
Tumors and Swellings, and to prevent threatened Mortification.

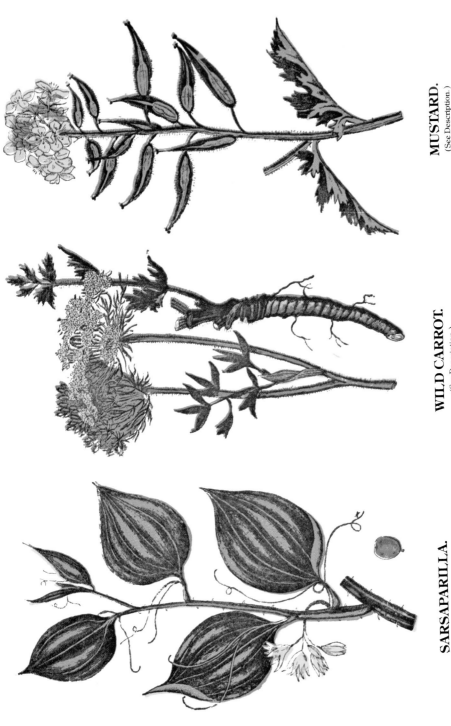

SARSAPARILLA.
(See Description.)
Used in all Diseases of the Blood,
Eruptive Skin Diseases, etc.

WILD CARROT.
(See Description.)
Used in Kidney and Bladder Complaints,
obstructed Menses, Dysentery, Chronic
Coughs, etc.

MUSTARD.
(See Description.)
Used externally to allay pain, and
internally as an emetic.

INDIAN TURNIP.

(See Description.)

This herb is used in Coughs, Consumption and Asthma, also in
Colic and Pains in the Bowels.

LOBELIA.

(See Description.)

This herb is exceedingly valuable in Asthma, Croup, Whooping Cough and Pulmonary Diseases generally, and is also used as an emetic.

SNAKE HEAD.

(See Description.)

This herb is a remedy for Costiveness, Dyspepsia, Loss of Appetite,
General Languor and Disorders of the Liver.

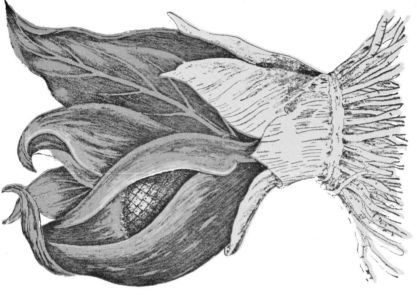

SKUNK CABBAGE.

(See Description.)

Useful in Asthma, Coughs, Catarrahs, Consumption, etc., also in the cough of old people.

SUMACH.

(See Description.)

This herb is useful in Scrofulous and Venereal Diseases, Skin Eruptions, Falling of the Bowels and Womb, Kidney Derangements and Sore Throat.

POKE WEED.
(See Description.)
This herb is used externally on Abscesses, Cancers and Ulcers, and is
given internally in Chronic and Syphilitic Rheumatism.

SENECA SNAKE ROOT.

(See Description.)

This herb is a valuable remedy in advanced stages of Chronic
Bronchitis and Pneumonia; also in protracted Whooping Cough and
the latter stages of Croup and Bronchitis in infants and children.

Properties.—Capsicum is an irritant and local stimulant. When taken internally in moderate doses, it produces a sense of warmth, increases the secretions of the stomach and thus aids digestion. It is often used to check the vomiting of drunkards and the condition present following an attack of delirium tremens. There are various forms for its administration. A very good one for the conditions just mentioned is to add a considerable quantity to some form of soup. It is recommended by some as one of the few remedies to stimulate the nervous system in those who are trying to break off the habit of alcoholic liquors. Its continuous local application is said to be strong enough to cause blistering. The Tincture of Capsicum is frequently used in liniments for rheumatism, neuralgia, headache, flatulent colic, etc. The powder is also much used to sprinkle over the surface of plasters applied externally.

Dose.—From 5 drops to ½ teaspoonful of Tincture of Capsicum, well diluted.

For Poisonous Bites, Hydrophobia, Dyspeptic Affections, Cholera Morbus, Neuralgia and Gout.

CEDRON SEED—*Simaruba Cedron.*

Native of South America.

Properties.—Reputed of value as a remedy for bites of insects and serpents; for hydrophobia; and of service in intermittent fever, spasm of the bowels and stomach, dyspeptic affections, cholera morbus, neuralgia of the face and gout. For serpent bites it is recommended to administer the fluid extract in 6-drop doses and to dress the bite with the fluid extract. It is rarely necessary to repeat the dose.

Dose.—From 1 to 8 drops of the fluid extract.

For Warts, Ringworm and Old Ulcers.

CELANDINE—*Chelidonium Majus.*—Grows in marshy places, stands two to three feet high, and has round, green, watery stalks with large joints, very brittle and transparent. The leaves are large, notched around the edges and very tender. The flowers are yellow and consist of four petals. After these come long pods which when pressed by the fingers instantly fly into pieces.

The juice of this plant rubbed on warts will remove them. It is also useful in curing ringworm and for cleansing old ulcers. The roots, boiled in hog's lard, make a valuable ointment for piles and salt rheum. At the same time a tincture of the Celandine should be taken. This is prepared by digesting 1 ounce of the plant in a pint of spirits (see TINCTURES).

For Pulmonary Consumption, Hysterics, Colics, Gout, Vomiting in Confinement, etc.

CHAMOMILE—*Anthemis Nobilis*, called also ROMAN CHAMOMILE.—This plant is not a native of this country, but is cultivated here for medical purposes. It grows nearly a foot in height, and has slender, trailing, hairy stems. The flowers are yellow in the center, surrounded by a ray of white petals. *See illustration.*

The flowers have a strong, spicy smell, and a bitter, nauseous taste. They are useful in pulmonary consumption, hysteria, spasmodic and flatulent colics, in gout, intermittent and typhus fevers, and in vomiting of women in pregnancy. For derangement of the stomach and digestive organs no better bitter can be given. They may be given in warm infusion, or in cases of debility may be made into a tincture with Wine. Boiled in milk or vinegar, they may be applied as a fomentation to painful swellings of the glands in any portion of the body.

For Bronchitis, Winter Cough, etc.

CHEKAN—*Eugenia Cheken.* ·
Native of Chili.
Properties.—Introduced from Chili as a remedy in chronic catarrhal inflammation of the mucous lining of the respiratory organs. Dr. Murrell, of London, especially commends it in winter cough, that annoying and obstinate affection of elderly people. Dr. Dessaur, of the German hospital of Valparaiso, speaks highly of its effects in the purulent form of bronchitis, and others who have tested its virtues recommend it as a valuable addition to the list of remedies in chronic bronchitis.
Dose.—From 1 to 3 teaspoonfuls of the fluid extract.

For External Application to Inflammatory Swellings.

CHICKWEED—*Cerastium Vulgatum.*—This is a common plant that springs up spontaneously and has to be weeded out of gardens.

It is principally used as an ointment for application to inflammatory swellings. Combined with Elecampane, the Germans consider it a specific for hydrophobia.

For Stomach Tonic and Bowel Complaints, and to disguise the taste and smell of other remedies.

CINNAMON—*Cinnamomum.*
Native of Island of Ceylon.
Properties.—Cinnamon is a very pleasant and grateful aromatic. It is stimulating and warming to the stomach, and

also produces a tonic effect. It is very useful in bowel complaints. It is much used in conjunction with other remedies to disguise their taste and smell, and is also commonly used as a flavoring extract.

Dose.—Given in powder in small ⅓-of-a-teaspoonful doses.

For Kidney and Bladder Troubles, Scurvv, Spitting of Blood, Tumors.

CLEAVERS—*Galium Aparine*, called also CLIVERS, CATCH WEED, GOOSE GRASS, etc.—Grows in moist places to a height of from three to eight feet, and creeps upon bushes and fences. Leaves small; flowers small and white.

This is an excellent remedy in gravelly disorders and inflammatory affections of the kidneys and bladder. It is taken in infusion, which should be made in cold water, 4 ounces to 1 quart of water, and drank freely and often. This infusion has also been found beneficial in the cure of scurvy and spitting of blood. The expressed juice of the plant mixed with oatmeal to the consistence of a poultice and applied cold over indolent (painless) tumors, keeping the bowels open in the meantime with Castor Oil and taking a tablespoonful of the juice every morning, will often disperse them in a short time.

For Nausea, Vomiting, Cholera Morbus, Toothache.

CLOVES—*Caryophyllus.*

Native of East and West Indies.

Properties.—A decoction of cloves is sometimes used to allay nausea and check vomiting. It will also relieve wind colic. It is made by boiling 2 or 3 teaspoonfuls of the ground cloves in ½ pint of sweet milk. This may be given in tablespoonful doses, as hot as can be borne, every fifteen to thirty minutes. This decoction is also valuable in cholera morbus. The Oil of Cloves may be given in place of the powder, and is also used in the cure of toothache, a little of the oil being put on batting and introduced into the cavity.

Dose.—Of the decoction, as above; of the oil, from 1 to 2 drops.

For Nervous Headache, General Debility, Typhoid Conditions.

COCA—*Erythroxylon Coca.*

Native of the Andes in Peru and Bolivia.

Properties.—Coca is fully represented by its well-known active principle, Cocaine. Cocaine is both a stimulant and a narcotic. Taken in small doses it first stimulates the heart action and respiration; if the dose is increased, it produces unconsciousness and dangerous symptoms. The continued use of cocaine produces sleeplessness, decay both of the mental and moral powers and, later, emaciation and death.

Applied locally, it is a powerful anesthetic to a limited area, hence is valuable in many forms of minor surgery. Combined with Carbolic Acid, it forms the well-known remedy for "painless extraction of teeth."

For Rheumatism, Sudden Colds, Nervous Debility, Dizziness, Headache, Pains of the Stomach and Bowels, Irregularity of the Menses.

COCASH—*Aster Puniceus*, called also MEADOW SCABISH, FROSTWEED, RED-STALKED ASTER, etc.—The Cocash grows in wet grounds. The stem is from two to three feet high, of a reddish color, covered with short, stiff bristles, is thickly branched at the top and easily broken. The leaves are rough on the margin and upper surface, tapering at both ends, and are bordered with teeth not set very close together. The flowers are of a light blue, and grow in spreading clusters at the tops of the stems and branches. They blossom about the first of September and remain in bloom until late in the autumn.

This plant is an agreeable stimulant and promotes perspiration. It is perfectly harmless and may be taken without regard to quantity. The infusion is prepared by steeping the fresh bruised roots and leaves in hot water, and is useful in rheumatism, sudden colds, nervous debility, dizziness, headache, pains of the stomach and bowels and irregularity of the menstrual discharges.

For Bronchitis ana Pulmonary Consumption.

COCILLANA—*Guarea.*

Native of Bolivia.

Properties.—Expectorant, tonic, laxative. This is a new remedy that acts on the respiratory organs in a manner similar to Ipecac, but said to be "superior in certain diseases of the air passages in which the latter is often used." Besides its excellence as an expectorant, it exerts a tonic influence upon the appetite and reduces the night sweats of chronic bronchitis and pulmonary consumption. Cocillana also gives promise of usefulness as a laxative.

Dose.—From 10 to 20 drops of the fluid extract.

For Ulceration of the Lungs.

COLT'S-FOOT—*Tussilago Farfara*, called also BULL'S FOOT, FLOWER VELURE, etc.—This is a common and very troublesome weed. The root is very long, frequently penetrating to a depth of several feet. The flower stem appears before the leaves. It is round, woolly, six to eight inches long, and covered with scales. Several stems generally rise from the same root, each stem supporting a single flower about one inch in diameter and of a bright yellow color. The seeds of the plant are provided with a feathery growth (something like the dandelion) which is carried by the wind and springs up wherever fitting soil is exposed.

It is usually taken in decoction, a handful of the leaves being boiled in a quart of water down to a pint, strained and sweetened with honey or coarse sugar. The dose is a teacupful. It is a pectoral, and sweetened with honey is recommended in ulceration of the lungs.

For Dyspepsia.

COLUMBO (Imported)—*Radix Columbo.*

Native of Island of Ceylon.

Properties.—This articles is found very useful, when administered in proper doses, in strengthening the digestive tract and giving tone to the stomach. In cases of dyspepsia it produces its best effects. If administered in too large doses, however, it is apt to nauseate. It is also sometimes combined with Ipecacuanha—10 grains of Columbo to 2 of Ipecacuanha—and administered in cases of dyspepsia.

Dose.—Of the powder, from 15 to 30 grains; or an infusion may be made by adding from 2 to 4 tablespoonfuls of the powder to a pint of boiling water and taken in three doses during the day.

See also AMERICAN COLUMBO.

For Consumption, Colds, Coughs, Diseases of the Bowels and Urinary Organs, Female Weaknesses.

COMFREY—*Symphytum Officinale*, called also HEALING HERB, GUM PLANT, etc.—Grows in gardens and meadows, blossoms in May and June and bears spikes of white or rose-colored flowers at the extremities of the branches. The root is large, blackish on the outside and white inside.

A decoction of from ½ to 1 ounce in a quart of water or milk is useful in diarrheas, dysentery, consumption, colds and coughs, female weaknesses and diseases of the urinary organs, owing to its mucilaginous properties. It may be drank freely. The fresh leaves, bruised and applied externally, are beneficial to sprains, wounds and ulcers. The fresh root makes an excellent poultice for white swelling.

For Gravelly Complaints, Gonorrhea, Suppression of Urine, Affections of the Liver, Dyspepsia.

COOLWORT—*Mitella Cordifolia*, called also MITRE WORT, etc.—This plant is found in shady places where the ground is not very wet. The leaves are heart-shaped, are hairy on both sides and bordered with roundish teeth, and have the taste and smell of cucumbers. The flowers are white and grow in spikes about an inch long on the top of a naked stem. The leaves are used as medicine, and should be gathered in July or about the first of August and dried without exposure to damp atmosphere.

An infusion of the leaves, which is prepared by steeping a handful in a quart of boiling water, may be employed freely as a drink, and is given with benefit in gravelly complaints, gonorrhea and suppression of urine. In all cases where the urine is acrid, or thick and highly colored, it may be used with advantage. Also in burning and scalding of the urine it rarely fails to afford relief in two or three hours. It is also taken with advantage in affections of the liver, in dyspepsia and sourness of the stomach. Women who are troubled with strangury soon after confinement will derive great benefit from the use of this plant.

COPAIBA.—(See BALSAM OF COPAIBA).

For Cramps, Spasms.

CRANBERRY, HIGH—*Viburnum Oxycoccus*, called also CRAMP BARK.—Grows in swamps to the height of eight or ten feet. The leaves resemble a goose's foot, the flowers are white and in clusters, and the berries, which resemble the common cranberry, are red, have a pleasant acid flavor and make a good drink.

The bark of the root possesses tonic and nervine properties and seldom fails to relax spasms or cramps of any kind. It may be taken in decoction, or a tincture may be made by putting an ounce of the pulverized bark into a quart of Wine, the dose being a wineglassful twice a day.

For Fevers, Pleurisy, etc.

CRAWLEY—*Corallorhiza Odontorhiza*, called also DRAGON'S CLAW, CORAL TEETH, FEVER ROOT, CHICKEN'S TOES, etc.—This curious plant has no leaves nor anything green about it. The root is a collection of small, jointed, irregular fleshy bulbs, branching like a piece of coral. From these rises a smooth, fleshy, striped flower-stalk to the height of ten inches, bearing a spike of from twelve to twenty brownish-green flowers which bloom in July and August. The fruit is a large, strong-ribbed box or capsule. It should be looked for in old woods, or where there is much decaying herbage.

This plant produces a gentle and copious perspiration, and is an excellent remedy in various kinds of fevers, pleurisy and similar diseases. An emetic should first be given, after which Crawley may be taken as a hot infusion, or teaspoonful doses of the powdered root can be given in warm tea. In some cases the powdered root is mixed with equal quantities of **Pleurisy** Root and given for the same purpose.

For Cathartic Purposes.

CROTON PLANT—*Croton Tiglium.*

Native of Java and Ceylon.

Properties.—The oil of this plant is a powerful and speedy purgative and is generally employed in cases of obstinate constipation. It is usually found successful when all other means fail. It acts with great rapidity, and will usually operate on a patient even in a comatose state, on which account it is sometimes given in apoplexy, or coma from other cause. Also used in dropsy and mania.

Dose.—From 1 to 2 drops. This may be placed on the back of the tongue, may be made into pills with bread crumbs, or administered in emulsion or capsule.

For Immoderate Discharges, Intestinal Putrefaction, Dvsenterv,
  Diarrhea, Cholera Infantum.

CROWFOOT—*Geranium Maculatum*, called also SPOTTED CRANESBILL, TORMENTIL, STORKBILL, etc.—This is a very pretty plant, blossoming from May to July. The root is thick, knobby, brownish in color and spotted with greenish-white inside. It is very brittle when dried. The branches come out in pairs, and the leaves and stems are hairy. It has purple flowers, and the fruit is a capsule in five sections, containing one seed each. The most suitable time for collecting it is in the fall. *See illustration.*

The general effect of this plant on the system is to give tone to the stomach and bowels, to arrest immoderate discharges and to prevent intestinal putrefaction. It is given in the secondary stages of dysentery, diarrhea and cholera infantum. *It should not be given in the first stages of these diseases.* The usual form of giving it is in decoction with milk. The Indians used it for wounds, gonorrhea, ulcers of the legs, diabetes, bloody urine, involuntary discharges of urine, immoderate menstruation, etc. In cases of severe bleeding from the womb the fresh root bruised in cold water and applied will arrest the hemorrhage. The decoction is also useful as a gargle in quinsy and apthous sores of the mouth and throat. A dose of the powdered root is from 15 to 25 grains; of the decoction, made by boiling from an ounce to 1½ ounces of the root in a pint of water, the dose is 1 to 2 tablespoonfuls.

For Inflammation of the Bladder and Urinary Passages, Incontinence of Urine and Discharges from the Genital Organs.

CUBEBS—*Cubeba Officinalis.*

Native of Japan.

Properties.—Their chief use is to relieve inflammation of the urinary passages. Also useful in incontinence of urine. They were long used in the treatment of gonorrhea, but have now been superseded by local treatment. Also used in leucorrhea, acute colds and catarrhal conditions of the air passages.

Dose.—From 10 grains upwards.

For Hysterical Diseases, Epilepsy, St. Vitus Dance, Spasmodic Asthma.

CUCKOO-FLOWER—*Cardamine Pratensis*, called also FIELD WATER CRESS, LADY'S SMOCK, etc.—This plant grows in damp situations all over the country. The flowers are a pale pink or flesh color. They have a slightly spicy odor, a biting, bitter taste, and are the part used in medicine.

The dried flowers are used in epilepsy, hysterical diseases, St. Vitus dance and spasmodic asthma. They are a very popular remedy for epilepsy in children. The dose is 1 to 3 teaspoonfuls of the powder several times a day; or it may be combined with English Valerian.

For Dyspepsia, Chronic Rheumatism, General Debility, Suppressed Menstruation.

CUCUMBER TREE—*Magnolia Acuminata.*—This is a common forest tree growing on rich hillsides and river bottoms. It is commonly called Cucumber Tree from the resemblance of the shape of its fruit to that of the garden cucumber. The fruit, or cucumber, has long been a domestic remedy in dyspepsia. Both the bark of the root and fruit have been used with success in that complaint, also with benefit in chronic rheumatism. They have tonic qualities, and may be given in general debility and in obstinate cases of suppressed menstruation. A dose of the recently dried bark in powder is from ½ to 1 teaspoonful. A better preparation is a tincture made by putting the cones into diluted Alcohol or Brandy.

For Bilious Fevers, Torbid Liver, Dropsy.

CULVER'S ROOT—*Leptandria Virginica*, called also BLACK ROOT, CULVER'S PHYSIC, TALL VERONICA, etc.—Found throughout this country growing in dry and open situations. Grows from three to seven feet in height, leaves being in whorls (growing in a bunch) along the stem, and stem ending in a spike of white flowers.

The root, which is used, is strong, bitter and nauseous, and a weak cold infusion is said to be the safest and best method of taking it. Or a heaping teaspoonful of the powder may be added to ½ gill of boiling water, sweetened, and the dose repeated in three hours if it does not operate before. It is an efficient cathartic without producing debility or prostration. In typhus and bilious fevers it is said to remove the black and morbid matter from the intestines, is given with great advantage in dyspepsia connected with torpidity of the liver and digestive organs, is a valuable agent in purifying the blood, and is of utility in dropsies.

For Impotency.

DAMIANA—*Turnera Diffusa*.

Native of California and Mexico.

Properties.—It has a local reputation as a stimulant tonic of the sexual organs among the natives of its habitat, and has been widely advertised as a remedy for sexual impotence. Medical dispensatories do not credit it with this property, and besides it has a tendency to derange the digestive organs.

Dose.—The average dose is ¼ to ½ teaspoonful.

For Chronic Inflammation of the Liver and Spleen, and Dropsical Affections of the Organs of the Abdomen.

DANDELION—*Leontodon Taraxacum*, called also MONKS-HEAD, etc.—The dandelion needs no description. A full grown fresh root is frequently more than a foot long, is as thick as the little finger, and is full of a milky, bitterish juice.

The dandelion has a direct action upon the liver and kidneys, and is valuable in derangement of the digestive organs generally. In chronic inflammation of the liver and spleen and abdominal dropsy it is very beneficial. The best form of giving it is an extract of the juice, from 10 drops to ½ teaspoonful taken before meals.

For Appetite, Stomach Complaints, Diseases of the Digestive Organs, Nausea and Vomiting, Weakness of the Generative Organs.

DEVIL'S BIT—*Helonias Dioica,* called also DROOPING STARWORT, UNICORN PLANT, BLAZING STAR, etc.—The proper botanical name for this plant is *Helonias* but through the common names that have been given to it, it is often confounded with the *Aletris Farinosa* (see STARWORT). They are somewhat similar in growth and appearance, but as their medicinal properties are very different, it is important not to make a mistake in their use.

The *Devil's Bit,* or *Helonias,* has a tapering, fibrous root about one inch long. It is furrowed, and ends abruptly as if it had been bitten off. A pretty story is told concerning its name: The Indians believed it to have been, originally, a cure-all, but that the evil spirit in a fit of anger bit it off and thus destroyed a portion of its power. The root and leaves continue green all winter, and spread upon the ground in the form of a star. They are four or five inches long and taper at the end. The plant ends in a long, graceful spike of flowers of a dirty white color.

The root of this plant improves the appetite and is beneficial in all stomach complaints and diseases of the digestive organs. It will check nausea and vomiting and, chewed and the juice swallowed, will relieve coughing. The Indian women believed it would prevent miscarriages, and its tonic qualities are considered especially applicable in debility of the generative organs of either sex. The root may be given in powder in doses of ½ teaspoonful, or may be chewed and the juice swallowed.

DIGITALIS.—(See FOXGLOVE).

For Dyspepsia, Flatulency.

DILL—*Anethum Graveolens,* called also GARDEN DILL or DILLY.—Cultivated in gardens. A smooth plant that rises to the height of two or three feet. Plant and seeds have a powerful, spicy odor and a moderately warm and pungent (biting) taste.

An infusion of the seeds in boiling water makes an excellent stomachic, good in dyspepsia and flatulency, and a grateful drink for women immediately after confinement.

For General Debility, Chronic Diarrhea and Dysentery.

DITA BARK—*Alstonia Scholaris.*

Native of India, Malay Archipelago, tropical Australia.

Properties.—Valuable in chronic diarrhea and in the advanced stages of dysentery. It is also prescribed during convalescence from fevers, etc., and generally as a bitter tonic.

Dose.—2 to 8 drops of the fluid extract before meals.

For Hysterics, Gout, Fevers, Dropsies, Bloody Urine.

DOUBLE TANSY.—Tansy may be cultivated in any common soil. The root is perennial, so that when a "tansy bed" is once started it will last for years. The stems of the plant are six-sided, striped, and grow to a height sometimes of two or three feet. The leaves spring from the stem one above the other on opposite sides, and are subdivided into deeply notched leaflets. The flowers are yellow and form flat-topped bunches. The seeds are small and oblong-shaped and covered with down. The whole shrub above the ground is used in medicine, and should be gathered when in bloom.

This is a powerful bitter and is used in the form of infusion to bring on menstruation; also used in hysteria, and as a preventive of gout when the paroxysms are coming on. Tansy tea is also a popular domestic remedy in fevers, dropsies and bloody urine, and a poultice of the leaves makes an excellent application for sprains and bruises. The infusion is made by adding an ounce of the plant to a pint of boiling water, of which the dose is a wineglassful two or three times a day.

For Fevers, Pleurisies, Inflammatory Affections, Headache, Asthma,
Hysteria, Nervous Derangements.

DROPSY PLANT—*Melissa Officinalis*, called also LEMON BALM and CURE-ALL.—This plant is cultivated in gardens. It grows about two feet high, and has spreading, egg-shaped leaves of a bright green color, deeply notched at the edges. The flowers are white. It has an agreeable smell, somewhat similar to that of the lemon.

A warm infusion of this plant may be drank freely, and is useful in fevers, pleurisies and other inflammatory affections; also in headache, asthma, hysteria and nervous derangements.

For Dropsy, Suppression of Urine, Piles.

DWARF ELDER—*Aralia Hispida*, called also BRISTLY-STEM SARSAPARILLA.—Grows on hemlock-timbered land. From each root rises a single stalk, which is thickly set with short thorns or prickles near the ground, grows from eighteen to thirty inches in height, and has many branches, terminating in a cluster of blossoms in July and August. The berries, which are ripe in September, are of a black color and are disagreeable to the taste.

Very valuable in dropsy, for which take the dried root, boil to a strong decoction and take a gill morning and night, or oftener if the stomach will bear it. An ounce of the inner bark and one of the roots in decoction may be taken in teacupful doses three times a day. Also valuable where there is suppression of urine. The extract of the inner bark is good in piles as well as in dropsy.

For Dropsical Diseases.

DYER'S BROOM—*Genista Tinctoria*, called also DYER'S WEED, GREENWEED, WOADWAXEN, etc.—This plant is not a native of this country, but is cultivated here in gardens. The flowering tops are employed to dye a bright yellow color, hence its name. It is a shrub that has numerous rush-like green twigs like brooms. Both the tops and seeds are employed in medicine, and are given freely in infusion in dropsical diseases.

For Blood, Erysipelas, Fevers, Rheumatism, Gout, Pleurisy, Chronic Cough, Eruptions, Bowel Complaints, Bruises.

ELDER—*Sambucus Canadensis*, called also SWEET ELDER and BLACK-BERRIED ELDER.—A common shrub, with a branched stem growing eight or ten feet high and containing a large, spongy pith. The leaves are of a dark, glistening green; the flowers are white and in clusters, and are succeeded by berries of a dark purple color.

The young leaves and buds are too strong for safe use, but a tea of the flowers or berries makes an excellent blood purifier, and is very useful in erysipelas, fevers, rheumatism, gout, pleurisy, chronic cough and eruptions, especially the eruptions to which children are subject. They make a good poultice for bruises, etc. They also impart a fine flavor to vinegar or wine. A syrup made of the berries is highly esteemed in bowel complaints. The bark of the roots may be used when the berries and flowers cannot be obtained. Also the bark and leaves given to sheep will cure the rot.

For Chronic Bronchitis, Dyspepsia, Catarrh of the Bladder, Suppressed Menstruation, Skin Eruptions.

ELECAMPANE—*Inula Helenium.*—This is a very common plant growing in meadows and by roadsides. It has a large, fibrous root, brown externally and white internally. The stem grows from four to six feet high, is branched toward the top and covered with a whitish down. The flowers are yellow and situated at the extremity of the branches. The root has a spicy smell, and the taste, bitter at first, afterwards becomes sharp and camphorated; it contains camphorated oil.

Inula (Elecampane) was one of the most famous of ancient medicines. It had a special reputation in all pulmonary affections, and as an external application in sciatica, gout, gravel, facial neuralgia, etc. It is now used in chronic bronchitis, dyspepsia, catarrh of the bladder, suppressed menstruation and other menstrual disorders, also in chronic eruptions of the skin. It is generally given in decoction, made by boiling from ½ to 1 ounce of the crushed root in a pint of water.

For Malaria and Septic (poisonous) Conditions.

EUCALYPTUS—*Globulus.*

Native of Australia.

Properties.—Eucalyptus is a powerful antiseptic and anti-malarial remedy. It is extensively used in the treatment of inter-mittent fevers, especially in those chronic varieties in which Quinine has failed; also in septic conditions, as consumption, or any lingering disease where fever is present. It may be given internally in all cases of ulcer of the stomach or bowels, typhoid fever, scarlatina, blood poisoning, fetid bronchitis, etc. It is employed in the treatment of fetid breath, ulcers (syphilitic or otherwise), purulent catarrhal affections of the bladder, urethra and vagina, spongy and bleeding gums, etc. Properly diluted and used in a steam atomizer, the inhalation from the spray is a valuable aid in the treatment of diphtheria, and also as a pallia-tive in purulent bronchitis, catarrh and consumption.

Applied externally in the proportion of 2 tablespoonfuls to a pint of warm water, it is a stimulant and disinfectant in the case of chronic ill-conditioned ulcers, removing the odor of the dis-charge and improving the character of the secretion. A mixture of half this strength may be used with excellent results as an injection in vaginal leucorrhea.

Dose.—From 5 to 20 drops of the oil.

For Colds, Coughs, Bronchial Affections.

EUPHORBIA—*Pilulifera.*

Native of Australia, West Indies, etc.

Properties.—This herb is becoming a favorite domestic remedy in Australia, where it is a common roadside weed. It is regarded as an infallible remedy for colds, coughs, bronchial affections, in short all diseases of the respiratory tract; but it is more especially esteemed for the prompt and complete relief it is said to give to sufferers from asthma.

Formula for Infusion of Euphorbia Pilulifera:

Fluid Extract Euphorbia Pilu-
    lifera .... 1 fluid ounce.
Hot Water............................. 15 "   "

Dose.—One tablespoonful.

For Affections of the Eyes.

EYE-BRIGHT—*Euphrasia Officinalis.*—This plant grows in sterile soil. It flowers in June and produces white blossoms. It has no odor, but is of a bitterish, astringent taste.

It is employed in decoction as a wash to weak and inflamed eyes.

For Liver Complaints, Contracted Sinews, Sores, Ulcers, Swellings.

FALSE BITTERSWEET—*Celastrus Scandens*, called also STAFF TREE, FEVER TWIG, etc.—A woody vine, sometimes attaining to a considerable height. The blossoms are of a greenish-yellow color and very fragrant, and the berries grow in clusters and remain on the vines all winter.

The bark of the root may be given in decoction in doses of a gill three times a day in liver complaints and as a blood purifier. The bark and berries also make an excellent ointment for contracted sinews, sores, ulcers, and swellings of every description.

For Dropsy and Heart Disease.

FALSE HELLEBORE—*Adonis Vernalis.*

Native of Southern Europe.

Properties.—It is employed in dropsy and heart disease. In action it resembles digitalis, but digitalis is not admissible in cases where the kidneys are affected, while this remedy has a good effect in cases where the heart disease is of a secondary nature, following chronic Bright's disease, etc.

Dose.—From 1 to 2 drops of the fluid extract three or four times a day; or an infusion may be made of ½ to 1 teaspoonful in 8 tablespoonfuls of water, of which the dose is a tablespoonful every one, two or three hours, according to effect.

For Dyspepsia, Disorders of Digestion, Colic in Children.

FENNEL—*Anethum Fœniculum.*—This plant is raised in gardens in this country. It grows about four feet in height and has a long root about the size of the finger. It blossoms in June and July and the fruit ripens in September.

Fennel seeds are given for dyspepsia, difficult digestion, flatulency, colic in children. Made into an infusion or tea, it may be given freely through the day; of the seeds pulverized, from ⅓ to 1 teaspoonful is a dose.

For Hysteria, Suppressed Menstruation, Worms, and in Sudden Attacks of Disease.

FEVERFEW — *Chrysanthemum Parthenium*, called also FEATHER-FEW, etc.—Found along roadsides, also cultivated in gardens. Grows from six inches to a foot in height, has numerous leaves of a yellowish green color, deeply cut into lobes or divisions and bordered with sharp teeth. Each of the branches end in a single flower which consists of a yellow center with a white border.

The flowers and leaves in infusion are given to strengthen the stomach, expel wind, promote the menses and destroy worms. The warm infusion is also an excellent remedy in colds, sudden attacks of disease, hysterical complaints and lowness of spirits. It should be prepared by steeping the leaves and flowers, or either, fresh or dry, in hot water. It is harmless and may be taken in almost any quantity. For the decoction, pour two quarts of boiling water on two handfuls of the leaves, of which a teacupful may be taken three or four times a day. The green herb in the form of a poultice is used externally for severe pains or swellings of the bowels.

For Fevers.

FEVERWEED—*Gerardia Pedicularia,* called also Louse-wort.—This plant, which is found only on barren, hilly or pine ridges, grows about two feet high, and resembles large bunches of Lobelia except that its branches are more numerous. The leaves are small with deeply cut edges. The stalks and leaves are like tobacco. The blossoms are yellow and about the size of the pink.

This plant given in infusion will produce a flow of perspiration in a very short time, and is a very popular remedy in fevers and inflammations of all kinds. The bowels should be evacuated before the infusion is taken.

For Sore Eyes, Epilepsy, Convulsions.

FIT ROOT—*Monotropa Uniflora,* called also Pipe Plant, Indian Pipe, Bird's Nest, Ice Plant, etc.—The juice of the fresh herb of this plant, mixed with water, is good for sore eyes. The plant also possesses nervine properties, and the pulverized root in teaspoonful doses is used in epilepsy and convulsions of children.

For Fevers, Fluxes and Excessive Menstruation.

FIVE FINGER—*Potentilla Canadensis,* called also Cinque-foil, etc.—This is grass, the stalks of which trail along the ground something after the manner of strawberries. Each stem has five leaves of unequal size, notched around the edges. The flowers are yellow and the root is small. It grows by roadsides.

It is taken in decoction, which may be made with milk. It is very beneficial in fevers, particularly when there is great weakness and night sweats. It is also serviceable in checking immoderate flow of the menses and flux. The decoction may be taken in wineglassful doses.

For Dysentery, Colic, Hemorrhage.

FLEABANE—*Erigeron Canadense*, called also CANADA FLEABANE, PRIDEWEED, BLOOD-STANCH, MARE'S TAIL, COLT'S TAIL, FIREWEED, etc.—This plant grows freely throughout all Canada and the northern and middle sections of the United States. It rises from two to six feet in height, is covered with stiff hairs and divided into numerous branches. It has narrow, lance-shaped leaves, and the flowers are small and white and grow in long clusters at the ends of the stems. For medicinal purposes the plant should be collected while in bloom—in July or August. It has an acrid, bitterish taste.

This plant possesses a high reputation as a remedy for dysentery. For this purpose it is steeped in hot water and a teacupful taken every hour or two until a cure is effected. It generally affords speedy relief in colic; for this purpose a teacupful may be given every fifteen to thirty minutes, and in obstinate cases an injection of the infusion may be given. The oil of this plant in doses of from 5 to 10 drops is a valuble remedy in hemorrhage.

For Dropsy of the Chest, Pleurisy, Inflammation of the Lungs, Inflammatory Affections.

FOXGLOVE, or DIGITALIS—*Digitalis Purpurea*, called also PURPLE FOXGLOVE, FAIRY'S GLOVE, etc.—The stem of the Foxglove is straight and hairy, and grows from two to three feet high. The leaves are very large, oval, whitish, and hairy on both sides. The flowers are a deep reddish purple. It is cultivated in America for its medicinal properties. *See illustration.*

It is a very valuable remedy in dropsy of the chest, pleurisy, inflammation of the lungs and all inflammatory affections, but is a poison and narcotic and should be administered with extreme caution. It is hardly safe to give it without a thorough understanding of its physiological effects, and the reader is therefore referred to *Digitalis* in A CHAPTER ON MEDICINE.

For Scrofula and Scrofulous Tumors.

FROSTWORT — *Cistus Canadensis*, called also ROCK ROSE.—This plant grows from six to twelve inches high and derives its name from its leaves, which are whitish like frost, and grow on small purple stalks. In early winter the bark near the root splits. The flowers are of a pale color and terminate in a pod containing very small seeds.

An infusion of this plant is very valuable in the cure of scrofula. It should be made by using 4 ounces of the dried leaves to a quart of boiling water, of which the patient may drink freely three times a day; scrofula sores should also be washed with it. Another external application for scrofulous tumors is made of a handful of the dried leaves to a tablespoonful of black Pepper and a quart of Rum. Simmer this for two hours, strain, add a handful or two more of the leaves, and again simmer for half an hour; then thicken by stirring in 2 ounces of the powdered leaves and apply as a poultice twice a day.

For Obstructions of the Liver, Eruptive Skin Diseases, Scurvy.

FUMITORY—*Fumaria Officinalis.*—This plant is culti- vated for medicinal purposes.

In large doses it is laxative, but as ordinarily given is a tonic. It is a valuable remedy for obstructions of the liver, erup- tive diseases of the skin and scurvy.

A decoction of the leaves, either fresh or dry, may be taken freely.

For Dropsy..

GAMBOGE—*Cambogia.*

Native of Siam, Cambodia and Cochin China.

Properties.—It is chiefly used as a cathartic in dropsical affections because of its power to produce large discharges of water from the intestines, and also because it stimulates the kidneys to increased action. It is sometimes given for consti- pation, but is not commonly used for general cathartic purposes because it produces such drastic effects. It should be taken only in small doses, and is more frequently combined with other remedies.

Dose.—A convenient formula is the following:

Gamboge, powdered.................... 10 grains.
Carbonate of Potash.................... 1 drachm.
Cinnamon Water........................ 2 ounces.
  Mix, and take 30 drops three times a day in water.

For Poulticing, Colds, Coughs, Asthma, Croup.

GARLIC—*Allium Sativum.*—Well known by its strong, disagreeable taste and odor. It is of the same genus as the onion, but much stronger and more powerful.

The bulbs roasted may be applied with advantage externally over the seat of almost any pain. They are often applied to the feet in inflammatory diseases, and to quiet and produce sleep in children. A syrup combined with honey is very serviceable in colds, coughs, asthma and croup, and in croup a poultice of garlic applied to the chest is one of the best things that can be used; also applied over the region of the bladder in retention of urine. A dose of the juice, to which sugar may be added, is from ⅓ to ½ teaspoonful.

For Stomach and Bowel Debility.

GENTIAN (Blue)—*Gentiana Catesbei*, called also SAMSON SNAKE ROOT, FLUX ROOT, etc.—This plant has a branching root, yellowish and fleshy, with a simple stem rising from one to two feet in height, and blue flowers. It is of the same genus as the yellow variety.

It is a tonic in cases of stomach and general debility, and is considered to have great value in affections of the bowels, as fluxes and severe diarrhea. The root and tops are used in infusion with Chamomile flowers, to which a little Brandy may be added. The dose is a tablespoonful, which may be increased as the stomach will bear it.

For Dyspepsia, Gout, Jaundice, Weakness of the Digestive Organs, Debility.

GENTIAN (Yellow)—*Gentiana Lutea.*—The root of the Yellow Gentian is long, wrinkled and twisted, and has numerous branches. It is brownish on the outside and yellowish and spongy on the inside. The flowers are handsome, showy, and grow in large clusters. *See illustration.*

Gentian root is a pure and simple bitter. In moderate doses it excites the appetite and strengthens the digestion, and does not constipate, therefore is of value in weakness of the digestive organs and debility attendant upon chronic diseases, in dyspepsia, gout, jaundice, etc. Of the powder the dose is about ⅓ teaspoonful. A better way of taking it is in an infusion made as follows: To ½ ounce of the root add 1 teaspoonful of Orange peel, ½ teaspoonful of Coriander, 2 ounces of Alcohol and 1 pint of water, of which the dose is from a teaspoonful to a tablespoonful three times a day before meals.

For Diarrhea, Colic, Cholera Morbus, etc.

GINGER—*Zingiber Officinale.*

Native of East Indies.

Properties.—Ginger is a useful remedy in diarrhea, dysentery, flatulent colic, cholera morbus, etc., and may be given in powder or tincture. The powder is mixed with hot water, but the tincture is preferable. Fomentations of Ginger are also applied externally to relieve colic, muscular rheumatism,

neuralgia, headache, toothache, etc., and the infusion is
in recent cases of relaxed condition of the uvula (the pa.
pendant from the soft palate), or loss of voice from a similar
condition of the larynx.

Dose.—Of the powdered Ginger, well diluted, what would
lay on a 5-cent piece; of the tincture, from 10 drops to ½ teaspoonful, also well diluted.

For Tonic, Nervine, Gravel.

GINSENG—*Panax Quinquefolium*, called also RED BERRY,
FIVE FINGERS, NINSIN, etc.—Scattered all over the Northern
and Western States from Canada to Missouri and Alabama; also
in the Alleghany mountains as far as the Carolinas. The plant
grows about a foot high, has five leaves to a main stem, and
bears small white flowers which are followed by red berries.
The root is white and fleshy.

The berries of this plant are not good to eat. The root,
tinctured in old Jamaica spirits, may be taken three times a day
on an empty stomach. It is found useful in gravel, general
debility, weakness from excessive venery, pain in the bones from
colds; and is a fine restorative medicine, strengthening the
stomach, invigorating the system and improving the appetite.
The decoction may be used in doses of a teacupful several times
a day as a nervine or tonic; or the powdered root taken in teaspoonful doses. The leaves make a grateful tea. The Ginseng
is greatly esteemed by the Chinese.

For Nausea, Pains in the Stomach and Bowels.

GOLDEN ROD — *Solidago Odora*, called also SWEET-
SCENTED GOLDEN ROD, etc.—There are a great many species of
the Golden Rod, but the medicinal plant may be identified by the
taste of the flowers and leaves, which is similar to that of Fennel
or Anise, and has been distinguished by the name of sweet-
scented Golden Rod.

Given freely in warm infusion (which should not be boiled),
it produces perspiration, and is useful to allay nausea, and pains
in the stomach and bowels occasioned by gas.

For Stomach and Liver Troubles, Sores, Ulcers, Proud Flesh, Piles.

GOLDEN SEAL — *Hydrastis Canadensis*, called also
ORANGE ROOT, YELLOW PUCCOON, etc.—This plant is found in
rich soils in shady locations. It blossoms in March and April.
The flowers are of a flesh or rose color, and the petals fall off
about as soon as the blossoms come out. The fruit is a red, oval
berry. The root is of a bright yellow color, is knotted and
wrinkled, and has many long fibers.

Golden Seal is an excellent tonic, and at the same time is laxative, which makes it a very appropriate remedy in dyspeptic disorders. For diseases of the stomach and liver it is given in infusion and tincture. A half ounce of the pulverized dried root is enough to infuse in a quart of spirits. It is also used as a wash for sore eyes, but should be used with caution. Also used as a wash for old sores and ulcers, and the dry powder may be applied externally to fungous growths or proud flesh. A dose of the powder, taken internally, is from 10 to 12 grains. It is one of the best correctives in piles and bilious habits that can be given.

For Stomach Tonic, Ulcers of the Mouth.

GOLD THREAD — *Coptis Trifolia*, called also MOUTH ROOT, VEGETABLE GOLD, etc.—This plant grows only in the northermost part of this country and Canada. It is found in mossy swamps and bogs and in evergreen woods. The root is of a bright yellow color and the flowers are yellow; the leaves are evergreen.

The roots only are used and should be collected in summer. They are easily dried, but are difficult to pulverize. They are a valuable tonic, particularly for the stomach, promoting digestion. They are useful in dyspepsia, debility, and in convalescence from fevers. The root is commonly given in infusion, sweetened with honey. The infusion also makes a good gargle in ulcers of the mouth. Of the powder, from 10 to 20 grains may be given three times a day; of the tincture, made by adding an ounce of the root to a pint of diluted Alcohol, the dose is a teaspoonful three times a day.

For Gravel or Stone, Dropsy.

GRAVEL PLANT—*Epigæa Repens*, called also TRAILING ARBUTUS, etc.—This is a small, creeping plant, found growing on shady rocks and in stony woods. Its flowers are white, tinged with red, and are very fragrant.

It incites the secretion and discharge of urine, and taken in decoction is a very beneficial remedy for gravel, stone in the bladder and kidneys, and dropsy. The dose is from 1 to 2 teaspoonfuls, which may be increased or diminished according to the strength of the decoction and the effect produced.

For Asthma, Bronchitis, Hay-Fever, etc.

GRINDELIA ROBUSTA.
Native of California.
Properties.—A useful remedy in asthma, and is recommended in bronchitis, pneumonia, hay-fever and coughs generally. It may also be applied locally in inflammation of the

eyes. For this purpose keep cloths wet with a solution of the fluid extract—one tablespoonful of the extract to 4 tablespoonfuls of water. It is also given internally and used externally, diluted with water as above, on ulcers, etc. It is sometimes prescribed in dropsical conditions.

Dose.—From ½ to 1 teaspoonful of the fluid extract.

GRINDELIA SQUARROSA.

Native of Mexico and West Coast of United States.

Properties.—This is the Spanish-American remedy for intermittent fevers, especially chronic cases of fever and ague, to check the lapsing chills. It has a very beneficial action upon the liver and spleen and glandular system. Also useful in inflammation of the bladder, and, combined with Yerba Santa, is used for that form of dropsy known as anasarca, or general dropsy. Also useful in chronic rheumatic affections.

Dose.—Should not exceed from 20 to 30 drops of the fluid extract.

For Stomach Tonic.

GROUND FLOWER—*Polygala Polygama*, called also BITTER POLYGALA.—This plant derives its name from its manner of flowering—an imperfect flower of a purple color grows close to, and in some instances under the surface of the ground. It is found in dry, sandy and gravelly soils. The stems are numerous and the leaves scattered.

An infusion of the dry plant imparts tone to the stomach; taken in large doses, it proves laxative.

For Catarrhal Headaches, Inflammation of the Eyes, Jaundice, Asthma, Coughs, Chronic Pulmonary and Urinary Affections.

GROUND IVY—*Glechoma Hederacea*, called also GILL-GO-OVER-THE-GROUND, ALE HOOF, CATFOOT, etc.—Grows wild along garden fences. The flowers are on short stems, grow in whorls, and are of a bluish color.

The powdered leaves of this plant are used as a snuff, which is very beneficial in catarrhal headaches. An ointment made of this herb is also used for chronic inflammation of the eyes. Taken internally, it is an excellent blood purifier, also an expectorant, and is much used in chronic affections of the lungs and urinary organs. It is a valuable remedy in jaundice and asthmatic coughs.

For Painful Swellings.

GROUNDSEL—*Senecio Vulgaris.*—This is an European plant which has been introduced into this country and grows in cultivated grounds. The whole plant is used, and should be gathered while in flower. When rubbed, it has a peculiar, unpleasant odor, and its taste is disagreeable and bitterish.

It is applied externally to painful swellings. It is not much given internally, but in large doses acts as an emetic.

For Rheumatism.

GUACO.
Native of Mexico.

Properties.—In Mexico the root of this plant is regarded as a specific in rheumatic affections. One part of the fluid extract to four parts of Whiskey, or two parts Alcohol, may be applied freely over the affected surface, which should then be well covered. This application is best made at bedtime and the parts kept covered all night.

Dose.—Taken internally, ¼ to ½ teaspoonful.

For Throat Troubles and Uterine Tonic.

GUAIAC—*Guaici Resina.*
Native of West Indies and the Northern Coast of South America.

Properties.—At one time it was much used as a remedy in syphilis, chronic muscular rheumatism and diphtheria. Its use now is largely confined to throat troubles, for which it is given in the form of lozenges. It has had some reputation in the treatment of consumption. It is a uterine tonic and used to increase the menstrual flow.

Dose—From 10 to 30 drops of the tincture.

For Headache, Asthma, Bronchitis, Diarrhea, Dysentery.

GUARANA, or BRAZILIAN COCOA.—*Paulinia Sorbilis.*
Native of Brazil.

Properties.—This remedy is used with almost unvarying success in sick headache, especially of nervous origin. A dose taken on the intimation of an attack is usually sufficient to abort it. It is beneficial in diarrhea and dysentery, also in asthma and bronchitis, the Wine of Guarana being especially beneficial in the capillary bronchitis of children. This remedy is also used both internally and in injections for leucorrhea, and has been employed with advantage in gonorrhea.

Dose.—From 5 drops to ½ teaspoonful of the fluid extract.

For Inflamed Conditions of the Throat and Stomach, etc.

GUM ARABIC—*Acaciæ Gummi.*

Native of West Indies.

Properties.—Gum Arabic is most frequently used as a vehicle for the administration of other remedies. It is a ready means of forming an emulsion for the administration of oils, principally Cod Liver Oil. Dissolved in water it serves as a protection to of the throat and stomach when in an inflamed condition. It is sometimes used in the preparation of lozenges containing certain remedies designed to be dissolved in the mouth and produce their effects along the mucous membrane of the throat.

For Chronic Coughs, Hoarseness, Ulceration of Mouth and Throat.

HEDGE MUSTARD—*Sisymbrium Officinalis.*—Grows from one to three feet high. The taste is somewhat sour and biting, especially of the tops and flower spikes, but not so biting as the regular Mustard.

A syrup is made by mixing an equal quantity of the juice of the plant with honey and sugar, and is very beneficial in chronic coughs and hoarseness; also in ulceration of the mouth and throat; or the seeds may be taken in substance.

For Dropsy, Epilepsy, Obstructed Menses.

HELLEBORE (Black)—*Helleborus Niger,* called also Christmas Rose.—This is a perennial plant, blossoming in winter or early spring. The root, which is the part used in medicine, is of the length and size of the little finger and of a blackish color externally. The stem, which springs from the root, grows horizontally under ground, the leaves appearing to grow out of the ground. The flower stalk bears from one to two flowers, consisting of five large round pinkish petals sometimes edged with purple. It is a poisonous plant and we do not recommend its use, excepting as it may be given in some reliable formula or under a doctor's direction.

For Uræmic Convulsions, also sometimes used in Epilepsy, Gout, and Acute Rheumatism.

HELLEBORE (White)—*Veratrum Viride,* called also ITCHWEED, INDIAN POKE, etc.—This is a poisonous, active plant, and is now made use of largely in the form of its active principle, "Veratrine," for the uses of which see "Veratrum Viride" in A CHAPTER ON MEDICINES.

For Falling of the Bowels and Womb, Rheumatic Affections, Sciatica, Lumbago, Rheumatism.

HEMLOCK TREE—*Pinus Canadensis*, called also HEM-LOCK SPRUCE, etc.—This tree, when full grown, is often seventy or eighty feet high, with a trunk two or three feet in diameter.

The bark in decoction makes an excellent wash for falling of the bowels and womb. The oil applied externally is valuable in rheumatic affections. The pith of the Hemlock dried makes an excellent plaster for lumbago, sciatica and rheumatism. The bark is never given internally alone as it is too astringent.

For Fistulas, Boils, Swellings of the Breast, Ulcers, Tumors, Inflamed Eyes, Cramps, Deep-Seated Inflammations.

HENBANE—*Hyoscyamus Niger*, called also BLACK HEN-BANE, FETID NIGHTSHADE, POISON TOBACCO, etc.—Cultivated in this country for medicinal purposes. It rises from one to two feet in height and has funnel-shaped flowers of a dingy yellow with bright purple streaks. It is a strong narcotic, very poisonous, and often proves fatal when taken by mistake. *See illustration.*

Applied externally, either as a poultice or by cloths wrung out of the hot decoction, it is useful in all cases of painful and obstinate inflammations, such as fistulas, boils, swellings of the breast, scrofulous ulcers, painless tumors, inflamed eyes and cramps in the bowels. In deep-seated inflammations the poultice is also very useful. It should be used with caution. Its action internally is the same as Belladonna. See A CHAPTER ON MEDICINES.

For Paralysis.

HOANG-NAN—*Strychnos Malaccensis.*

Native of Malacca and Cambodia.

Properties.—For leprosy, venereal and chronic diseases, serpent bites, hydrophobia, epilepsy, convulsions and paralysis. The most important use for which it is employed is in the treatment of paralysis. Where the paralysis is recent it is peculiarly efficacious. Also in rheumatism or syphilitic paralysis it achieves important results.

Dose.—From 3 to 10 drops of the Tincture of Hoang-Nan, concentrated. (This is a poison and should be carefully labeled).

For Inflammation of Mucous Surfaces, also Leucorrhea.

HOLLYHOCK—*Althæa Rosea.*—This is a showy, well-known plant. It is a native of Spain, and cultivated in this country for ornamental purposes and because of its medicinal qualities.

A tea made of the flowers is employed in inflammation of mucous surfaces, as the lining membrane of the throat, stomach, bowels, urinary passages, etc. Also useful in leucorrhea. The tea may be drank freely.

For Syphilitic Affections.

HONDURAS BARK—*Cascara Amarga.*

Native of Mexico and Honduras.

Properties.—Is an alterative, and is very useful in chronic cases of syphilitic eruptions, syphilitic tubercles, chronic eczema and gummy tumors. Especially recommended in the treatment of syphilis.

Dose.—From ½ to 1 teaspoonful of the fluid extract.

For Nervous Affections, Inflammatory Fevers, Pleurisy, Jaundice, Indigestion, Consumption, Hypochondria, Venereal Complaints, Worms.

HOPS—*Humulus Lupulus.*—Hops are cultivated in this country. The plant is climbing and ornamental. The stems twine around poles and reach to a great height. The flowers are of a greenish color.

A bag filled with warm hops and placed under the head is a popular remedy to quiet nervous irritation and produce sleep. They are also much used in fomentation to afford relief in inflammatory fevers, especially in pleurisies. They may be given internally in tincture, decoction or infusion. As a tonic, the infusion is the best preparation, of which a wineglassful may be taken at a time. It is given internally in jaundice, indigestion, consumption, hypochondria, venereal complaints, worms, in diseases attended with nervous irritation, and is very useful to give tone to the stomach and bowels. It is also given in the advanced stages of typhoid fever, where nervous tremors and twitching of the tendons of the muscles exist. It is also a useful drink in alcoholism and delirium tremens.

For Colds, Coughs, Affections of the Lungs.

HOREHOUND—*Marrubium Vulgare*, called also WHITE HOREHOUND.—This plant is found along fences and roadsides. It grows about a foot high. The leaves are deeply notched at the edges, are wrinkled and hoary, and stand in pairs upon long, thick, broad foot-stalks. The flowers are white. The plant has a musklike odor.

Horehound is usually given in the form of syrup or infusion, and is an excellent remedy in colds, coughs, and all affections of the lungs. The pure Horehound candy is very useful in troublesome coughs.

For Piles, Rheumatism, Catarrh, Gangrene.

HORSE CHESTNUT—*Æsculus Hippocastanum.*—This is a magnificent tree, too well known to need description.

A strong decoction of the bark is recommended as a wash in gangrene. For rheumatism and piles, a decoction of the nuts is highly esteemed, also an ointment of the powdered nut and lard for local application. Some people carry horse chestnuts in their pockets, believing they will ward off these diseases. In case of catarrh, a pinch of the powdered root or nut applied to the nostrils at night is said to clear the head nicely in the morning. A decoction of the bark may also be employed in intermittent fevers. The decoction is made of 1½ ounces of the bark to a pint of water, of which the dose is a wineglassful three times a day. The usual dose of the powder is from ⅛ to ½ teaspoonful every four hours.

For Urinary Disorders.

HORSE MINT—*Monarda Punctata*, called also ORIGANUM, DOTTED MONARDA, etc.—This plant is of the same genus as the Oswego Tea. It grows from two to three feet in height, has lance-shaped leaves and flowers in clusters.

A strong decoction, given warm and freely, is very beneficial in case of suppression of urine, difficulty in evacuating the same, or gravel.

For Dropsy, Rheumatism, Neuralgia.

HORSERADISH—*Cochlearia Armoracia.*—This plant is cultivated, or grows spontaneously in gardens, and is too well known to need description.

Externally, it produces irritation, and may be used in place of Mustard. A warm infusion of this plant, drank in sufficient quantity to produce perspiration, is an exceedingly valuable remedy in dropsy, also beneficial in rheumatism, neuralgia, etc. An infusion may be made by adding ½ to 1 ounce of the root to a quart of water.

HYOSCYAMUS.—(See HENBANE).

For Colds, Coughs, Pulmonary Catarrh, Phthisis and Lung Affections Generally.

HYSSOP—*Hyssopus Officinalis.*—This plant is a native of the south of France, but is cultivated in gardens in this country. It grows about one foot high, and has flowers of a blue or pink color.

It is very beneficial in colds, coughs, pulmonary catarrhs and all affections of the lungs. Infuse a handful of the herb in 2 quarts of boiling water and drink freely, or according to circumstances. It is also boiled with Figs and used as a gargle for sore mouth and quinsy.

HYSTERIONICA—*Haplopappus Baylahuen*.
Native of Chili.

Properties.—This plant has balsamic properties and is useful in the treatment of acute and chronic affections of the lungs and bronchial tubes, in flatulent colic and the diarrhea accompanying some forms of digestive troubles, in dysentery, and in diseases of the genital and urinary organs accompanied with purulent discharges. Also applied locally to wounds.

Dose.—From 5 to 15 drops of the fluid extract.

ICELAND MOSS—*Cetraria*.—This lichen is plentiful in Iceland, whence its name is derived. It is found throughout British America, and also grows as far south as the mountainous regions of North Carolina. It grows from two to four inches high and is irregularly branched. The upper surface is of a greenish-grey or olive brown, and the lower surface is whitish with depressed spots. Near the base it is reddish. Boiled with 20 parts water, it yields a liquid which on cooling forms a bitter jelly.

This plant increases the appetite, promotes digestion and improves nutrition. It does not excite the circulation nor constipate, but in large doses may occasion nausea or diarrhea. It is chiefly employed as a remedy for chronic pulmonary affections attended with cough and profuse expectoration and other symptoms belonging to consumption. It may be made in infusion by adding 3 ounces of the bruised plant to 1½ pints of water, steeping down to ½ the quantity and adding 1 drachm (teaspoonful) of the extract of Licorice. Of this preparation 2 tablespoonfuls may be taken every three or four hours if the cough is urgent.

For Tonic, Laxative or Cathartic Uses.

INDIAN PHYSIC—*Gillenia Trifoliata*, called also WESTERN DROPWORT, BOWMAN'S ROOT, etc.—The root of this plant is branching. The head of the root is a tuber from which proceeds numerous long, slender, brown branches, several stems rising from the same root and growing two or three feet high. They are of a reddish color and have large leaves. The flowers are small and white. It grows generally in hilly regions and sandy or gravelly soils.

The bark of the root is used as a medicine. Powdered and taken in doses of 1 to 2 teaspoonfuls, which may be repeated every twenty minutes until it operates, it acts as a mild emetic (producing vomiting) and also as a purgative at the same time. Taken in small doses, 5 to 10 grains, it acts as a laxative in cases of habitual costiveness. In somewhat smaller doses it acts as a tonic in dyspepsia arising from debility of the digestive organs. It may be given in decoction, but is preferable in the form of powder. Given in large doses it acts violently and brings on debility. A decoction of this plant is sometimes given to horses and cattle as a tonic.

For Coughs, Consumption, Asthma, Colic, Pains in the Bowels.

INDIAN TURNIP—*Arum Triphyllum*, called also WILD TURNIP, WAKE ROBIN, DRAGON ROOT, etc.—This plant has a tuberous root, which sends up in the spring a large colored spathe (an envelope-shaped or sheath-like leaf) that is flattened and bent at the top like a hood. The spathe or sheath has within it a fleshy spike of variegated flowers, round at the top, and surrounded at the base by stamens. The spathe and the spike of flowers enclosed in it is later converted into a bunch of scarlet berries. The leaves stand on long sheathing foot-stalks. There are several varieties of this genus, known by the different color of the spathe, which in one is white, in another dark purple, and in a third, green. It grows in swamps, along ditches, and in shady places. The root is the only part used. It loses its medicinal properties when old, but may be preserved fresh for a year by burying in dry earth or sand. *See illustration.*

In its fresh state it is a powerful stimulant of the secretions of the lungs and skin, and its expectorant properties are beneficial in coughs, consumption of the lungs and asthma. It is also an excellent remedy for colic and pains in the bowels. The root should be dried, pulverized and given in honey, or made into a paste with syrup. The syrup is also good for aphthous sore mouth and throat. Dose, from 10 to 15 grains.

IPECAC—*Ipecacuanha.*—(See A CHAPTER ON MEDICINES).

For Intermittent Fevers, Neuralgic Affections, Dyspepsia, Scrofula, etc.

IRONWOOD—*Astrya Virginica.*—This tree, which grows from ten to forty feet in height, is a native of the eastern United States. The bark of the tree is of a dark gray color, and the heart, which is the part used in medicine, is very dense and hard.

This remedy is used in intermittent fevers, neuralgic affections, dyspepsia, scrofula, etc. It may be taken in infusion made from chips of the tree, or in fluid extract, the dose of which is from ½ to 1 teaspoonful three times a day before meals.

JABORANDI.—(See A Chapter on Medicines).

For Affections of the Bladder.

JACOB'S LADDER—*Smilax Peduncularis.*—This plant consists of a single smooth, vine-like stalk, four or five feet high, which sends off branches that cling to shrubbery, fences, or anything within reach. It grows among bushes on rich soils. The root has many circular depressions in its sides like that of the Solomon's Seal.

An infusion of this plant, drank freely, is very useful in affections of the bladder; it is said to have the property of dissolving stone or gravel.

JALAP.—(See A Chapter on Medicines).

For Neuralgia, Whooping Cough, Muscular Rheumatism, etc.

JAMAICA DOGWOOD—*Piscidia Ervthrina.*
Native of West Indies.

Properties.—The Jamaica Dogwood resembles Opium in its physiological properties, but is less intense and without unpleasant after-effects. It relaxes the system, causes profuse sweating and a flow of saliva, and affords relief in neuralgia, whooping cough, nervous headache, muscular rheumatism, and other affections of a like nature. It is also sometimes used externally to allay the pain of burns.

Dose.—From ⅓ to ½ teaspoonful of the fluid extract.

For Diabetes.

JAMBUL—*Eugenia Jambolana.*
Native of East Indies.

Properties.—Useful in diabetes to arrest the formation of sugar.

Dose.—From 5 to 10 drops of the fluid extract.

For Worms, Asthma, Coughs, Suppressed Menstruation.

JERUSALEM OAK—*Chenopodium Botrys.*—Grows all over the United States by roadsides and in neglected fields, stands about a foot high, bears many small green flowers, and has an odor something like Wormseed, but not so strong and more fragrant. It is of the same genus as Wormseed.

It is used in infusion for worms, asthma, consumption, convulsive coughs, difficult breathing, etc., and is also useful in suppressed menses. The dose is 2 tablespoonfuls, repeated as necessary.

For Use Externally on Wounds, Sores, Swellings, Ulcers, Tumors;
Internally, for Diarrhea, Menorrhagia, Nervous Diseases.

JOHNSWORT—*Hypericum Perforatum*, called also ST. JOHNSWORT.—This plant grows in meadows and flowers during the early part of June. It rises about two feet high, has round, hard, upright stalks with spreading branches, and small leaves of a deep green color. The flowers are yellow and five-leafed, with many yellow threads in the middle, which, when bruised, yield a juice like blood, and produce small round heads, containing seeds. The seeds are black and smell like resin. The root is hard, of a brownish color, and has many fibers.

The tops and blossoms make a good ointment for wounds, sores, swellings, ulcers, tumors and rough skins. A tea of the leaves produces perspiration, and is beneficial in diseases of the lungs. It promotes the excretion of urine and is likewise useful for diarrhea, menorrhagia and nervous diseases. A syrup of Johnswort combined with Sage is a specific for coughs. The dose for a child twelve months old is ½ to 1 teaspoonful; for one six months old, ½ tablespoonful. An ointment made of Johnswort, Bittersweet, Elder bark and Stramonium, is valuable in hard, indolent tumors of the breast. For diarrhea or flux, put 2 ounces of the flowers into a quart of good Brandy, of which the patient may take a wineglassful night and morning, after first taking a good cathartic.

For Dropsical Complaints.

JUNIPER—*Juniperus Communis.*—This shrub rises to a height of about four feet. The leaves are long, sharp, pointed, of a dark green color, and stand three together without footstalks. The fruit consists of berries about the size of a pin, containing two or three small, triangular seeds. It flowers in June, and the berries, which are the part used, are ripe in August.

They are gently stimulant and diuretic, and are chiefly used in dropsical complaints. They have also been recommended in skin diseases, scurvy, etc. They may be given in infusion, prepared by steeping an ounce of the bruised berries in a pint of boiling water, the whole of which may be taken in the course of twenty-four hours.

For Worms, Itch, Herpes.

KAMALA—*Mallotus Philippinensis.*

Native of Southern Asia and Abyssinia.

Properties.—This remedy is used externally in various affections of the skin, particularly in itch and herpes, but its principal importance is its power to expel tapeworms. For this purpose it requires no preparatory treatment. In case the first dose fails to operate on the bowels, it may be repeated in four hours followed by a dose of Castor Oil.

Dose.—From 1 to 2 teaspoonfuls of the fluid extract.

For Gonorrhea.

KAVA KAVA—*Piper Methysticum.*

Native of South America and South Sea Islands.

Properties.—Kava Kava increases the secretion and discharge of urine, is a stimulant of the nervous system and a sedative of genital excitement. Taken in large doses it produces intoxication, which differs from that of alcohol in being without excitement, but rather of a quiet and sleepy nature. In smaller and moderate doses it resembles Coca in its action in allaying fatigue One of its principal uses is in the treatment of gonorrhea, and many experiments have been made with it along this line. As a remedy for this disease two or three doses should be taken during the day, each accompanied with a full glass of water. The gonorrheal discharge is at first increased, and an abundant and painless discharge of urine is usually produced by the first dose.

Dose.—From 2 to 4 grains of the solid extract.

For Colic, Tenesmus, Spasms.

KNOT GRASS—*Polygonum Aviculare.*—This is a pale green plant which usually grows where the ground has been made hard by being trampled. It has many branches spreading on the ground, so that the thrifty plant sometimes reaches a foot or more each way from the center. The leaves are short and small.

It is beneficial in colic and wind on the stomach, tenesmus (a straining of the bowels without effecting evacuation) and spasms in any part of the body. It is given in infusion in doses of about 1 cupful as often as appears necessary.

For Whooping Cough, Dysentery, Skin Diseases.

LABRADOR TEA—*Ledum Latifolium.*—This plant grows in damp places in the Northern part of this country and Canada. The leaves are broad, oblong, somewhat heart-shaped at the base, dark green and smooth above and rusty woolly beneath. They have an agreeable odor and taste and possess expectorant and tonic properties.

The leaves in infusion are useful in whooping cough, in dysentery, and may also be taken in cases of skin disease. It may be drank freely.

For Nervous Diseases, Hysterical Affections, Epilepsy, Tremors.

LADIES' SLIPPER—*Cypripedium Pubescens*, called also AMERICAN VALERIAN, YELLOW UMBEL, NERVE ROOT, MOCCASIN FLOWER, etc.—This plant is common in hills and swamps. It grows from twelve to eighteen inches high, and the flower is in the form of a purse or round bag with a small opening near where it joins the stalk. It somewhat resembles a moccasin or slipper, hence its name. The roots are fibrous and thickly matted together.

It is a nervine and anti-spasmodic, and is used in nervous diseases and hysterical affections to allay pain, quiet the nerves and promote sleep; it is beneficial in nervous headache, epilepsy, tremors, etc. A dose of the powdered root is a teaspoonful diluted in water. It may also be made in decoction.

For Use Externally in Ringworm, Itch and Other Skin Affections.

LAUREL—*Kalmia Latifolia*, called also MOUNTAIN LAUREL, CALICO BUSH, SPOON-WOOD, etc.—This is a shrub growing from four to ten feet high. The leaves are evergreen, of an oval lance-shape, pointed at both ends, and have a bitterish taste. The flowers, which are very beautiful, are of a rose color and shaped something like a cup. It grows on mountains and hills. The wood is soft when fresh, but becomes very hard and dense when cut and dried.

It is used externally rather than given internally. The powdered leaves made into an ointment with lard are an excellent application for ringworm and other eruptions of this nature. A decoction of it is used as a wash in itch and other skin affections. The powdered leaves are used as a snuff for catarrh. Taken internally, it is a powerful and dangerous medicine.

For Flatulence, Fainting, Nervous Affections.

LAVENDER—*Lavendula Spica*, called also BROAD-LEAF LAVENDER, etc.—This plant is cultivated for medicinal purposes. The stem is whitish and woody. The leaves are lance-shaped and pointed. The flowers are bluish and grow in spikes at the ends of the branches.

It is employed with advantage in flatulence, fainting and nervous affections. It is taken in the form of infusion or powder. Of the powder, a dose is from $\frac{1}{3}$ to $\frac{1}{2}$ teaspoonful.

For External Use in Inflammations.

LEEK, or HOUSE-LEEK—*Sempervivum Tectorum*, called also HEN-AND-CHICKENS, LIVE-FOREVER, SENGREEN, etc.—This singular plant is very well known by the name of " Hen-and Chickens."

The fresh plant is applied as a cold application to ulcers, stings of insects, etc. The juice, mixed with cream, is good as an application for inflammations, especially of the eyes and those of an erysipelatous character, also for burns. It is very beneficial taken internally for diseases of an inflammatory nature, also beneficial in dysentery. After cleansing the stomach and bowels with a good cathartic, give a tablespoonful of the syrup of this plant every two hours until the symptoms subside. To make the syrup, bruise the green leaves, press out the juice, and add to it its weight of white or loaf sugar.

For Scurvy, Colds, etc.

LEMON—*Citrus Limonum.*

Native of Asia.

Properties.—The juice of the lemon taken in small doses stimulates the stomach and facilitates digestion. The juice of one lemon in 1 pint of water, sweetened with sugar, is excellent for allaying thirst and, taken hot, is valuable for colds.

The lemon possesses slight antispasmodic properties. At one time it enjoyed some reputation in rheumatism and was recommended as a remedy in malarial fevers; but these claims and a number of others proved to be without foundation. It is of undoubted value in scurvy, and when that disease existed was used with most excellent results. Wonderful curative properties have been in some instances ascribed to it, but later investigations have proven these claims to be without foundation.

For Nervous Diseases, Chronic Rheumatism, Colic, Diarrhea, Coughs.

LETTUCE--*Lactuca Sativa.*—This plant is valuable as an article of diet in many diseases, as hypochondria, nervous complaints, etc., as it has sedative properties and conduces to sleep. Like Wild Lettuce, it contains a quantity of milky juice which is of a dark color and has in some degree the odor and taste of Opium. Lactucarium is a preparation made from the juice of the Lettuce, also sometimes called ''Lettuce Opium.'' The dose is from 3 to 5 grains. Lettuce is also employed with advantage in allaying the pain of chronic rheumatism and colic, checking the frequent stools attending diarrhea, and in relieving coughs.

For Colds, Coughs, etc.

LICORICE—*Glycyrrhiza Glabra.*

Native of Mediterranean Region and Western Asia.

Properties.—Licorice promotes the secretions of the congested mucous membrane of the air passages, and is a valuable remedy in the cure of colds, coughs, etc. Equal parts of this root, Lungwort and Iceland Moss, made into a strong decoction and sweetened with rock candy, of which as much may be drank as the stomach will bear, is said to cure colds bordering on consumption. It is also very valuable in pneumonia, and as a palliative in the cough of consumptives. Licorice root is also largely used in sweetening syrups, and in pharmacy to cover pills and give them a proper consistence.

Dose.—Of the powdered root, from 12 grains to 1 teaspoonful; of the extract, from ½ to 1 ounce.

For Disorders of Menstruation.

LIFE ROOT—*Senecio Gracilis*, called also UNCUM, NATQUA, MEQUOT, etc.—This is a native plant growing on the banks of creeks and low, marshy grounds in the northern and western parts of this country. The root is about the size of a common wheat straw, and has many short fibers. The flower stem rises from twelve to eighteen inches high and bears yellow flowers.

It is highly valued in lung affections attended with debility, especially the incipient (beginning) stages of consumption. One of its most important uses, however, is in cases of suppressed menstruation. It is said to be capable of restoring the secretion when suppressed, or restraining it if too profuse, and is known to many by the name of "Female Regulator." For this purpose it is given in the form of decoction, made by adding ½ ounce to a pint of water, the whole to be taken through the course of the day in divided doses. This treatment should be commenced five or six days before the expected time of menstruation, and if its purpose is not accomplished the first time, it should be repeated before the next expected period. In lung diseases, hemorrhages, etc., it is prepared by simmering a suitable quantity of the roots in a closely covered vessel until their strength is extracted and adding equal parts of honey and loaf sugar to form a syrup, to every pint of which may be added ½ gill of the best quality of Jamaica Spirits.

For Liver Complaint, Indigestion, Hypochondria, etc.

LIVERWORT—*Hepatica Triloba*, called also LIVER LEAF, NOBLE LIVERWORT, etc.—The leaves of this plant, which somewhat resemble a clover leaf, live through the winter, and the flowers appear early in the spring, sometimes when the snow is yet falling. They are small and white, and drooping at first, but spread out as they unfold. *See illustration.*

This plant has no smell and very little taste, but it is much employed in liver complaints, indigestion, hypochondria, etc. It is given in the form of infusion, either warm or cold, and may be drank freely without regard to quantity.

For Poultice to Inflamed and Sore Surfaces.

LIZARD'S TAIL — *Saururus Cernuus*, called also SWAMP LILY, etc.—The fresh root is applied in the form of poultices to inflamed and swelled surfaces. Roasted and applied as a poultice, it is very beneficial in lumbago, pains in the breast, sore nipples, etc.

For Asthma, Croup, Whooping Cough, Pulmonary Diseases Generally, as an Emetic.

LOBELIA—*Lobelia Inflata*, called also EMETIC HERB, INDIAN TOBACCO, WILD TOBACCO, PUKE WEED and ASTHMA WEED.—Grows in dry open places all over the United States, from one to two feet in height, and blossoms from June to October, bearing a small blue flower growing out of a capsule. The capsule contains two cells, and is very full of small black seeds. *See Illustration.*

Exceedingly valuable in asthma, croup, whooping cough and pulmonary diseases generally. The leaves, seeds and inflated capsules may be given in the form of powders or tincture. A dose of the powder is 1 to 5 grains; of the tincture, 10 to 20 drops. In asthma the dose should be repeated in about half an hour if the paroxysm continues. For croup, teaspoonful doses of the tincture are recommended to be taken in connection with warm drinks of some simple herb tea until vomiting occurs.

For Hysteria and Nervous Disorders, Eruptions.

LOVAGE—*Ligusticum Levisticum*, called also SMELLAGE and LAVOSE.—Has small oblong seeds, strongly ribbed and of a yellowish brown color.

The seeds may be given in powder, of which the dose is 10 to 20 grains, or infusion, and are considered valuable in hysteria and nervous disorders and to bring out the rash in eruptive fevers.

For Dysentery, Strangury, Urinary Affections.

LOW MALLOW—*Malva Rotundifolia*, called also CHEESE PLANT.—This is a very common, creeping plant, that bears a fruit popularly called "cheeses."

It is useful in decoction for dysentery, strangury and all urinary difficulties and complaints, also for injections. It makes a soothing poultice applied warm.

For Pulmonary Affections.

LUNGWORT—*Pulmonaria Officinalis.*—This is an European plant, but there are native allied plants, such as the Virginia Lungwort. It is an expectorant and used as an ingredient in cough mixtures. It is beneficial in the various pulmonary affections.

For Coughs, Hoarseness, Asthma, Tickling of the Throat, Pleurisy.

MAIDEN HAIR — *Adiantum Pedatum*, called also ROCK FERN.—This fern has a large brown root, which sends up a compound of tinted leaves and stem about a foot in height. The branches are of a shining chestnut color, forked upward, and each subdivided into from four to seven small ones. The color of the leaves is a pale green. It grows in rich soil and deep woods, and may be collected at any time. It may be given freely in decoction, or in syrup, and is useful in coughs and hoarseness; also in asthma and tickling of the throat, in pleurisies and all disorders of the bronchial tubes, larynx and breast. A decoction is prepared by pouring a pint of boiling water on an ounce of the plant, straining when cold and adding sufficient sugar to sweeten.

For Tapeworm.

MALE FERN—*Aspidium Filix Mas*, called also SHIELD FERN.—This plant grows in shady pine forests. The proper time for collecting it is during the summer. The dried root is externally of a brown color and internally of a yellowish white or reddish.

It is much used as a vermifuge in cases of tapeworm. A dose of the powdered root is from 2 to 3 drachms. Two hours after taking a purgative must be taken in order to expel the worm. Another form of giving it is the Oleoresin in doses of from 30 to 50 drops, half to be taken at night and the other half in the morning; to be followed in about an hour by 1½ ounces of Castor Oil.

For Venereal, Scrofulous and Dyspeptic Complaints, Dropsy, Incontinence of Urine.

MANDRAKE—*Podophyllum Peltatum*, called also MAY APPLE, INDIAN APPLE, etc.—The Mandrake has a jointed, running root, half the size of the finger. The stem of the plant grows about a foot high and is enveloped at its base by the sheaths which covered it when in bud. It divides at the top into two stems from three to six inches long, each one supporting a large leaf which resembles the hand spread out. In the fork of the stem is a large white flower. The fruit is of a yellowish color, and somewhat resembles a small apple.

The dried root of the Mandrake is easily reduced to powder. It is given internally, and is very valuable in chronic diseases, such as venereal, scrofulous, bilious and dyspeptic complaints, also in dropsy. It is also of the greatest service in incontinence of urine. For a cathartic, give from 15 to 20 grains of the powdered root; as an alterative, in chronic cases, from 1 to 3 grains twice a day. The resin of the Mandrake, called Podophyllin, may be substituted for the powdered root and given in grain doses. Podophyllin pills may be obtained at any drug store.

For Low Forms of Fevers, Scrofula, Jaundice, Suppressed Menstruation.

MARIGOLD — *Calendula Officinalis.*—This plant is well known in ornamental gardens. It has a peculiar, rather disagreeable odor, which is lost by drying. The taste is rough, bitter and salty.

The flowers are made into an infusion and daily given in low forms of fevers, scrofula, jaundice and suppressed menstruation. Also given in scarlet fever, measles, etc., to bring out the rash.

For External Application to Inflammatory Tumors and Swellings, especially those that threaten to run into a gangrenous state.

MARSHMALLOW—*Althæ Officinalis*, called also MORTIFICATION ROOT.—This plant grows plentifully along banks and rivers and in marshy places. The root is fleshy, about the size of the finger, and is of a white color. The plant rises from three to four feet in height, has smooth, downy, heart-shaped leaves, and large, single, light rose flowers. *See illustration.*

The most important use of the Marshmallow is in the form of a poultice, the application of which will subdue inflammation, and prevent mortification when threatened. Also applied to inflammatory tumors and swellings of every kind. For this purpose the root should be cut into small pieces, bruised as finely as possible and boiled in sweet milk, to which a small quantity of powdered Elm bark may be added from time to time until it becomes sufficiently thick. It should be applied as warm as can be borne, and renewed as often as it becomes dry. It is so valuable in inflammations that threaten to run into a gangrenous state that the name of "Mortification Root" is often given to it. It is made into an ointment and used in herpetic (See HERPES) affections to allay itching and burning. Take ½ ounce of the dried roots and boil in 2 pints of water down to 1 pint. This makes a valuable wash for canker of the mouth. It is given internally freely in the form of decoction, and is beneficial in diseases of the urinary organs, dysentery, gonorrhea and bronchitis.

For Relaxed Conditions, as of the Bowels, Falling of the Womb, Leucorrhea, Gonorrhea, etc., and Ulcerous Conditions, especially of the Mouth and Throat.

MARSH ROSEMARY—*Statice Limonium,* called also SEASIDE THRIFT, SEA LAVENDER and INK ROOT.—Is of the same genus as Thrift, elsewhere described, and grows in the salt marshes along our seacoast. The root is large, fleshy and branched, and of a purplish brown color. The flowers are blue.

The root is a tonic and a powerful astringent. Used as a gargle in ulcerous sore throat, in connection with a little Capsicum, it is considered a certain cure. Used also as a gargle in thrush of the malignant variety and all ulcerous conditions of the mouth and throat. Also used as a wash or injection in leucorrhea, gonorrhea, gleet and immoderate flow of the menses. It may be taken internally in the form of decoction, infusion or syrup in small, repeated doses, and is useful in hemorrhage, cholera infantum, chronic dysentery, and any relaxed condition of the bowels, falling of the womb, etc. Also much used in the putrid sore throat accompanying scarlet fever. A good way to make the decoction is with milk, an ounce of the root to a pint of milk, the dose in severe cases being a tablespoonful every hour. Or a tincture of 2 ounces of the root to ½ ounce of Cinnamon bark, to which is added 1 pint of Brandy, the dose being from 1 to 3 teaspoonfuls. The powdered root makes a good dust for old sores.

For Hemorrhages.

MATICO—*Piper Augustifolium.*

Native of Tropical America from Mexico as far south as Brazil and Peru.

Properties.—It is absorbed into the blood and appears to produce a constriction of the minute blood vessels, making it a valuable remedy in hemorrhages, as of the lungs, stomach, bowels, etc. In its native home the green leaves are applied direct to bleeding surfaces. This remedy has also been used in the treatment of bronchitis, leucorrhea, gonorrhea and various other diseases, but its chief use, as above stated, is in checking hemorrhages.

Dose.—Of the powder, from 1 to 2 teaspoonfuls several times a day; of the extract, from ½ to 1 teaspoonful.

For Rheumatism, Hysterical Affections, Epilepsy, Dropsy, Asthma, Scrofula, etc.

MAYWEED—*Anthemis Cotula,* called also WILD CHAMOMILE, DOG'S FENNEL, etc.—This plant is found in open fields everywhere; it never grows in the shade. The root is crooked and fibrous. The stem is from one to two feet high and very much branched, and both the stems and leaves are covered with short, woolly hairs.

The properties of Mayweed are similar to those of Chamomile, for which it may be substituted. It is weaker, however, and less pleasant to the taste. It is extensively used for rheumatism, hysterics, epilepsy, dropsy, asthma, scrofula and other complaints, both internally and externally. For rheumatism, hysterical fits, suffocations, swellings, pains and contusions, it is used externally in warm baths. Internally, the flowering tops are given in decoction or infusion for colds, fevers, rheumatism, asthma, etc. If given too strong, it produces vomiting, and even a weak infusion may nauseate the stomach. In small doses it is a gentle tonic. It produces a copious perspiration.

For Vitiated Blood and Eruptions of the Skin.

MEADOW FERN—*Myrica Gale,* called also SWEET GALE, BOG MYRTLE, DUTCH MYRTLE, etc.—This grows in beds or patches in wet meadows and about the edges of ponds and streams. The stem grows from two to five feet high, is much branched and covered with reddish bark. The leaves are narrow at the base, but increase in width toward the end. The flowers are succeeded by small green burrs or seed vessels, which grow in clusters on the branches. These burrs attain their full size about the middle of August, when they should be collected and carefully dried. This fern grows more abundantly in the New England States than others. It makes a valuable ointment for external application in itch and all troublesome humors or eruptions of the skin. A decoction of the burr, sweetened with honey and taken in the quantity of a teacupful three times a day, is beneficial in the above complaints to purify the blood and restore the skin to a healthy tone, and is sometimes used as an injection into the urethra in gonorrhea and gleet.

For Syphilis, Chronic Rheumatism and Skin Diseases.

MEZEREON—*Daphne Mezereum.*—This is a low shrub that grows in woods and shady places. Found plentifully in the vicinity of the Ohio River. It is also cultivated in gardens. The whole plant is so corrosive that six of its berries are said to kill a wolf. The bark of the root when chewed for some time causes great burning in the mouth and throat.

It is given in the form of decoction, as follows: 2 drachms of the bark with ½ ounce of Licorice Root, boiled in 3 pints of water down to 2 pints, of which a wineglassful may be given four times a day. It is principally used in syphilis; also used in chronic rheumatism and skin diseases.

For Dropsy, Catarrh, Scrofulous and Rheumatic Disorders, Worms.

MILKWEED—*Asclepias Syriaca*, called also SILKWEED.— This is a common and well known plant, growing in sandy places along roadsides. The stem grows from three to five feet high and has oblong, lance-shaped leaves which are downy on the under surface. The flowers are large, of a pale purple and sweet-scented. The pod is covered with short prickles, and contains a large quantity of silky down.

This plant is a valuable remedy in dropsy, and is also beneficial in catarrh, scrofulous and rheumatic disorders, disordered condition of the system generally and worms in children. A decoction is made by boiling 8 ounces of the dried root in 3 quarts of water, of which the dose for dropsy is a gill taken four times a day, the dose to be increased according to its effect. For other complaints a larger dose may be taken. A tincture of the root in Gin is also used in dropsy and gravelly disorders.

For Epilepsy.

MISTLETOE—*Viscum Verticillatum.*—This plant is found growing on various trees, usually on Oak. It has clusters of smooth white berries that remain on throughout the winter, each berry containing a single fleshy seed. It should be separated from the Oak about the last of November, carefully dried, ground into a fine powder and put into a well-stoppered bottle; it should not be left exposed to the air.

It is used as a remedy for epilepsy. To begin with the dose may be a teaspoonful four times a day taken in Valerian tea and increased to 2 or 3 teaspoonfuls, according to its effect.

For Nervous Affections of Women.

MOTHERWORT—*Leonurus Cardiaca.*—This valuable plant has a strong stalk, square and brownish, rising from two to four feet high and spreading into many branches. The leaves are broad and long, two at every joint, and notched about the edge. The flowers grow around the branches from about the middle to the top. They are of a red or purple color, and grow out of prickly husks or burrs.

This plant is a tonic and antispasmodic. It relieves hysterical symptoms, produces sleep, abates delirium and allays spasms of the womb. It is very beneficial to females who suffer from tenderness about the lower bowels and loins. It will also bring on the menses. It may be given in powder, a tablespoonful at a dose; or the expressed juice, ½ tablespoonful; or in infusion or decoction, which may be drank freely. The decoction may be made by adding 2 ounces of the dried herb to a quart of water and boiling down to 1 pint. The dose is from 1 to 2 tablespoonfuls every two hours during the day.

For Paralysis, Muscular Rheumatism, Nervous Affections.

MOUNTAIN ARNICA—*Arnica Montana*, called also LEOPARD'S BANE.—This plant has a woody, brownish root, which ends rather abruptly and sends forth slender fibers of the same color. It has a hairy stem, about a foot high, which ends in two or three flower stalks that bear a single large flower of a fine orange yellow color. The flowers, leaves and root are all employed as medicine, but the flowers are preferred.

It acts with great energy on the brain and nervous system, and may be given with advantage in paralysis, muscular rheumatism and nervous affections. It is given in substance or infusion. A dose of the powder is from 5 to 10 grains, frequently repeated. The infusion may be made by adding an ounce of the flowers to a pint of water, of which from 1 to 2 tablespoonfuls may be given every two or three hours. The infusion should always be strained through linen as otherwise the fine fibers of the plant might irritate the throat.

For Tonic Purposes, especially in Fevers.

MOUNTAIN ASH—*Sorbus Americana*, called also SERVICE TEA.—This is a small tree, reaching to the height of ten to twenty feet. It bears a fruit in the shape of a bright scarlet berry about the size of a pea.

The bark, which is the part used in medicine, smells and tastes like Cherry bark, but is more astringent. It is a fine tonic, and also possesses antiseptic properties, making it a valuable remedy in fevers. It is used in infusion, and may be drank freely, or according to its effects. The berries are used as a remedy in scurvy.

For Periodic Fevers, Rheumatism, Scarlet Fever, Diphtheria.

MOUNTAIN SAGE—*Sierra Salvia*, called also SAGE BUSH.—This plant is found in territory adjoining the eastern slope of the Rocky Mountains. There is a large variety of the genus known as Sage Bush found all over the western part of this country.

It is a valuable remedy in the treatment of periodic fevers, as remittent, intermittent, etc., for which purpose a teaspoonful of the fluid extract may be given in a glass of hot lemonade about an hour before the expected chill, and repeated in thirty minutes if sweating has not been produced. In rheumatism, scarlet fever, diphtheria, etc., it is also given hot, as above, and repeated every thirty minutes until sweating and free urination take place.

Dose.—From 1 to 2 teaspoonfuls of the fluid extract.

For Diarrhea, Colics, Scalding Urine, Consumption, Piles, Scalds, Wounds, Swellings, Sprains, Inflammation, Sores, Weak Eyes.

MULLEIN—*Verbascum Thapsus.*—Grows plentifully along roads and in old fields. Too common to need description.

An infusion of the leaves and flowers combined is given with advantage in looseness of the bowels and diarrhea, in colics and scalding urine, and is also useful in consumption. It may be drank freely. Also makes a good wash for piles, scalds, and wounds in cattle. In the form of a poultice the leaves and pith of the stalk are useful in white swellings, sprains and inflammations. The leaves boiled in vinegar are applied with advantage to offensive sores, swellings and contracted sinews. The blossoms saturated with rose water make an excellent wash for weak eyes.

For External Application to allay Pain.

MUSTARD—*Sinapis Alba.*—The flowers of this plant are small, yellow, and disposed in a terminal cluster. *See illustration.*

Ground Mustard seed makes an excellent external application in all cases of pain. It is used in the form of plasters, spread on cloth, and is excellent to relieve inflammation, to arouse the system in apoplectic conditions, in the last stages of low typhus fever, and to prevent the return of convulsions in adults and children it should never be omitted. It is also used in the treatment of cholera, cholera infantum, etc., applied in poultices to the abdomen. To make a Mustard plaster so it will not blister, beat the white of an egg, add a little flour, then enough of the Mustard to make a soft paste; it should not be stirred thick. Spread it on a cloth—a piece of old cotton or linen—large enough to fold back over it, apply, and lay several thicknesses of cloth above it to prevent soiling clothing. Mustard foot baths are given to induce sweating and to draw the blood away from the brain or other organs when in a congested state.

For Tonic, Gargle, Application to Ulcers and Sores.

NANNY BUSH—*Viburnum Lentago.*—A shrub growing from eight to fifteen feet high, usually in damp, rich soils.

The bark is dark gray and rough, and the berries, which are black, hang in clusters from the end of the limbs. Their taste is sweet.

An infusion of the bark of the root taken in tablespoonful doses makes an excellent tonic; and a decoction of the same makes a valuable wash for old ulcers and sores, and is particularly good as a gargle for the throat.

For Gravel, Hemorrhage, Diarrhea.

NETTLE—*Urtica Dioica.*—This common plant needs no description. The juice is astringent, and is good in gravelly complaints, internal hemorrhage and spitting of blood. The decoction is beneficial for those who make bloody urine and for consumption in its early stages. Also, sweetened with sugar, is much used in diarrhea and dysentery.

The better way to prepare it is to make a strong syrup of the Nettle, bark of the Wild Cherry and Blackberry root. These articles should be boiled and the liquid strained off, to each pint of which should be added from ½ to 1 pound of loaf sugar and a gill of good Brandy, together with a little Cinnamon, Allspice or Nutmeg. The dose for a child from one to two years old is a teaspoonful, often repeated; for an adult, from ½ to 1 wineglassful five or six times daily. Before giving this preparation a laxative should be given, as, for instance, Rhubarb. This is an effectual treatment in all bowel complaints, and is a valuable preparation in the summer complaints of children.

For Syphilis, Gonorrhea, Epilepsy, Asthma, Bronchitis, Coughs,
    Diseases of the Lungs.

NEW JERSEY TEA—*Ceanothus Americanus*, called also RED ROOT, WILD SNOWBALL, BOHEA, etc.—A shrub, bearing small white flowers in clusters. Found in New Jersey, Pennsylvania, New York and the Western States. The bark of the root has the smell and taste of Peach leaves and imparts a red color to water.

Given in decoction, it is esteemed a useful remedy in syphilitic complaints, in gonorrheal discharges, in epilepsy, asthma, chronic bronchitis, consumption and all diseases of the lungs. As an expectorant it is very valuable in coughs where there is no inflammation. The bark of the root may be employed in tincture in doses of from a teaspoonful to a tablespoonful three or four times a day; or the stems, leaves and seeds may be used in decoction or strong infusion, drank cold, about a pint in the course of the day.

For Heart Troubles, Dropsy, Threatened Apoplexy and Rheumatism.

NIGHT-BLOOMING CEREUS—*Cactus Grandiflorus.*
Native of West Indies.

Properties.—Especially useful in functional diseases of the heart attended with much irregularity of action, relieving or removing the symptoms—frequently giving prompt relief. It has been found serviceable in palpitation, angina pectoris and other affections of the heart, in rheumatism, dropsy and threatened apoplexy.

Dose.—From 10 to 20 drops of the fluid extract.

For Asthma, Colds, Fevers and Bowel Complaints.

NINE BARK—*Spiræa Opulifolia,* called also SNOWBALL, HARDHACK, etc.—This is a shrub with white flowers found in wet places. It grows from three to five feet in height. There are many shrubs called by this name, but are not the true Nine Bark.

It is used principally as an external application, either in fomentation or poultice, in burns, mortifications, swellings, etc. It is taken internally in warm infusion for asthma, colds, fevers and bowel complaints.

NUX VOMICA.—(See A CHAPTER ON MEDICINES).

For Gall-Stones, to Prevent Lead Poisoning, etc.

OLIVE—*Oleum Olivæ.*
Native of the Mediterranean Region.

Properties.—Olive Oil in the dose of 2 to 4 tablespoonfuls acts as a mild laxative, sometimes given to infants in teaspoonful doses for this purpose. It is extensively used by workmen in white lead factories to keep the bowels free and prevent lead poisoning. It is taken in large doses, say from 6 to 12 tablespoonfuls, in case of gall-stones. Large doses have also been known to kill and expel tapeworms. It is applied locally to the bites and stings of insects, also to wounds, burns, and, warmed, to bruises and sprains. It is employed as an article of food, and is put to many other uses.

Dose.—As above.

Note.—Most of the so-called Olive Oil on the market is Cotton-Seed Oil. Cotton-Seed Oil is comparatively inexpensive, and the public is unable to detect the difference. There may be many instances where this substitution offers no serious objection, but for internal use there should be some way of detecting the difference. This, however, is a difficult matter, and there are no simple means of accomplishing it.

For Poulticing, Colds and Croup in Children, Dropsies, Suppression of Urine, Gravel, etc.

ONION — *Allium Cepa.*—Roasted and split, onions are applied to boils and tumors in which pus is forming. They ease the pain and hasten the formation of the pus. The juice pressed out and made into a syrup with sugar is given to children for colds, croup, etc. As a food they are recommended in dropsies, suppression of urine, gravel, etc.

OPIUM.—(See A Chapter on Medicines).

For Debility after Sickness, Scalding Urine, Rheumatism, Colic, Paralysis, Piles.

OSWEGO TEA — *Monarda Didyma,* called also Moun-tain Balm, Square Stalk, Red Balm, etc.—Has many heads of flowers of a bright scarlet, and is a very handsome plant. It is of the same genus as Horsemint.

Much esteemed in protracted illness where stimulants are required for a long time. Said to be valuable in piles, scalding urine, rheumatism, colic and paralysis. Given in infusion freely.

For Diarrhea, Dysentery, Cholera Morbus, Colic, Night Sweats.

PARACOTO, or COTO, BARK.

Native of Bolivia and Brazil.

Properties.—This remedy is used in diarrhea, dysentery, cholera morbus and colic, its chief use being to check chronic diarrhea attended with general debility. It has also been success-fully used to check night sweats.

Preparations.—Cotoin and Paracotoin.

Dose.—Of Cotoin, from 1 to 2 or 3 grains three times a day, taken well diluted in water; of Paracotoin, from 2 to 3 or 4 grains, also well diluted.

For Dropsy, Bladder and Kidney Affections, Gravel, Obstructions of the Liver, Jaundice.

PARSLEY—*Angelica Petroselinum,* called also Rock Parsley.—A very common plant, rising about two feet in height and bearing small yellow flowers.

The whole plant may be used in infusion, or a decoction made of the roots and seeds, either of which may be drank freely. It is used in dropsy, affections of the bladder and kidneys, gravel, obstructions of the liver and jaundice. The bruised leaves make a good poultice.

For Kidneys and Bladder.

PARSLEY PIERT—*Aphanes Arvensis*, called also BREAKSTONE.—Found in the Southern States, particularly in Maryland.

A valuable remedy in gravel and all diseases of the kidneys and bladder. Take an ounce of the plant and pour on 1 pint of boiling water; steep, but not boil.

Dose.—A gill three times a day.

For Confinement, Dropsy, Gout, Suppression of Urine.

PARTRIDGE BERRY—*Mitchella Repens*, called also SQUAW VINE, CHECKERBERRY, ONE-BERRY, WINTER CLOVER. —A small evergreen vine, running along the ground, usually found among hemlock timber in swampy places. It has small, round green leaves, a white flower and a bright scarlet berry.

Famous among the Indians for lessening the labor of childbirth, the squaws drinking it for two or three weeks previous to and during delivery. It may be advantageously used in dropsy, gout and suppression of urine. It may be taken freely in infusion or made an ingredient in syrups. The herb and the berries are both used.

For Tonic Purposes.

PEACH TREE—*Amygdalus Persica.*—The dried fruit, stewed with sugar, is laxative, and is very wholesome for invalids who are troubled with costiveness. The kernel of the pit has a bitter, yet pleasant taste, and makes a very valuable medicine.

A syrup or cordial of the kernels is very useful to improve the tone of the stomach and bowels and invigorate the digestive powers. A tincture made of the kernels makes a powerful tonic, which is used in fever and ague, debility, etc., and is a valuable remedy in the treatment of leucorrhea. The dose of the tincture is a teaspoonful three times a day. An ounce of the flowers and kernels in equal proportions boiled in a pint of water, to which is added ¼ pound of sugar, is excellent, taken in teaspoonful doses, for children teething and suffering from worms.

For Suppression of Urine or Menses.

PENNYROYAL—*Hedeoma Pulegioides.*—This plant grows all over the United States and Canada in dry woods and plains. The root is small and yellowish. The leaves are small and of an oblong lance-shape. The flowers are a pale blue with purplish spots.

It is a popular remedy for suppressed urine and menses. For this purpose it is taken in infusion, which brings on a general perspiration. It should be made into a strong tea and taken warm freely and frequently.

For Nausea, Vomiting, Heartburn, Flatulent Colic, Bowel Complaints.

PEPPERMINT—*Mentha Piperita.*—The Peppermint grows from one to two feet high and bears spikes of purple flowers. It has a well known odor.

It is given in powder, infusion, essence or oil. Of the essence the dose is from 5 to 10 drops. The infusion is made by adding an ounce of the herb to a quart of boiling water, and may be taken freely. It is a very valuable remedy in complaints of the stomach. It is excellent to allay vomiting, sickness at the stomach, heartburn, flatulent colic, bowel complaint, cholera morbus, etc. The fresh herb, bruised and applied to the pit of the stomach, will cure nausea.

For Diarrhea, Chronic Dysentery, Hemorrhage of the Womb.

PERSIMMON—*Diospyrus Virginiana,* called also Seeded Plum.—The Persimmon tree is a native of the Southern States. It often grows to a height of sixty feet, and has a trunk eighteen or twenty inches in diameter. The farther north it grows, the smaller it becomes. An old tree is covered with a furrowed, blackish bark. It bears flowers of a pale orange color, and berries which are of a dark yellow color when perfectly ripe and contain numerous seeds in a soft yellow pulp. The flowers appear in May and June, but the fruit is not ripe until the middle of autumn. In a green state the fruit is excessively astringent, but after being touched by the frost it becomes sweet and pleasant to the taste.

The unripe fruit is used in infusion or syrup, prepared in the proportion of about 1 ounce of the bruised fruit to 4 tablespoonfuls of liquid, and given in the dose of a teaspoonful or more for infants, and a tablespoonful for adults, for diarrhea, chronic dysentery, and hemorrhage of the womb. The bark is employed in the form of a gargle in ulcerated sore throat.

PERUVIAN BARK.—(See A Chapter on Medicines).

For Diseases of the Bladder and Kidneys.

PHILADELPHIA FLEABANE—*Erigeron Philadelphicum,* called also Scabious.—This plant is generally called Scabious. It has a branching, yellowish root, and from one to five stems, which rise two or three feet in height and are much branched at the top. The whole plant is covered with short hairs. The lower leaves are supported on long foot-stalks; the upper are narrow, oblong, somewhat wedge-shaped, and slightly embrace the stem. The flowers are numerous.

This plant is of the same genus as the Scabious, elsewhere described, and is useful in dropsical and kidney affections, especially in irritability of the bladder. It is usually given in decoction made of an ounce of the herb to a pint of water, all of which may be taken within twenty-four hours.

For Hydrophobia, Old Ulcers.

PIMPERNEL—*Anagallis Arvensis*, called also RED CHICKWEED.—Has square stalks, lying on the ground, and the flowers, which are of a pale red color, stand singly. The root is fibrous.

The Germans esteem it infallible in hydrophobia, the dose being half a teaspoonful of the powdered herb repeated in eight hours. The decoction makes a useful wash for cleansing old ulcers. Applied as a poultice, it draws out thorns and other foreign substances from the flesh.

For Erysipelas, Tetter, Salt Rheum, Snake Bites and other Poisonous Wounds, Leucorrhea, Piles, Salt Rheum.

PLANTAIN—*Plantago Major*, called also LARGE PLANTAIN, ROUND-LEAVED PLANTAIN, etc.—Common in all parts of the country. Needs no description.

The leaves make an excellent ointment for erysipelas, tetter or salt rheum. Also remarkably effectual in poisons of all kinds. For snake bites take the expressed (pressed out) juice of Plantain and of Horehound, equal parts, in tablespoonful doses as often as the stomach will bear. If the fresh plant is not at hand, the dried leaves may be used, prepared by boiling in milk. It will be found useful in the treatment of wounds, leucorrhea and piles.

For Pleurisy, Pains in the Chest, Low Stages of Febrile and Inflammatory Diseases.

PLEURISY ROOT, or WHITE ROOT—*Asclepias Tuberosa*, called also BUTTERFLY WEED, ORANGE SWALLOWWORT, etc.—Grows in poor and gravelly soils in open situations; it is rarely met in rich soils. The root is large, fleshy, of a white color, and when dried is brittle and may be easily reduced to powder. The stems are round, hairy, and may be either green or red. The leaves are very hairy and pale beneath. The flowers are of a bright orange color, giving the plant a brilliant appearance. The seeds are contained in long, slender pods, to which is attached a kind of silk.

BLOOD ROOT.

(See Description.)

This herb is used internally as a Tonic or Emetic, and is applied externally to Ulcers, Ringworm and Ill-conditioned Sores.

CHAMOMILE.

(See Description.)

This herb is useful in Pulmonary Consumption, Hysteria, Colics, Gout, Vomiting in Confinement, etc.

BITTERSWEET.

(See Description.)

This herb is used in Scrofulous and Skin Diseases, in Liver
Complaint, and for Tumors and Ulcers.

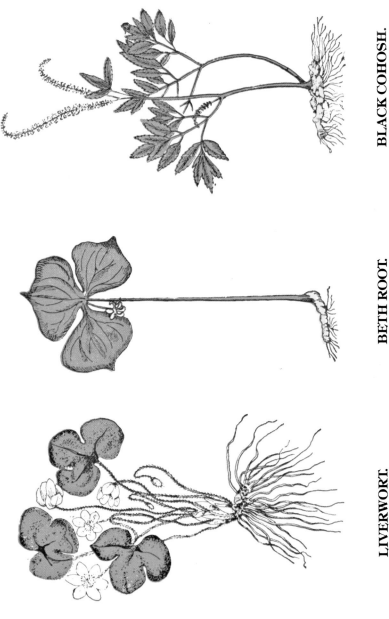

LIVERWORT.
(See Description.)
This herb is useful in Liver Complaints, Indigestion, Hypochondria, etc.

BETH ROOT.
(See Description.)
Useful in Hemorrhages, Lung Diseases, Asthma, Cough, Leucorrhea, Ulcers, Carbuncles, Snake Bites, etc.

BLACK COHOSH.
(See Description.)
Useful in Confinement, Disorders of Menstruation, Rheumatism and Bowel Complaints.

YELLOW GENTIAN.
(See Description.)
This herb is a valuable tonic, useful in Dyspepsia, Gout, Jaundice, Weakness of the Digestive Organs and Debility attendant upon Chronic Diseases.

HENBANE.

(See Description.)

Applied externally on Boils, Fistulas, Swellings of the Breast.
Ulcers, Tumors, Inflamed Eyes, etc.

CROWFOOT.

(See Description.)

This herb is a Stomach and Bowel tonic, useful in Dysentery, Diarrhea and Cholera Infantum; also used externally as a wash for Wounds, Ulcers, etc.

FOXGLOVE.

(See Description.)

This herb is useful in Dropsy of the Chest, Pleurisy and
Inflammatory Affections. (To be used with caution.)

This plant produces perspiration, and will relieve the difficult breathing of patients who are laboring under attacks of pleurisy, hence one of its popular names. It relieves difficulty of breathing in general, together with pains in the chest, and in low stages of febrile and inflammatory diseases it has been known to excite perspiration when other sudorifics (sweating medicines) had failed. It is given to infants who are teething, also in cholera infantum. It is used with advantage in affections of the lungs, also in acute rheumatism, in dysentery, colic and similar affections. It may be given in infusion or powder, a dose of the latter being from ¼ to ½ teaspoonful three times a day. A strong infusion of this plant may be given in chronic dysentery with great success.

For Cancerous Tumors, Epilepsy, Convulsions, Lockjaw, Hydrophobia.

POISON HEMLOCK—*Conium Maculatum.*—The stalks of this plant grow from six to seven feet in height, are branched near the top and furrowed near the bottom, and covered with a bluish exudation appearing like a fine powder. The roots grow about eight inches long and are of the size of the finger. It grows in New England and the North Central States, and is found in waste places and along streams. The lower leaves are about a foot long; the upper leaves are smaller. They are the part used in medicine, and should be gathered when the plant is in full bloom or when the fruit begins to form. In a fresh state they are of a dull dark green color, but on drying they become a grayish green and have a characteristic odor which has been compared to the urine of mice. It is a very poisonous plant, but is not dangerous in small doses often repeated and gradually increased.

The leaves are much applied externally to cancerous tumors. They are also given internally in affections such as epilepsy, neuralgia, convulsions, lockjaw and hydrophobia, and are said to relieve whooping cough, asthma and spasmodic laryngitis. Dose of the extract, from 3 to 5 grains twice a day; of the powdered leaves, from 2 to 3 grains. A fomentation may be made by adding an ounce of the leaves to a pint of boiling water. A plaster for application to tumors is made by taking 2 ounces each of Hemlock, Wax and Resin and 1 ounce of Olive Oil, melting and spreading on leather.

For External Application to Abscesses, Cancers and Ulcers, and Internal Use in Syphilitic Rheumatism.

POKE WEED—*Phytolacca Decandria*, called also GARGET, COAKUM, PIGEON BERRY, etc.—This plant has a very large root, often five or six inches in diameter, and is usually divided into three or four branches, which are whitish within and brownish outside. The stems of the plant grow to a height of six or eight feet. They are of a green color when young, but turn purple after the berries have ripened. The leaves are large. The flowers, which grow along the stem, something after the manner of grapes, are succeeded by dark purple berries. Each berry is divided into ten cells, and each cell contains one seed. It grows abundantly in all parts of the United States, flourishing along fences and by the borders of woods, and in appearance is a very striking plant. *See illustration.*

The root of this plant is covered with tow, roasted, and applied to scrofulous and hard abscesses to disperse them, and is very valuable for this purpose; or a poultice for the same purpose is made of the powdered and dried root mixed with Slippery Elm. The pulverized root is also combined with Blood Root as a snuff and used for polypus of the nose. The young shoots and leaves of the plant are eaten like asparagus and spinach, but the old leaves are not good to eat in this way. The juice of the plant is alterative, and beneficial in chronic and syphilitic rheumatism, 1 tablespoonful to be taken every four hours. A strong decoction of equal parts of this root, Blood Root and Sumach bark or berries makes a good injection for cancers and ulcers of the womb.

For Diseases of the Liver, Lungs and Skin.

POLYPODY—*Polypodium Vulgare.*—This is a well known fern, growing in large beds on the sides of rocks and shady hills. The root is about the size of a goose quill, is creeping, rough and irregular. The fronds or leaves are six or eight inches in length.

It is a valuable medicine. It appears to exercise a curative influence in diseases of the liver, both acute and chronic; also to relieve difficulty of breathing, tightness of the chest, and coughs either dry or loose, also dyspeptic symptoms; and is beneficial in diseases of the skin, such as salt rheum, erysipelas, and eruptions of a red color.

An infusion may be prepared by adding a teaspoonful of the powdered root or leaves to a pint of boiling water, sweetening with loaf sugar and taking in the course of twenty-four hours.

For Expulsion of Tapeworm.

POMEGRANATE—*Pumica Granatum.*

Native of Southwestern Asia.

Properties.—The principal use to which this remedy is put is the expulsion of tapeworm. For this purpose it may be taken in decoction made as follows: Take 2 ounces of the bark (the fresh is better than the dried), cut into small pieces, add 1½ pints of water and let stand over night, then boil gently down to 1 pint. Turn off the liquor, pressing out the grounds, and give it lukewarm in three doses at intervals of an hour, the patient not to take food. If the first dose is vomited, the other two may be given just the same and will usually be retained by the stomach. Two tablespoonfuls of Castor Oil may be given as soon as colic pains begin to take place.

Pelletierine, the active principle of Pomegranate, may be given for the same purpose, as directed under TAPEWORM.

For Chronic Rheumatism, Malignant Ulcers.

PRICKLY ASH—*Xanthoxylum Fraxineum*, called also TOOTHACHE TREE.—This tree is a native of the Southern States, but grows plentifully in the Middle States. It is found in low, moist ground. The bark, which is thin, is grayish outside and a yellowish white inside. Held in the mouth, it excites a flow of saliva.

The bark and berries are chiefly used in medicine, but the fresh leaves are also valuable. It is a remedy for chronic rheumatism, and is used both internally and externally. In cases of malignant ulcers it is a powerful blood purifier. The powder may be given in doses of from 10 to 20, or even 30, grains. Of the decoction, which is prepared by boiling an ounce of the bark in a quart of water until it is reduced one-third, the dose is from 4 to 6 tablespoonfuls in as many hours. A tincture made of the bark and capsules is a popular remedy in chronic rheumatism.

For Chronic Rheumatism, Gout, Sciatica and Gravel.

PRINCE'S PINE—*Chimaphila Umbellata*, called also PIP-SISSEWAY, GROUND HOLLY, RHEUMATISM WEED, etc.—This is an evergreen plant that grows on land thinly timbered with Chestnut, Oak and Pine. It rises from six to eight inches from the ground, where a number of thick, deep green leaves, notched about the edges, surround the stalk. On some of the plants the stem rises for five inches above the leaves, bearing on its top a loose cluster of blossoms which are succeeded by seed vessels like flaxbowls. The root is long, slender, white, and frequently supports a number of plants.

It is highly recommended for curing chronic rheumatism, gout, sciatica and similar affections. For this purpose a tincture should be made as follows: Put 1 pound of the dried herbs into a gallon of spirits, cover tightly, let stand in a dark place from eight to fourteen days and then turn off the top. Taken in decoction, it is very useful in curing gravel and gravelly obstructions of the urine, and for purifying the blood. Its use should be long continued.

For Uterine Tonic.

PULSATILLA—*Anemone Pulsatilla.*

Native of Europe and Siberia.

Properties.—The principal use of Pulsatilla is to relieve uterine pains and increase the flow at the menstrual period. For this purpose it should be taken a few days before the time.

Dose.—Of the tincture, 5 drops; of Anemonin, its active principle, $\frac{1}{100}$ of a grain every three hours.

For Urinary Difficulties.

PUMPKIN—*Curcubila Pepo.*—Pumpkin seed tea is a remedy for tapeworm. (See TAPEWORM). Also a valuable diuretic, relieving spasm of the urinary passages and scalding of urine. Pumpkin seed tea is one of the very best remedies for suppressing urine in infants.

For Diarrhea and Chronic Dysentery.

PURPLE WILLOW HERB—*Lythrum Salicaria*, called also LOOSE STRIPE, MILK WILLOW HERB, etc.—Found in meadows, swamps and along the banks of streams, growing from two to three feet high. The stem is soft and downy, and the leaves are downy on the under surface. It has showy purple flowers, and the fruit is a small capsule.

It is a popular remedy for diarrhea and chronic dysentery, but is to be administered after the proper cathartics have operated. The dose of the powdered herb is from ½ to 1 teaspoonful two or three times a day. The root may be taken in decoction in doses of from 2 to 4 tablespoonfuls.

For Affections of the Urinary Organs, Scrofula, Gonorrhea.

PURSLANE — *Portulacea Oleracea*, called also GARDEN PURSLANE, etc.—This plant grows spontaneously in gardens and is often used as greens, boiling it with other vegetables and meat. The leaves are thick and fleshy. The stalk is long and fine, is a foot or more in length, and has a smooth, reddish, brittle stem.

The plant may be taken freely in decoction, and is recommended for all affections of the urinary organs, scrofula and gonorrhea.

For Tonic Purposes.

QUASSIA—*Picræna Excelsa.*

Native of West Indies.

Properties.—Quassia is one of the most valuable of bitter tonics. It owes its effects to *Quassin*, its active principle. It increases the activity of the glands of the stomach and thus increases the amount of digestive fluid, aids in digestion, stimulates the appetite and makes a valuable remedy. It may be given in all forms of dyspepsia, and is especially valuable when there is loss of appetite, nausea, eructations and pain. It is a valuable remedy after protracted fevers or low physical conditions from any cause. Its use often relieves headache when due to digestive disturbances. During some forms of chronic dyspepsia, whether resulting from the prolonged use of alcohol or from other causes where the stomach contains a large amount of mucus, quassia, or its active principle, quassin, by its power to stimulate the normal secretions is a valuable aid in clearing up the mucous membrane, relieving the feeling of nausea and depression, improving digestion and giving tone to the stomach; in a word, restoring normal conditions. Quassia is usually obtained in the form of small chips. A few small pieces placed in a glass of water and allowed to stand several hours will yield the bitter principle, and the remedy may be taken in this way. The active principle, quassin, comes in small pills and may be taken without taste.

Dose.—Of the tincture, from ¼ to ½ teaspoonful; of quassin, the active principle, $\frac{1}{30}$ of a grain. This may be increased or diminished as needed. The infusion may be made as described above, is a convenient method, and costs comparatively nothing. Taken in this way, ½ tumblerful, more or less, may be drank before meals.

For Obstructions of the Kidneys and Urinary Passages.

QUEEN OF THE MEADOW—*Eupatorium Purpureum*,

called also PURPLE BONESET, GRAVEL ROOT, etc.—This plant grows in swamps and other low ground, flowering in August and September. It is five or six feet high, has a hollow stem of a purple color and purple flowers.

An infusion of the plant may be drank freely in gravel, stone in the bladder, and all obstructions of the kidneys and urinary passages.

For Rheumatism, Gravel, Diseases of the Kidneys, Gonorrhea, etc.

RED CEDAR—*Juniperus Virginiana.*—The wood of this

tree is of a reddish color, and is highly valued on account

of its great durabilty. It is a species of Juniper and seldom attains to a very large size. The leaves and tops are the parts used in medicine.

Given in infusion in wineglassful doses, they are useful in rheumatism, gravel, diseases of the kidneys, scalding of urine in gonorrhea, etc. The oil is used externally and also given internally in doses of 3 to 5 or 10 drops twice a day. The pulverized leaves may be given in doses of from 10 to 12 grains.

For Purifying the Blood, Correcting Acidity of the Stomach.

RED CLOVER—*Trifolium Pratense.*—This is the common variety growing in meadows. The roots in infusion, drank freely, will correct acidity of the stomach, and are valuable for purifying the blood. This infusion also makes a good wash for foul sores and ulcers. The blossoms boiled in water, which is then strained and simmered down to a thick syrup, makes a useful plaster for old sores, scrofulous tumors, sore lips, etc.

For Sore Mouths, Ulcers, Sores, Scalds, Burns, etc.

RED RASPBERRY — *Rubus Strigosus.*—The leaves of this shrub dried and made into a tea are good to remove canker from the mouth, throat, stomach, bowels, etc. The tea, thickened with Elm bark, pounded crackers or white bread, is often used as a poultice to remove canker and proud flesh. It makes an excellent gargle for children with sore mouths, and a good wash for ulcers, sores, scalds, burns, etc. In giving it to children it may be sweetened and milk added to make it pleasant to the taste.

RHUBARB.—(See A Chapter on Medicines).

For Leucorrhea, Menses, Vomiting in Pregnancy, Gleet.

ROSE WILLOW—*Cornus Sericea*, called also Red Rose Willow, Red Osier, Red Rod, Swamp Dogwood, etc.—About the size of a small apple tree, covered with a greenish bark and very red within. Flowers resemble a bunch of roses.

A powerful astringent that is very beneficial in leucorrhea, immoderate flow of the menses, etc., at the same time having a tonic and strengthening effect upon the system. It is also an excellent remedy for vomiting, particularly where it arises from pregnancy or diseased uterus. Mostly administered in the form of infusion. Or, a strong decoction may be made of 1 pound of the bark boiled to 3 quarts, to which is added 3 pints of Port Wine and 4 ounces of loaf sugar, the dose being a teacupful three times a day. Also useful in gleet, using the pure decoction (that is, without the wine and sugar) as an enema.

For Tonic Purposes, Hysterical Affections, Wind Colic.

RUE—*Ruta Graveolens.*—This plant is cultivated in gardens. The leaves, which are used for medicinal purposes, have a strong, disagreeable odor, especially when rubbed, and a hot, bitter taste.

Rue is a stimulant and appears to have a tendency to act upon the uterus. In moderate doses it promotes the menstrual discharge, and in larger doses it produces a degree of irritation in that organ which sometimes causes miscarriage. Taken in very large quantities it acts as an acrid, narcotic poison. It is also sometimes used in hysterical affections, wind colic and worms, but should be given with caution. A dose of the powder is from 10 to 20 grains two or three times a day. It is also given in infusion.

For Bringing out the Rash in Eruptive Diseases, Chlorosis, Hysteria, Menses, Spasms.

SAFFRON—*Crocus Sativus*, called also TRUE SAFFRON, SPANISH SAFFRON, etc.—The root is a small bulb standing upon a larger, with a multitude of fibers growing from the base. Four or five leaves rise from the root, dark green, narrow and grassy and about five inches long, and from the same root rises a stalk four inches high, sustaining a single flower that resembles a crocus. The orange colored, fleshy capillaments of this flower contain the medicinal properties of the plant.

The flowers in infusion are very valuable in bringing out the rash in measles, small-pox, scarlet fever and other eruptive diseases. It is useful to allay the lumbar pains which accompany menstruation in some females. It is useful also in chlorosis, in hysteria, and to promote the secretion of urine. It gives tone to the stomach and is an antispasmodic, *i. e.*, is given to relieve spasms.

Note.—There is another plant, called FALSE SAFFRON, the *Carthamus Tinctorius*, or SAFFLOWER, that is used for the same purposes as the so-called "TRUE" SAFFRON.

For Languor, Nervous Affections, Fevers, Colds and Coughs, Thrush, Quinsy.

SAGE—*Salvia Officinalis.*—Too well known to need description. An infusion of the leaves, or "sage tea," is good in languor, in nervous affections and fevers. Also used in summer complaints and worms in children. It produces perspiration, and is a popular remedy for colds and coughs. It is an excellent gargle in thrush or quinsy. In any disease where it is desirable to produce perspiration, Sage is a valuable remedy.

For Leucorrhea, Gonorrhea, Syphilis, Dysentery, Snake Bites.

SANICLE—*Sanicula Marilandica*, called also BLACK SNAKE ROOT.—Grows from two to three feet in height in forests, oak-timbered land and uncultivated fields. The blossoms are white, appear in June, and are succeeded by a small burr at the top of the stalk. The root consists of a number of small black fibers.

A decoction of the root, or whole plant, is useful in leucorrhea, gonorrhea, syphilis and dysentery. The root in poultice form makes an excellent application for snake bites and other poisonous wounds.

For Diseases of the Blood, Syphilitic Complaints, Chronic Rheumatism, Scrofula, Skin Affections, etc.

SARSAPARILLA (*wild*)—*Aralia Nudicaulis.*—For description of this plant, *see illustration*.

The roots in poultice are used for all kinds of wounds and ulcers, also for skin affections, erysipelas and ringworm. An infusion or decoction of the plant makes a good substitute for the foreign Sarsaparilla in all diseases of the blood, syphilitic complaints, chronic rheumatism, local pains, scrofula, skin affections, etc. Made into syrups and cordials it is useful in coughs, catarrhs and pains in the breast.

Note.—The root of the *Smilax Officinalis*, from which the Sarsaparilla of commerce is obtained, is a native of tropical America from the swampy forests of Mexico as far south as the northern part of Brazil. It is highly prized as a blood purifier.

For Rheumatic Complaints and Eruptive Diseases.

SASSAFRAS—*Laurus Sassafras.*—In the Northern States the Sassafras is shrubby, but in the Southern States it grows from 30 to 40 feet in height. The leaves, which are of various shapes, are green on the upper surface and whitish on the under. It has small yellow flowers. It grows in forests and along the borders of swamps. The dried root, which can be purchased at stores, is of a yellowish color, has a strong spicy smell and sweetish taste at first.

An infusion of the bark of the root is good in rheumatic complaints and eruptive diseases. It is made by infusing 1 or 2 ounces of the bark of the root in a quart of boiling water. This may be drank freely, according to circumstances. In cases of rheumatism, it must be continued for a long time to effect a cure. The pith of Sassafras put into rain water makes a very valuable eye water for inflammations of the eye.

For Menstrual Irregularities, Chronic Rheumatism.

SAVINE—*Juniperus Sabina.*—The stem of this plant rises from four to fifteen feet in height. Its branches are very large, and subdivided. The bark of the young branches is a light green; that of the trunk, reddish brown and rough. The fruit is a blackish purple berry, containing three seeds. The ends of the branches and the leaves are collected for medicinal use in the spring. They fade in color when dried.

It is a powerful and active medicine and heats and stimulates the whole system. It is held in high repute to produce determination of blood to the uterus and promote the menstrual discharges. It is also spoken highly of in chronic rheumatism where there exists a coldness of the surface, and especially of the lower extremities. Given in substance, the dose is from 2 to 5 grains three times a day. A decoction is prepared by boiling 1 ounce of the leaves in a pint of water down to half a pint and adding 2 ounces of syrup, of which the dose is a wineglassful three times a day.

For Wash in Eruptive and Skin Affections,

SCABISH—*Œnothera Biennis,* called also TREE PRIMROSE. —This plant is found in fields and along fences. It rises from two to five feet in height. The leaves are lance-shaped, quite broad at the base, and are minutely toothed and hairy. The blossoms are yellow and appear in July and August. They unfold at night and close in the daytime.

A decoction of the dried herb is used as a wash in tetter and other eruptive and skin affections.

For Cathartic Purposes.

SCAMMONY—*Scammonium Convolvulaceæ.*

Native of Syria, Asia Minor and Greece.

Properties.—The properties of Scammony are identical with Jalap (see A CHAPTER ON MEDICINES) with the exception that it is a little more irritating in its effects.

For Dropsy.

SCOTCH BROOM—*Spartium Scoparium.*—This plant is also cultivated in gardens. It grows from three to eight feet high, has very flexible branches and small, downy leaves. The flowers are of a golden yellow color, large and showy. The plant has a bitter, nauseous taste and, when bruised, a strong, peculiar odor. The tops of the branches and the seeds are used for medicinal purposes.

The Scotch Broom is employed to the best advantage in dropsical complaints. It is given in the form of decoction, made by boiling ½ ounce of the fresh tops in a pint of water down to ½ pint, of which 2 tablespoonfuls may be given every hour until it operates, either by stool or urine; or the seeds may be given in powder in the dose of from 10 to 15 grains.

For Tumors, Ulcers, Piles, Scrofulous Eruptions.

SCROFULA PLANT—*Scrophularia Nodosa*, called also Figwort.—This herb grows to a height of from three to seven feet. The leaves are opposite each other, are heart-shaped and notched at the edges. The flowers are small and of a dull purplish green or brown color. It has a very rank odor and a bitter taste.

The bruised leaves are highly esteemed as an application to painful tumors, ulcers, piles, skin eruptions, swollen breasts, etc. This plant has narcotic properties, but taken internally it produces nausea and vomiting before it becomes perniciously narcotic. The green leaves should be used when they can be obtained, or the leaves and roots may be dried and preserved and prepared for use by moistening them with warm water and bruising them. An ointment for external application is made by simmering the leaves in lard until they become crisp.

For Scurvy.

SCURVY GRASS—*Cochlearia Officinalis.*—This plant grows on the bank of streams. It reaches a height of about a foot, and has numerous tufts of flowers of a snow-white color. It has a warm, biting taste, and a rather unpleasant smell when bruised.

As the name indicates, it is a remedy for scurvy, for which purpose the expressed juice of the plant should be taken in the quantity of ½ to 1 pint a day, or the smaller leaves daily eaten as a salad.

SEAWEED.—(See *Iodine* in A Chapter on Medicines).

For Advanced Stages of Chronic Bronchitis and Pneumonia, Later Stages of Croup and Bronchitis in Children, Protracted Whooping Cough.

SENECA SNAKE ROOT—*Polygla Senega*, called also Mountain Flax, Milkwort, etc.—This plant is found growing in all the states of the Union. It rises to a height of from eight to ten inches. The leaves grow directly from the main stem, are long and narrow and of a light green color. The flowers are small, and grow in spikes at the top of the plant. The taste is sweet at first, but afterwards bitter, and provokes coughing and saliva. *See illustration.*

The Seneca Root is an energetic stimulant to the lungs, also an expectorant, and is a very valuable remedy in the advanced stages of chronic bronchitis, also in protracted whooping cough and the later stages of croup and bronchitis in infants and children. A dose of the pulverized root is from 5 to 10 grains. A decoction is made by adding an ounce of the bruised root to a pint of boiling water and simmering it in a closed vessel until the liquid is reduced to ⅓ of its original quantity, of which the dose is ½ wineglassful.

SENNA.—(See A CHAPTER ON MEDICINES).

For Scurvy, Tumors, Wens, Boils, Inflammations.

SHEEP SORREL—*Rumex Acetosa.*—A common, well known plant, usually found in old pastures and fields.

A decoction of it, freely used, is useful in scurvy and all inflammatory diseases. Poultices are also made of the leaves wrapped up and roasted, and these applied to tumors, wens, boils, inflammations, etc., will hasten the formation of pus. The leaves of the plant are often eaten for scurvy.

For Tonic and Nervine Uses.

SIDE-SADDLE PLANT—*Sarracenia Purpurea*, called also EVE'S CUP, WATER CUP, PITCHER PLANT, etc.—This plant generally grows in cold swamps where the ground is very wet and thickly covered with swamp moss. The leaves are oblong sacks which taper down to a short foot-stalk that connects them with the root. There are usually eight or ten of these leaves, and from the center of them a smooth stalk runs eight or ten inches in height and bears on its top a nodding purple flower.

The root, which is the part containing medicinal properties, is of a light red color and not so large around as the finger. It has both nervine and tonic properties. Given in infusion, the dose is from 1 to 2 tablespoonfuls. It has astringent properties and should not be taken in large doses.

For St. Vitus's Dance, Convulsions, Tremors, Nervous Affections.

SKULLCAP—*Scutellaria Lateriflora*, called also MAD WEED, HOODWORT, BLUE PIMPERNEL, etc.—This plant is found growing near water all over the United States. It has very little smell and a slightly bitterish taste. The root is yellow and fibrous. The stem grows from one to three feet high. The flowers are of a pale blue color and grow in long spikes.

The infusion is considered a valuable remedy in St. Vitus's dance, and is very useful in convulsions, tremors and nervous affections; also in lockjaw. The infusion may be drank freely.

For Asthma, Coughs, Catarrh.

SKUNK CABBAGE — *Ictodes Fœtida*, called also MEADOW CABBAGE, SWAMP CABBAGE, FETID HELLEBORE, etc. —Grows in boggy woods, swamps and other moist places throughout the United States. Its flowers are among the first that appear in the spring. It is stemless and somewhat resembles a cabbage head. *See illustration.*

A very useful remedy in asthma, especially in spasmodic asthma, in coughs, catarrhs, consumption, etc., also in the cough of old people. A dose of the powdered root is from 5 to 10 grains. A tincture or syrup may likewise be made from the root and seeds.

For Poultices, Drinks.

SLIPPERY ELM—*Ulmus Fulva.*—A native tree of North America.

As an external application, the bark in the form of a poultice is an excellent remedy for ulcers, tumors, gunshot wounds, chilblains, burns, skin diseases, erysipelas, felons, etc., and in sore mouth or thrush should be used as a wash. It makes a nutritious drink for consumptive patients and those who are recovering from illness.

For Suppressed Menstruation.

SMARTWEED—*Polygonum Punctatum*, called also BITING KNOT WEED, WATER PEPPER, etc.—This is a very common plant, known in every section of the country. It grows from one to two feet in height, is slender, smooth, branching and erect. The flowers are disposed in spikes, and are of a pale pink or white color. The plant itself is of a pale green.

This plant is used particularly in case of suppressed menstruation. It is a very successful remedy for such cases, it seldom being necessary to continue its use for more than six or seven days. It may be given in cold infusion. The plant should never be scalded, and long keeping also injures it. It is a perfectly safe medicine and may be taken freely until the desired effect is produced. Taken in the form of tincture, the dose is a teaspoonful two or three times daily; in the form of extract, from 5 to 8 grains may be given at a dose.

For Costiveness, Dyspepsia, Loss of Appetite, General Languor, Disorders of the Liver.

SNAKE HEAD—*Chelone Glabra*, called also BITTER HERB, BALMONY, FISH MOUTH, TURTLE BLOOM, etc.—This plant is found near the borders of streams or where the ground is wet. *See illustration.*

It is employed in costiveness, dyspepsia, loss of appetite, general languor or debility. It is a valuable medicine in disorders of the liver, and in jaundice it tends to remove the yellow tinge from the skin and eyes. A weak infusion of the leaves may be drank freely.

For Headache, Fresh Colds, etc.

SNEEZEWORT—*Helenium Autumnale*, called also FALSE SUNFLOWER, SNEEZEWEED, etc.—This is a native plant growing all over the country in moist locations. Its several stems rise from three to seven feet high, and both the stems and leaves are covered with short, dense growths of hair. The leaves are very much like cabbage leaves and are dotted by small pits. The flowers are of a golden yellow and are one or two inches in diameter. The disk or center is a greenish yellow, and the ray surrounding it bears from five to twenty leaves.

The whole plant may be reduced to a powder. The central parts of the flowers particularly are used as an errhine (snuff), a very small pinch of the powder causing prolonged sneezing.

It is used to relieve headache, the catarrhal condition of fresh colds, etc.

For Venereal and Scrofulous Affections and Skin Eruptions.

SOAPWORT—*Saponaria Officinalis*, called also BOUNCING BET.—This plant grows to a height of one or two feet, has smooth, lance-shaped leaves, and clusters of whitish or slightly purplish flowers which appear in July and August. The roots and leaves, which are the part employed as medicine, impart to water the property of forming a lather, the same as soap, which has given the plant its name.

It acts as an alterative, and is considered a valuable remedy in venereal and scrofulous affections and skin eruptions. The juice of the plant given in the quantity of ½ ounce in the course of a day is said to cure gonorrhea in about two weeks without any other remedy. It is also given in the form of decoction, made in the proportion of an ounce of the root to a pint of water, which may be taken freely.

For Female Weakness, Consumption, General Debility, Piles, Inflammations.

SOLOMON'S SEAL—*Convollaria Multiflora.*—Rises six or seven inches in height, has lance-shaped leaves of a dark green color, and flowers in clusters hanging to the sides of the stalks and producing red berries. Grows on the side of mountains and high banks.

The roots have an astringent property and are very useful in all cases of female weakness resulting in leucorrhea or immoderate flow of the menses. A syrup or cordial may be made of the roots of the Solomon's Seal and Comfrey combined which is very valuable in consumption and general debility. A poultice of the bruised roots is used for inflammations and piles.

For Worms, Skin Eruptions, Old Tumors, To promote Growth of Hair.

SOUTHERN WOOD—*Artemisia Abrotanum*, called also OLD MAN.—This plant is cultivated in gardens. It grows about three feet high and has small flowers of a grayish color which grow in close spikes, mixed with leaves, at the ends of the stems.

It is a species of wormwood, and is given to destroy worms, the dose being from 1 to 2 teaspoonfuls of the powder, given in molasses, morning and evening. It is also applied externally in ointment and fomentations for eruptions of the skin and hard tumors. Also to prevent hair from falling out and to cause it to grow. It may also be given in decoction and infusion.

For Dropsy.

SPANISH BROOM — *Spartium Junceum.* — Cultivated in gardens as an ornamental plant. The flowers are large, yellow, and have an agreeable odor.

The seeds of this plant may be used advantageously in dropsy. The dose for this purpose is from 10 to 15 grains, taken three times a day. They may also be given in tincture.

For Nausea, Vomiting, Gravel, Suppression of Urine.

SPEARMINT—*Mentha Viridis.*—The Spearmint is very similar to Peppermint in appearance and resembles it in its action. It is excellent to allay nausea and vomiting, and is also a valuable remedy in gravel and suppression of urine.

An infusion of this plant is made by bruising a handful of the herb in a quart of boiling water, and is useful to allay nausea and vomiting. A tincture may be made by bruising the green plant and adding Holland Gin. The dose of this preparation is a wineglassful, drank as often as the stomach will bear, and is a valuable remedy for gravelly affections, suppression of urine, etc. Cotton, saturated with this tincture and applied to piles, affords immediate relief.

For Tonic Purposes.

SPICE BUSH—*Laurus Benzoin.*—Grows from four to ten feet in height and is usually found in river bottoms and rich soils. The flowers, which are in clusters, appear before the leaves. Its berries are of an oval shape and are a shiny crimson color when ripe. All parts of the shrub have a spicy, agreeable flavor, particularly the bark and berries.

This plant makes a very pleasant tonic. It is given in fevers in the form of decoction, and is especially useful in intermittent fevers. The berries have been highly recommended as a stimulant in rheumatism. The dose as a tonic is from ½ to 1 teacupful of the infusion.

For Colds, Coughs, Asthma, Diseases of the Blood, Syphilis, Rheumatism, Dropsy.

SPIKENARD—*Aralia Racemosa*, called also SPIGNET, PETTYMORREL, PIGEON-WEED, etc.—Grows from two to five feet in height. Has a large root and a thick bark that is whitish on the inside. The main stalk is about the size of the thumb, is jointed and purplish. It has small, bluish flowers, and produces berries resembling elder berries.

An infusion or decoction of the roots and berries may be used in diseases of the blood, in syphilis, chronic rheumatism, etc. Made into a syrup by adding sugar, it is good in coughs, catarrh, pains in the chest and kindred complaints. Another manner of preparing it is to pour a pint of Brandy on the fresh berries, let them stand in a heated place for a week, and then add a pint of water and strain, of which the dose is a wineglassful three times a day. This makes an excellent remedy for languor, female debility and all pains in the stomach. A valuable poultice for the feet in general dropsy is made from the root combined with horseradish.

For Asthma, Incipient Consumption, Bronchitis.

SPINDLE BUSH—*Euonymus Atropurpureus*, called also INDIAN ARROW-WOOD.—A shrub growing from four to seven feet in height, having clusters of deep purple flowers, also bearing fruit in clusters of a bright red color about the size of a cherry which remains on the shrub nearly all winter.

It is beneficially used in diseases of the chest and lungs, in asthma, chronic inflammation of the bronchial tubes and incipient consumption. A strong decoction may be used, taken freely as the stomach will bear, or just sufficient to maintain moderate perspiration. Or a syrup may be made by boiling ½ pound of the bark of the root in a gallon of water down to a quart, straining and adding 2 pounds of sugar. Of the syrup the dose for an adult is from ½ to a wineglassful three or four times a day; and for children in proportion to their age.

SQUILLS.—(See A CHAPTER ON MEDICINES).

For Stomach Tonic, Female Complaints.

STARWORT—*Aletris Farinosa,* called also BLAZING STAR, FALSE ALOE, UNICORN ROOT, etc.—Grows in open fields and poor soils all over the United States. The root is a tuber lying nearly horizontal in the ground, with numerous fibers springing from its lower surface, and is of a very bitter taste. From six to twelve leaves of unequal lengths spring directly from the root and spread over the ground in the form of a star. The stem rises from one to two feet high and ends in a spike of small white flowers which blossom in June or July.

The root of this plant acts particularly as a tonic to the stomach, relieves colic, and is also very valuable in female complaints when attended with general debility—chlorosis, painful or suppressed menstruation, falling of the womb, etc. It is taken *in small doses only,* a tonic dose being from 4 to 15 grains. The root may be combined with Capsicum and orange peel in a Wine tincture; or another and perhaps better tincture is made by compounding it with Golden Seal, Prickly Ash and Seneca Snake Root. These tinctures should be given in small doses, about what the stomach will bear without producing nausea, dizziness or other unpleasant effects. An infusion of the root alone may be taken in the same way. (See DEVIL'S BIT).

For Syphilis, Gonorrhea, Gleet, Scrofula, Chronic Diseases of the Liver, Kidneys and Skin.

STILLINGIA—*Stillingia Sylvatica,* called also COCK-UP-HAT, QUEEN'S DELIGHT, YAW ROOT, etc.—This plant is usually found growing in dry, open woods. It has a large, thick, woody root and a light colored stem, which rises from two to three feet high. The leaves are oblong, taper somewhat at both ends, and are bordered with minute teeth. It bears a spike of yellow flowers. The plant when broken discharges a milky juice.

The bark of the fresh root is a valuable tonic, alterative and diuretic. Given in large doses it acts as a cathartic. It is much used in syphilis, gonorrhea, gleet, affections of the kidneys, scrofula, and chronic diseases of the liver and skin. Given in infusion or decoction, it should be combined with mucilaginous substances, as, for instance, Slippery Elm bark. A tincture may be prepared by macerating two ounces of the bark of the bruised root in a pint of Alcohol, the dose of which is a teaspoonful or more two or three times a day.

For Wounds, Sores, Cramps, Colic, Headache, Indigestion.

STONE ROOT—*Collinsonia Canadensis*, called also HORSE BALM, RICH WEED, KNOB ROOT, etc.—Found from Canada to Virginia. Grows from one to three feet in height. The root is hard and stonelike. Has numerous pale yellow flowers of a lemon scent. It habits rich woods.

It is used as a poultice and wash for wounds, sores, etc., and an infusion of the root is used in headaches, indigestion, cramps and colic, particularly in the colic that occurs after childbirth. Also highly spoken of in dropsy. In making the infusion, the root should be steeped in a covered dish.

For Diseases of the Bladder and Kidneys.

STRAWBERRY—*Fragaria Vesca.*—The Strawberry has many valuable medicinal properties. It is useful in diseases of the bladder and kidneys. Persons who suffer from any of these complaints should eat the fruit frequently when in season, and at other times use a syrup made from the berries.

For Wash for Inflamed and Ill-Conditioned Sores and Ulcers.

STRIPED MAPLE—*Acer Striatum*, called also WHISTLE WOOD, MOOSE WOOD, FALSE DOGWOOD, etc.—This is a small tree, attaining to the height of about fifteen feet and growing on cold timber lands. The bark is of a greenish stripe, and the leaves are large and of the form of those of the sugar maple.

A decoction of the bark of this tree is used as a wash for inflamed and ill-conditioned sores and ulcers. The fresh leaves are also applied in the form of draughts to reduce inflammations.

For Scrofulous and Venereal Diseases, Skin Eruptions, Gleet, Falling of Bowels and Womb, Kidney Derangements, Sore Throat.

SUMACH—*Rhus Glabra.*—A shrub growing from six to fourteen feet high, with a knotty stem usually much bent and divided into numerous branches; smooth, light-gray bark; reddish blossoms growing in spikes; leaves changing color to red in autumn; crimson berries growing in dense clusters. *See illustration.*

A decoction of the bark of the root makes an excellent injection or wash in venereal and scrofulous diseases and for falling of the bowels and womb. At the same time a decoction of the bark of the root together with Slippery Elm, White Pine and Blood Root may be taken freely; also valuable in gleet, eruptions of the skin, etc. An infusion of the berries sweetened with honey is used as a gargle in sore throat, or the infusion sweetened with loaf sugar may be given with advantage in diarrhea, dysentery and bowel complaints. Either the bark or the berries make an excellent poultice for ulcers and old sores. The decoction or fluid extract is also valuable in kidney derangements where there is suppression or incontinence of urine. From 10 to 30 drops of the fluid extract may be taken in a day.

For Diarrhea, Dyspepsia, Blood Purifier.

SWAMP SASSAFRAS—*Cornus Circinata*, called also Round-leaved Dogwood, Green Osier, etc.—A shrub with warty twigs and large, rounded leaves, woolly beneath. Grows in rich soil from Canada to the Carolinas and west to the Mississippi. It has white flowers growing in a thick cluster.

Much employed in the Northern States for diarrhea, dyspepsia, etc., but is too heating in fevers. Combined with Sarsaparilla, Burdock and Prince's Pine it forms an excellent blood purifier which is valuable in salt rheum, scrofula, cancerous humors and all skin diseases. Of the infusion of the bark, a wineglassful may be taken two or three times a day. The fresh leaves slightly bruised and wet with vinegar are an excellent application to a bruise or any inflamed part.

For Leucorrhea, Inflammations, Swellings.

SWEET CLOVER—*Melilotus Alba*, called also Melilot, King's Clover, etc.—There are two varieties of Sweet Clover, one bearing white and the other yellow blossoms. The odor resembles that of the Tonqua Bean. It frequently attains to a height of from four to six feet.

The leaves and flowers in decoction are useful in leucorrhea and coughs, but are more frequently applied as poultices, or made into ointments to allay inflammations and swellings.

For Colic, Diarrhea, Rheumatism.

SWEET FERN—*Comptonia Asplenifolia*, called also Sweet Bush.—This shrub grows on sterile and sandy soils from Canada as far south as Virginia. It has green flowers, which appear early in the spring before the leaves. The leaves, which are ten or twelve times as long as broad, are unequally notched on both edges. They have a strong, balsamic odor, which is increased by bruising, and a pungent taste.

The herb is a stimulant and astringent, and a decoction of the leaves is used to relieve colic and check diarrhea, and as a fomentation in rheumatism.

For Stomach Troubles, Wind Colic, Ague.

SWEET FLAG—*Acorus Calamus*, called also CALAMUS, FLAG ROOT, SWEET RUSH, etc.—Sweet flag is sometimes confounded with blue flag. The root of both is large, fleshy and horizontal, but while that of sweet flag is nearly round, that of blue flag is flattened at the top. The sweet flag root is also pinkish on the inside, has an agreeable odor and a pleasant taste; while blue flag root is grayish or brownish internally, has no particular odor, and is acrid and unpleasant to the taste. The sweet flag root is composed of a soft resin.

An infusion of the root is useful in disorders of the stomach, in flatulency, vertigo, dyspepsia, colic, etc., and a hot decoction is particularly good in wind colic. The tincture is beneficial in ague. An infusion for stomach troubles is made of 6 drachms of the bruised root to 12 ounces of boiling water, and in this form quickly relieves the distressing swelling of the abdomen in colic. The root is chewed by dyspeptics, and the juice swallowed when tonics are required.

For Strangury, Wasting Diseases of the Kidneys.

THIMBLE WEED—*Rudbeckia Lacinata*, called also CONE FLOWER, CONE DISK SUNFLOWER, etc.—This small plant is a native of this country and is very valuable in wasting diseases of the kidneys, being both diuretic and balsamic. Its properties were first learned by noticing its effect on a sheep that had lost the use of its hind legs. The animal daily dragged itself to this plant and ate of it, when, to the astonishment of all who noticed its situation, it recovered. By shepherds and herdsmen it has since been used with happy effects in strangury and similar diseases, taken freely in decoction.

For Asthma, Burns, Piles.

THORN APPLE, or STRAMONIUM—*Datura Stramonium*, called also STINK WEED, JAMESTOWN WEED, JIMSON WEED, etc.—Most commonly met with in old fields, along roads and old houses—never in woods and mountains. Bears a large white or bluish flower, and a thorny apple containing four cells, each of which is filled with black seeds. It is a strong poison, its action somewhat resembling that of Belladonna.

Smoking of the leaves mixed with tobacco is a popular remedy for asthma, but should be used with caution and the effects carefully noticed. An ointment of it is excellent for burns and piles, the claim being made that piles have been cured by rubbing the parts with the green leaves after each evacuation.

For Headache.

THYME—*Thymus Vulgaris*, called also MOTHER-OF-THYME, GARDEN THYME, etc.—Thyme is cultivated in gardens. The herb is cut while in bloom and dried for use as a domestic remedy.

It is used in the form of a warm infusion to promote perspiration, relieve headache, etc. Its principal use, however, is in liniments. By adding 1 pint of Oil of Thyme to 7 of Turpentine, or other means of adulteration, it forms the great bulk of the "Oil of Origanum" of commerce.

For Dropsy, Jaundice, Skin Eruptions.

TOAD FLAX—*Antirrhinum Linaria*, called also SNAP DRAGON, etc.—This herb grows from one to two feet high. Its leaves are very narrow, and the flowers are yellow and showy and grow in crowded spikes.

The herb should be collected when in flower, dried quickly and kept from the air. When fresh it has a heavy, disagreeable odor, but it loses this in a great measure by drying. It is used in dropsy, jaundice, and various eruptions of the skin. Given in infusion, it is especially valuable in skin diseases. An ointment made from it is much used in hemorrhoids.

For Spasmodic Cough, Asthma, Earache, External Application.

TOBACCO—*Nicotiana Tabacum.*—Tobacco has a powerful relaxing influence, but its active principle, Nicotine, is very poisonous, and makes it an unsafe remedy. *Nicotine is the second strongest poison known.*

The smoke of tobacco inhaled is a palliative of asthma, of the nervous cough provoked by tickling of the larynx, and is used in earache, etc. Tobacco was formerly much used for external applications, but if applied to broken surfaces symptoms of poisoning result, and it is now not much used as a remedy either externally or internally. It is the principal ingredient of TRASK'S OINTMENT. (See Index).

For Dysentery, Diarrhea, Amenorrhea, Leucorrhea, Palpitation of the Heart, Asthma, Apoplexy.

TREE OF HEAVEN—*Ailanthus.*

This tree, which grows to a height of from thirty to sixty feet, resembles an overgrown Staghorn Sumach. The wood is hard, heavy, and glossy like satin. The leaves are long and pointed. The flowers are small and of a greenish color, and are scattered along the stems. It is a native of China, but is now naturalized in this country.

The bark has been employed both dry and fresh as a remedy for dysentery, diarrhea, and as an injection in amenorrhea and leucorrhea. The tincture is used in doses of from 5 to 30 drops in palpitation of the heart, asthma and apoplexy.

For Tonic Purposes, Syphilitic Affections.

TURKEY CORN—*Corydalis Formosa.*—This is an early spring plant, sometimes making its appearance in March. The root is tuberous, the stem is from eight to ten inches high, and the flower stem bears a nodding, many-flowered cluster.

It promotes digestion and acts as a tonic, and is also used as an alterative in syphilitic affections. For this purpose a thorough purgative should first be given, and then followed with an infusion of this plant, which is made by adding from 2 to 4 teaspoonfuls of the plant to a pint of boiling water and taking the quantity in twenty-four hours, dividing the doses as the stomach will retain it. The ulcers should be washed several times daily with a decoction of the same, and the body bathed every night with an alkaline bath (water to which soda has been added).

For Chronic Rheumatism and Secondary Forms of Syphilis.

TWIN LEAF—*Jeffersonia Diphylla,* called also YELLOW ROOT, GROUND SQUIRREL PEA, etc.—Grows chiefly near streams and rivers, and is abundant in many parts of the Western States. It has a large, yellowish, fibrous root. Its leaves rise on long foot-stalks directly from the root. They are smooth, oval, and grow in twos, hence the name. The flower stem bears a single white flower, resembling that of the Blood Root. It blossoms in April. The root, which is the part used, has a biting, disagreeable taste.

It is usually given in the form of decoction, which is prepared by adding a pint of water to ½ ounce of the bruised root, boiling for fifteen or twenty minutes and straining. The dose is from ½ to a wineglassful three times a day. It is given in chronic rheumatism and the secondary forms of syphilis

For Stone in the Bladder or Kidneys, Incontinence of Urine, Painful Urination, Strangury, etc.

UVA URSI—*Arbutus Uva Ursi,* called also BEARBERRY, MOUNTAIN BOX, RED BERRY, etc.—The roots are creeping and slender. The stems spread over the ground, the young shoots tending upward. The leaves are variable in shape, some narrow and some broad. The flowers are of a flesh color and grow in small clusters, from six to twelve together. It has berries of a scarlet color, mealy and insipid to the taste and containing five seeds.

A powder or decoction of this plant may be used, the dose being from 5 to 25 grains of the powder or a wineglassful of the decoction three or four times a day. It is a tonic and astringent. It is valuable in all chronic disorders of the urinary passages—stone in the bladder or kidneys, incontinence of urine, painful urination, strangury, etc. It has also been used with advantage in chronic bronchitis and diarrhea, in leucorrhea and hemorrhage from the uterus. Inasmuch as these affections are all of a chronic nature, its use should be long continued. When used to increase the action of the kidneys in acute attacks, too frequent doses may prove unsatisfactory by reason of its irritating properties.

For Nervous and Hysterical Conditions.

VALERIAN—*Valeriana Officinale.*

Native of Europe from the Mediterranean northward.

Properties.—Valerian is not a cure, but is a palliative for nervous or hysterical conditions. It has been much used in the treatment of epilepsy. It will lessen the paroxysms of whooping cough, and has been successfully used for the relief of dysmenorrhea and diabetes insipidus. Its odor makes it unpleasant to use, and other remedies have largely taken its place on that account. The most pleasant preparation, and the one with the least odor, is the Elixir of Valerianate of Ammonia.

Dose.—Of the Elixir, 1 teaspoonful every three or four hours, or according to conditions.

For Colds, Early Stages of Fever, Fever and Ague, etc.

VERVAIN—*Verbena Hastata,* called also BLUE VERVAIN and SIMPLER'S JOY.—The blue Vervain grows commonly along roadsides. The root is woody and fibrous, and the stem, which is somewhat hairy, rises to a height of three or four feet. The leaves are narrow, rough, sharp at the point, and edged with sharp teeth. The flowers are blue or purplish and grow thickly upon slender spikes. They come out a few at a time from July to September.

A decoction of this plant produces nausea. From 1 to 2 teacupfuls will operate as an emetic (cause vomiting), for which purpose it is generally used. After the stomach has been thoroughly cleansed, however, nausea is not produced by it. It also produces perspiration, and may be given with benefit in severe colds, also in the early stages of fever where the stomach is much disordered. It is used in cases of fever and ague, the decoction being given as an emetic just as the paroxysm is coming on. A strong tea made of Vervain, sweetened with molasses and taken in tablespoonful doses once in thirty minutes to an hour is an excellent remedy in coughs.

For Debility, Worms, Venereal Diseases, Chronic Skin Diseases, etc.

VINE MAPLE — *Menispermeum Canadense*, called also YELLOW PARILLA, MOONSEED, etc.—This is a woody vine, usually found in moist land near streams, growing from three to six feet in length and twining around whatever it comes in contact with. The root is long, yellow and woody. The leaves somewhat resemble the maple leaf.

The root is a pleasant bitter tonic and laxative. It strengthens the nervous system, is useful in all cases of debility, especially the shattered condition resulting from syphilitic diseases, and is very good for worms. It also gives tone to the digestive organs and is serviceable in dyspepsia. It may be used in the form of a strong decoction or syrup, and may at the same time be applied externally. Of the syrup the dose is a wineglassful five or six times daily.

For Snake Bites, Bilious Complaints, Fevers, Colds.

VIRGINIA SNAKE ROOT—*Aristolochia Serpentaria.*— The root of this plant is knotted, brown, and very fibrous, the fibers being of a yellow color when fresh. The stems are slender, weak, jointed, and bear from three to seven leaves and from one to three flowers. The leaves are heart-shaped at the base, sharp at the end, and of a pale green color. The flowers are reddish or purplish. The seed capsule has six cells and contains many small seeds. The root has an agreeable, penetrating smell, and a warm, bitterish taste. It is the part used in medicine.

It first became known as a remedy against snake bites, having been used by the Indians for that purpose. It is now given in bilious complaints, fevers, colds, and in states requiring a stimulative action. It greatly increases the perspiration. In bilious complaints it checks vomiting and is soothing to the stomach. A dose of the powdered root is from 10 to 20 grains, which may be gradually increased to 30 grains or ½ teaspoonful. An infusion is prepared by adding 4 teaspoonfuls of the powdered root to a pint of water, of which from 2 to 4 tablespoonfuls may be given every four hours.

For Itch, Dropsy, Rheumatism, Gout, Syphilis.

VIRGIN'S BOWER — *Clematis Virginica,* called also Traveller's Joy.—This plant is a native of the United States. It grows from fifteen to twenty feet in height and blossoms in July.

The fresh bark, leaves and blossoms will cause blisters on the skin, and act as a corrosive poison when taken internally. The dried leaves in weak infusion have been used with advantage in cases of dropsy following intermittent fever, also in chronic rheumatism, syphilis and gout, and an application of an infusion or ointment of the leaves in oil will cure itch, for which purpose it is much used by the peasantry of Europe.

For Ulcers, Putrid and Spongy Gums, Scurvy, Skin Diseases.

WATER DOCK—*Rumex Aquaticus.*—A native of marshes. Rises about five feet in height and has narrow, pointed leaves nearly two feet long. The flowers are yellow and blossom thickly in spikes.

A decoction of this plant is especially used as a wash for foul ulcers and for putrid and spongy gums. It should be taken internally at the same time, drinking a small quantity of the decoction daily. Also good in scurvy and skin diseases. The dose usually given is a decoction of ½ ounce of the fresh roots in 1 pint of water.

For Irritability of the Stomach, Nausea and Vomiting.

WHITE COHOSH—*Actæa Alba,* called also Necklace Weed, White Beads, etc.—This plant very closely resembles Black Cohosh in appearance, but the berries are white instead of black, which distinguishes it from the other variety.

The medicinal properties of the two plants (see Black Cohosh) are nearly identical. The seeds of the White Cohosh, given in repeated doses of from 10 to 15 grains, are considered a specific for irritability of the stomach, nausea and vomiting, especially that of females arising from uterine troubles.

For Gangrenous Ulcers, Falling of the Womb and Bowels, Leucor-rhea.

WHITE OAK—*Quercus Alba*.—This tree rises from fifty to sixty feet in height, and has a cone-shaped fruit (acorns) surrounded at the base by a rough shell.

The bark of the Oak is very astringent, and especially so with the White Oak. The bark of the young branches is probably the best. It is used externally in the form of decoction, as a wash in gangrenous ulcers, or as an injection in falling of the womb or of the bowels, or in leucorrhea. A decoction of grated acorns, or roasted acorns mixed with cocoa or chocolate, is used as a remedy for diarrhea, flatulent dyspepsia and scrofula.

For Gonorrhea, Leucorrhea, Boils, Scrofulous Sores, Lockjaw, White Swellings, etc.

WHITE POND LILY—*Nymphæa Odorata*, called also Sweet Water Lily, Toad Lily, Water Cabbage, etc.— Found in ponds, ditches and rivers all over the country. The flowers shut at night. The seeds ripen in water. The perfume is similar to that of the magnolia. The roots of this plant are thick, notched and of a blackish color, and are the part chiefly used in medicine. They are useful in diarrhea, dysentery, and all complaints of the bowels; also in gonorrhea, leucorrhea and scrofula.

A dose of the powdered root is from ¼ to ½ teaspoonful taken in warm water; or a pint of the expressed juice of the root, to which is added ½ pint of Port Wine and 4 ounces of sugar, makes a better preparation, of which from 2 to 4 tablespoonfuls may be taken four times a day. Externally the roots and leaves are used for poultices in boils, scrofulous sores, lockjaw and inflamed skin. When employed as a poultice for white swellings, it is usually combined with Cohosh root and Slippery Elm bark. This poultice should be changed three times a day, the patient taking at the same time some blood purifying medicine. The fresh juice of the root, mixed with lemon juice, is said to be a good cosmetic and to remove pimples and freckles. A decoction of the leaves makes a good wash for old sores, ulcers and fresh wounds. It is also used as a gargle in putrid sore throat and asthma, and is a valuable wash for inflamed eyes.

For Dyspepsia, Dysentery, Chronic Rheumatism, Hysteria, etc.

WHITE POPLAR—*Liriodendron Tulipifera*, called also Tulip Tree, Whitewood, etc.—This tree is a native of the United States, growing sometimes to a height of over 100 feet.

It is allied to the Magnolia. It blossoms about the middle of May, the flowers being tulip-shaped, and of a greenish yellow color striped with orange red. These are followed by a cone-shaped fruit.

In dyspeptic states of the stomach and bowels this is an excellent remedy; also in low fevers, dysentery, chronic rheumatism, and, combined with a small quantity of Laudanum, is a certain, speedy and effectual remedy in hysteria. The bark of the root and trunk are both used. That of the root is more tonic and less stimulant than that of the trunk. A dose of the powdered bark is from ¼ to ½ teaspoonful. An infusion is made by adding from 2 to 4 tablespoonfuls of the bark to a pint of boiling water, of which the dose is 2 tablespoonfuls. The leaves were used by the Cherokee Indians in poultices for sores and headaches, and in ointment for inflammations and mortifications.

For Nervous Diseases, Pleurisies, Convulsions.

WHITE SNAKE ROOT—*Eupatorium Ageratoides,* called also WHITE SANICLE, POOL ROOT, etc.—This plant grows abundantly in nearly every part of the United States, rising from one to three or four feet in height and bearing a white flower. It has a white, fibrous root, which is the part used in medicine. For this purpose it should be collected in September or October. The stalk is furrowed, the branches are in opposite pairs, and the leaves, which are on long foot-stalks, are about the size of large apple-tree leaves.

It is used in the form of infusion and decoction, prepared by pouring a pint of boiling water on an ounce of the bruised root, of which from 1 tablespoonful to half a teacupful may be taken at a dose. It is a nervine and, taken to a sufficient extent, will overcome irritability of the nervous system. It also promotes freedom of expectoration and breathing in affections of the lungs, and is valuable in pleurisies and in diseases generally attended with nervous irritation and convulsions.

For Ailments of the Digestive Tract.

WILD CHERRY—*Prunus Virginiana,* called also BLACK CHERRY, RUM CHERRY, CABINET CHERRY, etc.— In open fields the limbs of this tree spread out into an elegant top, but in forests it often runs up to sixty feet or more in height with a few crowded branches. The flowers are white and grow along the stems from six to eight inches long. The fruit is black, with a bitter, astringent taste, similar to that of peach kernels.

The bark is the part used, that of the root being much better than that of the trunk of the tree. It should never be boiled, but is taken in the form of a cold infusion, which is made by adding cold water to the bark and letting it stand for forty-eight hours, an average dose being a wineglassful three or four times a day. It is particularly recommended in intermittent fevers, also in consumption. It is also excellent in dysentery, chronic diarrhea, colics, debility, dyspepsia, and most ailments of the digestive tract.

For Use Externally in Inflammations bordering upon Gangrene, Syphilitic Ulcers, etc.

WILD INDIGO—*Baptisia Tinctoria,* called also INDIGO WEED, HORSE-FLY WEED, YELLOW BROOM, etc. The root consists of a short, knotty head, two or three inches broad, with several long branches from its under surface. It is blackish on the outside and yellowish on the inside. The stems grow two or three feet high, are round and smooth and of a yellowish green color with black dots. The branches are thin and have small leaves of a bluish green color with a light green stripe on the midrif. The flowers are a bright yellow and come out in loose spikes at the end of the branches. They are succeeded by an oblong pod of a bluish black color, containing a row of small, rattling seeds. It blossoms in July and August, and the whole plant, even the flowers, often becomes black in the fall. It is usually found in dry, sandy soil, and grows more abundantly near the eastern coast. It is a native of Canada and the United States.

The outer layer of the bark is the part used. It is a general stimulant, and is used in decoction in protracted fevers, notably typhus or typhoid. Applied externally, it makes excellent poultices in inflammations bordering upon gangrene. Also good in syphilitic ulcers and malignant and ulcerous sore mouth and throat, sore nipples, chronic sore eyes, etc., in which case it is made into a strong decoction and used as a wash, or as a poultice, or made into an ointment with lard or cream. The decoction taken internally is made by adding an ounce of the fresh root to a pint of boiling water, of which the dose is a tablespoonful every three or four hours.

For Liver Derangements and Pulmonary Consumption.

WILD SUCCORY—*Cichorium Intybus,* called also ENDIVE. —This plant grows wild, and is found in neighborhoods which have long been settled. It grows one or two feet high, and has beautiful blue flowers which appear in July and August. The whole plant has a bitter taste, which is strongest in the root and weakest in the flower.

It is usually given in decoction, prepared by boiling one or two ounces of the root or a handful of the herb in a pint of water. It is useful in jaundice, and in congestion or obstruction of the liver in the early stages. The expressed juice taken in large doses, frequently repeated, has been found beneficial in pulmonary consumption and various other complaints.

For Bilious Colic.

WILD YAM—*Dioscorea Villosa*, called also COLIC ROOT.— This plant is a climber that is found growing in thickets in moist localities as far south as Florida and west as the Mississippi. The leaves are nearly smooth above, and downy beneath. The fruit is a triangular winged capsule that grows in pendant bunches. The root, which is of a pale yellowish brown color, is repeatedly forked and breaks with difficulty. It is the part used in medicine, and in Virginia is known as " Rheumatism Root."

Yam root is believed to have "a special action on the liver," and a celebrated botanic physician made secret use of it for many years as a remedy for bilious colic. For this purpose a decoction is made by pouring a pint of boiling water on 2 ounces of the bruised root, simmering it slowly for half an hour and straining, of which the dose is ½ teacupful every twenty minutes, as warm as the patient can bear it, until relief is obtained. It seldom fails to produce a beneficial effect within an hour after it has been taken. The application of a large Mustard plaster over the abdomen assists its action.

For Rheumatism, Neuralgia, Asthma, etc.

WINTERGREEN—*Gaultheria Procumbens*, called also MOUNTAIN TEA, TEA BERRY, etc.—This is a little evergreen with which nearly every one is familiar.

A tea may be made of the green plant, or the essence or oil may be purchased. The tea is used to relieve asthma, also to restore strength and promote menstruation. The oil contains Salicylic Acid and is used in rheumatism, also sometimes employed in neuralgia. A dose of the oil is from 5 to 10 drops every three to six hours, gradually increased until there is a ringing in the ears. The plant is a stimulant, restorative, cordial, and possesses antiseptic properties.

For Ulcers, Piles, Tumors, External Inflammations, Inflamed Eyes, Hemorrhages, Prolapse.

WITCH HAZEL—*Hamamelis Virginica.*—A shrub, rising from six to ten feet in height and blossoming in winter. The blossoms, which do not come out until the leaves fall, remain on from October to February, and the fruit, which is similar to a hazlenut, remains on until the next fall and then explodes, scattering the seeds about. Found in the damp woods of Canada and the United States,

The bark in the form of a poultice is applied externally to ulcers, piles, painful tumors of all kinds and external inflammations; a poultice made of the inner bark is excellent in treating inflammation of the eyes; an infusion of the leaves is a useful astringent in hemorrhages, and a strong decoction is used as an injection for falling of the womb or bowels. The extract is employed for many purposes. An excellent remedy in many cases of diarrhea, typhoid fever and other unhealthy conditions of the bowels, is made by adding 2 ounces of the extract to 1 ounce of Aromatic Sulphuric Acid, of which the dose is a teaspoonful every three or four hours, according to the severity of the case. Its value lies in its antiseptic and astringent properties.

For Inflamed Conditions of the Bladder and Kidneys, Fevers, Piles, etc.

WOOD SORREL — *Oxalis Acetosella*, called also SOUR TREFOIL, CUCKOO BREAD, etc. Found in mountain regions in the northern part of this country. The roots are white, juicy and creeping. The leaves grow on long, slender, hairy stems. The flowers are white with purple veins.

The leaves are used in decoction, and may be given freely in inflamed conditions of the bladder, urethra and kidneys, also in fevers, piles and putrid diseases.

For Worms.

WORMSEED—*Chenopodium Anthelminticum*, called also WORMSEED-GOOSEFOOT, STINKING WEED, etc.—Grows in all parts of the United States, rises from two to five feet in height, has leaves dotted beneath and small flowers of a yellowish green color. The whole plant has a strong, disagreeable odor.

It is used to expel worms from the intestines, for which purpose it must be given in small doses, repeated. From 5 to 10 drops of the oil mixed with sugar is a dose for a child. From ½ to 1 teaspoonful of the powdered herb and seed, united with powdered Peppermint, may be given to a child two or three years of age. In either form it should be given night and morning before eating for two or three days, and the last dose followed with a brisk cathartic.

For Tonic Purposes.

WORMWOOD — *Artemisia Absinthium.*—This plant is cultivated in gardens, or may be found growing wild in stony places. The stem is covered with a whitish down. The leaves are whitish on both sides. The flowers are small, yellowish, and form a long, pyramidal cluster. It has a strong smell and a bitter, spicy taste.

Wormwood is a valuable stimulant and tonic. In moderate doses it promotes the appetite and digestion, quickens the circulation and gives tone to the whole system. It is given in all cases requiring a tonic—in dyspepsia, suppressed menstruation, chronic leucorrhea and obstinate diarrhea and also as a vermifuge (to destroy worms). It has been given with advantage in nervous affections, such as epilepsy, hysteria, severe neuralgia and St. Vitus's dance. A dose of the powder is from ⅛ to ¼ teaspoonful. An infusion is made by adding an ounce of the herb to a pint of cold water, of which the dose is from 1 to 2 tablespoonfuls. It is also used externally as a fomentation for bruises and inflammations generally.

For Piles, Sores, Hemorrhages, Dysentery, Diarrhea, etc.

YARROW — *Achillea Millefolium*, called also MILFOIL, THOUSAND LEAF, etc.—This plant rises to a height of from 12 to 18 inches, and is distinguished by its double-winged leaves and leaflets, which are minutely divided and subdivided. Its flowers form a thick, flat bunch, and are white or rose colored. The whole plant has an agreeable taste and smell. It should be gathered when in bloom.

Milfoil is a general stimulant and tonic, and is especially valuable in relaxed conditions of the pelvic organs due to debility, giving rise to piles, leucorrhea, menorrhagia, amenorrhea, etc. Also good in dyspepsia and flatulent colic due to the same cause. The infusion is made by adding ½ ounce of the herb to 6 ounces of water and reducing by heat to 3 ounces, of which the dose is a tablespoonful every hour. The expressed juice may be taken in doses of 2 to 4 tablespoonfuls three times a day. The oil may be given in 20-drop doses.

For Blood Diseases, Bilious Diseases, Fevers, Skin Diseases, etc.

YELLOW DOCK—*Rumex Crispus*, called also NARROW-LEAF DOCK, GARDEN PATIENCE, SOUR DOCK, CURLED DOCK, etc. Grows from two to five feet in height. The leaves are long and curl in waves at the edges. The flowers are small and greenish and grow thickly on long stems. It has a large, spindle-shaped root, brownish yellow on the outside and yellow within. It grows abundantly in cultivated ground, also in damp places. Found in wet land, however, the root is white and woody and not fit for use.

Yellow Dock is a very old remedy, and it is said there is scarcely any disease where it may not be taken with advantage. A decoction of the root is found useful in dyspepsia and gouty tendencies, in bilious complaints, scrofula, syphilis, and all forms of scaly eruptions of the skin. In case of fever it will allay the internal heat and promote a moisture upon the surface. It is a gentle laxative and purifies the blood. The decoction is also considered beneficial in the case of cancers. An ointment of the powdered root and lard will cure the itch, and this ointment may also be used on cancers, tumors, etc. Sometimes the powdered root is stirred up with cream and applied in a paste. The root in powder makes an excellent dentifrice, especially where the gums are spongy. Of the decoction a tumblerful may be taken three times a day with safety, although it would be advisable to begin taking it in smaller quantities. Of the pulverized root 10 grains may be taken at a dose. The decoction may be made into a syrup if desired.

For Stomach Tonic, Worms.

YERBA BUENA—*Micromeria Douglasii.*

Native of Pacific Coast of America.

Properties.—It is a nervine, tonic and stimulant. In Chili the natives use it as a tea, drinking it the same as we do tea and coffee. It allays nausea and spasmodic pains in the stomach and bowels, and will lessen the force and frequency of the pulse in fevers. It is also adapted to the expulsion of round worms in children.

Dose.—From ½ to 1 teaspoonful of the fluid extract.

For Asthma, Bronchitis, Consumption, etc.

YERBA SANTA—*Eriodictyon Glutinosum*, called also Bear's Weed, Consumptive Weed, Mountain Balm, etc.

Native of California.

Properties.—This herb is a valuable remedy in all diseases of the respiratory organs. It may be smoked, as tobacco; the smoke inhaled gives relief in asthma; or the fluid extract in doses of ¼ to ½ teaspoonful affords relief in that disease. The natives esteem the tea a cure for consumption; hence one of its common names. It is valuable in consumption, chronic bronchitis, pneumonia and catarrh of the stomach, also chronic derangement of the kidneys. It possesses a resinous principle that has a soothing and alterative effect on mucous surfaces. It will soon relieve a cough, decrease the expectoration, and improve the appetite and the power to digest and assimilate food.

Dose.—Of the fluid extract, from ¼ to 1 teaspoonful. There are also a number of proprietary preparations of this herb.

Taken in the form of *Malto-Yerbine*, it is a specific for most cases of cough following influenza. This is a standard preparation and may be had at any drug store.

TIME TO GATHER AND METHOD OF DRYING.

The time to gather herbs is just as they begin to flower, as they possess the highest degree of medicinal properties at this time.

They should be dried in the shade. The best way is to hang them, tops down, in a corncrib or other airy place. If dried in the sun, they become too crisp, the leaves falling off, thereby losing the best part of the plant. Again, in drying in the sun they are liable to mould unless spread out. When perfectly dry, put them into paper bags, or else wrap well in paper to keep them from the air, and store in a dry place.

The time to gather roots is in the fall, after the leaves are dead; or, better, in the spring before the sap rises.

Barks should be gathered in the fall or early in the spring.

Berries or fruits may be spread thinly on papers on the floor in an unused room.

Department VI.

MISCELLANEOUS RECEIPTS.

ONE HUNDRED
VALUABLE PATENT AND SECRET PREPARATIONS.

In the following pages are given formulæ, or receipts for making, 100 of the best known patent medicines, face creams and lotions, etc., etc., any one of which preparations can be put up at a fraction of its cost bought under the manufacturer's label. These formulæ have been secured by analysis at great cost, and are substantially correct.

ALLEN'S LUNG BALSAM.

Blood Root, Tincture of	2	ounces,
Lobelia, Tincture of	2	"
Opium, Tincture of	1	"
Capsicum, Tincture of	3	drachms
Sassafras, Essence of	2	"
Anise, Essence of	2	"
New Orleans Molasses	1	pint.

Bring the syrup to a boil, add slowly the other ingredients and mix thoroughly.

ANTI-FAT.

Anti-Fat is the fluid extract of Bladder Wrack, or Seaweed. It is prepared from the fresh plant, 7½ pounds being used to make 40 ounces of the extract, with equal parts of Alcohol and water.

AYER'S CHERRY PECTORAL.

Acetate Morphine	3	grains.
Blood Root, Tincture of	2	drachms.
Antimony, Wine of	3	"
Ipecac, Wine of	3	"
Wild Cherry, Syrup of	3	ounces.

Mix together.

AYER'S HAIR VIGOR.

Lead, Sugar of	3	drachms.
Sulphur, Flower of	2	"
Glycerine	14	"
Water	5	pints.

AYER'S SARSAPARILLA.

Sarsaparilla, Fluid Extract of	3	ounces.
Stillingia, Fluid Extract of	3	"
Yellow Dock, Fluid Extract of	2	"
May Apple, Fluid Extract of	2	"
Sugar	1	"
Potash, Iodide of	90	grains.
Iron, Iodide of	10	"

Mix together.

BALM OF A THOUSAND FLOWERS.

Deodorized Alcohol	1	pint.
Bar Soap, nice and white	4	ounces.

Shave the soap when putting it in, let it stand in a warm place until dissolved, and then add the following:

Citronella, Oil of	1	drachm.
Neroli, Oil of	½	"
Rosemary, Oil of	½	"

BARREL'S INDIAN LINIMENT.

Alcohol	1	quart.
Capsicum, Tincture of	1	drachm.
Origanum, Oil of	½	ounces.
Sassafras, Oil of	½	"
Pennyroyal, Oil of	½	"
Hemlock, Oil of	½	"

Mix all together.

BAY RUM.

French Proof Spirit	1	pint.
Bay, Extract of	6	drachms.

Mix, and color with Caramel. Needs no filtering.

BEECHAM'S PILLS.

Saffron	1	grain.
Sodium, Sulphate of	1	"
Rhubarb	4	"
Aloes	20	"

Mix, and make into 3-grain pills.

"BIG G" INJECTION.

Berberine, Hydrochlorate of	15	grains.
Zinc, Acetate of	15	"
Glycerine	½	ounce.
Water enough to make	8	"

BLACK OIL LINIMENT.

Alcohol	2	ounces.
Arnica, Tincture of	2	"
British Oil	2	"
Oil of Tar	2	"

Mix together in a pitcher and slowly add

Sulphuric Acid	½	"

This will be found very useful as a liniment in cases where there is inflammation.

BORDET'S HAIR TONIC.

Carbolic Acid	30	drops.
Cardamon, Tincture of	30	"
Nux Vomica, Tincture of	2	drachms.
Cinchona, Compound, Tincture of	1	"
Cologne Water	1	"
Cocoanut Oil, enough to make	4	ounces.

BOSCHEE'S GERMAN SYRUP.

Tar, Oil of	1	drachm.
Ipecac, Fluid Extract of	½	ounce.
Wild Cherry, Fluid Extract of	6	drachms.
Opium, Tincture of	4	"
Magnesia, Carbonate of	3	"
Water	6	ounces.
White Sugar	10	"

Triturate the Magnesia first with the Oil of Tar, add the fluid extracts, mix thoroughly, then add the Tincture of Opium and water. Filter and form a solution with the sugar by shaking the bottle.

BRANDRETH'S PILLS.

Aloes	2	drachms.
Colocynth, Extract of	20	grains.
Gamboge	1	drachm.
Castile Soap	½	"
Peppermint, Oil of	2	drops.
Cinnamon, Oil of	1	drop.

Add a little Gum Arabic and a few drops of water, mix thoroughly and divide into 80 pills.

THE BRINKERHOFF SYSTEM.

Traveling "doctors" are too well known to need any introduction. A few years ago they claimed to possess secret methods for the successful treatment of many diseases, and even now there are those who claim to be specialists in the treatment of tapeworm and cancer. However, the so-called "secret methods" are secrets no longer, for with the advance of modern medicine the chemist has analyzed almost every preparation extant, and to-day the remedies applied by the traveling "doctor" are well understood. In justice to him, it may be said that occasionally some system of treatment possessed real merit. Not long ago the "Brinkerhoff's Secret Pile Remedy" was heralded throughout the country as the only sure cure for piles, and for a time the proprietors met with wonderful success—from a financial standpoint. Below we give the Brinkerhoff system in detail:

Brinkerhoff's Secret Pile Remedy.

Carbolic Acid	1	ounce.
Sweet Oil	5	"
Chloride of Zinc	8	grains.

Mix, and inject into the largest pile 8 drops; into the medium sized piles, from 4 to 6 drops; and into the small ones, from 2 to 3 drops; into club-shaped piles near the orifice, 2 drops.

He directs hot sitz baths for those cases where violent pains follow the injections. He also recommends an interval of from two to four weeks between each injection.

Brinkerhoff's Celebrated Ulcer Specific.

Distilled Extract of Witch Hazel.........	5 drachms.
Liquor of Subsulphate of Iron.................	1 "
Carbolic Acid Crystals..........................	2 grains.
Glycerine...................................	2 drachms.

Mix, and for fistula *in ano* inject 10 to 15 drops deep into the fistula, and press the track of the fistula with the fingers to force the fluid more deeply in.

In cases of recent ulcer, he gives the following treatment:

To 1½ ounces of water add ½ teaspoonful of the Ulcer Specific and ½ teaspoonful of starch, and inject into the rectum every night. Sometimes he recommends an injection of starch into the rectum in the morning after the bowels have moved.

The Brinkerhoff System as applied to fissures:

Once or twice a month as the "doctor" goes around on his circuit he inserts a small speculum, cleans out the ulcer and applies to it a solution of Nitrate of Silver—40 grains to the ounce. Between applications the patient uses a morning and evening treatment himself. Each morning he is to evacuate the bowels, then inject the rectum with lukewarm water, and finally insert into it a little ointment consisting of the following:

Carbolic Acid.......................................	3	grains.
Sulphur	8	"
Vaseline...	1	ounce.

or Lard may be used in place of Vaseline. For the evening treatment he uses the ulcer remedy containing the distilled Extract of Witch Hazel already given. Add ½ teaspoonful of this to the same quantity of starch and about 3 tablespoonfuls of water, and inject into the rectum every evening. In treating polypus, Brinkerhoff directs his patients to tie the pedicle close to the wall of the bowel with a waxed saddler's silk thread, then if the pedicle is long enough, to snip it off outside the knot; if it is short, to let it alone and it will fall off. Put the patient to bed, give something to constipate the bowels for three or four days, and then give a mild cathartic.

BROWN'S BRONCHIAL TROCHES.

Licorice, Extract of, pulverized...............	1	pound.
Sugar, pulverized.....................................	1½	"
Cubebs, pulverized.................................	4	ounces.
Gum Arabic, pulverized...........................	4	"
Conium, Extract of, pulverized...............	1	"

Mix.

BUCKLEN'S ARNICA SALVE.

Arnica, Extract of............................	1	ounce.
Resin Cerate.................................... ..	8	"
Vaseline	2	"
Seedless Raisins.................................	8	"
Fine-Cut Tobacco............................... ..	½	"
Water..	a sufficient quantity.

Boil the raisins and tobacco in 1 pint of water until the strength is extracted, press out the liquid and evaporate to 4 ounces. Soften the extract of Arnica with a little hot water and mix the liquid with it. Add this to the Cerate and Vaseline, previously warmed, and mix all thoroughly.

BULL'S COUGH SYRUP.

Morphine, Sulphate of	¾	grain.
Granulated Sugar	2	drachms.
Table Syrup	3	ounces.

Mix together.

CAMPHOR ICE.

Spermaceti	1½	ounces.
Gum Camphor	¾	"
Sweet Almonds, Oil of	4	teaspoonfuls.

Set this on the stove in an earthen vessel, heating it just enough to dissolve it. Then put into moulds and cover with tinfoil. This is used for chapped hands, lips, etc.

CARTER'S LITTLE LIVER PILLS.

Podophyllin	1½	grains.
Ground Aloes	3½	"

Gum Arabic, Mucilage of, enough to make a soft mass.

Divide into 12 pills and coat with sugar. Take at bedtime one or more as needed.

CASTORIA.

Senna	4	drachms.
Manna	1	ounce.
Rochelle Salts	1	"
Fennel Seed, bruised	1½	drachms.
Boiling Water	8	ounces.
Sugar	8	"

Oil of Wintergreen enough to flavor.

Pour the water on the ingredients. Cover and macerate until cool, strain and add the sugar, dissolve by agitation, and add Oil of Wintergreen to flavor.

CHAMBERLAIN'S COLIC, CHOLERA AND DIARRHEA REMEDY.

Capsicum, Tincture of	20	drachms.
Camphor, Tincture of	16	"
Guaiac, Tincture of	12	"

Mix together.

CHAMBERLAIN'S RELIEF.

Capsicum, Tincture of	1	ounce.
Camphor, Spirits of	¾	"
Guaiac, Tincture of,	¼	'
Color Tincture. to make	2	"

Mix together.

The color tincture is merely a solution kept in drug stores for the purpose of coloring mixtures.

COD LIVER OIL EMULSION.

Anæmic patients, those who have consumption or any form of wasting disease and wish to take Cod Liver Oil, will find the following preparation a most suitable one. It contains 50 per cent of Oil, and 50 per cent is all that is claimed for any preparation of this kind. It also contains Phosphate of Lime freshly precipitated. The Phosphate of Lime is made from Phosphate of Soda and Chloride of Lime, or Chloride of Calcium. In mixing the Phosphate of Soda and Chloride of Lime in water, the compounds are broken up and reunite, with the result that we have Chloride of Soda and Phosphate of Lime. Chloride of Soda is common salt, and remains dissolved in the water, while the Phosphate of Lime is precipitated. The Lime can be placed on a coarse filter, such as druggists use, and water poured over it, and as it passes through it will drain the salt and leave the Phosphate of Lime pure and fresh. This is the best preparation of the kind that can be had. It is made as follows:

Phosphate of Soda	12	ounces.
Chloride of Calcium	1	"

Dissolve separately in 1 or 2 pints of water; the amount is not particular. Then mix, stirring briskly while mixing, and filter as directed above. Dissolve 8 ounces of Gum Arabic in 24 ounces of water and add slowly 2 pints of Cod Liver Oil. Stir the solution of Gum Arabic with an egg-beater while adding the oil. If thoroughly mixed, these will make a perfect emulsion; the oil will not separate. Now add the Phosphate of Lime gradually and stir as above. Add a few drops of Cinnamon Oil or other flavoring to suit.

Dose.—One or 2 tablespoonfuls three or four times a day.

COKE DANDRUFF CURE.

The following is the formula of the Coke Dandruff Cure, so widely advertised throughout the country:

Resorcin	4	drachms.
Alcohol	4	ounces.
Water	4	ounces.

Mix all together and apply two or three times a week, rubbing the scalp lightly but for some time, with each application. Color, if desired.

CUTICURA OINTMENT.

The much advertised Cuticura Ointment has been found to consist of a base of Petroleum Jelly, colored green, perfumed with Oil of Bergamot and containing two per cent of Carbolic Acid, or 9 drops to the ounce.

CUTICURA RESOLVENT.

Aloes, pure	1	drachm.
Rhubarb, powdered	1	"
Iodide Potass	36	grains.
Whiskey	1	pint.

Macerate over night and filter.

DAVIS' (PERRY) PAIN KILLER.

Gum Myrrh	1	ounce.
Capsicum, powdered	2	drachms.
Gum Opium	1½	"
Gum Benzoin	1	"
Gum Guiac	½	"
Gum Camphor	2	"

Digest these ingredients in 1 pint of Alcohol for two weeks and filter.

ELY'S CREAM BALM.

Ely's Cream Balm is a catarrh remedy that is well known and for years has been sold throughout the country. The well-known *Kilmer's Modern Pharmacy* gives the following as the formula:

Thymol	3	grains.
Carbonate Bismuth	15	"
Oil Wintergreen	2	drops.
Vaseline	1	ounce.

ESPEY'S CREAM.

Cydonium	1½	drachms.
Boric Acid	4	grains.
Glycerine	2	ounces.
Alcohol	3	"
Carbolic Acid	10	drops.
Cologne water	2	drachms.
Rosewater	1	pint.

Dissolve the Boric Acid in 4 ounces of Rosewater, macerate the Cydonium in the solution for three hours, press through straining cloth, and add Glycerine, Alcohol, Cologne and sufficient Rosewater to make 1 pint. Lastly add the Carbolic Acid and shake well.

FAHNESTOCK'S VERMIFUGE.

Castor Oil	1	ounce.
Wormseed, Oil of	1	"
Anise, Oil of	½	'
Myrrh, Tincture of	½	drachm.
Turpentine, Oil of	10	drops.

Mix.

FELLOWS' HYPOPHOSPHITES.

Glucose (Grape Sugar)	1	pound.
Simple Syrup	1	pint.
Calcium, Hypophosphites of	128	grains.
Potash, Hypophosphites of	48	"
Iron, Sulphate of	48	"
Magnesia, Sulphate of	32	'
Strychnine, Sulphate of	2	'
Quinine, Sulphate of	14	'
Water		

Dissolve the Calcium and Potassium hypophosphites in 2 ounces of warm water. Add to 1 ounce of water 3 drachms of the Syrup, and dissolve in the mixture, by the aid of heat, the remainder of the sulphates. Mix the solutions and set by a few hours, covered, to deposit the Sulphate of Calcium which is formed. Filter into a bottle containing the remainder of the Syrup, wash the residue with an ounce of boiling water, and mix filtrate and washings with the Syrup. Dissolve the Glucose in the mixture, and add through the filter enough water to make 2 pints. The formula would be improved by substituting for the Glucose a refined extract of Malt like that prepared by Gehe in Germany.

FROSTILLA.

This is a preparation for chapped hands that is widely known throughout the country. The formula is as follows:

Quince Seed	1	drachm.
Glycerine	6	ounces.
Deodorized Alcohol	5	"
Water	21	"

Add the Quince Seed to warm water, let stand until it becomes quite thick, strain carefully and add the Glycerine and deodorized Alcohol. Perfume to suit.

This is a most satisfactory preparation, and will please all who use it.

GARGLING OIL.

Crude Petroleum	13	ounces.
Ammonia Water	6	"
Soft Soap	16	"
Benzine	16	"
Amber, Crude Oil of	2	"
Iodine, Tincture of	1	"
Water	5	pints.

Mix the Petroleum and Soap, add the Ammonia Water Oil of Amber and Tincture of Iodine, and mix thoroughly. Then add the Benzine and finally the water.

"GOLD CURE" FOR DRUNKENNESS.

We give below two systems of treatment. The first is that given by the well known Keeley Institute, the second is Dr. Wherrell's method. The two methods were recently investigated by two commissions appointed by the United States Government, and in each case Dr. Wherrell's was adopted and used in the National Military Home at Dayton, Ohio, where over one thousand old soldiers were cured. Perhaps people have heard more about the Keeley method because it was among the earlier used, and also because it has been more widely advertised; yet when analyzed, the Purge method, the Bromide method, Keeley method, Wherrell and various other methods used in sanitariums, are all one and the same. Any one taking either of the following "cures" must have an earnest desire to be cured, for experience has proven that the man who does not feel the necessity of a cure will not be benefited by the remedy.

The Keeley Cure.—

Gentian, Tincture of	2	ounces.
Columbo, Tincture of	2	'
Cinchona, Tincture of	2	"
Salicin	2	drachms.

Dissolve the Salicin in 4 ounces of boiling water and add to the tinctures. The dose is 1 teaspoonful every two hours, and should be taken with regularity for four or five weeks.

The Wherrell Treatment.—

Quassia, Tincture of	2	ounces.
Cinchona Compound, Tincture of	2	"
Hydrastis, Tincture of	2	"

Mix together and take a teaspoonful in water every three hours.

Either of these forms of treatment is a specific for the drink habit, and will effect a cure in nearly every instance where the patient desires to lead a sober life. Either remedy will antagonize and eliminate the alcohol from the system, and restore the brain to the natural condition so that there will be no desire for alcoholic stimulants. Either remedy must be taken regularly, and, if necessary, some one of the family or a nurse should see that the directions are fully carried out. Either of these remedies are for home treatment for patients who cannot spare the time to take such treatment at the institute. The bitter taste cannot be disguised. Neither remedy should be given without the full consent of the patient, for, as already stated, experience has proven that if the patient does not give his full consent and show an earnest desire to be cured, the treatment should not be undertaken. There will be no bad effects from taking these remedies according to directions, as the ingredients are harmless; on the contrary, they build up the nervous system and add strength and vigor to the whole body.

There are exceptional cases where, in addition to either of the remedies given, the injection method may also be needed. The injection consists of Chloride of Gold and Sodium, $\frac{1}{16}$ grain, and Apomorphine, $\frac{1}{15}$ to $\frac{1}{8}$ grain, for each injection. The injection is given under the skin with a hypodermic needle once or twice a day.

GOOD SAMARITAN COUGH SYRUP.

Muriate of Morphine	1	grain.
Cherry-Laurel Water	1	drachm.
Simple Syrup	2	ounces.

Mix. Take from 1 to 2 teaspoonfuls once or twice daily.

GOOD SAMARITAN LINIMENT.

Sassafras, Oil of	1	ounce.
Hemlock, Oil of	1	"
Turpentine, Spirits of	1	"
Capsicum, Tincture of	1	"
Opium, Tincture of	1	"
Myrrh, Tincture of	4	"
Origanum, Oil of	2	"
Wintergreen, Oil of	4	drachms.
Gum Camphor	2	ounces.
Chloroform	1½	"
Alcohol	4	pints.

Mix.

GREEN MOUNTAIN SALVE.

Resin	10	ounces.
Burgundy Pitch	4	drachms.
Beeswax	4	"
Mutton Tallow	4	"
Oil Hemlock	1	"
Balsam Fir	1	"
Oil Origanum	1	"
Oil Red Cedar	1	"
Venice Turpentine	1	"
Oil Wormwood	½	"
Verdigris, powdered	1	"

Melt the first articles together and add the oils. Rub up the Verdigris with a little oil, put it in with the other articles, stir well, and then put the basin containing the mixture into a larger vessel of cold water, and work with the hands until cold enough to roll.

GREENE'S NERVURA.

Cinchona, Tincture of	5	ounces.
Damiana, Tincture of	5	"
Coca, Tincture of	5	"

Mix.

GREEN'S AUGUST FLOWER.

Rhubarb	360	grains.
Golden Seal	90	"
Cape Aloes	16	"
Peppermint Leaves	120	"
Potash, Carbonate of	120	"
Capsicum	5	"
Sugar	5	ounces
Alcohol	3	"
Water	10	"
Peppermint, Essence of	20	drops.

Powder the drugs and macerate in the mixed Alcohol and water for seven days; filter, and add enough diluted Alcohol to make the whole measure one pint.

HAIR'S (W. B.) ASTHMA CURE.

Potash, Iodide of	1	ounce.
Tar Water	1	pint.
Caramel, about	30	grains.

Caramel is burnt sugar. Put the sugar on a hot stove and burn it until it is a dark brown.

Another.—

Tar, Wine of	14	ounces.
Potash, Iodide of	220	grains.

HAIR RESTORATIVES, LEAD IN.

There is a popular impression that the continued use of hair restoratives leads to paralysis. In the light of the facts below it is not strange that lead paralysis is caused by these preparations.

The following is taken from the report of Prof. C. F. Chandler to the New York Board of Health:

Mrs. S. A. Allen's World's Hair Restorer.

One fluid ounce contains:
Lead in solution............................ .... 5.26 grains.
Lead in the sediment.............................. 0.31 "

Hall's Vegetable Sicilian Hair Renewer.

One fluid ounce contains:
Lead in solution.......................... 6.45 grains.
Lead in the sediment.............................. 0.68 "

Ayer's Hair Vigor.

One fluid ounce contains:
Lead in solution.................................. 2.81 grains.
Lead in the sediment.............................. 0.08 "

Hoyt's Hiawatha Hair Restorative.—This is an Ammoniacal solution of Nitrate of Silver, containing 4.76 grains of the Nitrate to one fluid ounce. It contains no other metals.

Clark's Distilled Restorative for the Hair.

This preparation contains in one fluid ounce:
Lead in solution.................................. 0.11 grains.

L. Knittel's Indian Hair Tonic.

One fluid ounce contains:
Lead in solution.................................. 5.16 grains.
Lead in the sediment.............................. 1.13 "

Chevalier's Life for the Hair.

One fluid ounce contains:
Lead in solution.................................. 0.22 grains.
Lead in the sediment.............................. 0.80 "

Pearson & Co.'s Circassian Hair Rejuvenator.

One fluid ounce contains:
Lead in solution.................................. 1.40 grains.
Lead in the sediment.............................. 1.31 "

HALL'S CATARRH CURE.

Gentian Root, powdered........................ 1¼ ounces.
Orange Peel, powdered......................... 5 drachms.
Cardamom Seeds....................................100 grains.
Potash, Iodide of.................................. 1 ounce.
Alcohol ....
Water...................................... ....

Macerate the crude drugs in 12 ounces of diluted Alcohol for 48 hours, then transfer to a percolator and allow it to percolate slowly. When the liquid has ceased to percolate, pass enough menstruum through the percolator to make the finished product measure 16 ounces. In this dissolve the Potassium Iodide.

HALL'S HAIR RENEWER.

Precipitated Sulphur	1	drachm.
Lead, Sugar of	1	'
Common Salt	2	"
Glycerine	8	ounces.
Bay Rum	2	"
Jamaica Rum	4	"
Water	1	pint.

Mix together.

HARLEM OIL.

Sulphur	2	ounces.
Linseed Oil	1	lb.
Amber, Oil of	2	ounces.

Boil the Sulphur and Linseed Oil on a slow fire until the Sulphur is dissolved, then remove from the fire and, when the mixture has somewhat cooled take the Oil of Amber and enough Oil of Turpentine to bring the preparation to the consistence of molasses.

HOP BITTERS.

Hops, Tincture of	½	ounce.
Buchu, Tincture of	3	drachms.
Senega, Tincture of	3	"
Podophyllin (dissolved in Spirits of Wine)	10	grains.
Cochineal, Tincture of	20	drops.
Distilled Water sufficient to make	1	pint.

Mix.

HOSTETTER'S BITTERS.

Sugar	1	ounce.
Sweet Flag Root	1	"
Orange Peel	1	"
Peruvian Bark	1	"
Gentian Root	1	"
Columbo Root	1	"
Rhubarb	2	drachms.
Cinnamon	1	"
Cloves	½	"
Diluted Alcohol	1	pint.

HUNYADI JANOS WATER.

Lime, Sulphate of	72	grains.
Glauber Salts	2½	ounces.
Epsom Salts	2½	"
Potash, Sulphate of	6	grains.
Water	8	pints.

Mix together, and charge with gas if desired.

Dose.—One-half glassful more or less. This is an active cathartic and may be taken when needed.

INJECTION BROU.

Tincture Catechu (1 in 16)	1	drachm.
Cocaine Muriate	10	grains.
Lead Acetate	10	"
Zinc Sulphate	10	"
Water	6¾	ounces.
Alcohol	½	'

Dissolve the mineral salts (the Lead and Zinc) each in ½ ounce of water and mix them. Dilute the Tincture Catechu with 4 ounces of water. Add the minerals to the Catechu, then dilute the Cocaine Muriate in an ounce of water and add that. Lastly add the Alcohol and water.

If it is desired to color this the same as the Injection Brou, a small amount of Magenta may be added.

JAYNE'S EXPECTORANT.

Syrup Squills	2	ounces.
Tolu, Tincture of	1½	"
Camphor, Tincture of	1	drachm.
Digitalis, Tincture of	1	"
Opium, Tincture of	2	"
Wine Ipecac	2	"
Tartar Emetic	2	grains.

Mix.

KENNEDY'S MEDICAL DISCOVERY.

Bitter Root	4	drachms.
Sneezewort	1	ounce.

Mix and add:

Boiling Water	8	ounces.
Alcohol	5	"
Water	5	"
Licorice Root	½	"

Mix all together and let stand for two days, and add:

White Sugar	4	ounces.
Wintergreen, Tincture of	1	"

KING'S NEW DISCOVERY.

Morphine, Sulphate of	8	grains.
Ipecac, Fluid Extract of	½	drachm.
Chloroform	60	drops.
White Pine, Tincture of	2	ounces.
Water	7	"
Magnesia, Carbonate of	¼	"
Sugar	14	"

Rub the Magnesia with 1 ounce of the sugar in a mortar and triturate (stir rapidly) with the tincture of White Pine and the fluid extract of Ipecac; gradually add the water, and triturate with the mixture in the mortar. Filter, and dissolve the Morphia Sulphate in the filtrate. Mix the Chloroform with the rest of the sugar in a bottle and add the liquor above. Keep in a tight vessel.

LIEBIG'S CORN CURE.

Indian Hemp, Extract of	5	grains.
Salicylic Acid	30	"
Collodion	½	ounce.

Mix until dissolved. Apply with a camel hair pencil or brush four consecutive nights and mornings to form a thick coating. The Collodion protects the corn from irritation and rubbing, the extract of Indian Hemp acts as an anodyne, and the Salicylic Acid dissolves and disintegrates the corn.

LYDIA PINKHAM'S VEGETABLE COMPOUND.

Cramp Bark	4	ounces.
Partridge Berry Vine	4	"
Poplar Bark	2	"
Unicorn Root	2	"
Cassia	2	"
Beth Root	1½	"
Sugar	1½	pounds.
Alcohol	1	pint.
Water, a sufficient quantity.		

The drugs should all be reduced to a moderately coarse powder (what druggists call "Number 40"). Pour on boiling water, let stand until cold, then percolate with water until the percolate measures 5 pints, add the sugar, bring to a boil, remove from the fire and, when cold, add the Alcohol and strain.

Dose.—One or 2 teaspoonfuls of this may be taken three or four times a day.

LYON'S KATHAIRON.

Castor Oil	1	ounce.
Cantharides, Tincture of	1	drachm.
Bergamot, Oil of	20	drops.
Ammonia, Stronger Water of	1	"
Alcohol enough to make	3	ounces.

MADAME RUPPERT'S FACE BLEACH.

Corrosive Sublimate	1	grain.
Benzoin, Tincture of	7	"
Water	1	ounce.

Mix.

MALVINA CREAM.

"Warranted to remove freckles, beautify the complexion and preserve the smoothness of the skin." Used in conjunction with Malvina Lotion.

Saxoline	265	grains.
White Wax	50	"
Spermaceti	30	"
Bismuth Oxychloride	40	"
Mercuric Chloride	½	"
Rose, Spirits of (4 drachms of Oil to 1 pint)	20	drops.
Almonds, Bitter Oil of	$\frac{1}{10}$	"

Warm the Saxoline, White Wax and Spermaceti together until melted. While cooling, incorporate the Bismuth Oxychloride and the Mercuric Chloride, this last previously dissolved in a little Alcohol, and when nearly cool stir in the perfumes.

MALVINA LOTION.

"This lotion should be used as directed with the Malvina Cream, as it is of great importance in the cure of freckles, pimples, moth patches, liver mole, ringworm and salt rheum. It straightens wrinkles in the face, speeds the circulation of the blood, and cleanses and softens the skin to youthful freshness.''

Almonds, Oil of	2	drachms.
Rosewater	1	Pint.
Gum Arabic, best quality (dissolved in a little of the Rosewater)	4	drachms.
Corrosive Sublimate	2	grains.
Zinc, Oxide of	3	drachms.

MAGNETIC PAIN KILLER.

Laudanum	1	drachm.
Gum Camphor	4	"
Cloves, Oil of	½	"
Lavender, Oil of	1	"

Mix and add

Alcohol	1	ounce.
Sulphuric Ether	6	drachms.
Chloroform	5	'

Apply with lint; or for toothache, rub on the gums or upon the face against the gums.

MICAJAH'S MEDICATED UTERINE WAFERS.

Corrosive Sublimate	$\frac{1}{16}$	grain.
Zinc, Sulphate of	5	"
Bismuth, Subnitrate of	15	"
Gum Arabic	5	"
Carbolic Acid	3	"

Enough water to form a mass and make into suppositories. Each suppository contains the above amount.

ORANGE BLOSSOM.

Zinc, Sulphate of	1	drachm.
Alum	15	grains.
Cocoa Butter	3	drachms.
White Wax	½	"
Sweet Almonds, Oil of	1½	"
Henbane, Extract of	1	grain.

PAINE'S CELERY COMPOUND.

Celery Seed	2	ounces.
Red Cinchona	1	"
Orange Peel	¼	"
Coriander Seed	¼	"
Lemon Peel	¼	"
Hydrochloric Acid	15	drops.
Alcohol	5	ounces.
Glycerine	3	"
Water	4	"
Syrup	4	"

Grind the solids to No. 40 powder, mix the acid and the water, add the Glycerine and Alcohol, and in the menstruum so prepared macerate the powder for twenty-four hours; then percolate, adding enough water and Alcohol in the proportion to make 12 fluid ounces. Finally add the syrup and, if necessary, filter.

PERUNA.

Copaiba	6	drachms.
Cubebs	2	"
Calisaya Bark, ground	2	ounces.
Stone Root (Collinsonia) ground	2	"
Corydalis (Turkey Corn) ground	2	"
Deodorized Alcohol	1	pint.

Add all the ingredients to the Alcohol. Let stand one week. Shake the bottle frequently, and finally strain through several thicknesses of muslin, or filter through filtering paper, which may be obtained at any drug store. Sweeten and flavor to taste.

PETTIT'S EYE SALVE.

Olive Oil	4	drachms.
Spermaceti	1½	"
White Wax	½	"

Melt together and add gradually in a warm mortar the following in fine powder and thoroughly mix, stirring briskly while adding:

Zinc, Oxide of	30	grains.
White Precipitate	20	"
Benzoic Acid	2	"
Morphine, Sulphate of	¾	"
Rosemary, Oil of	½	"

Stir until cool, and preserve in a well covered vessel.

PIERCE'S FAVORITE PRESCRIPTION.

Savin	150	grains.
Cinchona	150	"
Agaric	75	"
Cinnamon	75	"
Water sufficient to make a decoction of....	8	ounces.

To this add the following:

Acacia	150	grains.
Sugar	75	"
Digitalis, Tincture of	½	drachm.
Opium	½	"
Anise, Oil of	8	drops.

Dissolve the gum and sugar in the strained decoction, and add the following:

Alcohol (in which the oil has previously been dissolved)	2	ounces.

PIERCE'S GOLDEN MEDICAL DISCOVERY.

Cinchona, Fluid Extract of	16	ounces.
Columbo, Fluid Extract of	4	"
Guaiac, Fluid Extract of	8	"
Licorice, Fluid Extract of	4	"
Opium, Tincture of	1	"
Podophyllin (resinoid)	120	grains.
Glycerine	6	pints.
Alcohol enough to dissolve the Podophyl- lin.		

Mix all together.

Dose.—One teaspoonful from two to four times a day.

PIMPLE LOTION.

Carbolic Acid	1	drachm.
Borax	4	"
Glycerine	2	ounces.
Tannin	2	drachms.
Alcohol	3	ounces.
Rosewater	10	"

Mix and dissolve. Apply night and morning.

PINK PILLS FOR PALE PEOPLE.

Iron, pure Sulphate of	½	ounce.
Potash, Carbonate of	140	grains.
Sugar	48	"
Tragacanth in fine powder	16	"
Glycerine	10	drops.
Water enough to make a mass.		

Mix all thoroughly and divide into 150 pills.
Coat with pink colored sugar.

PISO'S CURE FOR CONSUMPTION.

Tolu, Tincture of	½	ounce.
Lobelia, Fluid Extract of	2	drachms.
Indian Hemp, Fluid Extract of	2	"
Chloroform	1	"
Morphine, Sulphate of	4	grains.
Tartar Emetic	4	"
Water	8	ounces.
Sugar	14	"
Spearmint, Essence of	10	drops.

RADAM'S MICROBE KILLER.

Sulphurous Acid, U. S. P.	4	ounces.
Commercial Sulphuric Acid	½	ounce.
Muriatic Acid	from 2 to 10	drops.
Any kind of red wine	1	ounce.
Water enough to make	1	gallon.

Mix.

RADWAY'S READY RELIEF.

Soap Liniment	1½	ounces.
Capsicum, Tincture of	½	"
Ammonia, Water of	½	"
Alcohol	½	"

Mix.

RANSOM'S HIVE SYRUP AND TOLU.

Squills, Fluid Extract of	2	drachms.
Senega, Fluid Extract of	2	"
Tolu, Soluble Essence of	2	"
Tartar Emetic	4	grains.
White Sugar	4	ounces.
Water enough to make	4	"

It is readily prepared by rubbing the Tartar Emetic and sugar well together, adding the fluid extracts and essence of Tolu, and then enough water to make, after short slight heating and straining, 4 fluid ounces. Each fluid ounce of the syrup contains 1 grain of Tartar Emetic.

THE FAMOUS "RECAMIER" REMEDIES.

Recamier Moth and Freckle Lotion contains Corrosive Sublimate in Almond paste or emulsion with water. It is sold for $1.50. (Probable cost from ten to twenty cents.—PUB.)— *Boston Journal of Health.*

Recamier Powder contains Arrowroot and Oxide of Zinc. It is put up in a pasteboard box, and is sold for $1.00. Its cost is about *five cents.*—*Boston Journal of Health.*

Recamier Balm comes in a cheap glass flask, tied with a bit of ribbon and filled with water. It contains a white powder— the Oxide of Zinc—and Corrosive Sublimate. This preparation is sold for $1.50. To make it costs at most *ten cents.*—*Boston Journal of Health.*

Recamier Cream.—

Zinc, Oxide of...	2	ounces.
Glycerine..	6½	drachms.
Water	1	"
Rose, Spirits of (4 drachms to pint)..........	1	"

Triturate together until a perfectly homogeneous mass results.

SAGE'S CATARRH REMEDY.

Golden Seal, powdered...........................	1	ounce.
Borax, powdered....................................	10	grains.
Common Salt	10	"
Cyanuret of Iron	sufficient to color.	

Mix.

SANFORD'S RADICAL CURE OF CATARRH.

This consists of a distilled extract of Witch Hazel containing a little Alcohol and Glycerine, perhaps as much as 5 per cent of the latter and between 10 and 15 per cent of the former. Also an important constituent is Morphine. The "solvent" consists mostly of Nitre and Bicarbonate of Soda, with a small quantity of the yellow powder, insoluble or sparingly soluble in water, probably a vegetable powder.

SCHENCK'S PULMONIC SYRUP.

Wormwood..	½	ounce.
Catnip...	½	"
Tansy..	½	"
Hyssop	½	"
Horehound...	½	"
Hops...	½	"
Chamomile...	½	"
Comfrey	½	"
Senega..	½	"
Elecampane..	½	"

Boil with sufficient water to make, after straining, 1 quart. Then add:

Gum Arabic.................................. .... 1½ ounces.
Licorice .... 1½ "

Then add one good sized Indian Turnip, and finally add:

Sugar.. 3 pounds.
Brandy.. ½ pint.

And the juice of two lemons.

SEIDLITZ POWDERS.

Rochelle Salts.. 2 drachms.
Soda, Bicarbonate of............................. 2 scruples.
Tartaric Acid .... 35 grains.

Mix the Salts and Soda together and put in a blue paper; then put the Tartaric Acid in a white paper. When using, put the powder contained in the blue paper in about a half glass of water, then add the Tartaric Acid contained in the white paper, and drink quickly while effervescing. A little loaf sugar may also be added, if desired.

SEVEN BARKS.

Hydrangea, Extract of......................... 1 drachm.
Poke Root, " " .... 1½ ounces.
Culver's Root, " " .... 1½ "
Dandelion, " " .... 1½ "
Ladies' Slipper, " " .... 1½ "
Colocynth " " .... 1½ "
Bloodroot, " " .... 6 drachms.
Blue Flag, " " .... 6 "
Stone Root, " " .... 6¾ "
Golden Seal, " " .... 7½ "
Mandrake, " " .... 3 ounces.
Black Cohosh, " " .... 3 "
Butternut, " " .... 6 "
Spirits of Sea Salt .... 2 "
Aloes .... 10 drachms.
Borate of Sodium................................ 2 ounces.
Capsicum, Infusion of.......................... 4½ drachms.
Sassafras, powdered .... 11 "
Ginger .... 6 "
Syrup.. 1¼ quarts.
Water, sufficient to make..................... 3 "

SEVEN SUTHERLAND SISTERS' HAIR GROWER.

Distilled Extract of Witch Hazel............. 9 ounces.
Bay Rum .... 7 "
Common Salt.. 1 drachm.
Hydrochloric (Muriatic) Acid................. 1 drop.

Mix the Bay Rum and distilled Extract of Witch Hazel, add ½ ounce Carbonate of Magnesia and shake thoroughly, filter, add the salt and let it dissolve, and then add the Hydrochloric Acid. The agitation with the Magnesia causes the preparation to assume a yellow color, but by rendering it very slightly acid with 1 drop of Hydrochloric Acid, this color all disappears.

SHILOH'S CONSUMPTION CURE.

Morphine, Muriate of	3	grains.
Muriatic Acid	3	drops.
Henbane, Fluid Extract of	2	drachms.
Ginger, Fluid Extract of	3	"
Wild Cherry, Fluid Extract of	3	"
Alcohol	1½	"
Water	1½	"
Chloroform	1	"
Peppermint, Essence of	30	drops.
Tar, Syrup of	3	ounces.
Simple Syrup enough to make	8	"

SMITH BROS.' COUGH DROPS.

Average weight of each drop	36.5	grains.
Sugar (and glucose in small quantities)	35.5	"
Charcoal, powdered	.80	"

Licorice in small quantities.

Highly flavored with Oil of Sassafras with a little Oil of Anise added.

SOZODONT.

Castile Soap	75	grains.
Glycerine	75	"
Alcohol	1	ounce.
Water	5	drachms.
Peppermint, Oil of	sufficient quantity.	
Cloves, Oil of	"	"
Anise, Oil of	"	"
Cinnamon, Oil of	"	"

SQUIBB'S DIARRHEA MIXTURE.

Opium, Tincture of	1	ounce.
Capsicum, Tincture of	1	"
Camphor, Spirits of	1	"
Chloroform, purified	180	drops.
Alcohol enough to make	5	ounces.

Mix together.

Dose.—From 15 to 30 drops.

ST. JACOB'S OIL.

Gum Camphor	¼	ounce.
Chloral Hydrate	¼	"
Chloroform	¼	"
Sulphuric Ether	¼	"
Opium, Tincture of	1	drachm.
Origanum, Oil of	1	"
Sassafras, Oil of	1	"
Alcohol	1	pint.

STUART'S DYSPEPSIA TABLETS.

Each tablet contains the following:

Common Baking Soda	10	grains.
Morphine	$\frac{1}{10}$	"

"SUN" CHOLERA CURE.

Capsicum Tincture of	1	ounce.
Opium, Tincture of	1	"
Rhubarb, powdered	1	"
Peppermint, Essence of	1	"
Camphor, Spirits of	1	"

Mix—Dose: From 15 to 30 drops.

SWAIM'S VERMIFUGE.

Wormseed	2	ounces.
Valerian	1½	"
Rhubarb	1½	"
Pink Root	1½	"
White Agaric	1½	"

Boil in sufficient water to yield 3 quarts of decoction, and add:

Tansy, Oil of	30	drops.
Cloves, Oil of	45	"

Dissolve the Oils in a quart of rectified spirits.

Dose.—One tablespoonful at night.

SWIFT'S SYPHILITIC SPECIFIC.

Old Man's Gray Beard Root	1	peck.
Prickly Ash Root	4	ounces.
White Sumac Root	2	"
Red Sumac Root	2	"
Sarsaparilla Root	2½	"
Copper, Sulphate of	2	drachms.

Bruise the Gray Beard and Sumac roots, and put them with the Sarsaparilla into an iron pot sufficient to hold 2 gallons of water, or cover the roots completely with the water. Cover the pot with pine tops, and boil slowly until the liquid assumes the color of ink. Strain while warm, add the Sulphate of Copper and good Holland Gin sufficient to prevent fermentation.

Dose.—One wineglassful four times a day. Strictly abstain from horseback riding, butter or very greasy food, and all kinds of spirits or fermented liquors. The chancre must be treated in the usual manner.

SYRUP OF FIGS.

Senna Leaves	1¾	ounces.
Coriander Seed	6	drachms.
Figs	3	ounces.
Tamarind	2	"
Cinnamon Bark	2	"
Prunes	1½	"
Licorice, Extract of	1½	drachms.
Peppermint, Essence of	1½	"
Simple Syrup	1	pint.

THOMPSON'S EYE WATER.

Zinc, Sulphate of	5	grains.
Copper, Sulphate of	1¼	"
Saffron, Tincture of	½	drachm.
Camphor, Tincture of	15	drops.
Rosewater	2	ounces.
Pure Water	2	"

Mix together and filter through filtering paper kept by druggists.

TRASK'S MAGNETIC OINTMENT.

Hard Raisins, cut into pieces	2	ounces.
Fine Cut Tobacco	2	"
Lard	1	"
White Wax	1	"

Mix, and simmer together for one hour over a slow fire; or set the dish containing it into a pot of boiling water and let boil for that length of time.

The White Wax is added to give it the proper consistence, and may be used in greater or less proportion according to the season of the year, more being needed in summer than in winter.

UTERINE TONICS.

In the following preparation the whole drug is not used; the part employed is the active principle or medicinal quality only:

Buckley's Uterine Tonic.

Each pill contains:

Helonin	$\frac{1}{8}$	grain.
Caulophyllin	$\frac{1}{8}$	"
Macrotin	$\frac{1}{8}$	"
Hyoscyamine Amorphus	$\frac{1}{250}$	"

Dose.—Take 1 pill every three hours, or four times a day. If the throat becomes dry, or the face flushed, it is evidence that the dose should be lessened. If these symptoms do not appear, the amount can be increased if desired.

This prescription gives most satisfactory results, and has been used by many noted physicians.

Parke-Davis' Uterine Tonic.

Each pill contains:

Viburnum Prunifolium	1	grain.
Viburnum Opulus	1	"
Star Grass	½	"
Helonias	½	"
Squaw Vine	½	"
Caulophyllum	¼	"

Dose.—Take 1 three or four times a day whenever there is headache, backache, and a dull pain and feeling of weight in the pelvic organs.

VAN BUSKIRK'S FRAGRANT SOZODONT.
(*For the Teeth.*)

Alcohol	2	ounces.
Water	2½	"
Castile Soap, pure	½	"
Wintergreen, Oil of	5	drops.
Red Saunders enough to color		

But very little of the Saunders is required. Put all together in a bottle and allow the soap to dissolve.

WARNER'S SAFE KIDNEY AND LIVER CURE.

Lycopus Virg. (the herb), Extract of.....308   grains.
Hepatica, Extract of...............................232   "
Wintergreen, Extract of......................... 7½   "
Saltpetre.. 39   "
Alcohol... 2½   ounces.
Glycerine 10   drachms.
Water sufficient to make........................ 1   pint.

Mix all together, let stand one week. Filter if necessary.

WINSLOW'S SOOTHING SYRUP.

Morphine, Sulphate of........................... ½ grain.
Soda, Carbonate of................................ 1   "
Simple Syrup... 1½ ounces.
Pure Water.. ½   "
Fennel, Spirits of.................................. 1   drachm.

Note.—We have stated several times in this work that Opium in any form should not be given to children. Besides causing convulsions, it is liable to cause death. Just one drop of Laudanum has caused death in a babe. There are many more remedies more quieting and absolutely without danger.

DOSES OF MEDICINE FOR DIFFERENT AGES.

It must be plain to every one that children do not require such powerful medicine as adults, or old people, and therefore it is desirable to have some fixed method of determining or regulating the administration of doses of medicine. We will assume that the dose for a full-grown person is one drachm (60 grains, or 1 teaspoonful), then the following proportions will be suitable for the various ages given; keeping in view other circumstances, such as sex, temperament, habits, climate and state of general health.

AGE.	PROPORTION.	PROPORTIONATE DOSE.
7 weeks......................	one-fifteenth................	or grains................ 4
7 months.....................	one-twelfth.................	or grains 5
Under 2 years.............	one-eighth	or grains................ 7½
" 3 "	one-sixth....................	or grains 10
' 4 "	one-fourth...................	or grains 15
" 5 "	one-third	or scruple.............. 1
" 14 "	one-half	or drachm.............. ½
" 20 "	two-fifths....................	or scruples 2
Above 21 "	the full dose................	or drachm.............. 1
' 65 "	eleven-twelfths.............	or grains................55
" 70 "	five-sixths..................	or grains................50
" 85 "	two-thirds...................	or grains................40

Another Method of Averaging Doses for Children.—The following is very convenient inasmuch as it may be borne in mind and is thus always at hand. Add the age of the child to the number 12 and use as a denominator, then place the age of the child above the line and use as a numerator and the dose will be indicated by the fraction. To illustrate: If a child is three years of age, add 3 to 12, making 15 for the denominator; then use the child's age for the numerator and you have $\frac{3}{15}$, or $\frac{1}{5}$ of the adult dose. This plan of dosage is subject to variation, because some children are large and robust while others are physically weak. The dose should be regulated accordingly.

Alcohol, To Test Its Purity.—A simple means of detecting the purity of Alcohol is as follows: Take an equal amount of Alcohol and Castor Oil, put into a clean bottle and shake thoroughly. If the Alcohol has not been diluted with water, the mixture will be perfect. If the Alcohol has been so adulterated, the Oil will mix but partially.

Aqua Ammonia, or Water of Ammonia.—Water of Ammonia, when properly prepared, is made by adding 10 per cent of the stronger Water of Ammonia to pure water. In other words, to 1 pint of pure water add 1½ ounces of the stronger Water of Ammonia. The stronger Water of Ammonia may be had at any drug store. We have reason to believe that much of the Ammonia sold in department stores and other places is not of proper strength.

Asthma Remedy.

Stramonium, powdered	1	ounce.
Nitrate of Potash, powdered	½	"
Lobelia, powdered	½	"
Belladonna Leaves, powdered	½	"
Anise Seed, powdered	2	drachms.

The ingredients should be in fine powder and thoroughly dry before mixing.

This combination is used by burning a small amount on the tin cover of a can or pail and inhaling the smoke.

Asthma Remedy, Another.

Grindelia, powdered	4	drachms.
Jaborandi Leaves, powdered	4	"
Eucalyptus, powdered	2	"
Stramonium, powdered	4	"
Belladonna, powdered	4	"
Cubebs, powdered	4	"
Saltpetre, powdered	6	"
Cascarilla Bark, powdered	½	"

The ingredients should be in fine powder and thoroughly dry before using.

This combination is used by burning a small amount on the tin cover of a can or pail and inhaling the smoke.

BALSAMS.

For Pulmonary Affections and Coughs of Long Standing.

Spikenard root	2	ounces.
Horehound tops	2	"
Comfrey root	2	"
Wild Cherry bark	2	'
Blood root	2	'
Elecampane root	2	"

Add a suitable quantity of water and boil until the strength is all extracted; strain and reduce the liquid, by boiling, to 2 quarts or less; add 2 pounds of white sugar and 2 pounds of good honey and again boil down to 2 quarts. Let the mixture stand for twenty-four hours in order that it may settle, add 1 gill of spirits and bottle for use.

Dose.—A wineglassful three or four times a day.

For Pulmonary Affections.

Balsam Tolu...	2	ounces.
Balsam Fir..	2	"
Opium..	2	drachms.

Dissolve all in 1 quart of Alcohol.

Dose.—A teaspoonful occasionally.

BATHS—HOT OR COLD ?

We understand that "ice to the head," cold baths and even ice packs, have been recommended and used so long that the public has become more or less familiar with this form of treatment; yet we are prepared to state from actual experience that this is not only an unpleasant, and sometimes a dangerous form of treatment, but that it is entirely unnecessary. Warm packs and warm baths will accomplish all that is claimed for cold packs and baths, and are much more agreeable to the patient.

The cold application causes the vessels on the surface to contract and forces the blood to the internal organs, causing congestion and checking elimination. This is the very condition to be avoided. True, the cold is a stimulant after recovery from the first effects, or shock, and this aids the patient in overcoming what would otherwise be an increase of the trouble. Warm baths and warm packs cause the vessels near the surface of the body to dilate, thus bringing more blood to the surface, relieving the congestion and aiding in elimination. The first effects of a warm bath will not lower the temperature on the surface, but will lower it in the internal organs, relieving the liver, kidneys, stomach, lungs, heart and brain. The warm bath hastens resolution by producing the natural condition. A warm bath will also produce free perspiration, and for these reasons a warm bath will lower the temperature in a fevered patient sooner than a cold bath, and is why hot applications are so valuable in capillary bronchitis and cerebro-spinal meningitis, as mentioned under those heads.

It is well known that cold is especially dangerous to the young. Happily there are but few who apply cold to children and babies, yet the principle is the same whether applied to child or adult. The only reason the adult can sustain the shock is by reason of his greater vitality.

Someone says a hot bath is weakening. So is the disease. Fever may be caused by sunstroke, apoplexy, or some other condition or shock which paralyzes the nerves governing the size of the blood vessels, but, barring these, fever is the result of poison in the system. Apply a hot bath, sweat the patient, eliminate the poison, and note the improvement which is sure to follow. As already stated, we are in a position to advise from actual experience, and therefore wish to emphasize the statement that we *know of no condition where a hot bath is not superior to a cold one.*

In all forms of congestion or inflammation, whether in the digestive tract, lungs, liver or kidneys, a hot bath is more beneficial than a cold one. The bath improves the circulation, aids a sluggish liver, prevents congestion of the kidneys and relieves a clouded brain.

Beef Tea.—Take 1 pound of nice lean beef, cut fine, place in a clean basin or spider, add 1 pint of cold water and let stand for two hours, then place it over the fire and allow it to simmer for one hour. Now place in a coarse strainer, press out all the liquid and season to suit the taste.

This is a convenient way of making beef tea. It is always fresh, and is much more valuable than the expensive extracts of beef sold on the market.

Blackberry Cordial for Bowel Complaints.—The berries should be fully ripe before they are gathered. Mash them and let the juice and pomace remain together for eight or ten hours. Then add to 1 gallon of juice the following:

Loaf Sugar	2	pounds.
Cinnamon, finely pulverized	½	ounce.
Nutmeg, finely pulverized	½	"
Allspice, powdered	2	"

A few ounces of crushed raisins may be added if desired. Boil the mixture gently for 15 minutes, and when cold add ½ pint of Brandy or the best Rye Whiskey, then put into bottles with the corks cut off even with the top, and cover with wax or pitch of any sort to exclude the air. It is always better to store such cordial in small bottles, as half-pint size, because the contents of a small bottle can be used up before it will spoil; whereas, if a large bottle is opened and the cordial is not used in a few days, it is liable to lose the excellence of its flavor.

This cordial will be found highly beneficial in the bowel complaints of grown persons as well as children. It may be used freely, or in quantities to meet the requirements of the case. It is well to guard against constipation, however, by not continuing its use too long after the trouble has been corrected.

BLOOD PURIFIERS.

For Alterative and Blood Purifier.

Sarsaparilla, Fluid Extract of	4	ounces.
Stillingia, Fluid Extract of	4	"
Burdock, Fluid Extract of	4	"
Poke Root, Fluid Extract of	4	"
Prickly Ash, Tincture of	2	"

Mix together.

Dose.—1 teaspoonful three or four times a day.

For Impurity of the Blood, Venereal, Scrofulous and Skin Diseases, Ulcers, etc.

Honduras or Jamaica Sarsaparilla, sliced..	6	ounces.
Guaiac wood, rasped	3	"
Sassafras bark	2	"
Elder flowers	2	"
Burdock root or seed	3	"
Yellow Dock, bruised	3	"

To the above articles add dilute Alcohol or common spirits sufficient to immerse them. Digest with a moderate heat for one week, filter the liquor and set it aside. Add ½ gallon of pure soft water and boil gently to 1 quart. Mix the liquor and the decoction together, and boil again till 1 quart remains; then add 2 pounds of white or clarified sugar and simmer. Put the syrup into new or clean quart bottles, cork and seal tightly.

Dose.—A wineglassful three times a day, after having cleansed the stomach. The decoction may be used without the addition of sugar.

For Purifying the Blood.

Syrup	1	pint.
Alcohol	10	ounces.
Pure Water	12	"
Potash, Iodide of	2	"
Sarsaparilla Compound, Fluid Extract of..	6½	"
Dandelion, Fluid Extract of	3	"
Senna, Fluid Extract of	3	"
Stillingia, Fluid Extract of	3	"
Yellow Dock, Fluid Extract of	3	"
Rhubarb, Fluid Extract of	1½	"
Sassafras, Oil of	1	drachm.
Anise, Oil of	1	"

Mix together.

Dose.—One teaspoonful three or four times a day.

For Tubercular and Syphilitic Conditions.

Chloride of Gold and Sodium	2	grains.
Distilled Water	1	ounce.
Simple Syrup	2	drachms.

Mix, and form a solution.

Dose.—Twelve drops three times a day.

CASCARA CORDIAL LAXATIVE.

Cascara Sagrada, ground	4	ounces.
Senna Leaves, ground	2	"
Licorice Root, ground	2	"
Soda Sulphate of, powdered	1	"
Water	11	"

Macerate the drugs in the water for twelve hours. Place in a percolator and gradually pour on the following mixture:

Alcohol	8	ounces.
Water	4	"

After this has all drained through, add the following oils, dissolved in a little Alcohol.

Cardamon, Oil of	8	drops.
Anise, Oil of	4	"
Orange, Oil of	4	"

and to this mixture add:

Granulated Sugar	1½	pounds.

Dissolve by shaking the bottle.

Dose.—One teaspoonful night or morning. The dose may be increased or diminished.

CATARRH REMEDIES.

For use in an atomizer, or to snuff up the nose.

Pilocarpine, Hydrochlorate of	5	grains.
Rosemary, Oil of	½	ounce.
Cantharides, Tincture of	½	"
Glycerine	2	"
Bay Rum	2	"
Rose, Oil of	2	drops.
Camphor, Spirits of, enough to make	6	ounces.

To be snuffed up the nose several times a day.

Hydrastine, powdered	30	grains.
Indigo, powdered	5	"
Camphor, powdered	20	"
Carbolic Acid	20	drops.
Common Salt, very fine	1	ounce.

Mix the Camphor and Salt, the Carbolic Acid and the Indigo, and then add the Hydrastine.

To be sprayed up the nose with an atomizer.

Menthol	5 to 10	grains.
Eucalyptus, Oil of	½	drachm.
Alboline, liquid, add to	1	ounce.

Use in atomizer night and morning.

To be snuffed up the nose several times a day.

Bismuth, Carbonate of	10	grains.
Orris Root, powdered	3	"
Thymol, powdered	1	"
Milk, Sugar of	20	"
Gum Arabic, powdered	10	"
Soda, Bicarbonate of	2	"
Quinine, Sulphate of	10	"

Mix thoroughly.

Dobell's Solution for Nasal Catarrh.

Soda, Bicarbonate of	120	grains.
Borax	120	"
Carbolic Acid	24	drops.
Glycerine	½	ounce.
Water enough to make	1	pint.

Mix all together.

This is an excellent preparation for nasal catarrh. It should be sprayed up the nose with an atomizer.

Internal Treatment.

Potash, Iodide of.....................................	3	drachms.
Orange, Syrup of.......................................	1	ounce.
Cardamon Compound, Tincture of...........	1	drachm.
Quassia, Tincture of..............................	1	"
Alcohol	2	ounces.
Water enough to make............................	8	"

Mix.

Dose.—From 1 to 2 teaspoonfuls three times a day, taken in water between meals. While taking this remedy local treatment should also be applied by using a snuff or the atomizer.

For Chronic Catarrh of the Bladder and Chronic Mucous Discharges from the Vagina or Urethra.

Buchu, Tincture of................................	½	ounce.
Uva Ursi, decoction of...........................	7½	"

Mix.

Dose.—Half a wineglassful four times a day.

CAUSTICS.

Caustics are those substances which when applied to fungous flesh or to the skin, disorganize the same. Their operation, however, differs very much, according to the agents employed, some acting very mildly and others with great severity. They are derived from both the mineral and the vegetable kingdom, but the latter are always to be preferred when they answer the indication required.

Vegetable Caustic.

For Fistulas, Cancers, Scrofulous and Indolent Ulcers, and in all cases where there is proud flesh; also to excite a healthy action of the parts. It removes fungous flesh without exciting inflammation, and acts but little except on spongy or soft flesh.

Make a strong lye of hickory or oak ashes, put it into an iron kettle and evaporate to the consistence of thin molasses; then remove into a sand-bath, and continue the evaporation to the consistence of honey. Keep it in a sealed glass jar.

Wood Soot.

Wood soot is said to be excellent to remove fungous or proud flesh from ulcers and wounds.

CHILDREN'S PRESCRIPTIONS.

For Colds and Fever in Small Children.

Potash, Acetate of................................	1	drachm.
Dilute Nitro-Muriatic Acid.....................	40	drops.
Aconite, Tincture of..............................	10	"
Nitre, Spirits of...................................	40	"
Henbane, Tincture of.............................	40	"
Glycerine...	1	ounce.
Water, add to......................................	4	"

Dose.—One teaspoonful every hour until improvement, then less often.

For Colds and Fever in Small Children.

Ipecac, Fluid Extract of	10	drops.
Glycerine	½	ounce.
Squills, Syup of	3	drachms.
Senega, Infusion of, add to	4	ounces.

Mix.

Dose.—From 10 to 20 drops, taken as above.

For Feverishness and Restlessness in Teething Children.

Potash, Bicarbonate of	2	grains.
Potash, Bromide of	2	"
Syrup	40	drops.
Water, add to	2	drachms.

Dose.—From 5 to 10 drops every thirty minutes to one hour until quiet.

For Children threatened with an attack of Croup or Bronchitis.

Ipecac, Wine of	3	drachms.
Tolu, Syrup of	5	"
Gum Arabic, Mucilage of	1	ounce.

Mix.

Dose.—A teaspoonful every hour or two.

Carminative Mixture for Flatulency, Wind Colic, etc., of Children.

Ammonia, Aromatic Spirits of	16	drops.
Ginger, Tincture of	½	drachm.
Cardamon Compound Tincture	12	drops.
Dill Water, add to	1	ounce.

Dose.—From ½ to 1 teaspoonful every thirty minutes, or as needed.

Tincture for Stomach and Bowel Complaints of Children.

Alexandria Senna	4	drachms.
Jalap	2	"
Fennel Seed	1	"
Best Brandy, Proof Spirits of	1	pint.

Let it stand for one week and strain.

Dose.—One teaspoonful or more to keep the bowels regular.

For Cough Medicine for Small Children.

Ammonia, Carbonate of	30	grains.
Ipecac, Fluid Extract of	½	drachm.
Licorice, Syrup of	3	"
Glycerine	2	"
Simple Elixir, add to	4	"

Mix.

Dose.—One teaspoonful as needed.

For Cough Medicine for Children.

Ipecac, Fluid Extract of	½	drachm.
Liquor Ammonia Acetatus	1	ounce.
Potash, Bicarbonate of	1	drachm.
Tolu, Syrup of	1	ounce.
Water, add to	2	ounces.

Dose.—One teaspoonful as needed.

For Cough Medicine for Small Children.

Chloroform, Spirits of	1½	drachms.
Paregoric	3	"
Ipecac, Fluid Extract of	½	"
Glycerine	2	ounces.
Water, add to	6	"

Mix.

Dose.—One teaspoonful as needed. Each teaspoonful contains 5 drops of Paregoric therefore is not recommended for infants or very young children.

For Whooping Cough.

Potash, Bromide of	1	drachm.
Carbolic Acid	16	drops.
Belladonna, Tincture of	1	drachm.
Ipecac, Fluid Extract of	½	"
Tolu, Syrup of	1	ounce.
Water, add to	4	ounces.

Mix.

Dose.—One teaspoonful as needed.

For Whooping Cough.

Carbolic Acid	15	drops.
Belladonna, Tincture of	40	"
Ipecac, Fluid Extract of	½	drachm.
Glycerine	4	"
Water, add to	3	ounces.

Dose.—One teaspoonful as needed.

For Baby Powder.

Zinc, Oxide of	2	ounces.
Lycopodium	2	"

Mix thoroughly by passing several times through a fine sieve.

For Baby Powder.

Boric Acid	1¼	ounces.
Starch	2½	"
French Chalk, powdered	1½	pounds.
Rose Geranium, Oil of	1	drachm.

Mix together.

Soothing Syrup without Opium.

Syrup	1	ounce.
Deodorized Alcohol	2	"
Anise, Oil of	8	drops.
Caraway, Oil of	5	"
Potash, Bromide of	2	grains.
Water	1	ounce.

Dissolve the oils in the Alcohol, dissolve the Bromide of Potash in the water, add all to the Syrup and mix all together.

Dose.—From 5 to 15 drops, according to age.

Infant's Cordial.

Sassafras Bark	2	ounces.
Caraway Seed	2	drachms.
Coriander Seed	2	"
Anise Seed	2	"
Water	8	**ounces.**
Alcohol	8	"

Let stand several days, strain, and add of molasses 1¼ pints. Mix thoroughly. This cordial contains no Opium and is often valuable for restless and crying children.

Dose.—From ¼ to ½ teaspoonful.

Godfrey's Cordial without Opium.

Soda, Bromide of	24	grains.
Soda, Bicarbonate of	15	"
Sassafras, Oil of	1	drop.
Anise, Oil of	2	"
Chloroform, Spirits of	½	drachm.
Alcohol	1	"
Henbane, Tincture of	1	"
Molasses	2	ounces.
Water, add to	4	"

Dissolve the oils in the Alcohol and add the tincture of Henbane. Dissolve the Soda Salts in the water and mix all together. Shake the bottle occasionally for three or four days and carefully pour off the clear liquid.

Dose.—From ⅓ to 1 teaspoonful.

For Worms.

Santonine	1	grain.
Scammony, Compound Powder of	2½	"
Calomel	½	"

Mix all together and divide into four doses. Take one dose every night.

For Worms.

Pink Root, Fluid Extract of	1	ounce.
Peppermint, Essence of	1½	drachms.
Water	1	ounce.
Syrup	3¼	ounces.
Alcohol	½	ounce.
Wormseed, Oil of	8	drops.

Add the Pink Root, Peppermint and Wormseed to the Syrup; next add the Alcohol, shake thoroughly and add the water.

Dose.—From 10 drops to 1 teaspoonful.

For Worms.

Spigelia (Pink Root), Fluid Extract of	1	ounce.
Senna, Fluid Extract of	5	drachms.
Anise, Oil of	2	drops.
Caraway, Oil of	2	"
Syrup	1½	ounces.

Dose.—One or more teaspoonfuls.

COLDS AND COUGHS.

Hamburg's Breast Tea *for Colds in the Chest.*

Marshmallow Root, cut fine	2	ounces.
Licorice Root, cut fine	6	drachms.
Orris Root, ground	2	"
Colt's Foot Leaves, bruised	1	ounce.
Mullein Flowers, bruised	½	"
White Poppy Capsules, bruised	2	drachms.
Star Anise Seed, bruised	½	ounce.

Mix all together and use by putting a teaspoonful or two into a glass of boiling water. Let stand until cool. Carefully pour off the water and drink it.

For Coughs.

Ipecac, Fluid Extract of	½	ounce.
Chloroform	⅛	"
Pinus Canadensis, Tincture of	2	"
Water	7	"
Sugar	14	"
Magnesia, Carbonate of	½	"
Gelsemium, Tincture of	¼	"

Mix all together, and filter or strain if necessary.
Dose.—One teaspoonful every few hours as needed.

For Coughs.

Lemon, Syrup of	½	ounce.
Ipecac, Fluid Extract of	20	drops
Glycerine	½	ounce.
Codeine	4	grains.
Water, add to	2	ounces.

Mix together.
Dose.—One teaspoonful as needed.

For Coughs.

Squills, Syrup of	2	ounces.
Tolu, Syrup of	2	"
Ipecac, Syrup of	2	"
Paregoric	2	"
Chlorodyne	1	drachm.
Ammonia, Muriate of	2	"

Add the Chlorodyne to the syrups, dissolve the Muriate of Ammonia in as little water as possible, and mix all together.
Dose.—One teaspoonful as needed.

For Coughs.

Codeine, Sulphate of	4	grains.
Ammonia, Chloride of	2	drachms.
Ipecac, Fluid Extract of	2	"
Nitre, Spirits of	2	"
Squills, Syrup of	2	"
Wild Cherry, Syrup of	4	ounces.

Mix all together.
Dose.—One teaspoonful as needed.

CORN REMEDIES.

To Relieve the Pain of.

Sugar of Lead, powdered	1	drachm.
Myrrh, powdered	1	"
Camphor, powdered	1	"
Litharge, powdered	1	"
Sweet Oil	sufficient quantity.	
Saxoline	'	"

Make the powders into a stiff paste with Sweet Oil, then add Saxoline to bring to the consistency of an ointment. It is stated that this application gives almost instant relief.

To Remove.

Salicylic Acid	80	grains.
Indian Hemp, Extract of	40	"
Iodine Crystals	6	"
Sulphuric Ether	2	ounces.

Mix together by shaking the bottle. Paint a little on the corn and allow it to dry. Repeat the application for three successive days, then wait a few days until the corn loosens, when it may be readily removed.

DROPS.

Cholera Drops—for Cholera and Diarrhea.

Opium, Tincture of	1	ounce.
Camphor, Tincture of	1	'
Peppermint, Essence of	1	':
Capsicum, Tincture of	1	"

Mix, and take ½ teaspoonful in a little sweetened water, to be repeated according to the urgency of the symptoms.

Cough Drops—For Coughs, and Pains in the Breast.

Gum Guaiac	1	drachm.
Gum Camphor	1	scruple.
Castile Soap	12	grains.
Laudanum	20	drops.
Alcohol	1	ounce.
Balsam of Peru	12	drops.

Mix all together.

Dose.—Fifteen drops three times a day on a piece of loaf sugar.

Carminative Drops—For Flatulency, Wind Colic, Hysteria and Nervous Affections.

Angelica	4	ounces.
Ladies' Slipper	2	'
Sweet Flag	½	"
Anise	1	"
Dill	1	':
Fennel Seed	1	':
Catnip Flowers or Leaves	2	"
Motherwort	2	·
Pleurisy Root	4	"

Put the whole into 2 quarts of Brandy and digest for forty-eight hours; then press out and strain the liquid, and add to it ½ pound of loaf sugar; when dissolved bottle it for use.

Dose.—For children, from 10 drops to a teaspoonful, according to age; for adults, from 1 to 4 teaspoonfuls in a cup of warm tea. The dose may be repeated once in four to six hours.

DYSPEPSIA OR INDIGESTION.

Wheat Bran for Indigestion.—One of the best remedies for indigestion, and a very simple one, is to add a tablespoonful of common wheat bran to a glass of hot water and drink it the first thing in the morning.

For Dyspepsia.

Bismuth, Subnitrate of	1½	drachms.
Soda, Bicarbonate of	2	"
Calcined Magnesia, heavy	½	"
Rhubarb powdered	½	"
Ammonia, Aromatic Spirits of	2	"
Peppermint, Essence of	½	"
Dilute Hydrochloric Acid	10	drops.
Water, add to	6	ounces.

Mix all together. Shake before using.

Dose.—From 1 to 2 tablespoonfuls taken after meals. Smaller doses may also be taken between meals, if necessary.

For Indigestion with Nausea and Vomiting.

Carbolic Acid	4	drops.
Bismuth, Subnitrate of	2½	drachms.
Scale Pepsin (1 to 3000)	1	"
Gum Arabic, powdered	1	"
Glycerine	1	ounce.
Cinnamon Water, enough to make	2	"

Mix together.

Dose.—One teaspoonful after meals. Take a small dose between meals if needed. Shake the bottle before taking.

For Indigestion.

Scale Pepsin (1 to 3000)	2	drachms.
Hydrochloric (Muriatic) Acid, pure	½	"
Glycerine	2	ounces.
Fowler's Solution	2	drachms.
Simple Elixir, enough to make	4	ounces.

Mix, and take 1 teaspoonful after meals.

For Dyspepsia with Flatulency, or Wind on the Stomach.

Magnesia, Sulphate of	2	drachms.
Potash Bicarbonate of	1½	"
Chloroform, Spirits of	1	"
Nux Vomica, Tincture of	1	"
Capsicum, Tincture of	15	drops.
Gentian Compound, Infusion of, add to	6	ounces.

Mix and take 1 teaspoonful after meals.

For Indigestion with Pain.

Scale Pepsin (1 to 3000)	2	drachms.
Hydrochloric (Muriatic) Acid, pure	½	'
Bismuth, Subnitrate of	6	'
Fowler's Solution	2	"
Cascara, Aromatic	4	'
Glycerine	1½	ounces.
Simple Elixir, enough to make	4	"

Mix, and take 1 teaspoonful at meal times. Shake the bottle before taking.

EFFERVESCING DRINKS.

Effervescing Citrate of Magnesia.

Magnesia, Carbonate of	200	grains.
Citric Acid	400	"
Water	10	ounces

Add all together in a porcelain basin. When effervescing ceases, add the following:

Citric Acid, Syrup of	2	ounces.
Potash, Bicarbonate of	30	grains.

Drink while effervescing. This preparation is useful as an active cathartic, is pleasant to the taste and perfectly harmless in its effects.

If it is desired to keep this preparation, or to make more than the amount given, make as above, and add all to 12 ounce bottles except the Bicarbonate of Potash. Secure tightly fitting corks and a piece of strong cord, and to each bottle add 30 grains of Bicarbonate of Potash. Cork immediately, securing the corks with the cord to prevent their being driven out by the gas.

For Fever Patients, or for Summer Use.—To make an effervescing drink for persons suffering with fever, who always desire an abundance of cooling drinks, or for common summer use, take the carefully expressed and well strained juice of Raspberries, Strawberries, Currants or other small fruits, 1 quart, and boil it into a syrup with 1 pound of pulverized loaf sugar; to this add 1½ ounces of Tartaric Acid, and when cold put into a bottle and keep well corked. When required for use, fill a half pint tumbler three-fourths full of cold water and add 2 tablespoonfuls of the syrup. Then stir in briskly a small teaspoonful of Bicarbonate of Soda and a very delicious drink will be formed; drink while effervescing. The color may be improved by adding a very small portion of Cochineal to the syrup at the time of boiling.

The same may be done by taking 2 or 3 oranges, or lemons, if their flavors are preferred or if at seasons of the year when there are no small fruits. Take 3 oranges, or lemons, pare with a sharp knife and slice into water, 1 pint. Add sugar, 1 pound, and boil into a syrup as above. Strain and use in the same way.

Root Beer.

Sarsaparilla	1	pound.
Spice Wood	¼	"
Guaiacum Chips	½	"
Birch Bark	⅛	'
Ginger	¼	ounce.
Sassafras	2	"
Prickly Ash Bark	¼	"
Hops	½	"

Boil for twelve hours over a moderate fire with sufficient water so that the remainder shall measure 3 gallons, to which add

Ginger, Tincture of	4	ounces.
Wintergreen, Oil of	½	"
Alcohol	1	pint.

This prevents fermentation.

EYES, INFLAMED, REMEDIES FOR.

Eye Salve.

Mercury, Yellow Oxide of	5	grains.
Zinc, Oxide of	3	"
Vaseline	½	ounce.

Mix intimately and apply to the eyelids.

Eye Water.

White Vitriol	2	grains.
Alum	1	"
Common Table Salt, fine	3	"
Water	1	ounce.

Mix together and drop in the eye several times a day.

Fomentation for Application to Inflamed Eyes.

Take White Poppy heads or Henbane leaves, simmer them in water and spirits and apply.

Lime in the Eye—Remedy.

Quite often Lime gets into the eye of those who are working with it. As soon as possible, drop in water made very sweet with sugar.

FOMENTATIONS.

Fomentation to relieve pain and reduce inflammation resulting from contusions, sprains, dislocations and other causes. Usually employed in inflammation of the bowels. Beneficial in almost every species of inflammation.

Hops	3	ounces.
Double Tansy	3	"
Wormwood	3	"
Horehound	3	"
Catnip	3	"

Put into a small sack, large enough to cover the part, place in a kettle or pan on the stove, pour on water and boil to a strong decoction. Wring out the sack and apply hot. When cool, again dip it into the decoction, wring out and apply as before.

Poppy Fomentation for allaying pain.

Take White Poppy heads, or the flowers, a suitable quantity, add equal quantities of vinegar and water and simmer for a few minutes. Apply as above.

GARGLES.

For Sore Throat.

Sage Tea, strong	½	pint.
Honey, strained	2	tablespoonfuls.
Salt	2	"
Vinegar	2	"

Mix, strain and bottle for use, gargling from four to a dozen times daily, according to the severity of the case.

This is one of the very best gargles in use.

Gargle for Ulcerated Throat of long standing.

Sumach Berries	1	ounce.
Golden Seal	1	"
Water	1	pint.

Boil to make a decoction, strain, and add one drachm of pulverized Alum to every pint.

HEADACHE REMEDIES.

Capsules for.

Caffeine	60	grains.
Phenacetine	120	"
Soda, Bicarbonate of	400	"
Willow Charcoal	120	"

Mix and make into No. 2 capsules. Take one every hour until improvement.

Powders for.

Acetanilid	30	grains.
Caffeine	5	"
Soda, Bicarbonate of	30	"

Mix and divide into 10 powders. Take one every hour until improvement.

Powders for.

Soda, Bicarbonate of	10	grains.
Caffeine	5	"
Acetanilid	30	"
Soda, Salicylate of	20	"

Mix and divide into 10 powders. Take one every hour until improvement.

Effervescing Citrate of Caffeine for Headaches.

Caffeine, Citrate of	2	drachms.
Soda, Bicarbonate of	23	"
Tartaric Acid	12	"
Citric Acid	8	"
Granulated Sugar	5	"

The ingredients should be finely powdered and thoroughly mixed.

Dose.—One teaspoonful.

KIDNEY REMEDIES.

A Kidney "Cure."

Buchu, Fluid Extract of	2	ounces.
Pareira Brava, Fluid Extract of	1	"
Stone Root, Fluid Extract of	1	"
Potash, Acetate of	1	"
Holland Gin, best	8	"
Simple Elixir, add to	1	pint.

Mix all together, and take 1 or 2 teaspoonfuls three or four times a day.

Diuretic Mixture to Increase the Action of the Kidneys.

Potash, Acetate of	2	drachms.
Nitre, Spirits of	3	"
Juniper, Spirits of	3	"
Squills, Acetate of	2	"
Digitalis, Tincture of	1	"
Water, add to	6	ounces.

Dose.—One teaspoonful every two hours, more or less often, according to the urgency of the case.

Decoction for Gravel, Dropsy, etc.

Queen of the Meadow	2	ounces.
Milkweed	2	"
Juniper Berries	2	"
Dwarf Elder	2	"
Spearmint	2	"
Wild Carrot Seed	2	"

Put all into a mortar and bruise. Make a strong decoction.

Dose.—Half a pint to be taken often through the day.

Pills for Dropsy.

Jalap, pulverized	1	scruple.
Scammony	1	"
Gamboge	1	"

Add mucilage of Gum Arabic sufficient to form into 16 pills.

Dose.—One every hour or two.

Note.—This pill has cured cases of dropsy, and may be given when other means fail.

Pills for Gravel.

Soda, Carbonate of	2	drachms.
Castile Soap	2	"
Juniper, Oil of, sufficient quantity		

Form a mass and divide into 60 pills.

Dose.—Three pills three or four times a day.

LAXOL.

This is a preparation of pure Castor Oil with a little flavoring to disguise the taste. It is an elegant preparation, can be taken without any inconvenience and never causes nausea, but on the other hand may be taken in cases of biliousness and other derangements of the digestive organs. It is a proprietary preparation, put up in small bottles which sell for 25 cents each. The Castor Oil contains a little Saccharine – the sweet principle of sugar—and a trace of Cinnamon Oil. We have never made this preparation, but the following amounts of Saccharine and oils will be found nearly correct. More or less may be added as desired:

Castor Oil	8	ounces.
Saccharine	½	grain.
Cinnamon, Oil of	1 or 2	drops.

Dose.—The dose is the same as of the ordinary Castor Oil—from a teaspoonful to a tablespoonful. If the spoon is first dipped in milk, the oil will not stick to it.

LIME WATER, TO MAKE.

Get a hard piece of lime, of the kind that plasterers use, about half as large as a hen's egg. Put it into a porcelain or granite-lined basin and add a little water. After a few minutes the lime will begin to crack open. Now add a little more water, and after the lime falls to pieces add as much water as desired, say 1 pint. Stir well, allow the lime to settle, then pour off the clear water. The object of this is to get rid of any impurities that might be contained in the lime. Now add another pint of water, stir as before and allow it to settle. Repeat the stirring once or twice and it will be ready for use. Only a very small percentage of the lime is taken up by the water. The balance remains at the bottom. In using, pour off carefully and avoid stirring up the sediment.

It will be noticed that *fresh* Lime Water is advised. The reason for this is that Lime Water does not keep long. The oxygen of the air unites with the lime, forming Oxide of Lime. Oxide of Lime is insoluble and settles to the bottom, and the water continues to absorb impurities from the air, soon becoming unfit for use. Again, there is more or less decomposition of the vegetable products which are nearly always present to a greater or less extent. If kept in a tightly covered fruit can or in a tightly corked bottle, it will, of course, keep longer; but even then frequent exposure, as in preparing a baby's food, will sooner or later bring about the results mentioned.

Those using Lime Water should obtain from a druggist a few strips of *red* litmus paper and make frequent tests of the water to see that no change has taken place. To do this, simply dip one of the strips of paper into the water, and if the red color is immediately changed to a deep blue, it is evidence that the water is all right; if this change does not take place, the preparation should be thrown away.

LINIMENTS.

British Oil, *for general use.*

Turpentine, Oil of	4	ounces.
Linseed or Flaxseed, Oil of	4	"
Amber, Oil of	2	"
Juniper, Oil of	2	drachms.
Petroleum	1½	ounces.
Senega Oil	½	ounce.

Put all together into a bottle and shake thoroughly. This direction is applicable in the preparation of any liniment.

Brown's Liniment, *for general purposes.*

Gum Camphor	¼	ounce.
Alcohol	4	"
Linseed Oil	4	"
Turpentine, Spirits of	4	"
Aqua Ammonia	4	"
Capsicum, Tincture of	4	"
Origanum, Oil of	4	"

Very valuable.

Camphorated Oil, *for Counter-Irritant Purposes.*

Olive Oil	1	pint.
Camphor	2	ounces.

Mix, and dissolve by gentle heat.

In chronic rheumatism, sore throat, inflammation of the lungs, etc., this will be found a very powerful counter-irritant, or external stimulant, drawing the blood to the surface, and may be used over the chest in acute colds and in all other conditions where a counter-irritant is needed.

Camphor Liniment, *for Whooping Cough, Bronchial Affections, etc.*

Camphor, Spirits of	2	ounces.
Laudanum	½	"
Turpentine, Spirits of	1	"
Castile Soap, in powder	½	"
Alcohol	3	"

Set in a warm place for two or three days, and then if the soap is not all dissolved, strain it.

In bad cases of whooping cough, and for chronic bronchial affections, it may be applied warm to the throat chest and spine.

Cram's Fluid Lightning Liniment.

Mustard, Essential Oil of	1	drachm.
Cajeput, Oil of	1	"
Cloves, Oil of	1	"
Sassafras, Oil of	1	"
Ether	½	ounce.
Opium, Tincture of	6	drachms.
Alcohol	10	ounces.

Giles' Iodide of Ammonia Liniment.

Iodide Crystals	30	grains.
Camphor Gum	½	ounce.
Rosemary, Oil of	¼	"
Lavender, Oil of	¼	"
Ammonia, Water of	2	"
Alcohol	1	pint.

Dissolve the Iodine in the Alcohol, add the Camphor Gum, then the oils, then add the Water of Ammonia.

Lethian Liniment, *to relieve pain in swellings, rheumatism, bruises, pains, sore throat, etc.*

Turpentine Soap	1	ounce.
Gum Camphor	1	"
Alcohol	1	quart.

Put into a jug or bottle and stand in the hot sun, or a warm place, for two weeks, then add

Chloroform	2	drachms.

Shake often while cooling. Bottle.

Note.—If there is any difficulty in getting Turpentine Soap, take nice, white bar soap and add Oil of Turpentine, 1 ounce, with Camphor as above.

Soap Liniment, *for the same uses as the Lethian Liniment above.*

White Bar Soap	2	ounces.
Camphor Gum	1	"
Rosemary, Oil of	3	drachms.
Origanum, Oil of	2	"
Aqua Ammonia (3 F's strong)	1	ounce.
Alcohol	1½	pints.

Shave the soap fine and put into the Alcohol and keep in a warm place until the soap is dissolved, then add the other articles and put into wide-mouthed bottles. It cools to a soapy, half solid mass.

Stimulating Liniment, *for external or internal use.*

Alcohol	1	pint.
Origanum, Oil of	1	ounce.
Wormwood, Oil of	1	"
Camphor Gum	1	"
Cayenne, powdered	1	"
Aqua Ammonia	4	ounces.

Mix, cork, and shake daily for a week.

Dose.—Taken internally, the dose for an adult is from 10 to 30 drops, according to the severity of the pain.

Scarret's Liniment or Black Oil, *for Fistula, etc.*

Currier's Oil	5	ounces.
Oil of Spike	3	"
Vitriol, Oil of (Sulphuric Acid)	2	"

Directions.—This liniment will be of a dark or black color. An old pitcher is a good thing to mix the ingredients in, so that it can be poured into a bottle handily after mixing. First put in the Currier's Oil and Oil of Spike together, then from time to time put in a little only of the Oil of Vitriol; if all is put in at once it may foam over, or may break the pitcher or bottle in which it is made.

To apply to a fistula, dip a piece of cotton into the liniment and press it into the opening. This treatment should be repeated night and morning.

Stoke's Liniment, *for general use.*

Turpentine, Oil of	1½	ounces.
Acetic Acid	1½	"
Yolk of one Egg.		
Lemon, Oil of	20	drops.
Rosewater, add to	8	ounces.

White Liniment, *thick, for general use.*

Sweet Oil	2	ounces.
Aqua Ammonia	1	"
Turpentine, Spirits of	¾	"
Camphor, Spirits of	½	"

For Inflammatory Rheumatism, Gout, Quinsy, White Swelling, Inflamed Breasts, etc.

Hemlock, Oil of	1	ounce.
Gum Camphor	½	"
Gum Opium	½	"
Alcohol	1	quart.

For Rheumatism, Neuralgia, Sprains, etc.

Sassafras Oil	2	drachms.
Hemlock Oil	1	"
Red Cedar Oil	1	"
Turpentine Oil	1	"
Gum Camphor	1	"
Capsicum, pulverized	1	"
Alcohol	1	pint.

Mix. put all into a jug, and keep warm for five or six days, frequently shaking it until dissolved; then strain.

Bathe parts often and rub well in with the hand.

For Diseases of the Throat and Tonsils.

Castile Soap	½	ounce.
Sassafras, Oil of	1	"
Camphor	½	"
Hartshorn, Spirits of	1	"
Alcohol, enough to make	8	"

For Inflammatory Stiff Necks and Sore Throats.

Laudanum	1	drachm.
Camphor Gum	1	"
Castile Soap, scraped fine	1	"
Alcohol	4	ounces.

Put all together into a bottle and shake occasionally until dissolved.

For Chronic and Deep-Seated Pains, Acute Colds or Inflammation of the Lungs.

Turpentine, Spirits of	1	ounce.
Croton Oil	½	"
Olive Oil	1	"

A powerful counter-irritant. May blister.

For White and Glandular Swellings.

Henbane, Extract of	½	drachm.
White Soap	2	"
Linseed Oil	6	ounces.

LIVER MEDICINES.

For Liver Stimulant.

Dilute Nitrohydrochloric Acid	2	drachms.
Dandelion, Fluid Extract of	½	ounce.
Nux Vomica, Tincture of	2	drachms.
Nitre, Spirits of	2	"
Senna, Tincture of	1	ounce.
Gentian Compound, Infusion of, add to	8	"

Mix all together.

Dose.—One tablespoonful four times a day, or oftener if necessary.

For Liver Stimulant.

Dilute Nitrohydrochloric Acid	1½	drachms.
Podophyllin (Mandrake), Tincture of	80	drops.
Dandelion, Fluid Extract of	1	ounce.
Nux Vomica, Tincture of	80	drops.
Ginger, Syrup of	1	ounce.
Chloroform Water, add to	8	"

Mix all together.

Dose.—From 1 to 4 teaspoonfuls three times a day.

For Liver Invigorator.

Senna, powdered	4	ounces.
Mandrake, powdered	1	'
Rhubarb, powdered	1	"
Jalap, powdered	1	'.
Cloves, powdered	2	drachms.
Peppermint, Oil of	½	''
Alcohol	2	pints.
Water	1	"

Place the drugs in a bottle, mix the Alcohol and water and pour on. Let stand for ten days, shaking frequently, then strain or filter the liquid and add 1 pound of sugar. Dissolve without heat. More or less sugar may be added as desired.

Dose.—Teaspoonful, more or less, four times a day.

MILK OR WATER, BOILED.

During the past few years public opinion has been led to believe that boiled or scalded milk and boiled water are better than milk or water that has not been boiled. This applies especially to the feeding of infants and invalids. Such teaching is the result of certain theories that have evolved from what is often called "laboratory science," so-called because they are worked out in some laboratory with the aid of a test tube, microscope, etc. At the present time this theory is being opposed by many able men, as well as many noted physicians. The latter now claim that boiling milk not only renders it less valuable to the system, but that it is one of the great causes of scrofula and other diseases of a like nature. We deem it but fair to state both sides of the question, and those who then wish to boil the water and boil or sterilize the milk may do so. Personally, we believe that boiling milk interferes with its digestion, absorption and assimilation. We believe this because Nature designed milk to be drank in its natural state, and no amount of boiling or other artificial work can improve on Nature. Again, the fact that most people dislike boiled milk is strong evidence that boiling is a detriment and not a benefit.

In regard to boiling water, it should be remembered that boiling does not remove poisonous nor foreign matter of any kind. On the contrary, boiling will hasten decomposition of any and all organic matter, animal or vegetable. During the process of decomposition there are many poisonous gases and many other poisonous substances produced, and these taken into the system only add to the danger. Many suppose that pure water may be obtained by melting ice. This is not true. Every one has seen pebbles, leaves, twigs from the branches of trees and many other substances in ice. In like manner other kinds of foreign matter and filth of all kinds may be and undoubtedly are often present. When the ice melts, the foreign matter begins to decompose. Boil the water and you will hasten decomposition, as stated.

NEURALGIA REMEDIES.

For many years the following formulæ of Dr. Brown-Sequard and Dr. Gross have been famous in the treatment of neuralgia. They are relied upon by many physicians in treating this troublesome disease, and especially if the case is severe:

Brown-Sequard's Neuralgic Pills.

Each pill contains the following:

Hyoscyamus, Extract of	$\frac{1}{2}$	grain.
Conium, Extract of	$\frac{1}{2}$	"
Ignatia, Extract of	$\frac{1}{2}$	"
Opium, Extract of	$\frac{1}{2}$	"
Aconite Leaves, Extract of	$\frac{1}{3}$	"
Stramonium, Extract of	$\frac{1}{5}$	"
Indian Hemp, Extract of	$\frac{1}{4}$	"
Belladonna, Alcoholic Extract of	$\frac{1}{6}$	"

Dose.—One every three or four hours until improvement.

Gross' Neuralgic Pills.

Each pill contains the following:

Quinine, Sulphate of	2	grains.
Morphine, Sulphate of	$\frac{1}{80}$	"
Strychnine, Sulphate of	$\frac{1}{80}$	"
Arsenious Acid	$\frac{1}{80}$	"
Aconite Leaves, Extract of	½	"

Dose.—One every three or four hours until improvement.

Neuralgia Liniment.

Alcohol	½	ounce.
Turpentine, Spirits of	½	"
Sulphuric Ether	½	"
Laudanum	½	"
Camphor Gum	½	"
Cloves, Oil of	¼	"
Lavender, Oil of	¼	"

Mix, and keep corked.

This will be found a very valuable liniment for neuralgic pains. If the pain is not relieved by rubbing it on, wet a piece of brown paper with it and hold against the affected part as long as can be done without blistering. For decaying and painful teeth, apply with lint and rub upon the gums. For internal pains, as of colic, pains in the stomach, etc., take from 10 to 30 drops in a little sweetened water, or spirits and water, according to the severity of the pain, and repeat in fifteen to thirty minutes if necessary, or until relieved.

Ointment for Neuralgia.

Egg, White of	1	drachm.
Rhigolene	4	ounces.
Peppermint, Oil of	2	"
Collodion	1	"
Chloroform	1	"

Shake occasionally for twenty-four hours, which will harden the mass so that it will retain its consistency and hold the ingredients intimately blended for months.

" It will relieve facial or other neuralgia almost instantaneously." —*Georgia Medical Companion.*

Night Sweats—*To Relieve.*—After agues, fevers, etc., and in consumption, many persons are troubled with night sweats. They are caused by weakness or general debility. For their relief take the following:

Tansy, Essence of	½	ounce.
Alcohol	¼	"
Water	¼	"
Quinine	15	grains.
Muriatic Acid, pure	15	drops.

Dose.—One teaspoonful in a gill of cold Sage tea, which should be taken two or three times during the day and at bedtime. The cold Sage tea should be used freely as a drink also until cured.

OINTMENTS.

Carbolic Ointment.

Vaseline	2	ounces.
Carbolic Acid	20	drops.

Mix thoroughly.

Elder Flower Ointment and Oil.—Melt lard at the lowest possible temperature at which it assumes the fluid form, and introduce into it as many Elder flowers as the melted lard will cover. Steep them at the above temperature for twelve hours, and then strain off the lard through a piece of linen without the least pressure. By this means an ointment will be made when the lard is cold that is valuable in scalds and burns, and also in the treatment of erysipelas, etc. The manner of making it is applicable to making any ointment of flowers.

Mayer's German or Compound Lead Ointment, *for Cuts, Wounds, Ulcers and Skin Diseases.*

Olive Oil	2½	ounces.
White Turpentine	4	drachms.
Beeswax	2	"
Butter, unsalted	2	"
Honey	6	"
Red Lead	1	ounce.
Camphor, powdered	4	drachms.

Melt the Beeswax, White Turpentine, butter and Olive Oil together and strain. Then heat them nearly to the boiling point and gradually add the Red Lead, stirring the mixture constantly until it becomes black, or brown, then remove from the fire, and when it is somewhat cool, add to it the honey and Camphor, previously mixed together.

The Germans call this ointment Zusammengesetzte Bleisable.

Spermaceti Ointment, *for Chabs, Chafings, Dressing Blisters, etc.*

Spermaceti	3	drachms.
White Wax	1	"
Olive Oil	1½	ounces.

Melt over a gentle fire and stir until cool. Applied in any of the above cases, and to any irritable surfaces. It is not an ointment for long keeping, hence is made in small quantities at a time.

Chilbains, Ointment for.

Compound Turpentine Liniment	3	ounces.
Soap Liniment	3	"
Laudanum	1	"
Camphor Liniment	1	"

Mix together and apply locally.

Chilblains, Ointment for.

Lanolin	1	ounce.
Vaseline	2	drachms.
Cajeput, Oil of	2	"
Boric Acid	2	"
Carbolic Acid	20	grains.
Camphor	40	"

Mix intimately and apply.

For Frost Bites, Chilblains, etc.

Henbane Leaves, fresh	½	pound.
Stramonium Leaves	½	"
Bittersweet Leaves	½	"
Elder Bark	½	"
Lard	2	"

Mix, heat all together for two hours and strain.

For Painful Local Affections.

Balm-of-Gilead Buds, fresh	4	ounces.
Henbane Leaves	1	"
Poppy Petals	1	"
Belladonna Leaves	1	"
Bittersweet Leaves	1	"
Lard	12	"

Mix, and heat all together till the moisture has evaporated.

For Herpetic Affections, or Shingles.

Yellow Dock Roots	1	ounce.
Scabious	1	"
Swamp Sassafras	1	'

Boil down strong, add 1 pound of lard and simmer down to an ointment.

For Salt Rheum and Herpetic Affections.

White Turpentine	½	pound.
Butter, unsalted	½	"
Olive Oil	1	ounce.
Beeswax	2	"
Indian Turnip	1	"
White Lily Leaves	1	"
Plantain Leaves	1	"

Bruise the leaves and roots and slowly simmer them in spirits in an earthen vessel, which should be lightly covered; then strain, and when nearly cold add 2 drachms of yellow Ochre.

For Piles, Salt Rheum and Herpetic Affections.

Tobacco, cut fine	, ¼	pound.

Cover with spirits, and add

Lard	1	"

Simmer over a moderate fire until the herb is a little crisped, then remove and strain.

Note.—One of the best pile ointments in use.

For Salt Rheum and other Skin Affections, also Chronic Ophthalmia.

Fresh Butter	3	ounces.
White or Yellow Wax.......................	½	"
Red Precipitate...............................	2½	drachms.
Putty, prepared, or pure Zinc pulverized..	1	"

Melt, and mix all the other articles, and then add

Camphor, dissolved in Olive Oil..............	1	drachm.

For Piles, Itch, Tetter, Salt Rheum.

Lard or fresh Butter.............................	1	pound.
Sulphur	4	ounces.

Mix together and stir till cold.

For Scrofulous Ulcers, Scald Head, Itch.

Tobacco, best quality	1	ounce.
Yellow Dock........	4	"
Wood Soot....................................	4	"
Butter, unsalted	4	"
Tar..	4	"
Camphor, Spirits of..............................	2	"

Boil the tobacco, dock and soot in 2 gallons of water down to 1 gallon; then strain off and boil down to 1 quart. Add the butter and tar, and simmer over a fire of coals down to 1½ pints; then add the Camphor and stir till cold.

For Ulcers.

Verdigris...................................	5	drachms.
Honey, purified...................................	16	"
Vinegar, strong.................................	7	"
Alum, burnt...................................	½	"

Mix, and melt by gentle heat, stirring occasionally.

For Itch.

Sulphur, fine	1	ounce.
Venice Turpentine...............................	1	'
Lard......................................	½	pound.

Melt the lard and Turpentine, then add the Sulphur and stir till cold. Let it be applied two or three times a day.

For Sprains, Contusions, Dislocations, Swellings, Contracted Sinews, etc.

Double Tansy	1	ounce.
Wormwood	1	"
Horehound...	1	"
Catnip..	1	"
Hops	1	"

Bruise these and put them into a kettle, cover over with spirits and lard and let stand for two weeks; then simmer awhile and strain. Add 1 ounce of common Turpentine to every ounce of the ointment.

Pile Ointment.

Tannic Acid	20	grains.
Bismuth, Subnitrate of	40	"
Carbolic Acid	20	drops.
Morphine, Sulphate of	16	grains.
Vaseline	2	ounces.

Apply locally.

Pile Ointment.

Nut Galls, powdered	80	grains.
Opium, powdered	40	"

Mix intimately and add enough Vaseline to make 1 ounce. Apply locally once or twice a day.

Pile Ointment.—A patent was granted in 1844 (expired in 1868) to Wm. W. Riley, of Mansfield, O., for the cure of piles, as follows:

Flour of Sulphur	2	ounces
Nut Galls, powdered	1	"
Opium, powdered	1	grain.

Intimately mix with lard until the proper consistence is obtained. To be applied night and morning to the parts. A course of general treatment should be pursued that will restore general health, and especially overcome any tendency to constipation.

Ointment to Drive Away Swellings, Tumors, etc.

Bittersweet, Bark of the Root	1	ounce.
Stramonium Leaves	1	"
Water Hemlock Leaves	1	"
Belladonna Leaves	1	"
Yellow Dock Root	1	"
Poke Root	1	"
Venice Turpentine	1	"
Alcohol	½	pint.
Water	½	"
Lard	½	pound.

Bruise all of the roots and put into a suitable kettle for stewing; then put on the Alcohol and sufficient of the water to cover all of the articles well, and keep them moderately hot for twelve hours; then add the lard and increase and continue the heat until the roots and leaves are all crisped; then strain and add the Venice Turpentine, and keep it well stirred while cooling. The spirits are necessary to obtain all the properties of the articles.

Apply freely to any indolent swelling of the glands, or enlarging tumors, two or three times daily. Cover the parts with cotton, keeping it in place by bandaging; or otherwise, heat it in thoroughly for half an hour each time by means of a hot iron, or by the stove. Probably the most would be absorbed by covering it with the cotton and bandaging. It is reported to have cured even goiter.

Pain Killer, *for Bilious Colic and other Internal Pains.*

Alcohol	1	pint.
Opium	2	drachms.
Gum Camphor	½	ounce.
Gum Arabic	½	"
Gum Guaiac	½	"
Balsam of Fir	½	"
Balsam of Copaiba	½	"

Mix, and shake occasionally until all is dissolved.

Dose.—From ½ to 1 teaspoonful, according to the severity of the pain.

Painters' or Lead Paralysis of the Wrists—to Avoid.—Experience has shown that what is called lead paralysis, or loss of motion of the wrist-joints among painters, is largely owing to the habit they have of washing the hands in Turpentine to remove the paint. This dissolves the lead, zinc, etc., allowing it to be more freely absorbed than would otherwise occur; therefore, to avoid the paralysis, avoid the Turpentine.

Palpitation of the Heart, Immediate and Permanent Relief.—Hall's *Journal of Health* says that a lady of forty years who had been troubled for twelve years with periodical palpitation of the heart, found immediate and permanent relief in the use of soda water sold at soda fountains. The water is better drank clear, or containing but very little syrup.

Perspiration, Odor from.—This very great source of annoyance may be entirely removed as follows:

Mix a tablespoonful of the Compound Spirits of Ammonia in a small basin of water. By washing the arms, arm-pits and hands with this solution the skin will be left wholesome. It is cheap and harmless, and is much preferable to the perfumes and unguents which disguise the odor but do not correct the cause.

PILLS.

For Dinner Pills.

Aloes	4	ounces.
Jalap	4	"
Rhubarb	1	"
Wormwood, Syrup of, sufficient quantity.		

Mix, and divide into 3-grain pills.

Dose.—From 1 to 4 may be taken through the day.

Chapman's Dinner Pills.

Each pill contains the following:

Aloes	1½	grains.
Mastic	1½	"
Ipecac	1	"
Fennel, Oil of	1½	drop.

Dose.—One pill after dinner.

These will be found very satisfactory in many cases of constipation.

For Dyspepsia, to Give Tone to the Stomach, and Obstructed Menses.

Socotrine Aloes	4	drachms.
Castile Soap	2	"
Colocynth	2	"
Gamboge	2	"
Gentian, Extract of	4	"
Cloves, Oil of	2	drops.

Mix, and form into pills of the ordinary size.
Dose.—From 1 to 2, morning and evening, according to the way they operate.

For Regulating and Strengthening the Stomach and Bowels.

Compound Rhubarb Pill Mass	½	ounce.
Boneset, Extract of	½	"
Mandrake, pulverized	¼	"
Ginger, pure, pulverized	⅛	'

Mix, and form into pills of the ordinary size.
Dose.—From 1 to 2 to be taken morning and evening.

For Constipation, Deficiency of Bile, etc.

Inspissated Ox-Gall	1	drachm.
Gum Ammonia	1	"
Rhubarb, powdered	1	"

Mix into mass and form pills of 2 grains each.
Dose.—Five a day.

For Liver Complaint, Jaundice and Affections of the Kidneys.

Dandelion, Extract of	1	drachm.
Mandrake, pulverized	1	"
Blood Root, pulverized	1	"

Add a few drops of essential oil (Peppermint or Spearmint), and form the mass into pills of the common size.
Dose.—Take three night and morning.

For Coughs, Colds, Bronchial Affections, etc.

Henbane, Extract of	¼	ounce.
Canada Balsam	½	"
Ipecac	¼	"
Balm-of-Gilead Buds, Extract of	¼	"

Mix thoroughly together, add a few drops of the Oil of Anise, and form into pills of the ordinary size.
Dose.—One or 2 taken three or four times a day.

For Painful Nervous Affections.

Stramonium, Extract of	2	grains.
Henbane, Extract of	6	"
Hops, Extract of	½	drachm.

Mix, and divide into 12 pills.
Dose.—Give 1 every four hours, or until the pain subsides.

For Venereal and Skin Diseases.

Gold and Sodium, Chloride of	1	grain.
Mezereon, Extract of	1	drachm.

Mix, and form into 60 pills.
Dose.—One pill a day may be given.

PLASTERS.

For Strengthening Plaster.

Turpentine...	4 ounces.
Resin.....................................	sufficient quantity.
Mutton Tallow.......................................	" "
Vinegar.................................	" "

For Strengthening Plaster.

Henbane, Extract of...............................	1 ounce.
Cicuta, Extract of	1 "
Lead, Iodide of.....................................	½ "

Warm the extracts, then add the Lead and incorporate well together. Spread on a small piece of leather and apply to the parts, occasionally renewing it.

For Strengthening Plaster.

Yellow Resin..	8 ounces.
Beeswax	2 "
Cayenne Pepper	2 "
Spirits...	1 pint.

Simmer the pepper (enclosed in a linen bag) in the spirits and strain. Melt the other articles together, add the tincture, simmer till the spirits are nearly evaporated, remove from the fire, and when nearly cold add

Gum Camphor	2 ounces.
Oil of Sassafras...................................	3 drachms.

For Obstinate Ulcers.

Tar, thick	½ pound.
Gum Turpentine.......................................	¼ "
Burgundy Pitch	¼ "
Beeswax	¼ "

Melt, strain, and boil a few minutes; then remove from the fire, and, as it cools, stir in the following articles, finely pulverized, mixed and sifted, viz.: 3 ounces each of Poke Root, Mandrake, Blood Root and Indian Turnip. Stir it occasionally till the whole mass is well incorporated.

Directions.—Spread on a piece of soft leather and place over the part affected. Keep it on as long as it can be borne, then remove, and put it on again in a day or two. If the itching proves too troublesome, occasionally remove the plaster and wash the parts with spirits.

For Rheumatism, Cuts, Ulcers, etc.

White Resin...	12 ounces.
Beeswax	1 "
Burgundy Pitch	1 "
Mutton Tallow	1 "

Melt these together and add:

Olive Oil...	½ ounce.
Camphor	½ "
West India Rum......................................	1 gill.
Sassafras Oil	½ ounce.

When the latter articles have been incorporated with the former let the whole be poured into a vessel of water and kneaded with the hands until it is cold. In certain seasons and climates a little solution of Resin or of Olive Oil is required to render it of the proper consistence.

For Scrofulous, Cancerous and Hard Tumors.

The following is a very effective extract or plaster for scrofulous cancerous and hard tumors. It may be rubbed upon the parts affected, or a plaster of it applied:

Poke Root, Expressed Juice of................	½ gallon.
Gunpowder	1 gill.
Lard..	½ pint.

Simmer to the consistence of honey or molasses.

POULTICES.

Poultices should always be applied as hot as can be borne, and changed often enough to maintain a uniform temperature.

For General Inflammation, and especially of the Eyes.

Wheat Bread, stale	sufficient quantity.
Milk or Water.......................................	to moisten.

Soak the bread a short time in the milk or water and apply.

For Inflammation of the Eyes.

Common Potato, boiled and mashed soft..	sufficient quantity.
Slippery Elm Bark...............................	" "

Mix, and form a poultice.

For removing Inflammation in painful diseases, such as Pleurisy, Inflammatory Rheumatism, etc.

Lobelia, in powder	4	ounces.
Slippery Elm Bark...............................	4	"
Ginger..............	4	"
Whiskey, or other Spirits........................	sufficient quantity.	

Mix, and make into a poultice.

For Ulcerated Sores and Swellings of all kinds.

Garden Carrots, boiled and bruised	1	pound.
Flour...................	1	ounce.
Butter	½	ounce.

Mix, and make into a poultice.

For Scrofulous and Ulcerated Sores and Swellings.

Garden Carrot Roots	1 pound.

Wash them clean, scrape down to a pulp and apply.

For Rheumatism, Gout, Inflammatory Diseases, Fevers, etc.

Mustard, in powder......................	4	ounces.
Soft Bread, or Indian Meal.....................	6	"
Vinegar..	sufficient quantity.	

Mix, and make into a poultice.

POWDERS.

For Heartburn.

Quassia, pulverized	½	scruple.
Rhubarb	½	"
Calcined Magnesia	1	"

Mix, form a powder and divide it into twelve equal parts.

Dose.—Three powders a day.

For Hydragogue Purgative in Dropsy.

Jalap, pulverized	2	drachms.
Cream of Tartar	1	"

Mix, and divide into 12 powders.

Dose.—One powder every four hours, if needed.

For Diarrhea.

Rhubarb, powdered .... sufficient quantity.

Place in a shallow iron dish over the fire and brown, stirring constantly to prevent scorching.

Dose.—From 5 to 10 grains every two hours, or less often.

For Colds, Pain in the Stomach and Bowels, and to Promote Perspiration.

Bayberry	2	ounces.
Ginger	1	"
Cayenne Pepper	2	drachms.
Cloves	2	"

Pulverize finely and mix well.

Dose.—One-third teaspoonful in ½ glass of hot water every half hour until pain is relieved or until perspiration is produced.

For Piles and Skin Eruptions.

Flowers of Sulphur	½	ounce.
Cream of Tartar	1	"

Mix with molasses.

Dose.—A teaspoonful four or five times a day.

RHEUMATISM AND GOUT REMEDIES.

For Rheumatism.

Salicylic Acid	3	drachms.
Potash, Iodide of	160	grains.
Potash, Bicarbonate of	2	drachms.
Buchu, Fluid Extract of	1	ounce.
Gelsemium, Fluid Extract of	1	drachm.
Cimicifuga, Fluid Extract of	2	"
Alcohol	1	ounce.
Glycerine	3	"
Simple Elixir, add to	8	"

Mix all together and take teaspoonful every two hours until improvement, then less often.

Liniment for Rheumatism.

Ammonia, Water of	2	ounces.
Lavender, Oil of	1	drachm.
Camphor Gum	½	ounce.
Chloroform	1	"
Ether	½	"
Turpentine, Spirits of	1	drachm.
Alcohol	8	ounces.

Camphorated Oil Liniment(very powerful) *for Rheumatism.*

Camphorated Oil	2	ounces.
Turpentine, Spirits of	2	"
Laudanum	1	"
Aqua Ammonia	1	"

Shake well.

This will be found valuable in rheumatic pains of the loins, or for any chronic form of rheumatism about the joints.

For Rheumatism and Gout.

Potash, Bicarbonate of	5	drachms.
Potash, Iodide of	2½	"
Soda, Salicylate of	2½	"
Colchicum, Wine of	4	
Buchu, Infusion of, add to	8	ounces.

Dose.—One teaspoonful four to six times a day.

Liniment for Rheumatism and Gout.

Camphor Gum	2	ounces.
Origanum, Oil of	1	"
Hemlock, Oil of	1	"
Sassafras, Oil of	1	"
Cajeput, Oil of	1	"
Turpentine, Spirits of	½	"
Chloroform	½	"
Ether	½	"
Alcohol add to	1	pint.

For Gout.

Soda, Salicylate of	2	drachms.
Potash, Iodide of	2	"
Potash, Carbonate of	2	"
Cascara, Aromatic	2	ounces.
Simple Elixir, add to	4	"

Dose.—From 1 to 2 teaspoonfuls every two hours.

For Gout.

Potash, Bicarbonate of	2	drachms.
Potash, Iodide of	1	"
Soda, Salicylate of	1	"
Colchicium, Wine of	1½	"
Buchu, Infusion of, add to	6	ounces.

Dose.—One teaspoonful every two hours until improvement.

SALVES.

Bell's Salve or Ointment, *for Itch and other Skin Diseases.*

Lard	¼	pound.
Turpentine Spirits of	½	ounce.
Red Precipitate	½	"
Rosin	½	"
Corrosive Sublimate, powdered	2	grains.

Melt and mix.

This prescription has been successfully used for many years by a gentleman whose name it bears, in all eruptive diseases, as itch, salt rheum, etc.

Salve for Cuts, Bruises, Boils, etc.

Rosin	4	ounces.
Mutton Tallow	2	drachms.
Beeswax	1	"
Burgundy Pitch	1	"
Balsam of Fir	1	"
Venice Turpentine	1	"
Oil of Spike	1	scruple.
Hemlock, Oil of	1	"
Cedar, Oil of	1	"
Origanum, Oil of	1	"
Wormwood, Oil of	1	"
Laudanum	1	"
Camphor Gum, pulverized	1	"

The Oils, Balsam, Laudanum and Turpentine can all be put into one phial when purchasing. Melt the Rosin, Tallow, Beeswax and Pitch together. When a little cool, add the Oils, Laudanum, etc., stir in the pulverized Camphor and pour into cold water. By greasing the hands it can be pulled and worked as shoemaker's wax until it is all intimately mixed, when it can be rolled into suitable sized sticks for use or for sale.

For cuts, bruises, boils and all general purposes, this salve has no superior. It will remain upon the spot where it is placed, not shifting by motion nor heat of the body.

Salve for Strengthening and Stimulating Purposes.

In weak back, pains in the back or other parts, liver affections, etc., where it is desirable to apply a strengthening salve, or plaster, as usually called, add to the above very finely pulverized Verdigris, 1 drachm, at the same time the Camphor Gum and Oils are being added. The Verdigris is stimulating as well as detergent, *i. e.,* having a tendency to scatter or drive away disease from the parts.

For Scrofulous Ulcers.

Turpentine	2	ounces.
Bayberry Tallow	2	"

Dissolve together and form into a salve. If too hard or firm, add 1 tablespoonfnl, more or less, of Sweet Oil.

For Burns, Scrofulous, Fistulous and other Ulcers.

Olive Oil..	¼ pint.
Common Resin.....................................	1 drachm.
Beeswax	1 "

Melt these articles together, and raise the oil nearly to the boiling point; then gradually add of pulverized Red Lead, 1½ ounces, if it is winter; if summer, about 2 ounces. In a short time after the lead is taken up by the oil, and the mixture becomes brown or of a shining black, remove from the fire, and when nearly cold add ½ scruple of pulverized Camphor. It should remain on the fire until it forms a proper consistence for spreading, which may be known by dipping a knife into it from time to time and suffering it to cool.

Healing Salve.

Take a good sized handful of Comfrey root, wash and bruise and stew in about 1 pint of unsalted lard until crisped; then strain and add pulverized gunpowder, 2 tablespoonfuls, and Spirits of Turpentine, 1 tablespoonful, stirring as it cools to keep evenly mixed.

This makes a very valuable healing salve. The Comfrey root of itself, freshly dug and bruised, makes an excellent application to bruises, fresh wounds, sore breasts, ulcers, white swellings, etc.

SYRUPS.

Simple Syrup.—Simple Syrup is made by adding 2 pounds of granulated sugar to 1 pint of water, and dissolving by heat. It has been mentioned in many prescriptions given in this book.

For Coughs and Pulmonary Affections.

Spikenard Root.....................................	2	ounces.
White Root..	2	"
Blood Root..	1	"
Elecampane...	1	"
Coltsfoot	1	"
Boneset	1	"
Poplar Bark..	8	drachms.
Senega Snake Root..............................	4	"
Lobelia	4	"
Slippery Elm Bark................................	1	ounce.
Proof Spirits.......................................	3	pints.

Bruise, or pulverize all, and digest in the spirits for fourteen days; then strain, and add white sugar sufficient to form a syrup.

Dose.—A dessertspoonful occasionally in a mucilage of Slippery Elm.

For Epilepsy.

Peony Root..	8	ounces.
Peruvian Bark......................................	2	"
Virginia Snake Root..............................	2	"
Boiling Water......................................	1	quart.
White Sugar..	1½	pounds.

Extract the strength, simmer down to 1½ pints, then strain and add the sugar.

Dose.—A wineglassful three or four times a day.

For Scrofulous Affections.

Dandelion Root...............	¼	pound.
Sarsaparilla Root....................................	¼	"
Yellow Dock Root..................................	¼	"
Bittersweet, Bark of...	¼	"

Bruise, and boil till the strength is extracted; then strain, and simmer down to 1 quart. Add sugar sufficient to prevent fermentation.

Dose.—A wineglassful three times a day.

For Dysentery.

Blackberries, Juice of............................	8	ounces.
White Sugar.....................................	1	pound.

Mix, simmer and strain.

Dose.—A wineglassful four or five times a day.

TINCTURES.

For Rheumatism and other External Painful Chronic Conditions.

Gum Guaiacum....................................	2	drachms.
Nitre, Spirits of................................	2	"
Camphor	1½	scruple.
Balsam of Tolu.....................................	1½	"
Alcohol	½	pint.

Mix, and let stand one week. Strain or filter, and add ½ pint Glycerine.

Dose.—Take 2 teaspoonfuls three or four times a day in a tumbler of Prickly Ash tea.

For Pleurisy, Fever, Inflammation, etc., also in Dysentery.

Ipecac..	1	drachm.
Saffron	1	"
Camphor.	1	"
Virginia Snake Root.............................	1	"
Opium	10	grains.
Holland Gin or Jamaica Spirits...............	1½	gills.

Let it stand for two weeks, filter and bottle.

Dose.—One teaspoonful, given in a tumbler of Catnip tea every hour or two till it produces perspiration.

For Intermittent Fever, Fever and Ague.

Peruvian Bark.......................................	4	drachms.
Wild Cherry Bark.................................	2	"
Cinnamon..	1	scruple
Cloves	1	"
Nutmeg...	1	"
Sulphur...	2	drachms.
Wine	1	pint

Let it stand a sufficient time to extract the strength.

Dose.—A wineglassful every two or three hours.

TONICS.

Beef, Iron and Wine.

Iron and Ammonia, Citrate of	4	drachms.
Water	2½	ounces.
Simple Elixir	1	pint.
Beef, Extract of	½	ounce.
Good Wine	10	"

Mix all together in a large bottle. Shake occasionally and let stand for one week. Get two or three sheets of filtering paper, fold carefully and place in a funnel. Also get a little Wood Charcoal and carefully moisten it with a little of the solution, then pour the charcoal into the filter and filter the balance of the solution through the charcoal and paper. As a rule the beef extract is not added, because after standing for a time it becomes precipitated to the bottom of the bottle, and when shaken up makes a rather unsightly looking mixture.

Dose.—One teaspoonful at meal time. Larger doses may be taken.

Calisaya Bark and Iron.

Quinine, Sulphate of	20	grains.
Cinchona, Sulphate of	8	"
Citric Acid	5	"
Iron, Soluble, Citrate of	5	drachms.
Simple Elixir	1	pint.

Dose.—From 1 to 2 teaspoonfuls after meals.

Sweet Wine of Iron.

Cinchona, powdered	1	drachm.
Bitter Orange Peel, powdered	30	grains.
Citric Acid	30	"
Iron, Soluble Citrate of	2	drachms.
Water	3½	ounces.
Sherry Wine	7	"
Sweet Orange Peel, Tincture of	3½	"
Syrup	14	drachms.

Mix the tincture with the water, and with this percolate or mix the Cinchona and Orange Peel. Add to this the Citric Acid and Iron dissolved in the Wine, then add the Syrup and filter.

Dose.—One teaspoonful after meals and at bedtime.

Cordial for Tonic Purposes in all cases of nervous derangement and general debility, especially of that kind peculiar to females. Very useful in Leucorrhea, Consumption in its early stages, Dyspepsia, etc.

Comfrey Root	1	ounce.
Solomon's Seal	1	'
Spikenard Root	1	"
Columbo Root	½	"
Gentian Root	½	"
Chamomile Flowers	½	"

Bruise all together and add 4 quarts of the best Malaga Wine. Let it stand a week and strain.

Dose.—Half a wineglassful three or four times a day

TONIC BITTERS.

For General Tonic Purposes.

Red Cinchona Bark	2	ounces.
Gentian Root	2	"
Columbo Root	2	"
Juniper Berries	2	"
Glycerine	2	"
Alcohol	6	"
Water	10	"

Reduce the drugs to a moderately fine powder. Put into a large bottle, add the Alcohol and water and let stand for one week. Then get some filtering paper, place it carefully in a funnel, strain the liquid through it and add the Glycerine.

Dose.—One or two teaspoonfuls before meals.

For Dyspepsia, and Complaints Generally Requiring a Tonic.

Golden Seal	1	drachm.
Whitewood Bark	1	"
Bitter Root	1	"
Cayenne Pepper	1½	"

Bruise all and add 2 quarts of wine.

Dose.—From a tablespoonful to a wineglassful three times a day.

For Dyspepsia, Obstruction of the Menses, General Tonic Purposes.

Tamarack Bark	6	ounces.
Prickly Ash Bark	4	"
Wild Cherry Bark	3	"
Senega Snake Root	3	"
Tansy	1	"
Socotrine Aloes	½	"

Let these articles be pulverized and mixed, and take of the mixture ¼ pound, add 3 pints of boiling water, 2 quarts of Holland Gin and 1 pint of Molasses. Let stand a week.

Dose.—Half a wineglassful to be taken at morning, noon and evening.

VOMITING, TO CHECK.

Carbolic Acid	2	drops.
Bismuth, Subnitrate of	2	drachms.
Lime Water, add to	2	ounces.

Mix, and take from ½ to 1 teaspoonful every 20 to 30 minutes or one hour.

For Obstinate Cases.

Creosote	2	drops.
Mucilage of Gum Arabic	2	drachms.
Distilled Water	1	ounce.
Spirits of Nutmeg	2	drachms.

Mix. Let this draught be given at once, and repeated every other hour until the vomiting is checked.

COLD CREAMS.

Face Massage Cream.—Put 4 ounces of Sweet Almond Oil into the inside receptacle of a custard boiler. Put as much warm water into the outside boiler as though you were going to make a custard.

Set the two—one inside the other—over the fire. Have ready one good sized cucumber, which wash and cut into squares two or three inches in size. Do not remove the peel. When the Almond Oil begins to boil, put the sliced cucumber into it. Set the custard boiler on the back of the stove and let the water merely simmer for four or five hours. Strain. To 6 ounces of the strained liquid add 1 ounce of White Wax, 1 of Spermaceti and 2 of Lanoline (or wool fat). Heat until the Wax, Spermaceti and Lanoline have melted, then take off the fire and beat with an egg-beater until cold, adding during the beating process 2 teaspoonfuls of Tincture of Benzoin.

This is an excellent cream if properly and carefully made.

Another Face Cream.

White Wax	1	ounce.
Spermaceti	1	"
Almond Oil	3	"
Lanoline	1	"

Put these four ingredients into the inner vessel of the custard boiler. Fill the outer vessel about full of warm water and set over the fire. Place the inner vessel into the outer receptacle. When all the ingredients have melted, take the inner vessel out, stir the mixture constantly until cold, adding, little by little during the stirring, 3 ounces of Rosewater, 1 ounce of Witch Hazel and 1 drachm of Tincture of Benzoin. This will result in more than ½ pound of delightful cream for the purpose suggested.

An Elegant Cold Cream.

Glycerine	6	ounces.
Lanoline	1½	"
Petrolatum, white	4½	"

Mix the Lanoline and Petrolatum and then incorporate the Glycerine. Flavor with 3 or 4 drops of the Oil of Rose or other perfume. Put up in small jars or boxes. This is one of the finest preparations of its kind, easily made and keeps for any length of time.

Camphor Ice.

Petrolatum, white	2	ounces.
White Wax, pure	2	'
Camphor Gum	4	"
Rosin, white	4	"
Glycerine	16	"

Melt all together, stir well, and when nearly cold pour into jars or other receptacles.

Chapped Hands Preparation.

Quince Seed	½	ounce.
Borax, powdered	2	drachms.
Glycerine	1½	ounces.
Hot Water	12	"

Pour the hot water on the Quince seed and let stand until thick, which may require from twelve to twenty-four hours, then strain through a coarse cloth. Dissolve the Borax in a small amount of this, being careful to break up all of the lumps, and add it and the Glycerine to the mixture. Perfume can be added to suit.

FACE POWDERS.

Complexion Powder.

Bismuth, Subnitrate of	1	ounce.
Magnesia, Carbonate of	1	"
French Chalk	10	"

Add a few drops of Oil of Rose, or other perfume if desired.

Complexion Powder.

Zinc, Oxide of	3	ounces.
Precipitated Chalk	4	"
French Chalk	10	"
Magnesia, Light Carbonate of	1½	"
Rose, Oil of	2	drops.
Rose Geranium, Tincture of	10	"

Mix thoroughly by passing several times through a fine sieve. If desired, a few grains of Carmine may be added to give a pink color.

Borated Talcum.

French Chalk, powdered and purified	10	ounces.
Boric Acid, powdered	8	"
Violet, Tincture of	1	drachm.
Jasmine, Tincture of	½	"
Vanilla, Tincture of	½	"

Mix the French Chalk and Boric Acid, then mix the tinctures and add to the powder by means of an atomizer spray. Lastly mix by passing several times through a fine sieve.

HAIR, RECEIPTS FOR.

Hair Dye—In Three Numbers.

No. 1.	Distilled Water	4	ounces.
	Alcohol	1	"
	Pyrogallic Acid	1	drachm.

The Pyrogallic Acid is to be put into the Alcohol until dissolved, then the water added, and the preparation corked for use.

No. 2.	Aqua Ammonia	1	ounce.
	Water	1	"
	Nitrate of Silver	2	drachms.

Put the Nitrate of Silver into the Ammonia until dissolved, then add the water, cork and keep in a dark place.

No. 3. Distilled water 4   ounces.
          Sulphuret of Potash .... ½   "

Mix cork, and keep in cool place. This number loses its virtue in a month or two, but is not expensive to make.

To dye the moustache, whiskers or hair, be sure they are clean and free from soap, and only a little damp; then carefully apply No. 1, not getting it upon the skin and while it is still damp, but somewhat dried, apply No. 2, also avoiding the skin. In case any of either number touches the skin, it is best to have a damp sponge or a damp cloth and wipe it off immediately. Two or three minutes after No. 2 has been applied all over carefully, apply No. 3, which will "set" the dye and give it more depth of color, and also make it a more lively and natural black. If there is any of the silver number left on the skin, at the edges of the hair or whiskers, touch it with the No. 3, when it may be removed with a damp sponge. Be careful to take up all of the No. 3 with the damp sponge or cloth, otherwise it will give the skin a yellowish brown appearance from the action of the air upon it when you go out.

Pomade Hair Restorative—French.

Almond Oil .... ¼ pound.
White Wax .... ½ ounce.
Lard, clarified.. 3   "
Liquid Ammonia .... 2 drachms.

Add a few drops of Rose, Lavender, Bergamot or other perfume.

Place the Oil, Wax and Lard in a jar, and set the jar into boiling water until the wax is melted; then remove, and when nearly ready to set or stiffen, stir in the Ammonia and perfumes and put into boxes or jars for use, covering well. Apply the pomade at night only, not using combs nor harsh brushes during the growth of young hair.

The argument for the use of Ammonia is, that it contains nitrogen, which is one of the principal constituents of the hair, consequently affords nourishment. *It is utterly impossible for the animal economy to create hair out of any oil, because oil is destitute of nitrogen;* but if oil or grease is combined with *Ammonia*, which yields *nitrogen*, then great benefit will be derived from a pomade so made. All oils and pomades without Ammonia act only as polishers, affording no nourishment.

Another Restorative.—A very nice article of hair restorative and dressing is made as follows:

Rain Water .... 8 ounces.
Bay Rum 4   '
Aqua Ammonia .... ½   "
Glycerine.. ¼   "

Mix, bottle and keep corked.

The Glycerine gives it a glossiness, while the Ammonia and Bay Rum stimulate the surface to a healthy action.

Hair Invigorator.—A simple and pleasant article to invigorate the scalp, to remove dandruff and to prevent its return is the following:

Alcohol	1	pint.
Gum Camphor	2	ounces.

Apply daily, by means of a piece of sponge, for a month, or until the head is clean and free from dandruff; then once or twice a week only will keep it clean and healthy.

Another Invigorator.

Alcohol, of the best quality	1	pint.
Rain, or distilled, Water	1	"
Aqua Ammonia	1	ounce.

Mix. Wet the head thoroughly and rub well to the roots of the hair once daily.

This has brought out hair on absolutely bald patches on the head.

Hair Tonic.

Cantharides, Tincture of	2	drachms.
Quinine	½	"
Ammonia, Muriate of	2	scruples.
Glycerine	4	ounces.
Cologne	4	"
Water, distilled	4	"

When there is any irritation of the scalp, this preparation is especially valuable. It will be found very satisfactory as a stimulant or tonic to the scalp, while at the same time it acts as a hair dressing.

Another Tonic.

Glycerine	1	ounce.
Bay Rum	1	"
Cantharides. Tincture of	½	"
Aqua Ammonia	¼	"
Rosewater	½	pint.

Shampoo for Removing Dandruff and Scurf from the Head.

Alcohol	1	pint.
Water, soft	3	"
Cantharides, Tincture of	½	ounce.
Ammonia, Carbonate of	1	"
Potassa, Carbonate of	1	"
Bergamot, or Oil of Lavender	1	drachm.

Put the oils into the Alcohol, dissolve the carbonates in the water and mix all. It is used in cases where the dandruff in the hair has become so excessive as to fall out and keep the coat littered with it. Pour on sufficient to wet the hair completely, then with the ends of the fingers loosen the dandruff from the scalp thoroughly to allow the Ammonia, Alcohol and Cantharides, which are valuable correctives and stimulants to the skin, to have their full effect. In washing out it will be important to keep the eyes closed, as it would be a rather strong mixture for their comfort. Use any oily hair dressing after it. Any person whose condition of health is such that dandruff forms freely and readily should wash the head often with plain water and soap, and use one of the restoratives or invigorators above until a healthy state of the scalp is obtained, then as often as needed to maintain or keep it in a healthy condition.

Another Shampoo.

Alcohol	2	ounces.
Ammonia, Water of	1½	drachms.
Glycerine	1	"
Salts of Tartar (called also Carbonate of Potash	1	'
Castile Soap	10	grains.
Water, add enough to make	5	ounces.

Mix together. This application is pleasant to use and is very cleansing. If the head is rubbed briskly while applying it, a large amount of foam is produced. This disappears in a few minutes, leaving the scalp clean and fresh.

Hair Curling Liquid.

Borax, pulverized	1	ounce.
Gum Arabic, pulverized	½	drachm.
Water, scalding hot	1	pint.

Mix, and stir until dissolved; then add Spirits of Camphor, 2 tablespoonfuls, and bottle.

On retiring, moisten the hair with the above and paper in the usual style.

Hair Oils.—A cheap and good article is made suitable for a hair dressing, when there is no baldness nor call for a restorative, by clarifying lard oil, as follows:

Lard Oil	1¼	pints.
Alcohol	2	ounces.

Bottle, cork and shake, and shake frequently for two or three days; then let it stand and settle until clear, and pour off from the sediment for use.

This may be flavored with Oil of Citronella, Bergamot, Lavender or Rosemary, as preferred, ½ ounce; and if it is desired to give it color, tie Alkanet root, bruised, ½ ounce, in a bit of muslin, and put into the oil until a light purple shade is produced. Tumeric used instead of Alkanet gives a yellow shade.

Hen s Oil is a very fine oil, free from gumminess, and consequently makes an excellent hair dressing when flavored with Oil of Citronella, ½ ounce, and Bergamot, ¼ ounce, to 1 pint of the oil. This receipt is as good as it is short. Other flavoring oils may be used, if preferred.

Verbena Oil.

Cologne Alcohol	½	pint.
Otto, or Oil of Verbena	1	drachm.
Lavender, Oil of	20	drops.
Bergamot, Oil of	20	"

Mix all together.

Bay Rum Mixture.

Bay, Oil of	½	ounce.
Cloves, Oil of	½	"
Red Thyme, Oil of	1	"
Allspice, Oil of	1	"

Mix all together.

To make Bay Rum, add ¼ ounce of this mixture to 2 pints of Alcohol. Shake thoroughly and add 2 pints of water and 1 ounce of Carbonate of Magnesia, finely pulverized. Place it in a filter and filter the Bay Rum through it.

Another Bay Rum Mixture.

Bay, Oil of	1	ounce.
Cloves, Oil of	1	drachm.
Sweet Orange, Oil of	1	"
Neroli Petale, Oil of	30	drops.
Allspice, Oil of	30	"
Cardamon, Oil of	3	"

Prepare as above.

PERFUMES.

White Rose.

Rose, Oil of	15	drops.
Rose Geranium, Oil of	10	"
Patchouli, Oil of	2	"
Ambrette, Tincture of	2	ounces.
Orris, Tincture of	4	"
Deodorized Alcohol	12	"
Rosewater	1	pint.

Dissolve the oils in the deodorized Alcohol, add the tinctures, shake well, then slowly add the Rosewater and filter through filtering paper. If desired, a slight tinge of color may be given by adding a very small amount of Aniline.

Mary Stuart.

Rose, Oil of	15	drops.
Sandal Wood, Oil of	5	"
Bergamot, Oil of	½	drachm.
Orris Root, Tincture of	4	ounces.
Vanilla, Tincture of	1	"
Civet, Tincture of	1	"
Deodorized Alcohol	3	"
Rosewater	7	"
Magnesia, Carbonate of	½	"

Mix the oils and tinctures with 1½ ounces of the deodorized Alcohol, place the Magnesia in a mortar or some convenient vessel, pour on the solution of oils and Alcohol and mix thoroughly. Mix the remaining 1½ ounces of Alcohol and the Rosewater, add all together and filter through filtering paper.

Jockey Club.

Bergamot, Oil of	6	drachms.
Lavender, Oil of	15	drops.
Rose, Oil of	8	"
Orris Root, Tincture of	4	ounces.
Vanilla, Tincture of	1½	"
Cologne Spirits	4	"
Rosewater	7	"

Mix as above.

SACHET POWDERS.

Lavender.

Lavender Flowers	8	ounces.
Thyme, dried and powdered	½	"
Spearmint, dried	½	"
Cloves, powdered	¼	"
Caraway, powdered	¼	"
Lavender, Oil of	1	drachm.

Mix thoroughly, allow to stand for several days closely covered. then divide, place in several envelopes and seal.

Heliotrope.

Orris Root, powdered	6	ounces.
Vanilla, powdered	2	drachms.
Musk	3	grains.
Almonds, Essential Oil of	1	drop.

Mix thoroughly and divide as above.

Essence Bouqet.

Orris Root, powdered	2	ounces.
Grain Musk	8	grains.
Rose, Oil of	8	drops.
Bergamot, Oil of	20	"
Lemon, Oil of	5	"

Mix and divide as above.

TOILET WATERS.

Lavender Water.

Lavender, Oil of	2	drachms.
Bergamot, Oil of	1	'
Vanilla, Tincture of	4	"
Angelica, Tincture of	4	"
Cologne Spirits	10	ounces.
Rosewater	4	"

Dissolve the oils in the spirits, add the tinctures and let stand for three days, then add the Rosewater and let stand one week more, after which filter through a little Magnesia.

Florida Water.

Lavender, Oil of	¼	ounce.
Bergamot, Oil of	¼	"
Lemon, Oil of	¼	"
Sweet Orange, Oil of	½	drachm.
Cloves, Oil of	15	drops.
Cassia, Oil of	½	drachm.
Cologne Spirits	3	pints.
Rosewater	1	"

Mix and filter through Magnesia.

TOOTH POWDERS, ETC.

Precipitated Chalk	1	ounce.
Borax, finely pulverized	1	drachm.
Rose Oil	2	drops.

Intimately mix and keep in closely covered boxes for use.

Note.—If there is a tendency to sponginess or bleeding of the gums, dissolve 3 grains of Camphor Gum in a trifle of Alcohol and add to the above in place of the Rose Oil.

Antiseptic Tooth Powder.

Precipitated Chalk	4	ounces.
Orris Root, powdered	1	"
Boric Acid, powdered	½	"

Mix thoroughly by passing several times through a fine sieve.

Antiseptic Tooth Powder.

Precipitated Chalk	2	ounces.
Orris Root, powdered	2	drachms.
Camphor Gum, powdered	1	"
Boric Acid	2	"
Saccharine, powdered	1	grain.
Cloves, Oil of	1	drop.

Mix thoroughly by passing several times through a fine sieve.

Antiseptic Tooth Wash.

Alcohol, deodorized	6	ounces.
Boric Acid	½	drachm.
Thymol	8	grains.
Glycerine	½	ounce.
Eucalyptus, Oil of	5	drops.
Wintergreen, Oil of	8	"
Water	7	ounces.

Dissolve the Oils, Thymol and Boric Acid in the deodorized Alcohol. Mix the water and Glycerine, then add all together and filter through filtering paper.

CLEANING RECEIPTS FOR CLOTHING, ETC.

Cloth Cleaning Compound.

Glycerine.	1	ounce.
Sulphuric Ether	1	"
Alcohol	1	"
Ammonia	4	"
Castile Soap	1	"

Mix together and add sufficient water to make 2 quarts. Apply and rinse.

Scouring Balls, to Remove Grease, etc., from Cloth.

Soft Soap	1	pound.
Fuller's Earth	1	"

Beat well together in a mortar and form into cakes. The spot, first moistened with water, is rubbed with the cake and allowed to dry, when it is well rubbed with a little warm water, and afterwards rinsed or rubbed off clean.

Black Cloth, to Clean.

Ammonia, Bicarbonate of	1	ounce.
Water, warm	1	quart.

Dissolve the Ammonia in the water and rub the cloth with the solution, using a piece of flannel or black cloth for the purpose. After the application of this solution clean the cloth well with clear water, and dry and iron it, brushing it from time to time in the direction of the fiber.

Satins, to Clean.—Satins may be cleaned with a weak solution of Borax or Benzine when greasy. Care should be taken to sponge moderately and lengthwise, not across, the fabric. Iron on the wrong side only. White, cream and pink satins may be treated in the same way as light colored silks.

Black Satin, to Clean.—Boil 3 pounds of potatoes to a pulp in a quart of water, strain through a sieve, and brush the satin with it on a board or table, using a soft brush or sponge. The satin must not be wrung, but folded down in cloths for three hours and then ironed on the wrong side.

Black Silk, to Clean.—To bullock's gall add boiling water sufficient to make it warm, and with a clean sponge rub the silk well on both sides. Squeeze it out gently, and proceed in like manner until thoroughly cleaned. Rinse it in soft water, and

685

change the water until perfectly clear. Dry it in the air, and then dip a sponge in glue water and rub it on the wrong side, pin it out on a table and let dry before a fire.

White or Light Silk, to Clean.—Dissolve Naphtha soap in water, and add enough cool or lukewarm water to form the desired amount of suds. Dip the silk up and down in the water, gently rubbing any spots until they disappear—do not rub soap on the silk—rinse in lukewarm water and dry. Press on the wrong side.

Method Used in Cleaning Establishments.—The method used in establishments of this kind for cleaning silks, French flannels and other wool cloths, is to put the garment into a jar containing sufficient gasoline to cover it nicely, dipping it up and down, and rubbing soiled spots, or the entire garment, with Ivory soap. Rinse in clean gasoline. By shaking the garment in the air for fifteen or twenty minutes, or pinning it to a line with a good breeze blowing, the odor will be removed. It is not necessary to press it, unless it may be in much wrinkled parts, when the pressing should be done on the wrong side. Flutings, shirrings, etc., can be smoothed out with the fingers.

Ribbons, to Clean.—A good quality of ribbon, and especially in light colors, may be made to look like new. Wash with Naphtha soap, as above, or make a hot suds of other good soap, rub gently with the hands until clean, rinse and put into a clean white cloth to wring, for instance, into a sheet. This will leave the ribbon only a little damp. Do not press it, but lay it on the ironing board with the wrong side up, set a moderately warmed flat on it and *draw the ribbon through under the flat until smoothed.* The right side will look like new.

Lace, to Wash.—Cover an ordinary wine bottle with fine flannel, stitching it firmly around the bottle. Tack one end of the lace to the flannel, roll it very smoothly around the bottle and tack down the other end, then cover with a piece of very fine flannel or muslin. Now rub it gently with a strong soap liquor, and, if the lace is very much discolored or dirty, fill the bottle with hot water, place it in a kettle or saucepan of suds and boil it for a few minutes, then place the bottle under a tap of running water to rinse out the soap. Make some strong starch, and melt in it a piece of white wax and a little loaf sugar. Plunge the bottle two or three times into this and squeeze out the superfluous starch with the hands. Next dip the bottle in cold water, remove the outer covering from the lace, fill the bottle with hot water and stand it in the sun to dry the lace. When nearly dry, take it very carefully off the bottle and pick it out with the fingers. Lay it in a cool place to dry thoroughly.

Black Lace, to Revive.—Make some black tea, about the strength usual for drinking, and strain it off the leaves. Pour enough tea into a basin to cover the quantity of lace, let it stand ten or twelve hours, then squeeze it several times but do not rub it. Dip it frequently into the tea, which will at length assume a dirty appearance. Have ready some weak gum water, and press the lace gently through it; then clap it for a quarter of an hour, after which pin it to a towel in any shape which you wish it to take. When nearly dry, cover it with another towel and iron it with a cool iron. The lace, if previously sound and discolored only, will after this process look as good as new.

Plush, to Renovate.—To restore plush, hold the wrong side over steam arising from boiling water until the pile rises; or dampen lightly the wrong side of the plush and hold it over a pretty hot iron, not hot enough to scorch, however; or heat a clean brick, place upon it a wet cloth, hold the plush over it, and the steam will raise the nap.

To Raise the Pile on Velvet.—Put on a table two sticks of wood, place between them, bottom side up, three very hot flat-irons, and over these lay a wet cloth. Hold the velvet over the cloth, with the wrong side down and, when thoroughly steamed, brush the pile with a light whisk. The velvet will look as good as new.

Dark Furs, to Clean.—For sable, chinchilla, squirrel, fitch, etc., heat a quantity of new bran in a pan, stirring constantly so that it will not burn. When well heated, rub thoroughly into the fur. Repeat two or three times. Shake the fur and brush briskly until free from dust.

Light Furs, to Clean.—White furs, ermine, etc., may be cleaned in the following way: Lay the fur on a table and rub with bran slightly moistened with warm water. Rub until dry, then rub with dry bran. Use flannel for rubbing with the wet bran and book muslin for the dry. After using the bran, rub with Magnesia. Dry flour may be used instead of wet bran. Rub the wrong way of the fur, and afterwards shake and brush to place.

Glove Cleaner.

Castile Soap, white	3	ounces.
Javelle Water	2	"
Water	2	"
Water of Ammonia	1	drachm.

Dissolve the soap by the aid of heat in the water and, when nearly cold, add the Javelle Water and the Water of Ammonia. The preparation should form a paste, to be rubbed on the soiled part of the glove with a piece of flannel. This recipe is in use in many large cleaning establishments, and can be recommended.

Canteine—French Glove Cleaner.

Curd Soap (in small shavings)................	1	ounce.
Water....................................	3	"

Mix with heat and stir in

Essence of Citron....................	1	"

Saponine—French Glove Cleaner.

Duvignau Soap, in powder (or any good soap powder).....................	5	parts.
Water :..................................	3	"

Dissolve with heat and add

Eau de Javelle (Javelle Water)..............	3	"
Ammonia Water.....................	⅖	"

Directions.—A small portion of either of the above is rubbed over the glove with a piece of flannel (always in one direction) until it is sufficiently clean.

Kid Gloves, to Clean.—Put them, together with a sufficient quantity of pure Benzine, into a large stoppered vessel, and shake the whole occasionally, with alternate rest. If on removing the gloves there remain any spots, rub them out with a soft cloth moistened with Ether or Benzole. Dry the gloves by exposure to the air, and then place smoothly between glass plates at the temperature of boiling water until the last traces of Benzine are expelled. They may then be folded and pressed between paper with a warm iron.

Another way is to use a strong solution of pure soap in hot milk beaten up with the yolk of 1 egg to a pint of the solution. Put the glove on the hand and rub it gently with the paste, to which a little Ether may be added, then carefully lay by to dry. White gloves are not discolored by this treatment, and leather will be made thereby clean and soft as when new.

Kid Gloves, to Clean without Wetting.—Stale bread is sometimes used for this purpose. The gloves are put on, the softer part of the bread is broken up into crumbs, and the hands are rubbed one over the other as in the act of washing, the crumbs being thus rubbed over all parts of the gloves. Spongy rubber is often used for glove cleaning. It is applied in the same manner as in cleaning drawings, *i. e.*, it is rubbed over the soiled parts of the glove.

Straw, to Clean.—Wash in warm soap liquor, brushing well both inside and out, then rinse in cold water and it is ready for bleaching. Or, if the hat is not intended for bleaching, clean a small part only at a time and do not make it too wet, as otherwise it will destroy the sizing and give the hat a wilted look.

Note.—Preparations for cleaning straw may be purchased at a trifling expense.

Straw, to Bleach.—Put a small quantity of Salts of Sorrel or Oxalic Acid into a clean pan, and pour on it sufficient scalding water to cover the bonnet or hat. Put the bonnet or hat into this liquor, and let it remain in it for about five minutes; to keep it covered hold it down with a clean stick. Dry in the sun or before a clear fire. Or, having first dried the bonnet or hat, put it, together with a saucer of burning Sulphur, into a box with a tightly closing lid. Cover it over to keep in the fumes, and let it remain for a few hours. The disadvantage of bleaching with Sulphur is that the articles so bleached soon become yellow, which does not happen to them when they are bleached by Oxalic Acid.

Straw, to Finish or Stiffen—After cleaning and bleaching, white bonnets should be stiffened with parchment size. Black or colored bonnets are finished with a size made from the best glue. Straw or chip plaits, or leghorn hats and bonnets, may also be cleaned, bleached and finished as above.

White Manila Hats, to Clean.—Sprinkle with water and expose to the fumes of burning Sulphur in a tight box.

Panama Hats, to Clean.—To renovate white straw hats, the following method has been recommended. Prepare two solutions as follows:

I.—Sodium Hyposulphite	2½	drachms.
Glycerine	1	"
Alcohol	2½	"
Water	2¼	ounces.
II.—Citric Acid	½	drachm.
Alcohol	2½	"
Water	3	ounces.

First sponge the straw hat with solution No. I, and lay aside in a moist room (cellar) for twenty-four hours; then apply solution No. II and treat similarly. Finally the hat should be gone over with a flatiron, not too hot. If very dirty, the hat must be cleaned and dried before beginning the bleaching operation.

Felt Hats, to Clean.—Clean with Ammonia and water; if greasy, wash with Fuller's Earth. Size with glue size and block while warm. Glue size is made by diluting hot glue with hot water. Apply inside, not outside the hat. The thicker the glue, the stiffer the hat.

White Ostrich Feathers, to Clean.—Four ounces white curd soap cut small, dissolved in 4 pints water, rather hot, in a basin. Make the solution into a lather by beating. Introduce the feathers and rub well with the hands for five or six minutes. After the soaping, wash in clean water as hot as the hand can bear. Shake until dry.

Shoes, to Clean.—Defaced kid boots will be greatly improved by being rubbed well with a mixture of cream and ink.

Diamonds, to Clean.— Clean all diamonds and precious stones by washing them with soap and water with a soft brush, adding a little Ammonia to the water, and then dry in fine box-wood sawdust. A little Potash or Pearl Ash put in the water will answer the same purpose.

Sponges, to Clean.—Mix about a pint of water in a large basin, add 2 tablespoonfuls of Sulphuric Acid (common Oil of Vitriol), then steep the sponge about two hours, wringing it out several times in the acid, and finally wash out the acid in clean water. It will be just like new, regaining its former size, color and elasticity.

STAINS, TO REMOVE.

Stains from Acids, Vinegar, Sour Wine, Must, Sour Fruits, to Remove.— For white goods, simple washing, followed by Chlorine water if a fruit color accompanies the acid; for colored cottons, woolens and silks, carefully moisten with dilute Ammonia, applied with the finger ends. In case of delicate colors it will be found preferable to make some Prepared Chalk into a thin paste with water and apply it to the spots.

Note.—The Chlorine water mentioned above may be obtained at a drug store. *It should not be used on colored fabrics.*

Blood Stains, to Remove.—An accidental prick of the finger frequently spoils the appearance of work. Stains may be entirely obliterated from almost any substance by laying a thick coating of common starch over the place. The starch is to be mixed as if for the laundry and laid on quite wet.

Blood Stains, to Remove.—The free and early application of a weak solution of Soda or Potash, and the subsequent application of a solution of Alum, is also recommended.

Fruit Stains, to Remove.—Fruit stains, when fresh, may be removed by pouring boiling water through the stained portion until the spot disappears.

Grass Stains, to Remove.—Grass stains should be rubbed with molasses thoroughly and then washed out as usual. Another treatment is to rub with Alcohol and then wash in water.

Old Fruit Stains, to Remove.—Old fruit stains may be removed with Oxalic Acid. Wash the stained portion in the Oxalic Acid until clear, then rinse at once in rain water as the acid will attack the fabric if left upon it. Now wet the spot in Ammonia and give a final rinsing.

Milk and Coffee Stains, to Remove.—These stains are very difficult to remove, especially from light colored and finely finished goods. From woolen and mixed fabrics they are taken out by moistening them with a mixture of 1 part Glycerine, 9 parts water and ½ part Aqua Ammonia. This mixture is applied to the goods by means of a brush, and allowed to remain for twelve hours, occasionally renewing the moistening. After this time the stained pieces are pressed between cloth, and then rubbed with a clean rag. Drying, and if possible a little steaming, is generally sufficient to thoroughly remove the stains.

Linen, to Clean.—When linen is discolored by washing, age, or lying out of use, the best method of restoring the whiteness is by bleaching in the open air, and exposure on the grass to the dews and winds. There may occur cases, however, where this is difficult to accomplish, and where a quicker process may be desirable, for which the following is recommended:

Lay the linen for twelve hours in a lye formed of 1 pound Soda to a gallon of boiling hot soft water, and then boil it for half an hour in the same liquid. Then make a mixture of Chloride of Lime with eight times its quantity of water, which must be well shaken in a stone jar for three days, then allowed to settle and be drawn off clear, in which the linen must be steeped for thirty-six hours and then washed out in the ordinary way. This will remove all discoloration.

Rust and Ink Stains, to Remove.—Rust and ink stains should be rubbed with juice of lemon, the spot then covered with salt and the cloth placed in the sun. If this treatment does not serve to remove the stain, or if the fabric is colored and so cannot be treated with lemon juice, Oxalic Acid may be used as for old fruit stains.

Writing Ink Stains, to Remove.—Try Oxalic Acid followed by Chloride of Lime. Wash thoroughly with plenty of water afterwards.

Marking Ink Stains, etc., to Remove.—Apply Tincture of Iodine. The silver in the ink forms Silver Iodide, which is removed by a weak solution of Potassium Cyanide (deadly poison).

Printer's Ink Stains, to Remove.—Put the stained parts of the fabric into a quantity of Benzine, then use a fine, rather stiff brush, with fresh Benzine. Dry and rub bright with warm water and curd soap. The Benzine will not injure the fabric or dye.

Ink.—Ink that is freshly spilled upon a carpet should be covered with common or coarse salt or Indian meal. If the stain is not all absorbed, rub with lemon juice.

Broadcloth, to Remove Stains from.— Grind fine 1½ ounces Pipe Clay; mix with 18 drops of Alcohol and the same quantity Spirits of Turpentine. Moisten a little of this mixture with Alcohol and rub on the stains. When dry, rub off with a woolen cloth.

Color, to Restore.—When acid has accidentally or otherwise destroyed or changed the color of a fabric, Ammonia should be applied to neutralize the acid. A subsequent application of Chloroform restores the original color.

Mildew Stains, to Remove.—Mix well together a spoonful of table salt, 2 of soft Soap, 2 of powdered Starch and the juice of a lemon. Lay this mixture on both sides of the stain with a painter's brush, and then lay the article on the grass, day and night, until the stain disappears.

Mildew, to Prevent. — Housekeepers are often greatly troubled and perplexed by mildew from damp closets and from rust. By putting an earthen bowl or deep plate full of quick-lime into the closet, the lime will absorb the dampness and also sweeten and disinfect the place. Rats, mice, and many bugs that are apt to congregate in damp places have a dislike to lime. As often as the lime becomes slaked, throw it on the compost heap if in the country, or into the ash barrel if in the city.

GREASE, TO REMOVE.

Lightning Renovator, to Remove Grease.

Castile Soap	4	ounces.
Hot Water	1	quart.

When the soap is dissolved, add

Water	4	quarts.
Water of Ammonia	4	ounces.
Sulphuric Ether	1	"
Glycerine	1	"
Alcohol	1	"

Grease Spots, to Remove.—Put over the spot a piece of blotting paper and apply a hot iron.

Or, apply French chalk, put a piece of paper over it and apply the iron.

Or, try Ether or Benzine, and put blotting paper above and below the spot.

LAUNDRY RECEIPTS.

Jackman's Washing Compound.

Sal Soda	6	pounds
Borax	1	"

Dissolve in 1 gallon of boiling water and, when cold, add

Potassium Carbonate	⅓	pound.
Ammonia Water	3	ounces.
Alcohol	4	teaspoonfuls.

Boil for five minutes ¾ pound fresh unslaked lime in 1 gallon of water. Draw off the clear fluid when thoroughly settled, and add to this the other ingredients together with 9 gallons of cold water.

Directions for Using: Soak the clothes over night, after rubbing soft soap on the dirty places. In the morning add ½ pint of the compound, ½ pint soft soap and 4 gallons hot water. Boil not more than five minutes, and turn into a tub, putting into your boiler the same mixture as before. Wring the clothes into this and boil again ten minutes, suds them, blue them and hang them out to dry. Should the wristbands or parts that are very dirty need a little rubbing, it should be done while the mixture is boiling.

Washing Powder Compound.

Sal Soda, dried	1	ounce.
Muriate of Ammonia, powdered	1	"
Soda Ash	1	pound.

The ingredients should be well dried before mixing.

Directions: Put the clothes to soak over night in clear water. In the morning put the boiler on the stove half full of cold water, dissolve one tablespoonful of the compound in a little water and add to the boiler. Stir well. Now put in the clothes and boil twenty minutes, then take them out, rub lightly, rinse and hang out to dry, and you will be surprised to see how much labor is saved. The compound will not injure the clothes, and saves half the labor.

Wash Bluing.

Ferrocyanuret of Iron	1	ounce.
Oxalic Acid	¼	"
Water, distilled	3	pints.

Dissolve the iron and acid in a pint of the water, and add the remaining 2 pints. This makes a good article of bluing.

Indigo Wash Bluing.

Best Bengal Indigo	5	drachms.
Sulphuric Acid, strong	30	"

After five days place mixture in a tub and pour on ⅓ gallon boiling water.

Flannel Washing.—To wash flannel or flannel garments, prepare a good lather in hot water, and when just warm throw in your flannel and work it up and down, backward and forward. Scrubbing must be avoided, and no soap should be actually rubbed on it as this will induce further shrinkage. Rinse in warm water, twice if necessary. Never wash or rinse in hot or cold water, as either causes the flannel to shrink suddenly.

Flannels, to Iron.—Most flannels are the better for not being ironed, but in some cases it is necessary to do so. The proper way is to dry the flannels, then spread them on an ironing board, cover them with a slightly damp cloth, and iron over this, pressing down heavily. The iron must not be too hot.

Flannel Blankets, to Wash.—Put the soiled blankets to soak for fifteen minutes in plain soft warm water. Prepare a soft jelly with first-class laundry soap and boiling water, 1 pound of soap for every blanket. Pour this into a tub of warm water, let it melt and lather it well with the hand. Wring the blankets from the water, throw them into the lather, stir them about and leave to soak ten minutes, then hand-rub every inch of them paying especial attention to stains. Take them out and wring, then rinse in warm water twice. Dry well, but do not expose them to great heat. When dry, stretch them in every direction, and rub all over with a piece of clean rough flannel. This makes them fluffy and soft. If very dirty, a little Borax may be added to the water, but no Soda or bleaching powder should ever be used.

Blankets, to Cleanse.—Put two large tablespoonfuls of Borax and a pint bowl of soft soap into a tub of tepid water. When dissolved, put in a pair of blankets and let them remain over night. Next day rub and drain them out, rinse thoroughly in two waters and hang them up to dry. Do not wring them.

Blankets, to Cleanse.—Scrape 1 pound of Potash soap, and boil it down in sufficient water so that when cooling you can beat it with the hand to make a sort of jelly. Add 3 tablespoonfuls Spirits of Turpentine and 1 tablespoonful Spirits of Hartshorn, and with this wash the article well, and rinse in cold water until all the soap is taken off. Then apply salt and water and fold between two sheets, taking care not to allow two folds of the article washed to lie together. Smooth with a cool iron. Use the salt only where there are delicate colors that may run.

Gloss for Starch.

French Chalk	3	ounces.
White Soap, powdered............................	1	"

Directions: Take a piece of new dry flannel and dip it into the glaze powder, rub it well over the right side of the starched article and proceed to iron in the usual way, when a beautiful gloss will be obtained. Put in a little Borax in making the starch to give stiffness as usual.

Gloss for Starch, Another.

Borax, powdered..................................	1	drachm.
Spermaceti, powdered	1	"
French Chalk, powdered	6	"

Mix and sift.

Linen, to Polish.—To each pint of Starch add the following:

Wax, powdered	2	drachms.
Soap, powdered	2	"
French Chalk, powdered	4	"

Linen, to Stiffen.—Boil the starch after mixing it cold. Into 1 pint of starch drop a bit of White Wax, ½ the size of a small hazlenut, and 1 teaspoonful of Brandy. The Brandy is to retain the stiffness and increase it, and the Wax is to keep the starch from sticking to the iron.

Flatirons, to Remove Rust, to Make Smooth.—Pour coal oil (kerosene) on a folded newspaper, enough of the oil to spread over the paper, and rub the iron over it several times when it is taken from the stove. This will also prevent the starch from sticking to it. In ironing a starched garment a flatiron should not be so hot as for unstarched clothes.

Beeswax touched to a hot flatiron and the iron then rubbed on paper, is also good.

Scorches, to Remove.—Spread over the cloth a paste made of the following:

White Soap	¼	ounce.
Fuller's Earth	2	"
Vinegar	½	pint.
Juice of 2 Onions.		

Mix and boil well before using.

Towels, to Wash.—Towels with handsome, bright borders should never be boiled nor allowed to lie in very hot water. They should not be used until they are so much soiled that they need vigorous rubbing to make them clean. It is better economy to use more towels.

SILVER, BRASS, ETC., TO CLEAN.

Silver, to Keep in Good Condition. — Wash in hot soapsuds, then clean with a paste of Whiting and Whiskey. Polish with buckskin. If silver was always washed in hot suds, rinsed well and wiped dry, it would seldom need anything else.

Silver, Discolored, to Clean.—Silver articles discolored may be cleaned by rubbing them with a boiling saturated solution of Borax.

Note.—By "saturated solution of Borax" is meant as much Borax as the water will dissolve. But a small quantity of water would be needed.

Silver, Much Tarnished, to Clean.—Silver which has become much tarnished may be restored by immersion in a warm solution of 1 part Cyanide of Potassium to 8 parts of water. (This mixture is extremely poisonous). After washing well with water and drying, a somewhat dead white appearance will be produced, which may be quickly changed to a brilliant luster by polishing with a soft leather and Whiting.

Brass, to Clean.—There are many substances and mixtures which will clean brass. Oxalic Acid, Muriatic Acid, and several other acids will clean brass very effectively. Oxalic Acid is the best, but any acid must be well washed off, the brass dried and then rubbed with Sweet Oil and Tripoli, as otherwise it will soon tarnish again. Mixture to clean brass:

Soft Soap	1	ounce.
Rotten Stone	2	"

Another Method.—With a piece of rag put a coat of Nitric Acid over the part to be cleaned. As soon as it turns a light yellow, rub it dry and the brass will present a very clean appearance. If not satisfactory, repeat.

Another Method.—The Government method, in use at all the United States Arsenals, is to make a mixture of 1 part common Nitric Acid to ½ part Sulphuric Acid, in a stone jar, having also ready a pail of fresh water and a box of sawdust. The articles to be treated are dipped into the acid, then removed into the water, and finally rubbed with sawdust. This immediately changes them to a brilliant color. If the brass has become greasy, it is first dipped in a strong solution of Potash and Soda in warm water, which cuts the grease so that the acid has free power to act.

Fly Specks are also removed by this process.

Brass Gas Fixtures, to Restore.—Have the water clean and boiling in two vessels. Dip in one water and then in the other as soon as taken from the Nitric Acid bath (see above), so that there shall be no traces of acid on the fittings. Dry in sawdust while hot, and place upon a piece of hot sheet iron over a stove. As soon as all traces of water have left, quickly lacquer with very thin Shellac varnish, using a camel's hair brush. You can make the lacquer by dissolving Shellac in best Alcohol. Do not touch the metal with the fingers before lacquering.

Gilt Picture Frames, to Clean.—Fly specks can be cleaned off with soap and water used sparingly on the end of the finger covered with a piece of rag. When all cleaned off, rinse with cold water and dry with chamois leather. Next buy a pound of common size and two penny paint pans. Boil a little of the size in one of the pans with as much water as will just cover it. When boiled, strain through muslin into a clean pan and apply thinly to frames with camel hair brush. Take care not to give the frames too much water nor rub them too hard. On no account use gold size, as that is used only in regilding, and, if put on over the gold, would make it dull and sticky.

Gilt Frames, to Revive.

Eggs, White of	2	ounces.
Lime or Soda, Chloride of	1	"

Mix well, blow the dust from the frame and apply with a soft brush. Remove the paste, when dry, with a soft cloth or chamois skin.

FURNITURE POLISHES, STAINS, ETC.

Furniture Polish.

Acetic Acid	1	ounce.
Linseed Oil, raw	1	"
Alcohol, 188 per cent	2	"
Turpentine	2	"

Shake well before using.

The polish may be colored, if desired, by adding a little Aniline brown. If made in large quantities, keep well stirred while bottling.

Furniture Stains, Polish for Removing.

Alcohol, 98 per cent	1	pint.
Resin, ground	½	ounce.
Gum Shellac	1½	"

After the Resin and Shellac are cut in the Alcohol, mix in 1 pint of Linseed Oil and give the whole a good shaking. Apply with a cloth or newspaper, and polish with a flannel after applying the solution.

Furniture Polish—Simple and Cheap.—A very nice polish may be given to Furniture by using the following:

White Wax	1½	ounces.
Castile Soap	¼	"
Turpentine, Spirits of	½	gill.
Water	½	"

Shave the Wax finely into the Turpentine and let stand for twenty-four hours; then shave the soap very fine also, boil in the water and mix with the Wax and Turpentine. Keep covered when not in use. Apply to the whole surface, and polish with a chamois skin or old soft silk.

Furniture, to Fill Cracks and Pores in the Wood.—
Slack recently burned lime, and take one part of this lime powdered finely and two parts Rye Flour, mix into a stiff paste with boiled Linseed Oil, fill the cracks and color to suit the shade of furniture.

Patent Knot Filler.

Shellac, powdered	2	pounds.
Benzine	3¼	pints.

Dissolve and apply.

Waxed or Hardwood Floors, to Polish.

Beeswax, yellow.................................... 1   pound.
Potash .... ½   "

Boil one hour until well mixed, strain through a cloth, and put on with a wide, flat brush while hot. Brush as soon as dry. Have a brush made for the purpose—stiff and very heavy, with long handle put on the side. Use no oil. Keep the preparation on hand in case of any liquid touching and removing the wax. Wipe daily with dry flannel.

Floor Stain.

Linseed Oil 1   gallon.
Umber 5   cents worth.

Heat the oil hot in an iron kettle—soap will clean the kettle easily —then stir in the Umber, finely powdered, and with an old paint brush apply it as hot as possible. A mop wrung out of warm water will clean the floor nicely after being so oiled.

Cherry Stain.

Anatto 4   ounces.
Rain Water... 3   quarts.

Boil in a copper kettle until the Anatto is dissolved, then put in a piece of Caustic Potash the size of a walnut and boil gently half an hour longer.

Walnut Stain.—Dissolve 1 part Potassium Permanganate in 30 parts water, and apply twice in succession. In five minutes wash with clear water.

Ebony Stain.—Take a solution of Sulphate of Iron, wash the wood over with it two or three times, let it dry, and apply two or three coats of a strong decoction of Logwood. Wipe the wood when dry with a sponge and water, and polish with oil.

Mahogany Stain.

Dragon's Blood................... 8   ounces.
Benzine 6   pints.
Dissolve and apply.

Paint, to Clean.—Provide a plate with some of the best Whiting to be had, and have ready some clean warm water and a piece of flannel, which dip into the water and squeeze nearly dry. Take as much Whiting as will adhere to the flannel and apply it to the painted surface, when a little rubbing will instantly remove any dirt or grease. Afterwards wash the part well with clean water, rubbing it dry with a soft chamois. Paint thus cleaned looks as well as when first laid on, without injury to the most delicate colors. It is far better then using soap, and does not require more than half the time and labor.

If the paint has been varnished, boil 1 pound of bran in 1 gallon of water and wash with that, rinsing off with clear water and drying with a soft cloth.

Paint, to Remove.—Scraping or burning it off is extremely laborious, and too slow for general purposes. A more thorough and expeditious way is by chemical process, using for that purpose a solution of Soda and Quicklime in equal proportions. The solution may be made as follows: The Soda is dissolved in water, the Lime is then added, and the solution is applied with a brush to the old paint. A few moments are sufficient to remove the coats of paint, which may be washed off with hot water. The oldest paint may be removed by this paste. The wood should afterwards be washed with vinegar or an acid solution to remove all traces of the alkali before repainting.

Oil Cloth, to Clean.—Wash with a large soft woolen cloth and lukewarm or cold water, dry thoroughly with a soft cloth, and afterwards polish with milk or a weak solution of Beeswax in Spirits of Turpentine. Never use a brush, hot water nor soap, as any of these will be certain to take off the paint.

Paint Brushes, Care of.—Rinse all paint brushes, pencils, etc., in Turpentine, grease with a mixture of Sweet Oil and Tallow to prevent them from drying hard, and put them away in a close box.

Paint Brushes, to Clean.—When a paint brush is stiff and hard through drying with paint on it, put some Turpentine into a shallow dish and set it on fire. Let it burn for a minute until hot, then smother the flame and work the pencil in the fingers, dipping it frequently into the hot spirits.

VERMIN EXTERMINATORS.

Expelling Insects.—All insects dread Pennyroyal; the smell of it destroys some and drives others away. At times of the year that fresh Pennyroyal cannot be gathered, get Oil of Pennyroyal, pour some into a saucer, saturate in it small pieces of wadding or raw cotton and place in corners, closet shelves, bureau drawers, boxes, etc. Cockroaches, ants and other insects will soon disappear. It is also well to place some between the mattresses and around the bed. It is also a splendid thing for brushing off that terrible little insect, the seed tick.

Moth Exterminator.—It frequently happens that in spite of care moths are discovered in the middle of the summer in trunks or closets supposed to have been so impregnated with preventives that their existence there would be impossible. They hide in the crevices, and any attempts to dislodge them are futile. A simple and effective plan is to heat stove lids, or an iron shovel, red hot, pour vinegar upon the iron and let the fumes penetrate the cracks which can not be reached with a powder gun. Moths are particularly fond of new plaster, and the settling of the walls of houses affords them numberless hiding places which cannot well be reached except by fumigation. Sulphur is sometimes burned to rid walls of any sort of vermin, but the fumes of this are objectionable to many and they do not pass off so quickly as those of vinegar.

Bed Bug Exterminator.

Soft Soap	4	tablespoonfuls.
Water, hot	13	"
Oil Turpentine	1	"
Kerosene	2	"

Dissolve the soap in the water, add the Turpentine, stir until the latter is thoroughly mixed, and finally add the Kerosene, continuing the heat and stirring until a homogeneous mixture is obtained.

Wash the parts of the bedstead, let dry, and apply the mixture with a brush to all parts frequented by the bugs. The preparation may also be painted on walls, etc.

Bed Bug Exterminator, Another.—Corrosive Sublimate cut in Alcohol and applied with a brush to the parts is very effective. The Sublimate may be mixed with Turpentine, which makes a cheaper but not so effective a preparation. Corrosive Sublimate is a deadly poison and should be carefully labeled and put out of the reach of children. In applying, too, care must be taken not to get any of it into the eyes.

Cockroach Exterminator.—Mix 2 tablespoonfuls of Red Lead and Indian meal with molasses enough to make a thick batter, and apply the mixture at night where the insects frequent. They will eat it readily and it will poison them. Repeat the dose several nights in succession. Care should be exercised in the use of this poison.

Vermin Killer for Rats and Mice.

Strychnine, Sulphate of	½	ounce.
Sugar, powdered	1	"
Wheat Flour	14½	"
Anise, Oil of	½	drachm.
Aniline, Solution of		sufficient quantity.

Drop the Oil of Anise on the flour and stir thoroughly with the other ingredients. Spray with the solution of Aniline, or any other coloring desired, before mixing.

A Novel Rat Trap.—Take a barrel and fill it about one-third full of water, then place a log endwise in the water so that one end of it will just remain above the surface. Make the head of the barrel a little too small to fit, and sustain it by two pins to the inside of the top of the barrel, so that it will hang as if on a pivot, and easily tip by touching either side. On this head, thus suspended, secure a piece of savory meat. The first rat that

scents it will, to get the meat, leap on the barrel head. The head will tip, or tilt, precipitating him into the water, and resume its position. The rat in the water will swim to the log, get on the end of it and squeal vociferously. His cries will bring other rats, all of whom will be tilted into the water, and all of whom will fight for the only dry spot—the end of the log. As only one rat can hold it, the victor will drown all the rest, and can in the morning be drowned himself.

This is an old French plan which is still followed in Paris by men who make that their business; and if the contrivance is ingeniously arranged, and the fried pork, or cheese bait, is made sufficiently enticing, success will follow.

Sticky Fly Paper Mixture.

Yellow Resin	2	pounds.
Linseed Oil, boiled	2	"
Castor Oil	1	"
Molasses	¼	"
Beeswax	⅛	"

Melt the Resin and the Beeswax in the oils by the heat from a water bath. While still hot, mix in the Molasses and spread on sized parchment paper.

Sizing for Fly Paper.

Glue	¼	pound.
Water	¾	"

Dissolve the Glue in the water by the heat of a water bath, and while hot brush on to sheets of parchment paper. When the sizing has set on the paper, put on the sticky fly paper mixture (see preceding formula) with a brush, using a metal edge to keep the margin of the paper free from the mixture.

Note.—A **Water Bath** means one vessel set into another containing water, which is placed on a stove and kept hot or boiling. The ingredients contained in the inner vessel are thus heated without scorching or sticking to the vessel.

GARDEN AND ORCHARD INSECT ENEMIES.

To Discover Insects.—If the leaves of a plant turn reddish or yellow, or if they curl up, a close inspection will generally disclose that the plants are infested with a very small green insect, or else with a red spider, either of which must be destroyed. For this purpose scald some common tobacco with water until the latter is colored to a yellow, and, when cold, sprinkle the leaves of the plants with it; or a better plan is to pass the stems and leaves of the plant between the fingers, and then to shake the plant and water the bed well with the preparation immediately afterward. The latter operation destroys a large proportion of the insects shaken from the plant, and is the only infallible method.

Ants.—When these insects are troublesome in the garden, fill small bottles two-thirds full of water and add Sweet Oil to within an inch of the top. Plunge these into the ground near the nest or hills to within half an inch of the rim, and the insects coming for a sip will get into the oil and perish, as it fills the breathing pores. The writer once entrapped in a pantry myriads of red ants in a shallow tin cover smeared with lard, the vessel having accidentally been left in their track. Another means of entrapping them is to sprinkle sugar into a dampened sponge and place in their haunts. When they have swarmed through the sponge, it is squeezed in hot water and the trap is reset.

Cabbage Worms.—The same treatment (without using Paris Green) will prove effective in destroying the common cabbage worm.

Celery Pest, or Little Negro Bug.—The most effective remedy so far discovered is crude Carbolic Acid mixed with water, in the proportion of a tablespoonful of the former to 2 gallons of the latter, and sprinkled over the plants; or mix the acid with air-slaked lime or land plaster in the proportion of a teacupful of the acid to a bushel of the latter, and dust over the plants. Watch the young crop closely, and attack the insect with one of the above remedies when he first appears.

Cucumber Beetles, which are often so troublesome, can be kept away only by covering the plants with netting.

Currant Worms.—White Hellebore is an effectual remedy. This is a powder of a light greenish yellow color sold in drug stores. It should be thoroughly mixed with water in the proportion of a tablespoonful of the powder to 2 gallons of the water, and applied by means of a sprinkler to the leaves. Usually one application is sufficient; if not, the second may be made.

Cut Worm.—A little ring of wood ashes or lime about the plants will serve as a protection. By digging close to the roots of the plant they have eaten they may be easily found and destroyed, and thus prevented from continuing the mischief.

Cut Worms.—Where cut worms are troublesome in the field, a very old and at the same time a very good remedy is to entrap them in holes made near the plants; or hills, if in the cornfield. An old rake handle, tapered at the end so as to make a smooth hole five or six inches deep, or more, will answer very well for this purpose. In the morning the worms that have taken refuge in these holes may be crushed by thrusting the rake handle into them again, and the trap is set for the next night. It is always well in planting to make provisions for the loss of a stalk or two by cut worms or other causes, as it is easier to thin out than to replant.

May Beetles.—These are the perfect insects of the white grub, so destructive to lawns and sometimes to meadows. A French plan for destroying, or rather, catching the cockchafer, a very similar insect, is to place in the center of the orchard, after sunset, an old barrel, the inside of which has been previously tarred. At the bottom of the barrel is placed a lighted lamp, and the insects, circling around to get at the light, strike their wings and legs against the tarred sides of the barrel, and either get fast or are rendered so helpless that they fall to the bottom. Hundreds of beetles may be captured in this way in a single night.

Onion Maggot.—The use of chimney soot in the drills is the best known remedy for this troublesome little creature. Its ravages may be known from the dying of the tops.

Plant Lice.—These are readily destroyed by the use of tobacco smoke or tobacco in infusion. Where the roots have been attacked by the blue louse—a species of plant lice—water them with strong tobacco water. If the remedy is applied in season, it will save the plant.

Plant Lice, Another Remedy.—A remedy for plant lice upon the terminal shoots of rose bushes (or similar hardy plants), said to work like a charm, is as follows: Take 4 ounces of Quassia chips and boil for ten minutes in a gallon of soft water. Take out the chips and add 4 ounces of soft soap, which should be dissolved in the water as it cools. Stir well before using, and apply with a moderate sized paint brush, brushing upward. Ten minutes after, syringe the trees with clean water to wash off the dead insects, also the preparation, which would otherwise disfigure the rose trees.

Scale.—A French composition for destroying scale insects, plant lice, etc., on fruit and other trees, is as follows: Boil 2 gallons barley in water, then remove the grain (which may be fed to the chickens) and add Quicklime to the liquid until it approaches the consistency of paint. When cold, add 2 pounds of Lampblack, mixing it for a long time, then add 1½ pounds Flowers of Sulphur and 1 quart Alcohol.

The mixture is applied with a paint brush, first using a stiff bristle brush to remove moss, etc. It not only destroys the insects, but gives the bark greater strength.

Slugs.—English gardeners place handfuls of bran at intervals of eight or ten feet along the border of garden walks. The slugs are attracted to the bran, and in the morning each little heap is found covered with them. The ground is then gone over again, this time the operator providing himself with a dustpan, small broom and an empty bucket, when it is an easy matter to sweep up the little heaps and empty them, slugs and all, into the bucket. In this way many hundreds have been taken in a single walk. If a little salty water is placed in the bottom of the bucket, the slugs, coming in contact with it, are almost instantly destroyed.

Squash Bug.—Place clean white shingles on the ground around the vines. The insects will be found in the morning collected on the under side thereof, and may readily be destroyed.

Strawberry Slugs may be destroyed by the use of Pyrethrum, either dry or mixed with water. If this fails to remove all, the Paris Green mixture will finish them.

Strawberry Worm.—Dust the leaves of the plant with Quicklime when they are damp with dew or rain.

White Cabbage Butterfly.—This appears in the Northern and Middle States about the last of May or beginning of June, and deposits its eggs on the under side of the leaves of cabbage, turnip and radish plants. These butterflies may easily be caught in hand nets, as they fly lazily and are very tame. The second brood of the insect (the latter part of July or the first of August) may be circumvented by placing horizontal boards about one inch from the ground. Upon these the caterpillars will attach themselves for their change into the butterfly, and can easily be collected and destroyed.

Precautions to be Adopted in Spraying.—

1. Keep poison labeled, and out of the way of children.
2. Do not spray so far into the season as to affect the fruit.
3. In making emulsions remember the inflammable nature of coal oil.
4. Never spray trees in bloom.
5. Try solutions on a small scale, if likely to injure foliage, and watch results.

As copper compounds act upon tin and iron, it is well to prepare such mixtures in earthen, wooden or brass vessels.

For certain fungi and insects special mixtures must be used.

Preparations for Spraying.

No. 1. Copper Sulphate.................................... 6 pounds.
      Lime .... 4 "
      Water.. 22 gallons.

Dissolve the Copper Sulphate in 16 gallons of water. Slake the Lime in 6 gallons of water and, when the latter is cooled, pour it into the Copper solution and mix thoroughly.

No. 2. Copper Sulphate...................................... 1 pound.
Ammonia.. 1 pint.
Water.. 25 gallons.

Dissolve the Copper Sulphate in 2 gallons of hot water, and as soon as cool add the 1 quart of Ammonia and dilute to 25 gallons.

The mixture should be sprayed over the infected parts.

No. 3. The most useful insecticides are those containing, as a basis, Paris Green. This substance, being insoluble, does not injure the foliage. A good formula is, 1 pound of Paris Green to 200 gallons of water. This is very effective against leaf-eating insects. To destroy plant lice and scale insects, the following emulsion may be used:

No 4. Soft Soap.. 1 quart.
Boiling water.................................... 2 "

Mix, and while hot add 1 pint of coal oil.
When using, dilute with twice the amount of either hard or soft water.

Apple Tree Borer.—Keep the base of every tree liable to the attack of this insect free from weeds and rubbish, and apply soap to them liberally during the month of May. Examine the trees at the base in the fall, and also in the crotches, and cut out any insects which may have entered the bark.

Canker Worm.—This insect attacks apple and other trees and eats the leaves. The female insect is without wings, hence has to crawl up the trunk of the tree to deposit her eggs. Her passage up is usually very early in the spring. The remedy is to put a cloth band besmeared with tar, or a mixture of tar and molasses, about the trunk of the trees near the ground to prevent her passage, and apply kerosene oil to the bark of the tree below the strip to kill the eggs deposited there.

Grape Black-Rot.—Spray with Preparation "No. 2" six times at intervals of two weeks, commencing early in May.

Grubs.—These attack apple and peach trees, and may be destroyed by the method recommended for the apple tree borer. However, as they attack all parts of the tree, the examination and soft-soapings should be correspondingly extensive.

Pear-Leaf Blight, which appears on both leaves and fruit, giving the leaves a spotted appearance and causing the fruit to crack. Spray with "No. 2" as soon as the leaves begin to open, and repeat two or three times at intervals of two weeks.

Addenda.

A CHAPTER ON MEDICINES—THEIR EFFECTS AND USES.

By Samuel J. Wilson, M. D.

In giving treatment for the various diseases in this work, such remedies have been prescribed as are usually kept, and such methods recommended as may be easily and quickly applied. The object in presenting this chapter on medicines is to give such a clear description of the actions and symptoms produced by the use of the various drugs, that those who study it will not only understand the remedy needed in any given case, but will understand its effects so well that the most favorable results may be obtained. While no attempt has been made to describe all of the remedies mentioned, enough of the better known and more valuable are given to meet the requirements in nearly all cases.

No other family medical book has ever contained a chapter of this kind. It will not only prove interesting and instructive, but decidedly valuable to those who will familiarize themselves with it.

The older methods of preparing drugs consisted in using the whole plant, root, leaf or stem, either steeped and made into a tea, or ground and added to a quantity of alcohol and water, molasses and Holland gin, or some other menstruum. In most cases such preparations necessitated a large dose, which was extremely unpleasant and often nauseating. Later it was discovered that every vegetable used in medicine contains a small amount of *active principle*, upon which depends its effects. In most cases such active principle is without taste. Again, a dose of the active principle is exceedingly small, and always definite because it can be divided into exact amounts; while in the case of the older remedies, the dose varies for the reason that the percentage of the active principle varies in different specimens of the same drug, and for the further reason that the mode of preparation may or may not have extracted all of such active ingredient. It is true that what are called "standardized" tinctures and fluid extracts are now made which contain definite amounts of the active principle mentioned, but they also contain a large amount of extractive matter, which is quite as unpleasant to the taste as the older and cruder preparations. This extractive matter is waste material, which is not only worthless and unpleasant to the taste, but is often irritating to the stomach.

Another objection of equal importance is the fact that in using many of the preparations of extracts, powders, pills, etc., where the whole drug is employed, the fluids of the stomach, and perhaps those of the digestive tract, must perform a certain amount of chemical work in order to extract the active principle before it can take effect. Still another important feature—perhaps the most important of all—is found in the fact that many medicinal plants contain more than one active principle, and these principles often produce effects directly opposite to each other. Hence it follows that since an active ingredient can be selected in its pure state, it possesses marked advantages over all other forms of drug medication.

What we have called *active principles* are more properly called *alkaloids;* they are also sometimes called *concentrations.* The difference between an active principle and a concentration lies in the fact that an active principle, or alkaloid, is a substance possessed of definite chemical composition in an absolutely pure state, and of definite and unvarying effect; whereas concentrations include everything contained in the drug that is possessed of any activity, and from which the inactive constituents or waste material has been excluded to such an extent as to make the concentration more active and powerful than other preparations of the drug where the whole plant is used, but at the same time much less active than the alkaloids. As an illustration of the difference between an alkaloid and a concentration, we may state that the alkaloid of Coca leaves is Cocaine, whereas the concentration of Coca leaves would contain not only the Cocaine, but also other secondary substances, as the resin and tannin, contained in the leaves. Hence it will be readily understood that the administration of equal weights of the alkaloid Cocaine and the concentration of Coca leaves would be attended with quite differen results, because the Cocaine in its pure state would be much stronger than the concentration with its resin, tannin, etc.; yet the Cocaine represents the medicinal quality of Coca leaves. The same principle is true in many other cases,—in all cases, in fact, where the active principle or alkaloid represents all of the medicinal qualities of the drug. As already stated, some medicinal plants contain more than one active principle or alkaloid. In such cases it is understood, of course, that no single active principle would represent the whole drug.

The drugs given in the following list are fully represented by their active principles:

Aconite.—One grain of *Aconitine*, the active principle, is equal to 350 grains of Aconite root or 350 drops of the fluid extract of Aconite root.

Aconitine, the active principle of Aconite, occurs in two forms: One is called the *Amorphus*, and the other, the *Crystalline*. The Crystalline is four times stronger than the Amorphus. A dose of the Amorphus is $\frac{1}{100}$ of a grain, while a dose of the Crystalline is $\frac{1}{400}$ of a grain.

Blood Root.—One grain of *Sanguinarine*, the active principle, is equal to 40 grains of Blood Root, or 40 drops of the fluid extract of Blood Root.

Colchicum.—One grain of *Colchicine*, the active principle, is equal to 200 grains of Colchicum seed or root, or 200 drops of the fluid extract of Colchicum seed or root.

Gelsemium.—One grain of *Gelsemine*, the active principle, is equal to 200 grains of Gelsemium, or 200 drops of the fluid extract of Gelsemium.

Hyoscyamus.—One grain of *Hyoscyamine*, the active principle, is equal to 1,000 grains of Hyoscyamus, or 1,000 grains of the fluid extract of Hyoscyamus. The action of Hyoscyamus is the same as that of Belladonna.

Phytolacca, or **Poke Root.**—One grain of *Phytolaccine* (this is a concentration) represents 8 grains of Poke Root, or 8 drops of the fluid extract of Poke Root.

Pomegranate.— One grain of *Pelletierine*, the active principle, represents 30 grains of Pomegranate, or 30 drops of the fluid extract of Pomegranate bark. Pomegranate bark is a popular remedy for tapeworm.

Aletrus, Star Grass or *Unicorn Root*—a uterine tonic—*Aloes, Belladonna, Bryonia, Buchu, Capsicum, Coffee* — Coffee contains Caffeine, a heart-stimulant—*Chocolate*—Chocolate contains Theobromine, a heart tonic—*Golden Seal, Helonias, Hemlock, Indian Hemp, Jalap, Lobelia, Black Snake Root, Mandrake, Nux Vomica, Quassia, Squills, Strophanthus, Black Haw, Tea*—Tea contains Thein, a heart stimulant—*Viburnum*--a uterine sedative and antispasmodic—*Veratrum, Willow Bark, Wormseed*, and many other drugs, are fully represented by their active principles.

Note.—Tea and coffee, when used to excess, produce nervousness, sleeplessness, irregular heart action, indigestion and loss of appetite.

The foregoing is called alkaloidal medication. There are some who object to this system, claiming that the alkaloids are dangerous medicines because they are so powerful; yet the doctor who objects to alkaloids in known quantities still uses infusions, tinctures, fluid extracts and other preparations, each of which contains one or more of these same alkaloids in unknown quantities. A doctor cannot take a bottle of the Tincture of Aconite from the shelf and state exactly how much of the Aconitine, or active principle, is contained in a single dose, for, as stated at the beginning, the percentage of the active principle varies in tinctures and other preparations made from the entire drug.

Again, we have known some physicians to object to alkaloids because they are given in such small doses. They claim that it borders on homeopathy; yet from what has already been stated it will be readily understood that this claim is without foundation. We have also heard it argued against the active principles that those using them should understand their physiological effects, *i. e.*, the symptoms present when the system is being brought under the influence of the drug, as this would prevent giving too much; but this is equally true in using a drug in any form. It is also important because it is well known that some require larger doses than others, hence a minimum dose might be altogether too small in one case and a maximum dose altogether too large in another case. *The only safe way is to give a minimum dose and repeat at frequent intervals until there is evidence of effect.* Such evidence should not only be understood by the doctor, but should be explained to the patient or those in attendance. This not only insures safe dosage, but also insures the exact amount needed in each case. There are no exceptions to this rule.

In the following list of medicines no particular form or preparation has been selected. Those using the remedies can choose the infusion, tincture, fluid extract, pill, powder or active principle, although we might state that pills should not be given to a patient with a high fever, nor much medicine to one in a comatose state. During fever the mucous membrane of the stomach, like that of the mouth, may be dry, in which case the pills might not be dissolved; while the drowsy condition of the comatose state might prevent absorption until a number of doses had been taken, when improvement in the patient's condition might result in all being absorbed at one time, and might thus produce dangerous results.

What we have termed the "physiological effect," is a common term among physicians, but we shall substitute the word "symptom," meaning some evidence that a smaller dose should be given, or the same dose given at longer intervals. Following each drug we shall first state the symptoms of its effects, and second, its uses.

ACONITE—*Aconitine.*

Symptoms of Its Effects.—If a dose of Aconite in any form is taken on the tongue and allowed to remain there, there will soon be felt a tingling sensation of the lips, tongue and throat; if it is taken into the stomach and continued until effect, there will be felt the same tingling sensation in the hands and fingers, feet and toes, lips and face, and later a tingling or prickly sensation over the whole body.   With the tingling, or following it, there is a sense of numbness produced.   With the first evidence of this kind the dose should be lessened, or when perspiration follows its use, the dose should be lessened or stopped.   With children who are unable to explain the symptoms, the remedy should be lessened or stopped when the temperature is lowered or when perspiration is produced.   If a child has a high fever and is restless, nervous or delirious, the remedy should be discontinued when these conditions are overcome.

Aconite produces its first effects upon the distal or outer end of the nerve fibers, hence the tingling mentioned.   This paralyzes more or less the terminal fibers and they lose control.   Those nerve fibers supplying the small blood vessels are unable to govern the size of the arteries, and the arteries dilate.   It will be remembered that lying just beneath the skin is a large network of small vessels covering the whole outer surface of the body.   When these vessels dilate, a large amount of blood is brought to the surface, spread out in a wide sheet of superficial circulation, and then returned to absorb more heat from the internal organs.   The sweat glands become relaxed, perspiration follows, and by this process of evaporation and elimination the temperature is lowered.

The Use of Aconite in Fevers.—The most important use of Aconite is to relieve fevered conditions.   During fever the skin is dry and hot, the urine is scanty, the bowels are constipated, and the tongue is dry and often heavily coated.   By giving small doses of Aconite, frequently repeated, the skin is soon covered with perspiration, the quantity of urine is increased, the bowels become more active and the tongue more moist; thirst is also overcome. By closely observing the tongue of a fevered patient one is often able to judge of the progress of Aconite.   So long as the tongue remains dry, but little progress has been made upon the general secretions; when the tongue and throat become moist, general improvement soon follows.

In the use of Aconite it is unimportant concerning the kind of fever for which it is used, or the conditions which produce the fever.   It is understood, of course, that the greatest benefit is to be derived in acute attacks, such as pneumonia and the eruptive fevers.   While it is always easy to detect the presence of fever, it is not always easy to detect the cause, especially at the beginning; yet Aconite may be given without waiting for a positive diagnosis.   True, fever is only a symptom, yet Aconite may relieve the congested and inflamed organ or part, and thus abort the general storm which is gathering in the distance. Draining the blood from the congested area may prevent inflammation and thus ward off approaching disease. In many cases Aconite may be the only remedy needed besides thorough elimination of the bowels.

In Catarrhal Conditions.—Sometimes following measles the mucous membrane lining the air tubes presents a catarrhal condition, the exudate being unhealthy and irritating and accompanied by a chronic cough. Aconite is of value because it increases the eliminations and thins the tenacious mucus which clogs the small bronchial tubes, thus facilitating its removal. Ipecac will produce the same results and give the same benefit. For this particular purpose Ipecac is the better remedy for those who are physically weak or debilitated.

Aconite produces the same effect on all mucous membrane as that of the bronchial tubes, hence may be used in catarrhal conditions of the nasal passages, kidneys, stomach and digestive tract, and especially if fever is present. Aconite not only produces the local effect mentioned, but also aids by relieving congestion and thus removing the cause.

Other Uses.—Aconite is valuable in congestive headache, neuralgia, singing noises in the ears due to congestion, in tonsilitis and catarrhal sore throat.

Is Aconite a Dangerous Remedy?—We are aware that some physicians claim that Aconite is dangerous, but the great safe-guard in using Aconite, or any other remedy, is to note the symptoms of improvement and then gradually or entirely stop giving it. If the patient has been restless or delirious and becomes quiet, if thirst disappears, if the dry tongue and dry throat become moist, or if perspiration follows its use, *the remedy should be lessened*. In dilating the small vessels and bringing the blood to the surface, as already described, it follows that less blood is contained in the internal organs and that the heart has less work to do. It has been stated before that Nature never carries on any work without a purpose, and if the amount of blood in the heart is decreased, the action of this organ will be lessened in proportion. It is in this way that Aconite lessens heart action, and not because it has any paralyzing effects upon the organ directly. Aconite is not recommended, however, for those with a weak heart. We have used Aconite for many years in treating fevers, congestion and inflammation. If used according to directions, the remedy is perfectly safe for young and old, and will be found valuable in relieving many diseased conditions.

Dose.—Add 8 drops of the Tincture of Aconite to 4 table-spoonfuls of water, and give 1 teaspoonful of the solution every thirty minutes or every hour at the beginning; or about $\frac{1}{134}$ of a grain of its active principle, Aconitine Amorphus; or $\frac{1}{500}$ of a grain of Crystallized Aconitine. Either of the active principles may be taken in tablet form or in solution.

There are cases where Aconite, or any other remedy taken into the stomach, may produce vomiting. These cases are not evidence that the remedy does not agree with the patient, or that he may not be benefited by its use. It is evidence of disordered digestion, and the system rebels on general principles.

ALOES—*Aloin.*

Aloes is fully represented by its active principle, Aloin—in fact, Aloin is believed to produce more favorable results than when the whole drug is used. Aloes increases the circulation in the pelvic cavity, hence has a stimulating effect upon the uterus, and its use should, therefore, be carefully guarded, or restricted entirely, during pregnancy.

Effects and Uses.—The effects of this drug are mostly noticed upon the lower part of the digestive tract, and during constipation here is where the trouble usually exists. Aloes or Aloin is a tonic laxative, and its prolonged use does not diminish its activity. It is certain and mild in its effects, though not rapid, requiring from ten to twelve hours. It is usually given with other laxatives, and is one of the principal ingredients in the various forms of cathartic pills.

Larger doses can be given in solution than in pill form, but by reason of its bitter taste it is usually given in pills or tablets, and, as stated, is usually compounded with other remedies. What has proven the most satisfactory, hence a very popular combination, is the well known Aloin-Strychnine-Belladonna pills.

ANTISEPTIC REMEDIES.

An antiseptic is any agent or remedy that prevents putrefactive changes. Putrefactive changes can occur only in dead animal and vegetable matter, and then only under certain conditions of heat and moisture. There is also required a ferment to produce the change. Antiseptics act either directly upon the ferments, destroying and weakening them so as to prevent their action and development, or by forming in the substance undergoing decomposition such changes or compounds that the ferments produce no effect. Destructive changes going on in the lungs, liver, kidneys and other internal organs in the living subject, cannot always be reached with antiseptics, hence cannot always be checked; but external wounds and the digestive tract can be protected with much certainty. *Carbolic Acid, Corrosive Sublimate, Iodine, Salicylic Acid, Boric Acid, Salol* and the *Sulphocarbolates* are examples of antiseptics that are used internally; while

Carbolic Acid, Permanganate of Potash, Chloride of Zinc, Corrosive Sublimate and *Chromic Acid* are examples of antiseptics that are used externally.

ANTISEPTICS FOR THE DIGESTIVE TRACT.

There are many preparations used for this purpose. Some of them have been mentioned under the various diseases. We shall not attempt to enumerate all, but shall describe the two we believe to be the most valuable. These are Salol and the Sulphocarbolates. The Sulphocarbolates are the better of the two in the digestive tract. For this purpose they are undoubtedly the best antiseptics known.

Salol.—Salol is composed, in round numbers, of 64 per cent Salicylic Acid and 36 per cent Carbolic Acid. When taken internally, this combination is not broken up in the stomach, but upon entering the digestive tract below the stomach and coming in contact with the alkaline secretions, the Salicylic Acid and Carbolic Acid are separated. The separation takes place slowly, however, and this allows the antiseptic properties of the two acids to extend for some distance along the canal; just how far would depend upon the condition present. If constipation existed, their influence would not extend so far; on the other hand if the bowels were active, their antiseptic influence would extend much farther. The Carbolic Acid readily enters the circulation as a free agent, and is said to be eliminated as such; the Salicylic Acid combines with the soda salts present in the digestive tract and enters the circulation as Salicylate of Soda, after which it is separated from the Soda, and, like the Carbolic Acid, circulates in the blood as a free agent. Both the Carbolic and Salicylic Acid are eliminated by the kidneys, hence in large doses may irritate these organs.

Dose.—The dose in an ordinary case of constipation or unhealthy state of the digestive tract is 10 grains every four hours, or four times a day; in case of threatened typhoid fever and other serious conditions, 10 grains every two hours until improvement, then three or four times a day.

The Sulphocarbolates.—The Sulphocarbolates are composed of Sulphuric Acid, Carbolic Acid and a base of Soda, Lime or Zinc. The three bases are frequently combined together under the name of Sulphocarbolates. In round numbers the Sulphocarbolate of Soda contains 34 per cent Sulphuric Acid, 39 per cent Carbolic Acid and 27 per cent Soda; the Sulphocarbolate of Lime contains 31 per cent Sulphuric Acid, 37 per cent Carbolic Acid and 32 per cent Lime; the Sulphocarbolate of Zinc contains 29 per cent Sulphuric Acid, 33 per cent Carbolic Acid and 38 per cent Zinc. Practically, they all contain about 33⅓ per cent of each ingredient.

When the ingredients forming the Sulphocarbolates are separated in the digestive tract, the Sulphuric Acid unites with the soda and other salts present. The Carbolic Acid has less tendency to unite, and enters the circulation more readily, as stated under Salol. The reason is that the so-called Carbolic Acid is not an acid. It gives neither acid nor alkaline reaction to litmus paper; in this respect it is neutral. It has, however, the power to combine with a base and form salts, but has less tendency to do so than a true acid.

The Soda, Lime and Zinc aid in arresting putrefactive changes in the digestive tract. They aid in neutralizing the gases which have resulted from such changes, and thus relieve many painful colicky conditions of the stomach and bowels. They aid in relieving tympanitis, or bloating. They are absorbed into the circulation less readily, hence extend for a greater distance along the canal, and thus aid materially in producing antiseptic results; in other words, they aid in producing wholesome or normal conditions. The Lime is not absorbed, but passes off with the eliminations. This is also true of the Zinc, hence the influence of either is more certain in producing alimentary sanitation.

In the Sulphocarbolates the Carbolic Acid is the same as in the Salol, the Salicylic Acid in the Salol is replaced by the Sulphuric Acid, and there is still left the Soda, Lime and Zinc, which Salol does not contain; and as these aid in arresting putrefactive changes, we believe the Sulphocarbolates are the more valuable. The Salol is not soluble in water, is without taste, and the compound is not separated in the stomach. The Sulphocarbolates dissolve readily, and in some cases the patient prefers to take them in solution; whether taken in solution or tablet form, their effects are the same. The separation of the Sulphocarbolates in the stomach is not without its advantage, for the stomach is often unhealthy as well as the digestive tract, and the Sulphocarbolates produce the same purifying effects here as elsewhere.

Intestinal antisepsis is no longer a theory, but a *demonstrated fact*. This is admitted by physicians generally, and our own experience proves it true. The importance of such sanitation cannot be overestimated, for most diseases have their origin in the alimentary canal, and are the result of indigestion and constipation, which usually exist together. Antiseptics will not aid digestion directly, yet they will check the putrefactive changes due to constipation, maintain cleanliness, protect the system from many impurities and poisons, and allow the digestive organs to regain their normal condition. Thus they aid digestion indirectly, and at the same time ward off disease.

Drinking considerable quantities of water every day will also aid in maintaining a healthy condition. The benefits resulting from drinking mineral waters, or from the various water cures, *are not due to any virtues in the water, but to the large amounts the patient is required to drink each day.* This increases the fluid in the digestive tract, flushes the capillaries or small blood vessels throughout the system, and washes away many impurities, which are eliminated by the increased action of all of the eliminative organs—the digestive tract, kidneys, lungs and skin. This process of elimination explains why the constant use of mineral waters are of benefit in relieving corpulency.

In the treatment of diphtheria, scarlet fever, measles and other infectious diseases, intestinal antiseptics are of the greatest importance. Carbolic Acid is admitted to be the best known remedy in the treatment of diphtheria. Carbolic Acid or some other antiseptic is contained in all antitoxines. In treating diphtheria Carbolic Acid is now quite generally used in solution with clear water and injected under the skin, instead of injecting antitoxine, yet there is probably no better way of giving it than in combination with the Sulphocarbolates. In giving it in this way the patient not only receives the benefit of the Carbolic Acid, but also receives the other benefits described. In giving the treatment of diphtheria it was omitted to mention that the Sulphocarbolates should be given throughout the disease.

All of the bowel diseases, including typhoid fever, result from an unhealthy condition of the digestive tract. Congestion or inflammation of the liver, liver abscess, cancer, consumption, epilepsy, ulcer of the stomach and rheumatism also result from the same cause. Many cases both of Bright's disease and chronic inflammation of the spinal cord followed by paralysis are due to the same unhealthy condition. Many other important diseases could also be mentioned, to say nothing of the innumerable minor ailments, such as bad breath, coated tongue, headache, dizziness, palpitation, heartburn, mental stupor, nausea, vomiting, also jaundice, cholera morbus, cholera infantum, neuralgia, and the many emotional states known as nervousness, hysteria and other depressions and hallucinations. An unhealthy digestive tract may weave a web of disorders that will baffle human skill.

We are aware that we have carried the results to a considerable extent, but we have made a careful study of this question for many years and are confident that we speak the truth

Dose.—The same as given under SALOL.

ARSENIC.

Arsenic is one of the most valuable remedies in the whole list of medicines. It increases tissue change throughout the body and thus improves nutrition. It is also a powerful antiseptic. One grain, or part, will protect nearly seven thousand times its weight of tissue from degenerative or putrefactive changes. In many forms of indigestion, and in all forms of wasting or malignant disease, Arsenic is a valuable remedy.

Symptoms of Its Effects.—The *first symptom of the effect* of moderate doses of Arsenic is a little puffiness of the eyelids, or just beneath the eyes, followed by colicky pains and frequent elimination by the bowels. Some claim that when it is given it should be pushed until these symptoms appear. In our experience we have never found it necessary to give the remedy in such amounts, yet the results have always been most satisfactory. After entering the stomach and digestive tract Arsenic enters the circulation and is eliminated largely through the skin, hence is brought in intimate relation, not only with the various organs and tissues of the body, but with the individual cells constituting such organs and tissues. This process of elimination gives increased activity to every cell in the body. Such activity increases the strength and vitality of the individual cells and organs the same as physical exercise increases the strength and vitality of the whole body.

The *first effect* of Arsenic is upon the mucous membrane of the stomach and digestive tract. It increases the flow of the digestive ferments, and thus aids digestion and improves the appetite. For the same reason it will in many cases quiet any painful conditions of the stomach and bowels resulting from indigestion. Arsenic not only aids digestion, thus rendering the food elements appropriate for absorption, but by reason of its mode of elimination it increases tissue change throughout the whole body, thus improving nutrition and assimilation; and at the same time, as stated, it arrests putrefactive changes and checks morbid or diseased conditions.

It should be remembered that Arsenic produces the same nutritive changes in the nervous system as in other tissues, and perhaps herein lies its greatest power. The nervous system is the foundation upon which life and strength depend; to render it strong and active is to render the body strong and vigorous. This means increased vitality and freedom from disease. Every tissue, organ and muscle, and each individual cell in the body, is capable only in proportion to its nerve supply; hence to increase this supply is to increase vital force and physical power. Increase the strength of the fluid in the battery and you increase the power of the electric current; improve the nutrition of the nervous system and you increase the power and vital force of the individual. For the reasons enumerated, we believe that Arsenic stands at the head of the list as a reconstructive agent, meaning, of course, only those agents supplied by artificial means.

Uses of Arsenic.—The effect of Arsenic on the mucous membrane of the air passages is second only to its effect on the mucous membrane of the stomach and digestive tract, hence it is a valuable remedy in pneumonia, bronchial catarrh or chronic bronchitis, and in consumption. It is useful in catarrhal conditions of the stomach and bowels, in ulcer or cancer of the stomach, in heartburn, in the vomiting of drunkards, in constipation, and in chlorosis and other wasting diseases. It is of benefit in neuralgia, rheumatism, gout, asthma, hay fever and St. Vitus's dance. It is recommended in many forms of heart disease, including angina pectoris, or neuralgia of the heart. It is not recommended for the relief of an acute attack of pain in the last named disease, but its use should be continued between the attacks for some time. While its influence may not be so direct, its general effects are of far greater importance. This is true not only in diseases of the heart, but in all other disease and conditions for which it may be taken. We have stated that Arsenic is eliminated through the skin, therefore it should not be used in acute inflammatory skin diseases, but is beneficial in chronic forms.

Dose.—Its most common form of administration is Fowler's Solution, which contains one per cent of Arsenic. A dose of the Solution is from 3 to 5 drops, which is best given at meal time. It may also be given in tablet form, or is frequently combined with other remedies. Of these the Arseniate of Iron and Strychnine Arseniate are the most commonly used.

BELLADONNA—*Atropine.*

In whatever form Belladonna is used it is entirely dependent upon its single active principle, Atropine.

Symptoms of its Effects.—Dryness of the mouth and throat, a red flush of the skin, perhaps first noticed on the face and chest, and dilatation of the pupil of the eye. With children the symptoms may be noticed by the flush or by the dilatation of the pupil. It dries up the secretions of the breasts, therefore should not be given to those nursing infants.

Belladonna increases the heart action, increases respiration, dilates all the small vessels, thus bringing the blood to the surface and producing the flush mentioned, dilates the pupil of the eye, relieves or prevents spasmodic action of the involuntary muscles, *i. e.*, those not under the control of the will, or the muscles of the internal organs, and dries up the secretions of the body except those of the kidneys and the digestive tract. The effect upon the blood vessels and pupil of the eye is due to the paralyzing action of the drug on the terminal or outer end of the nerve fibers, which allows the arteries and the pupil to dilate. Regarding the secretions, it should be remembered that every gland that aids in furnishing these secretions is lined with a layer of cells which have terminating in them a nerve fiber, and when the drug paralyzes these terminal fibers, the secreting cells of the various glands fail to act. This is what makes the mouth and throat dry. Perspiration, or elimination by the skin, is checked in the same manner.

Uses of Belladonna.—Belladonna is one of the best remedies in coryza, or cold in the head, where there is considerable discharge from the eyes and nasal cavities. Such catarrhal discharge may be promptly checked by the action of Belladonna or its active principle, Atropine. It will check tyalism, or an increased flow of saliva. In many cases it will relieve the muscular spasm present in asthma. Its antispasmodic action renders it a valuable remedy in whooping cough. In capillary bronchitis (usually an affection of children), where the air cells and small tubes are being filled with the products of a catarrhal inflammation, and where suffocation may follow if relief is not had, Belladonna, or Atropine, is one of the safest and surest remedies to check the secretions and relieve the condition. It is especially valuable in these diseases in children since a child can take proportionately a larger dose than an adult. The catarrhal cough that follows measles may often be relieved by the use of Belladonna or Atropine, because this remedy dries the secretions and thus relieves the irritation.

Again, it is not a depressant, but a stimulant in its general effects. It not only checks the catarrhal condition present in the bronchial tubes, but it relieves the lungs of their congested condition by dilating the small vessels elsewhere and allowing the blood to drain away from them. Belladonna, or Atropine, is valuable in relieving any organ or part of congestion or inflammation. True, it does not produce sweating nor lower temperature, like Aconite, but it is a powerful remedy in these conditions; hence may be used not only in capillary bronchitis, as mentioned, but in the early stages of pneumonia, and other forms of inflammation from any cause, in inflammation of the middle ear, in tonsilitis and catarrhal sore throat. It is one of the best remedies to check night sweats in the latter stages of consumption, or when resulting from any other cause; it is valuable in collapse where the surface is pale and cold; by its power to bring the blood to the surface it is one of the best remedies in congestive chills; it aids in relieving colic by checking spasmodic muscular action; it may relieve torticolis, or wry neck; it is valuable in incontinence of children, because it is eliminated by the kidneys and relieves sensitiveness and spasmodic, or uncontrollable, action of the bladder; it is valuable in relieving the pain in dysmenorrhea, also in relieving ovarian pain. By its power to dilate the pupil of the eye it prevents adhesions in iritis, or inflammation of the iris. For this purpose it is best to use it locally. It is valuable in nose bleed, in hemorrhage from any cause, especially *post partum*, following confinement, or dangerous hemorrage during typhoid fever. It checks hemorrhage the same as it relieves inflammation,—by dilating the small vessels elsewhere and allowing the blood to drain away. It increases the action of the bowels and prevents pain. It is a physiological antidote for Opium, though it is not usually depended upon to any great extent in treating Opium poisoning; it is also an antidote for tyalism produced by too much Calomel. It is the best remedy to check the increased flow of all the secretions of the body following a large dose of Pilocarpine. Pilocarpine has been recommended as as important remedy in the treatment of uræmic poisoning or uræmic convulsions, especially those present during confinement; but the action of Pilocarpine is weakening, and the profuse perspiration that follows leaves the surface cold and chilly. Belladonna, or Atropine, checks the secretions, brings the blood to the surface and stimulates the patient. For the same reason it is *par excellent* in the treatment of cholera infantum or cholera morbus. It is the best remedy to dry up the secretions of the breasts, for which purpose some wet a thin cloth or thin layer of cotton with Belladonna liniment and lay over the breasts. Twelve grains of Atropine, the active principle of Belladonna, dissolved in four ounces of water, may be used in place of the Belladonna liniment.

Dose—A dose of the tincture of Belladonna is from 5 to 10 drops; of the fluid extract, 1 drop; of Atropine, $\frac{1}{250}$ of a grain every thirty minutes or one hour until effect. Any of these forms of dosage may be increased, if necessary, or under the doctor's direction.

THE BROMIDES.

The effect of the Bromides is much the same as that of Chloral, hence their most important therapeutic application is in the treatment of cerebral disorders, *i. e.*, where the brain is too active. In hypnotic power, or the power to relieve nervous conditions and produce sleep, Bromide of Lithium is said to be of first importance, Bromide of Soda second, and Bromide of Potash third, although the Bromide of Potash is the one most commonly used. The Bromides are useful in night terrors, convulsions, nervous headache, nervousness, sleeplessness, whooping cough, change of life, St. Vitus's dance, epilepsy, delirium tremens and acute mania.

Dose.—From 20 to 40 grains. This dose, or half the amount, may be repeated in two to four hours, if needed.

CASCARA SAGRADA.

Cascara Sagrada is as nearly a specific for chronic constipation as any medicine can be for any disease. It relieves constipation indirectly by restoring the tone of the digestive tract. It is one of the most important and best known of the newer remedies. Its use is not attended with the unpleasant after-effects which follow the employment of cathartics, neither does it cause griping nor any unpleasant symptoms. It is a mild tonic laxative, not an active cathartic, therefore should not be given in large doses, but in small and regularly repeated doses. It may be used in all forms of chronic constipation to relieve this condition, which often means the prevention of headache, neuralgia, rheumatism, typhoid fever, and many other diseases both acute and chronic. In case of hemorrhoids, which are usually due to obstructions in the digestive tract, it is superior to most remedies. Generally speaking, cathartics increase this trouble by their irritating effects; Cascara relieves by restoring the normal condition.

Preparations.—There are a number of preparations of Cascara that are used. The fluid extract, Aromatic Cascara and pills or tablets, are the principal forms. When used in pill form, it is generally combined with other laxatives, because of the Cascara alone it requires too many pills for a dose. The Aromatic is the most pleasant to take, because in this preparation the bitter principle which Cascara naturally contains is removed and aromatics are added. The bitter principle mentioned is claimed by some to be of benefit as a tonic to the muscle walls of the stomach and bowels, hence it follows that while Aromatic Cascara is pleasant to the taste and effectual in causing regular action, it would have to be continued for a longer time, because it does not give the "tone" resulting from the action of the laxative and bitter principle combined. The fluid extract contains both these principles, therefore, as stated, is believed by some to be the most valuable form of preparation. Our own experience has acquainted us with a number of cases where it was claimed that the Aromatic Cascara proved equally as valuable as the fluid extract.

Dose.—The usual dose of the Aromatic is from 10 to 20 drops, taken morning and evening; of the fluid extract, a little less. In either case the dose should be suited to the individual need. Some require only a light dose and prefer to take it at bedtime; others take it in the morning before breakfast.

CHLORAL—CHLORAL HYDRATE.

In case of poisoning from Chloral give a tablespoonful of Mustard in a glass of warm water. Repeat the warm water every ten minutes until the patient vomits, adding a little Mustard each time. Apply external heat in abundance. Give strong coffee or other stimulants, and artificial respiration, if needed, as described under DROWNING.

Uses of Chloral.—Chloral is used principally as a hypnotic— to relieve nervousness and produce sleep. It is a cerebral and spinal sedative and antispasmodic. It relieves exciting conditions of the mind, and is a valuable hypnotic in all nervous and hysterical conditions. It is sometimes used in asthma, whooping cough, after-pains, or those following labor, and uræmic convulsions. It produces but little effect upon the sensory nerves, therefore is of but little value in relieving pain.

Symptoms of Its Effects.—Its effects are usually rapid, producing natural sleep from which the patient can be easily aroused. Whenever sleep is produced or nervous conditions quieted, its use should be discontinued. It lessens the heart action, lessens respiration and lowers the pulse. While it is a perfectly safe remedy in the proper dose, and its effects are usually lasting, it is not recommended in cases of fatty heart or where the heart action is enfeebled from any cause. Its principal use, as stated, is to quiet nervous conditions and produce sleep. In most cases of insomnia Chloral is more satisfactory in its results than Morphine or Opium. The sleep produced by Chloral, as stated, is usually natural, and the patient on awakening feels refreshed, the mind is clear, and there are no bad after-effects.

Dose.—From 10 to 20 grains. Chloral is somewhat irritating, therefore should be taken largely diluted, and enough syrup added to cover the taste as far as possible.

CODEINE.

Codeine is one of the active principles of Opium, and, as stated under that head, is one of the most useful. Its narcotic powers are valuable, but its power to relieve severe pain is not equal to Morphine; yet it relieves many painful conditions, and is a most excellent remedy in states of irritability and nervousness. No bad after-effects follow its use as in the case of Opium or Morphine. Its strength is one-fourth of that of Morphine. It is a perfectly safe remedy to give to children, and in adults it will often meet all the needs. Some people cannot take Morphine, and in these cases Codeine usually produces excellent results. Codeine possesses another advantage: there is no danger of forming the habit.

Uses of Codeine.—In nearly all cases where either Opium or Morphine is used, Codeine may be substituted with advantage. In hysterical conditions, whether mild or bordering on delirium, it works like a charm. In diabetes mellitus it is one of the best remedies to check the elimination of sugar. Nearly all cases of pain in the stomach or digestive tract can be controlled by Codeine. In the weak and anæmic it is generally superior to Opium or Morphine. In those of nervous temperament it also possesses many advantages. It is of value in the ordinary cough following colds, and should be used in place of Morphine. It is especially recommended for children. If the effects of Codeine were better understood, it would be more generally used.

Dose.—From ⅛ to ¼ of a grain. Codeine is also used hypodermically.

COLCHICUM—*Colchicine.*

Colchicum is fully represented by its active principle, Colchicine. Its full effects may be obtained from its active principle,— in fact, better results may be obtained from Colchicine than when the whole drug is used. Colchicum increases the action of the liver and kidneys, the secretions of mucous membranes, and elimination by the skin.

Symptoms of Its Effects.—The first symptoms from the effect of Colchicum, or its active principle, Colchicine, are nausea and diarrhea. Colchicum increases the eliminations by all the avenues of the body,—the lungs, skin, digestive tract and kidneys. The elimination of uric acid is increased, and this clearly demonstrates the use of the remedy in neuralgia and rheumatism, especially the latter.

Uses of Colchicum, or Colchicine.—In rheumatism it is especially valuable in plethoric or fleshy subjects. It may be used in either the acute or chronic form of the disease, and is a valuable addition to Salicylate of Soda. Salicylate of Soda is almost universally recognized as the best remedy in the treatment of rheumatism. Colchicum is also valuable in stiff joints resulting from chronic rheumatism, and in that form of the disease frequently called sciatica. As the cause of neuralgia and rheumatism are much the same, it may be given in neuralgia with benefit.

Dose.—Of the tincture of the seed, 10 to 20 drops; of the wine of the seed, 10 to 20 drops; of the fluid extract of the seed, 2 to 4 drops; of the wine of the root, 5 to 10 drops; of the fluid extract of the root, from 1 to 2 drops; of the active principle, Colchicine, $\frac{1}{150}$ to $\frac{1}{100}$ of a grain.

Any of the foregoing doses may be given every three or four hours, more or less often as needed.

All fluid preparations of Colchicum are liable to vary greatly in strength unless made by standard manufacturers.

DIGITALIS—*Digitalin.*

Digitalis contains five active principles. One of these is an irritant and should not be used. Here we see the advantage of the active principle over the whole drug, or preparations including the whole drug, because such preparations include the objectionable principle. The four desirable active principles are combined under the head of Digitalin.

Symptoms of Its Effects.—Strong heart beat, which in some cases is noticed by the patient; full, strong pulse, which also may be easily detected by the patient or those in attendance; and full, strong and distinct heart sounds. Whenever these results are obtained, it is evidence that the dose should be lessened, or that the remedy should be stopped altogether, for a time at least. It is understood, of course, that where these conditions are already present, Digitalis, or Digitalin, is not needed.

Digitalis is a heart tonic, and perhaps occupies first place among the remedies of this kind. It produces its effects by increasing the power of the inhibitory, or restraining, nerves, and these gain control over the accelerators, or those nerves which otherwise would produce rapid heart action. Digitalis, or the combination of its active principles, Digitalin, also stimulates the nerves controlling the size of the small blood vessels, and these contract, producing an effect which is opposite to that of Aconite or Atropine. By slowing the heart action there is given a longer interval of rest between the beats, the cavities of the heart are more completely filled with blood, and the organ makes greater effort to force the blood out. This is another reason why its action is stronger. Again, it requires greater effort to send the blood through the circulatory system, because the small vessels are contracted, as stated, and the force of the heart beat increases in proportion to these extra demands made upon it.

Uses of Digitalis.—By reason of its power to improve the circulation Digitalis is sometimes given to relieve congestion and inflammation. Aconite, Veratrum and Belladonna relieve inflammation by dilating the small vessels elsewhere and allowing the blood to drain away from the affected area, while Digitalis is given with a view of *forcing* the blood through the diseased parts. This is the object when giving Digitalis in acute congestion or inflammation of the lungs. Digitalis is not advised in Aortic Regurgitation (see HEART, DISEASES OF), for in this case to slow the heart action would allow more blood to regurgitate from the arteries back into the heart cavity. Some forms of dyspepsia may be influenced by a sluggish circulation about the stomach.

These cases are improved by the use of Digitalis, because with increased heart action and contraction of the small vessels, it must follow that the blood is driven with greater force. In typhoid fever and other lingering diseases, where the heart naturally becomes weak from poisons and lack of nourishment, Digitalis is of benefit. By reason of the increased circulation and greater blood pressure following the use of Digitalis, it is of value in increasing the action of the kidneys, hence is an important remedy in dropsy, both in overcoming the pressure due to the dropsical conditions and in eliminating the fluid. When given to relieve dropsy, Caffeine, the active principle of Coffee, and Scillitine, the active principle of Squills, may be added with advantage. Caffeine is a heart tonic. It also stimulates the cells lining the collecting tubes of the kidneys and increases elimination. Squills, or its active principle, also stimulates the action of the kidneys. Neither of these remedies should be given in acute inflammation of the kidneys, because to increase their action at this time would be to increase the inflammation. This is more especially true of Squills. The action of Digitalis is slower than that of many other heart tonics, therefore is not so valuable in collapse and other conditions where immediate effects are required. Its effects are more lasting, however, thus making it more valuable where a longer effect is desired.

We have heard it argued against Digitalis, or its combination of active principles, Digitalin, that it may produce cumulative effects, *i. e.*, no results are produced for a time, and then the combined effects of a number of doses occur at once. This claim is not supported by the facts, however. If the drug is given in solution and the fluids of the stomach are normal, there will be no cumulative action. Neither Digitalis nor any other remedy circulates in the blood for days, and then suddenly takes effect with disastrous results. Opium is far more likely to produce cumulative effects, but Opium is a convenient remedy for so many conditions. It quiets the patient, saves the doctor so much time and often produces such immediate results, that cumulative action is not charged against it. Pills may lie in the stomach for days when there is a high fever, because the mucous membrane is dry and absorption is slight. Improvement in the normal secretions may dissolve the pills all at once, and they may enter the circulation rapidly and produce dangerous, results. This is why we stated in the beginning of this chapter that pills should never be given to a fevered patient, nor much medicine to one in a comatose state.

Dose.—Of the tincture of Digitalis, 5 to 10 drops; of the fluid extract, 1 drop; of Digitalin, $\frac{1}{100}$ to $\frac{1}{60}$ of a grain. May be given once in four hours until effect.

ERGOT.

Ergot is a powerful agent in contracting the uterus, therefore should not be given during pregnancy. It contracts the small blood vessels throughout the whole system, thus rendering it a valuable remedy in hemorrhage. Its effects upon the arterial system are the result of its action upon the muscular coats of the vessels.

Uses of Ergot.—It is sometimes of value in varicose veins, enlarged prostate and aneurism. Its effects upon aneurism, however, prove unsatisfactory if the tumor is situated on a large artery. It is also used in menorrhagia, nosebleed, hemorrhage from the lungs and hemorrhage resulting from typhoid fever. Ergot contracts all of the involuntary or internal muscles, contracts the bladder and increases the kidney action. It contracts the small vessels to such an extent that its continued use is said to have caused gangrene of the lower limbs. It is said to be useful in incontinence of urine and diabetes mellitus. Its special action, however, is upon the uterus, and this renders it valuable in subinvolution—where the uterus remains large after confinement—in uterine polypus and in fibroids or tumors of the uterus. It is also thought by many to be one of the best remedies to control hemorrhage following childbirth. In normal labor many physicians use Ergot after the child is born to aid in contracting the uterus. Regarding its effects in such cases, see note under LABOR.

Dose.—The fluid extract of Ergot is the preparation generally used. In menorrhagia, subinvolution, and other conditions where its use is continued for some time, give ½ teaspoonful of the fluid extract four times a day; to check hemorrhage, give 1 teaspoonful and repeat in thirty minutes. For dangerous hemorrhage it should be given with a hypodermic needle.

GELSEMIUM—*Gelsemine.*

Gelsemium is fully represented by its active principle, Gelsemine. This drug lessens heart action, lessens respiration, relaxes the muscular system and deadens sensibility. However, like Aconite, Veratrum, Belladonna and other remedies, if Gelsemium, or its active principle, Gelsemine, is used intelligently, it is a perfectly safe remedy. It is not recommended for weak subjects nor those with a weak heart.

Symptoms of Its Effects.—The first symptoms of its effects are a sense of languor, and drooping of the upper eyelids. If its use is continued, there will be dilatation of the pupils and nausea, and the weakness will be increased.

Gelsemium by its action on the heart slows circulation: the pulse is less rapid and blood pressure is lowered. This, together with its effects on respiration, lessens tissue change and lowers temperature; hence it is used in fevers, especially in the painful conditions sometimes met in rheumatism and neuralgia, in sciatic rheumatism, or rheumatism of the sciatic nerve, in ovarian neuralgia and in dysmenorrhea. In many of these cases it may be given with benefit. It is also recommended in remittent fevers. It relieves spasmodic muscular action in asthma and distressing coughs. It aids in relieving after-pains, or those following labor. It is sometimes used in whooping cough.

Dose.—Of the tincture, 5 to 10 drops; of the fluid extract, 2 to 5 drops; of the active principle, $\frac{1}{250}$ of a grain. May be given every three hours until effect.

GLONOIN—NITROGLYCERINE.

Glonoin is one of the most rapid and powerful stimulants known. Its effects are not lasting, however, but pass off within an hour. It is a powerful stimulant to the heart and respiration. It also dilates the small vessels, and thus brings the blood to the surface.

Symptoms of Its Effects.—Headache and flushing of the face. It may be used either in solution or in tablets. The tablets are the most convenient. Absorption takes place much more quickly from the tongue than from the stomach, and if a Glonoin tablet is dissolved on the tongue, its effects may be noticed in from two or three to five minutes. The effects can probably be produced more quickly this way than by giving it with a hypodermic needle, because in using the needle a little time is required to get the dose ready.

Uses of Glonoin, or Nitroglycerine.—By reason of its rapid and powerful action Glonoin, or Nitroglycerine, is one of the best remedies in emergency cases, *i. e.*, in accident or collapse. In cases of this kind where the face is pale and the surface cold, Glonoin often proves to be one of the most valuable of remedies. In fainting, in low conditions, in collapse during typhoid fever or pneumonia, or following the administration of Chloroform where the patient does not rally and where death seems imminent, Glonoin is the best stimulant and the one most likely to revive the patient. It should be remembered, however, that where vitality is low from any cause, so powerful a stimulant should be given in small doses. Overstimulation might paralyze the heart's action, and this would hasten death rather than afford relief. This is equally true of other stimulants. *Overstimulation will always produce death.*

Many cases of dysmenorrhea may be relieved with Glonoin. As stated, Glonoin, or Nitroglycerine, dilates the small vessels, and this relieves the congested uterus. Asthma, neuralgia, vomiting, dizziness, toothache and seasickness may often be relieved or benefited by the use of this remedy. In asphyxia from inhaling illuminating gas it is valuable. It is also a valuable aid in treating cases of suspected drowning.

Dose.—From $\frac{1}{250}$ to $\frac{1}{100}$ of a grain.

Note—Nitrite of Amyl produces a more rapid action than Glonoin. Its effects are more transient, however, and again, it is not so convenient a remedy.

IODINE.

Iodine is made from the ashes of Seaweed. It is never taken internally in its clear state. Poisoning from Iodine increases the flow of saliva, causes a catarrhal condition of the eyes, and, in fact, increases the secretions of all mucous membrane; also produces burning heat and pain in the stomach, nausea, vomiting, diarrhea and collapse.

Antidote.—A teaspoonful or two of starch taken in a little water forms Iodide of Starch and relieves the danger at once. This should be followed with a tablespoonful of ground Mustard in a tumblerful of warm water to produce vomiting. If results are not satisfactory, repeat the dose of warm water every fifteen minutes, but after the first tumblerful add only 1 or 2 teaspoonfuls of the Mustard. Iodine is absorbed from the stomach very rapidly, therefore the antidote must be given early. After vomiting, give mucilaginous drinks and allow only mild liquid food for a few days, or until the inflammation of the stomach has subsided.

Iodine is readily diffusible and, as stated, enters the circulation rapidly from the stomach. As a medicine its effects are those of a general disinfectant. It liquefies the products of inflammation, thus rendering them more readily taken up by the circulation and eliminated. It forms soluble iodides with metallic salts, hence is valuable in relieving the system of Mercury where this remedy has been taken for some time; also of lead in cases of chronic lead poisoning, sometimes found in painters and those who manufacture paints.

Symptoms of Its Effects.—Taken in medicinal doses, the first symptoms of the effects of Iodine are a catarrhal condition of the eyes and increased flow of saliva. By increasing the secretions of the mucous membrane along the digestive tract, diarrhea may result. Eruptions on the skin may also occur. It is also slightly diuretic, increasing the secretions of the kidneys. By reason of its effects on mucous membrane Iodine is sometimes used in chronic bronchitis. By its power to liquefy and eliminate inflammatory products it is a valuable remedy following pneumonia, pleurisy, typhoid fever, or inflammations from any cause. By reason of its antiseptic properties it has been highly recommended in consumption. By reason of its power to stimulate absorption it is frequently used externally in glandular swellings, swollen joints, etc. It is also applied externally to boils, carbuncles, ringworm and chilblains. When used in strong solution, it acts as a counter-irritant and is a frequent addition to liniments; also used externally in the form of ointments. It is a well known remedy in syphilis, especially in the latter stages. It is sometimes injected in strong solution into cavities, such as hydrocele, where it causes local inflammation, the new tissue growth uniting the inner surfaces of the sac and obliterating the cavity. Iodoform is only another means of using Iodine. This well known remedy is frequently used in dressing wounds. It is also taken internally in pill or tablet form. Iodide of Lime is highly recommended in spasmodic croup. There are several preparations of Iodine for internal use. Some prefer one form, some another; the object is the same in each case, and the different combinations are only different methods of administration. Any of the preparations should be taken *between meals*, because if taken with the meals, the Iodine unites with the starch in the food, forming Iodide of Starch, as stated, which destroys the effect.

For the rheumatic swelling of joints a most excellent application is Tincture of Iodine and Water of Ammonia, equal parts. After standing a few hours the mixture turns very light in color. This combination forms Iodide of Ammonia. The Ammonia is stimulating, and the Iodine renders the inflammatory products soluble, thus facilitating their ready removal.

Dose.—Syrup of Hydriodic Acid, 1 teaspoonful between meals. Tincture of Iodine, 5 to 8 drops taken in water or milk. Iodide of Ammonia, from 2 to 5 grains. Iodide of Soda, from 2 to 5 grains.

Iodide of Lime, when given to children for spasmodic croup, should be given in ¼ or ⅓ grain doses, dissolved in a little hot water, and the dose repeated every 15 to 30 minutes until relief is had.

Iodoform, 1 grain three or four times a day.

IPECAC—IPECACUANHA.

Ipecac is fully represented by its active principle, Emetine. Ipecac or its active principle is much used in unhealthy conditions of the mucous membrane of the air passages, stomach and digestive tract. It is also used in large doses as an emetic. For this purpose Ipecac is a perfectly safe remedy for adults or children. It produces vomiting by stimulating that part of the brain which controls the action. Its emetic effects are also said to be due to some extent to its local action on the mucous membrane of the stomach. The nerves that control the stomach have their origin in the brain, therefore, what is supposed to be the local action is in reality its effect on the nerves mentioned, the impulse thus produced being conveyed to the brain. When taken in moderate quantities, Ipecac relaxes the voluntary and involuntary muscles, and this allows the small arteries to dilate the same as described under Aconite and Belladonna.

Symptoms of Its Effects.—The first symptom is nausea. If its use is continued after this symptom appears, vomiting will result.

Uses of Ipecac.—Ipecac is a valuable remedy in catarrhal conditions of the respiratory organs and digestive tract. During the early stages of a cold where there is congestion of the membrane lining the bronchial tubes or air passages, the mucous membrane is often dry. This produces irritation and a hoarse cough. Ipecac increases the secretions of the mucous membrane, and this relieves the irritation and aids in relieving the trouble. The effects of Aconite in this condition are the same. In bronchitis, where the secretions are excessive, thick and tenacious, Ipecac is of value in draining the congested or inflamed vessels and in thinning the secretions mentioned, thus facilitating their elimination; hence it is of value in cough medicines. The same effects are produced in the stomach when a catarrhal condition is present. It frees the stomach walls of unhealthy exudate, relieves nausea and headache and improves digestion. When there is congestion and unhealthy eliminations in the digestive tract, the effects are the same. First, the engorged vessels are drained, thus relieving congestion and inflammation and increasing the fluids, which wash away the diseased products and restore the mucous membrane to a healthy condition. Here Ipecac acts both as a laxative and a disinfectant.

The great benefit to be derived from Ipecac in bowel troubles cannot be too strongly emphasized. If there is catarrhal jaundice present, that is, if the mucous membrane lining the duct through which the bile passes from the liver into the digestive tract is congested, swollen or inflamed, and more or less filled with unhealthy products, Ipecac gives the same relief and produces the same sanitary effects as elsewhere. Ipecac also stimulates the liver, increasing the flow of bile and thus aiding in clearing up unhealthy conditions. It also acts as a diuretic, increasing the action of the kidneys.

Ipecac is of value in amenorrhea when produced suddenly as a result of taking cold. By its power to relax spasmodic muscular action, it is of value in spasmodic croup. It aids in relieving bad breath, bad taste in the mouth and eructations when due to a disordered stomach. Ipecac is frequently used in large doses to produce vomiting; small doses have a directly opposite effect and aid in checking vomiting. Two or three drops of the Fluid

Extract of Ipecac stirred into half a glass of water and given in teaspoonful doses every ten or fifteen minutes, will often prove successful in relieving nausea or checking vomiting.

Dose.—The dose of the syrup is from 5 to 10 drops; of the fluid extract, 1 drop; of the active principle, Emetine, $\frac{1}{15}$ of a grain. The dose of any of the foregoing preparations may be increased or diminished, as required. As an emetic, the dose is 1 teaspoonful of the syrup, or from 10 to 20 drops of the fluid extract, every fifteen to twenty minutes. For other purposes Ipecac is combined with other remedies, as on pages 95 and 252.

IRON.

Iron is an astringent, contracting the small blood vessels. It increases the power of the red blood corpuscles to absorb oxygen while passing through the lungs, and is used in many low conditions to aid in building up the system.

Symptoms of Its Effects.—There are no immediate or early symptoms produced by medicinal doses of Iron. Iron is absorbed into the circulation mostly from the duodenum, or that part of the small bowel nearest the stomach, although it is also absorbed to some extent from the stomach and along the digestive tract.

Regarding the manner in which Iron enters the circulation, it may be stated that the inorganic salts, *i. e.*, the Iron given artificially, stimulates the absorption of the organic Iron, or that form contained in the food products, and at the same time the Iron taken artificially enters into combination with the sulphureted hydrogen which is present in the digestive tract, and then enters the circulation.

Uses of Iron.—By increasing the oxygen carrying power of the red blood corpuscles Iron increases oxidization, and this increases the tissue changes throughout the body. Iron in repeated doses not only increases the power of the red blood corpuscles, as stated, but increases their number also. This means increased nutrition and assimilation, and in this way Iron improves the condition of both the blood and tissues. It stimulates increased activity of the mental faculties, and at the same time increases the physical powers. Iron is of value in all forms of anæmia, in chlorosis, scrofula and Bright's disease. It is valuable in erysipelas where the subject is physically weak and the skin is pale. It is of value in neuralgia when the patient lacks "tone." It is an astringent, therefore is sometimes used in diarrhea. By reason of its astringent properties it is also sometimes used in hemorrhage, in nosebleed, and in menorrhagia, or hemorrhage from the uterus.

By reason of its power to contract the small vessels Iron is sometimes used in solution locally to check hemorrhage, although it is claimed that it coagulates the blood for some distance along the arteries and veins, and that such coagulum may undergo decomposition later and thus poison the system; hence its local use is not so frequent as in former years.

Preparations.—The Tincture of the Chloride of Iron contains Hydrochloric (Muriatic) Acid. This form has a more direct influence on digestion, because Hydrochloric is the natural acid present in the digestive fluid of the stomach. This is one reason why Tincture of Iron is the best form for internal use. What is called Dialized Iron is Iron in solution. Dialized Iron contains 16 grains of Metallic Iron to the ounce. This form is not injurious to the teeth, possesses an agreeable taste, and is harmless to the mucous membrane of the stomach and digestive tract. There are also many soluble Salts of Iron for internal use. Those containing Quinine and Strychnine are frequently used. Iron may also be conveniently used in pill or tablet form. Arsenic and Iron are frequently combined in pill or tablet form, called Arseniate of Iron. Iodide of Iron is another combination which may be given in pill or tablet form. Syrup of Iodide of Iron is also a popular form for internal administration.

Dose.—Of the Tincture of Chloride of Iron, 10 drops; of the Syrup of Iodide of Iron, from 10 to 30 drops; of Dialized Iron, from 10 to 30 drops; of Metallic Iron in pill form, from 1 to 3 grains. Any preparation of Iron should be taken after meals. It is absorbed into the circulation slowly, hence should be given in small doses and its use continued for some time.

JABORANDI—*Pilocarpine.*

The action of Jaborandi depends upon two active principles contained in the leaves: One is called Pilocarpine, and the other, Jaborine. When taken into the system, the effects of these two principles are directly opposed to each other. Pilocarpine increases the secretions of the glandular structures of the body, while Jaborine checks them. However, Pilocarpine is in excess, so that when the whole drug is used, or preparations made from the whole drug, the secretions are increased'; but it will readily be seen that a larger amount is needed than when the Pilocarpine is given alone. Thus we are continually reminded of the fact already stated, that when the active principles are separated and used singly, the effects are far more satisfactory.

Symptoms of Its Effect.—Jaborine is seldom used, therefore we shall give only the effects of Pilocarpine, which in some conditions is a very important and useful remedy. As stated, Pilocarpine increases the secretions of all the glandular structures of the body. The first effects are noticed by the increased flow of saliva. This one symptom is all that is needed to show that the system is being brought under its influence. Pilocarpine has been recommended in this work as one of the most useful remedies to produce elimination in uræmic convulsions. When given for this purpose, its full effects are usually desired, hence no attention is paid to the symptom given—increased flow of saliva. It is claimed that Pilocarpine produces contraction of the uterus, therefore should not be given in case of pregnancy. When a large dose, $\frac{1}{4}$ to $\frac{1}{3}$ of a grain, is given with a hypodermic needle, elimination is increased by all the avenues of the body—those of the lungs, digestive tract, kidneys and skin. The greatest amount of elimination takes place through the skin. To see a person thoroughly under the influence of Pilocarpine is to see a very uncomfortable individual. The water is pouring out over the surface of the body. The increased secretions of the mucous membrane lining the bronchial tubes and air cells cause free expectoration. Added to these are the secretions of the throat, of the salivary glands and of the nasal cavities. The result is a constant flow from the mouth and nose. The secretions of the stomach may be so profuse as to cause vomiting; those of the digestive tract may cause an active movement of the bowels; those of the kidneys cause an increased flow of urine; and the pores of the skin pour out large amounts of water. In this way from three to six pints of fluid may be eliminated in three or four hours, or the effects may last from three to five hours. The natural result of this experience is a weakened heart action, weak pulse, weak respiration, and a pale, cold surface; hence *Pilocarpine is not recommended for those with a weak heart or weak lungs.*

Uses of Pilocarpine.—In uræmic convulsions in confinement the patient is often unconscious, and in this condition may be unable to expel from the lungs all of the increased bronchial secretions; hence they may reach such proportions, fill the small air tubes and exclude the air to such an extent that the condition of the patient becomes serious. Should this condition present itself, it may be speedily checked by a hypodermic of Atropine. Atropine checks the secretions and further relieves the lungs by bringing the blood to the surface. It also stimulates the heart action and stimulates respiration. (See URÆMIC CONVULSIONS, also see BELLADONNA in this chapter). Besides its value in the treatment of uræmic convulsions, it is useful in smaller doses in other conditions. Following labor, when the secretions of the breasts are limited or entirely wanting, $\frac{1}{10}$ of a grain of Pilocarpine, more or less, given four times a day, will increase the secretions. It is one of the best remedies for this purpose, and in nearly every case will prove successful.

It will be noticed that the action of Pilocarpine is directly opposite to that of Atropine, therefore it is a physiological antidote for Atropine. Atropine checks the secretions; Pilocarpine increases them. Atropine dilates the pupil of the eye; Pilocarpine contracts it. And, *vice versa*, following a full dose of Pilocarpine, Atropine is one of the best remedies to check the secretions when they have gone far enough, to bring the blood to the surface and to increase the heart action and respiration.

A severe cough with no expectoration may be due to the dry condition of the mucous membrane which lines the air cells and small air tubes. One-tenth of a grain of Pilocarpine four times a day will increase the secretions, render the membrane moist, relieve the irritation and aid in checking the cough. For the same reason it is valuable in dry bronchitis. Pilocarpine is valuable in eliminating the poisons in diphtheria, in erysipelas in the strong and robust, and in relieving an attack of asthma. In cases of baldness where the hair follicles are not destroyed, Pilocarpine will produce a new growth of hair. (See BALDNESS.)

Dose.—$\frac{1}{10}$ of a grain four times a day. Also given hypodermically.

JALAP.

Jalap stimulates liver action and increases the flow of bile. It also increases the fluids of the digestive tract, hence is followed by large watery evacuations. This renders it especially valuable in the various forms of dropsy,—in abdominal dropsy from any cause, in cardiac dropsy, meaning water in the sac surrounding the heart, and other forms of dropsy in the chest cavity. In all of these conditions it rapidly removes the fluids from the body, and thus relieves difficult heart action and labored breathing. It is also valuable in bronchitis where the lungs are congested, and in all forms of congestion or inflammation of any organ or part.

Dose.—From 5 to 10 grains. Jalap is sometimes combined with Cream of Tartar, and this combination given in small and continued doses is perhaps equally as valuable in relieving the system. It is also sometimes combined with Calomel and other cathartics.

NUX VOMICA—*Strychnine.*

Nux Vomica possesses two active principles, Strychnine and Brucine. Strychnine is the principle generally used, and is believed by many to be one of the most valuable of stimulants. It increases the heart action, increases respiration, and stimulates the whole nervous system, both the motor and sensory, thus removing the sense of weariness and increasing the capacity for labor, both mental and physical.

Symptoms of Its Effects.—The symptoms resulting from the use of Strychnine are a slight nervousness, or slight muscular tremor, which may be first noticed in the hands; or there may be slight stiffness felt in the muscles of the throat, neck or else-where. If its use is continued, or the dose is increased after these symptoms are present, it may result in spasmodic and uncontrollable muscular action.

Uses of Strychnine.—Strychnine is one of the most powerful stimulants known. It increases the secretions of the stomach and digestive tract, and also increases peristalsis, or the action of the bowels. By stimulating the muscular coats of the bronchial tubes it contracts the air passages and aids in the elimination of unhealthy secretions; by stimulating the muscle walls of the small vessels it contracts the arteries, and this contraction, with the increased heart action, increases both the blood pressure and the circulation. It aids in contracting the uterus. By its power to produce muscular contraction it may be used in preventing distension of the abdominal cavity in peritonitis. Its stimulating and tonic effects are valuable in all cases where there is great prostration of the physical powers, or that condition commonly called shock, whether following an accident, an operation, or from any other cause. Its tonic effect renders it a valuable remedy in typhoid fever, capillary bronchitis and pneumonia, and relieves the necessity of any form of alcoholic liquors. Added to the Syrup of Hypophosphites, and this combined with Extract of Malt, it is valuable in consumption or enfeebled conditions from any cause. By some it is believed to have a special tonic effect on the lungs, and it is claimed that during its use the blood contains more oxygen. This claim is easily accounted for when we remember that the circulation through the lungs is increased. It is one of the best tonics for those who are trying to break off from the liquor habit. In small doses, $\frac{1}{100}$ to $\frac{1}{60}$ of a grain, taken before meals, it is a valuable stomachic, exciting an increased flow of the digestive ferments and increasing functional activity; by reason of its general stimulating and tonic effects it increases the amount of all the digestive ferments. Small doses may check the vomiting of pregnancy, cure sick headache and aid in relieving seasickness. It may be given with benefit during the passage of gall-stone or stone from the kidney. In this case results are obtained by the power of the Strychnine to contract the muscle fibers of the duct leading from the gall bladder, or those of the ureter leading from the kidney, such action aiding in expelling the stone. It also aids in relieving strangulated hernia by increasing peristalsis, thus helping to release the imprisoned bowel.

Nux Vomica in tincture or any other form of solution is not usually given, because its taste is so decidedly bitter. Its active principle, Strychnine, has been largely substituted. This can be taken in pill or tablet form without taste. The action of Brucine is the same as that of Strychnine, but the effects are much milder, hence the remedy is often used for children.

Dose.—A dose of the Tincture of Nux Vomica is from 5 to 20 drops; of Strychnine, from $\frac{1}{100}$ to $\frac{1}{20}$ of a grain; of Brucine, for children, from $\frac{1}{250}$ to $\frac{1}{20}$ of a grain. May be given three or four times a day.

OPIUM.—*Morphine.*

Opium contains a large number of active principles,—some eighteen or twenty. Some of them are valuable and some are not, in fact, some are believed to be injurious. However, Opium with its combined principles is an old and well known remedy. It is claimed by many that as a narcotic and hypnotic, Opium holds first place; yet in many conditions sleep may be produced equally as successfully with Chloral or the Bromides, or with a number of other preparations. In past years Morphine was believed to be the most valuable principle in Opium, but more recently Codeine has taken its place to a considerable extent. The principal use of either Opium or Morphine is in relieving pain. Either will relieve physical suffering and produce a state of quiet, ease and mental comfort.

General Effects of Opium.—Opium first stimulates heart action and the intellectual faculties. The thoughts are varied and pleasant, and care and suffering are past. This condition is followed by drowsiness, deadening of the mental faculties and profound sleep; following a large dose, the sleep deepens into coma. Sleep is induced by the deadening of the sensibilities to surrounding objects, but more especially by the anæmic condition of the brain resulting from the contraction of the small arteries. As the effects continue, the heart action becomes weakened and respiration lessened. In case of death from an overdose the brain is deeply congested. This condition is the result of dilatation or engorgement of the veins, which occurs during the last stage. One of the most serious objections to either Opium or Morphine is the danger of "forming the habit," as it is called.

Opium or Morphine lessens the flow of saliva, the secretions of the kidneys, the amount of bile and the secretions of the digestive tract, and also checks peristalsis, the natural action of the bowels, causing constipation; in a word, it may be said to lessen all the secretions of the body except those of the skin. These are increased, but such increase belongs more to the effect of Opium than of Morphine. The after-effects of either are unpleasant and often very unsatisfactory. Either causes dryness of the mouth and tongue, bad breath, loss of appetite, feeling of nausea, sense of dizziness, headache and general depression. Sometimes some of these conditions last for one or two days, and even longer. By prolonged use, however, the system can become so accustomed to either that enormous amounts can be taken without destroying life. Cases are reported where 320 grains of Morphine—nearly ¾ of an ounce—have been taken in one day, and from ½ to 1 pint of Laudanum.

Uses of Opium or Morphine.—The principal use of either of these remedies is for the relief of pain; it is their only legitimate use. In case of accident or injury where the pain is severe, enough of either may be given at a single dose to render the patient comfortable. It is seldom necessary to repeat the dose. From this the reader will understand that the only symptom needed is the one already given,—the relief of pain. It is not necessary to give enough to put the patient to sleep nor to produce any of the other symptoms mentioned.

Conditions Requiring the Use of Opium or Morphine.—Neither of these remedies should be given to infants nor small children, because they are liable to produce convulsions and even death. One drop of Laudanum has proven fatal to an infant. The cause of the convulsions is that in infants and small children the brain is but poorly developed and is easily overcome by the effects of the drug, hence the nerve centers situated along the spinal cord gain control over the cerebral centers, or those situated in the brain, and the spinal nerves set up convulsive action, according to their nature. When we remember that the nerves supplying the muscles of the body and extremities have their origin in the spinal cord, it is easy to account for the convulsions. Later, as the child grows, the brain develops and the centers in the cord mentioned are under the influence or control of the intellectual or higher centers in the brain. In adult life the weak and anæmic are also more susceptible. Opium or Morphine should never be given to nursing mothers, because it is eliminated by the milk.

As Opium and Morphine are the most certain remedies for the relief of suffering and pain, they are sometimes given in sciatica or sciatic rheumatism, to relieve the suffering in the late stages of cancer, and in severe colic. Morphine is perhaps the most certain remedy to prevent abortion. Opium is sometimes valuable in diarrhea where a good deal of pain is present. It may be needed in the intense pain present in peritonitis or pleurisy. A single dose of Opium and Quinine is sometimes given to break up a cold, the Opium producing free elimination through the skin. In case of severe cough Opium or Morphine is sometimes added to cough remedies, though in most cases Codeine is better. By reason of their power to dry the secretions they are sometimes given in small doses, together with Atropine, in coryza, or cold in the head. Morphine in $\frac{1}{30}$-grain doses is best for this purpose. It is sometimes given to check severe hemorrhage in typhoid fever, although we believe that Atropine is a better remedy for this purpose, and especially if the patient is low. Atropine not only possesses the power to check hemorrhage, but is a stimulant, therefore there would be less danger from its use. Opium or Morphine is sometimes needed, but should never be resorted to except in extreme cases.

Dose.—Of Opium, from ½ to 1 grain; of Laudanum, from 10 to 30 drops; of Morphine, from ⅛ to ¼ grain. These doses may be increased under the doctor's directions.

Dover's Powder is a convenient form for the administration of Opium. Dover's Powder contains ten per cent of Opium, ten grains of Dover's Powder being equal to one grain of Opium.

QUININE.

Calisaya Bark contains a number of active principles, of which Quinine is the most important, in fact, is the only one which is used to any extent. In small doses Quinine is a valuable tonic by reason of its effects on the digestive organs, particularly the stomach. Small doses are stimulating; large ones somewhat depressing. One of the principal uses of Quinine has been as a remedy for malaria.

Symptoms of Its Effects.—Singing in the ears. This is a result of its stimulating effect upon the auditory nerves. Quinine also stimulates uterine contractions, therefore should not be given during pregnancy. If taken by nursing mothers, it is partially eliminated in the milk. Large doses are said to lessen the amount of urea eliminated.

Uses of Quinine.—In small doses Quinine acts as a stomachic, increasing the flow of the fluids of the stomach and thus aiding digestion and improving the appetite ; hence it is frequently used for this purpose, both alone and with other bitter tonics. It is valuable in convalescence. It is frequently combined with Iron in anæmic conditions. Quinine is believed to exhibit an inhibitory effect upon the red blood corpuscles, and thus prevent, to some extent, their yielding up oxygen. This lessens tissue change and lowers temperature; hence Quinine is sometimes used in fevered conditions, though as a remedy for this particular purpose it is far less valuable than Aconite or Veratrum. During the inflammation preceding the formation of an abscess, and also during such formation, a large number of the white corpuscles which are in the circulation flow along to the inflamed and distended vessels, lodge there, and are converted into pus. Quinine is believed to prevent to some extent the migration of the white corpuscles and thus lessen the amount of pus formation. As stated, however, its greatest value is its tonic properties and power to check malaria. The latter is of less importance than in former years, because many sections of the country, once pervaded by the dread malaria, are now wholly free from that trouble.

Dose.—As a tonic, from 1 to 3 grains three times a day before meals; for malaria, large doses are sometimes given. See MALARIAL FEVERS.

RHUBARB.

Rhubarb contains two active principles, Chrysophanic Acid and Tannic Acid. When taken internally, it first acts as a laxative; this is due to the irritating effects of the Chrysophanic Acid. The secondary action is that of the Tannic Acid, which checks bowel movement. Rhubarb also increases the flow of bile. This aids in elimination and in rendering the digestive tract in a healthier condition. Rhubarb in small doses produces a tonic effect on the walls of the stomach, hence is useful in dyspepsia. Its effects upon the liver render it of value where jaundice is present. It is a well known remedy, perfectly safe, and much used in the bowel difficulties of children. One of the best combinations is the following, which has been given elsewhere:

Carbonate of Soda	1	drachm.
Ipecac, Fluid Extract of	½	"
Hydrastis, Fluid	6	"
Rhubarb, Syrup of	4	ounces.

Mix, and take 1 teaspoonful, more or less, every three hours, or as needed.

SEIDLITZ SALTS—SALINE LAXATIVE.

Seidlitz Salts, also called Saline Laxative, are a chemically pure form of Sulphate of Magnesia in effervescent combination. All irritants are removed, the taste is pleasant, and their effects are delightful and always satisfactory. Their value cannot be overestimated, and if made the basis of treatment in every home and used early, much sickness would be avoided. Seidlitz Salts are a prompt and sure relief in all forms of constipation, and in many forms of diarrhea. In diarrhea they remove all irritating substances, relieve congestion, and leave the digestive tract in a healthy condition.

Symptoms of Their Effects.—In the proper dose Seidlitz Salts act as a safe and harmless purgative, and can be administered to children and those with a delicate constitution. Taken on an empty stomach, their action is prompt and certain. They cause active transudation, or passing of water from the blood and tissues into the digestive tract. They also possess diuretic properties and increase the action of the kidneys.

Uses of Seidlitz Salts.—Seidlitz Salts are of value in fevers, acute or chronic, especially the former. Many acute fevers are due to the condition of the digestive tract, and may be wholly overcome by a liberal use of the Saline Laxative. During fever constipation usually exists, and with the increase in temperature putrefactive changes in the digestive tract take place more readily. The poisons resulting from such changes are absorbed and aid in lowering the vital powers, thus rendering the patient less able to ward off or withstand the threatened attack. A thorough flushing of the digestive tract at this time is of the utmost importance. This not only relieves the unhealthy conditions present, but drains the congested vessels which surround and supply the bowels. All forms of congestion or inflammation of the pelvic organs may be greatly benefited or cured by Saline Laxative. The drain upon the blood supply, both by the digestive tract and kidneys, aids in lowering blood pressure, and this slows the heart action. The internal vessels—those along the bowels—are continually being drained into the canal and refilled by draining the external vessels, or those nearer the surface. This flushing of the digestive tract lessens the heat along the inflamed canal, and at the same time the drain made upon the external vessels decreases their blood supply. This lessens tissue changes and lowers temperature, hence Seidlitz Salts are said to be cooling. This fact renders them of especial value during the summer months. In typhoid fever, attended with constipation, and in dysentery where the eliminations contain thick, tenacious secretions and pus, Seidlitz Salts are of especial value. The alkaline solution dissolves the unhealthy secretions along the mucous membrane, and thus facilitates their ready removal. The same is true in all other unhealthy conditions of the bowels where the mucous membrane is clogged and in an unhealthy condition. In chronic constipation a small dose of the Seidlitz Salts taken regularly, early in the morning on an empty stomach, or morning and night, will prove successful in overcoming the trouble.

Seidlitz Salts not only clear the digestive tract and render it healthy and free from disease, but they neutralize the excess of acids which are often present in the blood. It is the presence of these acids—uric and lactic acids—that cause headache, rheumatism, neuralgia, sciatica and other painful conditions. It is not claimed that Seidlitz Salts are the best treatment for these troubles after they have developed, but it is claimed that by a liberal use of the remedy many attacks might be prevented.

In all forms of catarrh of the stomach, whether the indigestion is the result of unwholesome food, overeating, or from an excessive use of alcoholic liquors, Seidlitz Salts dissolve the unhealthy secretions, drain the congested vessels and leave the mucous membrane clean and wholesome, the same as in the digestive tract. In eructations due to indigestion small doses of Seidlitz Salts will neutralize the gas and relieve the trouble.

The digestive fluid of the stomach is acid. It is well known that acid fluids are increased by the addition of an alkali, and if small doses—½ teaspoonful of Seidlitz Salts—are taken before meals, the digestive fluids of the stomach will be increased, digestion improved, and the bowels regulated at the same time.

The system of drainage resulting from Seidlitz Salts renders them a valuable remedy in dropsy, whether of the abdominal cavity, chest cavity, plural cavity or around the heart. Dropsical conditions during pregnancy may be quickly relieved. Congestion or inflammation of the brain may often be greatly benefited or entirely relieved by the use of Seidlitz Salts. In blood poisoning from any cause, in puerperal fever following childbirth and in uræmic poisoning, they offer one of the most effectual means of freeing the system. In uræmic convulsions resulting from pregnancy or following childbirth, Salts in any form should not be relied upon, because their action is too slow. In milk leg decided benefit follows the use of Seidlitz Salts. In that form of Bright's disease followed by dropsy in the abdominal cavity, producing pressure upon the heart and lungs and causing labored breathing and tumultuous heart action, small, continued doses of Seidlitz Salts, will give surprising results. The same is true in dropsy following rum drinker's liver.

In acne, or that form of rash about the forehead and face, if the surface is bathed with one or two teaspoonfuls of Seidlitz Salts dissolved in half a glass of water, the greasy appearance will be relieved and the skin made to appear healthier and more natural. If the practice is continued, much of the oily matter which clogs the skin will also be dissolved and removed.

Dose.—As a laxative, 1 heaping teaspoonful early in the morning on an empty stomach; as a cathartic, repeat the dose every hour until results; as a diuretic, or in dropsical conditions, take ½ teaspoonful in ½ glass of water every hour through the day.

Note.—The Abbott Alkaloidal Company of Ravenswood, Chicago, manufactures Saline Laxatives and the Sulphocarbolates.

SENNA.

Senna owes its well known cathartic action to an active principle called Cathartic Acid. Senna increases bowel action, causing free elimination. It is supposed to have a feeble action on the liver. It is always a safe and sure remedy, and produces satisfactory results. It is generally used in the form of tea or infusion made from the leaves. Senna leaves constitute the basis of the various teas sold throughout the country, such as *Garfield Tea*, *Lane's Tea*, *Rocky Mountain Tea*, etc. It is also the active ingredient in Syrup of Figs. When used alone, Senna tea sometimes causes nausea and griping pains, hence aromatics are usually added. Senna is frequently used with other cathartics, especially Rhubarb and Jalap. *Confection of Senna*, which is composed of Senna, Coriander seed, Licorice, Tamarinds and Cinnamon, is quite popular.

Cathartic Acid is seldom used. A dose of it is $\frac{1}{25}$ of a grain.

SQUILLS—*Scillitin.*

Squills owes its medicinal properties to an active principle called Scillitin. Squills is an expectorant and diuretic, *i. e.*, it increases the eliminations of the lungs and kidneys. When used in large doses, it acts as an irritant and produces vomiting and purging.

Symptoms of its Effects.—The only symptoms are those just given, but it should never be carried to the point of producing such results.

Uses of Squills.—Like Ipecac, Squills acts on the mucous membrane of the air passages, digestive tract and kidneys. In acute bronchitis it relieves the congestion present in the lungs and causes freer elimination. In health the mucous membrane of the bronchial tubes, like all other mucous membrane, furnishes just enough moisture to lubricate the surface and prevent friction. This moisture is thick like mucilage and is called mucus, hence the term *mucous membrane*. It is also sometimes called *secretions*. In chronic bronchitis the mucus is thick and tenacious and clogs more or less the air cells and small tubes, and this produces irritation and cough. By stimulating the action of the mucous membrane, Squills not only increases the amount of the secretions and drains the congested vessels, but such drainage thins the unhealthy exudate and aids in its freer elimination; hence it is a valuable expectorant in all forms of chronic lung affections. It stimulates the action of the kidneys, as stated, therefore should not be used in acute inflammation of those organs. In dropsical conditions not due to kidney disease, it aids in relieving the trouble by increasing the flow of urine.

Dose.—Of the syrup, 10 to 30 drops every three hours; of the fluid extract, 1 drop every three hours; of Scillitin, the active principle, $\frac{1}{30}$ of a grain every three hours.

STROPHANTHUS—*Strophanthin.*

Strophanthus is fully represented by its active principle, Strophanthin. Strophanthus is a powerful heart tonic. Its effects are the same as those of Digitalis, except that its action is more rapid and it does not contract the small vessels; Digitalis does. In case of feeble heart action where the pulse is irregular and wavering, Strophanthus will be found a valuable remedy. In typhoid fever, pneumonia, and in the so-called "tobacco heart,' it will prove of great service. See also DIGITALIS.

Dose.—Of the tincture, 5 to 10 drops; of the fluid extract, 1 to 2 drops; of Strophanthin, the active principle, $\frac{1}{500}$ of a grain. May be given every three or four hours until effect.

VERATRUM VIRIDE—*Veratrine.*

Veratrum Viride is fully represented by its active principle, Veratrine. This remedy is highly recommended in uræmic convulsions. It does not eliminate the poison, but aids in relaxing the spasms. Aside from this its effects are similar to Aconite, already described, and, like Aconite, it is not recommended for those with a weak heart. It relieves congestion and inflammation by dilating the small blood vessels and allowing the blood to drain away from the affected organ. It is claimed that it dilates the veins more than the arteries, hence it has been said that "Veratrum bleeds a person into his own veins."

Dose.—Of the fluid extract, from 1 to 2 drops every two to four hours; of the active principle, Veratrine, $\frac{1}{100}$ of a grain.

TO DISINFECT A ROOM AFTER A CONTAGIOUS DISEASE.

By SAMUEL J. WILSON, M. D.

Formaldehyde is the most convenient and at the same time the most satisfactory disinfectant in use. It is a gas, but for convenience it is used in liquid form, sixty per cent of water being added. Formaldehyde will not injure furniture, clothing, lace curtains nor other goods.

How to Use Formaldehyde.—First obtain a wide-mouthed bottle capable of holding six ounces. The cork should fit tightly, but should be perforated with a number of holes like those in a sprinkling can. Also make one large opening. Through this opening pass a glass tube long enough to reach to the bottom of the bottle. Now seal up all cracks around the windows, doors, and other places where there is a possibility for the Formaldehyde gas to escape. All bedding and clothing should be hung on a line or over chairs so that all parts will be exposed. Bureau drawers should be opened, and books, if present, should be stood upon end and partially opened. Next stretch a clothes line across the room and hang on it one or more sheets—one sheet and five ounces of Formaldehyde will be sufficient for a room containing not over one thousand cubic feet. The sheet should be hung so that it will nearly reach the floor. Lift up the bottom of it, and with the bottle containing the Formaldehyde and perforated cork, sprinkle the solution carefully over its surface. It will be noticed that when the bottle is turned bottomside up, the air can pass through the glass tube to the bottom, and this aids in forcing the liquid out. As soon as the sprinkling is finished, leave the room and immediately seal the door of exit, close the keyhole, and also any cracks or spaces at the top, bottom or sides of the door.

When exposed to air, Formaldehyde loses its strength rapidly, but it is customary to allow the room to remain closed for five hours, and then to open the doors and windows and admit fresh air in abundance. Also dissolve a few pounds of Copperas in a pail of water and pour through the sink or drain, if there is one present. This process, followed by thoroughly washing the floors and woodwork with soap and hot water, will make everything safe.

We are not unmindful of the fact that for many years it has been customary to burn Sulphur in rooms as a means of disinfection. There are many objections to Sulphur, notwithstanding

743

its popularity. Sulphur fumes cause a grimy deposit over the walls, furniture and other articles with which they come in contact, leave a disagreeable odor for days and sometimes for weeks, and often cause an irritating and disagreeable cough among those occupying rooms in which it has been burned. Again, *Sulphur will not destroy infection.*

Another objection to Sulphur is that it is apt to destroy more or less the various garments or clothing usually present. If the ceilings, walls, floor, carpet, furniture and other articles in a room were wet with water or steam and then exposed to the fumes of Sulphur, the results would be more satisfactory so far as destroying the poisons of the disease were concerned, but in this case everything in the room would also be destroyed. The Sulphur fumes would attract the oxygen from the water present, the increase in oxygen would change the fumes into strong Sulphuric Acid, and this acid would destroy every article of clothing, carpets, curtains, upholstered goods, etc., in the room. True, these might be removed, but in many cases they are not; and even if they were removed, the strong Sulphuric Acid would attack the woodwork, first destroying the varnish or paint and then more or less affecting the wood itself, leaving a black stain. Another important feature of Sulphur fumes in the presence of water is that they will also attract the oxygen from any and all kinds of colored goods, and this would destroy the colors at once as all colors contain oxygen.

Like Sulphur, Formaldehyde is irritating to the air passages— the throat and lungs—yet it possesses several important advantages. First, it is a more powerful germicide; second, it does not destroy, in fact, produces no effect upon the most delicate fabric; third, it leaves no evidence of its former presence.

After all, the principal advantage in using any disinfectant is found in the great abundance of fresh air which it is necessary to admit after its use.

INDEX.

NOTE: *Herbal remedies have not been included in index, as they are listed alphabetically within the herbal section beginning on page 505.*